MASTERPLOTS II

CHRISTIAN LITERATURE

MASTERPLOTS II

CHRISTIAN LITERATURE

1

A–Dre

Edited by
JOHN K. ROTH
Claremont McKenna College

SALEM PRESS
Pasadena, California   Hackensack, New Jersey

Editor in Chief: Dawn P. Dawson　　Manuscript Editor: Rowena Wildin Dehanke
Editorial Director: Christina J. Moose　　Production Editor: Andrea E. Miller
Acquisitions Editor: Mark Rehn　　Graphics and Design: James Hutson
Research Supervisor: Jeffry Jensen　　Photo Editor: Cynthia Breslin Beres
Research Assistant: Keli Trousdale　　Editorial Assistant: Dana Garey

Cover photo: "Virgin and Child," Simone dei Crossifissi
(The Granger Collection, New York)

Library of Congress Cataloging-in-Publication Data
Masterplots II. Christian literature / edited by John K. Roth.
　　p.　cm.
Includes bibliographical references and index.
　　ISBN 978-1-58765-379-7 (set : alk. paper) — ISBN 978-1-58765-380-3 (vol. 1 : alk.
paper) — ISBN 978-1-58765-381-0 (vol. 2 : alk. paper) — ISBN 978-1-58765-382-7
(vol. 3 : alk. paper) — ISBN 978-1-58765-383-4 (vol. 4 : alk. paper)
　　1. Christian literature—History and criticism. 2. Christian literature—Stories, plots,
etc. I. Roth, John K. II. Title: Masterplots 2. III. Title: Masterplots two.

BR117.M15 2007
230—dc22

2007024245

First Printing

PRINTED IN THE UNITED STATES OF AMERICA

LIST OF TITLES IN VOLUME

page

Publisher's Note ix
Contributing Reviewers xiii
Complete List of Titles in All Volumes xix

Editor's Introduction 1
The Bible in History 10

Abortion and Divorce in Western Law — *Mary Ann Glendon* 23
Acts of the Apostles — *Unknown* 27
(Ado)ration — *Diane Glancy* 31
"Advice to a Prophet" — *Richard Wilbur* 35
African Heritage and Contemporary Christianity — *J. N. K. Mugambi* 38
After the Lost War — *Andrew Hudgins* 41
Against Heresies — *Saint Irenaeus* 44
Agape and Eros — *Anders Nygren* 47
The Age of Anxiety — *W. H. Auden* 50
Aids to Reflection — *Samuel Taylor Coleridge* 54
Aké — *Wole Soyinka* 58
All New People — *Anne Lamott* 62
Amazing Grace — *Kathleen Norris* 65
"Amazing Peace" — *Maya Angelou* 69
And I Alone Have Escaped to Tell You — *Ralph McInerny* 73
The Angel of History — *Carolyn Forché* 77
Apocalypse — *Ernesto Cardenal* 80
Apocrypha — *Eric Pankey* 84
Apologia pro vita sua — *John Henry Newman* 88
Apology — *Tertullian* 92
Arena — *Karen Hancock* 96
Argument Against Abolishing Christianity — *Jonathan Swift* 99
The Arrival of the Future — *B. H. Fairchild* 103
Ascent of Mount Carmel *and* Dark Night of the Soul —
     Saint John of the Cross 107
The Augsburg Confession of Faith — *Philipp Melanchthon* 112
Awakening Mercy — *Angela Benson* 116

Baptismal Instruction — *Saint John Chrysostom* 120
Barabbas — *Pär Lagerkvist* 123
Basic Christianity — *John R. W. Stott* 127

page

The Beasts of Bethlehem — *X. J. Kennedy* 130
Belief or Nonbelief? — *Umberto Eco and Carlo Maria Martini* 133
Ben-Hur — *Lew Wallace* 136
Beowulf — *Unknown* 140
Beyond God the Father — *Mary Daly* 144
Bible and Theology in African Christianity — *John Samuel Mbiti* 147
Billy Budd, Foretopman — *Herman Melville* 150
Bioethics — *Gilbert Meilaender* 154
The Bishop in the Old Neighborhood — *Andrew M. Greeley* 157
The Bishop's Mantle — *Agnes Sligh Turnbull* 161
A Black Theology of Liberation — *James H. Cone* 165
Black Zodiac — *Charles Wright* 169
Blood Ties — *Sigmund Brouwer* 173
The Bloudy Tenent of Persecution for Cause of Conscience —
    Roger Williams 176
Blue Like Jazz — *Donald Miller* 180
Book of Common Prayer — *Thomas Cranmer* 184
Book of Divine Works — *Hildegard von Bingen* 188
The Book of God — *Walter Wangerin, Jr.* 192
The Book of Mormon — *Joseph Smith* 196
Book of Revelation — *John* 202
Books of the Prophets — *Isaiah , Jeremiah, Amos, and Micah* 206
Bread and Wine — *Ignazio Silone* 211
Bread for the Journey — *Henri J. M. Nouwen* 215
Brideshead Revisited — *Evelyn Waugh* 218
A Brightness That Made My Soul Tremble —
    Stella Ann Nesanovich 222
Broken Lance — *Michele Sorensen* 226
The Brothers Karamazov — *Fyodor Dostoevski* 229
The Burning Fields — *David Middleton* 233

Called to Question — *Joan D. Chittister, O.S.B.* 237
The Canterbury Tales — *Geoffrey Chaucer* 240
A Canticle for Leibowitz — *Walter M. Miller, Jr.* 245
A Capital Offense — *Gary E. Parker* 248
Care of the Soul — *Thomas Moore* 251
Casti Connubii — *Pius XI* 254
Catechism of the Catholic Church — *Council of Trent* 257
Catholics — *Brian Moore* 261
Centesimus Annus — *John Paul II* 265
The Cherubinic Wanderer — *Angelus Silesius* 268
Christ — *Jack Miles* 272

page

Christ Clone Trilogy — *James BeauSeigneur* 275
Christ in a Pluralistic Age — *John B. Cobb, Jr.* 280
Christ the Lord — *Anne Rice* 284
The Christian Faith — *Friedrich Schleiermacher* 288
The Christian Tradition — *Joseph Mitsuo Kitagawa* 292
Christianity and Democracy — *Jacques Maritain* 296
"A Christmas Carol" — *Charles Dickens* 299
Christy — *Catherine Marshall* 303
The Chronicles of Narnia — *C. S. Lewis* 307
The Church — *Jan Hus* 312
Church Folk — *Michele Andrea Bowen* 316
The Circle Trilogy — *Ted Dekker* 320
The City of God — *Saint Augustine* 325
The Cloud of Unknowing — *Unknown* 329
The Color of Faith — *Fumitaka Matsuoka* 334
The Color Purple — *Alice Walker* 338
Come Sweet Death — *Bunyan Davie Napier* 342
The Coming of the Cosmic Christ — *Matthew Fox* 346
A Complicated Kindness — *Miriam Toews* 350
Conferences — *John Cassian* 354
Confessio Amantis — *John Gower* 357
"Confession" *and* "The New Birth" — *Menno Simons* 361
Confessions — *Saint Augustine* 365
The Confessions of Nat Turner — *William Styron* 370
Constantine's Sword — *James Carroll* 374
The Country Parson — *George Herbert* 378
The Courage to Be — *Paul Tillich* 382
Crawl with God, Dance in the Spirit — *Jong Chun Park* 386
The Creation — *Bruce Beasley* 390
Credo — *William Sloane Coffin* 393
The Crucified God — *Jürgen Moltmann* 397
Cur Deus Homo — *Saint Anselm* 401
Cure for the Common Life — *Max Lucado* 405

The Da Vinci Code — *Dan Brown* 408
A Dangerous Silence — *Catherine Palmer* 412
The Dawning of Deliverance — *Judith Pella* 416
Dear and Glorious Physician — *Taylor Caldwell* 420
Death Comes for the Archbishop — *Willa Cather* 423
A Death in the Family — *James Agee* 427
The Death of Ivan Ilyich — *Leo Tolstoy* 431
Death on a Friday Afternoon — *Richard John Neuhaus* 435

page

A Declaration of the Sentiments of Arminius — *Jacobus Arminius* 439
The Destiny of Man — *Nicolai Berdyaev* 443
Devotions upon Emergent Occasions — *John Donne* 447
The Dialogue — *Saint Catherine of Siena* 453
"A Dialogue of Self and Soul" — *William Butler Yeats* 458
The Diary of a Country Priest — *Georges Bernanos* 462
Directed Verdict — *Randy Singer* 465
Divine and Human — *Leo Tolstoy* 469
The Divine Comedy — *Dante* 473
The Divine Conspiracy — *Dallas Willard* 477
The Divine Milieu — *Pierre Teilhard de Chardin* 480
The Divine Relativity — *Charles Hartshorne* 485
Divini Redemptoris — *Pius XI* 488
The Divinity School Address — *Ralph Waldo Emerson* 491
Doctor Faustus — *Christopher Marlowe* 496
Don't Throw Away Tomorrow — *Robert H. Schuller* 500
The Double Search — *Rufus M. Jones* 503
The Drama of Atheist Humanism — *Henri de Lubac* 508
"The Dream of the Rood" — *Unknown* 512
The Dream Songs — *John Berryman* 515

PUBLISHER'S NOTE

Salem Press's reference publications on literature fall into three broad categories: the *Masterplots* family, which contains 8 sets (47 volumes) organized around individual titles of great literary works; the *Critical Survey of Literature* family, which contains 4 sets (31 volumes) organized around individual authors; and 3 *Cyclopedias*: *Cyclopedia of World Authors*, *Cyclopedia of Literary Characters*, and *Cyclopedia of Literary Places*. Together, these publications cover literally thousands of works of literature.

The *Masterplots* series is divided into two groups. The original, core series is the 12-volume *Masterplots*, whose second revised edition was published in 1996. It covers more than 1,800 works of literature, from the classics to the great works of modern world fiction, nonfiction, drama, and poetry. In the mid-1980's, as the curriculum grew to include more diverse and world authors, Salem began the *Masterplots II* series to supplement and expand on the core titles covered in the original *Masterplots*. Sets in the *Masterplots II* series are organized around broad genres of literature—poetry, drama, long fiction, and short fiction—and on areas of interest—works by women, African Americans, juvenile and young-adult writers, British and Commonwealth writers, and American writers.

Scope and Content

The present set addresses one of the fastest-growing genres of literature as well as one of the oldest. *Masterplots II: Christian Literature* compiles summary-analyses of 502 titles. Of these, 45 have been updated from previous Salem publications. The remainder, 457 essays, are completely new, written for this publication.

Defining the genre of Christian literature can be, as Barbara J. Walker suggests in the first chapter of her *Librarian's Guide to Developing Christian Fiction Collections for Adults* (2005), a confusing task:

> A work can be correctly categorized as inspirational while not fitting into the category of what would be considered Christian, leaving librarians confused as to what is really meant by the phrase "Christian fiction." It does not help when they encounter patrons with totally different concepts about this category. Some don't consider a work as Christian at all unless it has a clear-cut presentation of a salvation message, while others look for the message in the story's content, whether it is overtly apparent or not. This can leave a librarian at a distinct disadvantage when trying to satisfy patron requests. The librarian may be of a different faith and unfamiliar with what is meant by the term "Christian," although Christianity is the claimed faith of four out of five Americans.

John Mort, in his invaluable collection-development tool *Christian Fiction: A Guide to the Genre* (2002), identifies at least twenty subgenres and nearly two thousand titles of Christian fiction "beyond romance." While focusing on the new wave of Christian writing that blossomed in the 1990's, he acknowledges the genre's vast reach:

> The [work's] content can be indirect, didactic, subtle, political, and multifaceted, but its Christian content is what turns Christian fiction into a genre. That is—at least in evangelical fiction—readers know the outcome to begin with; it is the details of the struggle that interest them. . . . Still, there are many fiction writers who don't fit the evangelical mold and yet are clearly Christian writers. To offer one example, since the 1950s, Frederick Buechner has written lyrically of suffering, exploratory Christians. Should evangelicals give him a try? Of course, but in any case, Buechner does not lack for readers, either "secular" or Christian. . . . [F]or many readers, what matters is a spiritual search that's made in Christian terms. For them, many evangelical novels will prove too rigid and unimaginative.

Layer the deep history of Christian nonfiction onto these definitions of imaginative Christian literature, and you have a broad genre indeed: While Walker and Mort are concerned solely with fiction, the foundational texts of Christian literature—from the Bible to the works of the church fathers to the key papal encyclicals and the rich philosophical, theological, and experiential archive of modern giants such as Dietrich Bonhoeffer, Reinhold Niebuhr, Pierre Teilhard de Chardin, and Cornel West—also testify to the rich and varied works addressing the Christian experience.

Masterplots II: Christian Literature captures the entire breadth of Christian literature—both fiction and nonfiction—by selecting more than 500 of the greatest and most representative works identified with the genre. At the core of this list are the fiction and nonfiction "classics" to which most students and general readers, Christian or secular, will be exposed at some time in their lives, from Saint Augustine's *Confessions* to John Bunyan's *Pilgrim's Progress* to Nathaniel Hawthorne's *The Scarlet Letter*, J. R. R. Tolkien's *Lord of the Rings* series, and C. S. Lewis's *Screwtape Letters* and Narnia chronicles. While several of the titles were not written exclusively for a Christian audience, all works covered in these volumes have been consulted, examined, taught, or analyzed from a Christian perspective. Many of the titles in our list, however, overtly emphasize the Christian experience, and often these works were written expressly for the purpose of addressing Christian concerns or simply providing a good "Christian read."

The scope is broad not only generically but also temporally and geographically, with works by authors as diverse as John Samuel Mbiti, Gustavo Gutiérrez, Immaculée Ilibagiza, J. N. K. Mugambi, and Fumitaka Matsuoka and dates of publication ranging from Christian times to the twenty-first century. Titles in all the major genres are included: drama, from *Everyman* to *Jesus Christ Superstar*; poetry, from "The Dream of the Rood" to Mark Jarman's *Questions for Ecclesiastes* and Scott Cairns's *Philokalia*; and representative titles from the best writers of Christian genre fiction, including romance, mystery, end-times, and science fiction. We have not avoided contemporary and often controversial blockbusters such as Dan Brown's

The Da Vinci Code and Tim LaHaye and Jerry B. Jenkins's *Left Behind* series; their best-seller status testifies to the continuing and growing interest in Christian spirituality and the Christian literature that supports it.

Clearly, any list defined as the "best" and most representative of the vast number of works now appropriated as Christian literature will be highly selective—and subjective. It is our hope that these titles will meet librarians' and readers' needs by offering commentary on works most likely to be known, asked for, and studied by both general readers and secondary and college-level students in a variety of courses, from literature to the history of religion.

Arrangement and Essay Format

The set is arranged alphabetically by title, and each essay (averaging approximately 1,650 words each, or 3-5 pages) is divided into sections in a predictable format that allows easy access to text discussions:

- *Title*: Title of the work (when originally not in English, the title best known in English publication).
- *Author*: Name by which the author is best known, followed in parentheses by years of birth and death.
- *First published*: Year in which the original work first appeared, usually a date of publication but also date of writing or transcription when publication does not represent first appearance. For late-twentieth and early twenty-first century works, publisher information is also included and "Edition used" (below) is omitted.
- *Edition used*: Edition and translation information for older or ancient works, as well as later editions of more modern works, where different from the original publication; provides access to accessible and well-known editions for English-language audiences.
- *Genre*: Drama, Nonfiction, Novel, Novella, Poetry, or Short Fiction.
- *Subgenres*: The subgenre or subgenres are listed, from Adventure and Apocalyptic Fiction to Theology and Thriller.
- *Core issues*: Subjects and themes of particular importance in the Christian experience, from Awakening to Faith to Union with God.
- *Abstract*: This key paragraph highlights the work's context and content, including its Christian significance.
- *Principal characters*: For works of drama, fiction, and narrative poetry, a list of major characters along with brief descriptions.
- *Overview*: A detailed summary of and commentary on the work's content (the meat of the essay).
- *Christian Themes*: A summary of the critical Christian issues addressed. For nonfiction works, this section summarizes the work's Christian focus and often evaluates it in the context of Christian history; for fictive works, this is a summary of the main Christian messages and motifs as illuminated by the plot and characters.

- *Sources for Further Study*: Offers a listing of readily available secondary reference material on the work and its author. Bibliographical annotations appear with each source.
- *Contributor byline*: Each essay is signed by the scholar or expert who wrote it.

Special Features and Finding Aids

Several appendixes and indexes are located at the back of volume 4:
- *Bibliography*: Lists secondary works important to the study of Christian and inspirational literature.
- *Electronic Resources*: Internet sources for reviews, readers' advisories, scholarship, and access to Christian literature.
- *Chronological List of Titles*: Titles covered in these volumes, arranged by first date of appearance, to form a time line for those interested in historical access.
- *Core Issues Index*: Titles by core issues with which the works are concerned, providing access by Christian themes.
- *Genre Index*: Titles arranged by subgenres.
- *Geographical Index*: Titles by author's country or region.
- *Title Index*: Titles arranged alphabetically for access to the full contents list.
- *Author Index*: Titles by author.

Acknowledgments

Such an undertaking would not have been possible without the invaluable editorial counsel and content decisions of Professor John K. Roth, Edward J. Sexton Professor of Philosophy and Director, Center for the Study of the Holocaust, Genocide, and Human Rights, Claremont McKenna College. We are also deeply indebted to the many academicians and experts who contributed the essays. Their names and affiliations are identified in the Contributing Reviewers list that follows this note.

LIST OF CONTRIBUTING REVIEWERS

Bland Addison
*Worcester Polytechnic
    Institute*

Linda Adkins
University of Northern Iowa

M. D. Allen
*University of
    Wisconsin—Fox Valley*

William Loyd Allen
Brewton-Parker College

Emily Alward
*Henderson, NV District
    Libraries*

Majid Amini
Virginia State University

Kathy Antonen
*South Dakota School of
    Mines and Technology*

Karen L. Arnold
Columbia, Maryland

Michael W. Austin
Eastern Kentucky University

Carl L. Bankston, III
Tulane University

Jack Barbera
University of Mississippi

Dan Barnett
Butte College

David Barratt
*Farnsfield,
    Nottinghamshire,
    United Kingdom*

Thomas Becknell
Bethel College

Tanja Bekhuis
TCB Research

Alvin K. Benson
Utah Valley State College

Chris Benson
Clemson University

Anthony Bernardo
Wilmington, Delaware

Cynthia A. Bily
Adrian College

Margaret Boe Birns
New York University

Nicholas Birns
*Eugene Lang College,
    the New School*

Franz Blaha
*University of Nebraska—
    Lincoln*

Devon Boan
Belmont University

Pegge Bochynski
Salem State College

Ellen Bosman
*New Mexico State
    University Library*

William Boyle
Brooklyn, New York

Trisha M. Brady
SUNY at Buffalo

Marie J. K. Brenner
Bethel College

Carol Breslin
Gwynedd-Mercy College

Matt Brillinger
Carleton University

Jean R. Brink
*Henry E. Huntington
    Library*

Howard Bromberg
Ave Maria School of Law

Brandon P. Brown
*Indiana University School of
    Medicine*

Mary Hanford Bruce
Monmouth College

Michelle M. Butler
University of Pittsburgh

Joseph P. Byrne
Belmont University

Harry James Cargas
Webster University

Henry L. Carrigan, Jr.
*Northwestern University
    Press*

Sharon Carson
University of North Dakota

Edgar L. Chapman
Bradley University

G. Clarke Chapman
Moravian College

C. L. Chua
*California State University,
    Fresno*

Bowman L. Clarke
University of Georgia

xiii

Douglas Clouatre
*MidPlains Community
    College*

David W. Cole
*University of Wisconsin
    Colleges*

John J. Conlon
*University of South Florida,
    St. Petersburg*

Julian W. Connolly
University of Virginia

Greg Cootsona
Butte College

Michael G. Cornelius
Wilson College

Lily Corwin
*The Catholic University of
    America*

Michael L. Coulter
Grove City College

Christopher E. Crane
*United States Naval
    Academy*

Marsha Daigle-Williamson
Spring Arbor University

Richard Damashek
*Calumet College of
    St. Joseph*

Frank Day
Clemson University

Kelly Denton-Borhaug
Moravian College

Joseph Dewey
*University of Pittsburgh—
    Johnstown*

M. Casey Diana
*University of Illinois at
    Urbana-Champaign*

Lesa Dill
*Western Kentucky
    University*

Marcia B. Dinneen
Bridgewater State College

Margaret A. Dodson
Boise, Idaho

Kim Dolce
Tecumseh, Michigan

William R. Drennan
*University of Wisconsin
    Center—Baraboo/Sauk
    County*

Thomas Du Bose
*Louisiana State University
    at Shreveport*

Scott M. Dutkiewicz
*Clemson University
    Libraries*

TammyJo Eckhart
*Indiana University—
    Bloomington*

Robert P. Ellis
Worcester State College

Priscilla E. Eppinger
Graceland University

Victoria Erhart
Strayer University

Thomas L. Erskine
Salisbury University

Patrice Fagnant-MacArthur
Spiritual Woman

Jo N. Farrar
San Jacinto College

Nettie Farris
University of Louisville

Jean H. Faurot
*California State University,
    Sacramento*

Thomas R. Feller
Nashville, Tennessee

Dale L. Flesher
University of Mississippi

Raymond Frey
Centenary College

Joy Gambill
Wake Forest University

Christopher E. Garrett
Texas A&M University

Mary E. Giles
*California State University,
    Sacramento*

Sheldon Goldfarb
*University of British
    Columbia*

Robert F. Gorman
*Southwest Texas State
    University*

Ryan R. Gorman
University of Dallas

Hans G. Graetzer
*South Dakota State
    University*

Jessica H. Gray
University of Rhode Island

Douglas H. Gregg
Occidental College

John L. Grigsby
*Appalachian Research &
    Defense Fund of
    Kentucky, Inc.*

Kenneth Hada
East Central University

LIST OF CONTRIBUTING REVIEWERS

H. George Hahn
Towson University

Elsie Galbreath Haley
Metropolitan State College of Denver

Nancy A. Hardesty
Atlanta, Georgia

June Harris
University of Arizona South

Mitchell M. Harris
Gustavus Adolphus College

John C. Hathaway
Strayer University

David Haugen
Western Illinois University

Jennifer Heller
University of Kansas

Thomas E. Helm
Western Illinois University

Diane Andrews Henningfeld
Adrian College

Paul K. Hesselink
Covenant College

Anna Dunlap Higgins
Gordon College

E. Glenn Hinson
Southern Baptist Theological Seminary

KaaVonia Hinton
Old Dominion University

Jen Hirt
Harrisburg Area Community College

Carl W. Hoagstrom
Ohio Northern University

Shannah Hogue
Cedarville University

David M. Holley
Friends University

Daryl Holmes
Nicholls State University

John R. Holmes
Franciscan University of Steubenville

Joan Hope
Palm Beach Gardens, Florida

Shaun Horton
Florida State University

James M. Houston
Regent College

William L. Howard
Chicago State University

John F. Hudson
West Concord Union Church

Robert Jacobs
Central Washington University

Elizabeth Jarnagin
Drew University

Edward Johnson
University of New Orleans

Keith Jones
Northwestern College

Leela Kapai
Prince George's Community College

Daven M. Kari
Vanguard University

Hideyuki Kasuga
Aichi Prefectural University

Kyle Keefer
Converse College

Sean J. Kelly
SUNY at Buffalo

Mara Kelly-Zukowski
Felician College

Howard A. Kerner
Polk Community College

Mabel Khawaja
Hampton University

Grace Ji-Sun Kim
Moravian Theological Seminary

Leigh Husband Kimmel
Indianapolis, Indiana

Anne Klejment
University of St. Thomas

Mary Kolner
University of Dallas

Paula D. Krueger
Duquesne University

Leah R. Krynicky
The Catholic University of America

Pam Fox Kuhlken
Arizona Western College

Wendy Alison Lamb
South Pasadena, California

Michael J. Larsen
Saint Mary's University

Eugene Larson
Los Angeles Pierce College

William Laskowski
Jamestown College

L. L. Lee
Western Washington University

William J. Leonard
Southern Baptist Theological Seminary

xv

Leon Lewis
*Appalachian State
University*

Sean Gordon Lewis
*The Catholic University of
America*

Thomas Tandy Lewis
St. Cloud State University

Martha Oehmke Loustaunau
*New Mexico State
University*

Bernadette Flynn Low
*Community College of
Baltimore County—
Dundalk*

Eric v. d. Luft
Gegensatz Press

R. C. Lutz
CII

Janet McCann
Texas A&M University

Joanne McCarthy
Tacoma Community College

Jennie MacDonald
University of Denver

Margaret H. McFadden
*Appalachian State
University*

James Edward McGoldrick
*Greenville Presbyterian
Theological Seminary*

Ian P. McGreal
*California State University,
Sacramento*

Ric Machuga
Butte College

John McLaughlin
Freed-Hardeman University

David W. Madden
*California State University,
Sacramento*

Mary Mahony
*Wayne County Community
College*

Lois A. Marchino
*University of Texas at
El Paso*

Hubert M. Martin, Jr.
University of Kentucky

Lee Roy Martin
*Church of God Theological
Seminary*

Tyler Mayfield
*Claremont Graduate
University*

Laurence W. Mazzeno
Alvernia College

Cecile Mazzucco-Than
Port Jefferson, New York

Gregory Mellema
Calvin College

Julia M. Meyers
Duquesne University

Michael R. Meyers
Pfeiffer University

Seth Michelson
*University of Southern
California*

Vasa D. Mihailovich
*University of North
Carolina*

Timothy C. Miller
Millersville University

Christian H. Moe
*Southern Illinois University
at Carbondale*

Bernard E. Morris
Modesto, California

Charmaine Allmon Mosby
*Western Kentucky
University*

Celia Neumayr
University of Dallas

Daniel J. Nodes
Ave Maria University

Erik Nordenhaug
*Armstrong Atlantic State
University*

Arsenio Orteza
*St. Thomas More High
School*

Sally B. Palmer
*South Dakota School of
Mines & Technology*

Robert J. Paradowski
*Rochester Institute of
Technology*

Deirdre Parsons
Duquesne University

David Partenheimer
Truman State University

Craig Payne
*Indian Hills Community
College*

Rodger M. Payne
Louisiana State University

Thomas R. Peake
King College

David Peck
Laguna Beach, California

Joseph P. Pendergast
Abingdon, Virginia

Jan Pendergrass
University of Georgia

LIST OF CONTRIBUTING REVIEWERS

M. Basil Pennington
St. Joseph's Abbey

Kimberly T. Peterson
Bethel College

David D. Pettus
Liberty Theological Seminary

John R. Pfeiffer
Central Michigan University

Amanda Porterfield
Syracuse University

Stanley Poss
California State University, Fresno

Jessie Bishop Powell
Lexington, Kentucky

Luke A. Powers
Tennessee State University

Maureen Puffer-Rothenberg
Valdosta State University

Tony Rafalowski
University of Missouri—Columbia

Paul A. Rainbow
North American Baptist Seminary

Patricia Ralston
Covenant College

Cat Rambo
Redmond, Washington

Lillian M. Range
Our Lady of Holy Cross College

Thomas Rankin
Concord, California

Paul L. Redditt
Georgetown College

Rosemary M. Canfield Reisman
Charleston Southern University

Thomas Renna
Saginaw Valley State University

H. William Rice
Kennesaw State University

Rodney P. Rice
South Dakota School of Mines & Technology

Betty Richardson
Southern Illinois University, Edwardsville

Edward A. Riedinger
Ohio State University Libraries

Dorothy Dodge Robbins
Louisiana Tech University

Kenneth Robbins
Louisiana Tech University

Joan A. Romano
The Catholic University of America

Joseph Rosenblum
University of North Carolina, Greensboro

John K. Roth
Claremont McKenna College

Donelle Ruwe
Northern Arizona University

Margaret T. Sacco
Miami University of Ohio

Scott Samuelson
Brigham Young University—Idaho

Todd Samuelson
Museum of Printing History

Vicki A. Sanders
Riverside Military Academy

Gary R. Sattler
Fuller Theological Seminary

Elizabeth D. Schafer
Auburn, Alabama

Kevin Schemenauer
The Catholic University of America

Reinhold Schlieper
Embry-Riddle Aeronautical University

Beverly Schneller
Millersville University

Rowland A. Sherrill
Indiana University

Martha A. Sherwood
University of Oregon

Bonnie L. A. Shullenberger
Trinity Episcopal Church

William Shullenberger
Sarah Lawrence College

Carl Singleton
Fort Hays State University

Joshua A. Skinner
University of Dallas

Brian Stableford
Reading, United Kingdom

Bradley Starr
California State University, Fullerton

August Staub
University of Georgia

Ingo R. Stoehr
Kilgore College

Fred Strickert
Wartburg College

Roy Arthur Swanson
*University of Wisconsin—
Milwaukee*

James Tackach
Roger Williams University

Nancy Conn Terjesen
Kent State University

J. D. Thomas
University of South Carolina

Susan E. Thomas
*Indiana University—South
Bend*

Richard P. Thompson
Spring Arbor University

Paul B. Trescott
Southern Illinois University

Jack Trotter
Trident College

Anita Tully
Nicholls State University

Mary Moore Vandendorpe
Lewis University

Joseph Van House, O.Cist.
*Cistercian Abbey Our Lady
of Dallas*

Suzanne Araas Vesely
*Maharishi University of
Management*

Steve Walker
Brigham Young University

Kathryn A. Walterscheid
*University of Missouri—
St. Louis*

Shawncey Webb
Taylor University

Carol Wayne White
Bucknell University

Charles White
Spring Arbor University

Thomas Willard
University of Arizona

Rosemary Gates Winslow
*The Catholic University of
America*

Clint Wrede
University of Northern Iowa

Scott Wright
University of St. Thomas

Jennifer L. Wyatt
Civic Memorial High School

Scott D. Yarbrough
*Charleston Southern
University*

Joanna Yin
University of Hawaii

COMPLETE LIST OF TITLES IN ALL VOLUMES

Volume 1

page

Publisher's Note ix
Contributing Reviewers xiii

Editor's Introduction 1
The Bible in History 10

Abortion and Divorce in Western Law — *Mary Ann Glendon* 23
Acts of the Apostles — *Unknown* 27
(Ado)ration — *Diane Glancy* 31
"Advice to a Prophet" — *Richard Wilbur* 35
African Heritage and Contemporary Christianity — *J. N. K. Mugambi*. 38
After the Lost War — *Andrew Hudgins* 41
Against Heresies — *Saint Irenaeus* 44
Agape and Eros — *Anders Nygren*. 47
The Age of Anxiety — *W. H. Auden* 50
Aids to Reflection — *Samuel Taylor Coleridge* 54
Aké — *Wole Soyinka* 58
All New People — *Anne Lamott*. 62
Amazing Grace — *Kathleen Norris* 65
"Amazing Peace" — *Maya Angelou*. 69
And I Alone Have Escaped to Tell You — *Ralph McInerny* 73
The Angel of History — *Carolyn Forché* 77
Apocalypse — *Ernesto Cardenal* 80
Apocrypha — *Eric Pankey* 84
Apologia pro vita sua — *John Henry Newman* 88
Apology — *Tertullian* 92
Arena — *Karen Hancock* 96
Argument Against Abolishing Christianity — *Jonathan Swift* 99
The Arrival of the Future — *B. H. Fairchild*. 103
Ascent of Mount Carmel *and* Dark Night of the Soul —
    Saint John of the Cross 107
The Augsburg Confession of Faith — *Philipp Melanchthon*. 112
Awakening Mercy — *Angela Benson* 116

Baptismal Instruction — *Saint John Chrysostom* 120
Barabbas — *Pär Lagerkvist* 123

page

Basic Christianity — *John R. W. Stott* 127
The Beasts of Bethlehem — *X. J. Kennedy* 130
Belief or Nonbelief? — *Umberto Eco and Carlo Maria Martini* 133
Ben-Hur — *Lew Wallace* 136
Beowulf — *Unknown* 140
Beyond God the Father — *Mary Daly* 144
Bible and Theology in African Christianity — *John Samuel Mbiti* 147
Billy Budd, Foretopman — *Herman Melville* 150
Bioethics — *Gilbert Meilaender* 154
The Bishop in the Old Neighborhood — *Andrew M. Greeley* 157
The Bishop's Mantle — *Agnes Sligh Turnbull* 161
A Black Theology of Liberation — *James H. Cone* 165
Black Zodiac — *Charles Wright* 169
Blood Ties — *Sigmund Brouwer* 173
The Bloudy Tenent of Persecution for Cause of Conscience —
    Roger Williams 176
Blue Like Jazz — *Donald Miller* 180
Book of Common Prayer — *Thomas Cranmer* 184
Book of Divine Works — *Hildegard von Bingen* 188
The Book of God — *Walter Wangerin, Jr.* 192
The Book of Mormon — *Joseph Smith* 196
Book of Revelation — *John* 202
Books of the Prophets — *Isaiah , Jeremiah, Amos, and Micah* 206
Bread and Wine — *Ignazio Silone* 211
Bread for the Journey — *Henri J. M. Nouwen* 215
Brideshead Revisited — *Evelyn Waugh* 218
A Brightness That Made My Soul Tremble —
    Stella Ann Nesanovich 222
Broken Lance — *Michele Sorensen* 226
The Brothers Karamazov — *Fyodor Dostoevski* 229
The Burning Fields — *David Middleton* 233

Called to Question — *Joan D. Chittister, O.S.B.* 237
The Canterbury Tales — *Geoffrey Chaucer* 240
A Canticle for Leibowitz — *Walter M. Miller, Jr.* 245
A Capital Offense — *Gary E. Parker* 248
Care of the Soul — *Thomas Moore* 251
Casti Connubii — *Pius XI* 254
Catechism of the Catholic Church — *Council of Trent* 257
Catholics — *Brian Moore* 261
Centesimus Annus — *John Paul II.* 265
The Cherubinic Wanderer — *Angelus Silesius* 268

page

Christ — *Jack Miles* 272
Christ Clone Trilogy — *James BeauSeigneur* 275
Christ in a Pluralistic Age — *John B. Cobb, Jr.* 280
Christ the Lord — *Anne Rice* 284
The Christian Faith — *Friedrich Schleiermacher* 288
The Christian Tradition — *Joseph Mitsuo Kitagawa* 292
Christianity and Democracy — *Jacques Maritain* 296
"A Christmas Carol" — *Charles Dickens* 299
Christy — *Catherine Marshall* 303
The Chronicles of Narnia — *C. S. Lewis* 307
The Church — *Jan Hus* 312
Church Folk — *Michele Andrea Bowen* 316
The Circle Trilogy — *Ted Dekker* 320
The City of God — *Saint Augustine* 325
The Cloud of Unknowing — *Unknown* 329
The Color of Faith — *Fumitaka Matsuoka* 334
The Color Purple — *Alice Walker* 338
Come Sweet Death — *Bunyan Davie Napier* 342
The Coming of the Cosmic Christ — *Matthew Fox* 346
A Complicated Kindness — *Miriam Toews* 350
Conferences — *John Cassian* 354
Confessio Amantis — *John Gower* 357
"Confession" *and* "The New Birth" — *Menno Simons* 361
Confessions — *Saint Augustine* 365
The Confessions of Nat Turner — *William Styron* 370
Constantine's Sword — *James Carroll* 374
The Country Parson — *George Herbert* 378
The Courage to Be — *Paul Tillich* 382
Crawl with God, Dance in the Spirit — *Jong Chun Park* 386
The Creation — *Bruce Beasley* 390
Credo — *William Sloane Coffin* 393
The Crucified God — *Jürgen Moltmann* 397
Cur Deus Homo — *Saint Anselm* 401
Cure for the Common Life — *Max Lucado* 405

The Da Vinci Code — *Dan Brown* 408
A Dangerous Silence — *Catherine Palmer* 412
The Dawning of Deliverance — *Judith Pella* 416
Dear and Glorious Physician — *Taylor Caldwell* 420
Death Comes for the Archbishop — *Willa Cather* 423
A Death in the Family — *James Agee* 427
The Death of Ivan Ilyich — *Leo Tolstoy* 431

page

Death on a Friday Afternoon — *Richard John Neuhaus* 435
A Declaration of the Sentiments of Arminius — *Jacobus Arminius* 439
The Destiny of Man — *Nicolai Berdyaev* 443
Devotions upon Emergent Occasions — *John Donne* 447
The Dialogue — *Saint Catherine of Siena* 453
"A Dialogue of Self and Soul" — *William Butler Yeats* 458
The Diary of a Country Priest — *Georges Bernanos* 462
Directed Verdict — *Randy Singer* 465
Divine and Human — *Leo Tolstoy* 469
The Divine Comedy — *Dante* 473
The Divine Conspiracy — *Dallas Willard* 477
The Divine Milieu — *Pierre Teilhard de Chardin* 480
The Divine Relativity — *Charles Hartshorne* 485
Divini Redemptoris — *Pius XI* 488
The Divinity School Address — *Ralph Waldo Emerson* 491
Doctor Faustus — *Christopher Marlowe* 496
Don't Throw Away Tomorrow — *Robert H. Schuller* 500
The Double Search — *Rufus M. Jones* 503
The Drama of Atheist Humanism — *Henri de Lubac* 508
"The Dream of the Rood" — *Unknown* 512
The Dream Songs — *John Berryman* 515

Volume 2

Drummer in the Dark — *T. Davis Bunn* 519

Early Christian Doctrines — *J. N. D. Kelly* 523
Early Theological Writings — *Georg Wilhelm Friedrich Hegel* 527
Economy of Grace — *Kathryn Tanner* 531
Edge of Honor — *Gilbert Morris* 534
Elmer Gantry — *Sinclair Lewis* 538
The Enneads — *Plotinus* 542
"An Epistle Containing the Strange Medical Experience of Karshish,
   the Arab Physician" — *Robert Browning* 545
The Epistle to the Romans — *Karl Barth* 549
Essays and Addresses on the Philosophy of Religion —
   Baron Friedrich von Hügel 553
The Essence of Christianity — *Ludwig Feuerbach* 557
Ethics — *Dietrich Bonhoeffer* 561
Ethics After Babel — *Jeffrey Stout* 565

page

Evangelium Vitae — *John Paul II* 568
Even in Quiet Places — *William Stafford* 571
Everyman — *Unknown* 574
Eve's Striptease — *Julia Kasdorf* 578
Evil and the God of Love — *John Hick* 582
Exclusion and Embrace — *Miroslav Volf* 586
An Existentialist Theology — *John Macquarrie* 590
Ezekiel's Shadow — *David Ryan Long* 594

The Face of the Deep — *Christina Rossetti* 597
The Faerie Queene — *Edmund Spenser* 601
"The Fall" — *Joseph Bottum* 606
Faust — *Johann Wolfgang von Goethe* 610
"Feet of Jesus" — *Langston Hughes* 614
Fifteen Sermons Preached at the Rolls Chapel — *Joseph Butler* 618
Figuring the Sacred — *Paul Ricœur* 621
Final Witness — *James Scott Bell* 625
Fire by Night — *Lynn N. Austin* 629
The First and Second Apologies — *Saint Justin Martyr* 633
The First Coming — *Thomas Sheehan* 636
Flabbergasted — *Ray Blackston* 640
Fools and Crows — *Terri Witek* 644
For the Time Being — *Annie Dillard* 647
"For the Union Dead" — *Robert Lowell* 650
Foundations of Christian Faith — *Karl Rahner* 654
Four Books of Sentences — *Peter Lombard* 657
Four Quartets — *T. S. Eliot* 660
The Freedom of a Christian — *Martin Luther* 664
The Friendly Persuasion — *Jessamyn West* 669

Gaudium et Spes — *Vatican Council II* 672
Ghost Pain — *Sydney Lea* 676
Gift from the Sea — *Anne Morrow Lindbergh* 680
Gilead — *Marilynne Robinson* 683
Go Tell It on the Mountain — *James Baldwin* 687
God and Philosophy — *Étienne Gilson* 691
God Has a Dream — *Desmond Tutu* 694
God Was in Christ — *D. M. Baillie* 698
The God Who Commands — *Richard J. Mouw* 704
Godric — *Frederick Buechner* 708
God's Silence — *Franz Wright* 712
God's Trombones — *James Weldon Johnson* 716

page

The Good Book — *Peter J. Gomes*. 720
The Gospel According to Jesus Christ — *José Saramago* 724
The Gospel of Christian Atheism — *Thomas J. J. Altizer* 728
Gospel of John — *Saint John*. 731
The Gospel of Mary of Magdala — *Karen L. King* 735
The Great Divorce — *C. S. Lewis* 739
The Great Exemplar — *Jeremy Taylor*. 743
The Great Mysteries — *Andrew M. Greeley*. 746
The Great Wheel — *Paul Mariani*. 749
The Greatest Story Ever Told — *Fulton Oursler*. 752

Hebrew Bible — *Unknown*. 756
"Here Follows Some Verses upon the Burning of Our House
    July 10th, 1666" — *Anne Bradstreet*. 768
Here I Stand — *John Shelby Spong* 772
The Hiding Place — *Corrie ten Boom* 775
Hinds' Feet on High Places — *Hannah Hurnard* 779
His Watchful Eye — *Jack Cavanaugh*. 783
A History of Christianity — *Paul Johnson*. 787
A History of God — *Karen Armstrong*. 791
Holocaust Politics — *John K. Roth*. 795
"Holy Sonnets" — *John Donne* 799
Home to Harmony — *Philip Gulley* 802
How Should We Then Live? — *Francis A. Schaeffer* 806
Humanae Vitae — *Paul VI*. 811
Humani Generis Redemptionem — *Benedict XV* 815
Hymns — *John Greenleaf Whittier*. 818
Hymns and Spiritual Songs — *Isaac Watts* 822

The Idea of a Christian Society — *T. S. Eliot* 826
The Idea of the Holy — *Rudolf Otto*. 830
The Imitation of Christ — *Thomas à Kempis* 834
"In Distrust of Merits" — *Marianne Moore* 839
In His Steps — *Charles Monroe Sheldon* 843
In Memoriam — *Alfred, Lord Tennyson* 847
In Memory of Her — *Elizabeth Schüssler Fiorenza* 851
In the Beauty of the Lilies — *John Updike*. 855
"In the Holy Nativity of Our Lord God" — *Richard Crashaw* 859
In This House of Brede — *Rumer Godden*. 863
The Infidel — *Joe Musser* 866
Inscribing the Text — *Walter Brueggemann*. 870
Insight — *Bernard J. F. Lonergan* 873

page

Institutes of the Christian Religion — *John Calvin* 877
The Instructor *and* Miscellanies — *Clement of Alexandria* 881
Interior Castle — *Saint Teresa of Ávila* 887
Interrogations at Noon — *Dana Gioia* 891
Introduction to Christianity — *Joseph Ratzinger.* 895
Isaiah — *Daniel Berrigan* 898

J. B. — *Archibald MacLeish* 902
The Jefferson Bible — *Thomas Jefferson* 906
Jesus Christ and Mythology — *Rudolf Bultmann* 909
Jesus Christ Superstar — *Tim Rice and Andrew Lloyd Webber* 913
The Jesus I Never Knew — *Philip Yancey.* 917
Jesus in History — *Howard Clark Kee.* 921
Jesus Through the Centuries — *Jaroslav Pelikan* 925
Journal of a Soul — *John XXIII* 928
The Journal of George Fox — *George Fox* 931
The Journal of John Woolman — *John Woolman* 936
The Journey — *Billy Graham* 941

The Keys of the Kingdom — *A. J. Cronin* 945
The Kingdom of God Is Within You — *Leo Tolstoy.* 948
King's Ransom — *Jan Beazely and Thom Lemmons* 952
Knowledge and Faith — *Edith Stein* 956
Kristin Lavransdatter — *Sigrid Undset.* 960

The Labyrinth of the World and the Paradise of the Heart —
    John Amos Comenius 964
The Ladder of Divine Ascent — *John Climacus.* 968
Lake Wobegon Days — *Garrison Keillor* 973
The Last Days of Pompeii — *Edward Bulwer-Lytton* 977
The Last Puritan — *George Santayana* 981
The Last Temptation of Christ — *Nikos Kazantzakis* 985
The Late Great Planet Earth — *Hal Lindsey* 989
Learning Human — *Les A. Murray* 993
Leaves of Grass — *Walt Whitman* 997
Lectures on Revivals of Religion — *Charles Grandison Finney.* 1001
Left Behind series — *Tim LaHaye and Jerry B. Jenkins* 1005
Left to Tell — *Immaculée Ilibagiza.* 1010
"Letter from Birmingham Jail" — *Martin Luther King, Jr.* 1014
Letters and Papers from Prison — *Dietrich Bonhoeffer* 1018
Letters from the Earth — *Mark Twain* 1021
The Letters of Saint Jerome — *Saint Jerome* 1024

page

Letters to a Young Catholic — *George Weigel* 1029
Life Abundant — *Sallie McFague* 1033
Life Is Worth Living — *Fulton J. Sheen* 1037
A Life of Jesus — *Shūsaku Endō* 1040

Volume 3

The Life of Jesus — *Ernest Renan* 1043
The Life of Jesus Critically Examined — *David Friedrich Strauss* 1046
The Lilies of the Field — *William E. Barrett* 1050
The List — *Robert Whitlow* 1054
The Little Flowers of St. Francis — *Unknown* 1058
Loaves and Fishes — *Dorothy Day* 1062
The Long Trail Home — *Stephen A. Bly* 1066
The Lord — *Romano Guardini* 1070
The Lord of the Rings — *J. R. R. Tolkien* 1073
The Lord's Prayer and the Beatitudes — *Saint Gregory of Nyssa* 1078
Love Comes Softly series — *Janette Oke* 1082

Magnificent Obsession — *Lloyd C. Douglas* 1087
A Man for All Seasons — *Robert Bolt* 1090
The Man Nobody Knows — *Bruce Barton* 1094
The Man Who Died — *D. H. Lawrence* 1098
The Marriage of Heaven and Hell — *William Blake* 1102
Mary Magdalene — *Ellen Gunderson Traylor* 1106
The Master and Margarita — *Mikhail Bulgakov* 1110
Mater et Magistra — *John XXIII* 1114
The Meaning of Persons — *Paul Tournier* 1118
The Meaning of Prayer — *Harry Emerson Fosdick* 1121
Meeting Jesus Again for the First Time — *Marcus J. Borg* 1125
Memoirs of Pontius Pilate — *James R. Mills* 1128
Memories, Dreams, Reflections — *Carl Gustav Jung* 1131
The Merchant of Venice — *William Shakespeare* 1135
Mercy's Face — *David Craig* 1139
Mere Christianity — *C. S. Lewis* 1143
The Metaphysical Demonstration of the Existence of God —
    Francisco Suárez 1147
Midquest — *Fred Chappell* 1151
The Mind of the Maker — *Dorothy L. Sayers* 1155
The Mind's Road to God — *Saint Bonaventure* 1159

page

The Miracle of the Bells — *Russell Janney* 1164

Misquoting Jesus — *Bart D. Ehrman* 1168

Mit brennender Sorge — *Pius XI* 1172

Moments of Grace — *Elizabeth Jennings* 1176

Morte d'Urban — *J. F. Powers* 1180

Music to Die For — *Radine Trees Nehring* 1184

My God and I — *Lewis B. Smedes* 1188

The Mystical Element of Religion — *Baron Friedrich von Hügel* 1191

Mystical Theology — *Pseudo-Dionysius the Areopagite* 1197

Mysticism — *Evelyn Underhill* 1200

The Name of the Rose — *Umberto Eco* 1204

The Nature and Destiny of Man — *Reinhold Niebuhr* 1207

A New Kind of Christian — *Brian D. McLaren* 1211

A New Song — *Jan Karon* 1215

New Testament Letters — *Saint Paul* 1219

Newpointe 911 — *Terri Blackstock* 1223

No Greater Love — *Mother Teresa* 1227

North of Hope — *Jon Hassler* 1230

The Nun's Story — *Kathryn C. Hulme* 1234

Octogesima Adveniens — *Paul VI* 1238

"Ode: Intimations of Immortality" — *William Wordsworth* 1241

Of Learned Ignorance — *Nicholas of Cusa* 1245

On Being a Christian — *Hans Küng* 1249

On Christian Theology — *Rowan Williams* 1252

On Divine Love — *John Duns Scotus* 1255

On First Principles — *Origen* 1259

On Listening to Another — *Douglas V. Steere* 1263

On Loving God — *Saint Bernard of Clairvaux* 1268

On Providence — *Ulrich Zwingli* 1272

On the Freedom of the Will — *Desiderius Erasmus* 1276

On the Incarnation of the Word of God — *Saint Athanasius
   of Alexandria* 1280

On the Truth of Holy Scripture — *John Wyclif* 1284

One Tuesday Morning — *Karen Kingsbury* 1288

The Orthodox Church — *Timothy Ware* 1291

Orthodoxy — *G. K. Chesterton* 1295

Out of My Life and Thought — *Albert Schweitzer* 1299

Out of the Red Shadow — *Anne de Graaf* 1303

Oxygen — *Randall Scott Ingermanson and John B. Olson* 1307

page

Pacem in Terris — *John XXIII* 1311
Paradise Lost — *John Milton* 1315
Paradise Regained — *John Milton* 1319
Passing by Samaria — *Sharon Ewell Foster* 1323
Paul — *Walter Wangerin, Jr.* 1327
Pearl — *Mary Gordon* 1331
Pearl — *Pearl-Poet* 1335
The Penitent Magdalene — *David Brendan Hopes* 1339
Pensées — *Blaise Pascal* 1342
Phantastes — *George MacDonald* 1346
Philokalia — *Scott Cairns* 1350
Philosophy of Existence — *Karl Jaspers* 1354
The Philosophy of Existentialism — *Gabriel Marcel* 1358
Piers Plowman — *William Langland* 1362
The Pilgrim's Progress — *John Bunyan* 1366
A Place Called Wiregrass — *Michael Morris* 1371
The Place of the Lion — *Charles Williams* 1375
A Plain Account of Christian Perfection — *John Wesley* 1378
The Poisonwood Bible — *Barbara Kingsolver* 1384
The Politics of Jesus — *John H. Yoder* 1389
Pontius Pilate — *Roger Caillois* 1393
Populorum Progressio — *Paul VI* 1397
The Power and the Glory — *Graham Greene* 1401
The Power of Positive Thinking — *Norman Vincent Peale* 1405
A Prayer for Owen Meany — *John Irving* 1408
Praying God's Word — *Beth Moore* 1412
The Presence of the Word — *Walter J. Ong* 1415
Prison Meditations of Father Alfred Delp — *Alfred Delp* 1419
Prison Meditations on Psalms 51 and 31 — *Girolamo Savonarola* 1423
The Problem of Christianity — *Josiah Royce* 1426
The Prodigal Girl — *Grace Livingston Hill* 1430
Prophesy Deliverance! — *Cornel West* 1434
The Protestant Ethic and the Spirit of Capitalism —
    Max Weber 1438
Psalms — *David* 1442
Purity of Heart Is to Will One Thing — *Søren Kierkegaard* 1446
The Purpose Driven Life — *Rick Warren* 1452

Quadragesimo Anno — *Pius XI* 1455
Questions for Ecclesiastes — *Mark Jarman* 1459
Quo Vadis — *Henryk Sienkiewicz* 1462

page

The Reasonableness of Christianity as Delivered in the Scriptures —
John Locke 1466
Reconciliation — *John W. de Gruchy*. 1470
The Red and the Black — *Stendhal* 1474
Redeeming Love — *Francine Rivers* 1478
Religio Medici — *Sir Thomas Browne* 1482
Religion — *Leszek Kołakowski* 1486
Religion in the Making — *Alfred North Whitehead* 1490
Religion Within the Bounds of Mere Reason — *Immanuel Kant*. 1494
Rerum Novarum — *Leo XIII* 1498
Resting in the Bosom of the Lamb — *Augusta Trobaugh* 1502
The Resurrection of God Incarnate — *Richard Swinburne*. 1506
Revelation and Reason — *Emil Brunner* 1510
The Rime of the Ancient Mariner — *Samuel Taylor Coleridge* 1514
A River Runs Through It — *Norman Maclean* 1518
The Robe — *Lloyd C. Douglas* 1522
Rose — *Li-Young Lee* 1525
Rule of St. Benedict — *Benedict of Nursia* 1529

Saint Joan — *George Bernard Shaw* 1533
Saint Manuel Bueno, Martyr — *Miguel de Unamuno y Jugo* 1537
Saint Maybe — *Anne Tyler* 1541
Sapphics and Uncertainties — *Timothy Steele* 1545
The Scarlet Letter — *Nathaniel Hawthorne* 1549
Scenes of Clerical Life — *George Eliot* 1553
Science and Health with Key to the Scriptures — *Mary Baker Eddy*. 1557
The Screwtape Letters — *C. S. Lewis*. 1560
The Seal of Gaia — *Marlin Maddoux*. 1564
The Second Coming — *Walker Percy* 1568
Secrets in the Dark — *Frederick Buechner*. 1571
The Secrets of Barneveld Calvary — *James C. Schaap* 1574
The Sense of the Presence of God — *John Baillie* 1578

Volume 4

A Serious Call to a Devout and Holy Life — *William Law*. 1581
The Sermons and Treatises — *Johannes Eckhart* 1586
The Seven Storey Mountain — *Thomas Merton* 1591
The Seventh Seal — *Ingmar Bergman* 1595
She Who Is — *Elizabeth A. Johnson* 1598

page

The Shepherd of the Hills — *Harold Bell Wright* 1602
The Shoes of the Fisherman — *Morris West* 1605
Showings — *Julian of Norwich* 1609
The Shunning — *Beverly Lewis* 1612
Silence — *Shūsaku Endō* 1616
The Silver Chalice — *Thomas B. Costain* 1620
Simply Christian — *N. T. Wright* 1624
The Singer Trilogy — *Calvin Miller* 1627
Sinners Welcome — *Mary Karr* 1631
Sir Gawain and the Green Knight — *Pearl-Poet* 1635
The Social Teaching of the Christian Churches — *Ernst Troeltsch* 1639
The Song of Albion Trilogy — *Stephen R. Lawhead* 1643
Song of the Sparrow — *Murray Bodo* 1648
Songbird — *Lisa Samson* 1651
Songs of Innocence and of Experience — *William Blake* 1655
Soon — *Jerry B. Jenkins* 1660
The Soul of Christianity — *Huston Smith* 1664
The Souls of Black Folk — *W. E. B. Du Bois* 1668
The Source of Human Good — *Henry Nelson Wieman* 1672
The Sparrow — *Mary Doria Russell* 1676
The Spiritual Exercises — *Saint Ignatius of Loyola* 1680
"Station Island" — *Seamus Heaney* 1685
The Stream and the Sapphire — *Denise Levertov* 1689
Strength to Love — *Martin Luther King, Jr.* 1693
The Subversion of Christianity — *Jacques Ellul* 1698
Suffering — *Dorothee Sölle* 1702
Summa Theologica — *Saint Thomas Aquinas* 1706
The Supplicating Voice — *Samuel Johnson* 1710
Sutter's Cross — *W. Dale Cramer* 1714
Synoptic Gospels — *Matthew, Mark,* and *Luke* 1717

The Tasks of Philosophy — *Alasdair MacIntyre* 1722
The Temple — *George Herbert* 1726
Their Eyes Were Watching God — *Zora Neale Hurston* 1730
Theodicy — *Gottfried Wilhelm Leibniz* 1734
A Theology for the Social Gospel — *Walter Rauschenbusch* 1738
A Theology of Liberation — *Gustavo Gutiérrez* 1742
A Theology of the Jewish Christian Reality — *Paul M. Van Buren* 1746
The Theory of Moral Sentiments — *Adam Smith* 1749
"They Are All Gone into the World of Light!" — *Henry Vaughan* 1753
The Third Spiritual Alphabet — *Francisco de Osuna* 1756
This Present Darkness — *Frank E. Peretti* 1760

page

The Thorn Birds — *Colleen McCullough*. 1764
Thr3e — *Ted Dekker* 1768
Three Essays — *Albrecht Ritschl* 1772
The Three Hardest Words in the World to Get Right —
  Leonard Sweet 1776
"Three Versions of Judas" — *Jorge Luis Borges* 1779
Tiger in the Shadows — *Debbie Wilson* 1782
Time Lottery — *Nancy Moser* 1786
To Kill a Mockingbird — *Harper Lee* 1790
To Scorch or Freeze — *Donald Davie* 1794
Transgression — *Randall Scott Ingermanson*. 1798
Traveling Mercies — *Anne Lamott* 1802
A Treatise Concerning Religious Affections — *Jonathan Edwards* 1806
Treatise on Divine Predestination — *John Scotus Erigena*. 1812
The Trip to Bountiful — *Horton Foote* 1816
The Triumph of Love — *Geoffrey Hill* 1820
True Honor — *Dee Henderson* 1823
The Truth Teller — *Angela Elwell Hunt* 1827
The Twilight of Courage — *Bodie Thoene and Brock Thoene* 1830
Two from Galilee — *Marjorie Holmes* 1834

Unattainable Earth — *Czesław Miłosz* 1837
Uncle Tom's Cabin — *Harriet Beecher Stowe* 1841
The Uneasy Conscience of Modern Fundamentalism —
  Carl F. H. Henry 1845
Unspeakable — *Os Guinness* 1849
The Unutterable Beauty — *G. A. Studdert Kennedy* 1853

The Varieties of Religious Experience — *William James* 1856
Velma Still Cooks in Leeway — *Vinita Hampton Wright* 1862
Veritatis Splendor — *John Paul II* 1866
The Vicar of Wakefield — *Oliver Goldsmith*. 1870
A View of the Evidences of Christianity — *William Paley*. 1875
Violence and the Sacred — *René Girard* 1879
Virgin Time — *Patricia Hampl*. 1883
The Vocation of Man — *Johann Gottlieb Fichte*. 1887

Waiting for God — *Simone Weil* 1891
Waiting for Godot — *Samuel Beckett*. 1897
Walking by Faith — *Angelina Emily Grimké*. 1901
War in Heaven — *Charles Williams* 1905
Warranted Christian Belief — *Alvin Plantinga* 1909

page

The Way of All Flesh — *Samuel Butler* 1913
The Way to Christ — *Jakob Böhme*. 1917
We Hold These Truths — *John Courtney Murray, S.J.*. 1923
What Are People For? — *Wendell Berry* 1927
What I Think I Did — *Larry Woiwode* 1931
What Jesus Meant — *Garry Wills*. 1934
When Jesus Came to Harvard — *Harvey Cox* 1937
While Mortals Sleep — *Jack Cavanaugh*. 1941
The Wind in the Wheat — *Reed Arvin* 1945
"The Windhover" — *Gerard Manley Hopkins* 1949
The Winter Garden — *Johanna Verweerd* 1953
Wise Blood — *Flannery O'Connor*. 1957
With Head and Heart — *Howard Thurman*. 1961
With the Grain of the Universe — *Stanley Hauerwas* 1965
The Woman of the Pharisees — *François Mauriac* 1968
Wonderful Words of Life — *Richard J. Mouw and Mark A. Noll* 1972
"A Word made Flesh is seldom" — *Emily Dickinson* 1976

Bibliography. 1979
Electronic Resources 1986
Chronological List of Titles. 1994
Core Issues Index 2007
Genre Index 2058
Geographical Index 2082

Title Index III
Author Index XIII

MASTERPLOTS II

CHRISTIAN LITERATURE

EDITOR'S INTRODUCTION

In the beginning was the Word. . . . (John 1:1)

More than two billion persons, about one-third of the earth's population, embrace Christianity, the largest of the world's religions. *Masterplots II: Christian Literature* illustrates and explores how people have used words to develop the Christian tradition. Without the variety of the writings discussed in this book, which include historic and contemporary works from many different genres, Christianity's existence and global reach would be inconceivable. The works selected provide a representative sample of the writings and styles of expression that have been the most influential in Christianity's ongoing development.

The Importance of Silence

Although words are indispensable for Christianity and other religious traditions, it is important in the beginning to consider some other aspects of human experience that provide the context out of which the words of religious traditions emerge. At their best, the words of religion orient people toward what is sacred and help them to act in ways that embody the highest values and ethical relationships. Such words encourage gratitude for the gift of life, reverence toward life's sources, and respect for the goodness that sustains human existence and the natural environment that is necessary for its thriving.

These attitudes of gratitude, reverence, and respect are often expressed in oral and written forms, but those dispositions also link religion with silence, a relationship reflected in the fact that all religious traditions make room for quiet reflection. Religions recognize that humble, meditative silence can be the most fitting response, at least at times, to the awe-inspiring reality of a universe that includes humanity.

Much of the Christian literature discussed in this book, including the Bible, the most fundamental text of the Christian tradition, emphasizes the importance of silence. Consisting both of the New Testament, which is explicitly and definitively Christian, and the Hebrew scriptures that are normative for Judaism, writings that Christians typically call the Old Testament, the Christian Bible's testimony about the importance of silence in spiritual life includes examples such as the following: Ecclesiastes (3:7) stresses that there is not only "a time to speak" but also "a time to keep silence." All the earth, says the Hebrew prophet Habakkuk (2:20), should keep worshipful silence before the Holy One, who creates and sustains the world. Psalm 46 urges men and women to "be still" (v. 10) so that the majesty and works of the Lord can be known. Such counsel is not found exclusively in Jewish and Christian scripture. Key writings from many other religions emphasize related themes too.

Experience leads people to wonder: Why does the world exist? Does human life have any ultimate purpose? What happens when a person dies? How can there be justice when people inflict so much pain, suffering, and death on one another? Both indi-

vidually and within the communities that shape human life, what should people do
with their fleeting time and finite energy? Religions respond to life's fundamental
questions in their own distinctive ways, but thoughtful religion rejects careless chatter
and cheap certainty about such matters and the passionate experiences of courage and
love, loss and grief, out of which they emerge. Instead, sound religion helps people to
cope with the silence encountered by their most heartfelt yearnings, which it does, at
least in part, by enabling them to see that there are times and places where nothing
substitutes for unpretentious stillness in response to life's impenetrable mysteries.

Religions speak about, describe, and interpret the sacred in multiple ways, but silence has places in them all because human beings are limited and fragile. Their experiences include fears and hopes; their minds and memories intensify needs and
questions. Humanity's religious expressions indicate that these hungers cannot be
satisfied or even addressed fully by human reason alone. Through its claims about
revelation or enlightenment and their sacred sources, which are said to transcend human finitude, religions offer access to reality and truth that is not constrained by the
limits of reason. Nevertheless, reality may not be grasped absolutely by any single religious tradition, and there is enough difference among those traditions that they cannot all be equally true or even reduced to a simple common denominator that is beyond questioning or criticism. More than likely, no religious tradition apprehends
truth infallibly, and reality eludes them all at least to some extent. As the New Testament's well-known thirteenth chapter of 1 Corinthians puts the point, "now we see in
a mirror, dimly, . . . now I know only in part" (v. 12). Ultimately, Christianity and
other religious traditions affirm, those circumstances may change, and perhaps beyond death enlightenment and fulfillment become more adequate if not complete.
Meanwhile silence—the presence of an absence of total enlightenment and fulfillment—remains.

The Words of Creation

Religion is a response to silence that calls for and recedes into silence in return.
That relationship and awareness of it, however, would not be imaginable without
words that identify and evoke, explore and communicate the multiple dimensions of
those realities. If people lacked language, if they could neither hear nor speak words
meaningfully, and in many cases write and read them as well, there would be relatively little, if anything, that human beings could recognize or remember as sacred
and holy. Without an evolving connection between silence and speech—written as
well as oral—the varieties of religious experience would be very different, if they
could be said to exist at all.

Religious traditions often link the very existence of the universe to words that
break through silence, even as words unavoidably bring dimensions of silence with
them. The opening words of Genesis, the first biblical book that Judaism and Christianity share, illustrate these themes. "In the beginning when God created the heavens
and the earth," says Genesis, "the earth was a formless void and darkness covered the
face of the deep, while a wind from God swept over the face of the waters. Then God

said, 'Let there be light'; and there was light. And God saw that the light was good; and God separated the light from the darkness. God called the light Day, and the darkness he called Night. And there was evening and there was morning, the first day" (Genesis 1:1-5).

In this narrative, one that stands at the heart of Christianity because it is at the core of Judaism, the tradition out of which Christianity emerged two millennia ago, God's word broke through and stood out against the silence of the formless void, bringing the world into existence through a process that linked silence and speech. On the sixth day, Genesis continues, God's voice called humankind to life, creating male and female in God's own image. As one version of that creation story stresses, God made humanity responsible for naming other living creatures, an action that involved words breaking through and standing out against silence in ways that symbolize humankind's ongoing accountability for the world.

Genesis makes clear that God's creation of the world led to human history. As that history unfolded, Jewish texts such as Genesis came into existence. Their breaking of silence eventually led to Christian writings. Looming large among them is the Gospel of John, one of four books in the New Testament that concentrate especially on the life of Jesus, a Jew from Nazareth. Jesus did not intentionally found the Christian religion. According to the New Testament book that is called the Acts of the Apostles, an early version of Christian history, the followers of Jesus were first called Christians in Antioch, an ancient city located in what is present-day Turkey. That first century designation came after Jesus' death. In fact, the term "Christian" appears only a few times in the New Testament. Without question, however, Jesus of Nazareth is the Christian tradition's foundational figure. Without him and his earliest disciples, all of whom were Jews, there would be no Christian religion.

Usually the scriptures of religious traditions are interpreted to have a divine and holy source. Their truth, these traditions often say, is revealed to human beings. Human minds and hands are inspired to speak and write what is revealed, but the words of scripture are not reducible to human thoughts and terms alone. Nevertheless, those writings, which frequently have origins in oral testimony and are edited and revised before they take authoritative written form, appear at particular times and places in history. For example, tradition identifies John, one of Jesus' original twelve disciples, as the author of the Gospel of John. However, scholars who study the development of scripture tend to affirm that this text probably was not written by that disciple. Their work suggests that this text was attributed to John by the early Christian community from which the narrative emerged late in the first century of the common era (C.E.). This dating places the Gospel of John some sixty years after the Roman authorities in Palestine crucified Jesus (c. 30 C.E.) because they considered him to be a political threat who would incite the Jews in Palestine, a Roman colony at the time, to rebel against their overlords. Whatever the precise date and exact origins of the Gospel of John may be, there is no question that it has long been a definitive and authoritative example of Christian literature.

The Word Made Flesh

None of the many significant features of John's gospel has been more central for Christianity than its opening or prologue, which echoes and augments the breaking of silence found in the creation accounts of Genesis. "In the beginning," the Gospel of John repeats. But then this Christian scripture adds that "the Word" was in that beginning. While the meanings of John's statement are among the key issues explored in *Masterplots II: Christian Literature*, three points related to that gospel's initial claim are worth noting here.

First, the opening words of the Gospel of John show that Christianity agrees with principal aspects of its Jewish heritage. Specifically, Christians reaffirm the Jewish testimony that God breaks silence and that, symbolically if not literally, God's word, a holy speaking, creates and sustains the world. As both of these traditions unfold, moreover, God's breaking of silence includes words that extend creation by conferring responsibilities and establishing boundaries for human beings. The responsibilities and boundaries include commandments not to steal or murder, to love one's neighbor as oneself, to relieve suffering, and to extend hospitality to the stranger. They also include an outlook that makes it imperative for men and women to love and honor God, the Holy One, with all their heart, soul, and strength. It is understood, moreover, that these requirements are inseparable. One cannot love and honor God apart from respecting and serving one's fellow human beings. Only through caring for life and respecting each and every member of the human family, all of whom bear God's image, does a person truly love and honor God. If people shirk their God-given responsibilities and boundaries, then they menace human existence and imperil the entire creation.

Second, while John depends on Judaism in vital ways, the opening of that gospel also identifies Christianity's most important and decisive departure from the Jewish ways that gave birth to the Christian faith. When John speaks about "the Word," the text still echoes Judaism by referring to God as the One who creates, orders, and sustains creation and its varied forms of life, separating light from darkness and ensuring that darkness does not overcome the light. But then John departs dramatically from Judaism by declaring that "the Word became flesh and lived among us" (John 1:14). According to John and the Christian tradition, this embodiment—Christians call it incarnation—is a breaking of silence that took place in and through the Jew named Jesus. Thus, Jesus is the person whom Christians call the Christ, the Messiah, Lord, Savior, and Son of God because, contrary to the Jewish tradition, they affirm that God is revealed distinctively in Jesus.

Christians believe that the resurrection of Jesus after he was crucified and buried is crucial to that revelation. For Christians, the resurrection of Jesus signifies not only God's power over every force and sin that wastes life, indeed over death itself, but also and especially God's gracious love for the world and humanity, a central conviction that Christians take to be supported by the life, teachings, and sacrificial death of Jesus. As one of the best-known passages of Christian scripture—it also comes from John—puts this point, "God so loved the world that he gave his only Son, so that everyone who believes in him may not perish but may have eternal life" (John 3:16).

According to Christianity, all men and women are sinners. No one fully succeeds in doing all that God expects and deserves from him or her. That failure is not simply the result of mistakes made in ignorance; it involves self-centered rebellion against God and refusal to obey God's word. Through Jesus, Christians say, God shows that humanity's fallen ways need not persist. By following and relying on Jesus as Lord, the Christian testimony claims, forgiveness, new life, and redemption can be found. Indeed, Christians affirm, the presence of God in Jesus Christ tells the world that the Kingdom of God is coming. Christians express that hope in the words of the Lord's Prayer, another foundational text, in which Jesus teaches his followers to say, "Our Father in heaven, hallowed be your name. Your kingdom come. Your will be done, on earth as it is in heaven" (Matthew 6:10-11).

Attracted to Jesus through the experiences they have had, which in the twenty-first century include a history of countless testimonies and narratives about his healing and saving presence in human lives, Christians are those who confess that Jesus is their Lord and Savior and who try to embody Jesus' ways in their own lives. Those ways are often mapped in stories told by Jesus. One of the finest examples of these parables, as Jesus' stories are frequently called, is about a good Samaritan (Luke 10:25-37) who saved a stranger who was robbed and nearly beaten to death by thieves. Jesus used this story to illustrate that love for neighbors requires caring for needy people who may be very different from one's family, friends, or community. When Christians truly practice what they preach, they try to be like the good Samaritan, working diligently and steadfastly to bring God's kingdom closer to reality on earth. Their efforts to follow Jesus typically affirm that faith in Jesus as Lord and faithfulness in living as Jesus taught ultimately save individuals from destruction and death and redeem the world from the dire straits into which it perpetually falls, as history's violence, corruption, and suffering so graphically and persistently show. The centrality of Jesus as the incarnation of God in history, as the embodiment of the Word that breaks the silence of darkness and death with light, love, and life, gives Christianity its particularity and distinctiveness among the world's religions.

Third, Christianity's emphasis on Jesus had crucial consequences that went beyond the fledgling religion's first century struggles to define itself in a primarily Jewish context. One of them was that even though Jews overwhelmingly rejected Christian claims about Jesus, his early Jewish followers, especially the apostle Paul, were convinced that they should share their Christian message with the world. In the words of Matthew, another of the New Testament's gospels, they were directed by Jesus himself to "make disciples of all nations" (Matthew 28:19). Thus, Christianity became and has continued to be a faith that takes seriously the importance of converting people to follow Jesus and to accept him as Lord, the saving Son of God.

Christianity's early evangelism in the Roman Empire frequently met resistance that led to repression of the new religion and deadly persecution of its adherents. Nevertheless, Christian influence grew and spread. By the end of the fourth century, not only had Christianity become the empire's official religion but also the religion's leaders had established key institutional, church structures, set normative teachings and doctrines into creedal forms, and identified the canonical contents of the New Testament, which included four Gospels, twenty-one Epistles (several of them authored by Paul), the Acts of the Apostles, and Revelation, which envisions what will happen when history ends and God's dominion over all will be revealed finally and completely. These steps enabled Christianity to gain increasing power to expand its mission and to multiply its impact in Western civilization and eventually throughout the world.

The Impact and Global Context of Christian Words

Opinions differ about how to evaluate Christianity's effects, but there is no doubt that they have been and continue to be enormous. As with all religions, Christianity's accomplishments and shortcomings are many and diverse. They range, for example, from sacrificial service, artistic grandeur, commitment to education, and resistance against tyranny and human rights abuses, on one hand, to dogmatism, intolerance, imperialism, and complicity in racism and violence, on the other. Christianity's long record of anti-Jewish hostility has been especially regrettable.

Christianity's antagonism toward Jews and Judaism had numerous roots. Some are in the Gospel of John. For instance, no sooner does John identify Jesus, a Jew, as the embodiment of the Word than the text states that "his own people did not accept him." For centuries, Christianity taught that Jewish rejection of Jesus contributed decisively to his crucifixion, but even more than that, Christians came to see that rejection as an act of deicide, the attempted murder of God.

More than sixty times, far more than in the New Testament's other three gospels (Matthew, Mark, and Luke) taken together, John uses the term *hoi Ioudaioi*—"the Jews," as that Greek phrase has typically been translated—and often "the Jews" are vilified as benighted disbelievers who rebel against God's grace and truth. In John, "the Jews" cry repeatedly for Jesus' death when he is put on trial before the Roman governor Pontius Pilate. One result is that John attributes a satanic character to those Jews who reject Jesus. At one point, John depicts Jesus as saying to Jews who challenge his authority, "If God were your Father, you would love me, for I came from God and now I am here. I did not come on my own, but he sent me. Why do you not understand what I say? It is because you cannot accept my word. You are from your father the devil, and you choose to do your father's desires" (John 8:42-44).

In recent years, biblical scholars—Christians and Jews alike—have worked carefully to produce translations and interpretations of John that are both more accurate and less destructive as far as that text's views about Jews are concerned. Their scholarship clarifies that John's negative rhetoric about "the Jews" should not be taken to refer to the Jewish people as a whole but only to some Jewish leaders and synagogue authorities in a particular historical context. Unfortunately, centuries-long reading and interpretation of John did not reflect those important qualifications, and the outcome meant that there has been no defamation of comparable severity by one religious tradition of another. That defamation, moreover, had tragic consequences because the ascription of a satanic nature to Jews had the effect of legitimating abuse against them. If every single man, woman, and child of the Jewish community is of the devil—and this is one implication of the defamation as it was typically understood—then no one needed to have many qualms about how Jews were treated. Even violence perpetrated against them could be defended as consistent with God's judgment.

Under Adolf Hitler and his Third Reich (1933-1945), the European Jews were nearly annihilated in the genocide that is called the Holocaust. Christianity alone did not cause the Holocaust, but its anti-Jewish hostility played devastating parts in making that catastrophe possible. Only after the Holocaust has the Christian tradition fundamentally revised its basic teachings about Jews and Judaism, a process that is still under way and full of difficulty because it raises anew primary questions about how John's claim that "the Word became flesh and lived among us" should and should not be understood.

Post-Holocaust revision and reformation of the Christian tradition are by no means the first of the watershed challenges and changes that have been part of Christianity's history. As the articles in *Masterplots II: Christian Literature* repeatedly show, there is no one-size-fits-all version of Christianity. Try as various "authorities" have tried to do over the centuries, Christians are of many and often contentious minds about what Christian faith means and Christian practice requires. Significant evidence to support that claim is found in Christianity's numerous churches, liturgies, biblical interpretations, and theologies. Their history and the implications of their development are traced in many of the essays that follow.

In Western civilization, the Roman Catholic Church long dominated with its papacy and hierarchical structure, but far from being uniform and unvaried, Roman Catholics, the largest Christian community, have been and continue to be remarkably diversified and differentiated. In the sixteenth century, Martin Luther, John Calvin, and other dissenters protested against Roman Catholic authority and launched what came to be known as the Protestant Reformation. Far from resulting only in a two-way split between Roman Catholics and Protestants, however, the Reformation multiplied churches and proliferated traditions. Christians periodically call for a restoration of unity, rightly suggesting that Jesus scarcely envisioned a world religion with a vast number of denominations and apparently unending divisions among them, but such calls appear unlikely to reduce the pluralism that has become one of Christianity's hallmarks.

Meanwhile, Christianity is situated more and more in a global context that contains inescapable interaction with the world's non-Christian religions. With the twenty-first century well under way, Christianity's influence wanes in Europe while it grows in Africa and Asia, but the Christian tradition, large and widespread though its presence continues to be, increasingly encounters Islam, Buddhism, Hinduism, Judaism, and other faiths in ways that make it less easy for Christianity to assume the triumphal superiority and exclusivism that it has often claimed for itself.

The Christian tradition is no exception to the rule that the identities of religious traditions are not fixed and settled once and for all. Each tradition has to locate the balance that combines strong continuity with its history and its fundamental beliefs and practices, on one hand, with sufficient flexibility and nimbleness, on the other, so that it can adapt to unfamiliar circumstances and to the fresh callings of its own spirit in ways that keep the tradition relevant, timely, and meaningful in a world of change. In the twenty-first century, these needs mean that Christians have to place priority on what their faith should say about the relationship between Christianity and the other major religions of the world. In addition, the contemporary Christian agenda includes the need to determine what Christianity should say about dilemmas such as global warming, abortion, gay marriage, HIV/AIDS, poverty, international relations, war, capital punishment, and much more. The decisions that are taken about these matters involve more than politics and public policy, although they are inseparable from those areas of human life because, in one way or another, Christianity, like every religion, mixes, mingles, and frequently collides with politics and culture. For Christians, the ethical stands that are taken have to be informed and defined by a sound grasp of God's will and sensitivity about what it means to follow Jesus. Honesty requires Christians to acknowledge that such insight and agreement about it are not likely to be achieved easily.

According to the New Testament, God sent Jesus "to bring good news to the poor, . . . to proclaim release to the captives and recovery of sight to the blind, to let the oppressed go free, to proclaim the year of the Lord's favor" (Luke 4:18-19). From the origins of the Christian religion until the present day, as the essays in *Christian Literature* help to make clear, Christians keep wrestling over and often disagreeing about what the followers of Jesus should make of those words, which keep breaking the silence of indifference and injustice.

The Affirmations of Christian Literature

Just as there is no one-size-fits-all interpretation of Christianity itself, there is no single definition that determines what does and does not count as Christian literature. As this introduction suggests, however, one could say that Christian literature basically includes writings that, in one way or another, affirm a version of the fundamental claim in the Gospel of John: "In the beginning was the Word, and the Word was with God, and the Word was God. . . . And the Word became flesh and lived among us, . . . full of grace and truth."

The word "affirm" does not mean, at least not necessarily, uncritical acceptance, unthinking belief, or uncontested commitment. To the contrary, affirmation is often hard-won; it may take place only after a critical sifting and sorting of experience, testimony, and tradition. Affirmation does not exclude questioning and argument, but may result from and even require those activities; it may be the outcome of encounters with silence that persists and remains. Nor is affirming limited to a specific form of expression. Affirmation can be voiced, for example, in multiple styles and patterns of writing. They can include fiction and poetry, philosophy and theology, prayer and hymn, history and the close reading and interpretation of religious texts and scripture such as the Gospel of John itself.

The acts of affirming often entail dialogue and disagreement with previous affirmations that have been made within a tradition such as Christianity. To affirm a version of John's fundamental claim about Jesus of Nazareth may entail rejection of what some earlier Christian interpretations have held; it may involve revisions and even the breaking of silence in new and creative ways. But literature will not rightly be called Christian if it strays too far beyond the claim that "the Word became flesh and lived among us." Where that line is crossed, however, is likely to remain debatable. Some writings will belong in the category of Christian literature more obviously than others. In some cases, the writings may be in a gray zone where the call could go either way. That fact means, as the pages to come bear witness, that Christian literature consists of genres, approaches, and perspectives whose historical sweep is as vast as their variety is immense.

"In the beginning was the Word." From that Christian claim so many words have flowed and will continue to do so. The essays that follow in these pages show how key examples of Christian literature—ancient, contemporary, and in between—have used words to develop a religious tradition that continues to offer its insight and help for encountering, coping with, and hopefully breaking open the silence that pervades the human journey.

John K. Roth

THE BIBLE IN HISTORY

No book has influenced history more than the Bible. Christianity's definitive text, the Bible is one book, but not in any simple way, because it contains numerous parts and exists in multiple versions. Their formation has a complex history. Christians regard the Bible as God's revealed word, but they also acknowledge that human beings wrote the texts and put them into a particular order. Furthermore, Christians have translated the original biblical writings into many languages and interpreted them in diverse and even conflicting ways. The Bible's influence on history is inseparable from the history of the Bible itself.

The Printed Word

Among the many points of departure that could begin an overview of the Bible's place in history and its essential significance for the Christian tradition in particular, one of the most important involves the German printer Johannes Gutenberg (1394/ 1399-1468). He invented movable metal type for each of the Western alphabet's twenty-six letters. This mass-produced type could be set in any sequence, making it possible for copies of previously hand-copied or block-printed manuscripts to be produced rapidly and in multiple copies. No result of Gutenberg's breakthrough would have greater significance than his printing of the Bible, which took place around 1455 in Mainz, Germany.

Gutenberg's Bible was the first major book to be printed in Europe. Of the approximately 180 original copies, about 50 still exist. Arguably, no books in the world are more famous or valuable. More important, since Gutenberg's watershed accomplishment, the Bible has always been in print. It remains the most widely distributed and best-selling book in the world. The Bible is widely accessible. In the twenty-first century, the entire Christian Bible exists in more than 325 languages, and parts of it have been translated into more than two thousand. The number of translations continues to grow as more than seventy-five Bible societies worldwide seek to make this book available in more of the world's estimated three to six thousand languages.

Whose Bible, Which One, Did Gutenberg Print?

Nothing in print tops the Bible's religious and cultural importance. Its impact, of course, did not originate with Gutenberg's revolutionary printing process. Centuries before his movable type multiplied and extended the reach of biblical words, the Bible had long affected history in ways that were no less significant than they would become in their post-Gutenberg phases. Both before and after Gutenberg, moreover, the Bible's historical effects have been inseparable from the history of the book itself. Those claims can be clarified and elaborated by inquiry about a tantalizing question: Whose Bible, which one, did Gutenberg print?

A first response to that question is that Gutenberg's Bible was Christian scripture. As will be seen in what follows below, Christians have not always agreed about all the

VERSIONS OF THE BIBLE

Tanakh/Jewish-Hebrew Scripture

Torah	Prophets	Writings
Genesis	Joshua	Psalms
Exodus	Judges	Proverbs
Leviticus	Samuel (1 & 2)	Job
Numbers	Kings (1 & 2)	Song of Solomon
Deuteronomy	Isaiah	Ruth
	Jeremiah	Lamentations
	Ezekiel	Ecclesiastes
	The Twelve:	Esther
	Hosea	Daniel
	Joel	Ezra-Nehemiah
	Amos	Chronicles (1 & 2)
	Obadiah	
	Jonah	
	Micah	
	Nahum	
	Habakkuk	
	Zephaniah	
	Haggai	
	Zechariah	
	Malachi	

Roman Catholic Bibles
Old Testament

Genesis	Judith	Daniel
Exodus	Esther (with the Additions)	Prayer of Azariah and the
Leviticus	1 Maccabees	Song of the Three Jews
Numbers	2 Maccabees	Susanna
Deuteronomy	Job	Bel and the Dragon
Joshua	Psalms	Hosea
Judges	Proverbs	Joel
Ruth	Ecclesiastes	Amos
1 Samuel	Song of Solomon	Obadiah
2 Samuel	Wisdom of Solomon	Jonah
1 Kings	Sirach (Ecclesiasticus)	Micah
2 Kings	Isaiah	Nahum
1 Chronicles	Jeremiah	Habakkuk
2 Chronicles	Lamentations	Zephaniah
Ezra	Baruch	Haggai
Nehemiah	Letter of Jeremiah	Zechariah
Tobit	Ezekiel	Malachi

(continued)

New Testament

Matthew	Ephesians	Hebrews
Mark	Philippians	James
Luke	Colossians	1 Peter
John	1 Thessalonians	2 Peter
Acts	2 Thessalonians	1 John
Romans	1 Timothy	2 John
1 Corinthians	2 Timothy	3 John
2 Corinthians	Titus	Jude
Galatians	Philemon	Revelation

Protestant Bibles (including King James Version)
Old Testament

Genesis	2 Chronicles	Daniel
Exodus	Ezra	Hosea
Leviticus	Nehemiah	Joel
Numbers	Esther	Amos
Deuteronomy	Job	Obadiah
Joshua	Psalms	Jonah
Judges	Proverbs	Micah
Ruth	Ecclesiastes	Nahum
1 Samuel	Song of Solomon	Habakkuk
2 Samuel	Isaiah	Zephaniah
1 Kings	Jeremiah	Haggai
2 Kings	Lamentations	Zechariah
1 Chronicles	Ezekiel	Malachi

New Testament

Matthew	Ephesians	Hebrews
Mark	Philippians	James
Luke	Colossians	1 Peter
John	1 Thessalonians	2 Peter
Acts	2 Thessalonians	1 John
Romans	1 Timothy	2 John
1 Corinthians	2 Timothy	3 John
2 Corinthians	Titus	Jude
Galatians	Philemon	Revelation

writings that properly belong within that category, but in Gutenberg's day and indeed throughout the tradition's history, Christians have usually concurred that scripture consists of two main parts: The Hebrew Bible, which Judaism calls Tanakh but is commonly called the Old Testament in Christianity, and the distinctively and definitively Christian writings that form the New Testament. The Bible that Gutenberg printed consisted of those two parts as their canonical (authoritative) status was understood at that time.

These writings, of course, were not just writings. They were *scripture*, words that Christians have taken to be the revealed word of God. According to that Christian understanding, these normative, canonical writings authoritatively anticipated and continue to testify to the Lordship of Jesus Christ. They have existed to govern the teaching and practice of the Christian faith, especially within the community known as the Church.

Complex Characteristics and Key Questions

Here it is important to note that both the Hebrew Bible and the Christian New Testament have complex characteristics. In some ways, each of these basic parts can be regarded as one book. Furthermore, the same can be said of the Christian Bible as a whole, which contains both parts. No less important, however, is the fact that the Hebrew Bible, the Christian New Testament, and the Christian Bible as a whole consist of many books as well. These features are reflected in the English word "bible" itself. It is derived from the Greek word *biblia*, a plural term that simply means "little books." However, as the Jewish and Christian biblical book collections came to be seen increasingly as one book, "Bible" (The Books) came to refer more and more to "The Book." In addition, already in the second century B.C.E., an adjective meaning "holy" was attached to Hebrew scriptural writings. "Holy Bible" indicated, then and now, a collection of sacred texts.

The answers vary and are often contested when key questions such as the following are raised: How many books does the Bible contain? Which ones properly belong in it? Which texts are considered canonical by some communities but not by others? Who made those decisions and with what authority were they taken? It will be necessary to deal with some of these questions later on, but at this point it should be noted that Tanakh, the title for the Hebrew Bible, is an acronym made from the first Hebrew letters of the names of the three parts of Jewish scripture: Torah, the five books of Moses (Genesis, Exodus, Leviticus, Numbers and Deuteronomy), which are also known as the Pentateuch; Nevi'im, the Prophets; and Kethuvim, the Writings. As for the contents of the New Testament, its writings include four Gospels (Matthew, Mark, Luke, and John), which concentrate on the life, teachings, death, and resurrection of Jesus, Christianity's foundational figure; the Acts of the Apostles, an account of the Christian church's earliest history; twenty-one Epistles, several of them authored by the apostle Paul; and Revelation, which envisions what will happen when history ends and God's dominion is revealed finally and completely.

Languages and Translations

Far from bringing closure to the question about Gutenberg posed above—Whose Bible, which one, did he print?—the initial response that Gutenberg's Bible was Christian scripture obviously raises more questions than it answers. They stretch back and forth in time. For instance, Gutenberg's Bible had to be printed in a specific language, but which one? In the mid-fifteenth century, the Bible had not yet been translated into his familiar German. Martin Luther (1483-1546), a key leader in Western civilization's sixteenth century Protestant Reformation, which eventually splintered Christianity into denominations that no longer accepted the authority of the Roman Catholic Church, did not finish his German translations of the New Testament and then the entire Bible until 1522 and 1534, respectively.

Gutenberg would have had no interest in printing an English version of the Bible, but in England the Oxford University philosopher and theologian John Wyclif (c. 1328-1384), a Christian reformer before Luther, had completed an English translation in 1382. Like Luther and other reformers who followed him, Wyclif thought that God's word should not be accessible only to priests, bishops, or scholars who were trained to read Hebrew and Greek, the original biblical languages, or Latin, the dominant and officially Church-sanctioned language of Christian scripture in Wyclif's time. Contrary to the Church's position that it was too difficult and even perilous for laypersons to read the Bible without the clergy's direction, Wyclif thought that people should be able to read God's word in languages of their own, for ultimately people were answerable to God alone, not to the intermediate authorities of the church or state.

When eventually coupled with Gutenberg's printing process, the idea that people could read God's word for themselves would lead to differences of biblical interpretation that made Christian communities increasingly pluralistic and often contentious, a trend that has been ongoing. In the meantime, the popularizing and unorthodox implications of Wyclif's translation of the Bible were not lost on the church establishment, which by 1409 had outlawed his English Bible. This ban against reproducing or even owning a Wyclif Bible without special permission remained in effect for more than a century. Violators could be convicted of heresy and executed. Copies of Wyclif's Bible were sometimes set ablaze, and in 1428 Wyclif's body was exhumed and burned as well.

In 1526, another Englishman, William Tyndale (1494-1536), produced the first English translation of the New Testament that was printed with the techniques Gutenberg had developed some seventy years earlier. Owing to the repressive conditions in England, Tyndale did his work in Germany, where he drew upon Luther's German edition as well as early Greek texts. Tyndale was working on an English version of the Old Testament when he returned to England only to be arrested for heresy, found guilty, strangled, and then burned at the stake.

Miles Coverdale (1488-1568) advanced Tyndale's project and completed a translation of the entire Bible into English. His edition was also printed in Germany, probably at Cologne in 1535, but when it was imported to England, the reception was different from the ones experienced by Wyclif and Tyndale. In 1534, the king of England, Henry VIII (1491-1547), had rebelled against the pope's Roman Catholic authority and become the head of the Church of England. Coverdale's translation of the Bible served Henry's interests, and it contributed importantly to the English version of Christian scripture that was officially authorized in 1539 for use in church services.

Important though they were for the development of Christianity and culture in the English-speaking world of their times, the biblical translations done by Wyclif, Tyndale, and Coverdale cannot compare with the King James version that appeared in 1611. Commissioned by King James I (1566-1625), for centuries it has been the best-known and most loved translation of the Bible. No text in the English language is more widely published, nor has any book influenced the English language and its literature more than the King James version of the Bible. By no means, however, did the King James version bring English translations of the Bible to an end. Among contemporary examples, the most widely used include *The New International Version* (1978), which is popular among conservative American Protestants; *The New Jerusalem Bible* (1985), which enjoys a following among Roman Catholics; *Tanakh* (1985), a translation of the Hebrew Bible published by the Jewish Publication Society; and the *New Revised Standard Version* (1989), a translation that is officially authorized by all major Christian churches: Protestant, Anglican, Roman Catholic, and Eastern Orthodox.

The Vulgate

All modern, national language translations of the Bible depended on much earlier texts in Hebrew, Greek, or Latin. Thus, the Bible that Gutenberg printed in the 1450's was the standard Roman Catholic version that had been dominant in Christianity for almost a thousand years. This edition of the Bible was called the Vulgate, a term indicating that its Latin language was vernacular, commonly used by people at the time that the translation took place. The Vulgate remained in use liturgically and in scholarship long after the use of Latin in daily life was supplanted by more modern languages.

The Vulgate edition of the Latin Bible remains in print and can be found on the Internet, but the translation project originated in 382 when Pope Damasus I (c. 304-384) commissioned an impressive scholar named Eusebius Hieronymus, better known as Saint Jerome (331/347-420), to carry it out. Jerome knew Hebrew and Greek, the original languages of the biblical texts, as well as Latin. Arguably the best scholar of his day, Jerome was well suited for the pope's translation project.

Already there were rough Latin translations of the New Testament Gospels: Matthew, Mark, Luke, and John. However, inconsistencies and errors corrupted those early Latin translations. These mistakes often crept into the texts as they were hand-copied by one scribe after another. Since these biblical writings were taken to be the revealed word of God, Pope Damasus wanted a reliable version. It needed to be not only as accurate as possible but also in tune with current Roman Latin, the language of government, commerce, and everyday life in the Roman Empire, where in 380 the

Byzantine emperor Theodosius (346/347-395) had proclaimed Christianity to be the state's official religion.

The Septuagint and Jerome's Dilemmas

Jerome's translation project took two decades, reaching completion in 405. Thereafter, he wrote commentaries on the biblical books, both continuing and anticipating a now extensive history of Christian biblical exegesis (interpretation) and hermeneutics (principles and theories of interpretation). Meanwhile, Jerome's translation work was complicated by the fact that he was unsatisfied by the standard Greek translation of the Hebrew scripture, which was called the Septuagint.

The Septuagint probably originated in Egypt during the early third century B.C.E. to meet the needs of Hellenistic Jews, those living in and influenced by predominantly Greek culture. The name Septuagint derived from the legendary claim that seventy-two elders from the traditional twelve tribes of Israel had completed the translation from Hebrew to Greek in seventy-two days. Those numbers were rounded to seventy—hence the name Septuagint, Greek for that number. An abbreviated title, LXX (the Roman numeral for seventy), was also used to designate this version of Hebrew scripture. The earliest fragments of the Septuagint that remain in existence date from the second century B.C.E.

The fact that the Septuagint was in Greek made it convenient for early Christians to use, since that language was familiar to them. When the New Testament, which was written in Greek, cited passages from the Hebrew Bible, those passages were taken from the Septuagint. These circumstances meant that the Septuagint's version of Hebrew scripture long enjoyed normative status in Christianity; it was this text that first became what Christians called the Old Testament.

Back to the Sources

Convinced that Christian scripture was God's word, not reducible to words that human beings wrote, Jerome believed that only the most original biblical manuscripts were thoroughly reliable. Translations of those texts could be made, but they would not be trustworthy unless they were carefully based on manuscripts that were as close to God's original inspiration as possible. This principle of biblical translation and interpretation, which Jerome did much to establish firmly, remains at the heart of contemporary biblical scholarship.

Compared to the Hebrew Bible, the New Testament is much shorter. Thus, Jerome was apparently able to finish his translations of the four Gospels in 384. He then revised other parts of the New Testament. By about 390 he was working on his translation of the Hebrew Bible, but he grew uneasy about relying on the Septuagint. To make his translation of the Old Testament as unerring as possible, he would have to go back to the original Hebrew sources. When he did so, however, more than language problems confronted him.

Jerome saw that the Septuagint included writings that were not found in the Hebrew Bible manuscripts that were available to him. This matter was not trivial. If scripture was God's revealed word, then it was crucial to identify correctly the writings that should and should not be included. To see how Jerome dealt with this problem and to discern the implications of his decisions requires discussion of an even more ancient past, with the numerous questions, ambiguities, and uncertainties that such exploration unavoidably encounters.

What Makes Writing Sacred?

How is it determined that a writing is a sacred text? At what point in the development and life of a text does that status become evident and achieve official confirmation within a community for which it is then authoritative? Each book in the Jewish and Christian Bibles has a history to which those questions are applicable, and there is no one-size-fits-all answer to them, for the biblical books were written—sometimes compiled and revised—one at a time and over a lengthy time as well. Nevertheless, the following points can be made.

The elements that make a text sacred are not exclusively divine. God may speak, as Jews and Christians claim, but if no one hears or receives God's word, literally or figuratively, there are not likely to be texts that are regarded as sacred or holy. Furthermore, unless what is taken to be God's word is written down, preserved, and proclaimed within a community that respects it as normative and gives it lasting life, then sooner or later the sense that a text is sacred or holy will probably wither away. For God's word to be revealed and received as such depends not only on God but also on a community for whom that word becomes religiously and culturally normative.

Why, however, do particular texts—and very few of them at that—obtain this status while the overwhelming majority of writing does not? Answers to that question are far from certain, but it is clear that specific experiences play a crucial part. In the Christian tradition, those experiences have everything to do with encounters between Jesus of Nazareth and his original Jewish followers, who, especially after Jesus was crucified by Roman authorities, became convinced that Jesus had been resurrected from death and that God's reality and truth were distinctively present in and through him. Early writings based on those formative experiences and their aftereffects came to be regarded by Christian communities as authoritative testimony about God's reality, nature, expectations and love for humanity, and relationship to history.

Without Jewish experience that preceded Christianity and gave it birth, the idea that God was revealed in what came to be known as the New Testament would have been incoherent and even inconceivable. Crucial to the Jewish understanding of revelation and the scripture that conveyed it was the unifying experience that God had delivered the Hebrew people from Egyptian captivity in an event known as the Exodus and then established a covenant with them that required faithful obedience to God's expectations. As these experiences were shared and communicated from one generation to another, they led to writings that, in particular, preserved and carried forward a normative understanding of what the covenant between God and the Jewish people entailed.

The Torah, which became the first five books of the Jewish scripture, loomed especially large because those writings set forth what God's most important requirements were taken to be. This part of the Hebrew Bible contains, for example, the famous Ten Commandments (Exodus 20:1-17). Various other writings, including those attributed to prophets such as Isaiah and Jeremiah, Micah and Amos, as well as poetic and reflective writings (Psalms and Job, for example), also came to be regarded as containing God's word or crucial insights about God, and thus they came to be regarded as revelational too.

As far as the identification of the canon, the officially recognized version, of the Hebrew Bible is concerned, the statement made by the historian Jaroslav Pelikan in *Whose Bible Is It? A Short History of the Scriptures* (2005) is a succinct and accurate summary:

> The safest generalization permitted is this: various collections of sacred writings were put together quite early in the history of Israel, . . . but they did not become a "canon" until much later. The name *canon* may properly be applied to the books that seem to have been adopted by the assembly of rabbis at Jamnia about 90 or 100 C.E. under the leadership of Rabbi Akiba [c. 55-132]. . . . Formally, the Jewish canon of the Bible came to include the three divisions of Torah, Nevi'im, and Kethuvim. . . . In this canon, however, the Torah has held, and holds, a special place as a "canon within the canon."

Jews and Christians, however, did not understand the revelational status of the Jewish scripture in the same way. Christian interpretations of the Hebrew Bible placed priority on the ways in which those texts prepared the way for Jesus Christ, the Messiah, and even foretold his coming. Although some Christians have contended that the Hebrew Bible is dispensable for Christianity—an early example is the Christian bishop Marcion (c. 110-c. 160 C.E.), whose arguments that the Old Testament was unworthy of scriptural status helped to force the issue of determining what the Christian canon should be—the ultimate decision was otherwise. In fact, as the early Christian leadership correctly saw it, one could scarcely make sense of the identity of Jesus, a faithful Jew, or the New Testament without the context provided by the Hebrew Bible. As an old Latin couplet identified Christianity's understanding of the relationship between the Old and New Testaments: "The New is in the Old concealed,/ The Old is in the New Revealed."

From Jewish perspectives, however, the relationship between the Hebrew Bible and the New Testament lacked such symmetry entirely. If Christians needed the Hebrew Bible to make sense of the New Testament, Jews did not need the New Testament to make sense of their sacred texts. Overwhelmingly, Jews who lived before, during, and after Jesus found nothing in their scripture that foretold the coming of Jesus, anticipated him as the Messiah promised in Jewish tradition, or, particularly foreign to Judaism, prefigured God's incarnation in human form.

For Jews, the revelation in their sacred texts focused sufficiently on what faithfulness to God's covenant with the Jewish people required. Those requirements did not at all entail belief that Jesus was the Messiah, the incarnation of God, as Christians came to affirm. From the mainstream Jewish perspective, such claims were and continue to be radical and unwarranted departures from what God's revelation truly contains. Much of the rivalry between the Christian and Jewish traditions, which has had immensely unfortunate effects for both, pivots around their divergent claims about God's revelation, sacred texts, and how to interpret their meanings and relationships.

The Christian Canon

It is not known exactly which Hebrew manuscripts of Jewish scripture were available to Jerome, but probably his comparison of the Septuagint with the more official canon of the Hebrew Bible codified by the late first century rabbis showed him that the former contained books such as the Tobit, Judith, Wisdom of Solomon, Sirach (Ecclesiasticus), Baruch, and 1 and 2 Maccabees, which had been eliminated from Jewish scripture. Therefore Jerome also withdrew these books from his Latin translation, assigning them apocryphal status, which meant that these writings were acknowledged as important religious writings that were linked with but not equivalent in authority to those that had canonical rank.

Jerome's translation of the Bible, especially its pruning of the Septuagint, was controversial, as has usually been the case when revised versions and translations of the Bible have appeared. By the time that the Latin Bible known as the Vulgate had been finalized and widely accepted as the official Christian version of the Bible, a process that took several centuries, Jerome's monumental work had been compromised. In particular, all the books he had downgraded to apocryphal status found their way back into the Christian canon, where they remained until the Protestant Reformation, which reemphasized the importance of original Hebrew sources, set them aside again.

The Old Testament

The net result for Christian understanding of scripture is that there are several versions of the Old Testament in terms of content and organization. In modern form, the Tanakh, Judaism's Hebrew Bible, includes twenty-four books, counting the Twelve Prophets as a single book. Upholding the decision taken at the Council of Trent (1546), which countered Protestant revisions by reaffirming that the Latin Vulgate was the only true Bible, Roman Catholic versions of the Old Testament include forty-six books, including the ones that Jerome had excised. Bibles in the Orthodox churches expand the Old Testament canon even further. Meanwhile, Protestant Bibles contain thirty-nine Old Testament books, counting 1 and 2 Samuel, 1 and 2 Kings, 1 and 2 Chronicles, each of the Twelve Prophets, and Ezra and Nehemiah as separate books. Some Protestant Bibles also include the apocryphal writings, which are found in the Roman Catholic and Orthodox scriptures but not in Jewish Bibles, placing them in a separate section.

The New Testament

Protestant, Catholic, and Orthodox Christians agree that the New Testament consists of twenty-seven books: four Gospels, the Acts of the Apostles, twenty-one Epistles, and Revelation. That fact does not mean, however, that the formation of the New

Testament canon came about easily. The list in an ancient document called the Muratorian Canon suggests that much of the New Testament had been defined, at least in some Christian communities, by the late second century, but it was not until late in the fourth century that the New Testament as it exists in contemporary Bibles gained general acceptance. Prior to that time, the books that eventually formed Christianity's official New Testament canon, as well as Jewish scripture, were variously but not uniformly read, studied, and used liturgically in the Roman Empire's diverse, scattered, but growing and only gradually unifying Christian communities.

In general, the writings that eventually formed the New Testament canon were those that could be traced back to the earliest Christian communities and had been useful within them. The writings that typically met such criteria were those credited to Jesus' disciples or very early apostles such as Paul. Absent that authorship identification, a writing's chances for inclusion were much more disputed if not eliminated altogether. The earliest of the explicitly Christian writings included letters written by or ascribed to Paul and addressed to various Christian communities, including those in Rome and Corinth. Among other things, these Epistles verify that early Christians were not of one mind. The New Testament's twenty-one Epistles show themselves to be part of a process to define Christian faith and identity, a work in progress ever since.

The centrality of Jesus in Christian experience and development meant that narratives about him were especially important. Biblical scholars usually assign a dating in the late 60's to Mark, which is thought to be the earliest of the Gospels, canonical or otherwise. Earlier oral traditions probably informed Mark and other written narratives about Jesus, but none of them is primarily an eyewitness account. Instead, they blend history, interpretation, and faith in ways that reflect the times, circumstances, and communities in which these texts were crafted. Numerous examples of the gospel genre existed, but only four gained canonical status. Among the others are gospels attributed to Bartholomew, Thomas, Philip, and Judas Iscariot. Even though these writings present themselves as authored by disciples of Jesus, that attribution was not sufficient for them to win canonical inclusion. Matthew, Mark, Luke, and John reflected most accurately the views about Jesus that had achieved mainstream status by the time the canon was settled in the second half of the fourth century.

In the twenty-first century, novels such as Dan Brown's *The Da Vinci Code* (2003) produced a surge of interest in the controversies and disputes that may have swirled around various gospels as their defenders strove to gain canonical status for them. As fact and fiction mix and mingle, it can at least be said that it took time and much sifting and sorting for the New Testament canon to form. Struggles for authority and power were at stake as Christians took decisive steps to determine and to close debate about what could count as God's revealed word.

The Embodied Word

The existence of Christianity is inseparable from the Bible's influences on and places within history. Significantly, in its Christian forms, the Bible places priority on the conviction that God's word was revealed not only, indeed not even foremost, in and through written texts, however much they may have been inspired by God. Even more primary is the claim that God's word and especially God's love for the world and humanity are revealed in and through a person, Jesus Christ. As the Gospel of John puts these points, "the Word became flesh and lived among us, . . . full of grace and truth" (John 1:14), and "God so loved the world that he gave his only Son, so that everyone who believes in him may not perish but may have eternal life" (John 3:16). In one way or another, all of the struggles to identify which writings should be canonical, how they should be translated, organized, and interpreted, are related to versions and implications of those beliefs, whose origins go back to the earliest followers of a Jew from Nazareth who lived two thousand years ago.

Christians are not of one mind when they say, as they commonly do, that the Bible contains God's revealed word, that the human authors or editors of its texts were inspired, led or influenced in decisive ways, by God. For some Christians, such claims entail that the Bible is literally true and even inerrant and infallible. For other Christians, biblical interpretation properly requires reflection that recognizes the presence of symbol, myth, and allegory in scripture and that necessitates philosophical exposition and critical analysis to discern and explicate scripture's meanings. Despite those differences, Christians of all kinds recognize that in vital and ongoing ways their faith depends largely on the Bible. That dependence is not simply on a book that has a history. It is also and most important a relationship that requires Christians to read and study scripture, to clarify what they believe God is still saying through its texts, and then to keep trying to the best of their abilities to embody the Bible's wisdom, it teachings and insights, in their daily lives.

Sources for Further Study

Ehrman, Bart D. *The New Testament: A Historical Introduction to the Early Christian Writings*. 3d ed. New York: Oxford University Press, 2003. Widely used in college and university courses, Ehrman's study includes insightful discussion about the controversies and decisions concerning which texts were included in or kept out of Christianity's most authoritative and essential writings.

Hamel, Christopher de. *The Book: A History of the Bible*. London: Phaidon Press, 2001. In a richly illustrated treatment, a scholar who studies ancient manuscripts analyzes the Bible in history by showing how it evolved from hand-copied texts to the multiple printed formats that have become commonplace.

Kee, Howard Clark, Eric M. Meyers, John Rogerson, and Anthony J. Saldarini. *The Cambridge Companion to the Bible*. New York: Cambridge University Press, 1997. Accompanying their analysis with helpful illustrations and maps, a highly qualified team of biblical scholars analyzes the historical, cultural, and political circumstances in which the writers of the biblical texts did their work.

Meeks, Wayne A., Jouette M. Bassler, Werner E. Lemke, Susan Niditch, and Eileen M. Schuller, eds. *The HarperCollins Study Bible*. New York: HarperCollins, 1993. In addition to containing the New Revised Standard Version of the Old and New Testaments with the Apocryphal/Deuterocanonical books, this edition includes

helpful introductions that identify the origins, structures, and themes of each biblical book as well as clear identifications of the names and order of the biblical
books in the Jewish and Christian traditions.

Metzger, Bruce M., and Michael D. Coogan, eds. *The Oxford Companion to the Bible*.
New York: Oxford University Press, 1993. Organized alphabetically by topic, this
book contains articles by more than 250 of the world's best biblical scholars, who
describe and analyze the historical development and interpretation of the Bible.

Pelikan, Jaroslav. *Whose Bible Is It? A Short History of the Scriptures*. New York:
Penguin Books, 2005. A leading historian of the Christian tradition shows how and
why the various versions of the Bible developed, paying special attention to the
ways in which Jewish and Christian scripture are alike and different.

John K. Roth

ABORTION AND DIVORCE IN WESTERN LAW

Author: Mary Ann Glendon (1938-   )
First published: Cambridge, Mass.: Harvard University Press, 1987
Genre: Nonfiction
Subgenre: Didactic treatise
Core issues: Abortion; ethics; justice; marriage; women

This academic study seeks to deepen understanding of American laws on abortion and divorce by comparing them with the analogous laws of Europe. In contrast to other Western nations' laws on abortion and divorce, American laws give scant support for the value of potential life and for the family as a unit, reflecting the American tradition of individualism and legal positivism.

Overview

Comparative law is the study of the laws and legal systems of different nations in order to deepen understanding of a particular nation's laws. This field was systematically developed by French and German scholars in the late nineteenth century. In *Abortion and Divorce in Western Law*, Harvard law professor Mary Ann Glendon uses the methods of comparative legal scholars to explain the distinctive elements of American laws regarding abortion and divorce. As she explains in the introduction, she also adopts the perspective taken in Plato's *Nomoi* (388-368 B.C.E.; *Laws*, 1804) that law is educational in purpose so that she can illuminate the differences between American and European law. Although Glendon does highlight provisions of abortion and divorce laws of European nations, in particular France and Germany, she does so largely to put American law in contrast and specifically to demonstrate that American law has embraced an extreme individual rights position on the legal spectrum.

Chapter 1 demonstrates how the laws regarding abortion in the Western world changed dramatically in the 1970's and 1980's. Of the twenty nations compared by Glendon (Austria, Belgium, Canada, Denmark, England, Finland, France, West Germany, Greece, Iceland, Ireland, Italy, Luxembourg, the Netherlands, Norway, Portugal, Spain, Sweden, Switzerland, and the United States), the great majority abandoned strict abortion laws dating from the nineteenth century and adopted more permissive ones. Although these countries widely allow abortion, the United States goes furthest in content and characterization in its abortion laws. Only American law rejects any effort to preserve the fetus before viability and severely restricts regulation after viability. In social policy, the United States provides almost no direct social benefits to mothers, married or unmarried. In constitutional law, although legislation protecting fetuses is permitted in countries such as West Germany, the United States Supreme Court decision *Roe v. Wade* (1973) prohibits any state or federal law limiting the right to abortion. Even in its language, the Court refused to acknowledge issues of developing life, avoiding such questions as whether the fetus is human or alive. In contrast to European nations, which emphasize the social interest in abortion law, the United States treats abortion as a constitutional right of legal interest only to private, autonomous individuals. Glendon states that the American laws regarding abortion would most likely tell a different story, placing higher importance on the value of life, if individual states were allowed to take a legislative role in balancing the interest in fetal life with a woman's liberty or privacy interests.

Like abortion, divorce—the topic of chapter 2—became more readily accessible in the 1970's and 1980's. Family law during this period was characterized by the withdrawal of legal control over the formation, benefits and burdens, and termination of marriage. The most striking pattern was movement in all twenty nations toward a system of no-fault divorce and away from a requirement of moral turpitude—adultery, desertion, cruelty—by one of the spouses as the grounds for dissolution of marriage. The United States, as it had with abortion laws, produced some of the most permissive divorce laws. Only Sweden rivals the United States in the ease of obtaining a unilateral, no-fault divorce, and the United States is alone in detaching its legal and social system from the economic consequences of divorce. Glendon writes that just as American abortion law tells the story of disregard for potential life, American divorce law communicates a message of the end of marriage with no blame attached, with almost reckless disregard for ensuring a fair level of child support, and with no public or private responsibility for the difficult economic circumstances that ensue.

In the third and final chapter, Glendon seeks to explain why in the transformation of abortion and divorce laws beginning in the late 1960's, the United States went the furthest among Western nations in removing regulation and public and private responsibility from its laws. Part of the explanation can be found in the American traditions of individualism, mobility, and self-reliance. While attractive qualities, these traditions tend to sap a sense of community and diminish the role of mediating institutions that in Europe have legal standing between the individual and the state. In addition, the Anglo-American tradition of legal positivism—beginning with Thomas Hobbes, gaining strength in the liberal philosophies of Jeremy Bentham, John Austin, and John Stuart Mills, and reaching culmination in Oliver Wendell Holmes, Jr.— draws a sharp distinction between law and morality. Thus the educational and persuasive value of law, always part of the continental tradition, was sheared from American jurisprudence, which described law as solely the external command of the sovereign. Finally, the United States, unlike Europe, lacks the tradition of explicit family policies and programs fostered by the government and by national private and semi-private organizations.

The final section of *Abortion and Divorce in Western Law* is the appendix, which summarizes the abortion laws of the twenty Western nations.

Christian Themes

Abortion and Divorce in Western Law is an academic study in comparative family law and is not an explicitly Christian work. However, its subject matter, abortion and divorce, are considered by most Christians to be crucial social questions relating to their religious faith. In addition, Glendon is a leading American lay Catholic, so it is not surprising that her study raises issues of critical importance to Christians and contains a certain Christian perspective.

The legalization of abortion is a relatively recent phenomenon in the West, but Christian ethics has always addressed this and other questions of human life and procreation. Few issues would seem to divide many Christians from contemporary legal norms as what is viewed as abortion on demand. Glendon criticizes America's disregard for the value of life or potential life in the name of abortion rights, and she contrasts the support pregnant European women receive, consistent with these nations' religious history of community support, with the lack of a family social net for pregnant women in the United States. Likewise, in questions of divorce, the Christian tradition has applied Jesus' command in marriage that "what God hath joined together, let no man put asunder" (Matthew 19:6). Certainly canon law and the law of most Christian nations forbade most forms of marital dissolution until contemporary times. Again, Glendon's critique of the modern "no-responsibility divorce" would be echoed by most Christian ethicists.

The extreme nonregulatory position in American abortion and divorce law cannot be explained in religious terms. However, the American emphasis on individualism and freedom from government interference is traceable at least in part to the Protestant Reformation with its emphasis on the individual relationship between each person and God without intermediaries, thereby de-emphasizing institutions that have a tradition of family support. Likewise, Glendon notes that Hobbes, to whom she traces the beginning of the Anglo-American philosophy separating morals from law, consciously broke with the traditional Christian view of humankind and society and with its idea of law as the perfection of reason. Glendon looks to the classical tradition of Plato's *Laws* as the epitome of law as educator of the citizenry regarding virtue. Her comparative study implies, however, that in the modern American equation of law as raw power from which the individual must be liberated, the American law of abortion and divorce has deviated not only from traditional ethics but also from the traditional legal ordering of Christian nations.

Sources for Further Study

Glendon, Mary Ann. *The Transformation of Family Law: State, Law and Family in the United States and Western Europe*. Chicago: The University of Chicago Press, 1989. In this later work, Glendon details the dramatic transformation of family law referred to in *Abortion and Divorce in Western Law*, particularly in England, France, the United States, and the former West Germany.

Santorum, Rick. *It Takes a Family: Conservatism and the Common Good*. Wilmington, Del.: ISI Books, 2005. By a United States senator, this book responds from a conservative perspective to Glendon's description of family law as a web of social, economic, and moral connections.

Shrage, Laurie. *Abortion and Social Responsibility: Depolarizing the Debate*. Oxford, England: Oxford University Press, 2003. This book calls for modification of America's abortion laws along the lines of other Western nations and endorses Glendon's encouragement of the establishment of a greater family security net in the United States.

Zweigert, Konrad, and Hein Kötz. *An Introduction to Comparative Law*. Translated by Tony Weir. Oxford, England: Clarendon Press, 1998. The definitive textbook in the field of comparative law, containing the methodology for Glendon's study.

Howard Bromberg

ACTS OF THE APOSTLES

Author: Unknown; early church tradition identifies author as Luke (fl. first century), a
ministry colleague of the apostle Paul

First transcribed: Praxeis Apostolon (Greek title), wr. c. 60 C.E. or c. 80-150 C.E. (English translation, 1380)

Edition used: "Acts," in *The Holy Bible, Containing the Old and New Testaments and
the Apocryphal/Deuterocanonical Books: New Revised Standard Version.* New
York: Oxford University Press, 1989

Genre: Holy writings

Subgenres: History; theology

Core issues: The Bible; church; discipleship; evangelization; God; Holy Spirit; obedience and disobedience; salvation; scriptures

*The Acts of the Apostles offers a picture of the earliest Christians that places them
within the overall purposes of God. Rather than understanding God's purposes only
in relation to the Jewish people as God's chosen people, this story includes both Jewish and non-Jewish persons within the realm of God's salvation. As part of the Christian canon, the book of Acts also provides a useful bridge between the Gospel stories
about Jesus and both Paul's letters and other early Christian writings.*

Overview

As the fifth book of the New Testament and a sequel to the Gospel of Luke (or the
second volume of what is often called "Luke-Acts"), the Acts of the Apostles continues
the story begun by Luke. Unlike the other three New Testament Gospels (Matthew,
Mark, and John), which end the narrative shortly after the crucifixion and resurrection
of Jesus, the Lukan story continues beyond these epical events. This ongoing story includes a wide range of scenes and situations: from the Jewish Temple in Jerusalem to
the Areopagus in Athens, from outlandish opposition to angelic intervention, and from
the utopian scenes among the Christian believers in early chapters to life-threatening
crises later on (see Acts 21:27-36). While the plot of Acts extends geographically and
thematically beyond the Gospel of Luke, both the repetition of numerous aspects of
Luke 24 (in the opening eleven verses of Acts) and the similarity between the depiction
of Jesus in Luke and key Christian characters in Acts support the conclusion that one
should read the Acts narrative as a continuation of the story begun in Luke.

As one reads the Acts, the words of Jesus in Acts 1:8 provide a general preview of
the story's progression: "But you will receive power when the Holy Spirit comes
upon you, and you will be my witnesses in Jerusalem, and in all Judea and Samaria,
and to the end of the earth" (author's translation). Thus, the first portion of the book
(1:1-8:3) focuses on persons and events in Jerusalem. The second portion of the book
(8:4-12:25) extends to the regions around or near Jerusalem. The action of the third
portion of the book moves to other places in the eastern Mediterranean world (13:1-
20:38). The last portion (21:1-28:31) focuses on the arrest and subsequent trials of

Paul, who in chapter 13 had become the leading figure of the Acts narrative.

Everything in the opening section of Acts (1:1-8:3) occurs in the city of Jerusalem. After Jesus' ascension to heaven, which is recorded only in Luke-Acts, Jesus' followers return to Jerusalem, as he had instructed them (1:4). These followers, numbering around 120 persons (1:15), gather consistently for prayer (1:14), probably in the temple courts (see Luke 24:52-53). The extraordinary event during Pentecost (Acts 2), when the Holy Spirit comes to these followers and enables them to proclaim the Gospel message in the native languages of those who have gathered at the Jewish Temple for that religious festival, represents God's fulfillment of his promise to the Jewish people as God's people. Thus, all the believers are Jewish, whom the author describes in utopian ways: enjoying God's presence among them; sharing possessions among the large, growing group of Christians; and proclaiming the Christian message about the resurrection of Jesus (see Acts 2:41-47, 4:32-37). However, these wonderful images of the Jewish believers stand in sharp contrast to the depiction of the Jewish religious authorities, who oppose the Christian message because they do not believe in any form of resurrection. The opposition and divisiveness of the Jewish leaders toward both the Christian message and their fellow Jews who embrace that message are epitomized by the ugly mob scene that ends in the savage murder of a believer named Stephen and the subsequent persecution that drives the Jewish believers out of Jerusalem.

The second portion of the Acts (8:4-12:25) occurs in the region around and near Jerusalem. Three characters take center stage, with their importance being their respective roles in taking the message of salvation to those considered outside the boundaries that define Judaism and Jewish understandings of God's purposes. First there is Philip, a leader in the Jerusalem church who proclaims the Christian message to persons in Samaria (whom Jewish persons considered as outsiders because of long-standing feuds and custom) and to a man who went to Jerusalem to worship but was an outsider to the Jewish people (no eunuch or castrated male could enter the Jewish Temple). Second, there is Saul, whom the resurrected Jesus confronted as Saul approached Damascus to arrest any Jewish believers he could find. This so-called conversion of Saul depicts the transformation of this staunch opponent of the Christian faith into its most ardent defender and proclaimer. Third, there is Simon Peter, the key figure in the early days of the Christian movement who took the Christian message of salvation to Cornelius, a pious but non-Jewish, Roman military official. For all three characters, the narrator of Acts makes it clear that the calling and purposes of God are behind their actions. These descriptions of God's actions with regard to these characters leave the reader with the distinct perspective that God's purposes extend beyond the Jewish people and include all people, even those considered outside Jewish boundaries and understandings. In other words, the narrative suggests a revision of the designation "people of God" to include not only the Jewish people but also all who truly receive the message of God's salvation, made available through the resurrected Jesus.

The third portion of the Acts narrative (13:1-20:38) depicts the spread of the Christian message throughout the eastern portion of the Mediterranean world. The main character is Paul (previously named "Saul" in chapter 9), whose ministry the narrative arranges in three separate journeys that lead to the acceptance of his message by both Jewish and non-Jewish persons. Questions about the status of non-Jewish believers resulted in the so-called Jerusalem Council of chapter 15, where the decision was reached that non-Jewish believers were not required to follow the Jewish law but needed only to heed a few matters that would facilitate fellowship with the Jewish believers. Nonetheless, the problems that Paul encountered in the synagogues of Corinth and Ephesus (Acts 18-19) imply that questions about who are and are not included among the people of God remained.

The final portion of Acts (21:1-28:31) describes the arrest and ensuing legal problems of Paul. Interestingly, Paul's arrest occurred as he followed the advice of the leadership of the Jerusalem church, who raised a serious question about Paul and his loyalty as a Jew but one that may have been a distortion of his ministry activities. His hostile capture by the stirred-up inhabitants of Jerusalem would have led to his murder, but Roman soldiers rescued him from the riotous mob. The rest of the book describes some of the legal troubles that Paul faced. When this section is compared to the whole book, it seems that the narrator has given disproportionate attention to these legal issues. Some suggest that these narrated scenes about Paul and these legal proceedings served to defend Paul against false charges against him. However, throughout these proceedings the focus is clearly on the call and purposes of God. Thus, the purpose here is not to defend Paul per se but to defend what this narrative presents. In other words, the purpose is to defend the understanding of God's purposes as presented in Acts—this narrative depiction of salvation and the revised concept of the "people of God." The final word in the original text, "unhindered," suggests that God's purposes are unstoppable and provides validation for this new understanding.

Christian Themes

Several related themes run throughout the narrative of the Acts. One of the most prominent themes has to do with God, who is the primary mover and agent of action in this story. The God of Israel fulfilled promises to Israel that God had made in an earlier day. At Pentecost, God enabled the followers of Jesus to overcome the obstacles to proclamation by giving them the Holy Spirit. God empowered these believers to overcome difficulties and opposition by filling them with the Holy Spirit. God moved both Cornelius and Peter to act when religious custom prohibited a faithful Jew like Peter from going to Cornelius's house. God provided direction and encouragement during Paul's ministry. Thus, the Lukan perspective makes it clear that behind everything in the narrative were the purposes and actions of God.

Closely related to the theme about God and God's purposes is the theme of salvation for all people. The quotation of the prophet Joel in Acts 2:17-21 emphasizes that "everyone who calls on the name of the Lord will be saved" (author's translation). While Jewish understandings of this declaration considered this to refer only to God fulfilling God's purposes to create and bless the Jewish people as God's people, the narrative offers a different understanding. In Acts, God directed persons like Peter and Paul to proclaim the message of God's saving purposes to persons both inside and outside the traditional Jewish categories. In addition, the narrated scenes made it clear that God blessed that proclamation because persons responded favorably. Thus, the narrative depicts salvation in universal terms.

Finally, the Acts narrative seems to focus significantly on the theme of the people of God. It is widely recognized that the vocabulary and style of Acts mimics the Jewish Torah, the first five books of the Old Testament, which tell the stories associated with God's establishment of the covenant with the Jewish people, thereby making them God's chosen people, or the "people of God." The different literary associations between these earlier texts and the book of Acts, as well as the usage of vocabulary in Acts that resembles the usage in these books, suggest a thematic connection. In addition, both the tensions among the Jewish people in the early chapters of Acts and the ongoing questions about the role of non-Jews with regard to salvation in the plot of Acts suggest a theological reorientation of the concept "people of God"—a reorientation that includes rather than excludes non-Jewish persons.

Sources for Further Study

Esler, Philip F. *Community and Gospel in Luke-Acts: The Social and Political Motivations of Lucan Theology*. Cambridge, England: Cambridge University Press, 1987. An appropriation of sociology and anthropology for the study of Lukan theology. Explores the social dynamics of the Christian community to which Acts (and Luke-Acts) was addressed.

Marshall, I. Howard, and David Peterson, eds. *Witness to the Gospel: The Theology of Acts*. Grand Rapids, Mich.: Wm. B. Eerdmans, 1998. A collection of twenty-five essays that highlight a variety of major theological themes in Acts. Takes seriously later developments in the study of Acts.

Pervo, Richard I. *Profit with Delight: The Literary Genre of the Acts of the Apostles*. Philadelphia: Fortress, 1987. A provocative study of the dramatic and entertaining aspects of Acts as a popular work of historical fiction or as a historical novel. Highlights the creative elements of the Acts composition.

Seim, Turid K. *Double Message: Patterns of Gender in Luke-Acts*. Edinburgh: T. & T. Clark, 1994. A reexamination of common assumptions about the Lukan perspective on women. Emphasizes a "double message" in Luke-Acts: one that preserves positive church traditions about women and another that limits their roles in the public proclamation and ministry of the church in Acts.

Spencer, F. Scott. *Journeying Through Acts: A Literary-Cultural Reading*. Peabody, Mass.: Hendrickson, 2004. Interprets Acts from both narrative criticism and the study of sociocultural dynamics. Underscores the element of surprise and its significance for a first-time reader.

Tannehill, Robert C. *The Narrative Unity of Luke-Acts: A Literary Interpretation*. Philadelphia: Fortress, 1990. A classic work emphasizing the unity of the two Lukan works. Interprets aspects of the Lukan writings in the light of their contribution to the whole Lukan narrative.

Richard P. Thompson

(ADO)RATION

Author: Diane Glancy (Helen Diane Hall; 1941-   )
First published: Tucson, Ariz.: Chax Press, 1999
Genre: Poetry
Subgenre: Lyric poetry
Core issues: African Americans; conversion; imperialism; Jesus Christ; Native Americans

In this collection of experimental, lyric poetry, the Cherokee-German poet Glancy reimagines the encounter between Old and New World spiritual traditions. She uses postmodern writing techniques such as darkly humorous wordplay and misspellings to emphasize the miscommunications between Western and Native sensibilities. She also collapses historical, contemporary, and personal perspectives to show the confluence of the past and the present in the unending spiritual struggle to come to an acceptance of God.

Overview

Helen Diane Hall was born in Kansas City, Missouri, to a mother of English-German descent and a father of Cherokee heritage. She married Dwane Glancy in 1964, the same year she received her B.A. from the University of Missouri. The couple had two children, David (b. 1964) and Jennifer (b. 1967), but the marriage was unhappy and ended in divorce in 1983. Glancy completed an M.F.A. from the prestigious creative writing program at the University of Iowa in 1988. In 1992, she became a professor at Macalaster College in St. Paul, Minnesota. Glancy's creative output is varied and prolific. In addition to poetry collections such as *(Ado)ration*, she has published novels, essay and short-story collections, plays, scripts, and literary criticism. She has received fellowships from the National Endowment for the Arts and the National Endowment for the Humanities as well as an American Book Award.

(Ado)ration is Glancy's most sustained interrogation of Native American and Christian spiritualities. The collection moves from an initial presentation of these spiritualities as a dichotomy to a new and richer hybrid or "syncretic" spirituality (literally "syn" meaning with or together and "cret" meaning creed or beliefs). This syncretic belief system is developed through a series of historical, personal, and metaphysical encounters.

Glancy's poetry defamiliarizes Christianity—not through a demonization of the conquerors and their religion, but through a struggle of faiths as seen from the Native American perspective that takes place across time, between cultures, and within the narrator. Particular Christian tenets that seem incomprehensible from the Native American perspective at the opening of the collection are recontextualized at later moments in the collection, showing how the narrator individually and Native Americans collectively are constantly struggling to understand and to re-create Christianity in a form that combines Old and New World perspectives.

One of the most striking ways in which Glancy reworks Christian tradition through Native sensibilities is in a series of poems that correspond to passages in the Old Testament. *(Ado)ration* opens with an epigraph taken from Genesis 27:5-19, the tale of Jacob and Esau. This passage, when perceived through Native American eyes, is a trickster story in which Rebekkah fixes a venison stew for her husband and teaches her favored son to behave like a skinwalker by wearing animal skins to change his identity. The opening poem of the collection further contextualizes the Genesis tale. "You Know Them by Their Stealing" recognizes that the Europeans came to the New World already prepared to take whatever they wanted, a thievery excused

> by the God who brought them
> (who had an eye like a suck hole
> for what he wanted).

After all, the narrator reflects, if they could steal from their own brother, they could take from anyone. Initially, then *(Ado)ration* presents Christianity as a conqueror's religion, one that condones and even promotes the theft of Native American lands and the destruction of Native American society.

Later in the collection, Glancy returns to the Jacob and Esau story in "They Came with a Bible." In this dramatic monologue about Christian missionaries and nineteenth century covered-wagon trains, Native Americans sit at a campground and talk about how the Christian Bible approves of theft, such as Jacob stealing Esau's birthright and Israel entering Canaan. They watch the wagons going by and recognize that each wagon, covered in white canvas like an angel's wing, represents the death of Native American culture. The poem ends with a startling juxtaposition that goes to the heart of the contrast between Native and Christian spiritualities: the Christian's "sacred ground was a building," but the Native Americans understood that all the earth was holy and that a man could worship anywhere and talk to the ancestors, the spirits, the animals, and even to the conquistadors who first "tore the flesh,/ drank the blood."

The final poem of the collection, "Stolen Blessing," returns one last time to the Jacob and Esau story. The poem's title alludes directly to the Genesis tale, which this poem recasts in the form of a lyrical meditation of a struggle between the "ancestral claim" and "the insert of new matter." This very pull and tug between the past and the present is the heart of a syncretic religious experience. As *(Ado)ration* suggests, a syncretic form of faith is not complacent but rather a continual and active process that continues through all life.

(Ado)ration's most powerful evocation of how the internal conflict between Native and European sensibilities leads to a religious conversion is "Well You Push Your Mind Along the Road." This poem presents the encounters of the opposing religious systems as Hegelian moments in which the tangible tribal religion confronts its antithesis, an intangible eclipse that is called God, and this collision creates a new being: "you lift your voice and say *praise to you nothing* and nothing begins to hear . . . nothing becomes something." The argument between the self and the other, the tangible

and the intangible, becomes an act of self-creation and the creation of a syncretic religious experience.

Christian Themes

(Ado)ration highlights several key differences between Christian and Native religions. One of Glancy's major preoccupations as a poet is how the visible relates to the invisible; she suggests that tribal peoples have special knowledge of the tangible world in contrast to the European emphasis on the intangible and the metaphysical. In "Ledger Book Drawing," for example, Glancy muses over an old Native American drawing of an Indian riding into battle: The artist draws the brave riding sidesaddle because he does not understand how to draw a leg on the other, invisible side of the horse. Glancy uses the ledger book artist to exemplify how the Native religious experience does not grasp the invisible. She later uses a poem about a conquistador riding a horse to exemplify how the Europeans do not respect the material world. In "You Know the Indian," Glancy reimagines the Indian's first view of a white conquistador on a horse. He seems to be a six-legged creature who can dismember himself. Glancy suggests that this violent separation of human from animal is emblematic of the European world and the "binary trail" of conflicting cultural and religious perspectives that Native Americans were ever forced to walk after the encounter.

Glancy suggests that a second, essential difference between Christian and Native traditions is in how each tradition approaches religious scripture and myth as authoritative and fixed or as fluid and infinitely variable. The history of Christianity has been marked by bloody, violent conflicts over determining whose version of Scripture or whose religious practices are the "true" ones. By contrast, in Native American spiritual systems, the idea of constant change is essential. A written and fixed text is the opposite of authoritative, for ceremonies and religious stories must be constantly told and retold, and each reimagining of a mythic tale or a spiritual narrative adapts old traditions to new understandings. If a ceremonial text cannot be reimagined, then it is a dead text and no longer provides spiritual healing. Not surprisingly, Glancy's religious poetry features images of journeys, travels, and transformations: a road trip across the Plains states taken by the narrator, Jesus as a street tough riding a Harley-Davidson, an Indian drawing a man riding a horse, a cross that is compared to a travois, a mind that is pushed along a road, the Cherokee Trail of Tears, the tracking of footprints, and Jesus giving a sermon from a rocking boat. As the titular poem "(Ado)ration" notes, the Native convert to Christianity can adapt to a new religion, for a spiritual sensibility that believes in the power of transformation can accept the "Spirit-world moving the boundaries of its yard chairs." But when the Christian faith insists on the Eurocentric and racist belief that the Great Spirit is "*white* as a sky on Sunday," it loses all validity.

Sources for Further Study

Allen, Paula Gunn. *The Sacred Hoop: Recovering the Feminine in American Indian Traditions*. Boston: Beacon Press, 1986. A foundational work in the study of Native American spirituality and women's writing.

Glancy, Diane, and Mark Nowak, eds. *Visit Teepee Town: Native Writings After the Detours*. Minneapolis: Coffee House Press, 1999. An anthology of postmodern writings; the preface and introduction are manifestos elucidating the editors' belief that subversive oral traditions are essential to Native American "survivance."

Rochon, Glenn. "Glancy's 'Well You Push Your Mind Along the Road.'" *Explicator* 61, no. 1 (Fall, 2002): 59-61. A lucid, close reading of Glancy's poem identifying how she uses a dialectic to present the religious transformation of a self.

Ruwe, Donelle. "Introduction." In *Dancing at the Altar: American Indian Literature and Spirituality*, edited by Donelle Ruwe. Special issue of *Religion and Literature* 26, no. 1 (1994): 1-7. A useful overview of Native American spirituality and literary criticism.

Donelle Ruwe

"ADVICE TO A PROPHET"

Author: Richard Wilbur (1921-   )
First published: 1959, in *Advice to a Prophet, and Other Poems*, 1961
Edition used: Collected Poems, 1943-2004. Orlando, Fla.: Harcourt, 2004
Genre: Poetry
Subgenre: Lyric poetry
Core issues: Beauty; connectedness; death; guidance; nature; sanctification

Written at a time when many feared destruction of the world by atomic bombs, Wilbur's "Advice to a Prophet" takes a different approach. Rather than focusing on the end of the human race in terms of numbers and cold statistics, Wilbur shows a world without common natural sights, enabling one to visualize and, therefore, comprehend the emptiness of a world without objects and, ultimately, without people to perceive them.

Overview

Richard Wilbur stated in "On My Own Work," reprinted in his book *Responses: Prose Pieces, 1953-1976* (1976), that his experiences serving as a soldier in Europe in World War II provoked him into becoming a poet. However, unlike other poets of his era who wrote about the war, such as Robert Lowell and Randall Jarrell, Wilbur did not focus on the horror of war but on the need to establish order in the world to restrain the chaos of war. His poetry has been characterized as bloodless, lacking a head-on confrontation with the problems characteristic of modern life. In addition, unlike many poets of his era, his voice is not "confessional" and does not address only how the world affects him as an individual. He is more of a classicist, seeing the world outside himself. Yet, in his close observation of nature, he echoes the Romantic poets, particularly William Wordsworth.

Wilbur is a master of the English language. With a translator's patience, Wilbur searches for the precise word to convey both the immediate meaning and a deeper connotation. Consequently, when he chooses a word, that word may have multiple meanings. As suggested by critic John Hougen, Wilbur uses wit "to surprise his readers," to shake them from traditional ways of seeing and thinking. Wilbur also uses allusions, providing layers of meaning to his poetry. In "Advice to a Prophet," Wilbur refers to Xanthus, the ancient city of Lycia in Asia Minor. The city was besieged by the Persians and, centuries later, by the Romans. In both instances, the inhabitants destroyed their city before surrendering. Using the word "Xanthus" underscores the theme of destruction as well as humankind's participation in its destiny. For some readers, Wilbur's specificity of word choice, classical allusions, and strict adherence to poetic form are daunting.

"Advice to a Prophet" was published in Wilbur's poetry collection *Advice to a Prophet, and Other Poems* (1961). The tone is conversational; the unnamed speaker is the poet. However, the speaker uses the first-person plural to indicate he is also part of the prophet's audience and that group's spokesperson. The concept of a prophet providing warnings to humankind is not uncommon. Biblical prophets such as Ezekiel and those of antiquity such as Cassandra tried to alert humankind to various destructive futures and were not heeded. Wilbur remarks that because of the state of the world created by nuclear fears, it is natural to assume a prophet, "mad-eyed" with stating the obvious and frustrated with the indifference of humankind, will issue warnings "When you come, as you soon must, to the streets of our city." What is uncommon in this poem is that the speaker will advise the prophet, stating that the prophet's words of doom will not be understood and, consequently, not heeded. "Spare us all word of the weapons, their force and range,/ The long numbers that rocket the mind;/ Our slow, unreckoning hearts will be left behind,/ Unable to fear what is too strange." How can people understand the unimaginable? Rather, why not provide examples from the "everyday" world, such as how "the white-tailed deer will slip/ Into perfect shade" or "How the dreamt cloud crumbles"? The disappearance of a deer and the breaking up of a cloud are things humankind has seen. Imagining the world without familiar natural sights provides insight into a world without people: "Speak of the world's own change."

By converting the abstract horror of nuclear destruction into the tangible loss of "the white-tailed deer" or the result of "the vines blackened by frost," Wilbur makes us understand. To him, the "things of this world" provide a way for us to communicate. "These things in which we have seen ourselves and spoken" are what make our world real, and humankind is a part of the world, not the center of it. In "Advice to a Prophet," the argument Wilbur proposes is that destruction by nuclear weapons is unimaginable, but the loss of people's dialogue with nature and the world around them can be comprehended. "Nor shall you scare us with talk of the death of the race./ How should we dream of this place without us?" Rather than warn us of the destruction of the planet, the end of humankind, the prophet needs to couch his warning in humbler terms, reminding us that who we are depends on "the live tongue" of nature. Since "we have seen ourselves and spoken" through the external world of nature, without the natural world, we cannot be human.

In *Responses, Prose Pieces 1953-1976*, Wilbur states that poets can be either "poet-citizens" or "alienated artists." Like the Romantic poets, he chooses to be involved in the human world and its concerns, and in "Advice to a Prophet" the poet counsels the prophet to show a way for the community to preserve itself not by dire, end-of-the-world warnings, but by describing a world without those things that people value, such as "the rose of our love and the clean/ Horse of our courage." And the poet-speaker asks the prophet whether humanity will fail itself or "come demanding/ Whether there shall be lofty or long standing/ When the bronze annals of the oak-tree close." The intimation is that humanity will not allow itself to become a victim of a nuclear holocaust. Like the residents of Xanthus, people will take charge of their own destiny.

Christian Themes

Although Wilbur is a lifelong Episcopalian, his poetry does not shout Christian doctrine. Instead, he reinforces the concept of finding "the invisible through the visible." Like the poet Wordsworth, he sees God (order) in nature, and through the perception of nature, people are able to understand and value both themselves and the world around them. Rather than focusing on the end of the world as being the end of humankind, Wilbur equates such a possibility with an end of the natural world. Like the Jesuit priest Pierre Teilhard de Chardin, Wilbur sees spirit within matter and the interdependence of all of life's parts, reflecting the divine working through the mundane. Much like the Metaphysical poets, whom he admired, Wilbur, as he remarked in "On My Own Work," favors a "spirituality that is not abstracted, not dissociated and world-renouncing." Looking at the "things of this world" and what they mean to humankind, Wilbur shows a reverence for all life and works to achieve a fusion between the tangible world, with its deer, roses, and trout, and the spiritual. To Wilbur the spiritual realm, the world of the Creator, exists united with the physical.

In "Advice to a Prophet," Wilbur alerts us to the necessity of balance between the two worlds. Although the poem speaks of the prophet's concern with the end of humankind, the poet is more troubled by the loss of the world outside humanity, the world of nature. It is this world that people can understand and that provides beauty and truths that are visible and, consequently, part of what defines humanity. Rather than people accepting the inevitability of the Apocalypse, Wilbur and the townspeople reject the doomsaying of the prophet and embrace the faith that people can save themselves and their world.

Sources for Further Study

Hill, Donald. *Richard Wilbur.* New York: Twayne, 1967. Each chapter concerns a book of Wilbur's poetry, focusing on subject categories such as war, nature, and daily life.

Hougen, John B. *Ecstasy Within Discipline: The Poetry of Richard Wilbur.* Atlanta, Ga.: Scholars Press, 1995. The focus in this volume is on Wilbur as a meditative poet, grounded in religion, who sees the spiritual in the natural world.

Michelson, Bruce. *Wilbur's Poetry: Music in a Scattering Time.* Amherst: University of Massachusetts Press, 1991. An extended study of Wilbur's poetry that shows his range of styles and how the poems relate to aesthetic and moral issues.

Salinger, Wendy, ed. *Richard Wilbur's Creation.* Ann Arbor: University of Michigan Press, 1983. Salinger discusses Wilbur's concept of the things of the world as "not merely a pretext for the ideal" but as a way to perceive truth.

Stitt, Peter. *The World's Hieroglyphic Beauty: Five American Poets.* Athens: University of Georgia Press, 1985. Stitt's essay "The Sacramental Vision of Richard Wilbur" discusses the poet's concern with "the unseen realm of spirit."

Marcia B. Dinneen

AFRICAN HERITAGE AND
CONTEMPORARY CHRISTIANITY

Author: J. N. K. Mugambi (1942-   )
First published: Nairobi: Longman Kenya, 1989
Genre: Nonfiction
Subgenre: Church history
Core issues: Africa; evangelization; pastoral role

Mugambi's book is intended for pastors and religious educators expressing the message of Christianity in Africa. His thesis is that Christian understanding and traditional African thought can be harmonized in such matters as views of God, spirits and angels, ancestors and saints, rites of passage, and eternal life. He looks at the history of Christianity in Africa, focusing on the interaction between numerous missionary movements and traditional African religions. He finishes with a prescriptive outline for African religious education that incorporates principles from both traditions.

Overview

J. N. K. Mugambi places the Christianization of Africa in its historical context to make the point that African Christians led the movement and that Christianity was not imposed on the continent by outside forces. Beginning with the rise of Islam in the seventh century, Africans were subjected to the slave trade across the Indian and Atlantic oceans, and Christians viewed the trade as justified. Primarily nonmainstream Christians and non-Christians worked to defeat slavery. Not until the twentieth century did liberation theology arise.

The rise of the missionary movement in the nineteenth century accompanied the colonization of Africa. Despite its flawed origins, the movement had a positive impact across the continent, and when the postcolonial era arrived, many African countries chose to retain their Christian faith rather than renounce it.

Mugambi points to a new wave of missionary organizations that focus on imposing their cultural norms as well as their religion and have an impact that he calls "alarming." He looks at the concept of mission, "going out to the world," and notes that early Christian missionaries had preached Christianity as the logical successor to the prevalent faith in their land, Judaism. However, missionaries in Africa introduced Christianity as a faith that had no connection whatsoever to existing religious worship and supplanted those traditions. The initial African converts were the first to begin to connect the Gospel to their everyday lives and make it more meaningful in the context of African traditions.

Christianity reached the East African interior in the early nineteenth century. The faith had been difficult to establish in this region because of ill-conceived strategies such as baptizing large numbers of people without training clergy to minister to them. In the nineteenth century, missionaries became more concerned with "teaching"

Christianity, seeing their mission as imparting civilization and economic well-being along with religion. An aspect of missionary activity that had immense impact was the establishment of schools teaching reading and writing along with simple trade skills. These schools became centers of diffusion for European culture.

The traditional African worldview is monosectional, meaning that there is no heaven or hell. Instead there is the world in which we live. When someone dies, they do not go elsewhere but instead change their physical mode of existence. This disconnect from the Eurocentric multisectional world makes transition from one belief to another difficult for native Africans. Other Africans raised to believe in scientific thought also may have difficulty with the Christian belief system. All these factors must be taken into account when attempting to communicate Christianity intelligibly to these disparate groups.

Many differences exist between the traditional African and Christian notions of God, although some syncretism has occurred. These differences include a lack of an equivalent for Satan and a notion of a God who is primarily disinterested in human affairs. African religion places a strong emphasis on the existence of spirits with whom peaceful and harmonious relationships must be maintained at all times. Spirit possession is not unknown in some African societies. This made the concept of the Holy Spirit difficult to translate from one culture to the other. The idea of possession by the Holy Spirit has ousted previous beliefs in a variety of spirits. This leads to a particularly strong emphasis in the East African Revival movement on the idea that once converts have accepted Jesus Christ as their savior, the converts' lives become ordered by the Holy Spirit and their activities are the fruit of that Spirit as well as to a focus on faith healing.

Traditional African thinking also maintains that the daily world is inhabited by ancestors with whom good relationships must be maintained. Ancestors were the mediators between God and humanity. In Christianity, belief in the power of Jesus, the Holy Spirit, and saints takes over this role.

Christianity is not a culture, but the Christian faith can be expressed and communicated only through cultural media. The need for cultural freedom and identity has factored into the establishment of most Christian denominations. An effort to meet this need led to the establishment of independent African churches during the colonial period. With the introduction of Christianity, new rites of passage, such as baptism and first communion, have arisen, and existing rituals have been adapted to accommodate them.

A central question is what aspects of African heritage must be retained as the society is inevitably transformed by contact with other forces. Mugambi feels it is important to remember that "every culture that has made significant impact on world history has done so only after rediscovering and reaffirming its roots."

Mugambi finishes by spelling out a complete colonial curriculum that incorporates traditional African values into Christian ones. It is based on principles such as moving from the known to the unknown, helping the learners relate their experiences to each other, providing for practical learning experiences, helping the learner discuss the knowledge gained, and facilitating positive character modification. Only in this way can a coherent program emerge that accommodates both African and Christian traditions and allows people to draw the best from both.

Christian Themes

A core concept for Mugambi is the idea of religious education and what form it should take in Africa. Because many Africans grew up when the conflict between traditional African religions and Christianity had a destabilizing effect on their spirituality, they may find themselves concerned about the moral welfare of their children. They may be unsure what to teach them, particularly when consensus has not emerged on the Christian values regarding morality. The churches need to draw from the traditional African approach to moral education, which is built on the limitedness of humans as compared with the limitlessness of God. Increasingly, traditional African values and norms should be incorporated in the Christian religious education curriculum.

For Mugambi, Christianity and African tradition are not incompatible or exclusionary. Rather he feels that a clash between Western cultural norms and the African worldview creates a dissonance that destabilizes the spirituality of the Christian converts when they attempt to explain and pass on the hybrid tradition to their children.

Another concern for Mugambi is the notion of mission, the idea of witnessing one's faith to the world in the hope that one's example will move others to follow. For some missionaries, the purpose was to baptize and therefore save as many souls as possible, but for others it was equally important to teach "the Christian way of life," moving Africans from a primitive state to a more civilized one. For yet other missionary groups, the importance of teaching people new trades and agricultural and industrial skills went hand in hand with the mission of saving souls. A central impulse of missionary work has also been the notion of saving people from suffering, whether physical, economic, or spiritual.

Sources for Further Study

Barrett, David B. *African Initiatives in Religion.* Nairobi, Kenya: East African Publishing House, 1971. Describes the establishment of independent African churches in Nairobi and their struggle with traditional norms.

Desmangles, Leslie G. "Africa's Syncretic Christianity." Review of *African Heritage and Contemporary Christianity. Cross Currents* 42, no. 1 (Spring, 1992): 122-123. Review of Mugambi's work examines the history of Christianity in Africa and notes that converts retain their African identity.

Gehman, Richard J. *African Traditional Religion in Biblical Perspective.* Kijabe, Kenya: Kesho Publications, 2001. Relates traditional African marriage practices, death rituals, and initiation rites to structures described in the Bible.

Imasogie, Osadolor. *Guidelines for Christian Theology in Africa.* Achimota, Ghana, West Africa: Africa Christian Press, 1983. Presents strategies for relating the Gospel to traditional African life, as well as listing places where the traditions reinforce each other.

Cat Rambo

AFTER THE LOST WAR
A Narrative

Author: Andrew Hudgins (1951-   )
First published: Boston: Houghton Mifflin, 1988
Genre: Poetry
Subgenre: Narrative poetry
Core issues: Death; healing; hope; nature; soul

Hudgins recounts the horror of the Civil War and the difficulties of physical and psychic survival afterward. Facing death as a soldier, as a prisoner of war, and as a lifelong consumptive, the poet's persona, Sidney Lanier, is fascinated with the idea of the soul but is unable to have faith in traditional Christianity. Though conscious of Christian explanations of life here and hereafter, he finally finds his primary hope in personal integrity, love, and nature.

Overview

The forty-four poems in *After the Lost War* by Andrew Hudgins are all spoken in the voice of the historical Georgia-born poet and musician Sidney Lanier. They are divided into four sections, ranging from chronicles of Lanier's Civil War experience to the personal aftermath of the war; from Lanier's state of mind during a time when his consumption threatened his life to the charting of the last days and thoughts of a man slowly dying of pulmonary tuberculosis. The poems follow a rough chronological order, and thematic leitmotifs unify the sections of the book.

Each section is introduced by a short biographical paragraph, and in the preface Hudgins informs the reader that the voice of the poems will not be familiar to those who know the poetry and prose of the historical Lanier. Thus, the poems are unified by an empathetic, artistic impulse rather than a historical one. Poetically, Hudgins explores narrative, dramatic monologue, and voice, but thematically he is interested in questions of how a man of talent and sensitivity confronts a life of brutality.

The brutal life of war is explored in "Burial Detail," in which Hudgins's Lanier tells of the grisly assignment of burying dead soldiers in a mass grave and scattering lime between layers of human flesh. At one point during the long night of burial detail, the soldier-poet faints and falls into the mass grave of rotting flesh. Ironically, the poet finds comfort in the acknowledgment that he too will rot, comfort because he sees the laws of nature redeeming man's inhumanity to man. This theme of nature's redemptive power is communicated in the climax of the poem when Lanier sees what he calls "the most beautiful thing I've ever seen:/ dawn on the field after the Wilderness. . . ./ In short, it looked like nothing human." Without saying so directly, the persona communicates his disgust with human endeavor and yearns for something more—the immutable laws and cycles of nature.

The book confronts readers with questions of human violence and invites them to ponder what they will do to compensate for the blood and sins of this generation. One of the answers arrived at by Lanier is that minor redemption can be found in human empathy and personal expiation. In "Post Cards of a Hanging," Hudgins's Lanier sends nine numbered postcards to his brother Clifford, who served with him in the war. He reports seeing a black man lynched by a mob for insulting a white woman. Deeply troubled by this cruelty, Lanier describes the scene through the image pattern of shoes, feet, and boots. A passer-by asks if he might have the dead man's boots. Lanier goes home and blacks all his own boots and then walks five miles into the woods, sits down, and sobs "until my stomach hurt." He then shoulders his boots and walks barefoot back home. "When I got there/ my feet were sticking to the ground with blood./ It helped a bit." The poet is deeply troubled by this socially sanctioned murder and, not being able to intervene, wishes to make some kind of personal expiation. There is no talk of vicarious bearing of burdens, but the persona attempts, in a not wholly logical way, to right the wrongs of the world with the offering of his own personal suffering.

Hudgins's Lanier is very much interested in the nature of the soul and the proof from everyday experience that the soul exists. For example, in "The Yellow Steeple," Lanier describes a day when, walking home, he cuts across a cemetery. A worker, painting the church's steeple yellow, drops the can of paint, raining the persona with coat-ruining drops. The poet then looks up to the sky and sees an unmoving hawk, a point of "predatory grace." He then "barks [his] shins on a marble angel" and falls into a creek. The poem concludes, "It was one of those sustaining days/ when you're absolutely sure you have a soul." The poem's religious allusions to death, manifestations of Holy Spirit and grace, angelic influence, and baptism are all ironic, and yet lead the speaker to profess belief in the soul. Whether the confession is straight or ironic, for the speaker, grace is predatory but remains an insistent reality.

At the thematic center of the book lies the theme of death—how it is to be met and what happens afterward. The dying Sidney Lanier lies in a tent in the woods in the poem "The House of the Lord Forever." A preacher starts quizzing the man on his deathbed with questions such as "Where will you spend eternity?" and "Where is God?" The poem describes their conversation/debate. The persona says, "I won't/ debate my soul with strangers—not/ when I have family who pray/ for me so urgently." The poem ends, "How can they be so sure? They are so sure." The "they," no doubt, refers both to the sympathetic, desperate family members who yearn for their husband/father's survival and to the preacher who offers facile, clichéd sentiments. The persona is not unconcerned with matters of the soul and eternal habitation, but he is put off by surety, by blind faith. He favors imagination as prompted by observation of nature.

Christian Themes

Though *After the Lost War* is deeply spiritual, it mostly remains shy of an explicit connection with Christianity. Hudgins seems to believe that war's brutality and the constant threat of death inform the human condition and constitute its central realities.

Nevertheless, a simultaneous spiritual impulse, every bit as real, works in humanity and connects people to their inner selves, to each other, and to the world. Traditional Christianity constitutes one version of that impulse, but though the poet-persona flirts with it, he is more inclined to a spirituality committed, personal view of nature.

The book explores with unabashed honesty the range of human nature, in various stages of pain, healing, and forgiveness. The book implicitly asks whether people heal and forgive because that is part of their natures or because human nature is redeemed by some higher power. The book affirms the redemptive power of human kindness, which at times preserves or prolongs life but ultimately remains powerless to stop death. In the face of that death, one hopes for God's grace but sees clearly only the metaphors for it reflected in nature. Hudgins's Lanier says "It's strange/ how everything I say becomes/ a symbol of mortality, a habit I cannot resist/ and don't care to." The poet seeks symbols of mortality, not symbols of divinity or symbols of the connectedness between God and humanity.

One of the poet's chief symbols of mortality is the hawk. In one poem a hawk feints attack; birds rise into flight, and then the hawk takes a slow bird. The persona remarks, "I sat shaken—astonished and afraid,/ but also moved—by this assurance that/ God keeps his eye on everyone/ and snatches even those who flee his grace." The hawk proceeds to eats the fallen bird on the spot, and the poem concludes, "In that, he wasn't much like God/ —I hoped as I walked deeper in/ the darkening marshes past my home,/ through clover, chamomile, under heaven." The poet finds himself, finally, "under heaven" in the world of the "darkening marsh," where the hawk is both like and unlike God. The poet's awe at God's watchfulness is matched by his conviction that violence informs not only the human and the natural worlds but also the world of God. However, hope redeems that reality.

Sources for Further Study

"Andrew Hudgins." In *Contemporary Southern Writers*, edited by Roger Matuz. Detroit, Mich.: St. James Press, 1999. A short biography of the poet that describes his works and life.

Hudgins, Andrew. *The Glass Anvil*. Ann Arbor: University of Michigan Press, 1997. In this collection of essays, the poet explains why parts of his earlier biography, *The Glass Hammer*, were fictionalized. Includes discussions of religion, language, and narrative poetry.

_____. *The Glass Hammer: A Southern Childhood*. Boston: Houghton Mifflin, 1994. Hudgins describes his childhood in a series of narrative poems.

Reynolds, Clay. "Crossing the Line of Poetic Biography: Andrew Hudgins' Narrative of the Life of Sidney Lanier." *Journal of American Studies Association of Texas*, 20 (October, 1989): 27-40. Examines the issue of Hudgins taking the Lanier voice in *After the Lost War*.

Scott Samuelson

AGAINST HERESIES

Author: Saint Irenaeus (120/140-c. 202 C.E.)
First transcribed: Adversus haereses, c. 180 C.E. (English translation, 1868)
Edition used: Against Heresies, translated by Alexander Roberts and James Donald-
  son, vol. 1 in the Ante-Nicene Christian Library. Edinburgh, Scotland: T &T Clark,
  1880
Genre: Nonfiction
Subgenres: Biblical studies; didactic treatise
Core issues: Catholics and Catholicism; church; Gnosticism; salvation; truth

In this treatise, Irenaeus, a bishop in Lyons, combats various groups he considers he-
retical, in particular, the Gnostics. In his opposition to these groups, Irenaeus focuses
on the unity of Christianity by emphasizing apostolic succession and canonical Chris-
tian works.

Overview

The main goal of Saint Irenaeus's *Against Heresies* was to counteract Christian
teachings he believed to be false and insidious. Most of those doctrines fell under the
category of Gnosticism, a second century Christian movement that emphasized
knowledge (from the Greek word *gnosis*) as the key to salvation. Irenaeus set out not
only to show the absurdity of the Gnostic systems but also to warn against the ethical
dangers of such systems. He did so in five books addressed to an anonymous reader.

Book 1 is largely a catalog of various heresies. Foremost among these is Valentin-
ianism, a movement begun by Valentinus, a prominent Christian teacher in Rome in
the middle of the second century. He expounded an elaborate cosmology in which the
creator of the world was evil and thus all material things—including human bodies—
were also evil. Those people who realized that they were spiritual and not material
(including Valentinus and his followers) were the only ones who would experience
salvation; the others (the majority of Christians) had an incomplete understanding of
the truth. Irenaeus's argument against the Valentinians takes two directions. First, he
shows that the Valentinians pervert Scripture by taking it out of context and ignoring
the plain sense of the text. Second, and more important, he argues that the Valen-
tianian system attacks the unity of the church. Irenaeus emphasizes that the church
must stand as a whole, "as if she had but one soul and heart." Valentinians, however,
extol individuality. Irenaeus's stress on the unity of the church is the most prominent
polemical aspect of the entire work. The rest of book 1 is a long catalog of other prominent Christian heresies, each of which Irenaeus describes and then attacks.

In book 2, Irenaeus elaborates on many of the points he made in the first book, arranging his discussion under theological topics. He confines himself primarily to the
Valentinians, but he claims that the arguments against them are damning of other heresies. Irenaeus favors absolute monotheism over the polytheism of the Valentinians,

stating that to believe in polytheism is logically absurd. He presents arguments against the many deities in which the Valentinians believe and chastises them for their numerological speculation and their distorted belief in the afterlife. In this book, Irenaeus first uses the phrase "rule of truth." This phrase encapsulates the unity he emphasizes in book 1: Only one truth exists for Christians, and it is the one truth that has always provided guidelines for Christians.

Irenaeus turns to Scripture in books 3 and 4. Book 3 divides into two sections, one that highlights the monotheism taught in the Old Testament and one that emphasizes the unique manifestation of God in Jesus Christ. Before quoting Scripture, however, Irenaeus lays the foundation for its authority. What is crucial for Irenaeus and what helps illuminate his concept of Scripture is that the apostolic succession of church leaders, especially the episcopate at Rome, ensures the veracity of Christian teachings. It therefore provides parameters within which Scripture can receive proper interpretation. For Irenaeus, Scripture and apostolic succession form a conjoined stream. In this work are the earliest delineations of the two main sources of revelation in Catholicism: Scripture and tradition.

An important historical aspect of book 3 is Irenaeus's argument for the completeness of the four Gospels. He is the first to argue for the authority of Matthew, Mark, Luke, and John alone. In a fairly elaborate narrative, he states that just as there are four winds of the earth and four corners of the earth, so also there should be four Gospels. As a corollary of this argument, he chastises Christians who read only one to the exclusion of the other three.

After he makes the case for apostolic and scriptural authority in book 3, Irenaeus shows in book 4 that the teaching of Jesus and his apostles meshes perfectly with the story of the Old Testament. The Valentinians, along with others in early Christianity (namely Marcion), made a sharp division between the person of Jesus and the God of the Old Testament. Irenaeus, in an important development for the early church, states that the God of the Old Testament and Jesus are inseparable and, furthermore, that they are incomprehensible apart from one another. Irenaeus marshals evidence for both ideas. He demonstrates that figures such as Moses and Abraham looked forward to the coming of Jesus as the Son of God. Conversely, he shows that Jesus himself adhered to the stories of the Old Testament and the God proclaimed there. Irenaeus elegantly displays the continuity between both testaments and shows how both are authoritative for Christianity.

Central to book 5 are the topics of incarnation and salvation. Referring often to Paul's letters, Irenaeus shows that Jesus became fully human while losing none of his divine qualities. Because of the Incarnation, death, and Resurrection of Jesus, humans will also experience resurrection after death. This book contains the most pastoral passages of *Against Heresies*. Irenaeus's disagreement with the heretics is not simply a matter of being proved correct. He believes that Gnostic teachings will lead unknowing Christians to their eternal damnation. In book 5, he explicitly states that Valentinus and other Gnostics are minions of Satan and that their doctrines, which are bereft of salvific power, will ultimately destroy those who follow them.

Christian Themes

The importance of Irenaeus's *Against Heresies* transcends its historical polemics against Gnosticism. In making a case against Valentinians, Irenaeus developed the theological groundwork for what would become orthodox Christianity. He desired to make the church truly "catholic" (universal) and, in doing so, formulated important principles, especially creed, canon, and apostolic succession. Apostolic succession was necessary to create a common discourse among Christians. A definite canon was important for having a shared set of texts from which all could draw. A creed was vital for summarizing what bound Christians together. Behind all Irenaeus's polemics lay an intense pastoral desire for the welfare of the church.

It would therefore be misguided to see Irenaeus as a bullying bishop trying to force his beliefs on others. What he disliked about Gnosticism was its dual tendencies toward rampant individualism and toward elitism. Although superficially inclusive—Gnostics seemingly put few constraints on their adherents—they clearly thought of themselves as a superior minority. Irenaeus's catholicism attempts to clear out a space whereby all can be a part of the church, not just a select few.

Irenaeus's desire for unity within the church shapes his understanding of both Scripture and salvation. At a time in Christian history when the Old Testament could easily have been discarded, Irenaeus advocates its role within Christianity. Because he believes God to be eternal and singular, the story of God's relationship with humans cannot begin with Jesus. Rather, Jesus functions as the climax and fulfillment of God's work on earth. Humans participate in that story by believing in Jesus and experiencing salvation. When Irenaeus claims that salvation occurs through the church alone, he highlights the uniqueness of Christian teachings. If God is one, then God must have one method of relating to humans, and this is through Christ. Irenaeus's exclusive claim for Christianity comes from his conviction of the unity of God. What might strike the modern reader as vitriol should not overshadow Irenaeus's pastoral aims. Behind all his harsh language, he exhibits a capacious vision of what an ideal church might be.

Sources for Further Study

Donovan, Mary Ann. *One Right Reading? A Guide to Irenaeus.* Collegeville, Minn.: Liturgical Press, 1997. A book-by-book reading guide to *Against Heresies*, with outlines and commentary.

Grant, Robert M. *Irenaeus of Lyons.* New York: Routledge, 1997. English translations of selected portions of *Against Heresies* with some useful introductory essays.

Norris, Richard A., Jr. "Irenaeus of Lyon." In *The Cambridge History of Early Christian Literature*, edited by Frances Young, Lewis Ayres, and Andrew Louth. Cambridge, England: Cambridge University Press, 2004. A nice, brief overview of Irenaeus's work within the context of early Christianity.

Osborn, Eric Francis. *Irenaeus of Lyons.* Cambridge, England: Cambridge University Press, 2001. The most comprehensive study in English of Irenaeus's life and theology, with an emphasis on his rhetorical and aesthetic skills.

Kyle Keefer

AGAPE AND EROS

Author: Anders Nygren (1890-1978)
First published: Den kristna kärlekstanken genom tiderna: Eros och Agape I, 1930;
  Den kristna kärlekstanken genom tiderna: Eros och Agape II, 1936 (English trans-
  lation, 1953)
Edition used: Agape and Eros, translated by Philip S. Watson. New York: Harper &
  Row, 1969
Genre: Nonfiction
Subgenres: Biblical studies; church history; theology
Core issues: Agape; Catholics and Catholicism; Gnosticism; God; Gospels; grace;
  love; Protestants and Protestantism; religion

The first part of Nygren's work compares the Christian idea of love, agape, *with the
Hellenistic idea of love,* eros. Agape *is identified with the Christian God's unqualified
and unmotivated love for human beings, which humans may learn to show to each
other.* Eros *is identified as the desire of human beings for things of the world or for
God. In the second part of his work, Nygren provides an intellectual history of* agape
and eros *from the earliest times of Christianity through the Reformation.*

Overview

Anders Nygren identifies his purpose in writing this work as to investigate the
Christian idea of love and to examine the changes this idea has undergone throughout
the history of Christianity. He describes his approach as "motif research." This means
that he looks at the essential ideas that characterize Christianity and Hellenism, the
cultural and spiritual orientation of Greco-Roman antiquity. The essential ideas about
love can be distinguished by the Greek words *agape* and *eros.*

Through study of the Gospels, Nygren finds that the characteristic feature of *agape*
is that it is God's love for humans. *Agape* comes down from God to humanity as a sacrificial giving. It is a matter of grace, in which salvation comes from God. *Agape* is
unselfish; God gives freely and abundantly without seeking anything. When human
beings love according to *agape*, they are patterning themselves on God. *Agape*, further, is spontaneous and unmotivated, and it does not consider whether those who are
loved deserve to be loved. Finally, *agape* creates value in the object of love: Those
who are loved become worthy because they are loved.

Nygren finds a different and unrelated kind of love in non-Christian, Greco-Roman
antiquity. He traces this kind of love to Plato and to Plato's heirs and followers. Plato
distinguishes between two kinds of love, described as varieties of *eros.* The first is
"vulgar" *eros*, love for things of the world and of the body. The second is "heavenly"
eros, love for heavenly things. Nygren spends little time on vulgar *eros*, because its
difference from Christian love seems immediately evident to him. In his view, heavenly *eros* is also quite different from *agape. Eros*, whether vulgar or heavenly, is a
matter of desire and longing.

While *agape* involves a downward movement from God to humanity, heavenly *eros* is an upward movement and an attempt to ascend from humanity toward God. Although salvation depends on grace from the perspective of *agape*, from the perspective of *eros*, people achieve their own salvation through their own efforts. According, even heavenly *eros* is egocentric. It involves the self-assertion by individuals of what is best and highest in themselves. Because *eros* springs from desire, it is a matter of lacking; it depends on want and need, rather than on the abundance of *agape*. For this reason, *eros* is an expression of the will to get and to possess, rather than to give. This Hellenistic conception of love is at core a human love. Even when it is directed toward God, it is the human being's love of God. *Eros* loves its object because the object is worthy of that love. Accordingly, *eros* does not create value but recognizes it.

Following nineteenth century German philosopher Friedrich Nietzsche, Nygren acknowledges *eros* as the center of the value system of antiquity. Accordingly, *agape* introduced what Nietzsche had referred to as a transvaluation of all values. However, Christianity did not completely overthrow the value system of antiquity but coexisted with it, so that *agape* and *eros* were combined and confused. The second part of Nygren's book deals with the history of this confusion.

To the motifs of *agape* and *eros*, Nygren adds a third motif, that of *nomos*, or the Judaic conception of the law. The earliest church fathers tended to blend *agape* with Hellenistic and legalistic conceptions of faith and love in varying ways and to varying degrees. The Hellenistic motif of *eros* made its greatest inroads to Christianity with the Alexandrian school, particularly in the work of the philosopher Origen, who was heavily influenced by Neoplatonic ideas of the return of the multiplicity of created beings to the One. Even Saint Augustine, one of the central figures in Christianity, mixed *agape* and *eros* in his concept of *caritas*, or Christian love.

The Neoplatonic motif of *eros*, of love as the upward movement toward God, flowed into the mainstream of the medieval Christian tradition through the writings of Pseudo-Dionysius. Heavily influenced by the Neoplatonic philosopher Plotinus and by Plotinus's follower Proclus, this anonymous writer identified himself as Saint Paul's disciple Dionysius the Areopagite, but actually probably lived and wrote about 500 C.E. Pseudo-Dionysius became the source of much of the mystical tradition in medieval Christianity, which Nygren associates with Hellenistic *eros*. Pseudo-Dionyisus also passed on the Neoplatonic image of the heavenly hierarchy between God and the human, by which people ascend to God.

The Neoplatonic idea of ascent to God was one of the dominant strands of medieval Christianity even in the poetry of Dante. The Augustinian *caritas*, blending ideas drawn from *agape* and *eros*, was another strand, one that was developed through medieval theology. Nygren interprets the teachings of Martin Luther, based on the idea that salvation comes from God's grace and love alone, as a turning back to Christian *agape*.

Christian Themes

The most fundamental theme of Nygren's work treats one of the central questions of the Christian tradition: How much of this tradition is uniquely Christian and how much of it is a product of the classical culture in which Christianity developed and out of which the intellectual heritage of Western civilization emerged? A related question is whether the values of Christianity are essentially the same as those held by pagans such as Plato and Aristotle or whether Christianity introduced a radically new set of values. Nygren answers that from the very earliest years Christianity has absorbed non-Christian ideas. Moreover, as the values associated with the Christian and non-Christian are utterly different, the values and views of Greco-Roman antiquity have introduced alien elements into Christianity.

In addition, Nygren identifies the concept of love as a fundamental motif, the distinguishing idea of Christianity. He recognizes that it is not always clear just what love means, though, and that dissimilar kinds of forces are identified by the use of the single English word. His contribution is to carefully consider the nature of Christian love and to distinguish it from other views of love.

The attempt to identify the uniquely Christian idea of love and to trace the intellectual history of this idea involves Nygren in a central confessional dispute. One of the Protestant objections to Catholicism was that the Catholic intellectual tradition had absorbed non-Christian influences and had therefore moved away from true Christianity. The Catholic hierarchy, similarly, was seen as a human effort to create a link to God through the Church structure, in place of the immediate descent of God's love and grace to each individual. While Nygren does not explicitly criticize Catholicism, the ultimate characterization of Luther's teachings as the return to *agape* makes Nygren a sophisticated advocate for the Protestant side of the Catholic-Protestant debate.

Sources for Further Study

Hall, Thor. *Anders Nygren*. Reprint. Makers of the Modern Theological Mind series. Peabody, Mass.: Hendrickson, 1991. The best available examination of Nygren's thought, written by the foremost expert on Nygren.

Johnson, William A. *On Religion: A Study of the Theological Method in Schleiermacher and Nygren*. Leiden, the Netherlands: E. J. Brill, 1964. Consists of two parts. The first looks at the conception of religion by the late eighteenth and early nineteenth century German theologian Friedrich Schleiermacher. The second looks at Anders Nygren's conception of religion and then discusses the relation of Nygren's ideas to Schleiermacher's.

Kegley, Charles W., ed. *The Philosophy and Theology of Anders Nygren*. Carbondale: Southern Illinois University Press, 1970. A collection of essays on the work of Anders Nygren. The first chapter is an intellectual autobiography; the last is Nygren's reply to his interpreters and critics. The seventeen other chapters cover Nygren's philosophy of religion, his method of motif research, the meanings of love in his work, his theology, his ethics, and cultural and ecumenical concerns in his work.

Carl L. Bankston III

THE AGE OF ANXIETY
A Baroque Ecologue

Author: W. H. Auden (1907-1973)
First published: New York: Random House, 1947
Genre: Poetry
Subgenres: Allegory; narrative poetry; parables and fables
Core issues: Acceptance; alienation from God; compassion; despair; loneliness; regeneration

Modern people suffer alienation from God and estrangement from each other. Seeking to understand the world through reason and experience, they see much, but they encounter futility when they try to discover meaning in life. Increases in knowledge through scholarship and science only make the human predicament worse, and the tragedy of war demonstrates the breakdown of political effort. Only by encountering others and becoming aware of their anxiety and despair do Auden's protagonists find a measure of hope through their recovery of a vision of life with God at its center.

Overview

After flirting with romantic fascism like that represented by the thought of D. H. Lawrence and then dabbling in left-wing ideologies such as communism, socialism, and various liberal movements in the 1930's, W. H. Auden rediscovered the Christianity of his boyhood and returned to the Anglican church in 1939, not long after emigrating to the United States. Influenced by his conversion (or regeneration) after a meeting with Charles Williams and a reading of his history of Christianity, *The Descent of the Dove* (1939), Auden was also energized by reading Reinhold Niebuhr's books and by his discovery of Søren Kierkegaard's work.

Moreover, Auden had been disillusioned by political ideologies during his visit to Spain during the Civil War (1936-1937) and by encounters with both fascism and human cruelty in the slaughter of animals. Finally, the invasion of Poland by Adolf Hitler's Germany shocked Auden into a vivid awareness of human evil, although he had expected that German aggression would create war. Feeling that liberal humanism did not offer an adequate explanation for the problem of evil, Auden chose to return to Christianity—in large part because it offered a coherent vision of life. However, although Anglican Christianity became for Auden both an intellectual and an emotional commitment, his adherence to this faith did not prevent him from continuing in a lengthy homosexual relationship with Chester Kallman, an American Jewish intellectual, nor from occasional involvement in other sexual liaisons, including at least one relationship with a woman (Rhoda Jaffe, a New York intellectual and a possible model for Rosetta in Auden's poem).

The Age of Anxiety: A Baroque Ecologue, which won the Pulitzer Prize, is one of three long poetic works that Auden wrote mainly during World War II, which, following his decision to leave England, he spent in the United States as a freelance reviewer, lecturer, and instructor. In these poetic works, Auden moved away from his earlier political stances to define himself as a Christian humanist poet, while continuing to comment memorably on the social conditions of his age.

All three poems were composed as dramatic dialogues for numerous voices, a method reflecting Auden's collaboration with Christopher Isherwood during the 1930's in writing satirical plays (such as *The Dog Beneath the Skin: Or, Where Is Francis?*, pb. 1935). These ambitious long poems were *For the Time Being* (1944), a re-creation of the Nativity story, which Auden called an "oratorio"; *The Sea and the Mirror* (1944), an imaginative meditation on the characters and events of William Shakespeare's *The Tempest* (pr. 1611), which was itself a dramatic romance that emphasized forgiveness and new beginnings, themes that understandably held great interest for Auden in the 1940's; and *The Age of Anxiety*, where the chance meeting of four lonely individuals leads to an anatomy of the evils and the malaise of Auden's contemporary era and its secularism.

Auden's subtitle, *A Baroque Ecologue*, seems intended as modernist irony (somewhat in the manner of T. S. Eliot, one of the poetic leaders of modernism and a major influence on Auden). A traditional ecologue was a romantic pastoral poem, usually in dialogue, celebrating nature, simple rural life, and passionate love, although such poems were written by accomplished poets for sophisticated readers, with their tone of innocent naïveté being a pose. In addition, the Baroque era was known for a grand assertion of religious and political certainties. Unlike the literary ecologues of the seventeenth and eighteenth centuries, however, *The Age of Anxiety* is an urban poem, in essence an ironic "antipastoral," commenting on an age of uncertainty—but in a manner of extravagant language and metaphor that can be called baroque.

Most of the poem is set in a Manhattan bar, where its four speakers meet casually and soon repair to a booth for serious discussion. This quartet includes Malin, a medical officer from the Royal Canadian Air Force; Quant, a middle-aged Irish emigrant employed as a clerk; Rosetta, a Jewish buyer for a department store; and Emble, a young American sailor on shore leave. In sections called "The Seven Ages" (referring to human life) and "The Seven Stages" (divisions of history), the quartet present their vision of the human condition and its discontents, including the failure of science to provide a satisfactory explanation of the meaning of life, the failure of politics to produce utopias or even rational societies, and the mundane frustrations of everyday existence.

Eventually, the four go to Rosetta's apartment, where Emble's infatuation with Rosetta becomes apparent; but after the others leave, the inebriated Emble falls asleep instead of making love to Rosetta. Nevertheless, despite its seriocomic action, the poem ends in a tone of forgiveness and hope, as both Rosetta, meditating over her sleeping sailor, and Malin, going home alone, experience epiphanies acknowledging God's existence and goodness.

Christian Themes

Auden's poem is best approached from the context of modernist and existential theology, where "anxiety" (or unfocused concern) about the apparent meaninglessness of life (akin to the angst or "dread" of Kierkegaard and later existentialists) is an overriding concern, as Paul Tillich describes in *The Courage to Be* (1952). As the characters voice their disillusionment with modern industrial society and with the world of scientific rationalism, each reveals bitter loneliness as well as an abiding estrangement from all sources of meaning.

The four characters are presented both as individuals with personal needs and as symbolic types, for most Auden scholars agree that the quartet represents the four faculties of the mind described in the theoretical psychology of C. G. Jung. In this interpretation, Malin embodies reason; Quant, intuition; Rosetta, emotion; and Emble, sensation or experience attained through the senses. Such a scheme may indicate that Auden saw humanity as afflicted by a "divided consciousness." However, such allegorical symbolism also shows Auden's desire to endow his questing characters with a universal or "everyman" quality, as intended in traditional Christian allegories, such as John Bunyan's *The Pilgrim's Progress from This World to That Which Is to Come* (part 1, 1678; part 2, 1694).

Obviously, Auden's speakers are driven by a longing for a true community of vital human interaction, whereas the intrusive radio and other media provide only a spurious sense of authentic community. Their awareness of the futility of life lived on a purely naturalistic level should be seen as the basis for a quest for faith. The separate epiphanies of Rosetta and Malin at the poem's conclusion establish the importance of faith as a bulwark against the contingencies of temporal existence.

The two recognitions of the Divine Power are different, however. In her meditation, Rosetta returns to acceptance of the God of Judaism, while acknowledging that the experience of her people must continue to contain unmerited suffering. While Auden clearly sees Jewish religious experience as a valid alternative to Christian faith, he gives Malin an explicitly Christian view of meaning. Seeing the failure of reason to make sense of life, Malin, following the model of Kierkegaard, envisions human hope as lying in acceptance of the irrational or "absurd" paradoxes of God's assumption of humanity in the Incarnation and suffering in the Crucifixion, an unreasonable sacrifice of divine love aimed at the redemption of an irrational species known as human beings.

Sources for Further Study

Carpenter, Humphrey. *W. H. Auden: A Biography*. Boston: Houghton Mifflin, 1981. A thoroughly researched biography, this massive work offers judicious comment on Auden's many literary enterprises.

Davenport-Hines, Richard. *Auden*. New York: Pantheon Books, 1995. Vividly written biography by an able critic, who focuses on major themes in Auden's life.

Mendelson, Edward. *Later Auden*. Reprint. New York: Farrar, Straus and Giroux, 2000. A meticulous analytical study of Auden's work from 1939 through 1973, a fine companion to this author's *Early Auden* (1981), which offered first-rate analysis of Auden's poetry of the 1920's and 1930's. Mendelson devotes twenty pages to a careful analysis of *The Age of Anxiety*.

Smith, Stan, ed. *The Cambridge Companion to W. H. Auden*. New York: Cambridge University Press, 2004. Anthology of nineteen essays by significant scholars assessing Auden's life and career. Included are studies of Auden's religious views, his sexuality, and the various genres of his poetry and prose.

Spears, Monroe K. *The Poetry of W. H. Auden: The Disenchanted Island*. New York: Oxford University Press, 1968. Published in Auden's lifetime, this book remains one of the better interpretations of the Christian themes in Auden's verse.

Wright, George T. *W. H. Auden*. Boston: Twayne, 1981. This revised and expanded edition of Wright's literary study, first published in 1969, is still a reliable guide to Auden's career.

Edgar L. Chapman

AIDS TO REFLECTION

Author: Samuel Taylor Coleridge (1772-1834)
First published: 1825
Edition used: Aids to Reflection. New York: Cosimo Classics, 2005
Genre: Nonfiction
Subgenres: Meditation and contemplation; spiritual treatise; theology
Core issues: God; morality; Protestants and Protestantism; reason; self-knowledge

This spiritual treatise exemplifies Coleridge's most mature period of theological reflection, in which he moves away from the Unitarianism and materialism found in earlier poems and writings. Drawing from the works of German Idealists and British seventeenth century Anglican divines, Coleridge drafts a philosophic and didactic treatise differentiating between prudential, moral, and spiritual religion, and associates each with, respectively, the understanding, the conscience, and the will and reason, hoping to revise Anglican orthodoxy to incorporate intellectual reflection.

Overview

Aids to Reflection is considered one of Samuel Taylor Coleridge's most influential theological writings. His purpose is not only to revise Anglican orthodoxy and revive the writings of seventeenth century divines such as Archbishop Robert Leighton, whose writing on spiritual truth and religion Coleridge thought invaluable, but also to reveal the shortcomings of many religious and spiritual tenets and beliefs of contemporaries, especially those associated with evidence writing (particularly the work of Archdeacon William Paley), Socinianism (or Unitarianism), and rational theology, three religious trends that Coleridge alleged to be undermining Anglican orthodoxy.

Coleridge begins his treatise by explaining that his intention is didactic in nature; he hopes that his readers will be largely young intellectuals aspiring to greater reflective spiritual discipline, particularly those entering a clerical life. He sets forth various objectives in his preface: to acknowledge the value of words; to establish and distinguish the meanings of prudence, morality, and (spiritual) religion; to authoritatively differentiate between reason and understanding; and to do all of this within the context of a specifically Christian framework. *Aids to Reflection* is the result of the amalgamation of the author's personal transcendental philosophy with more traditional Protestant doctrine. Above all, he stresses the importance of thinking, particularly reflective thinking, considering its end, self-knowledge, to be the individual Christian's duty and purpose. Religion, Coleridge asserts, is the ultimate reality of life.

Aids to Reflection is written primarily in an aphoristic style, with the aphorisms categorized according to prudence, morality, or spirituality. Many of the aphorisms are derived from the work of Anglican divines such as Robert Leighton, Jeremy Taylor, Richard Hooker, and Henry More; however, some of Coleridge's own aphorisms are interspersed throughout the text. Coleridge's lengthy commentary on the work of the divines dominates the latter half of the book, particularly the section entitled "Aphorisms on That Which Is Indeed Spiritual Religion," and it is this work that highlights Coleridge's significance as a religious thinker.

Coleridge's aphorisms are loosely organized into the tripartite division of prudence, morality, and spiritual religion, though there is some overlap, particularly in the moral aphorisms, some of which would also fit in the division of spiritual religion. However, the three are closely related, as each successive religion builds on the former. Prudence, according to Coleridge, is necessary for there to be both moral and spiritual religion. Prudence enables virtue and holiness; though it is lesser than morality, it is still necessary, as it functions as a protector of virtue and a preventer of the sensual ("Thou shalt not").

Beyond religious prudence is religious morality, which refers to the transformation of the conscience and the heart by religious faith. This transformation is essential for the full development of spiritual religion. In this second stage of religious development, religion truly becomes a matter of personal conviction and commitment.

Spiritual religion, the highest level of religious attainment, is primarily concerned with reason and the will. For Coleridge, the will is the ultimate transcendent, transcending nature and the laws of cause and effect. Coleridge's approach refutes doctrines of Calvinism as espoused by the American philosopher Jonathan Edwards, who promulgated the notion of a completely passive will. Coleridge's active view of the will encourages a decidedly more cooperative relationship with the divine.

All of Coleridge's methods and assertions in *Aids for Reflection* are aimed at subverting the popular trends of evidence writing and rationalism in theology in the early part of the nineteenth century. Evidence writing worked to "prove" Christian beliefs and mysteries, using the idea of their "reasonableness" as proof of their veracity. Paley, Coleridge's theological archrival, wrote what is considered to be the most well known of these, *Evidences of Christianity* (1824). Coleridge abhorred this type of religious writing, finding it denied the spiritual and active aspects of religion and faith. Coleridge hoped to revitalize religion not by explaining or "proving" all its dogma, but rather by encouraging thinking and reflection on the Christian dogmas and mysteries through not a spiritual but a rational context.

Coleridge makes a distinction between reason and understanding in Aphorism 8 of the "Spiritual Religion" section. Though the influence of Immanuel Kant's critiques of reason is implicit, this precise distinction is unique to Coleridge, and he uses understanding in connection with his more negative arguments against the uninspired theology of his day, while reason is posited in connection with his positive arguments; it is the organ of a more intellectual, reflective theology. Reason precipitates complete awareness of the self and its freedom.

Coleridge ends *Aids to Reflection* by looking closely at some specific Christian beliefs and how they are matters of spiritual religion and thus are suited to be objects of the reason and cannot be sufficiently considered through Paley's philosophy. Coleridge offers a discussion of the concept of Original Sin in relation to the will and grounds his argument in the etymology of the word "original," concluding that since the sin is "original" it must have its "origin" in the individual will; that is, it is something derived internally, not something externally inflicted or inherited. With this view, Coleridge once again found himself at odds with Calvinist theology.

Coleridge's idea of a free and active will is crucial to understanding his theology as put forth in *Aids for Reflection*. The individual will is independent of a higher power, he argues, because that higher power (the spirit) would communicate only with a free will. Coleridge believed that religion, particularly Christianity, was not merely a belief system, but also a way of life, a "living process," and so it is by the will and the reason that human beings are rendered capable, through reflection, of fully realizing their spirituality. It is this effect that Coleridge hopes his aphorisms will have on the serious reader.

Christian Themes

As a didactic and spiritual treatise, *Aids to Reflection* aimed to guide those looking for a more theological and spiritual Christianity than that offered through strict adherence to orthodoxy, or an overreliance on rationalism to "explain" the Christian mysteries.

Coleridge's condemnation of contemporary divinity is striking, but especially so is his call for a revised theology and the challenge for greater reflection on spirituality. He casts himself as singular among his contemporaries, a lone prophet heralding a need for revitalization of doctrine that merely follows the letter of the law rather than the spirit.

Coleridge holds that the two greatest mysteries of Christianity are Original Sin and redemption. His linguistic argument concerning Original Sin as originating with the individual will requires that individuals alone take responsibility for their sins. Yet it is still a mystery, and its concept is not unique to Christianity—a similar philosophy can be found in almost every patriarchal faith. Yet it is Christianity alone, Coleridge concludes, that provides redemption from the power of sin. Through Christ's voluntary sacrifice for the sins of humanity, the power of sin is conquered by the power of the spirit, and thus though the individual will is separate from this higher spirit, the will and the spirit become partners through the saving grace of the redemptive spirit.

Redemption, for Coleridge, is something truly transcendental. Since the Resurrection of Christ, redemption has been an overriding state; that is, it is not something that occurs at a certain point, but rather is an ongoing condition of the Christian soul. It is the absolute that complements the reason of the individual will, and it is what enables the will to cooperate with the higher spirit. The transcendental redemption is a purifying and personal experience, and so it is most important for the true Christian to attest to the truth of religion, rather than "prove" the redeeming power of Christ through the evidence of miracles. These evidences, Coleridge vehemently argues, must not be substituted for the truth of Christian grace, which is realized through reflection and by reflection cooperating with the higher spirit of God.

Sources for Further Study

Boulger, James D. *Coleridge as Religious Thinker*. New Haven, Conn.: Yale University Press, 1961. A thorough examination and analysis of the growth and scope of Coleridge's theology, in both poetry and prose, published and unpublished. Extensive coverage of *Aids to Reflection*. Contrasts ideas in *Aids to Reflection* to those in Coleridge's theological *Notebooks* (1957-1986) and his Opus Maximum. Places Coleridge's theology within the context of his contemporaries.

Hipolito, Jeffrey. "'Conscience the Ground of Consciousness': The Moral Epistemology of Coleridge's *Aids to Reflection*." *Journal of the History of Ideas* 65, no. 3 (2004): 455-474. Situates Coleridge's theology within the greater Kantian philosophy of morals.

Perkins, Mary Ann. "Religious Thinker." In *The Cambridge Companion to Coleridge*, edited by Lucy Newlyn. Cambridge, England: Cambridge University Press, 2002. Provides a brief overview of Coleridge's religious development within his writing, with particular emphasis on his influence on later philosophers and theologians.

Jessica H. Gray

AKÉ
The Years of Childhood

Author: Wole Soyinka (1934-   )
First published: 1981
Edition used: Aké: The Years of Childhood. New York: Vintage International, 1989
Genre: Nonfiction
Subgenre: Autobiography
Core issues: Africa; innocence; memory; religion; women

In this autobiographical account of the first ten years of his life, Soyinka, the 1986 winner of the Nobel Prize in Literature, re-creates the day-to-day life in a small town in western Nigeria, where the Christian and pagan world coexisted peacefully. He depicts the personalities, events, beliefs, and ideas that shaped his thinking and nurtured his creative spirit.

Overview

The eldest son of a primary-school headmaster and a devout Christian mother, Wole Soyinka lived a comfortable life in the Aké parsonage in Abeokuta. Soyinka's father, called "Essay" by his son (for his initials S. A.), belonged to a tribal elder's family, and his mother, whom he names "Wild Christian," came from an influential family.

Soyinka was a self-confident, inquisitive, precocious child who started schooling when he was only three. The books, maps, and posters in the classroom seemed to make it the best playground he could imagine. Because his family lived in the walled church compound, it was only gradually that the little boy discovered the existence of a colorful and noisy world beyond the walls. His presence of mind and fearlessness astounded everyone when Soyinka, then four years old, became lost after following a street parade for miles. His incessant questions and self-reliant attitude set him apart from other children. Listening to the animated discussions about political and theological issues of his father and his friends—many of which were beyond his understanding—exposed him early to a rich world of ideas.

Like all autobiographies, *Aké* records interesting anecdotes, childhood adventures, and fond memories of friends and numerous relatives. However, what stands out in the narrative is the child's perspective of the illogicality of the adult world. Soyinka's devout Christian mother, his intellectual father, and his learned uncle, all strict interpreters of the Bible, firmly believed in character building by following the precept "Spare the rod and spoil the child." Physical punishment and public humiliation were administered generously for the good of the miscreants. Much to his woe, the boy realized that what he considered inhumane treatment would continue even in the next school in the distant city. The students there were not permitted to wear shoes (his parents did not allow this either) nor permitted to have pockets in their school uniform.

The connection between these strictures and character building escaped Soyinka's understanding.

The environment in which young Soyinka grew up offered an interesting mix of Christian and native Yoruba beliefs. The children were admonished to reject native superstitions and follow Christian beliefs, yet Soyinka could not help notice that spirits and native deities always played a significant part in most of his mother's tales. She tried to exorcise *emi esu*, a native demon she held responsible for her son's stubbornness and adventurous spirit, with her Christian prayers. The children were warned to stay away from *egúngun*, the masked figures representing the ancestral spirits, yet her narratives invariably conceded their mysterious power. In one of her stories, a pastor did not interrupt the church service in honor of the *egúngun* procession passing by. In anger, the leading *egúngun* tapped the church door three times with his wand. Soon after the procession passed, the church building crumbled; miraculously, the walls fell backward saving all worshipers. However, the tale narrated to celebrate the force of Christian faith failed to diminish the power of the *egúngun*.

Soyinka's memories of childhood in *Aké* reveal constant superimposition of Christian imagery on the native objects and beliefs. He thought of the saints in the stained glass window as the much revered *egúngun*. The orchard on the church property became an extension of Scripture classes. Because the children saw no apple tree in the orchard, the exotic pomegranate replaced the forbidden fruit responsible for Adam and Eve's fall from Eden.

The last three chapters of *Aké* depict the ten-year-old Soyinka as an observer and a participant in the rise of the women's movement in his hometown. The intent of the Christian wives of the professionals, a group that included his mother, to initiate young married women into the responsibilities of their position in society, turned into an effort to organize working-class women to revolt against the corrupt officials who arbitrarily imposed taxes. Beere Ransome-Kuti, the wife of the principal of Abeokuta Grammar School, became the spokeswoman for the group demanding the abolition of taxes on women's small businesses. The predictable response of the authorities— both colonial administrators and the community elders and tribal chiefs—was to ignore the women and treat them as troublemakers, but the intensity with which the rebellion spread eventually brought the authorities to their knees and forced them to negotiate.

The Egba Women's Union eventually expanded into the Nigerian Women's Union. The historic rebellion did not win the women all the concessions they sought, but it rocked the administrative authorities. The *ogboni*—the conclave of elders—lost its mysterious hold and the *Alake*—the local king in Abeokuta—lost his "throne." The district officer who failed to stem the revolt was transferred. Soyinka, in his words, "an odd job man" carrying messages between the main organizers, observed the political power play at work and learned the value of collective action. The narrative ends with Soyinka's entering his eleventh year and preparing to attend the government college in Ibadan.

Christian Themes

The relationship of Christianity and the ancient Yoruba beliefs forms the backdrop of events in *Aké*. A prevailing theme is how the African beliefs combined and conflicted with the beliefs of Christianity. Since Soyinka's parents and relatives from his mother's side were devout Christians, Christian imagery from scriptures abounds in the narrative. The converts preached emphatically against the superstitions and ignorance of the general masses, yet the native beliefs were deeply ingrained in their daily lives.

The reminiscences of the elders were replete with their own or their friends' encounters with the denizens of the spirit world. Soyinka's uncle was believed to be an *oro*—a reincarnated spirit—who was befriended by the spirits in the woods where the children gathered firewood and edible plants. When he suffered from a mysterious ailment, the cure suggested by a convert acquaintance was to offer an appeasement feast to the offended spirits. It is hard to miss the irony in Soyinka's mother's admission that the sick child recovered after the unseen spirits had devoured the feast.

Similarly, no one in *Aké* challenged that the daughter of the bookseller—a family friend—was an *abiku*, someone who, under the spell of spirits, goes through a repeated cycle of birth and death. Her occasional trancelike state was attributed to these malevolent spirits who could be appeased only with a feast to honor them. These practices, in direct contradiction to Christian beliefs, remained unquestioned.

Even Beere Ransom-Kuti, the leader of the emerging women's movement, was believed to possess supernatural powers. The word went around that it was her stern look at the haughty, disrespectful chieftain that brought on his stroke, bringing him literally to his knees. The power of the voodoo objects sneaked into the Kuti family compound was neutralized by the prayers of a church official. Similarly, the young aspirants for admission to the government college often resorted to voodoo practices to improve their chances, and ironically, if confronted by such an object, chanted SMOG (an acronym for Save Me O God) to ward off its evil effects. This juxtaposition of native practices and Christian remedies permeates the narrative and accounts for Soyinka's subsequent loss of faith in his parents' beliefs.

Sources for Further Study

Gibbs, James. "Wole Soyinka." In *Twentieth-Century Caribbean and Black African Writers*. Vol. 125 in *Dictionary of Literary Biography*, 2d ser. New York: Gale Group, 1993. Provides an exhaustive overview of Soyinka's activism and an analysis of his major works with their contemporary critical reception. Also available online.

Gordimer, Nadine. "The Child Is the Man." Review of *Aké*. *The New York Review of Books* (October 21, 1982): 3, 6. A perceptive analysis of the strengths and weaknesses of *Aké* in the context of autobiographies written by African writers. While admiring Soyinka's sensual evocation of the place where he grew up, Gordimer raises questions about the credibility of the total recall and the remarkable ripostes of a three- to four-year-old child.

Wright, Derek. "History and Fiction: The Autobiographies." In *Wole Soyinka Revisited*. New York: Twayne, 1993. This chapter in Wright's detailed study of Soyinka's works discusses *Aké* in the context of his two other autobiographical works, *"The Man Died": Prison Notes of Wole Soyinka* (1972) and *Ìsarà: A Voyage Around "Essay"* (1989). Wright's analysis of *Aké* provides a valuable insight into Soyinka's developing sense of self. Also useful is the "Glossary of Yoruba and Other African Terms and Names" for readers unfamiliar with the dialect.

Leela Kapai

ALL NEW PEOPLE

Author: Anne Lamott (1954-   )
First published: San Francisco: North Point Press, 1989
Genre: Novella
Subgenres: Literary fiction; meditation and contemplation
Core issues: Acceptance; African Americans; alienation from God; awakening; confession; forgiveness; illumination; psychology

Reflecting its author's emergence from a troubled past of insecurity occasioned by her father's premature death from brain cancer, Lamott's fourth novel depicts the journey of her protagonist, Nanny Goodman, from the darkness of drug addiction, alcoholism, and a profound depression and alienation into a quiet, joyful, quasi-Christian acceptance of what may come.

> *Principal characters*
> *Nanny Goodman*, the skinny, frizzy-haired protagonist and narrator
> *Casey Goodman*, Nanny's slightly older brother
> *Robbie Goodman*, Nanny's witty and talented father
> *Marie Goodman*, Nanny's Christian mother
> *Uncle Ed*, Robbie's appealing but ne'er-do-well alcoholic brother
> *Aunt Peg*, Uncle Ed's wife
> *Natalie*, Marie's best friend

Overview

All New People closely follows Anne Lamott's life, a major event of which was the early death of her father, also a writer. The novel begins with a prologue in which the protagonist, Nanny Goodman, is undergoing hypnosis therapy. She says that her life is a mess and her mind is broken. Affairs, drugs, alcohol, depression, anxiety, fears of suicide, madness, and death constitute an insupportable burden. Nanny is in her twenties, but the therapist requires her to regress to childhood, reminding one both of Carl Jung's admonitions about the need to go back in order to go forward and of Christ's words about suffering little children.

The narrative proper begins with a largely idyllic picture of a pre-Yuppie Marin County across the Golden Gate Bridge from San Francisco and moves chronologically to Nanny's present, wherein she has presumably learned to shoulder the burdens under which she was sinking. Over the course of this narrative, the Edenic green and golden Marin County that Nanny loved disappears, along with its most famous landmark, mythic Mount Tamalpais, known as the Sleeping Woman. The landscape is a major presence in the novel, but it is gradually submerged by present reality as it becomes one of America's most sought-after and costliest pieces of real estate. The transformation of the beautiful prelapsarian rural county into an upscale world of high-priced shops, expensive restaurants, architect-designed houses, luxury cars, and wealthy people parallels Nanny's loss of innocence and her slide into a slough of despond, now that she has no anchors.

As the 1950's become the 1960's, the social and political upheavals of the Vietnam War infect all the characters with a pervasive unease. Fathers abandon families, families break up, people break down, and drugs, insecurities, and anomie proliferate. Nanny's brother Casey is setting a course for trouble with drugs and appears to be thinking about fleeing the draft to Canada. Uncle Ed and Aunt Peg separate. One of Nanny's friends is raped and murdered. Marie's best friend, Natalie, pregnant by Ed, moves to San Diego with her brood. Marie is in a car accident on her way to Carmel to offer succor to Peg, and as the national and local and personal centers cannot hold, even Peg—the only one to possess a Christian faith—finds herself hard pressed to sustain it.

Politics offers no hope for these characters, all of whom are liberal and lean to the left as a matter of course, in this liberal era. The novel is peppered with references to the Bay of Pigs, George McGovern, Eugene McCarthy, and Pat Brown of California—but these progressive leaders all lose in their respective elections. Conversely, to vote for Richard Nixon or "Ronnie the Rat" Reagan is to be contemptuously dismissed as a political troglodyte. As W. B. Yeats proclaimed in his prophetic poem "Slouching Towards Bethlehem," the best lack all conviction while the worst are full of a passionate intensity. The only solace is the bitter knowledge that in a hundred years the world will contain "all new people"—hence the title, with its multiple significances.

The evidence of an ever-present redemptive grace is nevertheless alluded to all along, usually wittily or with what would seem to many irreverence in a novel formed by equal parts of offbeat humor and serious purpose. Marie, a Christian, has shaken her fist at a God she calls a "retard" and a "cheese-dick" for allowing such disasters as the Vietnam War, with its pain and death, to happen. A Presence follows her around, an inescapable scent of a stray dog or cat, until Marie thinks she might end her life wearing a sandwich board for Jesus in downtown San Francisco.

This Presence manifests itself chiefly in an African American church in a black working-class neighborhood that appears frequently in Lamott's writings. It is far from accidental that the movement forward and upward toward the reintegration of the disintegrated lives of the novel—principally the narrator's—is symbolized at the end of the novel by a sermon in this church on the Crucifixion, followed by Nanny's dream of a newborn baby taken from a coffin and handed to her as the infant calmly and alertly looks around, just taking in the world. Nanny knows who it is. The last scene, confirming the reassembling of the scattered lives, takes place at a wedding of Casey's old school friend, who is now a Republican banker and wears a hairpiece. Like all true comedies, the novel ends in this marriage and its celebration—preceded in this case by a death and a birth to complete the cycle.

Christian Themes

Lamott has devised a new kind of religious writing comprising reverence and wise-cracks. A word that means both "wit" and "seriousness" is needed to describe La-mott's religious views. She might be called a literal Protestant, although in college she wanted to be a Jew, and to that end her clever, funny Jewish friends bat-mitzvahed her at her request. Her Christianity did not appear in her novels, however, until *All New People*, her fourth. It is much more evident in her nonfiction and in the columns she contributed to Salon.com starting in 1999. In them, she puts herself on the line as un-equivocally as Flannery O'Connor (though 180 degrees removed from that writer ex-cept for her acceptance of the reality of God and Jesus, whom she says she encoun-tered as a real presence in an airplane lavatory thirty-five thousand feet up). She is a single mother, uninhibited and outspoken, an ex-hellraising drug user and alcoholic and a fierce and angry leftist activist who hates George W. Bush and the war in Iraq, including what she recognizes as the injustice, poverty, sybaritic affluence, blindness, insularity, and indifference it fosters.

Lamott believes that American conservatives are deeply wrong and fears that an American theocracy is a real and terrifying possibility. Her version of Christianity would cause mass apoplexy among American fundamentalists, who, she believes, consider heaven to be a great fortress created just for them and barring outsiders from entry. By contrast, Lamott holds that those who have created God in their own image are likely to be off track if it turns out that that God hates the same people they do. Pro-fane and sarcastic and funny, Lamott nevertheless takes absolutely seriously her Christian faith. She believes fervently that the center of Christianity is to try to do well by as many people as one can manage, no matter how antipathetic. She finds sublim-ity in the daily, materially aided in this by her black church in "non-Yuppie" Marin City ("No MBA. No condo. No BMW"), of which she is a regular communicant and which plays an important part, perhaps a central part, in her life and works. This church, she has noted, taught her to have hope, because if there is hope for someone like her—who did not leap but rather staggered into faith—there is hope for everyone.

Sources for Further Study

Lamott, Anne. *Plan B: Further Thoughts on Faith*. New York: Riverhead Books, 2005. Essays on what it means to live a Christian life in the confusion and stresses of a present even more problematic that that of Lamott's earlier nonfiction.

_____. *Traveling Mercies: Some Thoughts on Faith*. New York: Anchor Books, 2000. Lamott thinks of these essays as a handbook for people trying to live faithfully against long odds. A number of them are not specifically religious.

Tennant, Agnieszka. "'Jesusy' Anne Lamott." *Christianity Today*, January 21, 2003. A sympathetic perspective on an iconoclastic and challenging writer whose radical Christianity is, perhaps surprisingly, rooted in tradition.

Stanley Poss

AMAZING GRACE
A Vocabulary of Faith

Author: Kathleen Norris (1947-   )
First published: 1998
Edition used: Amazing Grace: A Vocabulary of Faith. New York: Riverhead Trade, 1999
Genre: Nonfiction
Subgenres: Autobiography; meditation and contemplation; theology
Core issues: Church; conversion; grace; monasticism; self-knowledge

In this work, Norris describes her journey from a religious upbringing in her childhood, to rejection of the Church as irrelevant in her early adulthood, and to her gradual conversion to a life of faith based on participation in a Christian community. Along the way, she struggled with the special vocabulary used by church people. After personal experience enabled her to interpret such terms, she decided to share her insights with others who may be having the same kind of struggle.

Overview

Kathleen Norris has written in detail about her personal quest for a mature religious faith. *Dakota: A Spiritual Geography* (1992) described her move from New York City to a small town in South Dakota where she rediscovered her religious roots after attending her grandmother's church. A personal crisis in her marriage brought Norris to a retreat at a Benedictine monastery in Minnesota. After several periods of residency, she described the eye-opening experience of living in a community of monks and nuns in *The Cloister Walk* (1996). The third book in this series is *Amazing Grace: A Vocabulary of Faith.* It contains short essays, meditations, anecdotes, and historical commentary about the sometimes forbidding vocabulary used in Christian churches. What is meant by "salvation," the Incarnation, or the Apocalypse? Norris wants to share her personal insights with other people who also may have found such words to be obstacles in their journey of faith.

The Bible is the foundational document for the Christian church. In the essay "Bible," Norris is not concerned with any intellectual arguments about symbolic versus literal interpretation of the Scriptures. Instead, she tells the story of a South Dakota rancher who had received a Bible from his grandfather as a wedding gift. He had laid it away on a closet shelf while he struggled to make a living. Toward the end of his life, he finally looked into it and discovered that his grandfather had placed a twenty-dollar bill in each book of the Bible. Altogether the money added up to more than a thousand dollars, which could have helped him through some hard times. This anecdote is a simple reminder that the Bible needs to be read. If it is just kept on a shelf, it is of no value. Norris credits her monastery experience with making her aware that the Bible conveys a sacred perspective that is genuinely helpful in dealing with the problems of daily life.

In the essay "Prayer," Norris recommends the Psalms to readers as a helpful starting point to approach God. She rejects the selfish kind of prayer that asks God for material things or for personal success in some enterprise. From her observation, she says, "Even many Christians seem to regard prayer as a grocery list we hand to God, and when we don't get what we want, we assume that the prayers didn't 'work.'" She has come to view prayer as a dialogue in which one needs to listen for God's voice. The outcome of prayer might well be an unanticipated, surprising change in oneself rather than the elimination of the problem that one is facing.

The word "evangelism" brings to mind an image of someone on a street corner with a Bible in hand, accosting people to ask if they "know the Lord." Norris rejects the idea of forcing one's faith on someone else. She expresses appreciation to her local congregation in South Dakota for giving her time to grow in faith without being pressured. It took several years until she was able to make a commitment to join the Christian community. At a later occasion, she had a conversation with a woman who also was attempting to find her way back to the Church. By sharing her personal journey of faith, she was able to help this woman see the way ahead more clearly. Norris was grateful for the opportunity to fulfill the role of evangelist in this situation by friendly discussion rather than confrontation.

In the essay entitled "God-Talk," Norris expresses exasperation with sermons that stick to biblical language without translating its abstract concepts into concrete human experience. The jargon, or specialized vocabulary used by professionals in a field of study, may be useful within that circle of experts, but it often fails to communicate to the general public. Norris feels strongly that doctrinal language, the jargon of Christian faith, needs a recognizable human interpretation to become meaningful. She identifies with outsiders who are turned off by pastors who talk in generalities about faith and grace without demonstrating how such concepts find application in people's lives.

The word "Pentecost" refers to an event in the book of Acts, fifty days after Easter, when the Holy Spirit came to the disciples. They received the gift of speaking in foreign languages so that people from many nations miraculously could hear the Gospel message in their native tongue. Norris notes that in modern times, Pentecostal churches are at odds with mainline Protestant denominations because of their apocalyptic theology and their style of worship. Pentecostal worship generally is characterized by personal testimonies, revival hymns, raising one's arms to God, and sometimes speaking in tongues. Coming from a Presbyterian background, Norris confesses that such emotional displays make her feel uncomfortable. However, after she became friends with an Assembly of God pastor and went to some worship services, she came to admire the diversity of people who attended. A successful businessperson and a person recently released from a mental hospital somehow bonded together in this fellowship. Norris wondered if people who live on the margins of society would feel as welcome in her home congregation as they evidently did here. After recalling how Jesus provided healing and acceptance for a tax collector, a leper, a rich young man, and a prostitute, she developed an enlarged vision of Pentecost, where people with different wounds and a variety of gifts spoke in different languages but were able to be understood.

Christian Themes

Norris gives a personal interpretation of some eighty terms used in Christian worship. Her vocabulary list includes essays on salvation, incarnation, repentance, grace, apocalypse, and the Trinity. One can imagine an adult Sunday school class reading any of these essays to provide a starting point for group discussion. People with diverse backgrounds would be able to contribute different perspectives to bring about a greater appreciation for the wide variety of individual religious experiences.

A major theme to which Norris returns several times in her book is conversion. One of her grandmothers was a "born-again" Christian who had committed her life to Jesus when she responded to the altar call at a revival meeting. Conversion was a one-time, emotional event that she would remember for the rest of her life. Her other grandmother had been brought up by her parents to read the Bible and to memorize and recite important verses. Conversion for her was not a spectacular moment of decision, but a continuation of her inherited faith expressed in kind deeds done for others.

Norris was in her mid-thirties, living in New York as a writer, when she began to feel that she was drifting along rather aimlessly. Her conversion was a very gradual process. She credits her conversion to friends in her small-town congregation, the Benedictine monks and nuns at the monastery, meditative reading in the Bible, and inspiration received from the writings of saints in the early Christian church. She did not follow in the path set by either of her grandmothers. Her story provides readers with reassurance that conversion can take place in a multitude of ways.

Sources for Further Study

Borg, Marcus J. *Reading the Bible Again for the First Time: Taking the Bible Seriously but Not Literally.* San Francisco: HarperSanFrancisco, 2001. Recounts the author's journey of faith, from literal acceptance of Bible stories in childhood toward a more mature understanding based on the stories' historical context and metaphorical meaning.

Cooper, David D. Review of *Amazing Grace. Fourth Genre* 6, no. 2 (Fall, 2004): 147-149. Examines how the concept of the lived experience of faith permeates the work.

Norris, Kathleen. *The Cloister Walk.* New York: Riverhead Books, 1996. Describes the author's personal experiences during her extended visits to a monastery, where she learned to appreciate the significance of ritual and liturgy in creating the sense of community for which she had been searching.

_____. Interview by Dick Staub. *Christianity Today* (July 15, 2002). http://www.ctlibrary.com/ct/2002/julyweb-only/7-15-21.0.html. Transcription of a radio interview in which Norris expresses regret at succumbing to peer pressure during the late 1960's and experimenting with sex and drugs and describes how she gradually was able to change her lifestyle.

Shurr, William H., ed. *New Poems of Emily Dickinson*. Chapel Hill: University of North Carolina Press, 1993. Contains poems, letters, and other writings by Emily Dickinson, whose vivid imagination, unorthodox style, and religious insights are greatly admired by Norris.

Taylor, David. *The Myth of Certainty: Trusting God, Asking Questions, Taking Risks*. Grand Rapids, Mich.: Zondervan, 1992. A thoughtful analysis of the tension between traditional Christian faith and intellectual inquiry, using an unusual format of essays interspersed with delightful, fictional anecdotes.

Hans G. Graetzer

"AMAZING PEACE"
"A Christmas Poem"

Author: Maya Angelou (Marguerite Johnson; 1928-　　)
First published: New York: Random House, 2005
Genre: Poetry
Subgenre: Lyric poetry
Core issues: African Americans; Christmas; connectedness; friendship; hope; peace

In a world of hatred, natural disasters, and war, the poem laments the abuse of our environment and of one another, urging humanity to work actively for peace and appealing to God to remember his covenant.

Overview

Maya Angelou's books of poetry, like her groundbreaking autobiographies, have topped best-seller lists. The first printing of the 32-page *Amazing Peace* was 230,000—a record for a book of poetry. Readers who are impatient with the ambiguity and complexity of much modern verse find Angelou's poetry disarmingly casual and accessible on the first reading.

Although Angelou (then known as Marguerite Johnson) received only a modest public education in Stamps, Arkansas, and San Francisco, she overcame sexual and spousal abuse and prostitution to become an autobiographer, poet, and teacher. She has become nationally known and respected for her work, which is more political and populist than that of many writers.

The political overtones in her work reflect her long history as a civil rights activist. She was appointed coordinator for Martin Luther King, Jr.'s Southern Christian Leadership Conference (1959-1960) and worked on civil rights committees for Gerald Ford (1975-1976) and Jimmy Carter (1978-1979).

Angelou's prominence in the arena of civil rights led to her being called on to create special occasion verse for political events. For Bill Clinton's presidential inauguration on January 20, 1993, Angelou composed and performed "On the Pulse of Morning." At the time, the United States poet laureate was the scholarly African American poet Rita Dove, but Angelou's triumphant spirit more broadly represented the Democratic platform. Angelou received a Spoken Word Grammy for the White House reading. Two years later, Angelou delivered "A Brave and Startling Truth" for the United Nations' fiftieth anniversary.

During the White House's Sixty-Third Annual Pageant of Peace on December 1, 2005, Angelou read "Amazing Peace" before President George W. Bush lit the national Christmas tree. Peace on Earth has been the theme of the tree-lighting ceremony since President Calvin Coolidge began the Pageant of Peace tradition in 1923.

Angelou's "Amazing Peace," influenced by the rhetoric, rhythm, and imagery of Southern black preachers and gospel choirs, generated meaning through her performance of the poem and was imbued with significance because of the preeminent setting at the White House and the momentous occasion. However, "Amazing Peace" does not stand on its own as a spectacular piece of literature. Critical responses to "Amazing Peace," described as an "antiwar" poem, were largely unfavorable, with one critic describing it as being "memorable" only for being "unmemorable." In fairness, however, it is important to remember that the main purpose of national, special occasion verse is not to be ambiguous, profound, and intricate, but to function as a rousing call to a mass of listeners.

Angelou, a charismatic seventy-seven-year-old when she read her poem at the White House, was a mature matriarchal figure who had weathered many personal storms. She began her poem with a tribute to the thousands of victims of Hurricane Katrina, which had ravaged New Orleans and the southern United States just months before her reading. Wielding power from the first word, "Thunder," to the last phrase, "Peace, my Soul," "Amazing Peace" opens with a clap of thunder and a flash of lightning that by the end of the 480-word, 13-stanza poem, is subdued by the jubilant shouts of the masses, crying for peace.

"Amazing Peace" depends on counterbalance for its structure: tempest and peace, shouts and silence, warring and waiting, fear and security, believers and nonbelievers, brother and sister, as well as heaven and earth. The audible, visual storm is the only extended metaphor, functioning as a literal storm and figuratively as despair. Otherwise, the imagery is manipulated arbitrarily: an avalanche becomes a raised platform, a tabula rasa for a peaceful world to reach higher ground.

"Amazing Peace" dreams big, but realistically; it acknowledges that peace is not here yet, so it incants the word into being, expectant that peace will fall on the platform as if it were the landing pad for a space shuttle. In the 62-line poem, the first mention of "peace" appears at the midpoint. This "true Peace"—"Not just the absence of war"—becomes the dominant theme. At first a whisper, it increases and becomes louder than exploding bombs. Somehow it creates a majestic world of harmony and security. As a poet, Angelou hoped to be more than a "peacemaker"; she wanted to speak to hearts of every "hulk or dove" as a "peacebringer" and urge them to pursue peace in their daily movements.

Christian Themes

The title of the poem immediately calls to mind the hymn "Amazing Grace," in which the speaker comes through "many dangers, toils, and snares," and the earth ultimately dissolves like snow. Yet the hymn proclaims that God offers a life of "joy and peace" after trial and tribulation, a theme echoed in Angelou's "Amazing Peace."

Like prophecies in the Bible, Angelou's poem is an oracular revisioning of the future conceived of as a return to creation out of a formless void, as in Genesis 1 and 2. In the wake of Hurricane Katrina and amid growing fears of global warming, the first two stanzas of the poem strip Everytown, USA, as bare as winter and forecast coming disasters in what appears to be the apocalypse. The Job-like speaker questions God: "Are you there? Are you there, really?" God is pressed to remember his covenant, which could refer either to the promise he made to Noah that he would never destroy the earth with water—disqualifying twenty-first century hurricanes and avalanches—or to the covenant made with Abraham that countless descendants would inherit a promised land.

The poem describes a present-day Babel, partitioned according to religions, nations, and tribes, wherein communication is predominantly argument and accusation. Angelou, a Protestant, impartially addresses members of all major religions and sects: Baptists, Methodists, Catholics, Jews, Muslims, Buddhists, Jainists, and Confucians. These "believers and nonbelievers" alike have failed peace or simply have no alternative vision.

Into this purgatory, shifting between the negative forces of natural disaster, war, and hatred, "Christmas enters." In a passing reference, the "Holy Instant" of Jesus' birth is credited as being the universal source of trust, hope, and peace. Jesus alone is responsible for the "Glad Season," a time of Yuletide friendship "streaming lights of joy," "ringing bells of hope," and "singing carols of forgiveness."

"Amazing Peace," read before the lighting of the national Christmas tree, returns Christianity to the meaning of this holiday symbol. The poem unapologetically acknowledges that the birth of Christ is ecumenical and impartial, the only reason to commemorate December 25 and the only means of initiating peace on earth. This Christmas poem boldly offers the world an oblique invitation to accept the advent of light, Jesus Christ, and the peace he wants to bring to earth. "Amazing Peace" echoes the utopian vision of "On the Pulse of Morning" when it urges "all the earth's tribes" to stop hating one another and "look beyond complexion and see community." Angelou envisions everyone joining hands and together seeking peace in these often-quoted lines: "We, Angels and Mortals, Believers and Nonbelievers,/ Look heavenward and speak the word aloud./ Peace."

Sources for Further Study

Angelou, Maya. *Collected Autobiographies*. New York: Modern Library, 2004. A compilation of Angelou's six acclaimed autobiographies, unabridged.

_____. *Conversations with Maya Angelou*. Jackson: University Press of Mississippi, 1989. Reprinted interviews from 1971 to 1988 reveal Angelou's indomitable, nonconformist spirit and insistent survivor's drive as she created her identity and found her place in America.

Hagen, Lyman B. *Heart of a Woman, Mind of a Writer, and Soul of a Poet: A Critical Analysis of the Writings of Maya Angelou*. Lanham, Md.: University Press of America, 1996. Hagen aspires to validate Angelou's prominent status in his effusive presentation of "layers and depth" within her eclectic canon of messages or "sermons." Bibliography, index.

Lupton, Mary Jane. *Maya Angelou: A Critical Companion*. Westport, Conn.: Greenwood Press, 1998. Lupton discusses the structural and literary development in each volume of Angelou's five-volume autobiography, arguing that Angelou transcends both the genre and the African American experience. Bibliography, index.

McPherson, Dolly. *Order Out of Chaos: The Autobiographical Works of Maya Angelou.* New York: Peter Lang, 1990. A critical study that comprehensively examines topics including the circuitous journey, homecoming, maternal angst, personal chaos, and epiphanies in five autobiographies. Bibliography.

Saher, Annette D., Sebastian M. Brenninkmeyer, and Daniel C. O'Connell. "Maya Angelou's Inaugural Poem: 'On the Pulse of Morning.'" *Journal of Psycholinguistic Research* 26, no. 4 (July, 1997): 449-463. A technical, fascinating linguistic analysis charting how the inaugural poem's true meaning is conveyed only through the unpredictably rich sounds and rhythms of Angelou's performance.

Pam Fox Kuhlken

AND I ALONE HAVE ESCAPED TO TELL YOU
My Life and Pastimes

Author: Ralph McInerny (1929-   )
First published: Notre Dame, Ind.: University of Notre Dame Press, 2006
Genre: Nonfiction
Subgenres: Autobiography; church history
Core issues: Catholics and Catholicism; faith; knowledge; truth

McInerny's autobiography comprises twelve chapters that address key themes in his life. In addition to providing sketches of his upbringing, education, and family life, these chapters gradually move into a direct defense of McInerny's lifelong loyalty to the philosophy of Thomas Aquinas, a philosophy grounded in respect for the authority of the Church. Despite his prodigious accomplishments as a writer of detective fiction and scholarly works, his autobiography is modest about his talents and courteous in its strong indictments of modernism.

Overview

In his brief and readable autobiography *And I Alone Have Escaped to Tell You*, Ralph McInerny traces the events that led him away from a life as a priest to the life of a professor of philosophy at the University of Notre Dame and a parallel career as the author of more than sixty-five Father Dowling mysteries. Arranged chronologically, the book clusters events around themes expressed in the chapter titles. McInerny traces his growth from his Irish Catholic boyhood and early education through his appointment at Notre Dame. He describes his success as a writer of popular fiction, then addresses more directly the passions of his intellectual and religious life. Two of these are the life and teachings of Saint Thomas Aquinas and the erosion of the Catholic Church's traditional identity through the effects of Vatican II.

McInerny's family members were firmly and deeply committed to the practice of Catholicism. His parents were strictly observant believers; his mother, in fact, was a lay member of a religious order. McInerny's studies at a Catholic college-preparatory school were the same as those offered to young men planning to enter the priesthood. McInerny assumed his life would lead to ordination, but before leaving high school, he had turned his sights toward scholarship and university teaching. His undergraduate and graduate work culminated with a Ph.D. in philosophy from Laval University.

At his university, McInerny immersed himself in the study of Aquinas and the foundations of Scholasticism. These interests followed him throughout his career, the entirety of which (except a brief stint at Creighton University) was spent at Notre Dame. The location of many of his mystery stories on campus suggests that for McInerny, Notre Dame made possible a seamless integration of his family, his two careers, and his spiritual life.

A major focus of the later chapters of McInerny's memoir is the shift at Notre Dame from the sacred toward the secular in education generally, but in the philosophy department specifically. This shift he attributes to the misguided desire of Notre Dame, like the ancient Israelites, to be like its neighbors. To achieve this competitive likeness with secular institutions such as Stanford or Brown, McInerny believes that Notre Dame gradually gave away a significant part of what made it unique—its Catholic heritage. In its place came a "culture of dissent," made up of faculty eager to prove to the world that even though they worked at Notre Dame, they answered to no one, most especially the Vatican. Much of his life was spent in rallying students and faculty to resist these trends and preserve their heritage.

Obedience to authority is a key element of McInerny's Christian values. Despite the Church's lapses over the centuries, McInerny separates the incorrect or even evil acts of individuals from the "magisterium" of the Church: its authority to define and teach doctrine. That authority is larger than individuals and even that of entire eras, McInerny affirms. As his autobiography progresses, McInerny expresses his concern for the Church more forcefully. Vatican II is the central cause of these concerns. The changes reflected in the documents of Vatican II were not simply stylistic, McInerny feels, but substantial and damaging. McInerny points out the influences of liberal theologians like Karl Rahner and the even greater impact of a manipulative world press. Authors of the documents that came out of this council caved in to pressure from clergy and laity alike, he says, to make the Church "relevant" to modern life. The resulting downshift in interpretation of doctrine into the lives of laity has produced confusion and rudderless drifting by a generation reared on these revisions. McInerny feels this loss to be deep and grievous, a feeling that may have inspired the title of his book. Like the servant in Job, McInerny announces to his readers what they may expect to experience next as their weakened Church attempts to respond to its challenges.

Increasingly marginalized in his own discipline and relegated to the sidelines by modernist philosophers, McInerny made subtle use of his popular fiction as a pulpit for his understated views. Father Dowling, a recovering alcoholic, became a genial spokesperson for McInerny's conservative beliefs. Liberal in compassion and forgiveness, this character is nonetheless thoughtful and regretful about much of what has happened to the Church. It is one of McInerny's best strategies as a writer to make this priest gracious and urbane rather than didactic. As a result, Father Dowling became a comforting figure for many Catholics, especially those mourning the loss of traditional features of their faith.

McInerny acknowledges that he is better known for his career as a writer of popular fiction, but he has not gone unnoticed as a scholar and teacher. Holder of two Fulbrights for study abroad, he also served on the President's Committee for the Arts and Humanity and received several honorary degrees and numerous awards from philosophical societies. His students have gone on to major appointments at universities in the United States and abroad, and their scholarly work keeps the contributions of Aquinas, Maritain, and McInerny alive. Indeed, this volume of reflections on scholarship, family life, and contemporary Catholicism is, despite its title, confident and hopeful. Its judgments are rueful instead of gloating, and its celebrations of the stream of good people through McInerny's life are filled with gratitude and hope.

Christian Themes

McInerney's autobiography, as well as the body of his scholarship, focuses primarily on tradition, specifically the usefulness and relevance of the thought of Thomas Aquinas to modern Christianity. Like Aquinas, McInerny considers it self-evident that the human mind is a meaning-making device. An innate desire to know, humanity's defining trait, not only motivates the mind's practical, secular curiosity, which has produced a wide range of accomplishments in the arts and sciences, but also drives the human being to know God. One's innate logical powers, McInerny feels, can lead one to respect the hard-won truths of tradition and apply their guidelines to contemporary life.

While it does not have the ecstasy of mysticism or the fire of dramatic conversion, McInerny's experience of Christianity does not lack joy or depth. McInerny does find in his examination of the details of his ordinary life an intriguing element of mystery. Particularly where self-knowledge is concerned, he finds himself, like Saint Paul, unable to say with certainty at some moments whether he is in a state of grace. McInerny's definition of faith is, in part, the willingness to rest within occasional uncertainties, comforted by similar experiences expressed by saints and mystics throughout the history of Christianity.

As his autobiography progresses, McInerny's concern for the future of Christianity emerges as an overriding theme. In the latter chapters, McInerny sees modern philosophers and theologians as those who, in the abandonment of authority and tradition, have set on a clear path toward disaster. In his arguments, McInerny repeatedly relies on common sense and elementary logic to show that the dismantling of faith and ethics through pluralism, relativism, or simple wrongheaded dissent is for him fraught with peril. In this domain, McInerny presents himself candidly as a prophet calling on church officials, scholars, and laity to review their faith and return to its core values.

Sources for Further Study

Gorman, Anita G. "Ralph McInerny." In *American Mystery and Detective Writers*. Detroit, Mich.: Gale, 2005. An overview of McInerny's detective fiction with analyses of individual novels and an exhaustive survey of critical reactions to his work in this genre. McInerny's Father Dowling series draws its vitality from its deft depiction of social mores of Catholic society, according to Gorman.

Hibbs, Thomas, and John O'Callaghan, eds. *Recovering Nature: Essays in Natural Philosophy, Ethics, and Metaphysics in Honor of Ralph McInerny*. Notre Dame, Ind.: University of Notre Dame Press, 1999. A collection of essays analyzing the leadership of McInerny in opening a dialogue among competing interpreters of the intellectual heritage of Catholicism.

Labrie, Ross. "Ralph McInerny." In *The Catholic Imagination in American Literature*. Columbia: University of Missouri Press, 1997. Labrie cites McInerny's record of creativity, both in fiction and in scholarship, as evidence of a uniquely Catholic sensibility tied to the artist's self-conscious identification with his religious
tradition.

Anita Tully

THE ANGEL OF HISTORY

Author: Carolyn Forché (1950-   )
First published: New York: HarperCollins, 1994
Genre: Poetry
Subgenre: Lyric poetry
Core issues: Despair; doubt; good vs. evil; knowledge; social action

In this collection of socially conscious poems, activist poet Forché discusses the accommodations that people make with life and their memory of that life. Drawing on her own experience of war in El Salvador and Beirut, she explores moral disasters such as the Holocaust, war, and Hiroshima, piecing together the compromises that human beings make in order to survive the unimaginable. The book received the Los Angeles Times *Book Award in 1994.*

Overview

The title of Carolyn Forché's book is drawn from Jewish German Walter Benjamin's essay "Theses on the Philosophy of History" (1940), in which Benjamin talks about the power of history to overwhelm human memory and understanding. The angel of history, Benjamin says, watches events hurtle past, while debris from disaster after disaster piles at his feet. History can be lived meaningfully only through redemptive vision and practice, and otherwise is only a dead set of facts. The angel hopelessly yearns to reassemble the smashed fragments of the past but is rendered unable to engage in that task because of the pressures of the future. Benjamin says, "The angel would like to stay, awaken the dead, and make whole what has been smashed. But . . . the storm irresistibly propels him into the future to which his back is turned, while the pile of debris before him grows skyward."

Benjamin's angel, who records history as he witnesses it, is the being to whom the multitude of voices in Forché's book speak. Many of the voices making up the poems are deliberately ambiguous, without gender, and unknowable, mere fragments that swirl past in the whirlwind of history. Others are more developed and specific, allowed to speak at length: Forché's paternal grandmother Anna, a Czech immigrant; a suicidal mental patient in Paris whose experiences with the Nazis have led him to believe that God is a psychopath; Hungarian poet Miklos Radnoti, found buried in a mass grave of concentration camp victims, his poems crumpled in his pocket; and a survivor of Hiroshima who has become a tour guide in the Garden Shukkei-en, telling a tourist: "We have not, all these years, felt what you call happiness/ But at times, with good fortune, we experience something close."

The accomplished and moving poems rely on verbal as well as visual fragments to display the historical entities too large to be shown in any other fashion: a boy pedaling a bicycle, blank-eyed, a broken doll in the basket before him; a flock of crows descending on a dead child, pulling at its hair in order to feather their nests; and a hungry baby crawling over its mother's corpse, crying for milk. Again and again, the poems present individual visual fragments that, collected into a mosaic, show the landscape of death, devastation, war, and horror that makes up the twentieth century. In a similar strategy, Forché presents the group of individual voices speaking at each moment as a means of encapsulating the experience of a group of survivors who become representative of humanity overall and the suffering to which all human beings are subject.

This collection of voices contemplating history in retrospect makes up the voice of the soul, the angel of history seems to insist, as voice after voice passes like a witnessing ghost through the pages of the book. These are the voices that must make sense of the events that they have lived through, as people's individual souls must make sense of the storm of history whirling around them in their daily lives.

In this way, the narrator of the poems becomes not a single "I," but rather a collection of history's voices over the course of the twentieth century, witness after witness to suffering and evil who insist on asking the question, "What place does God have in such a world as this?" From the launching point of this question, Forché posits poetry as a force that enables us to contemplate the sacred. The act of iterating the events, of contemplating horror and transmuting it into something, elevates the soul, and that is the duty of those trying to make sense of this world.

Like Benjamin, Forché sees history, particularly twentieth century history, as an epic story of catastrophe that shows no sign of ever coming to an end. Calamities like the Holocaust, Hiroshima, World War II, the Russian invasion of Czechoslovakia, Chernobyl, and atrocities in El Salvador appear over and over again like haunting presences in the book, the repetition bonding the past and the present together, as the survivors themselves are haunted by the events that they have been forced to witness.

Forché deals with the intersection of poetry and politics in the poems and says in her foreword:

> *The Angel of History* is not about experiences. It is for me the opening of a wound, the muffling and silence of a decade, and it is also a gathering of utterances that have lifted away from the earth and wrapped it in a weather of risen words. These utterances issue from my own encounter with the events of this century but do not represent "it." The first-person, free-verse, lyric-narrative poem of my earlier years has given way to a work which has desired its own bodying forth: polyphonic, broken, haunted, and in ruins, with no possibility of restoration.

Indeed, it is the broken nature of history that contains much of its appeal for the writer, and it is the acknowledgment of the brokenness that is created by wanting to fix history that forms the hypnotic maze of fragments that holds the angel of history's gaze so fixedly and unwaveringly.

Christian Themes

One of the central questions that the multitude of suffering voices that speak in the poems ask in their interrogation of history is "Where is God's place in a world that is filled with so much suffering?" How, the poems ask, are we to regard a God who seems content to witness suffering rather than alleviate it?

Another core theme of *The Angel of History* is the responsibility of the Christian poet who witnesses suffering: Should the poet embrace it or keep a distance that allows objective testimony? Where is the dividing line between the impulse to record and the movement to take suffering and transform it for the entertainment of others? Forché writes, "Surely all art is the result of one's having been in danger, of having gone through an experience all the way to the end," and she goes further to ask what the ethical implications are of art arising from such acts.

One of the poems with which *The Angel of History* is often compared is T. S. Eliot's *The Waste Land* (1922), which attempted a similar task of making sense out of unimaginable horror and its coexistence with the vacuity of modern life and what part faith or spirituality should play. Like Eliot before her, Forché contemplates the position of the spiritual person when confronted with the banality and horror that make up modern existence and tries to determine whether the effort should be to distance oneself from or fully engage with the horror.

In the end, the act of witnessing and the art created by that act of witnessing become the only coherent and meaningful narrative that can be rescued from the chaos of history and the only sign of God's presence in a world that seems a collision of catastrophic moments. The horrors can be transformed, or so Forché seems to insist, and that act is the only possible spiritual practice in the face of evil.

Sources for Further Study

Ashton, Jennifer. *From Modernism to Postmodernism: American Poetry and Theory in the Twentieth Century*. Boston: Cambridge Studies in American Literature and Culture, 2006. This exhaustive collection includes Forché and many of her contemporaries, placing them in their individual spiritual and political traditions.

Forché, Carolyn, ed. *Against Forgetting: Twentieth-Century Poetry of Witness*. New York: W. W. Norton, 1993. This collection of political poetry was put together by Forché to showcase 140 poets from five continents.

Mark, Alison, and Deryn Rees-Jones, eds. *Contemporary Women's Poetry: Reading/ Writing/Practice*. New York: St. Martin's Press, 2000. This anthology discusses the intersection of women's political practice and spirituality in the twentieth century.

Cat Rambo

APOCALYPSE
And Other Poems

Author: Ernesto Cardenal (1925-   )
First published: New York: New Directions, 1977, edited and selected by Robert
  Pring-Mill and Donald D. Walsh, translated by Thomas Merton, Kenneth Rexroth,
  Mireya Jaimes-Freyre, and the editors
Genre: Poetry
Subgenres: Epigrams; lyric poetry; meditation and contemplation
Core issues: Apocalypse; capitalism; compassion; conscience; good vs. evil; justice;
  Latin Americans; suffering

Fusing politics with religion, Apocalypse, and Other Poems *conveys Cardenal's belief in Christian liberation theology and social justice through beautifully crafted,
lyric, and memorable verse. Among the dominant Christian themes are resurrection,
renunciation, love, and justice, and an Augustinian sense of sin as absence pervades
the writing.*

Overview

Leading Latin American poet Ernesto Cardenal is also an ordained Roman Catholic priest and an avowed Christian-Marxist. After his ordination in 1965, he moved to
the island of Mancarrón on Lake Nicaragua, where he founded a Christian-Marxist
commune called Our Lady of Solentiname. There he began preaching his revolutionary form of Pauline Christianity, which aims to cultivate a distinctly Christian
sociopolitical awareness. In this way, Our Lady of Solentiname is linked to the larger
Latin American Christian movement, *concietización*, to which Cardenal contributes
his advocacy of Christian liberation theology and social justice. Both ideas pervade
Apocalypse, and Other Poems, a selection of English translations from Cardenal's
major short poems from the late 1940's to 1973.

The poetry in *Apocalypse, and Other Poems* enacts many of Cardenal's major
Christian themes, including resurrection, renunciation, love, and justice. Certainly his
interpretations of such themes are informed by his Marxist politics, but one must remember that the practice of Marxism and the practice of Christianity are equivalent
for Cardenal. Thus, his remonstrations against political corruption and murder, for
example, are exegetic articulations of the sins of humankind, and the poems ultimately transmit to the reader a sense of Cardenal's belief in God's love as transforma-
tional and transcendent. In other words, just as Jesus is able to heal because he loves,
so might these poems aspire to similar achievement.

Likewise, if one accepts the notion from Augustinian Christianity of sin as a form
of absence, then *Apocalypse, and Other Poems* is a profoundly Roman Catholic book.
More specifically, Cardenal repeatedly explores the catastrophic consequences of
God's absence from the lives of people, and nowhere is this more clear than in the

book's title poem, "Apocalypse," a free-verse, bleak, and violent depiction of nuclear winter as the consequence of humankind's failure to live through God's love and teachings. However, with typical resilience of spirit, Cardenal concludes the poem on a magisterial note by prophesying humanity's replacement: a gloriously new, spiritually unified being made of humans but definitively improved.

Like "Apocalypse," Cardenal's epigrams elucidate the sin of absence. Translated from *Epigramas: Poemas* (1961; *Epigramas*, 1978), his first collection of mature, distinctive poems, the epigrams in *Apocalypse, and Other Poems* ostensibly explore Cardenal's love for two women, Claudia and Myriam. The epigrams excite in him a succinct poetry of remarkably deep and conflicted feelings, ranging from euphoria and valor to humiliation and fear. They also lend themselves to multilayered readings, whereby the beloved can symbolize both the state and the divine. Here again the link between politics, love, and spirituality becomes clear, centering these well-wrought homages to Catullian epithalamia.

For example, in Cardenal's epigram 8, the speaker learns of his beloved's infidelity, which drives him to excoriate the government in writing until somewhat suicidally (and therefore sinfully) landing himself in jail. In other words, the speaker is stripped of love, and its sudden absence drives him to self-destruction, with the amorous, the political, and the spiritual invoked. This is compounded in epigram 10, where the speaker upbraids his beloved for her inadequate love for him. Again, the absence of love might be read on the literal, romantic level. It can also, however, represent an irreverent challenge to God for failing to love his followers more perceptibly. Simultaneously it can symbolize the Nicaraguan state's lack of love for its people, whom it neglects and murders with seeming indifference throughout Cardenal's book. Thus the absence of love ultimately resounds as a metonymic reminder of Jesus' teachings of unconditional love for God and his creation.

Like the epigrams, the book's "psalms" are beautifully crafted explorations of the intersections of faith, time, love, and politics. Translated from *Salmos* (1967; *The Psalms of Struggle and Liberation*, 1971), these poems are Cardenal's lively reinterpretations of biblical Psalms by casting them in modern context and idiom. Rhythmically driven, they range in tone from the ecstatic to the outraged, and a fine example of the former is "The Cosmos in His Sanctuary (Psalm 150)," where Cardenal exhorts everyone on Earth to celebrate God and his goodness with unbridled euphoria. In startling juxtaposition, the Psalm "Unrighteous Mammon (Luke 16:9)" is a fierce, twenty-two-line Marxist-Christian manifesto of Cardenalian renunciation, in which private wealth ranks among the most egregious and execrable sins of injustice.

Like renunciation, resurrection is explored with tremendous force. Poems like "Behind the Monastery" and "The Lost Cities" elicit the anguish and impatience in awaiting Christ's return. Equally poignant, the poem "Night" offers a violent, resonant depiction of life in a despoiled world unready for Christ's return. Nevertheless, even in this case, Cardenal's faith buoys the poem, suffusing it with an ultimately unconquerable strength. This strength is explicit in poems such as "Katun II Ahau," which forecasts the triumph of the Scriptures over political and spiritual evil. Similarly, "The Arrival" quickly transcends its political details to evince an indestructible fraternal love uniting God's children. Thus, whether impatient, terrified, battered, or ecstatic, Cardenal's belief in God is absolute and essential to this powerful collection of poetry.

Perhaps the most moving and masterful poem in the collection is its longest one: "Coplas on the Death of Merton." Written in eulogy of monk and poet Thomas Merton, who was Cardenal's novice-master at the Trappist Monastery at Gethsemani, Kentucky, from 1956 to 1959, the poem creates a quintessentially Cardenalian collage of personal memories, geopolitical history, theological wonder, and much more to generate equanimity in the face of death, grief, and suffering. This peace amid the terror can be read as nothing less than Cardenal's belief in the triumph of God's love over mortal agonies, and the careful crafting of such a notion in fresh, plangent poetry is what distinguishes this book.

Christian Themes

The dominant Christian themes in *Apocalypse, and Other Poems* are resurrection, renunciation, love, and justice. Most often these themes are approached through indirection, whether in the form of historical commentary, social allegory, or political vision. Regardless, Cardenal's Christian ethic never falters. Instead his belief in God's love prevails over multifarious challenges.

Furthermore, through lyrical, vernacular poems, the book enacts Cardenal's unique Christian-Marxism, which aims to cultivate sociopolitical awareness through a revolutionary form of Pauline Christianity fusing liberation theology with social justice. To understand this, one must understand Cardenal's belief in the practice of Marxism as equivalent to the practice of Christianity. Thus, to create a Marxist economy for Nicaragua would be to create a Christian utopia for Nicaraguans. This is evident throughout the book, whether Cardenal is joyously rewriting a biblical Psalm or hauntingly prophesying the Apocalypse.

Likewise, one must recognize Cardenal's belief in the Resurrection. That belief never abandons him, however terrifying his portrayals of a world despoiled by misbehavior (both political and personal). God's love always circumscribes human life, and always his love is posited as salvific and indomitable. Thus the work of the poems is the work of readying oneself for God.

Similarly essential to the book is an Augustinian notion of sin as a form of absence. For example, the cardinal sin of avarice is frequently portrayed as the absence of Christian morality from the political domain. Nevertheless, implicit in such absence is its potential refilling: through devotion to God in thought and deed. Thus the book becomes a means for healing the damaged world by redressing the injustices among people, cultures, and countries.

Sources for Further Study

Cardenal, Ernesto. *Cosmic Canticle*. Translated by John Lyons. Willimantic, Conn.: Curbstone Press, 1993. A long poem (almost 500 pages) exploring the intersections of Christianity and science.

_____. *Love: A Glimpse of Eternity*. Translated by Dinah Livingston. Brewster, Mass.: Paraclete Press, 2006. Prose from Cardenal's religiously formative years of study to become a Trappist monk; apolitical both in content and by monastic order.

Elias, Edward. "Prophecy of Liberation: The Poetry of Ernesto Cardenal." In *Poetic Prophecy in Western Literature*, edited by Jan Wojcik and Raymond-Jean Frontain. London: Associated University Presses, 1984. Good introduction to scholarship on Cardenal's fusion of religion with poetics.

Field, Les W. "Constructing Local Identities in a Revolutionary Nation: The Cultural Politics of the Artisan Class in Nicaragua." *American Ethnologist* 22, no. 4 (November, 1995): 786-806. Scholarly, succinct introduction to the sociopolitical landscape of Cardenal's work.

Merton, Thomas. *Courage for Truth: The Letters of Thomas Merton to Writers*. Edited by Christine M. Bochen. New York: Farrar, Straus and Giroux, 1993. Includes letters to Cardenal from his Trappist novice-master; their friendship and correspondence spanned more than a decade and inspired Cardenal to create Our Lady of Solentiname.

Seth Michelson

APOCRYPHA

Author: Eric Pankey (1959-   )
First published: New York: Alfred A. Knopf, 1991
Genre: Poetry
Subgenre: Meditation and contemplation
Core issues: Catholics and Catholicism; doubt; faith; Jesus Christ; nature; reason

Pankey's poetry shows a struggle between faith and doubt and explores the human desire for clarity and assurance in a universe that offers none. These mostly short, free-verse poems examine religious and secular subjects with the desire to ascertain what is true. The poems find the secular in the spiritual and the spiritual in the secular. They use the language of Christianity to interrogate it. Their intense engagement with Christianity together with their probing nature and original imagery make them memorable.

Overview

Eric Pankey was born in Kansas City, Missouri, in 1959, and after graduating from the University of Missouri-Columbia, he received an M.F.A. from the University of Iowa. His first book, *For the New Year* (1984), won the Walt Whitman Award. He has received many awards, including a National Education Association fellowship and an Ingram Merrill Foundation grant. From his earliest poems, his work has been rich with Christian, particularly Catholic, imagery and thought; however, his is not standard-issue theology. Pankey explores Christianity in a lively way that makes it remain the background of his work while he is questioning and reinterpreting it.

Apocrypha as a title suggests his direction, as the Apocrypha are books that some believe to be inspired and some do not, so that the tales are not included in most Bibles. The book consists of six sections, "Nocturnes," "Illuminations," "Depositions," "Arguments," "Departures," and "Reconstructions." The sections can be taken as phases of faith and doubt, or as different perspectives on the same issues. "Nocturnes" features landscapes; "Illuminations" are discoveries, spiritual and otherwise; "Depositions" discusses Christ's life and death; "Arguments" defines art; "Departures" are elegies; and "Reconstructions" are experimental revisions, or reinterpretations, of the world.

In Pankey's vision, religion has a ghostly presence, and his poems are examinations of these ghosts and attempts to express and explain them. The speaker in *Apocrypha* is alienated from his childhood religion but cannot banish it entirely; its emblems and its vocabulary are part of him. Indeed, the titles and the subjects suggest a collection of traditionally religious poetry: "Vespers," "Triptych," "Exegesis," "Icon," and "Te Deum Laudamus." However, the poetry is anything but traditional: It searches, revises, and probes the Christian story. "The Allegory of Doubt" seems to crystallize the position in that the speaker "looks to edges" to see the two visions, "disturbed choppy air of mirage." The sure faith of the past and the current doubts of the speaker are represented in the scene as a fragmented image, as two scenes that do not quite align. The speaker leaves without submission or dismissal, but with a certain reluctance:

> As he turns to leave, he moves his hands
> Along a doorframe. Puts one hand through.
> Still rehearsing the rudiments of ontology.

These poems ask questions, often deep questions with no answers; however, the Bible stories and Christian mind-set—Eden, the Crucifixion and the tomb, even the parables—are a major presence in them. There is no getting away from Christianity and no yielding to it. Guilt, atonement, contrition, and submission dominate the poetry, but often as queries. The questions are often hidden in the poems: Who is Jesus? What is the Resurrection? What has faith to offer us? Yet the scenes and images of the poems presuppose a deep and lasting engagement with the Christian faith, one that doubt cannot undo. A fundamental sense of loss—of people, childhood, certainties, and faith—dominates this collection. The elegiac tone echoes that of Wallace Stevens, who pursued a similar course in his own work and whom Pankey admires.

The opening poem to *Apocrypha*, which does not fall into one of the six groups, expresses sorrow and longing. The poem, "Prayer," reflects on loss, or "the fugitive/ released as easily as a breath" and ends "Sweet,/ Sweet anchor, how long/ Your hook held."

Pankey's poetry is in part a search for a lost metaphysic. Pankey's work, like that of the poet Stevens, is permeated by a search for the truly spiritual. Stevens walked a short way down a number of spiritual paths before electing in old age to join the Catholic Church, which he did on his deathbed. Pankey has stayed with Christian ideas and images in his search. *Apocrypha* provides a close examination of what was once for him the container of the spiritual, the Church. He painstakingly reviews all the images and events of Catholicism, perhaps still looking for hooks.

Christian Themes

One of the major themes in *Apocrypha* is the conflict among the grand narrative of Christianity, historical facts, and the observances of ordinary life. This work is defined by, even bound by, the most Christian of thoughts and images: icon, Bible, church music, and church art. Yet the speaker does not find the items of faith to be fruitful in the production of faith. They deceive him; they turn into other things. There is a sense that the speaker has in some way been let down by his faith; things that once were filled with joy are empty. The speaker is haunted by his lost faith and its forms.

The book is one of three by Pankey that explore the nature and difficulty of the Christian faith, the other two being *The Late Romances* (1997) and *Cenotaph* (2000). In an interview, Pankey once stated that he thinks of the three as panels in a triptych, rather than as works in a sequence. Each panel examines a particular perspective on the Christianity that molds and haunts him and examines its promises and its failure to fulfill them. The poems together suggest a spiritual vacancy in the speaker's life, a nostalgia for lost belief, and an unwillingness to turn completely away from the past.

The doubt in the poems seems locked into step with an unwillingness to let Christianity go. The poems begin with Christian images and sometimes with the baggage of literary allusion. For instance, "The Tomb in Palestine" suggests the famous skeptical Stevens poem "Sunday Morning"; at one point, the woman of the poem, hovering uneasily at the edge of faith, is assured that she will do well to accept the world as enough and realize that "the tomb in Palestine" is not, as she had once believed, a "porch" or threshold of "spirits lingering." Instead it is "the grave of Jesus." When Pankey invokes the tomb—that of Jesus as seen by Stevens—he finds questions, not answers. Less conclusive than the Stevens poem, "The Tomb in Palestine" raises some of the same issues. However, it seems that the answer given by Stevens, "Death is the mother of beauty," is not quite enough for Pankey. He goes back again and again to the images, the stories, and the sacraments. Pankey's version of the Catholic sacramental vision is different from that of most poets, who tend to find the sacramental in the elements of daily life, thus endowing the normal with the sacred. Pankey tends to start with the sacred and deconstruct it. Yet after all the demythologizing, something stubbornly remains. In this work, the residue, or remains, of Christianity are still indeterminate in nature. The last poem in *Apocrypha*, "Eschatology," suggests directions for new explorations:

> It is not the lure of a past,
> . . . not exile from that garden
>
> That instills nostalgia and brooding,
> But a belief that joy will come,
> That joy is relief and not a homecoming.

The poem concludes

> Go on. The mockingbird's song and the lily,
> Fragmented and fragrant, respectively, fill
> The last days as they filled the first.

Few poets struggle so hard with Christianity, and few have internalized it so deeply. In poems of skill and craft, Pankey describes the Christian in a post-Christian age. His poems examine the gaps and blurs that the microscope finds in the Christian fabric, but they cannot turn away from it or toss it aside.

Sources for Further Study

Collins, Floyd. "Body and Soul: Three Visionary Poets." *Gettysburg Review* 13, no. 2 (Summer, 2000): 314-329. Study of contemporary visionary poetry precedes *Apocrypha* but provides a fine introduction to Pankey's thematic preoccupations.

_____. "Mythic Resonances." *Gettysburg Review* 11, no. 2 (Summer, 1998): 344-361. Explores Pankey's work together with that of others. Gives a sense of how he uses stories.

Gurley, James. "*Apocrypha* by Eric Pankey, *Mercy* by Kathleen Pierce, *Riddles for a Naked Sailor* by Mary Azrael, and *Looking for Luck* by Maxine Kumin." *Poet Lore* 87, no. 3 (Fall, 1992): 53. A review that sets *Apocrypha* in the context of other concurrently published poetry books.

Pankey, Eric. "The Form of Concentration." *The Iowa Review* 19, no. 2 (Summer, 1998): 175-187. Study of Charles Wright that gives much insight into Pankey's own poetics.

Janet McCann

APOLOGIA PRO VITA SUA

Author: John Henry Newman (1801-1890)
First published: 1864 (English translation, 1870)
Edition used: Apologia pro vita sua, edited by David J. DeLaura. New York: Norton, 1968
Genre: Nonfiction
Subgenres: Autobiography; church history; theology
Core issues: Catholics and Catholicism; conversion; obedience and disobedience; Protestants and Protestantism; reason

Newman presents a history of his religious opinions to prove his lifelong sincerity in seeking to find the true church, which for him— after a long struggle as an Anglican attracted to Catholicism—was the Catholic Church. He emphasizes the importance of dogma and the sacraments in Christian belief, supports the infallibility of the Catholic Church, and criticizes the Protestant Reformation for creating schism and lawlessness when what was most needed was unity.

Overview

In his *Apologia pro vita sua* (literally, "a justification of his life"), John Henry Newman set out to defend himself against charges of dishonesty and deceitfulness. In the January, 1864, issue of *Macmillan's Magazine,* an article by the popular writer Charles Kingsley had questioned Newman's honesty. On the surface, this allegation involved Newman's supposed view that it was acceptable for Catholic clergymen like himself to resort to cunning and not necessarily adhere to the truth.

The deeper issue, however, involved Newman's conversion to Catholicism twenty years earlier. Newman had long served as a vicar within the Anglican Church before becoming a Catholic, and the real charge that he felt compelled to answer was that he had been a secret Catholic within the Protestant Anglican Church long before he announced his conversion and that his conversion was simply the culmination of a deliberate plan to lure Protestants out of their faith and into the Catholic one.

In the *Apologia pro vita sua,* Newman decided that it would be more effective to present a narrative of his own life than to attempt to answer specific charges. Instead of rebutting false ideas, he would present true ones, so that the bulk of the book became a sort of spiritual autobiography explaining how he came to convert to Catholicism and attempting to show that he was sincere in this change and had not merely hidden his true Catholic beliefs beneath a Protestant disguise.

This central part of the book goes back to Newman's earliest childhood and his attraction to Arabian tales and magic. It also mentions his early habit of crossing himself in the Catholic fashion and describes a cross he drew when young. His point seems to be to indicate that from a young age he was drawn to Catholicism even before he really knew what it was. He also emphasizes his growing belief in the unreality of the material world and his corresponding belief in angels and other spirits, views that he would later feel accorded best with Catholicism and its emphasis on the sacraments and their connection with the unseen world.

Newman also notes his brief interest in the skeptical writings of Thomas Paine and Voltaire and his temporary adherence to the extreme Protestant beliefs associated with Calvinism, notably predestination and the notions of heaven and hell. He mentions at this time developing a belief in probability as the basis of life, a belief he notes can be dangerous for its encouragement of skepticism.

This account of Newman's early life sets the stage for later internal struggles, for in it Newman seems to be suggesting an almost inborn attraction to Catholicism while at the same time suggesting an attachment to views, such as skepticism, not usually associated with Catholicism. Along the same lines he notes two conflicting ideas he was drawn to as early as the age of fifteen, one that the early Catholic Church was quite admirable, the other that the current pope was the antichrist.

Newman next recounts how he became involved in the Tractarian or Oxford movement to stem the advance of liberalism in the Anglican Church by emphasizing the importance of dogma and the sacraments. At this point in his life, Newman says, he felt invigorated and full of a sense of mission to save the Anglican Church from the liberals and rationalists who would make religious belief a matter of mere opinion.

Newman next recounts how this period of confidence came to an end, in part because the bishops of the Anglican Church condemned one of his tracts for going too far in the direction of Catholicism. At the same time his own belief in the viability of the Via Media, the middle way between Catholicism and Protestantism, which he hoped the Anglican Church would adopt, crumbled in a most unusual manner.

Newman was studying an early period of Church history having to do with the Monophysite heresy, in which the Monophysites had seceded from the Church over a doctrinal dispute. In the *Apologia pro vita sua*, he comments that as he studied this period, he suddenly became overwhelmed by the notion that he was a Monophysite. He saw the Monophysites as being parallel to the Anglican Church of his day, but since the Monophysites had clearly been wrong to separate from the early Church, so must the Anglicans have been wrong to separate from the Church of Rome.

This sudden revelation plunged Newman into intellectual crisis, and for the next half dozen years, he wrestled with his doubts before finally deciding that Rome was right and the Anglicans wrong. He describes this period as a painful one in which he was forced to leave his home in the Anglican Church and at Oxford and venture onto the open sea. He also compares the situation to a deathbed, as if leaving the Anglican Church was a sort of death, creating a somber, elegiac tone in the second to last section of the *Apologia pro vita sua*.

However, in the final section of the *Apologia pro vita sua*, the tone lightens and Newman describes his arrival in the Catholic Church as being like coming into port after a voyage on rough seas. He says that by becoming a Catholic, he freed himself from doubts, and he then proceeds to describe some aspects of his Catholic beliefs.

The *Apologia pro vita sua* is generally hailed as a literary masterpiece in which

Newman succeeds in defending his integrity by presenting a portrait of himself as a sincere seeker after truth who, far from planning his conversion, struggled mightily against it before at last accepting it.

Christian Themes

Newman says that his aim in the *Apologia pro vita sua* is not to present doctrine but to trace his own personal religious history. The most important Christian aspect of the work, therefore, is its autobiographical conversion story, which places it in the tradition of Saint Augustine's *Confessiones* (397-400; *Confessions*, 1620) and John Bunyan's *Grace Abounding to the Chief of Sinners* (1666), though in contrast to those works, Newman's *Apologia pro vita sua* is not about a sinner wrestling with demons, but about a bookish man undergoing an intellectual crisis that causes him to shift from one church to another.

Newman does take up some doctrinal matters, however, notably the question of the infallibility of the Catholic Church. He argues that in a sinful world in which human reason can easily run amok and lead to skepticism, it is necessary to have a strong institution like the Catholic Church, which can issue infallible decrees in matters of faith and which must be obeyed on those matters and also on matters beyond faith.

However, Newman argues that this does not mean an end to free inquiry and private judgment; rather, he sees such inquiry flourishing in fruitful interaction with the infallible Church. He argues that Protestants are wrong to say that they have a monopoly on private judgment; he sees it as operating within the Catholic Church as well.

Newman also emphasizes the importance of unity or universality (what he sometimes calls "Catholicity") within the Church. In the end, he decided that unity was so important that no error within the Catholic Church could have justified the Protestant Reformation, which he saw as introducing lawlessness and schism.

Another issue Newman deals with is the position of the Virgin Mary and the saints in the Catholic Church. For many years, this remained the main stumbling block keeping him from converting, because he feared that Catholic worship of Mary and the saints as intercessors with God was a deviation from true Christian teachings. However, he recounts that he eventually was reassured that despite popular misconceptions, Catholic doctrine did not allow anyone, even Mary, to intercede between individuals and God. For Newman, the individual soul must be able to connect directly with God, and he was satisfied that this view was consistent with Catholicism.

Sources for Further Study

Barros, Carolyn A. *Autobiography: Narrative of Transformation*. Ann Arbor: University of Michigan Press, 1998. Distinguishes Newman's gradual conversion from the more sudden ones of Saint Paul and Bunyan.

Henderson, Heather. *The Victorian Self: Autobiography and Biblical Narrative*. Ithaca, N.Y.: Cornell University Press, 1989. Compares Newman to Job, Saint Paul, and Moses. Sees his conversion story as a journey and the *Apologia pro vita sua* as an almost legal defense in a trial.

Peterson, Linda H. *Victorian Autobiography: The Tradition of Self-Interpretation.* New Haven, Conn.: Yale University Press, 1986. Says the *Apologia pro vita sua* follows the model of Saint Augustine rather than that of the Protestant John Bunyan.

Tirumalesh, K. V. "Autobiography's Search for Truth: Newman and Gandhi." *Centennial Review* 40 (1996): 99-123. Sees binary oppositions in the *Apologia pro vita sua* between feeling and reason, faith and church, and Rome in theory and Rome in action.

Sheldon Goldfarb

APOLOGY

Author: Tertullian (Quintus Septimius Florens Tertullianus; c. 155/160-after 217 C.E.)
First published: Apologeticus, 197 C.E. (English translation, 1642)
Edition used: The Fathers of the Church, vol. 10, *Tertullian: Apological Works and Minucius Felix—Octaviuis,* edited by Roy J. Deferrari. New York: Fathers of the Church, 1950
Genre: Nonfiction
Subgenres: Church history; instructional manual; theology
Core issues: Catholics and Catholicism; daily living; faith; justice; religion; theology

Tertullian's Apology, *addressed as an open letter to Roman provincial governors, is his explanation of the content of the Christian faith. Tertullian argues that Roman officials should embrace Christianity, once it is truly understood, rather than attempt to stamp it out throughout the Roman Empire.*

Overview

Tertullian, a highly educated Roman citizen and lawyer from Carthage in North Africa, converted to Christianity in 193 C.E. because he was so impressed by the behavior and faith shown by Christian martyrs. He was convinced that the one true religion was Christianity, not one of the various philosophical systems and cults then widely practiced in the Roman Empire. Tertullian thought that if he could explain the content of Christian belief to other educated non-Christian Romans, they would see the truth of Christianity, convert, and cease to persecute Christians. Tertullian, not a man of moderate temperament, offers a fiery defense of Christianity in his *Apology.* He not only advocates forcefully in favor of Christianity but also seeks to discredit traditional Roman polytheism and emperor worship, calling them nothing more than idolatry and baseless superstitions.

Apology, in the Latin sense of *apologia,* means to explain, which is what Tertullian does in his *Apology.* Speaking to Romans very similar to himself in culture and education, he explains why all the accusations of atheism, incest, and cannibalism against Christianity were ludicrous and why Christians should be thanked rather than persecuted for expounding the truth to their fellow citizens. He argues that Christianity was a benefit rather than a liability to the Roman Empire and that only bad emperors would persecute a good religion.

Tertullian was writing at the close of the second century C.E. when Christianity, though a fragile and discontinuous presence in the Roman Empire, had begun to come to the attention of Roman authorities who regarded it as just another unauthorized organization with potentially dangerous overtones. The authorities suppressed it as seditious and prosecuted members of the quasi-secret society for treason. They neither knew nor cared about Christianity as a belief system; it was not a recognized religion and therefore was banned.

Arguing like the lawyer he was, Tertullian examines the accusations made against Christianity and Christians. He demonstrates the moral integrity of Christians who are exercising their liberty of conscience, an idea Romans claim to value. According to traditions of Roman justice, Christians must be found guilty of crimes before they can be punished. Try as they might, the accusers of Christianity have neither the legal nor logical grounds to substantiate their accusations. Christians cannot be atheists because they believe in a deity. Every other ethnic and geographical group within the empire is allowed to worship particular deities, which Tertullian claims are nothing more than human mental and physical creations. He asks why Christians alone are forbidden to worship their deity, which he claims is above all tribal and geographical deities.

Christians do not engage in cannibalism and incest in their *agape* or fellowship meals together. Tertullian gives a rather complete description of early worship services and meetings that took place in members' homes: Christians met to read Scripture, sing hymns of praise to God, agree to treat one another with honesty and charity, and share a meal together. When Christians say they love one another, Tertullian explains, they mean as friends and members of a community. Because Christians had to meet in secret for fear of persecution, outsiders accused Christians of engaging in various sexual perversions. When Christians commemorated the Last Supper by sharing the body and blood of Christ with one another, their accusers took this quite literally and thought Christians were practicing cannibalism. Tertullian debunks this false understanding as well.

Tertullian also defends Christians against the charge of treason, based on the idea that the continued existence of Christianity is a threat to the continued existence of the Roman Empire. Accusers tried to claim that Christianity was offensive to the gods and that all the bad events in the empire were signs of the gods' displeasure. Therefore, Christianity must be eliminated for the good of the empire. In answering this charge, Tertullian reviews a number of negative events in recent history and explains their causes, which are revealed to be something other than the existence of Christianity. He challenges the accusers to actually prove, rather than merely state, a causal connection between Christianity and negative events. Tertullian gives an account of the prayers used in Christian worship services, prayers offered not only for the emperor but also for the members of the government and for peace throughout the empire.

Tertullian further writes that Christians voluntarily assume a code of conduct that requires them not to harm one another or engage in any socially destructive behavior and to provide social services for the poor and vulnerable among them. Tertullian challenges those in authority to investigate charges against Christians in an unbiased manner. He asserts that the governors will find that Christians, far from being a threat to society, are unlikely to be on the wrong side of the law because they hold themselves to high moral standards. Christianity forbids its members from joining secret political and religious organizations, engaging in frivolous lawsuits that waste the governors' time, and attending the public spectacles and athletic contests that often degenerate into violence and riots. Governors will conclude they would rather have a larger Christian population to govern, Tertullian argues.

Christian Themes

The predominant theme of Tertullian's *Apology* is that Christianity is not only a true religion but also the truth, unlike all the different idolatrous religions and man-made philosophies known throughout the Roman Empire. Christianity is not just one more religious option; it replaces all other religions and philosophies. Despite superficial similarities between those religions and aspects of Christianity, those other religions are inherently false because they originate from human minds, not from God. It was the insistence on the divine origination of Christianity that caused Tertullian to hurl his famous question at the accusers of Christianity: What has Athens to do with Jerusalem? What does all the knowledge of this world matter when one should live life for the sake of eternal salvation?

Tertullian was not a systematic thinker or theologian. His writings were controversial, both within the Christian community and in wider non-Christian circles in the empire. The *Apology* is addressed to non-Christian Roman governors, so there is no doctrinal development in it. Nonetheless, the *Apology* was quickly translated into Greek for the benefit of Christians in the Eastern Roman Empire. They modeled their defense of Christianity after Tertullian's *Apology*.

In later writings, Tertullian returned to ideas mentioned in passing in the *Apology*. His "Letter to Scapula" discusses in detail the fact that religious belief cannot be coerced and that only bad officials seek to compel assent. His writings against heretics, "Against the Heathens" and "Against the Valentinians," reinforce his contention that other religions are merely human constructs. The respect due to believers who die as martyrs is detailed in "Scorpiace," and the reasons Christians are forbidden to attend public festivities forms the basis for "Spectacles."

There is little evidence that Tertullian's logically rigorous defense of Christianity made any difference to Roman authorities. Persecution of Christians continued for another hundred years until Emperor Constantine issued the Edict of Toleration in 312 C.E. Regardless of the effectiveness of his explanation and defense of Christianity, Tertullian is considered the father of Latin theology because he provided the theological vocabulary for later Latin Christian writers.

Sources for Further Study

Barnes, Timothy. *Tertullian: A Historical and Literary Study*. Oxford, England: Clarendon Press, 1995. In addition to a discussion of the important points of Tertullian's theology, Barnes provides an in-depth presentation of Tertullian's contribution to the development of a specifically Christian Latin.

Osborn, Eric. *Tertullian: First Theologian of the West*. Cambridge, England: Cambridge University Press, 2002. Osborn analyses the influence of Tertullian's vocabulary and theology on later Latin Christian writers, despite the fact that Tertullian spent the last years of his life outside the mainstream Christian community.

Sider, Robert, ed. *Christian and Pagan in the Roman Empire: The Witness of Tertullian*. Washington, D.C.: The Catholic University of America, 2001. This volume contains selections from many of Tertullian's writings and serves as a good introduction to the range of topics on which Tertullian wrote.

Victoria Erhart

ARENA

Author: Karen Hancock (1953-   )
First published: Minneapolis, Minn.: Bethany House, 2002
Genre: Novel
Subgenres: Allegory; romance; science fiction
Core issues: Conversion; doubt; guidance; psychology; self-knowledge; trust in God

Life does not always progress as people desire. When several humans are given a chance to change their lives by alien kidnappers, they fight their way out of the arena around and inside them as they discover their own strengths and weaknesses and the possibility of having faith in others.

> *Principal characters*
> *Callie Hayes*, a woman who undergoes a profound personal enlightenment
> *Meg Riley*, Callie's best friend
> *Pierce*, guide of the Witnesses
> *Rowena*, Callie's opposite
> *Garth*, leader of another Arena group
> *Elhanu*, leader of the Aggillon, aliens who kidnap humans

Overview

The *Arena* is an investigation of how much some people have to go through to learn enough about themselves to make the changes needed to improve their lives. The protagonist, Callie Hayes, is an artist trapped in a world in which her friends and family believe that art can never be more than a fun hobby. Armed with an unwanted bachelor's degree, Callie has been taking poorly paying jobs that bore her. For extra cash and from a desire to do something different, she agrees to join her best friend, Meg, and volunteer for a college psychology department experiment.

The experiment is merely a cover for aliens who are battling among themselves for influence over the galaxy in a place they call the Arena. After rejecting the advice of her experimenter, Callie is dumped rather unceremoniously into a hostile alien environment. Armed with a bag of small items and a manual describing how to leave the Arena, she begins a journey that will last more than a year in her life but less than half a day back on Earth.

Callie is unprepared to use the manual and unwilling to fully trust the aliens, so she tries to find her way out on her own. She fails and teams up with a man named Pierce, who has been in the Arena for five years. He has thrown out his own manual and seems very rough, but throughout the novel, he helps Callie and receives help from her in return. Together they find his old group of survivors and continue to search for the gate, which will let them out and allow them to return home.

The Arena is a complex place. Throughout, there are animals, planets, and people corrupted by their own desires and by the Tohvani, the enemies of the Aggillon, the aliens who kidnapped the earthlings. While the humans fight for a way out, they also seem to be fighting one another and themselves, suggesting that this battle is not so much between the aliens and the humans as it is within the individual men and women.

The Arena has three layers. One can easily leave the first layer by following the manual, using the tools given, and simply asking to be let out. It takes Callie six months of hardship to figure it out. She, Pierce, and a few others leave this first area only to find themselves in a safe haven where Meg and others have been waiting all this time for a guide to finish reading the manual and lead them to the next exit.

Pierce turns out to be this guide, even though he has been in the Arena for five years and has survived some horrifying experiences. While he reads and communes with the Aggillon leader, Elhanu, the humans train as though they are preparing for war. In a way they are, because once they leave the safe haven, they must find the next exit, which is guarded by the Trogs, corrupted humans who have given in to the dangers and pleasures of the Arena's wild areas.

After this exit and the loss of some of their group members, Callie and Pierce find themselves in another safe haven, this one headed by Elhanu himself. Here they study the manual, learn from the Aggillon ruler, and prepare to fight their way through hostile cities to the final exit. Through the kind encouragement of the Aggillon, Callie and Pierce together discover love and an inner strength to lead the rest of their team, now called Witnesses, through the most dangerous regions of the Arena.

The cities they must cross have placed bounties on their heads and are hunting them down. Meanwhile, their former teammates have been living a bit like Trogs, their bodies and minds growing a touch more corrupted as they try to find the exit on their own. This corruption leads to the Witnesses being captured by one city whose ruler possesses one of the old team's members in an attempt to scare Callie and Pierce into submitting to their own physical desires and personality weaknesses. It is only by remembering the promises of Elhanu and trusting in him that they are able to escape from the cities. In the end, though, only Callie makes it through the final exit, while Pierce sacrifices himself for her.

The changes in Callie allow her to remember and fully use all the lessons she learned in the Arena to a degree that no one else she met there can. She embraces her art, moves to another part of the country, and starts to stand up for herself against her family and friends. She learns to rely on herself and her faith in Elhanu to guide her life, which includes a possible reunion with Pierce.

Christian Themes

The predominant theme of *Arena* is that human beings must acknowledge their doubt in God, confront it, and learn more about themselves to survive. They are placed in dangerous situations that they must survive as individuals and as a group. They can read the manual that they each have received, but after a certain point, they can no longer understand the texts and must wait for someone to guide them through them. Before the humans can use the manual, however, they must be aware that they need it; most of the main characters are so angry at being kidnapped that they toss the manual away or ignore it. They must realize that they need help and guidance to deal with their psychological issues.

These psychological issues are not the only hurdle the humans in the Arena have. Almost all of them have been betrayed by their families, their jobs, or their own desires. They have stopped trusting others and sometimes themselves. Slowly, over the course of months, they learn to trust each other, the manual, and Elhanu, who has given them the manual and provided the safe havens throughout the Arena. Their growth and their conversion, by which they come to accept the help and opinions of others, are slow and steady, constantly pushed by both the dangers of the Arena and Elhanu's refusal to let them just relax for too long.

The greatest message of the novel is the importance of self-knowledge and the choice to trust in God. While Elhanu never allows anyone to just stay in his safe havens, he also offers them ample opportunities to choose other paths and switch group alliances. Those who become the most self-aware return to Earth with more of their memories intact and a new purpose in life that allows them to pursue their dreams in positive ways.

Sources for Further Study

May, Stephen. *Stardust and Ashes: Science Fiction in Christian Perspective.* London: Society for Promoting Christian Knowledge, 1998. While older than Hancock's *Arena*, this still provides a good overview of the state of science fiction and Christianity and could be used to compare Hancock's work and earlier works.

Nelson, Marcia Z. "Karen Hancock: Fantasy Serving Truth." *Publishers Weekly* 249, no. 24 (June 17, 2002): 523. Brief interview with Hancock about her philosophy and background.

Seed, David, ed. *Imagining Apocalypse: Studies in Cultural Crisis.* New York: St. Martin's Press, 2000. Several articles that focus on different aspects of Christian science fiction, especially those that examine modern attitudes toward sex, science, and government.

TammyJo Eckhart

ARGUMENT AGAINST ABOLISHING CHRISTIANITY

Author: Jonathan Swift (1667-1745)
First published: An Argument to Prove That the Abolishing of Christianity in England
  May, as Things Now Stand, Be Attended with Some Inconveniences, and Perhaps
  Not Produce Those Many Good Effects Proposed Thereby, 1708
Edition used: Jonathan Swift, edited by Angus Ross and David Woolley. New York:
  Oxford University Press, 1984
Genre: Nonfiction
Subgenre: Didactic treatise
Core issues: Church; Protestants and Protestantism

*This short treatise ironically makes a case that the British government should not re-
peal Christianity as the state religion. The author of the argument defends only nominal Christianity because real Christianity has "been for some time wholly laid aside
by general consent, as utterly inconsistent with all our present schemes of wealth and
power." One of several works Swift wrote in defense of the Church of England, this
treatise also reveals the futility of a religion that is only nominal.*

Overview

The *Argument Against Abolishing Christianity* by the Irish clergyman and satirist
Jonathan Swift presents itself as a case for maintaining Christianity as the official religion of England. The author undertakes this task hesitantly, acknowledging that he is
going against popular opinion and the wisdom of the age. Early in the work, however,
he makes it clear that he is defending only nominal Christianity; to try to restore real
Christianity would be a "wild project" that would destroy wit and learning, ruin trade,
and disrupt the entire frame of society.

Having thus limited the scope of his argument, the author describes and dismisses
eight proposed advantages of abolishing Christianity. First, it would considerably
"enlarge and establish liberty of conscience." His reply is that nominal Christianity is
useful as a subject of mockery for "great wits" who would otherwise target an important institution such as the government. A second supposed advantage is that freethinkers would no longer be required to believe things they find difficult. The response is that the English can already believe and publish whatever they please
without endangering their careers or being prosecuted for blasphemy.

The third and fourth points are more pragmatic. Abolishing Christianity would free
up the funds devoted to supporting ten thousand parsons plus the bishops; it would
also gain another usable day in the week. The rebuttals are equally pragmatic. The income of the clergy would support only one hundred or two hundred fashionable
young gentlemen, and the country needs the clergy as "restorers of our breed" rather
than the sickly offspring of dissipated gentlemen. As for Sunday, its observance is no

"hindrance to business or pleasure," and churches are fine places to meet for business or gallantry or to sleep.

The author finds the fifth advantage attractive: Abolishing Christianity would eliminate the party differences "of High and Low Church, of Whig and Tory, Presbyterian and Church of England," which interfere with the functioning of government. The author argues, however, that the party spirit is so deeply engrained in human hearts that people would soon find other labels to maintain divisions in society.

The sixth advantage is that abolishing Christianity would get rid of the practice of hiring men to "bawl" on Sundays against the practices by which others pursue recognition, wealth, and pleasure the rest of the week. The author replies that prohibiting something simply gives it a greater relish. A seventh and greater advantage of "discard[ing] the system of the Gospel" would be the disappearance of religion and all its "prejudices of education" such as virtue, conscience, and honor. The author responds that the current methods of education seem to leave young gentlemen with little trace of such notions anyway and that it may be useful to keep the lower orders of society in some fear of a higher power; religion also gives the common people material for scaring their children or amusing them on a long winter night.

The last advantage is that abolishing Christianity would unite Protestants because Dissenters would be able to participate in all spheres of church and state. The author answers that the spirit of opposition will always motivate some to differentiate themselves "from the reasonable part of mankind." Every nation has its allotted "portion of enthusiasm," and it is best to give this an outlet through religion rather than in disturbances of civil society. If Christianity were to disappear, the government would have to find some other diversion for such people.

The author concludes his "proof" by pointing out a few "inconveniences" of repealing the Gospel. If the unfashionable and impoverished parsons were to disappear, wits would need some other target of mockery. Similarly, freethinkers would lack religion as the ideal topic for flaunting their mental abilities. Abolishing Christianity might put the Church in danger and force Parliament to find another supporting vote. Lastly, abolishing Christianity would lead to the introduction of "popery," for Jesuits have been known to disguise themselves as Dissenters and even freethinkers, and people will seek some method of worship.

Allowing that his arguments may not have convinced those intent on repeal, the author concludes by humbly recommending that the bill substitute the word "religion" for the word "Christianity."

> For, as long as we leave in being a God and his Providence, with all the necessary consequences which curious and inquisitive men will be apt to draw from such premises, we do not strike at the root of the evil though we should ever so effectually annihilate the present scheme of the Gospel.

The real goal of the abolishers being freedom of action, not just freedom of thought, religion in any form must be eradicated.

Even so, the author suggests that the repeal be postponed until a time of peace, for the allies are all Christians and a potential alliance with the Turks would be unlikely, because they are strictly religious and "what is worse, believe a God; which is more than is required of us even while we preserve the name of Christians." Finally, the "extirpation of the Gospel" might cause stocks to fall 1 percent, much more than the age would spend to preserve Christianity.

Christian Themes

What should a reader make of this "proof," with its shallow, silly, and shocking arguments? Why would Swift defend nominal Christianity? Have Christianity and the Church of England been defended? One way of approaching an answer is to consider the historical context. In 1708, when the *Argument Against Abolishing Christianity* was written, Swift was in England representing the interests of the Irish (Anglican) Church. At this time the Whig government was considering relaxation of the Test Act, a 1673 law requiring all persons holding office to receive the Eucharist according to the rites of the Church of England. The act effectively barred Catholics and Dissenters from the government and the universities. Swift, a strong supporter of the state church, opposed the Whig position and wrote several treatises defending the established church. Some of these are straightforward; the *Argument Against Abolishing Christianity* is not, though it was published with the other treatises.

The work can be seen either as a cynical or purely pragmatic defense of even a nominally Christian established church (positions held by some modern scholars) or as an ironic exposure of the weakness of nominal Christianity and the real motives of the Dissenters and freethinkers eager to weaken the position of the state church. Readers later in Swift's century tended to see it in this latter way. Some saw it as laughing readers into religion, and Samuel Johnson, a conservative churchman and Tory himself, called it "a very happy and judicious irony." In other works Swift identifies the Church of England with apostolic Christianity. Also, in the *Argument Against Abolishing Christianity*, he names prominent freethinkers and refers to "Presbyterians, Anabaptists, Independents, and Quakers." Therefore it seems reasonable to believe that for him any attack on the established church was an attack on Christianity, whether the offenders were Dissenters or freethinkers.

Yet the irony and satire of the *Argument Against Abolishing Christianity* make it a problematic text that literary scholars have interpreted in various ways. Some see its "author" as one of Swift's masks, like Gulliver or the narrator of *A Modest Proposal for Preventing the Children of Poor People of Ireland from Being a Burden to Their Parents or the Country, and for Making Them Beneficial to the Public* (1729), and the satiric target as the kind of person who would think nominal Christianity worth defending. Other scholars reject the idea of a consistent mask but argue that Swift was demonstrating the kinds of reasoning one would use to defend the state church from such a person. What seems clear is that Swift was more concerned with exposing a false Christianity than edifying those who held to "real" Christianity.

Sources for Further Study

Fox, Christopher. *The Cambridge Companion to Jonathan Swift*. Cambridge, England: Cambridge University Press, 2003. A collection of essays providing overviews of many topics related to the author, including religion.

Hoppit, Julian. *A Land of Liberty? England 1689-1727*. New York: Oxford University Press, 2000. The chapter "Faith and Fervour" surveys the social, political, and theological conditions of the church in this era.

Phiddian, Robert. *Swift's Parody*. Cambridge, England: Cambridge University Press, 1995. Discusses the *Argument Against Abolishing Christianity* as an instance of "open" and hence "anarchic" parody that eludes definitive interpretation.

Robertson, Mary F. "Swift's *Argument*: The Fact and the Fiction of Fighting with Beasts." *Modern Philology* 74 (1976): 124-141. Considers the *Argument Against Abolishing Christianity* in the light of Swift's sermons and political/ecclesiastical pamphlets and offers a sophisticated reading of the work.

Rosenheim, Edward W., Jr. *Swift and the Satirist's Art*. Chicago: University of Chicago Press, 1963. This provocative discussion of Swift's masks sees the nominal Christian "author" as the satiric victim.

Paul K. Hesselink

THE ARRIVAL OF THE FUTURE

Author: B. H. Fairchild (1942-   )
First published: 1985
Edition used: The Arrival of the Future. Farmington, Maine: Alice James Books, 2000
Genre: Poetry
Subgenres: Lyric poetry; narrative poetry; stories
Core issues: Daily living; life; nature

Fairchild focuses on the daily lives of characters from his past to depict a world in which religion outwardly consists of churchgoing and hymn singing but inwardly manifests in deep spiritual feelings that are seldom expressed in words but are evident in people's unquestioning and unwavering faith in a higher power that directs their lives and provides meaning and support. The poems portray people for whom the Judgment Day, Christ, and everlasting life are as real as the physical reality of their lives.

Overview

In the forty poems in *The Arrival of the Future*, B. H. Fairchild dwells on scenes in the Midwest and South: an Oklahoma farm, a wheat field, a potato patch, a small-town cafeteria, a highway in west Texas, a grocery store, a movie house, a tavern, a barber shop, a machine shop, and a hotel. Each is evoked in such vivid, descriptive detail that one assumes the poet is recalling early boyhood experiences. Yet the portraits of those who people these locales and the scenes themselves lack sentimentality, however fondly the poet remembers, and the images have a sharpness that delivers meaning without excess emotion.

Structurally, the poems reveal considerable artistry. Fairchild employs enjambment to regulate not only the rhythms of his lines but also the meaning. Shorter lines break meaning into fragments of thought, suggesting the discontinuity of scattered remembrances, as though the material of thought is present but the connectedness of meaning is still missing, as in these lines from "The Girl in the Booth."

> new car, string of trout,
> holidays in Hawaii—
> bending palm and floral
> background—then weddings
> and funerals, same bright
> bleached faces and some kid
> frowning into the ground.
> Sometimes, though, the odd
> shot: . . .
> old guy in the attic
> window.

The pauses at a line's end to suggest a thought that is modified in the next line also suggest that the poem's persona remains uncertain of the meanings that accumulate as he remembers. This give-and-take is managed by the ebb and flow of the lines' rhythms and lengths, and the poem concludes when meaning itself has achieved coherent shape.

Stanzaic structures are used to give a poem both symmetry and balance: three stanzas of seven lines each; three unrhymed quatrains; a single, lengthy stanza; a single stanza of short lines that looks like a linguistic totem; and a series of irregular short stanzas and lines that scatters meaning like exploded emotion. Many of the poems have stanzas of equal length and number of lines (unrhymed), suggesting that the poet's ideas are conceived more fully before they are written or that his thoughts form a more coherent and larger whole than do the shorter, broken-up lines. Sometimes, the lines form units of thought or images that play against one another. In the following stanza from "A Cafeteria in Pasadena," each of the four lines ends on a pause, and at the conclusion, the words seem to spiral upward.

> In that stare is the word within the word,
> The white cup, empty, on the white tablecloth,
> An old man's speech, rising,
> The spiraling song.

Each line has its own subject—word, white cup, speech, song—so each length contains a part of the meaning that develops from "word" to "song." The last line not only concludes the poem but also emphasizes the final image by its brevity.

Among Fairchild's other poetic strengths is the ability to evoke both atmosphere and emotion in descriptive passages while subtly giving a religious context and meaning to the whole poem. His poem "Angels" seems at first to have little to do with heavenly figures. The angels appear in a vision as "four flaming angels crouched on the hood" of a tractor trailer that has crashed and put the driver in the hospital. Friends sit around the bed laughing, drinking, and singing a country song, missing the religious significance of the man's words. As he leaves the hospital, however, the driver shouts, "*Behold, I come like a thief!*" (from Revelation 16:15). The moment is rife with religious overtones, suggested by the image of nurses waving good-bye to the man, their "white dresses puffed out like pigeons/ in the morning breeze." The flaming angels have been transformed into billowing white figures.

By injecting biblical quotations and religious language into many of his poems, Fairchild conveys the sense that Christian principles play a large role in the lives of his characters, the Bible's teachings are never far from their minds, and the Bible gives them a moral reference point and even a language. The poet is one of them, too, for in "Describing the Back of My Hand," his drooping, curled fingers bring to his mind the image of "Adam reaching out to God." Perhaps this point is nowhere more evident than in the book's climactic poem, "The Arrival of the Future," which returns to the poet's early years in Oklahoma. An especially hot summer has made people fear that the end of the world is at hand and that "Christ would ride in on a cloud." The poem follows the boy's grandmother as she works in the potato patch, "*Rock of Ages/ running through your head*," and goes about her life, expecting the Second Coming with the full faith of a Christian soul. At the conclusion, however, the boy's vision supervenes. Having absorbed his grandmother's faith, he sees that death gives life, that the future has arrived, and that it "was forever now and new and holy." The book's final lines demonstrate the essence of Fairchild's ability to shape his meaning into a vision that is both poetic and religious.

Christian Themes

Fairchild's poetry describes a world that is mainly southern and rural, a world that is peopled by characters who believe in basic Christian principles and who could be characterized as God-fearing and Bible quoting. For them, Jesus is real and always close by, and the hierarchy of their thinking runs from the earth they till to the animals they tend, through their own humanity to Heaven, which overlooks their world and guides them in it, finally judging them. The lives of Fairchild's characters are filled with labor, be it driving a semitruck or working on the farm, in a cafeteria, or in a tavern. Churchgoing is a regular activity, as are visits to the tavern. Death is viewed as the end of an earthly life and the beginning of a life hereafter.

These people expect to be judged by their actions on earth and punished for their sins, which are defined by the fundamental precepts of Christianity and which are taught in their churches. For them, sin and salvation are not questioned or analyzed. These people know what sin is and what salvation requires of them. As humans, they are tempted to sin, and they often do, but they also believe in the spirit and God's mercy, so as they live, they hope, and as they sin, they pray for forgiveness. Their faith is more implicit than overt, despite their churchgoing ways. Their values express their beliefs, the value of daily labor and of constancy, the value of earth's creatures in the scheme of nature, and the importance of the whole natural realm in which they live and breathe. Many of the characters are boisterous and profane, but one senses that beneath the rough exterior, they harbor and are sustained by a simple, strong faith that, in times of crises or strong emotion, rises to the surface.

Sources for Further Study

Christophersen, Bill. "The 'I' and the Beholder: Negotiating the Shoals of Personal Narrative." *Poetry* 182, no.1 (April, 2003): 35. A number of well-illustrated insights into the nature of Fairchild's poetry are linked to the early collections, beginning with *The Arrival of the Future.*

Hentoff, Nat. "A Poet with the Pulse of Jazz." *The Wall Street Journal*, August 19, 2004, p. D8. A profile of Fairchild that deals with one of his poetry collections and the poet's relationship with jazz.

Mason, David. "Seven Poets." *The Hudson Review* 57, no. 2 (Summer, 2004): 325-335. Contains discussion of Fairchild and his poetry, which the author feels deserves more attention.

Phillips, Robert. "Lines Brief and Bountiful." Review of *The Arrival of the Future*. *Hudson Review* (Spring, 2001): 169-175. Fairchild's first collection is given a brief appreciative review that is set amid a survey of several other poetry books, with some comparison among them.

Bernard E. Morris

ASCENT OF MOUNT CARMEL *and*
DARK NIGHT OF THE SOUL

Author: Saint John of the Cross (1542-1591)

First transcribed: La subida del monte Carmelo, 1578-1579 (English translation, 1864); *Noche oscura del alma*, c. 1585 (English translation, 1864)

Editions used: Ascent of Mount Carmel, translated and edited, with a general introduction, by E. Allison Peers. New York: Image Books, 1958. *Dark Night of the Soul*, translated and edited, with an introduction, by E. Allison Peers. New York: Image Books, 1959

Genre: Nonfiction

Subgenres: Meditation and contemplation; mysticism; spiritual treatise

Core issues: Illumination; purgation; soul; union with God

The intellectual, poetical, and mystical were graciously fused in these works of the most celebrated of Catholic mystical theologians, Saint John of the Cross.

Overview

The sixteenth century Carmelite monk Juan de Yepes (canonized in 1726 as Saint John of the Cross) drew upon the long tradition of apophatic mysticism to chart the ascent of Mount Carmel, which is his image for the ascent of the soul to God. There is reason to believe that Saint John was familiar not only with the writings of the early apophatic mystic, Pseudo-Dionysius the Areopagite, but also such later ones as Eckhart and Ruysbroeck. Saint John, however, provides a precise, comprehensive, and elegant description of the way of unknowing that is missing in preceding texts.

Although the *Ascent of Mount Carmel* and *Dark Night of the Soul* appear as two volumes with different titles, they constitute a single treatise on one poem. The recommended order for reading them is:

(1) Active purgation of the senses: *Ascent*, book 1

(2) Passive purgation of the senses: *Dark Night*, book 1

(3) Active purgation of the spirit: *Ascent*, books 2 and 3

(4) Passive purgation of the spirit: *Dark Night*, book 2

It is well to begin the "ascent" with chapter 5 of book 2 of the *Ascent of Mount Carmel*, wherein Saint John defines substantial union and mystical or transforming union. The former is natural union with God whereby the soul is able to exist; the latter is supernatural in that the transformation of the soul, whereby the will is brought into conformity with the will of God, is effected through grace. *Substantial* union is the union of essence, while *transforming* union is the union of likeness. Saint John suggests that the purpose of the Christian life is to experience mystical union; all Christians, therefore, are called to ascend the mount.

Saint John's mystical map assumes that God is totally other than the soul and yet can be known by the soul. Granted that God is not like the soul, the soul cannot rely on what is like her to know and love God. Since all means must be proportioned to the end, and since the end is the unknown, the soul must travel by the unknown to the unknown. Thus the ascent is a leaving behind and being detached from that which is known, meaning that which is like the soul, in order to travel by the unknown (the unlike) into the unknown (the unlike) which is God. Night is the image for the journey wherein the soul is deprived of desire for worldly things, dispossessed of natural understandings of God and plunged into Divine Darkness.

There is only one night, but there are stages in the night. In the first part of the night, the Active Night of the Senses, the soul strives actively to rid herself of desires that come in a natural way through the five exterior senses and the interior senses of the imagination and fancy. Unless desires are purged, the soul will suffer *privative* desire: The more she fills herself with desire for things, the more she is deprived of God. She will also suffer five *positive* effects: She is wearied, tormented, darkened, defiled, and weakened. The main point that Saint John makes is that it is our craving for things rather than the things themselves that hinders the ascent.

The soul is unable to accomplish the purgation of the senses. God perfects the work in a more intense darkness known as the Passive Night of the Senses. Saint John describes passive purgation in terms of the spiritual imperfections that afflict beginners: pride, avarice, luxury, wrath, gluttony, envy, and sloth. These chapters reveal the author's spiritual perceptiveness, sharpened not only by reflection on his own journey but also by years of service as spiritual director to novices, brothers, priests, and nuns. He knew firsthand, for example, the grave obstacle of pride that blocked the ascent of beginners who flaunted their piety, looked to confessors for praise, and were impatient with their own faults; or the extremes of bodily penance in which the gluttonous indulged while in pursuit of spiritual sweetness.

Spiritual sweetness, that is, the good feelings the soul experiences in meditation and devotion, must cede to dryness if the ascent is to continue. In a chapter of stunning clarity Saint John sets forth three signs by which to discern if the absence of sweetness in spiritual activities is caused by the soul's own lukewarmness or is God's way of leading her into a more delicate mode of prayer. Had Saint John left no more than this one chapter (nine), his place in mystical literature would be assured. The first sign is that the soul finds no pleasure in God or things created; the second is that the soul is anguished because without spiritual sweetness she thinks she is not serving God but backsliding; the third is that she cannot meditate or use her imagination in prayer, devotion, and reading. If the three signs exist together, they mark the transition from meditation to contemplation, from active consciousness to passive, from the natural to the supernatural, from the known to the unknown. The proper response to the experience of aridity that is indicated by the coexistence of the three signs is to rest in peace and do nothing except remain attentive to the darkness. God infuses love into the soul in ways too subtle for the senses to grasp. Infused loving, however, is discernible in the effects of humility, charity, increased virtue, remembrance of God, and liberty of spirit. Now, as the poem sings, the house (of the senses) is at rest.

The climb becomes steeper and darker as the soul becomes ever more aware of the need to cleanse herself of attachments, not only to natural understandings but also to supernatural ones. Chapter 10 of the second book of the *Ascent of Mount Carmel* is the necessary introduction to all of book 2, which treats purgation of understanding, and book 3, purgation of memory and will.

Saint John's explanation of the two kinds of understanding, natural and supernatural, derives from the process of knowing wherein we gather information about an exterior reality through the senses, store the data in the imagination as images, and conceptualize the images. If the elements of exterior reality, senses, imagination, images, understanding, and concepts are present or active, the mode and content of knowing/understanding are natural. If one of more of the elements are absent, the mode of understanding is supernatural, but the content is not necessarily supernatural.

For example, if a person is present at the crucifixion of Jesus Christ, sees the event with the eyes, stores images in the imagination, and conceptualizes the images as the execution of a man, the knowing is natural in mode and content. This knowing John calls corporeal natural understanding. If the exterior reality of the crucifixion is absent, the phenomenon is a corporeal supernatural understanding, supernatural in mode in that the first element is missing but not in content because that which is seen in a supernatural way is nonetheless specific and distinct, hence natural (that is, a man executed by crucifixion).

If the image of the crucifixion is impressed directly on the imagination without benefit of the exterior reality or use of senses, the phenomenon is a supernatural imaginary vision, supernatural in mode in that the elements of exterior reality and senses are absent but not in content because that which is seen in the imagination (a man executed by crucifixion) is nonetheless specific and distinct, hence natural.

If the exterior reality of the crucifixion, the senses, the imagination, and the understanding are absent or not active, and if the understandings are given to the understanding in the form of distinct, clear visions, revelations, or locutions—that is, they can be articulated in the form of concepts—the phenomenon is a supernatural spiritual understanding, supernatural in mode in that said elements are absent, but not in content because that which is understood in the understanding in the guise of a vision or revelation or locution is nonetheless specific and distinct, hence natural.

If, however, the vision or revelation or locution is not distinct—as, for example, in the case of an angel or an event prophesied—but is dark and confused, and if the dark, confused understanding leaves the soul quiet, desirous to do God's will, and inwardly convinced of being present to God, even though she does not see or imagine or understand anything clear and specific, then the content as well as the mode of understanding is supernatural.

The summit of Mount Carmel is dark, confused, and general understanding, for the summit is God; to human reason God is darkness. All that is not dark, confused, and general is to be dispossessed in the ascent; the soul is not to depend on anything specific, hence natural, to mediate that which is not specific, hence supernatural.

Throughout the rigorous treatment of these kinds of understandings, Saint John states repeatedly the case against depending on specific and distinct knowledge. Surely he was painfully aware of the precipitous plunges suffered by contemporaries who mistook their visions of angels and prophecies of the future for the Divine Darkness that, for Saint John, must overwhelm the traveler if God is to be met in the transforming love of mystical union.

The structure of understanding outlined in the second book of the *Ascent of Mount Carmel* is the foundation for the active purgation of memory and will that follows in the third book. Just as one acquires knowledge, so it is remembered; hence the purging of memory of natural and supernatural understandings in the order established in the preceding book. The rest of book 3 is devoted to cleansing the ill of affections of joy, hope, grief, and fear. Saint John breaks off discussion after defining temporal, natural, sensual, moral, supernatural, and spiritual joys, describing the evils of attachment to them and benefits of purging attachment. Saint John has made his case against attachment so thoroughly that by this time further explanation would be tedious. The point of purgation is clear.

Night, however, is not over. The mount is steeper and darker than ever. The soul feels bound for desolation. If she was disconsolate in the Passive Night of the Senses, what she is made to endure in the Passive Night of the Spirit leaves her gasping and groaning. Gone are consolations: The understanding is dark; the will, dry; memory, empty. In vain she labors to meditate and read; in vain she seeks comfort from spiritual directors. She feels abandoned by friends, books, devotions, by whatever once served to bring alive God's presence; and she feels abandoned by God, cast into a cell of dark solitude, her only companion Darkness itself. She cannot see that God is dispossessing her of cravings, desires, and attachments, whatever form they take—and Saint John hastens to advise that the way is individual, beset with unique difficulties such that no person, only God, can illumine the way. However, God's illumination the soul cannot see in the blackness of night, as God blinds the eyes of natural understanding, annihilating her with respect to how and what she knows, remembers, and wants.

Thus God secretly instructs the soul, lighting her with divine wisdom. However, the more she is illumined by God with God, the more her natural faculties are darkened. She cannot see the Light that is darkness to her faculties.

So the soul suffers. She undergoes. She is passionate. Paradoxically, her suffering—her passion—is her love for God and God's love for her, for she would not suffer if God were not present to her beyond her natural understanding and if she did not yearn with all her being to love and know God as God is. In the awful darkness come moments of relief, fleeting yet sufficient to sustain her, when she discerns God in the sudden enflaming of her will to love. Emboldened, she runs in search of her Beloved.

In darkest night, faculties and senses purged, freed from attachments to the natural, the soul is freed to love God and know God, not as she thought or expected God to be, but as God is. Securely, secretly, joyously, she runs up the dark slopes to be touched again and again by God, to seize him, hold him fast and be held, to soar upward to her Beloved, the house of her spirit and senses now at rest.

Christian Themes

A summary of the main Christian concerns of Saint John's treatises would include the following points:

- In the apophatic way, also known as the via negativa, the soul increasingly detaches herself and is detached from the specific and knowable until in utter detachment she knows only that which is dark, confused, and general, which is God.
- The journey is traced in terms of the sensual and spiritual parts of the soul as well as active and passive consciousness.
- Night is the image for the journey of purgation or detachment.
- The stages of night are active purgation of the senses, passive purgation of the senses, active purgation of the spirit, and passive purgation of the spirit.
- Actively and passively purged in the sensual and spiritual parts, the soul is transformed by God so that her will is conformed to God's will.

Sources for Further Study

Dicken, E. W. Trueman. *The Crucible of Love*. New York: Sheed & Ward, 1963. This study remains the indispensable introduction to the mystical theology of Saint John of the Cross and Saint Teresa of Ávila.

Feldmeir, Peter. *Christianity Looks East: Comparing the Spiritualities of John of the Cross and Buddhaghosa*. New York: Paulist Press, 2006. A Roman Catholic priest considers Saint John's dialogue with Buddhaghosa to explore the similarities and differences between Christian and Buddhist paths toward liberation. Bibliography, index.

John of the Cross, Saint. *The Collected Works of St. John of the Cross*. Translated by Kieran Kavanaugh, O.C.D., and Otilio Rodgríguez, O.C.D. Washington, D.C.: ICS Publications, 1979. Contains Saint John's *Spiritual Canticle* and *Living Flame of Love* in two excellent translations.

May, Gerald G. *The Dark Night of the Soul: A Psychiatrist Explores the Connection Between Darkness and Spiritual Growth*. New York: HarperSanFrancisco, 2004. Psychiatrist May draws on the Carmelite mystics Saint John and Teresa of Ávila, along with pscyhological research and biblical scripture, to address the mysterious "dark night of the soul" as necessary to overcome depression, addiction, and other mental afflications. Bibliography, index.

Mary E. Giles

THE AUGSBURG CONFESSION OF FAITH

Author: Philipp Melanchthon (1497-1560)

First published: Confessio Augustana, 1530 (English translation, 1536)

Edition used: The Book of Concord: The Confessions of the Evangelical Lutheran Church, translated and edited by Theodore G. Tappert in collaboration with Jaroslav Pelikan, Robert H. Fischer, and Arthur C. Piepkorn. Philadelphia: Fortress Press, 1959

Genre: Nonfiction

Subgenre: Theology

Core issues: Evangelization; faith; Lutherans and Lutheranism; Protestants and Protestantism

The Augsburg Confession of Faith *presents all major tenets of Lutheran belief and lists objections to perceived corruptions and abuses in the late medieval Roman Church. Melanchthon, principal author of the document, enumerated the doctrines of the Evangelicals (Lutherans) in a manner so as to emphasize agreements with Rome, while affirming clearly Protestant understanding of the Gospel where it conflicted with the papal position. The reformers presented their confession to Emperor Charles V in German and Latin texts.*

Overview

By 1530 Germany had become divided into Catholic and Lutheran states over which the Holy Roman Emperor exercised an ineffective rule. To promote imperial unity in the face of the Turkish military threat in Eastern Europe, the monarch asked the princes of the empire to meet. Because religious dissension impaired concerted military and political action, Charles V was eager to achieve a resolution. Concerned officials met in Augsburg, Bavaria.

Before receiving the imperial summons to Augsburg, the German Evangelicals had adopted the Schwabach Articles to express their understanding of the Christian faith, and they soon drafted the Torgau Articles, a list of complaints against practices of the papal church that they deemed abusive or corrupt. Philipp Melanchthon, a professor at the University of Wittenberg and close collaborator with Martin Luther, combined the two documents for presentation to the Imperial Diet on June 25, 1530. It thereafter became *The Augsburg Confession of Faith.*

To combat accusations of heresy, Melanchthon stressed the historical character of Lutheran beliefs by linking them to ancient creeds and writings of the church fathers, especially Saint Augustine. This reformer argued that nothing the Evangelicals affirmed conflicted with the teachings of Scripture and the faith of the ancient church.

The twenty-eight articles that make up *The Augsburg Confession of Faith* consist of twenty-one statements of doctrine and seven long declarations about abuses, together with demands for reforms. Although Melanchthon and his associates compiled the confession, Luther approved it as an accurate account of his doctrine. Luther could not attend the diet because he was under the ban of the empire and subject to arrest.

Public presentation of the Augsburg confession was the work of Christian Beyer, chancellor of Saxony in the employ of Prince-Elector John. Some time before the convocation, the Protestants had agreed to present a German rather than a Saxon front before the emperor, as the margrave of Brandenburg-Ansbach and the landgrave of Hesse joined with the city government of Nuremberg in endorsing the effort. Soon five other princes and municipal officials from Reutlingen also signed the confession.

Aligning the Evangelicals with historic orthodoxy, the confession begins by affirming a trinitarian view of God and scorns all who reject the doctrine of Original Sin. It emphatically declares the deity and humanity of Christ in the manner of ancient creeds, while asserting that Jesus died as a sacrifice for all sin, original and volitional.

Article 4 declares justification through faith alone in opposition to the common medieval belief in salvation by grace plus works of merit. This article is the cornerstone for the rest of the confession, for it specifies the arch distinctive in the Protestant understanding of salvation as an undeserved gift from God. That is, sinners cannot merit divine favor, but God requires perfect righteousness from them nevertheless. Justification *sola fide* (through faith alone) means that God confers on unworthy people who embrace Christ by faith the very righteousness he demands. In a transaction of imputation, the righteousness of Christ becomes the possession of believers as a gift of grace. Article 6 of the confession cites Saint Ambrose in support of this doctrine, thereby connecting it with ancient Catholic teachings.

Article 6 rebuts the charge that the Evangelicals' doctrine of justification disparages good works by teaching that such deeds follow as fruits of justification. While such works contribute nothing to justification, they flow from it as necessary consequences. This conflicts with the Roman Catholic view that good works form faith and make it acceptable to God.

The Augsburg Confession of Faith is explicit in defining the church as the body of all true believers in Christ, the context within which the preaching of the Gospel and the proper administration of the sacraments occur. This church does not require hierarchical government, as Rome contended.

In addition to its teachings contrary to Catholicism, the Augsburg confession condemns the Anabaptists for rejecting infant baptism and for disdaining Christian participation in civil government as incompatible with true faith. The confession, on the contrary, calls for Christians to regard civil rulers as agents of God, and it urges believers to enter civil service if they have the opportunity. In making these assertions, the Evangelicals dissociated themselves from radicals, some of whom had engaged in violent social revolts.

A bitterly contested subject in the debates of that era pertained to the effects of sin on the human will, a matter that had engaged Luther against Desiderius Erasmus in 1524-1525. The confession upholds Luther's teaching that the fall of humans into sin robbed them of genuine freedom in their relationship with God. Article 18 admits that people possess free will in their contacts with one another and they are able to achieve a sort of civic righteousness by deeds that benefit society. They cannot, however, please God unless his Holy Spirit regenerates them and empowers them to believe the Gospel and trust in Christ for forgiveness. Only as justified believers can they will to love God and obey his commandments.

Beginning in article 22, the Augsburg confession identifies specific practices of the Roman Church that the Evangelicals deemed contrary to Scripture and therefore were matters for reform. Prominent among them was the imposition of celibacy on the clergy, the contention that the Mass is a sacrificial reenactment of Calvary, and the inviolability of monastic vows. The confession rejects all these teachings as without biblical foundation. The controlling position of justification *sola fide* in Lutheran theology made rejection of such practices inevitable. At the root of the controversy with Rome was the issue of authority, because the Evangelicals insisted on the supremacy of Scripture as the arbiter in all matters of doctrine and practice. Although the Roman Church had, to that point, issued no official pronouncement about the relative authority of the Bible and the papacy, it became clear that this was the fundamental issue between Rome and Wittenberg. Melanchthon addressed that matter in his *Treatise on the Power and Primacy of the Pope* in 1537.

Christian Themes

The desire of Charles V to achieve unity at Augsburg was not to be; Catholic theologians perceived correctly that, despite Melanchthon's conciliatory language, the Catholic and Lutheran positions were incompatible, and while the diet was still in session, several more German states endorsed the Augsburg confession. The emperor then allowed a team of Catholic scholars to compose a confutation of the confession, which, he declared, had refuted the errors of the Evangelicals. He would not permit the dissidents to have a copy of the confutation, but they took notes during the reading, and Melanchthon soon produced *Apologie de Confession aus dem Latin verdeudschet* (1531; *The Apologie*, 1536). When the Protestants presented this to the emperor, he refused to accept it. *The Apologie* appeared in print in 1531 and quickly gained acceptance in Lutheran states. In 1537, Lutheran theologians meeting in Smalcald formally endorsed it as another confession of their church. In contrast to the pacific language of the Augsburg confession, that of *The Apologie* is polemical, even belligerent, evidence there was no longer any expectation of reconciliation with Rome. Luther often extolled Melanchthon's confessional works as accurate summaries of Christian doctrine.

The history of the Augsburg confession after 1530 reflects the seriousness with which the Evangelicals regarded doctrinal precision. Melanchthon made several revisions of the confession, some of them relating to the condition of human nature as a consequence of the Fall. Rigorist Lutherans considered such revisions compromises with Rome, and they therefore insisted on adherence to the unaltered edition of 1531. When, in 1580, to heal intramural disputes about doctrine, Lutheran scholars and officials published their theological documents as the *Konkordienbuch* (1580; *The Book of Concord*, 1882), they included only the unaltered version of the Augsburg confession. It thereby became the primary statement of Lutheran orthodoxy, which it remains.

An English translation of the *Confessio Augustana* appeared in 1536, evidence of Luther's broadening influence. When English and German theologians met at the request of King Henry VIII in 1538, they referred to the Augsburg confession as a basis for possible collaboration against Rome, and the Thirty-nine Articles of Religion, which became the official declaration of the Anglican Church in 1563, shows the influence of the Augsburg confession. Luther maintained all who adhere to that document are brothers in Christ, and it is worthy to note that John Calvin was among numerous Protestant reformers to sign the confession, even though Lutherans and Calvinists became critical of one another after their mentors died.

Sources for Further Study

Bergendoff, Conrad. *The Church of the Lutheran Reformation*. St. Louis, Mo.: Concordia, 1967. This historical survey of Lutheranism is of great value for placing theological disputes within their contexts and showing how and why church leaders found it necessary to draft statements of faith.

Burgess, Joseph A., and George Lindbeck, eds. *The Role of the Augsburg Confession: Catholic and Lutheran Views*. Philadelphia: Fortress Press, 1980. This collection of essays by distinguished scholars, Lutheran and Catholic, who seek a basis for reconciliation between their churches, contains much valuable historical information.

Junghans, Helmar. "Augsburg Confession." In *Oxford Encyclopedia of the Reformation*. Oxford, England: Oxford University Press, 1996. This succinct yet substantial article presents events leading to adoption of the Augsburg confession in chronological sequence and demonstrates the concern for precise doctrine characteristic of the Evangelical reformers.

Kolb, Robert. *Confessing the Faith*. St. Louis, Mo.: Concordia, 1991. Written from a confessional point of view, this is a helpful examination of Lutheran beliefs in general and the role of the Augsburg Confession in particular.

Kolb, Robert, and Timothy J. Wengert, eds. *The Book of Concord*. Minneapolis, Minn.: Fortress Press, 2000. This contains all historic doctrinal statements of the Lutheran Church in a fresh translation together with insightful introductions that relate each item to its context in history.

James Edward McGoldrick

AWAKENING MERCY

Author: Angela Benson (1959-   )
First published: 2000
Genre: Novel
Subgenre: Romance
Core issues: African Americans; faith; forgiveness; healing; love; prayer; responsibility

Ashamed by her past behavior, Cecelia (CeCe) Williams feels unworthy of God's love, loses her faith, and distrusts men. Working two jobs to repay a substantial debt, she rushes through her daily obligations. When she forgets to pay the fines for numerous parking violations, a judge assigns her to community service. CeCe meets Genesis House director Nate Richardson, who helps her rediscover her spirituality through church attendance and prayer. Falling in love, she learns to forgive herself and others, deal with a secret that has troubled her, and trust in God's unconditional acceptance and the possibilities of love.

> *Principal characters*
> *Cecelia "CeCe" Williams*, the protagonist
> *Nathaniel "Nate" Richardson*, the director of Genesis House
> *Gertrude "B. B." Brinson*, CeCe's mentor
> *David Williams*, CeCe's son
> *Shay Taylor*, a founder of Genesis House
> *Anna Mae Wilson*, a staff member at Genesis House
> *Marvin Taylor*, a founder of Genesis House
> *Stuart Solomon*, a judge

Overview

In love with her hometown boyfriend, Eric Bradshaw, twenty-one-year-old Spelman College senior Cecelia (CeCe) Williams is devastated when he rejects her to marry another woman, Yolanda, despite CeCe's having told him she is pregnant with his child. Five years later, CeCe is working as an accountant in Atlanta, Georgia, living with her son, David, and former Spelman dorm adviser, sixty-five-year-old Gertrude (B. B.) Brinson, who is CeCe's closest friend and spiritual mentor. CeCe also sells real estate to earn extra income. Unsure of most men's intentions, she rarely dates.

When CeCe is summoned to court regarding more than forty unpaid parking tickets, Judge Stuart Solomon, who believes in social accountability, assigns her 150 hours of community service at Genesis House, a Christian-oriented service, in downtown Atlanta. Canceling real estate tours on a Saturday afternoon, CeCe is annoyed when the Genesis House director does not show up for their appointment to discuss how she will complete her hours. CeCe arrives at their rescheduled meeting, expecting to dislike the director. Thirty-three-year-old Nathaniel (Nate) Richardson regrets having missed CeCe the previous Saturday; their meeting had coincided with his ex-wife Naomi's wedding, which had distressed him. He feels like a failure because Naomi left him and their marriage.

Nate apologizes to CeCe and suggests she count eight hours of her service for Saturday. He tells her that Judge Solomon is his friend and admires the social work done at Genesis House. Nate explains the purpose of Genesis House, revealing that a couple, Marvin and Shay Taylor, grief-stricken when their young son was killed several years earlier, established the center to assist people living in Atlanta's inner-city Robinwood community. Nate describes the needs of those residents, suggesting that CeCe could plan teen pregnancy or unemployment programs. She offers to help people learn job-hunting skills.

At home, CeCe contemplates how she will manage her time and complete her remaining 142 hours of community service. Sorting through her mail, CeCe impulsively rips up a letter from David's paternal grandparents, the Bradshaws, and throws away the pieces unread, despite B. B.'s urging CeCe to consider the Bradshaws' feelings. CeCe defends her decision to refuse the Bradshaws access to their grandson because they negatively reacted to news of her pregnancy.

During the next weeks, CeCe forms friendships with Shay Taylor and Anna Mae Wilson at Genesis House, developing employment workshops. CeCe and Nate tentatively begin a romance. She divulges information about Eric while visiting a spot where Nate likes to pray in Stone Mountain Park. Nate takes David to youth baseball games and is nurturing toward him, even buying a toddler car seat for his car. CeCe and David begin to worship at Nate's church. Nate sits with CeCe on her porch swing most evenings after eating dinner. They confide their fears to each other and speak frankly regarding intimacy and marriage, agreeing to proceed cautiously and not rush physical expectations. Nate hopes to sustain his relationship with CeCe and marry her, buying an engagement ring, which he hides, waiting for the best time to propose. When Nate's parents visit Atlanta, they meet CeCe and express approval of her as a possible wife for Nate. He asks CeCe to introduce him to her parents, but she stubbornly refuses his request. CeCe withdraws emotionally from Nate, who is frustrated by her distrust.

When CeCe's parents call to tell her that her grandfather is dying, CeCe asks Nate to accompany her and David to her Alabama hometown. Nate meets her parents in the hospital and stays at their home. He is disturbed by her unfriendly reception of the Bradshaws when they arrive at the Williamses' house with a gift for David. Questioning CeCe about her continuing anger toward Eric, Nate suggests she might still love him, telling her she needs to resolve her emotions concerning David's father before they can continue their relationship.

Returning to Atlanta, CeCe admits her secret to Nate, revealing that she blackmailed Eric to pay her twenty thousand dollars for her silence, keeping her pregnancy concealed from Yolanda. CeCe had used that large sum as a down payment on her house and for other expenses but, feeling guilty, had been working to earn money to reimburse Eric in one large payment (she never mentions his legal obligation to pay child support). Remarking that earning twenty thousand dollars might take years, Nate tells CeCe they cannot be married until she asks Eric for his forgiveness and arranges to pay the twenty thousand dollars in smaller amounts.

When CeCe meets Ronald, a teenage boy whose girlfriend is pregnant, she reassures him and offers advice. CeCe realizes her experiences might help teenagers dealing with unplanned pregnancies. She travels home to Alabama to apologize to her family and the Bradshaws, explaining her anguish when they did not support her emotionally during her pregnancy and inviting them to visit David. Returning to Atlanta, she tells Nate she has forgiven Eric and the Bradshaws, her parents, and herself. CeCe and Nate reconcile, forgiving each other and bonding through prayer. CeCe decides to continue volunteering at Genesis House even though she has completed her 150 hours of service. She plans to develop a program to assist pregnant teenagers. CeCe and Nate vow to trust themselves, and their relationship, to God.

Christian Themes

Awakening Mercy was the first novel in Angela Benson's Genesis House series. Although in some respects it is representative of a new generation of romances and novels written specifically for a Christian audience, *Library Journal* deemed it a "breakthrough Christian romance" for addressing universal issues featuring contemporary African American characters. The novel won Best Multicultural Romance from *Romantic Times* magazine and Best Contemporary Ethnic Romance from *Affaire de Coeur* magazine; it was a finalist for the coveted RITA Award (awarded by the Romance Writers of America), Christy Award (given by the Christian Booksellers Association), and Gold Pen Award (from the Black Writers Alliance). Benson, a graduate of Spelman College who majored in mathematics and industrial engineering before becoming a novelist, has said of her novel: "This book is close to my heart. . . . First, because I consider it an honor to write for the Christian market. Second, in many ways, CeCe's story—about living with the consequences of our bad choices, and finding forgiveness—is my story, too." Forgiveness, self-acceptance, trust, and community service are the key themes of *Awakening Mercy*.

Service and social work help CeCe, Nate, and other characters in the novel heal from emotional wounds inflicted by themselves, others, and fate. Although she is devoted to caring for her son, CeCe reluctantly serves her community as a punishment. Finding comfort and connections with others helps CeCe recover and sustain her faith. By performing good deeds, she realizes her Christian responsibilities, viewing her work as valuable not only to the people she helps but also as a gift to strengthen her belief in herself and God.

Prayer is an important aspect of the characters' relationships with one another and acceptance of themselves. When she was conflicted about her pregnancy, CeCe prayed in college with B. B., who guided her to seek comfort from God despite feeling spiritually alienated. Prayer brings Nate and CeCe together as they form their relationship and face issues that test their love. Although leery of commitment after previous partners' shortcomings, they patiently listen to and respect the fears and doubts each expresses, seeking help from God to provide comfort and ease pain the other is experiencing.

Family, whether biological or formed through friendship, community, or church, is essential to the characters. Nate invites CeCe and David to meet his parents and friends and includes them in his life. The trio attend church together, where the congregation views them as a family. CeCe and Nate help their friends fix broken relationships and find love. CeCe realizes that by feeling empathy and giving her time and assistance to people suffering personal crises, she also can heal her heart. Such kindnesses awaken CeCe from her despair and anger, connecting her to God and her community.

Nate insists that CeCe learn to forgive David's father and grandparents. Most important, he states she needs to forgive herself. He assures her that God forgives her. CeCe must overcome her sense of shame and unworthiness to regain her faith and accept herself. By freeing herself of her guilt and self-loathing, CeCe can open her heart and feel redeemed and deserving of being loved. She can then begin to accept and trust others. Her personal revival transforms her into a person who has a sense of belonging and can commit to herself, Nate, her family, friends, and God.

Sources for Further Study

Benson, Angela. *Telling the Tale: The African-American Fiction Writer's Guide.* New York: Berkley Books, 2000. Writing at about the same time she created *Awakening Mercy*, Benson discusses how she became a writer and appropriated aspects of her life for her stories.

Black Issues Book Review 2, no. 1 (January/February, 2001): 18. Reviews *Awakening Mercy* and other novels.

Duncan, Melanie C. Review of *Awakening Mercy. Library Journal* 125, no. 14 (September 1, 2000): 184. Identifies the novel as a "breakthrough Christian romance featuring African American characters and universal themes. . . ."

Frederick, Marla F. *Between Sundays: Black Women and Everyday Struggles of Faith.* Berkeley: University of California Press, 2003. Useful for understanding CeCe's attitudes, this study examines how spirituality impacts southern African American women's reactions to problems. Describes varying religious views of gender and sexuality.

Nelson, Timothy J. *Every Time I Feel the Spirit: Religious Experience and Ritual in an African American Church.* New York: New York University Press, 2005. Sociological study exploring how southerners similar to Benson's characters develop individual and communal relations with God to sustain and comfort them in their daily lives.

Elizabeth D. Schafer

BAPTISMAL INSTRUCTION

Author: Saint John Chrysostom (c. 354-407 C.E.)
First transcribed: Catecheses ad illuminandos, 388 C.E. (English translation, 1889)
Edition used: Instructions to Catechumens, edited by W. R. W. Stephens and T. P.
   Brandram. Grand Rapids, Mich.: Wm. B. Eerdmans, 1978
Genre: Nonfiction
Subgenres: Exegesis; sermons
Core issues: Baptism; repentance; women

In these two sermons, Chrysostom instructs people preparing to be baptized into the Catholic Church on the importance of baptism and its meaning and importance for them as Christians in this life and the next.

Overview

Two sermons by Saint John Chrysostom survive from among the hundreds he preached in Antioch in the late fourth century. Though brief, each sermon covers a plethora of theological points. John was born into a wealthy Christian family in Antioch and prepared for a career in law, but ran away from home to begin a career in the Church. His pronounced ascetic practices and his remarkable eloquence caused him to be appointed chief preacher in Antioch, where he acquired the nickname "Chrysostomus," or "Golden Mouth." He was consecrated patriarch of Constantinople, the imperial capital, in 398. He immediately began to make powerful enemies for publicly rebuking both clergy and imperial officials for their corrupt and unchristian behavior. After he called Empress Eudoxia a thief to her face during a Sunday service, she had him banished from the city, and Chrysostom died en route to his place of exile.

Most of Chrysostom's vast literary output exists in the form of sermons on the books of both the Old and New Testaments. Writing and preaching in flawless Greek, he left behind hundreds of sermons from his period as chief preacher in Antioch. Unfortunately, only two of the sermons on baptismal instructions for catechumens survive. They were preached during Lent of 388. Though brief, these two sermons give indications of many topics of which Chrysostom preached in more detail on other occasions. One of these sermons is addressed to male catechumens; the other is addressed to female catechumens. Both groups would have been making final preparations to be baptized into the Church during Easter.

The first sermon is addressed to the male catechumens, who Chrysostom refers to as "those about to be illuminated." He dwells on the image of baptism as illumination, as a new way of seeing, at length. He wishes the catechumens to be very clear that baptism is not some sort of magic ritual for the forgiveness of sins. Accepting baptism involves a fundamental reorientation of one's entire existence. One is baptized into the death of Christ. Chrysostom takes this quite literally. On becoming a Christian, one's former self, one's previous lifestyle, dies. One now lives not for the possibility of material advantage, but in hope of eternal life. Baptism also entails participation in the resurrection of Christ. Christians reorient their lives to live for the sake of heaven. While the promise of forgiveness of sins is a component of the baptism into the death and resurrection of Christ, it is not an end in itself. Chrysostom wants to be certain the catechumens recognize that baptism is a permanent, life-changing decision.

All of Chrysostom's theological opinions are grounded in a very close, literal reading of the biblical text, a method of biblical interpretation particularly practiced in Antioch, his hometown. Chrysostom rarely waxed poetic or philosophical in his sermons. He was not a speculative thinker. He was a very careful and thorough reader of the Bible. All the material in his sermons and all of his examples are taken directly from Scripture, rather than from philosophical or literary texts, though Chrysostom and his audience certainly knew these secular texts. He was always trying to impart an immediately practical benefit or point of guidance to his audience. The sermons on baptismal instruction are no exception to his policy. Every statement he makes to the catechumens and every image he invokes has its antecedents in Scripture. In the midst of their instruction on the meaning of baptism, the catechumens are exposed to a tour through the entirety of Scripture.

The catechumens are praised for their decision not to wait until their deathbed to request baptism, still a common practice in the late fourth century. By preparing for baptism while in good health, the catechumens will immediately begin to enjoy the benefits of eternal life while still on earth. Such current benefits, however, do not come without responsibilities. One such responsibility is to refrain from swearing any oath, even if the oath is one that can be kept easily. Chrysostom takes quite literally Jesus' teaching equating oath taking with works of the devil in Matthew 5:35. Jesus said not to do it, and for Chrysostom, that is the end of the discussion. Scripture is clear, and becoming a Christian means living by the Scriptures in both thoughts and deeds.

In his baptismal instructions to the female catechumens, Chrysostom dwells at length on Christian modesty. Specifically, Chrysostom objects to women using makeup, wearing gold jewelry, or arranging their hair in fancy styles. Such behaviors are of this world, precisely the world the women are preparing to leave behind them through baptism. Refraining from stylish ornamentation will mark a Christian woman for all to see. A woman's true marks of beauty are her modesty and devotion, not household wealth or costly clothing. Chrysostom was preaching this sermon in Antioch, but this attitude toward women caused him many problems when he tried to preach a similar message to the wealthy and powerful women of Constantinople, many of whom competed with one another is ostentatious displays of wealth and social standing.

Chrysostom takes issue with women's continued reliance on folk medicine, particularly as folk healers used magic amulets and incantations as part of their remedies. Christians should rely on prayer to the Lord, the giver of life, not pagan superstitions. Again, Chrysostom is trying to impress on the catechumens that the consequences accompanying baptism require a fundamental reorientation of all aspects of life.

Christian Themes

Despite their brevity, the baptismal instruction sermons are packed with meaning. Chief among the important ideas conveyed by Chrysostom is the notion that baptism is a permanent, life-altering event, the consequences of which last into the next life. Baptism into the death and resurrection of Christ sets a Christian apart from the rest of society in both thought and action, both in this earthly life and in the world to come. Because of baptism's tremendous consequences, catechumens should be aware of exactly what type of covenantal relationship they are agreeing to enter.

To help them navigate their new lifestyle, the baptized should constantly refer back to Scripture, Chrysostom says. The literal meaning of the Scriptures is straightforward. A thorough knowledge of Scripture will provide one with plenty of examples of how to think and act for the sake of heaven. Jesus himself provides the perfect example for Christians to emulate.

Chrysostom asks Christians to pay less attention to their social and physical selves, and much more attention to their spiritual selves. He asks them to forgo previous patterns of thought and behavior, to give attention to the poor and the vulnerable in society, to turn away from anything that gives power to Satan, to act in the grace of the Lord, and to give glory to God.

Sources for Further Study

Chrysostom, John. *Commentary on Saint John the Apostle and Evangelist.* 2 vols. Fathers of the Church series. Reprint. Washington, D.C.: Catholic University of America Press, 2000. Contains eighty-eight sermons on the Gospel of Saint John. These sermons are from the time when Chrysostom was in Antioch.

Kelly, J. N. D. *Golden Mouth: The Story of John Chrysostom, Ascetic, Preacher, Bishop.* London: Duckworth, 1995. A detailed biography of John Chrysostom. Includes numerous translated passages from his sermons and the historical context in which these sermons were preached.

Mayer, Wendy, and Pauline Allen. *John Chrysostom.* New York: Routledge, 2000. A useful introduction to the importance of John Chrysostom's preaching to later biblical exegesis.

Victoria Erhart

BARABBAS

Author: Pär Lagerkvist (1891-1974)
First published: 1950 (English translation, 1951)
Edition used: Barabbas, translated by Alan Blair. New York: Random House, 1951
Genre: Novel
Subgenre: Biblical fiction
Core issues: The divine; faith; Jesus Christ; love

Lagerkvist depicts the Christian message "Love one another" as a secular fulfillment of life, a message that is wrongly taken to extend to the love of God. Like his character Barabbas, Lagerkvist believes in, or acknowledges, the existence of God, but he does not have the belief in God that constitutes faith, which entails the expectation of reward or benefit. In this context, humans are seen to forfeit their existential reality by translating their love of each other into a love of God. Barabbas is shown to be most alive in his momentary acts of love for a harelip girl and his companion Sahak and least alive in his desire to share the faith that each has in Jesus Christ as God.

> Principal characters
>> *Barabbas*, the protagonist, the criminal whose life was spared when the populace chose Jesus for crucifixion
>> *Sahak*, Barabbas's closest friend, a fellow-prisoner in a copper mine, who becomes a Christian martyr
>> *Harelip girl*, Barabbas's former mistress, who becomes a Christian martyr
>> *Fat woman*, Barabbas's second mistress
>> *Big man with red hair and blue eyes* (unnamed, but identifiable as the apostle Peter)
>> *Man who was raised from the dead* (unnamed, but identifiable as Lazarus)
>> *Roman procurator* (governor), who takes on Barabbas and Sahak as field slaves

Overview

With *Barabbas*, Pär Lagerkvist initiated a series of novels that illustrate his personal doctrine of religious atheism, a profound nurture, through human love, of the divinity that lies within individuals.

The story has three geographical settings, each of which features a dramatic contrast of light and darkness and a graphically depicted crucifixion. In Jerusalem, Barabbas comes out of the darkness of prison into light to witness the crucifixion of Jesus; on the island of Cyprus, Barabbas and his fellow-prisoner Sahak come out of the darkness of a mine into sunlight, and Barabbas witnesses the crucifixion of Sahak;

in Rome, Barabbas ascends from the darkness of the Catacombs into the firelight of Rome and is himself crucified.

Emerging from the darkness of prison, Barabbas sees Jesus in a blinding light. His eyes become accustomed to the light, and although he discerns a strangeness in Jesus, he sees him as only a man standing in the light: He will not come to see Jesus as the God who is the Light. Lagerkvist's chiaroscuro plays on darkness as death and on light as both truth and falsity—the truth of love and the falsity, or delusion, of faith.

His life having been spared at the expense of the life of Jesus, Barabbas returns to his former habitat and to his coarse and rowdy companions, among them the fat woman, who, as his mistress, welcomes the heightened sensuality with which he tries to efface the memory of Jesus and to ignore the claims made by Jesus' followers, including the big red-haired, blue-eyed man, that Jesus is the Son of God. His former mistress, the harelip girl, likewise claims that Jesus is the Son of God and the Messiah.

Uncertain and disturbed by their claims, Barabbas seeks from the disciples information about the nature of their faith, and they reluctantly attempt to instruct him. They send him to a man whom Jesus resurrected. The man, clearly the Lazarus of the Gospel according to John, assures Barabbas that Jesus has brought him back to life and explains that the realm of death exists but is, in fact, nothing. Barabbas had not believed that Jesus rose from the dead but instead assumed that Jesus' followers had simply removed their master's body from the tomb; he does not, however, dispute the reality of Lazarus's resurrection. The reader is free to infer that Lazarus has been in a coma: The four days and four nights in the tomb are mentioned, but not the putrefaction (John 11:39). Barabbas accepts Lazarus's return to life as a fact but is unsettled by the account of the nothingness of death and by Lazarus's insistence that, for one who has been dead, everything else is also nothing. The episode may be interpreted as follows: Leaving a life not fully lived and being reborn into it is to exist in a void.

The harelip girl is stoned to death for her faith. Barabbas buries her and returns to a life of brigandage in the hills. It is revealed that he, when young, had killed his own father, whose name, Eliahu, contains the element *Eli-*, meaning "God." Barabbas, whose name means "son of the father," may be seen, figuratively, as a patricidal son of a father/God, reversing, in a kind of balance, the figure of Jesus as a son of a father/God who has abandoned him to death.

In his apathy and alienation from his former associates, Barabbas himself becomes a kind of Lazarus, for whom nothing is anything any more. They are relieved when he leaves them.

The narrative then jumps to the later life of Barabbas. On Cyprus, he is condemned to work in the perpetual darkness of a copper mine, chained to an Armenian Christian named Sahak, the name being a variation of Isaac and recalling another significant father-son relationship. Sahak's prayerful Christianity wins the interest of a replacement supervisor, who brings him, along with Barabbas, up to the light to work in a flour mill. Once again, Barabbas is spared death's darkness as the result of a connection with Jesus. The procurator, whose slaves they then become, orders Sahak to be crucified because he will not deny Jesus as his God. Barabbas readily does so, and is spared.

The procurator, taking Barabbas with him, retires to a luxurious estate in Rome. Barabbas gets to see the city during marketing errands. He explores the Catacombs, another realm of death, and emerges from them to the light of the city in flames. Lending his help to the arsonists, whom he mistakenly thinks to be Christians lighting the way for Jesus' return, he is apprehended and, along with many Christians, including Peter, crucified. His arson is a would-be act of faith, as opposed to his acts of love in burying the harelip girl and sorrowfully witnessing Sahak's execution. As the faith of the harelip girl and that of Sahak led to their deaths, so the momentary faith of Barabbas leads to his. As he dies, he commits his soul, ambiguously, either to Jesus or to the darkness.

The ambiguity of the commission owes to a complex of four words: *som om* (as if; as though), *själ* (soul), and *andan* (breath, spirit):

> When he sensed the approach of death, that of which he had
> always been so afraid, he spoke out into the darkness, as [*som*]
> though [*om*] he were addressing it:
> —To thee I surrender my soul [*själ*].
> And then he gave up the ghost [*andan*].

The idiom *andan* may mean "gave up the spirit" or simply "expired." Barabbas, thinking that he was surrendering his soul, merely died in the darkness. At the beginning of the novel, Jesus is shown to give up the ghost (*andan*) after crying out to the God who has forsaken him. If Lagerkvist emphasizes Jesus' dying without his God and Barabbas's dying without his Jesus the Light, then in his narrative, both Jesus and Barabbas may be seen to expire as humans and not as, respectively, divine savior and one who wishes to be divinely saved.

Christian Themes

Barabbas establishes the secularism and the limitations of two key passages from the New Testament: Luke 17:21, . . . [T]he kingdom of God is within you; and John 13:34, . . . [L]ove one another.

Lagerkvist posits the need for God as an untenable one that, in its sustained intensity, is its own satisfaction (wanting something so much that one can taste it). The satisfaction must be within the self, not in another world; it is not a satisfaction that nullifies the self. The harelip girl and Sahak die secure within a religious faith that entails abandonment of the self. Barabbas cannot elude his abhorrence of an abandonment of his self. In this he is right, but he is wrong to reject the doctrine of love. The holiness of mutual love is the love of humans for each other. The harelip girl and Sahak err in extending this love to God.

Barabbas and the pentalogy it initiates illustrate a position stated by Lagerkvist in *Den knutna näven* (1934; *The Clenched Fist*, 1982). In an apostrophe to Jesus, Lagerkvist says:

Your lesson of love is not your own, it is in the human heart. . . . My inner being has never exalted you to some mystical position, and it will never do so. But the love of man for which you became the voice I feel to be the foundation of my being.

In his next four novels, *Sibyllan* (1956; *The Sibyl*, 1958), *Ahasverus död* (1960; *The Death of Ahasuerus*, 1962), *Pilgrim på havet* (1962; *Pilgrim at Sea*, 1964), and *Det heliga landet* (1964; *The Holy Land*, 1966), Lagerkvist develops the theme of the existence and untenability of true love and the Holy Land, which are ultimately one and the same, and the unrelenting striving that constitutes the divinity within the human heart and the fulfillment of the human self.

Sources for Further Study

Barnett, Anthony, trans. *"Evening Land" by Pär Lagerkvist.* East Sussex, England: Allardyce, Barnett, 2001. Poetic complement (1953) to *Barabbas* and the pentalogy. Repeats themes of darkness.

Lagerkvist, Pär. "The Clenched Fist." In *Pär Lagerkvist: Five Early Works*, translated by Roy Arthur Swanson. Lewiston, N.Y.: Mellen, 1988. Lagerkvist states his positions on belief, faith, and Christianity as they will come to be presented in his pentalogy.

Polet, Jeff. "A Blackened Sea: Religion and Crisis in the Work of Pär Lagerkvist." *Renascence* 54, no. 1 (Fall, 2001): 47-65. Places *Barabbas*'s expression of "the ambiguous 'No' to faith" within the developmental context of the pentalogy and shows Lagerkvist to be suspicious of any claim to having solved the mystery of existence.

Scobbie, Irene. "Contrasting Characters in *Barabbas*." *Scandinavian Studies* 32, no. 4 (November, 1960): 212-229. Explicates the physical and psychological contrasts of Barabbas with the other characters in the novel.

Weathers, Winston. *Pär Lagerkvist: A Critical Essay.* Grand Rapids, Mich.: Wm. B. Eerdmans, 1960. Concise introduction to Lagerkvist's works; shows Lagerkvist anticipating "radical Christians . . . by envisioning a human Christ" and opposing institutional religion.

Roy Arthur Swanson

BASIC CHRISTIANITY

Author: John R. W. Stott (1921-   )
First published: 1958
Edition used: Basic Christianity. Downers Grove, Ill.: InterVarsity Press, 1972
Genre: Nonfiction
Subgenre: Spiritual treatise
Core issues: The cross; Incarnation; Jesus Christ; redemption; sin and sinners

Focused on Christ and his unique relationship in regard to God and humanity, Basic Christianity *holds the doctrine of Christ as the most important factor in Christian teaching and explores this doctrine with biblical exposition and carefully reasoned explanation. Stott moves from the reality of Jesus of Nazareth to the meaning of his life and death and to the claims that these realities place on his followers. He concludes with the basic evangelical message: that the claims deserve a response. He leaves it to the individual reader to assess what the response might be, while never letting slip his own assumptions of what those claims require.*

Overview

John Robert Walmsley Stott was born to Sir Arnold and Emily Stott on April 27, 1921. He was educated at Rugby School and Trinity College, Cambridge. At Cambridge, he earned a double first (an extraordinary honor) in French and theology. While a student at Rugby, he had undergone a conversion experience because of the preaching of Eric Nash and determined to devote his life to the Gospel. He was ordained in the Church of England in 1945 and went on to become curate at the Church of All Souls, Langham Place, London, from 1945 to 1950, then rector there from 1950 to 1975, and then rector emeritus beginning in 1975. He was appointed a chaplain to Queen Elizabeth II (1959-1991). One of his major involvements in Christian action was through the 1974 International Congress on World Evangelization held at Lausanne, Switzerland. Stott acted as chair of the drafting committee for the Lausanne Covenant, a significant milestone in the evangelical movement. As chair of the Lausanne Theology and Education Group from 1974 to 1981, he contributed greatly to the growing evangelical understanding of the relation between evangelism and social action. He has also been active in the Tear Fund, an evangelical British charity, for many years. He has written more than forty books, including *Basic Christianity* and *The Cross of Christ* (1986), and founded the London Institute for Contemporary Christianity in 1982. He never married. He was awarded the CBE in the New Year's honors list, 2006.

Basic Christianity is exactly what its title suggests, an exposition of the central themes of Protestant Christianity. "Christianity is a rescue religion," Stott declares midway through the book, but this is his theme in one form or another throughout. He begins with God's central activity in creation. The Creation and God's word given through the prophets and through Christ call for a response from humankind.

The proclamation of God's word through Christ begins with what Stott calls Jesus' "self-centered teaching." He contrasts this to other great religious teachers. They proclaimed truth to be apart from themselves; Jesus called himself "the way, the truth and the life" (John 14:6). His claims for himself were both direct and indirect, both spoken and dramatized. His feeding of the five thousand is an example of a dramatized claim.

Stott then turns to the issue of the character of Jesus as a person. He notes that Jesus believed himself to be in complete harmony with the will of God; that his followers, exemplified in the epistles of Peter and John, viewed him as without sin; and that even his enemies were reduced to petty legalisms to find fault with him. The perfection of his character is clear from both his self-observations as preserved in the Gospels and those made by his contemporaries.

From this, the examination turns to the Resurrection. Stott has four observations here: First, the body of Jesus was gone; second, the burial garments were undisturbed (Stott's emphasis on this is forensic); third, there are various accounts of his having been seen and spoken to after his death; and fourth, serious changes in personality and behavior could be observed in Jesus' followers. From these Stott concludes the veracity of the Resurrection.

Stott now turns back to the death of Christ and its meaning. He calls this section "Man's Need" and begins with a subheading, "The Fact and Nature of Sin." Sin, Stott notes, is an unpopular subject. People prefer not to hear about it, but it is ever present. There would be no need for door locks were it not for sin, but locks are a universal of human experience, and thus it can be seen that sin is universal as well. Stott spends some time on the Ten Commandments, examining the far reaches of their implications. Stott's interpretation of the commandment against theft is illustrative: "What the world calls 'scrounging' God calls stealing. To overwork and underpay one's staff is to break this commandment."

Sin has consequences. The death of Christ is interpreted as the intervening factor in the consequences of sin. To explain this, Stott must turn to the centrality of the cross, that is, the death of Jesus, for explanation. While he acknowledges the death of Christ as an example for his followers, Stott makes clear the central evangelical doctrine of substitutionary atonement, that Jesus Christ died as an offering for sin and not for the sins of a few, but for the sins of the whole world. Stott admits that this is a stumbling block in some ways for Western civilization, but he sees it as the sole means of human salvation.

"What must we do, then?" Stott asks. His answer is frank. "We must commit ourselves, hearts and mind, soul and will, home and life, personally and unreservedly to Jesus Christ." Intellectual consent is not enough: "We have to translate our beliefs into deeds."

Stott's vision of Christian belief is one of active self-analysis and active concern—both inner-directed and other-directed. His understanding of Christian belief is focused and substantial, with the life, death, and resurrection of Jesus of Nazareth as incontrovertible claims that humanity must either accept or deny. To accept is to acknowledge God's call to humanity; to refuse is to refuse humanity itself. The choice is essential, and Stott is not one to let his reader off the hook.

Christian Themes

Basic Christianity is precisely what it promises: an overview of the premises of basic Protestant Christianity. It begins with the person of Jesus Christ and his claims and those of his followers. Having established what he feels is certitude regarding the claims of Christ, Stott turns to the question of sin and its profound role in human life. Evangelical theology does not skirt the problem of human wrongdoing, and Stott places sin firmly at the center of the work of Jesus Christ and also at the center of the transformation required of his followers. Because the human condition precludes any possibility of making up for sin on one's own account, the question of an acceptable offering for sin arises. This leads to the doctrine of substitutionary atonement, the view that the death of Jesus Christ on the cross has fulfilled for all humanity the sacrifice necessary for sin. When the gravity of this self-sacrifice is understood, it will create in the believer a constant sense of gratitude and wonder. From this sense of gratitude and wonder should come a transformation of life, marked by humility, self-sacrifice, and joy. The life of the Church follows on this, as the Church is not only the acceptable sphere for faithful interaction, but also the outward and visible sign of God's ongoing activity in the world.

Sources for Further Study

Dudley-Smith, Timothy. *John Stott: The Making of a Leader—A Biography, The Early Years*. Downers Grove, Ill.: InterVarsity Press, 1999. The authorized biography of John Stott's early years.

_____. *John Stott: A Biography of the Later Years*. Downers Grove, Ill.: InterVarsity Press, 2001. The authorized biography of John Stott's later years.

Stott, John R. W. *The Cross of Christ*. Downers Grove, Ill.: InterVarsity Press, 1986. A thoughtful, well-rounded approach to the central Christian dilemma of the death of Jesus Christ.

Stott, John R. W., and David L. Edwards. *Evangelical Essentials: A Liberal-Evangelical Dialogue*. Downers Grove, Ill.: InterVarsity Press, 1988. An informed, intelligent conversation between Stott and a "liberal" colleague on the essentials of the Christian faith: the authority of Scripture, the cross of Christ, miracles, and evangelism.

Bonnie L. A. Shullenberger

THE BEASTS OF BETHLEHEM

Author: X. J. Kennedy (Joseph Charles Kennedy; 1929-   )
First published: New York: M. K. McElderry Books, 1992, illustrated by Michael
    McCurdy
Genre: Poetry
Subgenres: Lyric poetry; narrative poetry
Core issues: Christmas; humility; innocence; Jesus Christ; simplicity

The voices in the poems in The Beasts of Bethlehem *are the those of the animals—predator and prey, domestic and wild—who were in the stable on the night of Jesus' birth. The Gospels mention the presence of a cow, an ox, a donkey, and camels among other beasts, but Kennedy adds others, including a snail, hawk, goat, and worm. Through the varied perspectives that the animals bring to the event, the poet reflects individual Christians' varied knowledge of God.*

Overview

The American poet Joseph C. Kennedy adopted the pseudonym X. J. Kennedy to separate himself from from the family of Kennedys active in politics in his native Massachusetts. He has written nearly three dozen books of poetry for adults and children, published essays and novels, and compiled anthologies of verse for children as well as college literature textbooks.

The Beasts of Bethlehem comprises nineteen poems spoken by mammals, birds, and insects that Kennedy places in the stable on the night of Jesus' birth. In keeping with the folktale that holds that the animals could speak on the night Christ was born, each creature voices its individual reaction to the birth. This enables children to engage in the story of the Nativity through the eyes and voices of the creatures who were there. Some of the creatures are benign or even prey, and others are predators who stop their killing for just this night. All are given the opportunity to ponder the mystery of Jesus' birth and to apply it in some way to their own lives, thus mirroring the experience of Christians.

Kennedy maintains that poetry for children should be intellectually challenging, use language in vivid and memorable ways, and present a means through which children can grasp the relationship of form to meaning. He favors iambic meter, rhyme, and stanzaic variety: twelve poems are rhymed couplets, one is rhyming quatrains, one is unrhymed, and the remainder are cinquains (five lines) or sestets (six lines) with no consistent rhyming patterns. The shortness of the verses with their rhyme and meter or wordplay permit easy memorization, another attribute Kennedy asserts should be present in poetry for younger readers.

Kennedy, who feels that teachers and poets often downplay children's ability to understand complexities, uses irony, puns, and paradox to emphasize the magnitude of God becoming a person. For example, in "The Bat," the bat speculates that its part in the stable is to eat the mosquitoes that might bite the infant Jesus. In "The Mosquito," the insect counters with the epigram: "Who but a blind bat swaddled in his wings/ Could dream that I might bite the King of Kings?" Here Kennedy plays off the idiom "blind as a bat" to challenge the bat's sense that the mosquito is only out to harm and has no judgment or sense of right and wrong.

The first speaker in the book is the cow, which, like the donkey who is the last to speak, is said to have warmed the baby with his breath. Other beasts not usually considered in the Nativity story but given voice here are the snail, the hawk, the ant, the goat, the worm, and the beetle. These other animals help complete the portrait that all creation was present at the moment of Jesus' birth and also encourage the reader to think beyond the limits of the Gospel narratives when it comes to the inhabitants of the stable.

A central theme in each beast's poem is the paradox that the birth of Christ presents. The cow, for instance, contemplates how small the baby is compared with the size of his mission on Earth. The owl, accustomed to praise for its proverbial wisdom, wonders why this child is the one that people and animals will revere. The horse, though given the chance to speak, is dumbstruck with awe. The camel's poem, divided into a sestet and a quatrain, tells how he and his rider, Gaspar, one of the three kings, followed the star to the stable, and the camel ponders how this infant will bring an end to Christian longing. The camel's sentiments reappear in the words of the ant and the hummingbird. The sheep, which warms people with its wool, humbly asks, "Who cares/ What sheep think of the Lamb of God?" Like the disciples, the sheep promises to watch over the baby faithfully and says that it will be happy knowing that Jesus will know of its love for him, even if no one else does. Similarly, the snail and the hen offer their gifts of comfort, despite the opinions of people about their relative worth.

With the mouse, Kennedy presents a different theme about the things that people reject and God embraces. The mouse wonders why ordinary people flee from things that do not disturb Mary and the baby. The mouse suggests that Jesus will bring peace to all nations on earth. Similarly, the bat, the cat, and the hawk all promise not to prey on other animals on this night, suggesting that nature can be altered by the application of will. The goat and the ox, like the cow before them, pledge their faith to the newborn baby, while the worm provides the image of death in an otherwise celebratory atmosphere. The final poems of the beetle and the donkey contrast the low with the high: The beetle realizes that God loves it even if people do not, and the donkey, who brought Mary to the stable, experiences a renewal and rejuvenation of spirit in the presence of the divine. It is clear to the reader that the beasts are on a quest to find their place in the presence of God and to interpret the experience of Christ's coming to renew Earth.

The poems display coherence internally in theme and externally in form. Each theme is addressed by an animal, a bird, or an insect, and Kennedy uses witty allusions, wordplay, and irony to move the narrative forward. For instance, the goat builds his poem on clichés that make him a scapegoat and an old goat before asking readers to put themselves before the Christ Child to see who is the innocent one, the person who calls people names or the goat whose name is taken in vain.

Christian Themes

The coming of Christ began a cycle of life, death, and rebirth. The poems in *The Beasts of Bethlehem* address how his coming presented a sense of wonder and how his presence among people created a promise, or a fulfillment, of life. Each beast teaches the reader how to approach the mystery of Jesus as it meditates on the importance of Jesus as the one who brings peace, love, innocence, and wisdom to people. The beasts' faith is ideal and pure. Though an undercurrent of strife is present, it does not limit their joy at the chance to see themselves in a new light.

Kennedy's approach to the Nativity focuses on individual faith, not on organized religion. By having each creature relate to Christ's birth, he emphasizes how rational creatures can know God, though some believe blindly and others struggle to understand what they have seen. The animals' lives gain meaning in the presence of Jesus, and they come to appreciate themselves more as a result of being in his presence.

Sources for Further Study

Collins, Michael J. "The Poetry of X. J. Kennedy." *World Literature Today* 61, no. 1 (Winter, 1987): 55-58. Examines his use of wordplay and attention to couplet form in an analysis of selected poems.

Kennedy, X. J. "'Go and Get Your Candle Lit!': An Approach to Poetry." *The Hornbook Magazine* (July, 1981): 273-279. Presents Kennedy's ideas on how to write for children and how to teach them to analyze poetry effectively. Includes his definition of poetry as "passionate thought persuaded into form."

_____. "Strict and Loose Nonsense: Two Worlds of Children's Verse." *School Library Journal* (March, 1991): 108-112. Discusses two types of nonsense writing for children with a concentration on the contributions of Edwin Lear to the development of nonsense verse.

Morris, Bernard E. *Taking Measure: The Poetry and Prose of X. J. Kennedy.* Selinsgrove, Pa.: Susquehanna University Press, 2003. A full-length study of Kennedy's work that includes chapters on Christianity and writing children's verse.

Prelutsky, Jack. "Talking with X. J. Kennedy." *Instructor* 102, no. 2 (September, 1992): 26. An interview in which Kennedy discusses his writing process, his favorite children's books, and the importance of poetry to various readers.

Beverly Schneller

BELIEF OR NONBELIEF?
A Confrontation

Authors: Umberto Eco (1932-   ) and Carlo Maria Martini (1927-   )
First published: In cosa crede chi non crede? 1997 (English translation, 2000)
Edition used: Belief or Nonbelief? A Confrontation, translated by Minna Procter, with
    an introduction by Harvey Cox. New York: Arcade, 2000
Genre: Nonfiction
Subgenres: Critical analysis; letters
Core issues: Catholics and Catholicism; doubt; ethics; faith; morality; reason; women

*In this collection of letters, nonbeliever Eco, a noted novelist and professor of semi-
otics, and believer Martini, former archbishop of Milan, discuss questions of significance concerning morality, worldview, and human life. This correspondence, suggested and published by the Italian newspaper* La Correra de la Sera, *seeks to find
common ground for dialogue between Christians and secularists on topics fundamental to an understanding of the world and humanity.*

Overview

This collection consists of eight letters—four from Umberto Eco, four from Carlo
Maria Martini—in which they deal with the following topics: the contemporary secular understanding of the Apocalypse, the question of when human life begins, the role
of women in the Catholic Church, and the possibility of ethics without God.

Eco begins with "Secular Obsession with the New Apocalypse," in which he probes
the various cultural visions of the end of the world (imagined as occurring through such
means as ecological disasters and diseases) and the sense of history they entail (one of
progress, end, and meaning). Eco raises the question of whether a notion of hope exists
that could be held in common by both believers and nonbelievers: If we have a sense of
history through the idea of its end, we may hope for progress in the future by learning
from past events and trying to better society. Martini responds with "Hope Puts an End
to 'The End,'" explaining how Christian hope looks beyond this life to the next and how
it is precisely this relation to the divine that provides value for human life on earth. Martini does not so much reject Eco's hope for social progress as point out that the Christian
Apocalypse is not merely destructive but also productive: The end is eternal life.

The next topic begins with Eco's "When Does Human Life Begin?" He raises the
bioethical question of when human life begins and asks whether the state should have
any say in these mysterious matters. (Eco recognizes the "miraculous" nature of human life and is personally opposed to abortion, though he thinks it improper to limit it
through legislation.) Eco argues that since many of Aristotle's ideas have been rejected, the precise beginning of human life has become a mystery, a threshold with a
perhaps unknowable location, and he asks how contemporary theologians understand
the question. Martini's answer, "Human Life Is Part of God's Life," gives a good

overview of the Catholic position on the matter, noting that a sense of "genetic determination" (teleology—that every living thing has a natural end implicit in its design, an aspect of Aristotle's thought that many Catholic thinkers are trying to preserve) leads Catholic theologians to argue that human life begins at conception and thus should be legally guarded. Furthermore, Martini says each human life is called by God to be with him forever in heaven, granting each human being, from conception to death, an inestimable kind of dignity that is lacking in merely secular understandings of human life.

The third topic for debate—the role of women in the Catholic Church—is heavily prefaced by Eco in "Men and Women—According to the Church," in which he explains that he does not seek to criticize the Catholic Church's position on ordaining women (since he himself is not Catholic and does not think it fit to criticize the internal workings of an institution of which he has chosen not to be a part), but rather simply to understand the Church's rationale. His analysis of previous arguments against female ordination—including that women are naturally inferior to men—reveal the internal problems that the Church has and its inadequacy in explaining its position. Martini responds in a fascinating manner in "The Church Does Not Fulfill Expectations, It Celebrates Mysteries." He bases the Church's position on the fact that Christianity is a historical religion: The Catholic and Orthodox Churches do not ordain women because they believe that Jesus Christ, the Son of God, instituted the priesthood through his apostles. All twelve apostles were men, and all of their orthodox successors have been men; the reason for this practice is a mystery that theologians must continue to seek to understand.

Martini begins the final exchange with "Where Does the Layman Find Illumination?" He asks a genuine question: Where do secularists find ground for their ethics without the divine? If ethics have no basis in transcendental, universal principles, what saves a conscientious secularist like Eco from complete relativism? Eco's reply, "Ethics Are Born in the Presence of the Other," is an eloquent and compelling explanation of secular ethics. Eco argues that universal principles on which to base ethics do exist, but these principles can be found solely in the physical realm: We are embodied creatures that have certain needs, experience pleasures and pains, and live in communities. Thus, Eco's basis for an ethics in which God is unnecessary is a recognition that others like us exist in this world. Since humans are communal creatures, other individuals are, in a way, a part of us. Helping others helps ourselves, while hurting others hurts ourselves. This realization of otherness provides Eco with a universal principle that prevents his pluralism from becoming relativism.

Christian Themes

While some of the issues raised in this exchange are particular to Catholic and Orthodox Christianity (specifically, the rationale behind an all-male priesthood), most of the themes in this collection are of interest to Christians of all denominations. Perhaps the most central Christian theme raised by this debate is that of faith: how faith in God must necessarily change one's worldview in a radical way. In this dialogue between a philosopher and a theologian, it becomes clear time and again that Eco and Martini are profoundly similar men (their dialogue is laudably cordial), with the difference that Martini has faith in Christian revelation and Eco does not. One gets the sense that the fulcrum on which each of their arguments turns is whether a God exists and whether he sent his Son to redeem the world. If he does and did, Martini's point is correct; if he does and did not (or if we simply cannot know), Eco's viewpoint is. This is, admittedly, an overly neat dichotomy (some of their cultural observations hold regardless of the nature of metaphysical reality), but it may provide a way of understanding the dynamics of the dialogue. The reality of faith as a gift from God comes up quite plainly in Eco's last letter: One gets the sense that he in some way regrets having lost his faith as a young man and appreciates belief in something more than secular philosophy (though that is all he can hold on to in good conscience at this point).

More vitally, this exchange provides a praiseworthy model of Christian witness in the contemporary world. In the twenty-first century, Christians and non-Christians, believers and nonbelievers, find themselves, by necessity, living and dealing with one another. If debates between the two groups were more like this dialogue—seeking common ground and mutual understanding, clarifying the positions of the other and the reasons for these positions—believers and nonbelievers might find a more harmonious existence. This dialogue seems to suggest that Ecumenism need not be limited to relations between and among Christian churches; it should be extended to a discussion that includes all of humanity and probes the value and meaning of human life and how the presence of the Gospel challenges one's perspective of the world.

Sources for Further Study

Eco, Umberto. *Foucault's Pendulum*. Translated by William Weaver. London: Secker & Warburg, 1989. One of Eco's best novels, this tale of mystery and the occult works out many of the epistemological musings found in Eco's letters.

_____. *A Theory of Semiotics*. Bloomington: Indiana University Press, 1975. Eco's scholarly masterpiece on symbols and communication ranges over a wide variety of signs, how they are produced, and how they are understood culturally.

Gane, Mike, and Nicholas Gane, eds. *Umberto Eco*. Sage Masters of Modern Social Thought series. London: Sage, 2005. A collection of essays that examines Eco's works and their impact on society, culture, and philosophy.

Martini, Carlo Maria. *Communicating Christ to the World*. Translated by Thomas M. Lucas. Kansas City, Mo.: Sheed and Ward, 1993. These pastoral letters by Cardinal Martini to the parishioners of his diocese give perspective on Martini's views of communication in a variety of media.

_____. *The Joy of the Gospel: Meditations for Young People*. Translated by James McGrath. Collegeville, Minn.: The Liturgical Press, 1994. Martini introduces *lectio divina* (meditative readings of scripture) to a young lay audience, revealing some of Martini's scholarship and popular outreach.

Sean Gordon Lewis

BEN-HUR
A Tale of the Christ

Author: Lew Wallace (1827-1905)
First published: New York: Harper, 1880
Genre: Novel
Subgenres: Adventure; biblical fiction; historical fiction (first century)
Core issues: Awakening; the cross; Jesus Christ; redemption; regeneration; submission

Ben-Hur *may be the most widely known work by any American author. It sold more than two million copies by 1944 and was made into a stage production and two epic movies. Wallace's historical romance is sometimes clumsy, melodramatic, and turgid, but at its best, the tale is swift-moving and gripping. The author's reverent, if sentimental, depiction of Christ, his nature and his sufferings, helped legitimate the novel form in the eyes of an occasionally philistine reading public.*

> *Principal characters*
> *Judah Ben-Hur*, the protagonist, who forsakes revenge and revolt
> against Rome when he learns the true nature of Jesus Christ
> *Ben-Hur's mother* and
> *Tirzah*, Ben-Hur's sister, who are cured of leprosy by Christ
> *Messala*, a Roman patrician, enemy of Ben-Hur
> *Jesus Christ*, the Messiah

Overview

Lew Wallace's novel sets the story of Judah Ben-Hur, a wealthy Jewish prince unjustly condemned to be a galley slave and robbed of his inheritance, against the birth, ministry, and crucifixion of Christ. Embittered by the betrayal of his Roman friend Messala and enraged by what he perceives as the arrogance of Rome, Ben-Hur slowly comes to the realization that the kingdom offered by the miracle worker and Messiah Jesus is spiritual, not political.

The novel begins with a meeting in the desert of the Three Wise Men. Gaspar, the Greek, has learned from study and his country's philosophers that each human being has an immortal soul and there exists one God. Melchior, the "Hindoo," is moved by compassionate love for the suffering. Balthasar, the Egyptian, has performed good works. The three's spiritual journeys lead them to Bethlehem and the cave in which Jesus is born.

The story moves forward twenty-one years. Ben-Hur runs into his childhood friend Messala after the latter has spent five years in a Rome that is beginning to lose reverence for the gods and religious absolutes. Hurt and angered by Messala's pragmatic cynicism, Ben-Hur returns to the family mansion, where his mother soothes him by speaking of Jewish history and achievements. However, the loving family life of the Hurs—mother, son, sister Tirzah, and Amrah the servant—is shattered when Ben-Hur, watching the Roman governor of Judea ride by, accidentally dislodges a roof tile that strikes the administrator and knocks him from his horse. Messala identifies Ben-Hur as the would-be assassin. Condemned to the galleys, he is taken to the coast by a detachment of Roman soldiers. In a little village called Nazareth, the exhausted prisoner is given water by the local carpenter's son, whose loving and holy face Ben-Hur will never forget.

He is made an oarsman in the ship of Quintus Arrius, a Roman given the task of extirpating pirates from the eastern Mediterranean. Quintus notices the youth and comeliness of Ben-Hur and resolves to know more about him. He orders that the young Jew not be chained to his bench before the engagement with the pirates, thus enabling Ben-Hur to save the Roman's life when the ship is struck. In gratitude, Quintus adopts Ben-Hur and makes him his heir.

Rich and free, Ben-Hur visits the decadent city of Antioch, where he meets Simonides, a former agent of his father who has become immensely wealthy through trade, using money of the Hurs that the Romans had not been able to find and confiscate. He also sees Messala, who is to compete in a chariot race, the highlight of the Antioch games. Ben-Hur is accepted by Sheik Ilderim, a nomadic desert leader and the possessor of splendid thoroughbreds, as his charioteer. Ben-Hur decides to humble Messala by publicly defeating him and to bankrupt the Roman by causing him to bet his entire fortune on the race. In the race, Messala wrecks his chariot. He survives but is penniless and has a broken back. Ben-Hur has now obtained the for revenge he has longed for, but he has still not been able to learn the fate of his mother and sister, dragged away after the roof tile struck the Roman governor.

The scene shifts to Jerusalem. Pontius Pilate has recently become procurator and ordered an inspection of all prisons and their inmates. A secret cell in the Tower of Antonia is found to hold two hideously leprous women, a mother and her daughter, who are released. Ben-Hur's mother and Tirzah visit their former house and see their recently returned son and brother asleep on its step. Afraid of infecting him, they wretchedly move on. Amrah, their former servant, learns of their survival and state, and brings them food and water every day.

Ben-Hur's adventures have taken place against the background of a defeated people, fiercely resentful of foreign control and dreaming of a liberating Messiah. Simonides has read to him the Old Testament prophecies of a king who will restore the ancient glories, a Messiah who will be a king of this world. However, the now aged Balthasar sees the Messiah's power as spiritual. Ben-Hur first inclines to the former interpretation ands secretly trains Galilean legions to fight for the king of the Jews when he so declares himself. However, at Bethabara a gaunt man dressed in camel's hair acknowledges a delicately handsome young man as the Lamb of God. Ben-Hur recognizes the face of the carpenter's son who had earlier given him water and decides to follow and observe him. He is thus able to narrate to Simonides and Balthasar the miracles he witnesses, including the curing of lepers. Hearing this, the devoted

Amrah leads her former mistress and Tirzah to Jesus as he triumphantly enters Jerusalem. Seeing the mother's faith, he makes them clean.

Still hoping for a military rebellion, Ben-Hur dogs the Nazarene's footsteps. He is present at the betrayal in Gethsemane, then at the Crucifixion. The words Jesus speaks to the repentant thief—"Verily I say unto thee, To-Day shalt thou be with me in Paradise!"—finally illuminate to him Christ's true nature. Ben-Hur takes his fortune to Rome and uses it to build the catacombs that will shelter Christians during the persecutions. He is thus instrumental in Christianity's survival and eventual triumph.

Christian Themes

The subtitle of the novel, *A Tale of the Christ*, is misleading in that Christ, far from providing the novel's focus, appears only rarely and speaks only toward the end. However, it is against the backdrop of Christ's divine sorrow at human sin and pain that the all-too-human Ben-Hur comes to realize that the world needs a redeeming savior of souls rather than a king of the Jews who will bring about military dominion.

Ben-Hur has been given good reason to hate the Romans and to long for revenge. He does gain revenge against the Roman Messala. However, he continues to wish for the defeat and humiliation of the world power that occupies his country. Like Simonides, who wishes to bankroll Jesus as a military commander, Ben-Hur also thinks and desires in human, not divine, terms, dreaming of the Messiah as a military leader. Even after Christ's arrest in Gethsemane, he trails the bound man, asking if he will accept help if Ben-Hur brings it. He stumbles along until he reaches an awakening to Christ's true nature and God's plan, and learns to submit to that plan and forsake revenge. In the end, only the cross can bring him to that awakening.

Christ's regenerating power is most vividly made concrete in the curing of Ben-Hur's mother and sister, who feel a spiritual as well as physical purification after their cleansing.

It takes a brave writer to attempt to portray Christ in a novel. The otherworldly nature of Christ's kingdom is reflected in a depiction of the Savior that is conventional and unsatisfying and has the concept of "gentle Jesus, meek and mild" as its apparent source. His Christ has long-lashed blue eyes; words like "pallor," "gentleness," "delicacy," "tenderness," and "softness" are applied to him. Little attempt is made to capture the slow agony of the Crucifixion.

Sources for Further Study

Allmendinger, Blake. "Toga! Toga!" In *Over the Edge: Remapping the American West*, edited by Valerie J. Matsumoto and Blake Allmendinger. Berkeley: University of California Press, with UCLA Center for Seventeenth- and Eighteenth-Century Studies and the William Andrews Clark Memorial Library, 1999. Wallace's depiction of the decline of barbaric Rome and the birth of Christianity helps justify United States expansion in the West. *Ben-Hur* also resembles the formulaic Western.

Eddings, Dennis W. "Lew Wallace." In *Nineteenth-Century American Fiction Writers*, edited by Kent P. Ljungquist. Vol. 202 in *Dictionary of Literary Biography*. Detroit, Mich.: Gale, 1999. Brief biography and criticism of Wallace's works, especially *Ben-Hur*. Contains lists of Wallace's books and selected periodical publications as well of lists of biographies and further references.

Gutjahr, Paul. "'To the Heart of the Solid Puritans': Historicizing the Popularity of *Ben-Hur*." *Mosaic: A Journal for the Comparative Study of Literature* 26 (1993): 53-67. New historicist attempt to explain the contemporary reception of *Ben-Hur* as the Protestant response to scientific challenges to the literal truth of Bible.

McKee, Irving. *"Ben-Hur" Wallace: The Life of General Lew Wallace*. Berkeley: University of California Press, 1947. Biography with an account of the writing of *Ben-Hur*. Useful listing of itineraries (1899-1920) of the play based on the novel; brief account of first movie (1925).

Morsberger, Robert E., and Katherine M. Morsberger. *Lew Wallace: Militant Romantic*. New York: McGraw-Hill, 1980. Biography with a chapter recounting the writing of *Ben-Hur*, its critical and popular reception, its sales, the reasons for its success, and a three-page synopsis of the plot.

Theisen, Lee Scott. "'My God, Did I Set All of This in Motion?' General Lew Wallace and *Ben-Hur*." *Journal of Popular Culture* 18 (1984): 33-41. Account of the writing of *Ben-Hur*, its sales, Wallace's activities on the lecture circuit, the stage version, the first and second movie versions (1925 and 1959), and reasons for the novel's success.

M. D. Allen

BEOWULF

Author: Unknown

First transcribed: c. 1000

Edition used: Beowulf: A Verse Translation—Authoritative Text, Contexts, Criticism,
  edited by Daniel Donoghue, translated by Seamus Heaney. New York: Norton,
  2002

Genre: Poetry

Subgenres: Epic; narrative poetry

Core issues: Death; friendship; good vs. evil; responsibility; stoicism; virtue

*The young warrior Beowulf, a nobleman from the land of the Geats, travels to the
kingdom of the Danes, where he saves the people of King Hrothgar by slaying the
monster Grendel and his mother. In his later years, after becoming king in his homeland, Beowulf loses his life in a fight with a dragon who is guarding a hoard of treasure and terrorizing the Geats.*

> *Principal characters*
> *Beowulf*, a warrior from the land of the Geats
> *Hrothgar*, king of the Danes
> *Unferth*, a retainer in Hrothgar's court
> *Wiglaf*, a Geat in service to Beowulf

Overview

Commonly thought of as an English epic poem, *Beowulf* actually celebrates the
deeds of a Norse hero. In fact, all the characters in the poem are from the region of
northern Europe from which the Danes, Swedes, and other Norse tribes originated.
This should not be surprising, however, because Norse warriors invaded the British
Isles in the early sixth century and remained there for nearly three hundred years. That
Beowulf is written in a language now called Old English may be a testament to the
popularity of the story; while it takes place between 600 and 800 C.E., the one surviving version of the poem was transcribed centuries later, probably by a Christian
monk. The manuscript was preserved in the collection of an English man until the
seventeenth century, when it was donated to the British Museum. Despite its damaged
condition, the manuscript has been examined repeatedly by scholars interested in the
historical background and literary qualities of this unique poem.

Beowulf opens with a brief account of some of the great heroes of Norse history and
legend, setting the stage for a narrative that establishes Beowulf's place among these
men of valor. The principal story is divided into three segments, with brief interludes
linking them. In the first major episode, the young Beowulf, a noble from Geatland
(southern Sweden), leads a party of his countrymen to Denmark. His intent is to rescue the Danish king Hrothgar and his household from a fierce monster, Grendel. This

demon has been terrorizing the population in a series of nightly visits to Heorot, Hrothgar's palace, dismembering and devouring warriors in the king's service.

Before Beowulf can fight Grendel, however, he must establish his credentials among the Danes. His fitness for the confrontation is challenged by Unferth, one of Hrothgar's retainers. Beowulf defends himself against this verbal attack, explaining how his past behavior reflects both personal bravery and concern for his fellow warriors. Having successfully answered Unferth's challenge, Beowulf settles down for the night and lies in wait for Grendel. The two engage in a horrific struggle, during which Beowulf wrenches Grendel's arm from its socket. Mortally wounded, the monster slinks back to its home in the nearby mere.

Hrothgar celebrates Beowulf's victory, bestowing on him gifts of gold and armor. The feeling of joy is short-lived, however; that night, Grendel's mother emerges from her lair in the swamp to avenge her son's murder. Her vicious attack on one of Hrothgar's favorite subjects drives Beowulf on a second quest, to slay the she-devil. He descends into the underwater den where he finds Grendel's mother and the body of her slain son. Although she proves an even stronger foe than her son, Beowulf manages to defeat and slay her, and he brings back Grendel's head to show that he has once again been victorious.

At the evening victory celebration, Hrothgar offers Beowulf some advice regarding the necessity to restrain his pride and to recognize his responsibility to act not simply for personal gain. Acknowledging the wisdom of Hrothgar's advice, Beowulf departs for his homeland, where he is welcomed by his uncle Hygelac, the king of the Geats. Once home, he reports his adventures to his uncle, who honors him still more for his selfless acts of bravery. Once again, stories of other heroes and villains from Norse history and legend are inserted into the narrative to demonstrate how much Beowulf deserves the praises given him.

For years, Beowulf continues to support Hygelac and his successors, until a series of events leads to his installation as ruler of the Geats. Late in his life, Beowulf learns that his country is being terrorized by a dragon that is guarding a treasure horde. He assembles a raiding party to assault the dragon at his lair. Unfortunately, all but one of his warriors deserts him at the battle; only the faithful Wiglaf remains to help slay the dragon. The fight is costly for Beowulf; the dragon inflicts a deadly wound, and the renowned chieftain knows he will not survive. Before he dies, he gives instructions to Wiglaf regarding the disposition of his possessions and the organization of his funeral. Beowulf's body is carried to a peak overlooking the sea and is burned on a magnificent pyre on which numerous precious objects have been placed.

Christian Themes

Since the early nineteenth century, critics have debated the extent to which Christianity plays an integral role in the poem. Some have argued that the original poem simply celebrated the virtues of the society that existed in northern Europe before missionaries brought Christianity to the region. These critics contend that overt references to a Christian God were added by later transcribers, who adapted the original tale by giving it a Christian coloring. Others, among them the distinguished medieval scholar and fantasy novelist J. R. R. Tolkien, have argued that the Christian elements have been woven skillfully into the text; they claim that the poem in its present form celebrates Christian virtues as they were understood by a medieval audience.

The most obvious Christian reference is the designation of the monster Grendel and his mother as descendants of Cain, the son of Adam who kills his brother Abel. Less direct references include frequent acknowledgement by characters in the poem that their lives are in the hands of God, who determines their destiny and who will reward or punish them for their deeds.

Additionally, *Beowulf* celebrates those who exhibit friendship, self-sacrifice, concern for their community, and generosity, virtues shared by Germanic peoples and by the Christians who converted them. The idea of gift giving, a holdover from pre-Christian tradition, figures prominently in the poem, as evidenced by Hrothgar's sharing of valuable treasures with Beowulf to honor his bravery and Beowulf's sharing of the gifts he receives from the Danish king with his own sovereign, Hygelac. The hero of the poem is venerated not simply for his bravery, but also for his concern for those whose welfare has been entrusted to him. In the Danish kingdom Beowulf puts his own life at risk to relieve Hrothgar's people from the scourge of the monster that has been threatening their safety. Similarly, when he has become king of the Geats, he takes it on himself to lead a band of warriors in combat against the dragon to retrieve the treasure that will benefit his people once it is rescued from the serpent's clutches.

In several ways the poem presents a value system consonant with Christian principles that would have resonated with a medieval audience that saw personal bravery and combat in service to kingdom and church as noble. The monsters in the poem are clearly embodiments of evil forces that must be overcome for society to be safe and prosperous; the hero who takes on the quest of freeing the land from such monsters fights as the representative of good. Beowulf does not believe he can conquer these forces on his own; rather, he recognizes that he will succeed only as long as God allows him to do so. He also knows that he will eventually die, and he accepts that knowledge stoically. Throughout the narrative, he measures his success by his ability to make life better for those he serves. The idea of fatalism that permeated northern European religions is transformed into a version of divine providence that stresses God's control over human events. All people, even heroes, have to face the inevitable fact that death awaits them at the time God has chosen to call them.

While it would be unwise to make specific links between Beowulf and Christ, there is one parallel that can be seen in the poem; both are aware of their mission to take responsibility for and act with love toward their fellow men and women. This is the great lesson of Beowulf's life, and it is brought home to readers by the contrasts the poet sets up between Beowulf's actions and those of many of the other leaders described in the poem. At three points in the narrative, the stories of Norse rulers and fighting men are highlighted: first in the opening prologue; again by the scop, or poet, at the banquet given by Hrothgar to honor Beowulf after he has slain Grendel; and once more in the section that follows Beowulf's return to his homeland. In all three instances, one reads of leaders who take vengeance on their neighbors and even on their own kinsmen, perpetuating blood feuds that lead to social unrest. By contrast, Beowulf is presented always as a peacemaker—albeit of a distinctly medieval character. He fights against the monsters not to gain personal favor but to first to rid Hrothgar's kingdom of the monsters menacing it, and then to save his own people from the threat of the dragon. The audiences that would have listened to the poem in the eleventh century would have accepted the notion that violent behavior was compatible with Christian principles. In fact, most devout Christians believed in the idea that "might makes right"—at least in the sense that a just God would not allow those fighting in his service to fail.

Seen in this light, Beowulf's actions speak of selfless sacrifice; if he is violent, it is because, like people of his age, the times required violent action to secure peace and bring about prosperity. His own words throughout the narrative and the advice he receives from Hrothgar before departing the land of the Danes stress the importance of avoiding the sin of pride and recognizing that victory comes not from personal prowess but from the hand of God. In a sense—though it is important to emphasize that the parallels are not exact—Beowulf is like Christ, working on earth to further the eternal Father's plan for humankind. Like the knights of Arthurian legend, whose stories would replace the Norse tales as favorite readings among English audiences within a century after the surviving version of *Beowulf* was transcribed, Beowulf is the model Christian hero.

Sources for Further Study

Bjork, Robert E., and John D. Niles, eds. *A "Beowulf" Handbook.* Lincoln: University of Nebraska Press, 1997. Includes an essay explaining how overtly Christian and Germanic pre-Christian elements are blended in the portrait of the hero and throughout the narrative.

Bloom, Harold, ed. *Modern Critical Interpretations: "Beowulf."* New York: Chelsea House, 1987. Collection containing important essays by J. R. R. Tolkien and Fred C. Robinson establishing the importance of Christianity in shaping the themes of the poem.

Davis, Craig R. *"Beowulf" and the Demise of Germanic Legend in England.* New York: Garland, 1996. Discusses ways that Christian elements are blended with Germanic religious traditions.

Pulvel, Martin. *Cause and Effect in "Beowulf."* Lanham, Md.: University Press of America, 2005. Interweaves commentary about the Christian elements of the poem throughout a discussion of the forces that motivate characters in the narrative.

Staver, Ruth Johnston. *A Companion to "Beowulf."* Westport, Conn.: Greenwood Press, 2005. Series of essays providing background on the poem, including one focusing on religious elements.

Laurence W. Mazzeno

BEYOND GOD THE FATHER
Toward a Philosophy of Women's Liberation

Author: Mary Daly (1928-　　)
First published: 1973
Edition used: Beyond God the Father: Toward a Philosophy of Women's Liberation,
　with "Original Reintroduction" by the author. Boston: Beacon Press, 1985
Genre: Nonfiction
Subgenre: Theology
Core issues: Church; ethics; freedom and free will; homosexuality; self-knowledge;
　women

Daly, a longtime controversial professor at Boston College (a Jesuit Catholic university), wrote Beyond God the Father, *a work of metaphysics or ontology (philosophy of being) in 1973. She both critiques the traditional canon—from Aristotle and Saint Augustine through Thomas Aquinas, Gottfried Wilhelm Leibniz, and Karl Barth to Teilhard de Chardin and Paul Tillich—and proposes her own understanding of Being, using God as verb, for the liberation of women from the all-encompassing patriarchy. In 1985, she added a more radical introduction to the second edition, revising many of her earlier positions.*

Overview
"If God is male, then male is God." This clichéd tagline about the connection between Christianity and patriarchy might be the thesis of Mary Daly's first book, *The Church and the Second Sex* (1968), but in her second and most theological book, *Beyond God the Father*, Daly finally refuses "God-talk" and renames the Ultimate as the verb of verbs, Be-ing.

The chapter titles give a good overview of Daly's thesis and method in this work: "After the Death of God the Father," "Exorcising Evil from Eve: The Fall into Freedom," "Beyond Christolatry: A World without Models," "Transvaluation of Values: The End of Phallic Morality," "The Bonds of Freedom: Sisterhood as Antichurch," "Sisterhood as Cosmic Covenant," and "The Final Cause: The Cause of Causes." In each of these, Daly is careful to give evidence from the theologians of the past (all male of course). As the holder of Ph.D.'s in both philosophy and theology from the University of Fribourg in Switzerland, she is very familiar with the scholarship of the canon, and thus can critique it without resorting to hasty generalization or *ad hominem* arguments.

In the first chapter, Daly posits God as a verb, not a noun, a verb of verbs, which is intransitive, thus not taking an object, and therefore getting beyond the subject-object dualism that has plagued both religion and philosophy. For women, this step is the refusal to be objectified. Using the language of Martin Buber's *Ich und Du* (1923; *I and Thou*, 1937), Daly says that women can pioneer new ways of being in the world that refuse I-It relationships for themselves and others; instead they can treat others as thou, another subject, not an object. When women do this, they move into new space and new time, "on the boundary of the institutions of patriarchy," and use their anger as a positive creative force beyond the "inauthentic structures" of the patriarchal church.

The next section analyzes the problem of Eve—the association of evil with women from the time of Genesis forward. Because of the millennia of belief in women's sin at Creation, women themselves have become psychologically paralyzed with guilt and hopelessness, complicit in this view of themselves. Daly is relentless in her analysis of various institutions, from the Church to the university and the peace movement, and their co-opting of women. She analyzes the "scapegoat syndrome" or society's need to create "the Other," and gives historical examples from witch burning to persecution of prostitutes to psychosurgery such as lobotomies on women. Even the Catholic Church's sanctification of Mary (and the Protestant church's refusal of Mary's near deification) cannot erase the guilt and anxiety foisted on women.

Daly's method in all her subsequent work was first used in this book: She deconstructs Christian concepts and terms such as "Christology" (which becomes "Christolatry," the reification and idolatry of Jesus) and "re-member," looking at the etymologies of various parts, or she makes up new words ("cosmosis") to reflect the complete break from patriarchal theology that she envisions. Although she is much influenced by Paul Tillich, she proposes a new way for women, communally "verbing," which works not through an individual decision but a collective one made by all women together. Freedom for women comes with the power to name, not accepting all the words and names given to women by men for millennia. The "Power of Be-ing" for women means taking their future into their own hands, stepping out communally, refusing the old patriarchal structures, and creating new worlds for themselves.

The "Original Reintroduction" to the second edition uses Daly's "new" language and rejects the terms "androgyny" and "homosexuality" as well as "God." However, she correctly notes that the main ideas in *Beyond God the Father* are still relevant, and without this foundation, her later works (*Gyn/Ecology*, 1978, and *Pure Lust*, 1984) could not have been written. She applies her incisive language to some earlier concepts, such as asserting that "the Courage to Be is the Courage to Sin," using etymological evidence that "sin" is connected to the Latin *est* and the Indo-European *es* or "to be." "Sinning" in the patriarchy is really "Be-ing" in her vision of the new world. Quoting from the end of the 1973 work, she rephrases the liturgical wording (from Acts 17:27-28): "The Journey can and does continue because the Verb continues— from whom, in whom, and with whom all true movements move." Thus, even in her radical revised version of *Beyond God the Father*, Daly still posits an ultimate reality beyond the individual.

Christian Themes

Daly's 1973 work (and 1985 republication) has had an enormous influence on every part of the women's movement, not least in Christian circles. Even though Daly has since become a "post-Christian," her work was the catalyst for many feminist theologians working to reform the Church from within. Such movements as the ordination of women priests and pastors (in Episcopal and other Protestant denominations), the textual work on noncanonical parts of the New Testament (the so-called Gnostic Gospels), and the movements for acceptance of same-sex couples, divorce, and birth control all were strengthened by Daly's work.

Daly's view of God as verb which has no object is both transcendent and immanent. Her conclusion for women ("The Final Cause") is that they must find freedom within: That the Ultimate not only transcendent but also immanent. In her later work, she makes clear that the plural, "Power-s of Be-ing" (in *Beyond God the Father*, she used the singular, "Power of Be-ing"), is the proper way to understand the principle of unity as metaphor: "[W]omen can and do speak of different Powers and manifestations of Be-ing, which are sometimes imaged as Goddesses."

Daly's ethics are powerful. Although she writes before the development of a feminist ethics, she presciently analyzes many of the areas that have since become contested: the connection of rape, genocide, and war; the ecological significance of the misuse of the earth, water, and nature and its connection to oppressive attitudes toward women; the affluent consumerist society's complicity in the destruction of nature; and the oppressive sexual revolution that has brought about a more violent society toward women.

Sources for Further Study

Berry, Wanda Warren. "Feminist Theology: The 'Verbing' of Ultimate/Intimate Reality in Mary Daly." In *Feminist Interpretations of Mary Daly*, edited by Sarah Lucia Hoagland and Marilyn Frye. University Park: Pennsylvania State University Press, 2000. Emphasizes *Beyond God the Father*, the concept of Be-ing, and the critique of Paul Tillich's *The Courage to Be* (1952).

Heyward, Carter. "Ruether and Daly: Theologians Speaking and Sparking, Building and Burning." *Christianity and Crisis* 39 (1979): 66-72. Contrasts the theology of Rosemary Ruether and Daly as of 1979, asserting that both the reformist (Ruether) and the radical (Daly) positions are necessary.

Hoagland, Sarah Lucia, and Marilyn Frye, eds. *Feminist Interpretations of Mary Daly*. University Park: Pennsylvania State University Press, 2000. Anthology of articles on all Daly's works and various themes: metaethics, evil, Be-ing, essentialism, myth, and language. Includes bibliography of secondary sources.

Ratcliffe, Krista. *Anglo-American Feminist Challenges to the Rhetorical Traditions: Virginia Woolf, Mary Daly, Adrienne Rich*. Carbondale: Southern Illinois University Press, 1996. Analyzes Daly's use of rhetoric, etymologies, and neologisms.

Tong, Rosemarie Putnam. *Feminist Thought: A More Comprehensive Introduction*. Boulder, Colo.: Westview Press, 1998. Helpful overview and analysis of Daly's work in section on radical feminism, pages 45-93.

Margaret H. McFadden

BIBLE AND THEOLOGY IN AFRICAN CHRISTIANITY

Author: John Samuel Mbiti (1931-   )
First published: Nairobi: Oxford University Press, 1986
Genre: Nonfiction
Subgenres: Church history; theology
Core issues: Africa; faith; Gospels; healing; knowledge; prayer

Anglican priest and canon Mbiti broke new ground with his studies of the Bible's influence on African Christianity. Based on the results of his massive field research, he challenged the notion that traditional African religious ideas were driven by sheer superstition and were, therefore, inherently un-Christian. In Bible and Theology in African Christianity, *he examines the contributions made by traditional African religions to Christian faith and practice.*

Overview

There is a widespread notion that Christianity in Africa has been merely an instrument of colonization. Conversely, some have believed that Christianity brought progress to African peoples by supplanting traditional religions that were bound by superstition. To a committed African Christian such as Anglican priest John Samuel Mbiti, both of these notions are too simplistic to be of any value. He states that "aided by the biblical revelation and faith in Jesus Christ," Africans built their approach to Christianity on a foundation that already existed in traditional African religions. However, African cultures that have adopted Christianity view religious practice and salvation quite differently from European cultures. Mbiti holds that a respectful understanding of the differences can help to ensure the viability of the Christian church in Africa.

According to Mbiti, European and American Christians tend to separate mind and body and to view salvation as a phenomenon solely of the afterlife: Jesus died on the cross so that we might have everlasting life. African Christian cultures, in contrast, view salvation as a phenomenon both of the hereafter and of the here and now. Earthly life and the afterlife are parts of the same continuum; far less emphasis is placed on the afterlife than in Western Christian cultures. Africans look for evidence of God's love and protection in their daily lives, for example, in the form of deliverance from present evil. The evils from which African Christians ask God to deliver them include earthly tribulations such as illness, injury, infertility, starvation, and lack of rain for crops or water to drink—reflections of life's hardships on that continent. African Christians also hope for earthly peace and deliverance from enemies as well as protection against curses and malevolent spirits. Historically, Africans have looked to religion for practical demonstrations of protection against these ills.

It is helpful to know this background, says Mbiti, when one is trying to understand specific tenets of African Christians' faith, such as their approach to prayer. Mbiti explains how this approach is rooted in religions that preceded the introduction of Christianity in Africa. Indeed, traditional African religions have a rich heritage that deepens their understanding of Christian faith. It is, says Mbiti, "a spiritual practice which readily takes root in the fertile soil of the biblical world." Thus, African prayer asks for blessings that encompass the entire journey of life. "Man is a whole, his body and spirit belong together. The welfare of one part is subsequently the welfare of the other." However, Mbiti reminds readers that prayer is addressed to the spirit world in the most literal sense.

Mbiti makes a distinction between mission churches (established by colonists) and independent churches (established by Africans who have accepted Christianity). Mbiti says it is the independent churches that continue to convey the tradition of prayer in Africa. Mission churches may be reluctant to do so because to them Africans seem to be dealing in superstition. The traditional approach to prayer helps explain the growth of the independent churches in Africa. "Many independent churches practise faith healing, which includes exorcisms of unwanted spirits. They pray for people to be protected against witchcraft and sorcery or the use of mystical power against them." Generally, Mbiti points out, African society believes that illness, accidents, and disappointments are brought about by people who invoke mystical powers against their targets—individuals or the entire community. Prayer is viewed as a powerful defense against spiritual assault. A church that fails to acknowledge this urgent fact of spiritual life, calling it superstition, is not fully serving its faithful. Prayer is and should be a powerful instrument to secure the blessings of life from a loving God.

Another major point of difference between African and European Christianity is their perspectives on health and healing. Like other everyday challenges in Africa, disease is a religious concern. Mbiti reports that traditional African churches practiced faith healing, and of course some denominations in the West have done likewise. However, he makes two further points about African tradition. First, it has included exorcisms of unwanted spirits, witchcraft, and sorcery. When feeling beset by spirits, Christians from mission churches often secretly consult "traditional religious experts" for remedies. These African Christians have nowhere else to turn as long as Western Christianity remains skeptical. Drawing on his own massive field research, Mbiti cites the role of testimony about the cure of serious illnesses, through God's love, in the attraction of new members to some indigenous churches.

Second, faith in healing can be confused with belief in magic, which Westerners may dismiss as superstition. In a religious context, varying beliefs about healing can become polarized. Those who turn to Western or African medicine—physical remedies—may be seen as lacking faith in spiritual healing. On the other side, those who rely on pure faith to resolve health problems may be forgetting "that God also uses physical agents to heal the sick." Mbiti advises a balanced perspective, adding, "Perhaps the churches are moving in this direction."

Christian Themes

Mbiti's research has shown him that the people of Africa have much to contribute to the meaningful practice of Christianity. Traditional Africans have long had a practical religion that permeates all aspects of their daily life. Their all-encompassing view of life does not see people as exclusively spiritual beings or physical beings, but as both at once, without any contradiction. Therefore, in practical matters such as health and healing, Mbiti counsels that there be no opposition between the spiritual and the physical, between faith healing and the acceptance of physical remedies.

Mbiti says that the traditional view of prayer allows African Christians to draw together into a community and experience the living presence of Christ ministering to them "in mighty ways." These can include healings, exorcisms, divine revelations, the gift of fertility to childless women, and more. Above all, he says, these prayerful communities are experiencing the "presence of the risen Lord."

Reading Mbiti's description of this total approach to religion by traditional Africans, one senses how he might regard them as potentially ideal Christians in that they see their lives as a religious whole and not as a random assortment of experiences leading to conflicted attitudes. In any case, Mbiti's discussion lends itself to the concept of inclusive religion, respectful of coreligionists whose experience may have fostered significantly different worldviews.

Sources for Further Study

Mbiti, John S. *Introduction to African Religion*. Westport, Conn.: Praeger, 1993. A well-organized survey of traditional African religion, based on Mbiti's extensive research but intended for a nonspecialist readership.

Olupona, Jacob K., and Sulayman S. Nyang, eds. *Religious Plurality in Africa: Essays in Honor of John S. Mbiti*. Berlin: Mouton De Gruyten, 1993. A collection of essays by other scholars honoring Mbiti's work as academic research and Christian ministry. Includes biographical information on Mbiti.

Partain, Jack. "Christians and Their Ancestors: A Dilemma of African Theology." *Christian Century*, November 26, 1986, p. 1066. Briefly surveys the scholarly work done by African scholars, including Mbiti, on traditional African concepts of life after death and the challenge these concepts present to Christianity.

Thomas Rankin

BILLY BUDD, FORETOPMAN

Author: Herman Melville (1819-1891)
First published: 1924
Edition used: Billy Budd, Sailor (An Inside Narritive), edited by Harrison Hayford
    and Merton Sealts, Jr. Chicago: University of Chicago Press, 1962
Genre: Novella
Subgenres: Allegory; historical fiction (eighteenth century)
Core issues: Good vs. evil; innocence; justice; sacrifice; submission

Critics debate the significance of Billy Budd. Is it an allegory expressing Melville's final acceptance of God's unfathomable but necessary justice, or a satire using its fictional narrator ironically to disguise a bitter protest against a cruel and arbitrary divinity? Or is the allegorical content secondary to a sociohistorical critique of class-based oppression? All these readings have been persuasively argued; the text, which was still evolving when Melville died, is ambiguous.

> Principal characters
> *Billy Budd*, sailor, the protagonist
> *The Honorable Edward Fairfax Vere*, captain of HMS *Bellipotent*
> *John Claggart*, master-at-arms (a naval police chief)

Overview

In *Billy Budd, Foretopman* (also known as *Billy Budd, Sailor*), the HMS *Bellipotent*, a seventy-four-gun ship of the line, intercepts the British merchantman *Rights of Man* and impresses seaman Billy Budd. Billy is the handsome sailor—extraordinarily attractive, able, well-intentioned, and amiable. He is flawed only by a sometimes severe speech impediment and—if flaws they be—by illiteracy and a total ignorance of human malice. When Billy is mustered into the king's service, he reveals that he is a foundling, discovered in a silk-lined basket at the door of a good man of Bristol.

Soon after arriving on the man-of-war, Billy witnesses a flogging and resolves never to deserve such punishment. His good looks, his manifest good intentions, and his ability as a seaman win him ready acceptance among his shipmates but also the enmity of John Claggart, a petty officer charged with disciplining the crew. Claggart is as intelligent as Billy is innocent, and as pale as Billy is tanned. Claggart is also handsome but innately evil. Like Billy, he has obscure origins but possibly culpable ones, and like Billy, he is new to the *Bellipotent*, having been transferred from another ship. Claggart recognizes Billy's virtues and resents them because he cannot duplicate them. His envy manifests itself first in trivial ways and then in an abortive attempt to entrap Billy in a bogus mutiny plot. Billy is too innocent to understand the proposal at first, too loyal to acquiesce, and too honorable to report the ambiguous solicitation.

Mutiny has particular significance in the summer of 1797, a few months after the mutinies at Spithead and the Nore, when all London had feared that rebellious crews would bring the fleet up the Thames. The mutinies had been put down and some of the sailors' grievances addressed, but discipline in the fleet still seems tenuous in the midst of Britain's war against revolutionary France.

Commanding the *Bellipotent*, Captain Edward Fairfax Vere, widely known as "Starry" Vere, is an accomplished officer—brave, modest, conscientious, and unusually intellectual for a naval officer. As the ship's captain, he is remote from his crew—and even, to an extent, from his officers—and his habits of mind make him more abstracted still.

While the *Bellipotent* is on detached duty, far from the fleet, Claggart approaches Captain Vere and accuses Billy of fomenting mutiny. Vere instinctively distrusts Claggart and trusts Billy, but such a charge demands attention. Vere arranges that Billy confront his accuser privately, in the captain's cabin. Shocked by the accusation, Billy is absolutely tongue-tied and finally can respond only with a powerful blow. Claggart drops to the deck, dead.

Vere tells the ship's surgeon that Claggart's death is "the divine judgment on Ananias," adding "Struck dead by an angel of God! Yet the angel must hang!" He directs the surgeon to inform the ship's officers of the event and of his intent to empanel a drumhead court. The surgeon privately questions the wisdom and propriety of such haste and indeed doubts Vere's sanity but accepts perforce his commander's decision. In the trial, all the participants including the captain recognize Billy's essential moral innocence but also the legal fact of his striking a superior. However, Vere, while nominally only a witness in the case, uses his status as captain to force the officers of the court not to delay the case until it can be regularly considered in the fleet but instead to affirm Billy's guilt and to pronounce a sentence of death, all in the overriding interest of naval discipline. In his arguments, Vere is intensely regretful but decisive.

After the trial, Vere visits Billy for a long, private interview, not described in detail. During the night, Billy is also visited by the chaplain, a sensitive and compassionate man who withdraws when he sees that Billy's simple purity of soul is a better guarantee of heaven than any doctrinal sophistication. At dawn, Billy is hung from the cruciform main yard. His last words, spoken without impediment, are "God bless Captain Vere!" The crew, called up to witness punishment, echo him. At the moment Billy is suspended, "the vapory fleece hanging low in the East . . . [is] shot through with a soft glory as of the fleece of the Lamb of God seen in mystical vision," and Billy "takes the full rose of the dawn."

In the aftermath, the *Bellipotent* engages a French ship of the line, the *Athee* (the *Atheist*), and takes her. Captain Vere receives a wound that proves mortal. He dies with Billy Budd's name on his lips. A distorted account of Claggart's death and Billy's execution appears in "a naval chronicle of the time," vilifying Billy and eulogizing Claggart. However, the sailors of the fleet believe something else. An anonymous sailor memorializes Billy in a ballad, "Billy in the Darbies," and the sailors of the fleet keep track of the yardarm from which Billy was hung, following it from ship to ship and finally to a dockyard hoist. They venerate pieces of it as devout Christians venerate relics of the cross.

Christian Themes

Melville began the composition of *Billy Budd, Foretopman* with a vision of a sailor condemned to hang for mutiny. Over time, the sailor evolved into an embodiment of innocence compared by the narrator to Adam before the Fall and to the unsophisticated and unspoiled "savages" of Tahiti. Captain Vere calls Billy "an angel of God," and his execution has clear parallels to the Crucifixion. Billy's exceptional physical beauty and social popularity are matched by his moral virtue, which is paradoxically defined by what Billy is not—not intellectual, not sophisticated, not envious, not suspicious, and not malicious.

As Billy's character evolved in the process of composition, his antagonist emerged—a dialectical opposite but harder to characterize. Claggart is intellectual, rational, deferential, and self-controlled. Where does he get his preoccupation with Billy? The narrator refers to "natural depravity" and "the mystery of iniquity." Captain Vere identifies Claggart with Ananias, whose sin was falsehood. He is also compared to a serpent, recalling "the envious marplot of Eden." Claggart, recognizing Billy's virtue, despairs of achieving it for himself; perhaps this is the source of his enmity.

Captain Vere's character was the third to emerge in the process of composition and is subject today to the most critical debate. Even his name is ambiguous. In Latin *veretas* is "truth," and *vir* is "man," but "veer" in English suggests a course that is less than true. Independent but self-effacing, well read and thoughtful, sensitive and compassionate, a maintainer of order and a father figure, Vere is seen by some critics as a dispenser of justice—even an allegorical representation of God the Father. Others see him as an arbitrary, oppressive, and cruel aristocrat—a proto-fascist—casting any allegory in a quite different light.

Vere insists on a drumhead court, a guilty verdict, and the maximum penalty because of his perception of naval necessity. He must have absolute control of the crew—"the people," he calls them—men for whom he is responsible but from whom he is always remote. To maintain control and fulfill his duty, he believes he must sacrifice Billy, regardless of personalities. Vere is compared to Abraham and Billy to Isaac, and there is no ram in the story. Billy is also like the second Adam, Christ. Whatever may have passed in his private interview with the captain, Billy trusts him and submits. Billy's final words ensure the necessary harmony of the captain and his people—peace in the midst of war. Billy's apotheosis follows.

Sources for Further Study

Bryant, John, ed. *A Companion to Melville Studies*. New York: Greenwood Press, 1986. Includes an important essay by Merton Sealts, Jr., "Innocence and Infamy: *Billy Budd, Sailor*," and a general article by Rowland Sherrill called "Melville's Religion." Bibliography and index.

Duban, James. *Melville's Major Fiction: Politics, Theology, and Imagination.* De-Kalb: Northern Illinois University Press, 1983. The last chapter, "The Cross of Consciousness: *Billy Budd*," treats among other subjects Melville's relationship to his narrator. Index.

Marvel, Laura, ed. *Readings on "Billy Budd."* New York: Greenhaven Press, 2003. A collection of essays, often excerpted, from a variety of viewpoints. Bibliography and index.

Milder, Robert, ed. *Critical Essays on Melville's "Billy Budd, Sailor."* Boston: G. K. Hall, 1989. Another wide-ranging collection of essays. Index.

Yanella, Donald, ed. *New Essays on "Billy Budd."* New York: Cambridge University Press, 2002. Three of the four essays in this volume deal with questions of religion in *Billy Budd, Foretopman.* Bibliography and index.

David W. Cole

BIOETHICS
A Primer for Christians

Author: Gilbert Meilaender (1946-   )
First published: 1996
Edition used: Bioethics: A Primer for Christians. 2d ed. Grand Rapids, Mich.: Wm.
    B. Eerdmans, 2005
Genre: Nonfiction
Subgenres: Didactic treatise; handbook for living
Core issues: Abortion; ethics; life; morality; regeneration; virtue

Although much of biomedical ethics can seem to consist merely of competing textbook "principles" and quality-of-life calculations, Meilaender's compact work, Bioethics, *has cast these difficult issues in a more complete and accurate context, especially for the Christian reader. Lest modern bioethical judgments become too narrow and calculating in their vision, Meilaender reminds his reader to maintain "a more expansive vision."*

Overview

There are many texts cataloging the broad concerns of modern bioethics; this book is not merely another. Gilbert Meilaender does not attempt to involve all perspectives in presenting the key issues in bioethics. Instead, he presents a more specific focus in *Bioethics*; he avoids catering to one segment of the populace and instead engages what he calls "the truth that has claimed us in Jesus."

Meilaender begins at procreation, investigating the language and mentality behind the modern approach to making babies. The beginning of life, as he tells us, is not a matter of the exercise of rights or the self-fulfillment of parents, but rather an engagement of and cooperation with God's love. This book first analyzes the controversial topic of abortion. Meilaender engages all the familiar questions surrounding the beginning of life, personhood, the woman's right to privacy, and other concerns surrounding human attitudes toward unwanted pregnancy and people's ability to accept the unbidden. He reminds the Christian reader that this topic, though controversial for some, should be largely straightforward despite the difficulties that some pregnancies might entail.

Meilaender also looks at medical testing and treatment of fetuses, as the advances of the Human Genome Project bring society closer to genetic diagnosis, treatment, and even enhancement at the fetal stage of life. The wonders of genetic knowledge contain a dark side, he warns, which may lead away from an unconditional commitment to children and toward an attitude of "quality control."

Other difficult questions confronting modern medicine that Meilaender discusses include suicide and euthanasia, the rejection of life-prolonging treatment, the extent of patient autonomy allowed, and the donation to medicine of organs and embryos.

The issues surrounding death and the relief of suffering are opportunities for the author to point out that physicians must not become too enamored of their own abilities. Although pain may be numbed, in the truest sense, real human suffering will continue beyond the reaches of the most advanced medical science. Meilaender points out that death presents no guarantee of relief of suffering for Christians. While medicine can prolong life and hasten death, it cannot control the larger accountability by which each life is bound.

The author comes full circle in his considerations by returning at the end to prenatal life and the embryo. It is, as he says, "the smallest of research subjects," and it also is a very real embodiment of the Christian duty to "the least among us." Involved here are artificial fertility, stem cell research, and cloning, at once the most hailed and the most disputed aspects of medical science. Meilaender argues that although embryos may be considered "spare" or destined to die anyway, this status does not serve to justify their use to further scientific progress. He repeatedly asserts that the more vulnerable and hopeless their condition, the greater our duties toward them.

This book takes neither a too suspicious nor too embracing approach toward each discussion of a topic regarding medical progress and bioethics. Medical technology and progress involve important work and achieve valuable goals, yet they are not in themselves an end for which even the smallest human life can be degraded or sacrificed, Meilaender says. It is a mistake to view the efforts of biomedical science as a fight to conquer vulnerability and human nature in the cause of promoting human longevity and satisfying human desire. The author argues for medical science that promotes health in a way that is respectful of the larger needs and responsibilities of humans, body and soul. A particularly useful image is the emphasis on "maximizing care," as opposed to seeking the end of all suffering. The book follows by saying that if the elimination of suffering were the entirety of the goal, it would often be most efficient to eliminate the sufferers themselves. He shows that the purpose of bioethics, then, is to distinguish between a desire for self-fulfillment through power and control over the physical self and a careful bodily stewardship that allows for "an attentiveness before a good and nurturant God."

The theme of bioethics as more than a competition between moral perspectives never rings more true than in the area of human suffering. Meilaender sets up an encounter with and contemplation of such suffering as a deeper role for bioethics. It is far too banal an assessment to write off suffering merely as an impediment to true fulfillment. As the author puts it, "our way of life is shaped by the fact that we trust in a God who suffers for our redemption." Hope is a crucial factor in the contemplation of suffering, a hope that goes beyond the so-called positive attitude. Hope as an encounter with Jesus Christ is what Meilaender offers as the key to Christian bioethics, mindful of the good of the body yet aware of existence beyond it.

Christian Themes

At the beginning of this book, Meilaender clearly indicates his belief that bioethics is not merely for bioethicists but also part of the role of all citizens—physicians, patients, and philosophers alike. In the same way, his approach is not simply to write an apologetic for one viewpoint among the many. This author firmly insists that to speak of "Christian bioethics" is to broaden one's ethical focus, not narrow it. Only an ethical approach that is mindful of human history can hope to find wisdom in such decisions. This approach invites the reader to consider the larger context of human life, beyond any agenda to simply advance science or technology, in which a decision about medical treatment or research involves recognition of the limits of human nature. The Christian especially should be aware of how the cosmological implications that follow from bodily decisions can be more significant than any physical results.

The fact that Christianity centers on the Incarnation and is sustained by the Resurrection of Christ means that we can neither regard the human body as a mere tool at the mind's disposal, nor stake too much hope in medical progress and relief. This author emphasizes throughout the book that the satisfaction that medical science purports to offer is not ultimately a true source of fulfillment. The vulnerability of bodily decay, while difficult to grapple with, is an important reminder of the fact that we also are creatures. We are not our own creators, nor are we in full control of human events. The hope for physical health and satisfaction that drives modern medicine and often creates bioethical dilemmas is not an inappropriate desire, as long as it remains subject to the Christian hope that looks beyond physical well-being. Meilaender begins and ends his primer on bioethics affirming Christ as the true source of hope, and highlighting the difference between the responsibility to protect physical health and a misguided desire to find wholeness through medical knowledge.

Sources for Further Study

Eberl, Jason T. *Thomistic Principles and Bioethics*. New York: Routledge, 2006. An in-depth look at bioethical dilemmas of the beginning and end of life, using the philosophy of Saint Thomas Aquinas as a practically applicable guide.

Elliot, Carl. *Better than Well*. New York: Norton, 2003. This exploration of the biological pursuit of happiness is an interesting analysis of the problems that may be encountered on the road to genetic enhancement.

Kass, Leon R. *Toward a More Natural Science*. New York: Free Press, 1985. In this seminal work for Christian bioethics, Kass explores what it means to be human in an era of medical advance and challenge toward human nature.

May, William E. *Catholic Bioethics and the Gift of Human Life*. Huntington, Ind.: Our Sunday Visitor, 2000. A look at the spectrum of bioethical issues and how modern approaches both derive and deviate from Catholic teaching on humans.

Meilaender, Gilbert. "The Politics of Bioethics." *The Weekly Standard* 9, no. 30 (April 12-19, 2004): 13-14. Contains a discussion of the President's Council on Bioethics and the politics that affected it.

Brandon P. Brown

THE BISHOP IN THE OLD NEIGHBORHOOD

Author: Andrew M. Greeley (1928-   )
First published: New York: Forge, 2005
Genre: Novel
Subgenres: Catholic fiction; mystery and detective fiction
Core issues: African Americans; Catholics and Catholicism; church; confession; forgiveness; justice; marriage

In his attempt to find out who murdered three undocumented aliens, Bishop John "Blackie" Ryan encounters a variety of characters attempting to gain or retain power in St. Lucy's parish. At the same time, he investigates a mass murder that occurred sixty years earlier and discovers a link between the old and recent cases that reveals the guilty parties. In the process, Blackie guides others without judgment and teaches the power of confession, forgiveness, and love.

> *Principal characters*
> *Bishop John "Blackie" Ryan*, the protagonist
> *Declan O'Donnell*, an Irish police sergeant
> *Camilla Datillo*, a state's attorney and beach-volleyball champion
> *Mikal Wolodyjowski*, a charismatic monsignor
> *Pablo*, leader of the West Lords gang
> *David Crawford*, an alderman
> *Tim O'Boyle*, an architect
> *Marshal O'Boyle*, O'Boyle's adopted son

Overview

The Bishop in the Old Neighborhood is one of Andrew Greeley's Christian mysteries in the Bishop Blackie Ryan series. The Old Neighborhood of the title, St. Lucy's parish, has always been at the center of Chicago's Austin district. Over the years, the neighborhood and its church have been crumbling under the influence of narcotics and resultant high crime, but now a movement toward gentrification is promising to restore the parish's former stature. With the charismatic Polish monsignor Mikal Wolodyjowski as its leader, St. Lucy's has attempted over the years to care for its diminishing Catholic parishioners, and now Wolodyjowski looks forward to revamping the neighborhood, providing his parish with a long overdue facelift. To this end, he retains the architects Tim O'Boyle and his adopted son Marshal.

However, three mutilated bodies have been discovered in the sanctuary of St. Lucy's church after an attempt to blow up the church. Declan O'Donnell, an idealistic young Irish police officer, and the voluptuous Sicilian state's attorney Camilla Datillo arrive on the scene to investigate. A romantic subplot emerges as they discover that they knew each other in grade school. They soon find themselves remembering old times—and planning new times. They wonder whether the killings are a warning to the monsignor to leave well enough alone and not proceed with his plans to refurbish the neighborhood.

Central to the action is longtime Chicago resident Bishop John Blackwood "Blackie" Ryan, an Irishman who has been ordered by Archbishop Sean Cronin, on his way to the Vatican, to investigate the murders. Bishop Blackie has known the aristocratic Father Wolodyjowski for years and feels the Polish man should have been promoted in his place. Soon, Blackie finds himself traveling by train all over Chicago. He visits the O'Boyles' office and learns that they have been receiving threats designed to force them to stop rebuilding in the neighborhood. Blackie's visit to the home of Pablo, the young leader of the West Lords gang, ends in the young man's promise to find out who is responsible for desecrating the Church, where he attends Mass and where his children attend school. Alderman David Crawford is next on Blackie's list. He believes the gentrification of St. Lucy's will result in the flight of his African American constituents. The more people Blackie interviews, the more puzzled he becomes about the identity of whoever killed the three victims—who appear to be undocumented Mexicans. Especially important is how the killers entered the church: without tripping its state-of-the-art burglar-alarm system.

With the help of former superintendent of police Mike O'Casey and Blackie's brother Packy, Blackie learns about a letter—written more than sixty years ago, near the end of World War II, by his long-dead attorney father—regarding a horrific accident involving six young parishioners and Monsignor Wolodyjowski, who was a seminarian at the time. Father Wolodyjowski had spent the day with the teenagers touring the countryside; they had happened upon a Wisconsin farm that was experimenting with lethal gas. Later that day, the teens were hit by a truck containing flammable material and were incinerated, dying on the spot. Particularly devastating was the death of the beautiful young Annie Scanlon, who was beloved by all, including Wolodyjowski. However, the investigative letter written by Blackie's "Old Fella" (as he called his father) reveals that the deaths were no accident: Someone in the U.S. Navy had ordered the murders of the young people, whose discovery of the gas facility threatened to endanger national security.

As Blackie continues to search for the identity of whoever ordered the killings so long ago, O'Donnell, a computer expert, and Datillo, a beach-volleyball champion, continue their search for the present-day killers. As they work together, the couple cannot deny that they are in love, despite their fear of marriage and prospective in-laws. After Blackie gives him a name to investigate, O'Donnell discovers that a band of mercenaries—former Green Berets and agents of the Central Intelligence Agency— were responsible for the church killings and that the church burglar-alarm system was hacked into by someone who turns out to have a Web site with a URL in Poland.

Another attempt to blow up St. Lucy's is foiled when it becomes clear that Tim O'Boyle was behind the old killings: He was a naval lieutenant at the time and ordered the deaths of the Old Neighborhood teens. He had been rebuffed by the beautiful Annie Scanlon (whose ghost has recently been spending time at Blackie's rectory). The elder O'Boyle breaks down and confesses, deeply relieved to shed his sixty-year-old burden of guilt. He dies soon after, having received the Sacraments, and enters heaven with Annie Scanlon as a guide. His adopted son, Marshal, is simultaneously arrested for the more recent murders at St. Lucy's. The malicious man had been intent on taking over his father's office, but when he found out how much money he stood to lose on rebuilding St. Lucy's, he went to great lengths to put an end to the project, even allowing the deaths of three innocents.

The novel ends with the engagement of O'Donnell and Datillo and the promotion of Blackie to auxiliary archbishop upon Archbishop Cronin's return from Rome.

Christian Themes

The Bishop in the Old Neighborhood—the fifth Bishop Blackie Ryan book by prizewinning priest, sociologist, and author Andrew Greeley—is rich in Christian themes: primarily the healing power of confession and forgiveness and the sacred power of love. Early in the novel, O'Donnell goes to a retreat where he comes to terms with the fact that he bullied a young Sicilian girl when he was in grade school. He finds her, confesses, apologizes, and asks forgiveness. Because she recognizes his sincerity, she forgives him and in the process feels the first flushes of love. By asking forgiveness, O'Donnell opens himself up to true love that is spiritual in nature.

The themes of confession and forgiveness continue throughout as the elderly Tim O'Boyle confesses to arranging the deaths of the Chicago teenagers during the summer of 1944. Rebuffed by the beautiful Annie Scanlon, the young naval lieutenant O'Boyle arranged for her and her friends' deaths under the pretext of safeguarding national security when the youngsters stumbled across the secret military installation. He has lived a life of horrific guilt that led to his adopting Marshal, the younger brother of one of his victims, as his son. Tim O'Boyle—in the end relieved to be found out—abjectly confesses his sin and finds forgiveness and redemption.

Greeley, a professor of social sciences at the University of Chicago and the University of Arizona, interweaves these spiritual themes of forgiveness and redemption into highly readable, entertaining fiction. Side plots—such as that of the love affair between O'Donnell and Datillo—advertise the importance of other Christian themes, here the need to gain perspective on physical and spiritual love: Blackie acts as O'Donnell and Datillo's spiritual adviser when they call on him for help navigating their physical and spiritual longings. Both fear making a commitment to marriage (having seen their friends suffer severe consequences), but Blackie asks the right questions and provides them with the confidence that what they feel is real love that will grow and mature into a truly intimate, lifelong bond.

Sources for Further Study

Greeley, Andrew. *Priests: A Calling in Crisis*. Chicago: University of Chicago Press, 2004. Examines the sexual abuse crisis of the clergy from a sociological point of view and forecasts the scandal's impact on the future of the Catholic Church.

_____. *White Smoke: A Novel About the Next Papal Conclave*. New York:

Forge Books, 1996. Father "Blackie" Ryan leaves Chicago for Rome with Cardinal Cronin, where he addresses the vicious politics behind the selection of a new pope.

Shafer, Ingrid, ed. *Andrew Greeley's World: A Collection of Critical Essays, 1986-1988*. New York: Warner Books, 1989. A wide variety of essays, positive and negative, that provide insights into Greeley as a priest, sociologist, and novelist. Highlights Greeley's propensity to write about renewal.

M. Casey Diana

THE BISHOP'S MANTLE

Author: Agnes Sligh Turnbull (1888-1982)
First published: New York: Macmillan, 1947
Genre: Novel
Subgenre: Evangelical fiction
Core issues: Clerical life; connectedness; devotional life; pastoral role; Protestants and Protestantism; self-knowledge

Written more than fifty years ago, during a simpler, more innocent time, the novel addresses age-old conflicts between love and reason, parents and children, and doubt and faith. Set in 1939-1941, it reflects the spirit of a nation and its people as they first view the beginnings of World War II from a distance and then are forced to become directly involved. Popular appeal made it a best selling novel in 1948, with close to a million copies sold. Today's readers may find the novel dated and simplistic.

> *Principal characters*
> *Hilary Laurens*, the protagonist, a young, newly married Episcopal priest
> *Lexa "Lex" McColly*, Hilary's wife, a wealthy socialite, fond of the party scene
> *Dick Laurens*, Hilary's brother and best friend, an adventurer who embraces danger

Overview

The Bishop's Mantle is a coming-of-age novel in which the main character, Hilary Laurens, is tested by a variety of circumstances; it is also a novel that reflects a particular time and place in American history. At the beginning of the novel, Hilary, a minister in his early thirties, must face the death of his grandfather, who has been Hilary's sole support since his mother and father died. His grandfather was a nationally known bishop of the Episcopal church whose guidance over the years and his insight, recorded in a bound scrapbook, are the "mantle" protecting and guiding Hilary. The young minister will often turn to that scrapbook in his first professional appointment as priest to the prestigious St. Matthews, a high Episcopal church in an unnamed eastern city.

As he assumes his role of priest to this community, Hilary is attempting to win Lex, a beautiful young woman whom he loves passionately. Although Hilary is certain how he feels, Lex worries that becoming the minister's wife may not suit her fun-loving nature. Her uncertainty about marriage to a minister and her desire not to be tied down contrast with Hilary's certainty in his choice not only of Lex but also of vocation. His ardor for Lex and his alternating delight and despair over their relationship help to show his human, vulnerable side.

The bulk of the novel details Hilary's encounters with various situations and personalities. Of importance are the minor characters who play an evolving role in assisting or becoming an obstacle to the new priest. By showing Hilary reacting to these characters, Agnes Sligh Turnbull gives insight into his personality. His instinctive compassion is evident in how he consoles Morris, the black servant of his grandfather, the bishop. Sensing how lost the elderly man feels and how uncertain he is about future employment, Hilary announces that he cannot do without Morris in his new parish and asks him to come with him to the new city. At the new parish, Hilary must deal with a different kind of character, the prickly church sexton Hastings, who, during his forty years at St. Matthews, had become the bulwark of the previous pastor. Showing acumen beyond his years, Hilary asks for Hastings's advice, consequently winning him over. Mrs. Reed, another memorable character, catches Hilary swearing and discerns that he may be a high Episcopal priest, but he is, indeed, a man.

Hilary's first services as a priest are memorable; his gift as a speaker is remarkable. However, Hilary is not content with success within St. Matthews; he looks beyond the church property and the regular, moneyed parishioners to the tenements and cheap apartments around the church and to the poor who live there. He is conscious of others not being served by the church: young intellectuals from the university and young professionals. The vestrymen who hired him and "held great corporations in the hollow of their hands" are pleased with his effectiveness as a preacher but hesitant concerning his desire to share the beauty of St. Matthews with the poor. Senior Warden Henry Alvord, in particular, wants to keep things as they are, serving only the "right kind" of people: the wealthy who pay a suitable sum of money to rent their pews.

As Hilary begins to learn his way around his new church, he encounters a variety of situations. His tremendous effectiveness as a preacher attracts the lonely widow Diana Downes; she is no temptation to Hilary, who is completely in love with Lex, but she is a danger to his reputation. A situation for which he did not plan was Lex's attitude toward her position. The antithesis of the stereotypical minister's wife, the vivacious Lex plans a cocktail party, eager to show her large group of socialite friends her new home, the rectory, and to display her handsome new husband, the priest.

So engrossed is Hilary in implementing his plans for the parish, he "gives scant attention to the seething problems beyond the sea." However, the "growing black cloud of war" becomes more intrusive and finally a reality to Hilary when his brother Dick volunteers to drive an ambulance in Europe, and some of the young male parishioners go to Canada to enlist.

As the war escalates in Europe, Hilary's personal wars come to a head. He learns that Alvord not only owns the tenements close to the church but also two brothels. Having a senior warden, a pillar of the church, engaged in this type of commercially profitable activity is abhorrent to Hilary; his efforts to make Alvord divest himself of these "immoral" sources of income come to naught. True to his sense of what is right, Hilary calls a meeting of the vestry and announces that he must resign if Alvord continues on the board. Awakened by their priest's social consciousness, the vestrymen support him. At home, Lex, unhappy with her quiet lifestyle, gets drunk and blurts out a hurtful truth to the assistant pastor's wife. Hilary cannot forgive her.

The climax of the novel begins with the death of Hilary's brother and the crisis of faith Hilary suffers. As he works through his grief and finds a deeper faith, he matures. He forgives Lex. After hearing the radio broadcast announcing the Japanese had bombed Pearl Harbor, Hilary resolves to continue to serve as a priest but, again, to a wider community as a chaplain in the war.

Christian Themes

Love and forgiveness are central to the novel. In the principal love story between Hilary and Lex, their loving relationship develops from the initial physical delights into a deeper love, promoted by their transcending a number of obstacles. Subplots show how love can grow and change between parents and children and how Christian love is expressed as people sacrifice themselves to benefit others.

Concerning the church and its role in the community, the novel is ahead of its time. Rather than embracing tradition and focusing on the customary, elite members, Hilary leads the church to become more than a building. He tries to show that Christianity is not restricted to a specific church service but can extend not just spiritual but also concrete aid, such as dances for young people, outings to a farm, and even recipes on how to make a soup bone stretch into more than one meal. However, he always promotes these specific projects as a gateway to the stronger values of membership in the church community.

Principally, the novel is centered on the spiritual development of a priest. At the beginning of the novel, Hilary's faith has not yet been tested. The death of his parents occurred when he was young, and although he is saddened by the bishop's death, what causes Hilary to despair is the death of his young, vibrant brother, whom he had always counted on and who seemingly led a charmed life. He feels as if all his "foundations were crumbling," and the words he so often uses to comfort others are now just words. Hilary begins to doubt there is a caring God. Again his grandfather's scrapbook provides help with the bishop's thoughts on immortality and faith. Reflecting on Saint Paul, who wrote on the mortal body and the spiritual body, of perishing and of immortality, the bishop shows how his own doubts renewed his faith. Hilary, under the bishop's mantle, finds a deeper faith. "And he knew that there was law here, and order; there was purpose and design," and his faith became "impregnable."

Sources for Further Study

Hart, James D. "Platitudes of Piety: Religion and the Popular Modern Novel." *American Quarterly* 6, no. 4 (Winter, 1954): 311-322. An overview of how religious subjects are treated in popular novels, focusing on Hilary's human dilemmas.

Morey, Ann-Janine. "Blaming Women for the Sexually Abusive Male Pastor." *Christian Century* 105, no. 28 (October 5, 1988): 866-869. A study that details the dynamics of the relationship of Hilary and his wife, as well as discussion of the fictionalized portrayal of ministers' wives by Turnbull and others.

Paige, Judith. "St. Matthew's." Review of *The Bishop's Mantle. The New York Times,*

October 26, 1947, p. 24. A favorable review that stresses the importance of character development of the main characters and also notes the "wonderful" minor characters.

Turnbull, Agnes Sligh. *Dear Me, Leaves from the Diary of Agnes Sligh Turnbull.* New York: Macmillan, 1941. Turnbull's diary provides a glimpse into her life and the woman behind the novels.

Marcia B. Dinneen

A BLACK THEOLOGY OF LIBERATION

Author: James H. Cone (1939-   )
First published: New York: Lippincott, 1970
Genre: Nonfiction
Subgenres: Critical analysis; theology
Core issues: African Americans; the divine; ethics; faith; Jesus Christ; racism; social
   action

*Cone outlines a revolutionary theology of liberation, providing both a harsh critique
of white Christian theology and society and a radical reappraisal of Christianity from
the perspective of the oppressed African American community in North America.*

Overview

In 1970, James H. Cone—who later became Charles A. Briggs Distinguished Professor of Systematic Theology at Union Theological Seminary in New York City—published *A Black Theology of Liberation*, which features a scathing critique of Western theological traditions and reinterprets the Christian faith and the entire biblical revelation in the light of African Americans' struggles against oppression and their quest for justice. When it was first published in 1970, *A Black Theology of Liberation* sparked much controversy and debate within North American theological circles. Since then, it has been lauded as a classic text on which other black and liberation theologians have drawn to construct their own brand of liberation discourse.

Cone's theological formulations in this work derive from the social conditions of African Americans of the 1960's and 1970's, which gave rise to the Civil Rights and Black Power movements. Cone advanced the revolutionary thesis that Christian theology is not simply a rational inquiry into the nature of the divine but also a study of God's liberating presence in the world, or of God's activity on behalf of the oppressed. In seven compact chapters, Cone outlines major elements of this new black theology, imbuing basic Christian doctrines with new meaning. These include the nature and content of Christian theology and its primary sources; God's ongoing revelation to the world and its connection to biblical writings; the nature of human beings; the concept of divinity (or God); the doctrine of Christology; the role of theology in the world; and the doctrine of eschatology. Throughout the text, Cone argues in a passionate, sometimes angry, tone that the historic and current forms of racism in Western civilization (especially within Christian cultures) mandates a radically new understanding of Christian theology as a theology of liberation from oppression. Some of the general ideas Cone treats in this work were introduced in an earlier one, *Black Theology and Black Power* (1969). In both, Cone articulates the themes that God is on the side of the oppressed and that Jesus is the quintessential symbol of liberation. *A Black Theology of Liberation* moves beyond the earlier text in its systematic reworking of the major Christian doctrines based on Cone's assessment of the experiences of African Americans in North America.

For Cone, a black theology of liberation must have a starting point different from that of traditional Western theology in perspective, content, and style. He unmasks the purported universalism of Eurocentric theology in the United States, pointing to its failure to address the existential, historical realities facing African Americans. He states that white Christian theology is influenced by its social thought and that any social environment functions as a mental grid, deciding what will be considered relevant in a given inquiry. Furthermore, Cone argues, the dominant Western European Christian theology in the United States actually serves the interests of those in power. Thus, in a society where individuals are oppressed because of their blackness, Christian theology must become black theology; that is, it must be a theology through which African Americans can validate their quests for liberation and justice. Cone is also careful to note that the patterns of meaning found in his articulation of black theology are not confined to the experiences of blacks in North America but extend to oppressed communities everywhere, adding that blackness symbolizes oppression and liberation in any society.

Cone identifies key sources for doing black theology, such as the historical and religious experiences of black people in the United States, the revelation of God at work in the black experience, the witness of Scripture, the truth in Jesus Christ, and church tradition. When addressing the black experience, Cone universalizes oppression as the main feature of African American lives, displaying a rhetorical, political discourse that addresses the prevalence and pernicious effects of institutionalized racism in the daily lives of African Americans. In his discussion of black liturgy or worship, another key source, Cone speaks of the sermon as the proclamation of Gospel disclosed in black idiom, and of prayer as rejection of whites' religious outlook initiated by slaves. Furthermore, Cone introduces the notion of hymns or songs as singing the "truth" as lived by the people. Cone's black theology of liberation includes other aspects of black experience as important theological sources: namely, folklore, humor, the blues, the narratives of slaves' and ex-slaves' triumphs and defeats, and the black literary tradition.

With this new theological approach, Cone asserts that one's social and historical context decides not only questions that communities of faith address to God but also the mode or forms of the answers given to those questions. This epistemological insight has become an important feature of all liberation theologies, whose adherents hold that (theological) ideas do not have a separate existence from life but arise out of a framework of reality constructed by people. Equally important in Cone's liberation discourse is the primacy given to a certain type of biblical hermeneutics, which emphasizes a God who is not neutral regarding oppressive forces and institutions. The concept of "liberation" is chosen by Cone to augment his religious reflection on the divine-human relationship, which he draws from biblical revelation. Thus, for Cone, the social, a priori basis of black theology is closer to the axiological perspectives of biblical revelation than to traditional white theology because black theology centers attention on a liberating deity who addresses human suffering. For Cone, theology loses its integrity within the North American context when it is abstracted from—or opposed to—God's will to do justice for the racially oppressed.

Christian Themes

A dimension of Cone's Christian discourse that warrants attention is his assertion that God must be "black." Rejecting the very notion of a colorless deity in a society where human beings suffer precisely because of their color, Cone insists that God must be black in order to correlate the truth of divine reality with oppression. Any inkling of God's connection with the white oppressor contains an implicit approval of their actions. In announcing God's blackness, Cone is virtually saying that the concept of the divine must not, in any form or symbolic ordering, be intimately associated with the racist-inflected white theology that grounds much of mainstream Christianity in North America.

Closely linked to the provocative theme of a "black God" is Cone's Christocentric focus. He asserts that the proper subject of black theology is Jesus the Liberator. Cone's Christological theory views Jesus as the Event of liberation—a monumental happening in the lives of oppressed black peoples seeking freedom from the distortion and sins of racist forces. Cone associates the freedom that Jesus offers with the existential notion of authenticity. In other words, oppressed black bodies are set free to be what they genuinely are, without the harmful distortions promoted by white racism and power. Cone adds that any interpretation of the Gospel that fails to see Jesus as the Liberator of the oppressed is heretical. Accordingly, any message that is not related to the liberation of the poor in a society is not Christ's message, and any theological system that is indifferent to the theme of liberation is not Christian theology.

Another theme in Cone's liberation theology that remains provocative is his doctrine of eschatology. Cone rejects what he terms the "white lie" that Christianity is concerned primarily with life in the next world and that God is indifferent to the suffering of the oppressed in this world. His black theology affirms hope for this life—the here and now. Here one sees the usefulness for Cone of European existential philosophy, with its emphasis on the concreteness of human experience and on self-determination. In the final analysis, however, Cone's theological discourse necessarily parts ways with the humanistic, atheistic veins found in Jean-Paul Sartre and other existentialist philosophers, with its unabashedly confessional articulation of an objectively true God who acts in history on behalf of the poor and the oppressed.

Sources for Further Study

Burrow, Rufus, Jr. *James H. Cone and Black Liberation Theology.* Jefferson, N.C.:
   McFarland, 2001. Discusses the significance of Cone's theological canon, explaining the systematic development of his themes: social and economic analysis, black sexism, and relations between black, feminist, and Third World theologies.
Cone, James H. *A Black Theology of Liberation: Twentieth Anniversary Edition.* New
   York: Orbis Books, 1990. This commemorative edition is enhanced by Cone's re-

flections on the evolution of his own religious quest for liberation and by critical essays by other leading liberation theologians.

Thomas, Linda E., ed. *Living Stones in the Household of God: The Legacy and Future of Black Theology*. Minneapolis, Minn.: Fortress Press, 2004. Numerous scholars and theologians assess the influence and significance of black theology in the past and for the future. Includes two chapters by Cone.

Carol Wayne White

BLACK ZODIAC

Author: Charles Wright (1935-   )
First published: New York: Farrar, Straus and Giroux, 1997
Genre: Poetry
Subgenres: Lyric poetry; meditation and contemplation
Core issues: The divine; God; nature; recollection; soul

Wright examines the relationship between God and the human from a distinctly personal perspective through a poetic re-creation of meaningful moments in his life, intermixed with invocations of immediate present experience. Identifying himself as one of "God's word-wards," he understands the practice of his craft as an attempt to describe the universe as a map of meaningful mysteries, difficult to discern but crucial for the survival of the soul.

Overview

Charles Wright's extensive and informative discussions of the shape and structure of poetry—his own and the work of the artists he admires—are an indication of the importance of these elements for him, but at least as important is his emphasis on the spiritual dimensions of a poem. In one of the first entries in "Improvisations on Form and Measure" (which he published in 1987 as an explanation of his aesthetic intentions in the form of a series of brief statements and quotations), he declared, "Form is nothing more than a transubstantiation of content." This assertion forms a gloss on a familiar theme that combined the linguistic invention, which is a central feature of his work, with a vocabulary redolent with religious implications. Several entries later, again casting formal concerns within a religious context, he states, "Each line should be a station of the cross."

These assertions seem to derive from a traditional Catholic foundation, but Wright has considerably complicated this impression with his observation that he "was formed by the catechism in Kingsport [Tennessee], the evangelical looniness at Sky Valley Community in North Carolina, and by songs and hymns," and through his juxtaposition of High Renaissance depictions of religious icons (derived from the work of Dante Alighieri and other European classical masters) with the gospel music of American legends such as the Carter family, near Kingsport. Calling their music "God-haunted, salvation-minded and evangelical," and identifying its theme as "death, loss, resurrection, salvation," Wright has, in his poetry, developed a distinctly personal version of a powerful spiritual vision from seemingly disparate components.

The poems in his Pulitzer Prize-winning volume *Black Zodiac* form a polished, nuanced expression of this vision. The volume is divided into five sections, beginning with the classic "Apologia Pro Vita Sua," in which the poet accepts as a matter of being that "The love of God is the loneliest thing I know of," wondering "Who can distinguish darkness from the dark, light from light." The poems are designed as an exploration of a cosmos that has come into existence through a divine verbal declaration of light, but a cosmos that remains wreathed in shadow and darkness, its outlines and substance often obscure and untenable. "Apologia Pro Vita Sua" serves as an explanation, after the well-known poem of the same title by Cardinal John Henry Newman (1801-1890), for an individual's progress on a spiritual journey, a journey that continues to be marked by, as reviewer Carol Muske put it, the "'dark stars' that guide our fate and provide the contrast that shapes us; the shadow, the photographic's negative, the mirror's reversals."

"Apologia Pro Vita Sua" is divided into three sections, followed by an "Envoi" in which Wright offers some tentative conclusions about what matters most to him at this stage in his life. The first part is a philosophic excursion regathering ideas and insights that Wright has assimilated into a philosophic overview of a cosmos he describes as a "shapeless shape of darkness." Asserting as one of his core precepts that "Landscape's a lever of transcendence" (with the image "The dew bead, terminal bead, opens out/ onto a great radiance" as an example of an infinitely intriguing terrain to be explored), Wright asks "St. Stone" to "say a little prayer" as an offering of assistance drawn from the divinity of the substantive world. The second section is a recollection of instances of insight, each moment linked to a specific geographic location that corresponds in an emblematic fashion to a counterpart of the human psyche. "What I remember redeems me," Wright asserts here. The third section continues the mode of transport through inner consciousness in an exploration of the poet's essential self, a series of queries carrying a search forward and inward. The concluding section, the "Envoi," is an expression of acceptance, Wright observing, "I'll take as icon and testament/ The daytime metaphysics of the natural world," reaffirming his faith in the possibilities of profundity within the "metaquotidian landscape."

"Apologia Pro Vita Sua" forms a frame for the volume, whose last section, "Disjecta Membra" (or "scattered parts"), is a meditation in the mode of Guido Ceronetti's commonplace book *Il silenzio del corpo* (1979; *The Science of the Body*, 1993), which Wright notes is a compendium of "elusive, coveted and vaguely scented knowledge." "Disjecta Membra" is designed as a means of establishing a pattern of coherence, relying on the fundamental principles of Wright's aesthetic credo, which are epitomized by the statement near the close of the poem, "I think of landscape incessantly."

The three sections within the frame all, in some way, attend to this guiding principle. This middle section of the book includes a group of poems linking the landscape near Charlottesville, where Wright has been a distinguished professor at the University of Virginia, with his travels in Europe. It includes several poems in which he "seances with the great dead" (including Li Ho, Robert Johnson, Giacomo Leopardi), while the fourth group moves toward the title poem, in which the volume's central concerns are intensified and summarized. Wright's quest for understanding in a cosmos depicted as a "Black Zodiac," where nothing is ultimately fixed, stable, or permanent, is portrayed as "A pilgrim's way" outlined by "a sidereal roadmap." As he considers "Unanswerable questions, small talk/ Unprovable theorems, long-abandoned arguments—" his ultimate wisdom is that "You've got to write it all down."

Christian Themes

Throughout his writing life, Wright has made his deep and driving interest in theological issues a major focus of his poetry, expressing a belief that "the true purpose of poetry is a contemplation of the divine and its attendant mysteries." In a revealing interview with Morgan Schuldt in 2002, he proclaimed that "Poetry is a matter of 'soul making' as John Keats said," and for Wright, the human soul is illuminated through the "contemplation of the divine." In *Black Zodiac*, this is primarily a contemplation of landscape, the "lever of transcendence" that elevates the human above the profane. Given the disparate sources of Wright's religious background, the poetry here depends on a search for God's presence within every aspect of the landscape he encounters. In the opening lines of "Apologia Pro Vita Sua," Wright sees the blossoming dogwood trees doting the landscape as a "via Dolorosa," the path Christ walked on his way to the cross, with individual trees as "part-charred cross points." Such images link the local with the manifestation of God on earth in human affairs, leading toward this image in the third section:

> The Unknown Master of the Pure Poem walks nightly among his roses,
> The very garden his son laid out.
> Every so often he sits down. Every so often he stands back up.

The wry humor of this conception—a sort of shield against the awesome implications of God's actions—does not detract from its awareness of God's existence. The heart of the whole volume is a record of the poet's responses to this phenomenon, an attempt to convey in language something he feels profoundly, if somewhat abstractly. Quoting Saint Augustine with approval, the poet acknowledges that "God is neither imaginable nor conceivable, but is the ground and condition of all existence and knowledge"—thus, the image of "The Unknown Master" and the quest for evidence of the Master's work.

That word is written in many languages, such as (in the poem "Meditation on Summer and Shapelessness") the "cloud-ragged, cloud-skutted sky," which Wright calls "God's wash"; or as the "respirations of the divine," in the poem "Lives of the Saints," which concludes with the admonition, "God says, watch your back"; or (in "Disjecta Membra") as an image of "God's blue breath," which he calls a "compulsive cameo" that is "so light on the skin, so infinite." These, and many other images and invocations throughout the volume, testify to the presence of God, if glimpsed aslant, or through shadows. "Is *this* the life we long for?" Wright asks in a kind of summation in the last section of "Disjecta Membra," and then answers, "Well, yes, I think so." The conclusion might seem like a step down from the exalted; it is actually a characteristically subdued capstone, bringing the vivid, intense images of the divine back to the level of everyday human existence.

Sources for Further Study

Andrews, Tom, ed. *The Point Where All Things Meet: Essays on Charles Wright.* Oberlin, Ohio: Oberlin College Press, 1995. A wide range of essays on Wright's work, representing many different critical perspectives and judgments.

Muske, Carol. "Guided by Dark Stars." *The New York Times*, August 31, 1997. A discerning review of *Black Zodiac* by a fellow poet.

Wright, Charles. *Halflife: Improvisations and Interviews, 1977-1987.* Ann Arbor: University of Michigan Press, 1988. Illuminating comments about his art by the poet, with revealing interviews. See also the companion volume *Quarternotes: Improvisations and Interviews, 1988-1995* (Ann Arbor: University of Michigan Press, 1995).

Leon Lewis

BLOOD TIES

Author: Sigmund Brouwer (1959-   )
First published: Dallas, Tex.: Word, 1996
Genre: Novel
Subgenres: Evangelical fiction; mystery and detective fiction; thriller/suspense
Core issues: Good vs. evil; Native Americans; redemption

A stalker who has been pursuing Kelsie McNeill for twenty years circles closer and closer to her life, which is already in shambles. Kelsie's husband, former FBI agent Clay Garner, plays a mind game with the stalker in an attempt to capture him before harm comes to Kelsie. Clay's pure motives clash with the stalker's irredeemably evil mind in a spiritual parable of the monumental struggle between good and evil.

> Principal characters
> *Kelsie McNeill*, the protagonist
> *Taylor*, Kelsie's son
> *Clay Garner*, Kelsie's husband, a former FBI agent
> *The Watcher*, the antagonist, who is stalking Kelsie
> *George Samson*, Clay's Native American friend and spiritual
>   companion
> *Doris Samson*, Samson's granddaughter
> *Flannigan*, Clay's FBI forensics colleague
> *Russ Fowler*, the sheriff of Kalispell, Montana
> *Nick Buffalo*, a ranch hand and friend of Kelsie

Overview

In a brilliant follow-up to his medical thriller *Double Helix* (1995), Sigmund Brouwer creates in *Blood Ties* a world where physical evil lurks around every corner and where metaphysical evil confronts the good in the small town of Kalispell, Montana. In 1973, Clay Garner, an agent of the Federal Bureau of Investigation (FBI), is called to Kalispell to investigate a suspicious train derailment on property that abuts the federal reservation land where Native American George Samson lives. When George's granddaughter, Doris, is found dead in a local hotel, Clay's assignment takes on new dimensions. Although the local sheriff, Russ Fowler, ridicules Clay and his urban training, he reluctantly allows Clay to work on the case after Clay threatens to report Fowler for obstruction of justice. Clay believes the clues that he finds at Doris's murder scene—especially an eagle feather that the murderer has left as a calling card—indicate that a serial killer may be at work in the community.

Meanwhile, Kelsie McNeill has troubles of her own. The daughter of one of the town's wealthiest ranchers, she is headstrong and beautiful, especially as the 1973 teenager first presented to the reader. She has a crush on Nick Buffalo, one of her father's ranch hands, but someone else is watching and pining for Kelsie from afar. This stalker leaves Kelsie notes about his love for her, and an eagle feather accompanies each note. Sheriff Fowler is no more help to Kelsie than he is in finding Doris Samson's murderer, so Clay and Kelsie's father, along with some other men in the town, set a trap to try to catch the stalker, who is called the Watcher. During this botched attempt, the Watcher shoots and wounds Clay. Kelsie visits him in the hospital every day, falls in love with him, and marries him.

Readers learn about the Watcher's life through his interior monologue and stream-of-consciousness reflection on his past life. At a young age he was physically and sexually abused, and his abuser sliced off the head of the Watcher's beloved kitten. From that day forward, the Watcher killed his share of animals, drawing power and ecstasy from the act of killing. He soon graduated to humans: He killed Doris Samson, watching her die a slow death and reveling in the excitement and power he felt. The Watcher has plans for Kelsie McNeill.

Twenty years later, Kelsie and Clay's marriage is on shaky ground and starts to fall apart. Kelsie leaves Clay to start a new life in Denver, but she leaves behind their son, Taylor, with his father. Once in Denver, she is vulnerable to the ways and wiles of the Watcher, who has not left her alone since his early notes to her. One day after work, she opens the glove compartment of her car and a rattlesnake lunges at her. Inside the glove box are another love note and an eagle feather. In Kalispell, Taylor disappears, and a worried Kelsie and Clay get back together momentarily. When she returns to Denver after this night with Clay, the Watcher is waiting for her in her apartment and kidnaps her. Although bound in the trunk of his car, she manages to free her hands to use a cell phone to call Clay and leave a message for him before the phone loses its signal.

The Watcher whisks Kelsie and Taylor to a house that he has specially prepared for them. In his misguided love for Kelsie, the Watcher believes that she loves him and wants to be with him as much as he wants to be with her. Frantically putting all the clues together, Clay, with the help of his friend George Samson, frenetically searches for his wife and son. When he discovers the Watcher's hiding place, Clay rushes in to rescue his family and defeats the Watcher in a life-and-death struggle.

The novel's surprise ending reveals a small Montana town full of corrupt political and legal officials that provided an opportunity for the development of the Watcher's evil ways. Although good trumps evil in the end, Clay's spiritual goodness fails to be as interesting or as convincing as the Watcher's evil.

Christian Themes

One of the great themes of Christian literature is the monumental struggle between moral evil and moral good. The earthly conflict between good and evil stands as a symbol for the cataclysmic battle between metaphysical forces of evil and good; thus, God and the sons of light battle against Satan and the sons of darkness in catastrophic skirmish out of which the forces of God emerge triumphant. Dante, John Milton, Johann Wolfgang von Goethe, and other great poets and writers depicted this struggle in their epic works, and many other writers have addressed this theme—whether in an explicitly Christian context or not. Brouwer's novel captures the very real conflict that every person experiences in choosing good over evil.

Clay Garner is a good man repulsed by the evil in the world around him. He struggles with spirituality, asking questions about why God allows suffering in the world. Although he acts as a force for good in the novel in his actions toward Kelsie and Taylor, his good is more moral than spiritual. He is unconvincing as a force of God's goodness in the world. His name, Clay, indicates this in two ways. God is shaping him like clay in the struggle with evil, and his clay feet make him human in his failures.

The Watcher, much like Milton's Satan and Goethe's Mephistopheles, is powerfully attractive in his evil ways. He is utterly convincing as a soul consumed by evil and in his commitment to acting out his moral evil in the community. It is only in the last moments—and not entirely because Clay is a good man—that good triumphs over evil in the novel. The Watcher stands as a symbol for Satan, and Clay Garner stands as a symbol for the frailty of humankind and its need to be constantly in God's presence in order to overcome evil.

Sources for Further Study

Carrigan, Henry L., Jr. "Blood Ties." *Library Journal* 121, no. 14 (September 1, 1996): 163. In this positive book review, Carrigan compares Brouwer's novel to John Grisham's thrillers and points out Brouwer's brilliant storytelling skills.

Mort, John. "Blood Ties." *Booklist* 93, no. 1 (September 1, 1996): 65. In this generally positive book review, Mort points out that Brouwer effectively uses suspense to capture his readers and to produce an unusual Christian novel.

Schriefer, Kirk. "Mystery Novel Disappoints." *M.B. Herald* 36, no. 14 (July 18, 1997). In his mostly negative book review, Schriefer observes that *Blood Ties* lacks sufficient suspense and mystery to be an effective thriller.

Henry L. Carrigan, Jr.

THE BLOUDY TENENT OF PERSECUTION FOR
CAUSE OF CONSCIENCE

Author: Roger Williams (c. 1603-1683)
First published: 1644
*Edition used: The Bloudy Tenent of Persecution for Cause of Conscience: Discussed
in a Conference Between Truth and Peace, Who, in All Tender Affection, Present to
the High Court of Parliament (as the Result of Their Discource) These, (Among
Other Passages) of Highest Consideration,* edited by Richard Groves. Macon, Ga.:
Mercer University Press, 2001
Genre: Nonfiction
Subgenres: Didactic treatise; spiritual treatise; theology
Core issues: Church; conscience; faith; obedience and disobedience; persecution;
predestination; Puritans and Puritanism

*Christians had traditionally believed that because they knew the truth and that this
truth was universal, then those who publicly maintained differently should be punished,
in extreme cases even by death. Williams's conviction that individuals should be
granted freedom of conscience in their religious beliefs thereby set him in opposition to
the Church of England, and he argued his position intensely, especially in a long exchange with John Cotton, a leading clergyman of the Massachusetts Bay Colony.*

Overview

Roger Williams graduated from Cambridge University in 1627, took holy orders in
the Church of England, and arrived in the Massachusetts Bay Colony in 1631. Regarded as a young man of great promise, he was quickly offered a ministerial post in
the church in Boston. When he declined the appointment, explaining that he could not
minister to a congregation that followed the Church of England, he identified himself
as a separatist. At the same time, he asserted his conviction that the civil authorities
had no right to punish colonists who held dissenting religious beliefs.

Williams next stopped briefly in Salem before moving on to Plymouth, but his
charge that the colonies were stealing land from the Indians contributed to the controversy that followed him. Meanwhile, in 1634 the General Court of Massachusetts
responded to worry about the colony's enemies in England by requiring an oath of
loyalty, a commitment that Williams refused to abide by, and when he learned in January, 1636, that he was about to be shipped back to England, he hurried south to
Narragansett Bay in what was to become Rhode Island. Concerned about the mother
country's threats to his new settlement in Rhode Island, in 1643 Williams returned to
England right in the middle of its civil war.

Among the contending religions in England, the Presbyterians were strongest,
while their main rivals were another Calvinist group, the Independents, or Congrega-

tionalists, who rejected the hierarchy of Presbyterian Church governance. The publication in 1644 of *An Apologeticall Narration* was intended by its Independent authors to present their faith as a middle way, but it was attacked by virtually all parties. Alert to these doctrinal issues, Williams seized the opportunity to offer the principles of his Rhode Island settlement as the answer to England's theological strife, and in 1644 he laid out his beliefs in *The Bloudy Tenent of Persecution for Cause of Conscience*. This "messy book," as Williams's biographer Edwin S. Gaustad calls it, argued the convictions that had grown in Williams's mind during his years in the New World.

Two interrelated issues dominate Williams's argument. A central point was his insistence on the total separation of church and state, denying secular officials any role in spiritual matters; from this position derives the "bloudy tenent." The Massachusetts Bay rulers had said they were not banishing Williams for his religious convictions but for inciting civil unrest. Given the establishment of a state church in Massachusetts, however, it mattered little whether he was hounded for his religious beliefs or oppressed by civil authorities for supposedly stirring up trouble among the citizens. The church had its own members, the elect, to whom the state had civic responsibilities but, in Williams's mind, no warrant to interfere with their spiritual lives.

The Bloudy Tenent of Persecution for Cause of Conscience was published in London in July and publicly burned in August, but it had a wide readership, and as Irwin H. Polishook notes, it "became one of the most noted books of the English Revolution." Although the Presbyterians liked elements of the book that they saw as critical of the Independents, they came out strongly against any freedom of conscience. In this way Williams inserted his New World experience into the controversies of the English Civil War, but the strongest response came from John Cotton in Massachusetts, an old opponent of church-state separation. In *The Bloudy Tenent, Washed, and Made White in the Bloud of the Lambe* (1647), Cotton replied that humankind's only religious freedom was the freedom to obey God's will. The debate went on tediously in Williams's *The Bloudy Tenent Yet More Bloudy: By Mr. Cotton's Endeavor to Wash It White in the Bloud of the Lambe* (1652). By the time Williams left for America again, the issues were clearly outlined.

Christian Themes

Williams stuffed *The Bloudy Tenent of Persecution for Cause of Conscience* full of any materials he found relevant to his cause. It opens with three prefaces and three chapters from a 1620 work purportedly from a former inmate of Newgate prison pleading against persecution for cause of conscience. A broad response from John Cotton follows, and the bulk of the first part of this book of about 265 pages comes in "A Reply to the Aforesaid Answer of Mr. Cotton," a reply couched in the form of a dialogue between Truth and Peace.

In various formulations, accompanied by references to the Scriptures and to church fathers such as Tertullian, Cotton had pounded away at one theme: that a man may be granted liberty of conscience if he fears God because it is certain that he will repent of his errors once he learns the truth, but there remains the question of should a "heretic, after once or twice admonition . . . be tolerated . . . without such punishment as may preserve others from dangerous and damnable infection." Cotton's answer, of course, is no. Against Cotton's talk of punishment, Williams pleads for toleration, citing "the cry of the whole earth, made drunk with the blood of its inhabitants, slaughtering each other in their blinded zeal for conscience, for religion, against the Catholics, against the Lutherans, etc." As for Cotton's "admonitions," Williams replies that "the worship which a state professes may be contradicted and preached against, and yet no breach of civil peace."

Williams had referred to Matthew 13:30, 38, in which Christ had commanded that the tares be allowed to grow together with the wheat. To this, Cotton had responded that the tares were "partly hypocrites, like unto the godly, but indeed carnal," and that the good and the bad are so intertwined that the persons in whom the tares grow "cannot be rooted out but good wheat will be rooted out with them." However, Williams disagrees, saying that no evidence suggests that tares represent persons. This exchange of exegeses of the wheat and the tares—and of other scriptural passages—continued repetitiously in *The Bloudy Tenent Yet More Bloudy*.

A Calvinist himself, Williams slyly turned Cotton's own Calvinist tenets against him. Because one never knows whom God has chosen for his elect, one cannot be sure that a persecuted sinner does not enjoy God's grace. Furthermore, the doctrine of predestination disproves the logic of forcing sinners to convert when they have no free will to exercise on their spiritual fate. Williams asked what the point was anyway, as after all, "The souls of all men are either naturally dead in sin or live in Christ." Indifference to these points of theology incurs a "three-fold guilt" on the part of those civil authorities who meddle forcefully with an individual's faith, Williams says.

The Bloudy Tenent of Persecution for Cause of Conscience is a long, repetitious work, organized according to a private vision inscrutable to most readers, replete with biblical references, and exhausting to read. Its greatness lies not only in its arguments but also in the fervor of its composition by a man whose courage was exemplary. Polishook concludes that Williams's ideas today "appear unmistakably fitting and correct, because the accumulation of years has made them familiar and acceptable," whereas "Cotton's monument was the untold influence of his thought on the New England way of life."

Sources for Further Study

Coyle, Wallace. *Roger Williams: A Reference Guide.* Boston: G. K. Hall, 1977. An indispensable guide for Williams researchers.

Gaustad, Edwin S. *Liberty of Conscience: Roger Williams in America.* Valley Forge, Pa.: Judson Press, 1999. A biography that elucidates the theological issues clearly and includes a valuable note on sources.

Miller, Perry. *Orthodoxy in Massachusetts, 1630-1650.* Cambridge, Mass.: Harvard University Press, 1933. A standard overview of the period and its controversies.

Morgan, Edmund S. *Roger Williams: The Church and the State.* New York: Harcourt, Brace & World, 1967. An illuminating account of Williams as a separatist.

Polishook, Irwin H. *Roger Williams, John Cotton, and Religious Freedom. A Controversy in New and Old England.* Englewood Cliffs, N.J.: Prentice-Hall, 1967. Contains a thirty-five-page introduction that is excellent on the background of the dispute in Puritan England and includes selected discussions from the time not only by Williams and Cotton but also by other clerics.

Frank Day

BLUE LIKE JAZZ
Nonreligious Thoughts on Christian Spirituality

Author: Donald Miller (1971-   )
First published: Nashville, Tenn.: T. Nelson, 2003
Genre: Nonfiction
Subgenres: Autobiography; handbook for living; spiritual treatise
Core issues: Connectedness; discipleship; forgiveness; grace; hope; love; redemption

Many postmodern Christians—who practice their religion indifferently, who confine their religion to traditional institutions that are restricting and unfulfilling, who feel that God has become distant and impersonal, and who yearn for a compelling emotional relationship with Christ and the love that the New Testament promises—are particularly challenged to explore the spiritual, rather than the doctrinal, expression of Christianity by seeking the forgiveness of an embracing God and being enveloped by his acceptance and love. This acceptance strikes the willing soul with the impact of free-flowing jazz music.

Overview

A nationally known evangelical minister, Donald Miller has tirelessly promoted what he terms postmodern Christian spirituality specifically directed to a generation of disaffected and disinterested Christians fostered by an institutional expression of a religion that, at its beginning, was intended to be a compelling emotional experience. Miller, positioning himself as a kind of contemporary Christian Everyman, recounts his own spiritual journey in a series of essays that, although not strictly linear, track with evident care his movement toward embracing a spirituality that makes the Christian Gospel message of love and the presence of Jesus immediate and relevant.

Miller employs an archmetaphor: the rich emotional impact of jazz, which defies explanation and compels the deepest sort of intimacy. He argues that Christian redemption on earth begins not with cheerless fidelity to church attendance, rigorous scriptural study (Miller himself acknowledges he has read only parts of the Bible), or the self-loathing and guilt that attend an unexamined assumption of a punishing God who acts largely as a bookkeeper for the soul. Rather, redemption begins with the emotional conviction that each person is a sinner, that each person is part of the fallen world commandeered by Satan as recorded in Genesis, and that only by approaching God with the earnest intention to seek forgiveness for their sinful nature and for their indifferent reception of the Christian message can people finally open themselves to the intuitive conviction that Jesus is love, that Jesus intended his creatures to love themselves and each other, and that salvation is a heartfelt joy. Thus, love of Jesus is both a decision and a revelation. Miller's argument is presented in an invitatory second person: You must apologize to God before you experience the happiness ransomed on Calvary.

The message is straightforward evangelical Christianity (Miller was raised a fundamentalist Baptist). There is only a passing acknowledgment of the triune God (his focus is principally on the redemptive love of Jesus) and of the Old Testament (his focus is principally on the evangelists and the wisdom of Jesus). The presentation, however, distinguishes Miller's traditional argument. Forsaking the homiletic voice of the preacher and the scholarly voice of a theologian, Miller tells his own story, his own journey toward the epiphanic conviction of Jesus' love, which begins with a childhood without a father (he suggests his lifelong pilgrimage is in part a search for a comforting Father) and finds its landmark moments when Miller ends up, after a cross-country odyssey, in Oregon within a small, resilient, and unorthodox Christian community named Imago Dei (or Image of God) that ministers around the campus of Reed College, a small liberal arts campus known nationally for its liberal thought and its irreverent promotion of nontraditional expressions of intellectual freedom.

There amid a raucous campus environment that indulges the excesses of the fleshly life (alcohol, promiscuity, drugs, atheism), Miller begins to explore his own commitment to Christianity. His anecdotal essays—each of which centers on a Christian principle (grace, love, redemption) and ordinary experiences that unexpectedly reveal critical aspects of his ongoing quest to tap the emotional center of Christianity—are rendered in an approachable, encouraging voice rather than one that insists on its lessons. Miller comes across as Don, a fallible Christian (he smokes dope, he drinks, he doubts, he watches too much television, he is socially awkward) who comes to determine that contemporary Christianity faces two problems: fallen humanity's stubborn egotism and contemporary Christianity's institutional expression, which encourages bigotry, political activism, and paranoia by targeting specific groups (often gays and liberals) for directed hate. Like Christian allegorists since John Bunyan, Miller is accompanied on his quest by stock characters—Andrew the Protester, Tony the Beat Poet, Mark the Cussing Pastor, Penny the Doubter—to illustrate the frustrations and challenges of the Christian journey.

Happiness, Miller contends, begins with accepting others unconditionally, returning to Jesus the forgiving God, and accepting the love God intends his creatures to enjoy. To accept, rather than understand, Jesus, and to believe in, rather than know, God are the foundation of what Miller sees as Christian spirituality. Miller pictures Jesus as a friend who joins us at a campfire, listens patiently, and then offers love as the sole avenue to authentic freedom. Miller argues that Christianity was never intended to encourage monastic isolation but demands the energy of witnessing and the commitment to community.

Miller's journey toward Christian conviction—that ultimate affirmation of complete dependency on Jesus and the absolute depravity of the individual person who has been redeemed by the awful sacrifice at Calvary—is rendered contemporary and immediate by Miller's postmodern, cool style: The writing is conversational and hip, the voice self-deprecating and ironic, the narrative multigeneric (part memoir, part sermon-essay, part parable, part Christian handbook, and even part comic book), and the argument rich with allusions to pop culture (including *The Simpsons*, Starbucks, *South Park*, Nintendo, infomercials, and rap). Regardless of such referents, Miller's message ultimately draws its resonance from its rediscovery of the Christian message, all but lost in those contemporary churches where congregations gather without emotion and feel estranged from God. That message is: Respond to the joyful dependency that sustains human beings as creations of a God who has designed a universe to reflect his unfathomable love. Not surprisingly, Miller finds great appeal in the counterculture avant-garde leftovers of the 1960's and the hippie lifestyle of love and acceptance. He rejects only the flower children's misdirected exploration of controlled substances and the chic, trendy New Age spiritualism that developed out of their youthful idealism.

Christian Themes

Although Miller's book was dismissed as shallow and misleading by some church leaders, it has found an enthusiastic audience. His message affirms conservative evangelical Christianity's faith in the Gospel message of redemptive love; at the same time, his unconventional voice and his unrelenting criticism of institutional Christianity have led to a cultlike embrace, specifically among the disaffected Christians of Generation X, who have responded not only to the free-spirited college environment in which Miller's spiritual journey unfolds but also to his comforting assurance that religious conviction can have the same emotional impact as music.

What concerns Miller ultimately, however, is how conviction must contend inevitably with doubt. Inspired by a PBS documentary on mother penguins—which abandon their newly laid eggs in the nest for a month and still manage, by some inexplicable radar, to return to the nest in time for the eggs to hatch—Miller argues that Jesus returns unfailingly even to the souls most grievously cut by doubt. Humanity, thus, can be fixed only one soul at a time. Resisting the rich pull of God's love generates much of the world's misery and mayhem.

Although the argument can seem naïve, the core of Miller's conviction rests on his argument that the heart craves awe, that worship was intended to be centrally a mystical experience, and that centuries of Christian theology, obscure doctrinal disputes, and fierce territoriality have distracted the Christian Gospel. Miller moves contemporary Christianity beyond judgments, beyond intolerance, beyond distrust, and beyond the walls of churches to offer the unconditional love of God as a way to free the soul from the burden of the self. Miller liberates Christianity from function-specific buildings and documents how contemporary Christians in the most mundane circumstances—shopping at the Safeway, watching *South Park* with a friend, camping on the floor of the Grand Canyon—can experience the tectonic immediacy (and consequent serenity) of Christian spirituality, which offers nothing less than a tangible interaction with a loving God. The collection closes with an offer extended to the reader to ask Jesus for forgiveness and to fall in love with Jesus.

Sources for Further Study

Lamott, Annie. *Traveling Mercies: Some Thoughts on Faith*. New York: Anchor Books, 2000. A bittersweet collection of essays that are each a reflection on pivotal, if everyday moments of the author's journey toward enlightenment. Miller has often cited this as his model for *Blue Like Jazz*.

Miller, Donald. http://www.donaldmillerwords.com. Miller's Web site, regularly updated with an ongoing journal of his Christian experience. Includes biography, book reviews, contact numbers, and a helpful chapter-by-chapter study guide to *Blue Like Jazz*.

_____. *Through Painted Deserts: Light, God, and Beauty on the Open Road.* 2000. Rev. ed. Nashville, Tenn.: Nelson, 2005. Miller's first work, updated after the success of *Blue Like Jazz*. In the American road trip genre, influenced by John Steinbeck and Ernest Hemingway, it tells of the trip taken by Miller and a friend from Texas to Oregon. An indispensable prequel to the essays in *Blue Like Jazz*.

Joseph Dewey

BOOK OF COMMON PRAYER

Editor: Thomas Cranmer (1489-1556)
First published: 1549
Edition used: The Book of Common Prayer and Administration of the Sacraments and Other Rites and Ceremonies of the Church, According to the Use of the Church of England. Oxford, England: Oxford University Press, 1936
Genre: Nonfiction
Subgenre: Prayer book
Core issues: Baptism; Eucharist; prayer; Protestants and Protestantism

The Book of Common Prayer prescribes rules and services for public worship in the Church of England and serves as a liturgical model for the member churches of the Anglican communion. It also gives a catechism and sets forth Articles of Religion, and so is normative for Anglican doctrine. Many Christians other than Anglicans have drawn from its wealth. Second only to the Bible itself, it has had an incalculable impact on the language of theology, worship, and devotion in English-speaking lands around the world.

Overview

The Book of Common Prayer is the greatest liturgical treasure of the English language. Produced by several generations of ecclesiastical leaders for more than a century after the English Reformation and the political severance of the Church of England from papal control, it establishes a style of churchmanship midway between Western Catholicism and Protestantism: reformed in doctrine, yet episcopal in polity and formal in worship, hence at once Evangelical and Catholic. In Elizabethan cadences of the same era as the King James Bible (1611), it teaches worshipers how to approach God directly, boldly, and reverently.

Thomas Cranmer was the archbishop of Canterbury when King Henry VIII in 1533 claimed that he, rather than the pope, was head of the English national church. Under Edward IV (1547-1553), Cranmer achieved his ambition to provide the English people with a liturgy in the vernacular, in place of the Latin services that had been in use hitherto. The first prayer book of 1549—compiled, edited, and translated by Cranmer and others from ancient sources (with a few prayers composed fresh) and enforced by a parliamentary act of uniformity—pleased neither those conservatives who hankered for Rome nor the Puritans, who favored more ambitious reforms. Cranmer oversaw a major revision in 1552. Despite continuing power struggles between parties, during the rule of Charles II (1660-1685), the edition of 1662 appeared, and it stood for three centuries.

The 1662 prayer book became the basis for adaptations in other provinces of the Anglican communion: in Scotland (1764), America (1789), Ireland (1877), South Africa (1954), India (1960), and Canada (1962). More recent updates—in Australia

(1978), America (1979), Ireland and Wales (both 1984), Canada (1985), and South Africa and New Zealand (both 1989)—have often diverged more freely, while preserving the spirit of the original. Officially the Book of Common Prayer remains the standard for public worship in the Church of England, though in practice it is now superseded in many parishes by alternative liturgies in current idiom. The right to print the text belongs solely to the Queen's Printer, together with the university presses at Oxford and Cambridge.

The unstated framework for all the service material in the Book of Common Prayer is the church year, a calendar of seasons and high days that gradually took shape over the course of centuries, based on the analogy of the Jewish festival cycle. Three complexes of observances flowed together to round it out: one centered on Holy Week and Easter (associated with the Jewish Passover), prepared for by Lent and flowing into Ascension and Pentecost; one centered on the Feast of the Nativity of Christ (Christmas), preceded by Advent and followed by Epiphany; and one that distributed commemorations of the lives of saints throughout the year. Thus the calendar affords adherents an annual opportunity to traverse the main events of the Gospel: the long period of prophetic expectation (Advent); the coming of God's Son in the person of Jesus (Christmas); his manifestation to the nations in infancy, at baptism, and through public ministry (Epiphany); his self-denial and march into danger (Lent); his betrayal, crucifixion, and burial (Holy Week); his rising from the dead (Easter); his exaltation to heaven as Messiah and Lord (Ascension); and his pouring out the end-time gift of the Holy Spirit (Pentecost). Anglicans, like Lutherans, largely retained this inherited structure. In the Book of Common Prayer, Scripture readings and short prayers appointed for the Sundays of the year reflect themes of the changing seasons.

Chief among the services is the Order of the Ministration of the Holy Communion, as the set readings and collects are meant to be integrated into precisely this service week by week. In broad outline the Communion service follows the order of the Western Mass: After a recollection of God's commandments, driving congregants to plead for mercy, there follow readings from an Epistle and a Gospel (the people standing), a recitation of the Nicene Creed, a sermon, and a pastoral prayer embracing people of all degrees and conditions; then the preparation of the table, the invitation to partake of Christ's body and blood, and closing prayers. Yet specialists in liturgy, on comparing the Book of Common Prayer communion with the missal, note numerous shifts both of phrase and in the ordering of the elements, intended to bring the service into conformity with the doctrines of the Reformation. For example, the communion is described as "a perpetual memory" of the "full, perfect, and sufficient sacrifice, oblation, and satisfaction, for the sins of the whole world" offered "once" at Calvary, in contrast to the Roman Catholic belief that the Eucharist is a representation of Christ as victim to the Father. Instead of holding forth objectively transubstantiated bread and wine, the Book of Common Prayer bids participants, "feed on him in thy heart by faith with thanksgiving." Besides the weekly Eucharist, the Book of Common Prayer provides for daily morning and evening prayer, that is, services of public worship involving the ministry of the Word without sacrament, and intercessions.

Corresponding nearly to the seven sacraments of Catholicism, the Book of Common Prayer lays down forms for six ceremonies: baptism, confirmation, the Holy Communion (as described above), matrimony, the visitation of the sick, and the consecration of bishops, priests, and deacons—Penance being omitted—though it defines only two of these, Baptism and Holy Communion, as "sacraments of the Gospel."

The Articles of Religion, or Thirty-nine Articles as they are popularly known, bear the stamp of the continental Protestant Reformation, with a few adjustments to suit a middle-of-the-road English temperament. In common with Christian antiquity, they uphold the doctrines of the Trinity, of perfect godhead and manhood united in Christ, of his atoning death and bodily resurrection (articles 1-5). In distinction from medieval Catholicism, they affirm the sufficiency of the Scriptures for salvation (article 6), an understanding of justification as sinners' being accounted righteous before God solely for the sake of Christ's merits, which they appropriate by faith (article 11), and the right of the king of England to function as the chief ecclesiastical power, free from foreign jurisdiction (article 37); also they maintain that councils have erred (articles 19, 21), they subordinate the authority of the church to that of the scriptures (article 20), call the doctrine of purgatory "a fond thing vainly invented" (article 22), deny that sacrifices of masses can satisfy for sins of the deceased (article 31), and so on in the same vein. However, they differ from Reformed Christianity in a few particulars: They allow for the apocryphal books of the Old Testament to be read "for example of life and instruction of manners," albeit not "to establish any doctrine" (article 6); the robust article on predestination omits mention of the reprobation of the nonelect (article 17); and they uphold the power of the church to establish traditions and ceremonies "which be not repugnant to the Word of God . . . only by man's authority" (article 34).

Many felicitous turns of phrase in the Book of Common Prayer have found their way into common parlance: "We have left undone those things which we ought to have done; And we have done those things which we ought not to have done" (Morning Prayer, general Confession); "to have and to hold from this day forward, for better for worse, for richer for poorer, in sickness and in health, to love and to cherish, till death do us part" (Solemnization of Matrimony, giving of their troth); and "ashes to ashes, dust to dust" (Burial of the Dead, at graveside, casting of earth).

Christian Themes

Unlike many works of literature, the Book of Common Prayer comes into its own not when perused by an individual in silence, but when performed orally over and over by an assembly meeting regularly for worship, hence the words "common prayer" in its title. As a manual meant for such a setting, it brings to expression virtually all the great themes of the Christian religion, organized and packaged for public rehearsal. The deeds of God in history, from creation to the consummation, pass in review on an annual basis in the readings of the lectionary and the homilies based on them, and are compressed into each recitation of the Apostles' or the Nicene Creed. At every weekly Eucharist there is a special focus on proclaiming, by word and sacrament, the death of Jesus for the sins of the world, his resurrection on the third day, his present reign, and his awaited return as judge and savior, together with an appeal to put personal faith in him for salvation.

Also implied by the words "common prayer" in the title is the network of Anglican churches at the levels of parish, diocese, and national province, bound together by the collegiality of their bishops. Churches for centuries tapped into essentially the same resource, this book of prayers, each time they gathered to render divine service. Although Anglicans in the twenty-first century tolerate a lesser measure of uniformity from place to place than they did in the past, there remains a family resemblance among the various national and local liturgies, which enables a traveler to feel oriented even in a parish away from home.

From another perspective, the Book of Common Prayer surrounds an individual with the truths and graces of the Gospel at every stage of life, from birth (Baptism), through adolescence (Confirmation), marriage (Matrimony) and childbearing (Thanksgiving of Women after Child-birth), to death (Burial of the Dead).

Sources for Further Study

Clarke, W. K. Lowther, and Charles Harris, eds. *Liturgy and Worship: A Companion to the Prayer Books of the Anglican Communion.* New York: Macmillan, 1932. Topical essays by experts on all facets of the Book of Common Prayer. Older but very thorough.

The Common Worship Lectionary. New York: Oxford University Press, 2006. This annual work in 2001 replaced the *Alternative Service Book 1980*, which was valid until 2000 in England, as the official standard for contemporary liturgies in the tradition of the Book of Common Prayer.

Hatchett, Marion J. *Commentary on the American Prayer Book.* New York: Seabury, 1980. A companion to the former without parallel, tracing the sources of elements old and new, and explaining the reasons for changes. Full bibliographies.

Packer, J. I. "For Truth, Unity, and Hope: Revaluing the Book of Common Prayer." *Churchman* 114 (2000): 103-113. A sermon commending the evangelical qualities of the Book of Common Prayer to a congregation of Canadian Anglicans.

Procter, Francis. *A New History.* London: Macmillan, 1901. One of three or four classic accounts of the origins and vicissitudes of the successive versions of the Book of Common Prayer.

Paul A. Rainbow

BOOK OF DIVINE WORKS

Author: Hildegard von Bingen (1098-1179)
First published: De operatione Dei, 1163-1173 (English translation, 1987)
Edition used: Hildegard of Bingen's Book of Divine Works, with Letters and Songs,
    edited and introduced by Matthew Fox. Santa Fe, N.Mex.: Bear, 1987
Genre: Nonfiction
Subgenres: Meditation and contemplation; mysticism; theology
Core issues: Catholics and Catholicism; clerical life; Creation; justice; mysticism;
    nature

In the year 1163, Abbess Hildegard von Bingen of Rupertsberg, Germany, began re-
cording visions that she had experienced; during the next decade she constructed her
Book of Divine Works *in Latin, describing and interpreting her ten visions. The text*
was illuminated, around 1200, with paintings depicting Hildegard's visions. Draw-
ings of these are printed in the Fox edition; the color images are also available in sev-
eral places online. Hildegard was recognized by contemporaries as a wise and holy
woman; today she is revered as a Christian mystic, whose work encourages personal
holiness and harmonious interplay between humans and the natural world.

Overview

In "The World of Humanity," part 1 of *Book of Divine Works*, Hildegard von
Bingen affirms that her visions are from God, who has instructed her to write them for
the benefit of others. This section includes four visions. Part 2, "The Kingdom of the
Hereafter," contains the fifth vision, and part 3, "The History of Salvation," concludes
with five visions.

In the first vision, Hildegard describes a complex image of a winged human being.
Her descriptions are very clear, and the illustrations help explicate the descriptions.
She records the accompanying voice, which identifies the figure as love, co-eternal
with the Trinity. This vision emphasizes the importance of the Catholic faith and of
love for God and for one's neighbor. She briefly describes God's unfolding plan of
salvation for humans through Adam's fall and Abraham's obedience. Also, Hildegard
contrasts Eve's disobedience with the Virgin Mary's obedience, which will result in
the salvation of body and soul.

The second vision begins with a medieval focus on the cosmos and the four elements that make up all things: fire, air, water, and earth. Hildegard explains that God,
in Creation, has caused these alien elements to cooperate with one another to make
humans and all the other creatures. An important image here is that of balance; humans must aim for constancy by experiencing repentance, trust, and faith to accomplish God's will. In addition, Hildegard identifies six periods in world history in
which love guides the elements and humans to live in balance and justice.

In the third vision Hildegard discusses the ways in which the natural world affects human beings, and following the medieval model, she describes the circulation of humors through the body and the effects these have on well-being—both physical and spiritual. She discusses the seven gifts of the Holy Spirit, which guide one toward holiness. Christians must learn to cooperate with the Holy Spirit in good deeds and prayer so that God will bless them. By strongly renouncing the sins of the flesh, Christians can move past depression and other ills of the body to find joy and hope.

The human being as microcosm in harmony with the macrocosm of Creation is delineated in the fourth vision. The four elements, as well as the planets, are related to the physical components of the body. In addition, Hildegard describes the soul as having three powers—"understanding," "insight," and "execution"—by which it can accomplish good works. Being composed of both body and soul, humans live in disharmony because of sin; to gain salvation, the soul must, through spiritual obedience, call the body to discipline and repentance. In this vision, Hildegard also includes an exegesis of John 1:1-14.

In the fifth vision, Hildegard recognizes that the five senses are influenced by the knowledge of both good and evil. She describes a globe divided according to the senses and discusses each in turn. Also included is exegesis of Revelation 6:2-8 and 12:13-14, as well as a brief history of the fall of Satan and the fall of humanity.

The sixth vision describes the heavenly city and the angelic choirs, as well as the fall of the devil and his angels. The human race was created to replace the fallen angels—to make up the perfect number of God's creation.

The seventh vision details the history of three eras on earth: before the Flood, after the Flood when humans were under God's Law, and after the coming of Christ, when the new covenant is instituted—a covenant of grace. Hildegard recognizes three "signs" before Christ's advent: animal sacrifice, circumcision, and the Mosaic law. These all prepared the way for redemption.

In the eighth vision, Hildegard identifies humans as rational beings, created and brought to truth by wisdom through love. The prophets and evangelists were inspired by wisdom so that humans could be brought by love to redemption, and humans should live in peace and harmony.

In the ninth vision, one complex character indicates God himself; Hildegard references his creative work, his love expressed in the Old and New Testaments, and his coming judgment of rebellious humans. All elements of the cosmos work together to accomplish God's work.

The tenth vision depicts Old Testament symbols of the Roman Catholic Church: the obedience of Noah and Abraham, as well as the law given to Moses. However, in Christ the law and obedience are combined, resulting in justice and peace. The Church is served by believers in many different circumstances—both religious and lay, both celibate and married. In this vision, Hildegard relates the history of several of the apostles, showing how their lives were examples of the work of the Holy Spirit in people of different temperaments. She exhorts religious and lay persons to work in harmony because they both work for Christ to bring those outside the Church, regardless of ethnic group, to salvation. Hildegard warns that divisions among Christians will precede the coming of the Antichrist and the final judgment, but those who remain faithful will be blessed by God.

Also included in this edition are forty-one letters documenting Hildegard's interaction with and advice to several secular and religious leaders as well as individual religious persons. Finally, Fox has included twelve songs with notation and original Latin lyrics as well as modern English translations.

Christian Themes

Hildegard envisions the unfolding of God's plan throughout history. She describes the divine work of Creation, in which God brings the four elements into harmony and obedience to create the cosmos. Humans are a special creation, made in the image of God, separated from the rest of creation by reason. However, human beings have fallen and now must choose between obedience to God or punishment with the devil. Right faith, in the redemptive sacrifice of Christ, leads to freedom, harmony, and joy.

While Hildegard often speaks of the soul being weighed down or led astray by the body, she does not completely follow a neo-Platonic philosophy; she is emphatic that both body and soul will experience salvation and a glorious eternal life if humans, through virtue and holiness, are obedient to God.

She teaches that right faith leads to right living, which honors and creates harmony in the physical earth. All creation is important and affected by human behavior; we are responsible to know, love, and care for the earth and its creatures. If our sinful acts and attitudes cause disharmony in the earth, we will suffer as a result.

Humans must learn to live in moderation, which Hildegard recommends as the way to live healthy, productive lives in harmony with God, the earth, and other people. While she values a disciplined life, she asks Christians not to lead lives of too rigorous asceticism, which can lead to deteriorated health and inability to do God's work.

Hildegard recognizes that God's grace allows humans to desire and to do good, and she encourages good works as grateful expressions of love and obedience to God. She is especially concerned with justice, recommending attitudes and actions that lead to justice in the state and Church, as well as in individual matters. Her emphasis on justice works in conjunction with her concept of cosmic harmony. Even small instances of injustice can lead to disharmony. In her understanding of the connectedness of all creation, any lack of harmony affects the whole and distracts from our understanding of and praise to God.

To understand Hildegard's vision is to recognize the solidarity Christians must feel with each other, the earth, and the cosmos as a whole as they mature in their faith and love for their Creator Redeemer and his divine works.

Sources for Further Study

Baird, Joseph L., and Radd K. Ehrman, trans. *The Letters of Hildegard of Bingen*. 3
    vols. New York: Oxford University Press, 1994-2004. Letters ranging from advice
    and encouragement to rebuke, to and from Hildegard to church leaders, including
    popes, as well as monks and nuns.

Fox, Matthew. *Illuminations of Hildegard of Bingen*. 1985. Reprint. Rochester, Vt.: Bear, 2002. Provides insight into Hildegard's spiritual message. Includes color plates of twenty-one visions from Hildegard's *Scivias* (1141-1151; English translation, 1986) and three from *Book of Divine Works*.

King-Lenzmeier, Anne H. *Hildegard of Bingen: An Integrated Vision*. Collegeville, Minn.: Liturgical Press, 2001. Explores Hildegard's mysticism, spirituality, and theology. Includes excerpts from her writings and discusses her music and the morality play, *Ordu Virtutum*.

Pernoud, Regine. *Hildegard of Bingen: Inspired Conscience of the Twelfth Century*. Translated by Paul Duggan. New York: Marlowe, 1998. A thorough biography that examines Hildegard in the political and religious context of her age.

Patricia Ralston

THE BOOK OF GOD
The Bible as a Novel

Author: Walter Wangerin, Jr. (1944-   )
First published: Grand Rapids, Mich.: Zondervan, 1996
Genre: Novel
Subgenres: Biblical fiction; epic; saga
Core issues: God; Gospels; Jesus Christ; scriptures

In his fictionalized reshaping of the story of the Bible, Wangerin sweeps from the primitive shepherd Abram to the central event of Christianity: the life, death, and resurrection of Jesus. Biblical events and people come alive in vivid and earthy portrayals as Wangerin adds his imagination to his faith. He spans millennia with this sweeping account, covering Old Testament ancestry, the covenant between God and the Israelites, wars, kings, prophets, and the Exile, and crowns them all in the final section, "The Messiah."

> *Principal characters*
> *Abram/Abraham*, first of the ancestors to receive God's covenant
> *Moses*, leader who takes the enslaved people of God home to Canaan
> *David*, king of Israel who exhibits excellence and human failings
> *Zechariah*, father of John the Baptizer
> *Jesus*, God's son, the fulfillment of the covenant and the yearning
> *Mary Magdalene*, a disciple of Jesus who is healed by him
> *Simon Peter*, a brusque and loyal disciple of Jesus

Overview

While remaining faithful to the contours of the Bible, Walter Wangerin combines faith and imagination in a selective retelling of the major biblical stories. He begins with the story of Abraham, showing him worrying about his nephew Lot's involvement with Sodom, trying to sidestep Sarah's complaints against Hagar, and willingly obeying God's command to sacrifice his son Isaac.

After exploring the human side of Isaac's love for Rebekah and their family life as well as several stories involving Joseph, Wangerin moves from these ancestral figures to Moses, who ultimately receives God's covenant with Israel. As Wangerin tells the story of Moses leading the Israelites out of Egypt, he embellishes the account with a fictional backstory about Achan, who is born during the crossing of the Red Sea. Achan eats manna in the wilderness and learns that his father, Carmi, dreams of having his own land in Canaan. When the twelve spies return from reconnoitering the homeland, Achan hears his father crying angrily that God has led them to a dead end rather than a homeland. This fictionalized episode is designed to put a human face on the many bitter complaints and the faithlessness generalized in the Bible. Achan first appears in the Bible in Joshua, chapter 7, as a forty-year-old culprit who is condemned to death for looting after the Battle of Jericho and thereby causing the Israelites to lose a subsequent battle.

After the Israelites fight off the other tribes and settle in Canaan, they ask the prophet Samuel to anoint a king to rule in their land. Wangerin depicts the nation's growing sophistication by describing how the nation evolved from using primitive bronze weapons to more powerful iron arms during the reign of the first king, Saul. Next, Wangerin examines all the facets of King David: shepherd, musician, warrior, rebel, friend to Jonathan, king, father, adulterer, and frail old man. The author ends his description of the United Kingdom period with an account of Solomon, described as an archetypal wise man ultimately besotted with Sheba's beautiful Egyptian princess.

The prophets of God continue to warn, teach, bless, and threaten the Israelites. Elijah, Elisha, Amos, and Obadiah all differ in their attempts to remind the people of their covenant with God. Assyria ultimately crushes the Northern Kingdom of Israel, amazing the Israelites with the use of horses in battle. Later, Isaiah, a young nobleman, promises Judah's King Hezekiah: "Unto us a child" will come; a "son" will come to redeem the people. Jeremiah follows, but his prophecies are ignored, and the Southern Kingdom of Judah goes into exile for seventy years.

Wangerin then outlines the plight of the exiled Jews and their yearning to return to their homeland. Finally, Nehemiah and Ezra are allowed to return to rebuild Jerusalem. God's word is once again taught in the temple, and Ezra reads to the faithless Jews the stories of Creation, the Fall into sin, Cain and Abel, and Noah. Wangerin inserts these early stories of the Bible here, as he closes his retelling of the Old Testament.

"The Messiah," Wangerin's final chapter, opens with a fictionalized backstory for Zechariah, the father of John the Baptizer. Zechariah, a nail smith, makes spikes to sell to Herod, who uses them to crucify criminals in the Roman manner. After Zechariah delivers spikes to Herod's palace, he serves in the temple. He is visited by the angel Gabriel as a "spilling of brilliance," and the angel tells him that he will father a son. In the meantime, in Nazareth, after losing his first wife, Joseph courts Mary. Mary's father, Joachim, settles on house repairs as an appropriate dowry, and he approves of Joseph's ancestry, traced back to David and to Abraham.

Wangerin, unlike many writers, sets the Annunciation outdoors on the crown of a hill. He shows Mary's mix of girlish delight, fear, and confusion as she is told she will bear the Son of the most high God. Because she is worried about how Joseph will feel, she suddenly leaves and stays three months with her cousin Elizabeth. When Mary returns to Nazareth, Joseph, having been enlightened in a dream, tells her, "I know who is sleeping in you and I love him too."

Jesus' birth is recounted in visceral detail, but the only description of his childhood is a brief account of his precocity in the temple at age twelve. Wangerin next develops Jesus' temptation in the wilderness, imagining the third temptation to occur with an icy-bright Satan on a glacial icecap. Jesus establishes his authority with miracles and teachings and is followed by ever increasing numbers of disciples. Shy Andrew is the first disciple, and his blunt brother Simon is the next. Wangerin conflates various events and teachings as Jesus moves through the countryside. The disciple Mary of Magdala, who is thankful to Jesus because he cast out her demons, plays an intimate role, washing Jesus' clothes, providing him with food, and comforting him as he grows increasingly intense, leaner, and filled with a heaviness no one understands.

The whole novel has been building to the Crucifixion, even as the Bible itself finds fulfillment in Jesus' sacrifice and resurrection. Jesus is taken outside Jerusalem's walls and crucified. Three days later, his disciples realize that Jesus is alive. The Resurrection is joyously announced; the good news is spread by the apostles. Wangerin's brief "Epilogue" announces that every continent has now heard the story and "innumerable hearts . . . have been shaped by it."

Christian Themes

This novel is based entirely on the themes and narratives of the Bible and on the covenant that God made with his chosen people: They are to worship and serve him, and he will protect and provide for them. Of course, there are many side themes and peripheral accounts, but in his novel Wangerin focuses on the covenant, which is ultimately realized in God's Son, Mary's child, Jesus, who gives his life, as his heavenly father wills, for the salvation of all people.

Wangerin's intimately drawn portraits of biblical characters bring passion and vitality to the original narrative. Readers are shown humanized portraits of figures only thinly sketched in the Bible: Leah, Jacob's second-best wife; Saul, conflicted between loving David and jealously fearing him; Tamar, David's daughter, raped by her half-brother and impoverished in exile; and Judas, sadly wrong about the role Jesus would play in saving his people.

Occasionally, Wangerin develops or expands a character beyond what is stated in the Bible, as he does with Ahikam, an exile in Babylon. He provides a biblical reading guide to supplement his text, offering the relevant books, chapters, and verses in the Bible. In addition, he suggests supplementing his story with other biblically based novels, including *Ruth: A Love Story* (1986) by Ellen Gunderson Traylor and Lew Wallace's *Ben-Hur: A Tale of the Christ* (1880).

The overriding purpose of Wangerin's work is to point to the need for God's Son and to make real the covenant established with Abraham. While staying faithful to the biblical contours, he adds imaginative nuance and color. The first seven chapters of *The Book of God* are based on the Old Testament and move chronologically and artistically to the fulfillment of the covenant in Jesus Christ. The last chapter is dominated by Jesus and begins with the familiar Gospel narratives of the birth in Bethlehem. Wangerin shows Jesus revealing more and more of his wisdom and power. As his death approaches, his followers notice his increased intensity, his thoughtfulness, and his withdrawal. However, God's promise is to be kept, for his covenant is faithful. Wangerin writes movingly of Jesus' death, resurrection, and ascension, then closes with a few pages concerning the early church, the apostles' martyrdoms, and Saint Paul's spreading of the Gospel.

Sources for Further Study

Distel, Joan McIntyre. "Religious Storytelling." *Christianity and the Arts* (August-October, 1997): 56-57. Provides background on the author's career and other literary works; examines use of first-person narration, humor, and the creative conflation of multiple events.

Ryken, Leland. "Bible Stories for Derrida's Children." *Books and Culture* (January/February, 1998): 38-41. Examines four recent literary approaches to the Bible, focusing on Wangerin's reshaping of the Bible's varied genres written over centuries into one focused, fluid narration.

Wilson, John. "The Greatest Story Ever Retold." *Christianity Today* 40 (1996): 75. Describes Wangerin's ability to show the big picture of God's providence; also comments on the author's fully human, fully divine Son of God.

Marie J. K. Brenner

THE BOOK OF MORMON
Another Testament of Jesus Christ

Translator: Joseph Smith (1805-1844)

First published: 1830

Edition used: The Book of Mormon: Another Testament of Jesus Christ. Salt Lake
City, Utah: Church of Jesus Christ of Latter-day Saints, 1981

Genre: Holy writings

Subgenres: History; sermons; theology

Core issues: Atonement; Baptism; faith; Jesus Christ; Mormons and Mormonism;
obedience and disobedience; redemption; repentance

*The Book of Mormon is the holy book of the Church of Jesus Christ of Latter-day
Saints, presented as a record of the early inhabitants of the American continent. It
tells the story of two separate founding groups inspired by God to leave the Old World
to begin a new life in a promised land. Tracing the development of these two great civilizations, the book illustrates repeatedly the promise that those who are righteous
prosper in the land, while the wicked perish. The record's pinnacle is the appearance
of the resurrected Christ to these early American peoples.*

Overview

The Book of Mormon: Another Testament of Jesus Christ presents itself as a translated record of ancient American peoples detailing their dealings with each other and
with God. The book as a whole received its name from its primary editor, identified as
Mormon, who is said to have delivered the record to the concluding author, his son
Moroni, around 400 C.E. Mormon's record, compiled from four sets of metal plates,
resulted in a book of direct historical narrative, expansive summary, and theological
editorial observations. The Book of Mormon stands with the Bible as scripture for the
Church of Jesus Christ of Latter-day Saints. Interpreted as God-inspired, its text offers an account of the history and culture of two separate founding groups who leave
the Old World to begin a new life in a promised land. The earlier community, the
Jaredites, came to the Americas around the time of the biblical Tower of Babel. The
other group left from Jerusalem around 600 B.C.E. and eventually divided into opposing factions: the Nephites and the Lamanites.

The Book of Mormon comprises fifteen books, each named after its principal
writer. Mormon included in his compilation the first six books as they were written.
Nephi starts the record (1 Nephi) by recounting his father Lehi's vision warning the
family to leave Jerusalem to escape pending destruction. Against complaints of the
two oldest sons, the family struggles its way across the wilderness. Following two return trips to retrieve religious records and to invite another family for marriage prospects, the expanded family treks until it reaches the sea. Nephi builds a ship under
God's direction, and the family sails to the Americas—the "promised land." While

traveling through the wilderness, Lehi has another vision, in which he sees a path leading to the Tree of Life, which contains fruit "desirable above all other fruit" (1 Nephi 8.12). Nephi petitions God and is shown the same vision, learning of God's love and condescension.

Some time after they arrive in the Americas (2 Nephi), the tension between Nephi and his brothers becomes so intense that they split into two groups: the Nephites and the Lamanites, named for the eldest brother. Nephi keeps the record until his death, when his younger brother Jacob becomes the new religious leader.

Jacob records the society's progress (Jacob) and his own preaching regarding purity and Christ's atonement. Jacob's son Enos briefly shares his own powerful conversion (Enos), and his fervent prayer secures God's promises for his own salvation as well as that of fellow Nephites and even enemy Lamanites. Enos's son Jarom (in the Book of Jarom) succinctly summarizes the continuing battles between the two warring civilizations and describes the saving spirituality of his own Nephite people.

Passing of the plates to sons or to brothers results in desultory entries from Omni, Amaron, Chemish, Abinadom, and Amaleki (Omni), who describe vacillations of violence and peace among the Nephite people. Amaleki mentions how one Nephite man, Mosiah, was inspired to take followers to the land of Zarahemla, where they discover a group of people who migrated from Jerusalem at the same time that Lehi and his family left. The joyful reunion results in the unification of the Nephite band and the people of Zarahemla, with Mosiah as spiritual and temporal leader. The people of Zarahemla possess the record of the ancient Jaredites, which is passed down with the other sacred records until Moroni later abridges it. Mosiah's son Benjamin succeeds as king and gains advantage in the continuing battle against the Lamanites. A small group of King Benjamin's subjects journey back to repossess the land of Nephi. Amaleki closes his record with a testimony of Christ's saving power.

Having no family, Amaleki gives the record to King Benjamin. The plates are handed down until they come into Mormon's hands. In a brief editorial interjection ("The Words of Mormon"), Mormon explains that the next part of the record will be his own abridgment of the other metal plates.

Mormon reviews the difficulties of King Benjamin's reign as he struggled to promote righteousness through moral reprimands and peace through military struggle (Mosiah). After selecting his son, also named Mosiah, to be the next ruler, the weakening King Benjamin offers a moving sermon to his beloved people. His discourse recounts his just reign, reminding his followers of their obligation to serve God and others. His powerful witness of God's mercy moves his people to sincere repentance.

Under Mosiah's reign the people beg their king to discover the whereabouts of the group that left to find the land of Nephi during Benjamin's reign. A search party discovers these lost Nephites in bondage to the Lamanites. Recounting their history, the oppressed people explain that their first leader, Zeniff, made a treaty with the Lamanites to repossess the land of Nephi, an agreement broken when the flourishing of the Nephite people triggered Lamanite jealousy.

Eras of uneasy peace and fierce fighting alternated until Zeniff's son Noah became king. Wicked Noah's slothful and extravagant reign stirred up a prophet named Abinadi to bear testimony so compelling that he was burned at the stake. Unprepared for a Lamanite invasion, Noah was killed and the people enslaved under the burden of a 50 percent tax. When the search party discovered them, they got the Lamanite guards drunk, allowing escape back to the land of Zarahemla. Meanwhile one of Noah's priests, Alma, who believed the prophet's words and secretly organized a church, escaped with his newly organized church to the safety of Mosiah's reign.

Alma's son and King Mosiah's four sons persecute believers, seriously frustrating the church's growth until the miraculous appearance of an angel turns them to repentance. In a stunning transformation, these men become a powerful influence for good. In the Book of Alma, it is related that Alma the Younger is chosen first chief judge under the new government system until iniquity and dissensions make his spiritual responsibilities so demanding that he appoints a new chief judge. Alma the Younger and his companion Amulek work unceasingly to regain righteousness among the Nephite people.

Meanwhile, the four sons of Mosiah take the Gospel to the Lamanites. Ammon begins his ministry by offering himself as a servant to Lamanite King Lamoni. He heroically defends the king's flocks against an enemy band, hacking off the sword arms of multiple opponents. Lamoni wants to know more about the source of Ammon's power. After Lamoni's dramatic conversion while in a coma, Ammon's brother Aaron teaches Lamoni's father, king over all the land. Seven cities in the lands of the Lamanites become converted to the church and call themselves the Anti-Nephi-Lehis.

Making a covenant never to shed blood again and burying their weapons deep in the earth, these steadfast converts allow themselves to be killed rather than break their covenant to fight. Their martyrdom results in the conversion of more Lamanites. Continued threat from hardened Lamanite bands, however, encourages Ammon to take the people to Zarahemla, where they can be protected by the Nephites.

In the heat of battle, Alma continues to preach doctrinally packed sermons. Along with Alma's sermons to the crowded masses, Mormon includes the tender teachings of this loving father to his three sons. Molded to the spiritual maturity of each son, Alma's instruction includes profound theological insights into immorality, repentance, atonement, and the resurrection.

Warfare escalates, complicated by much internal dissension from Antichrists and more Nephite dissensions to the Lamanites. Moroni, a mighty war captain, becomes the Nephite leader, rallying his people by tearing off his shirt and inscribing on it causes worth fighting for: God, religion, freedom, peace, wives, and children (Alma 46.12). Dissenting Nephite Amalickiah becomes the fierce leader of the Lamanites, luring away many apostate Nephites. Moroni's power as a leader results from his vigilant strategy, defensive focus, and unwavering dependence on God.

Upset at the burden they are placing on the weakening Nephites, the Anti-Nephi-Lehis contemplate breaking their covenant of peace. In this crisis, their young sons offer to fight under the command of Helaman, Alma the Younger's son. These courageous warriors, true to their mothers' faith, prove to be a crucial asset in the war. Miraculously, though almost all are wounded, none is killed.

The advantage alternating between Nephites and Lamanites, the two great societies become increasingly blended as Nephite dissenters migrate northward and converted Lamanites ally themselves with the Nephites (Book of Helaman). Eventually most of the Nephite peoples abandon the church and the Lamanites become more righteous. Samuel, a Lamanite prophet, warns the Nephites regarding their wickedness and prophesies the signs of Christ's birth. Many believing Nephites are baptized, while wicked Nephites persecute those who trust Samuel. Heavenly portents of Christ's birth arrive barely in time to save believers from threatened destruction.

Despite the fervent efforts of Nephi, Helaman's son, the Nephites become progressively more wicked, their wickedness compounded by the arising of a lawless secret band, the Gadianton Robbers (3 Nephi). At the height of their Mafia-like wickedness come the vivid signs of Christ's crucifixion: Earthquakes, fires, storms, and floods leave the landscape dramatically destroyed. Silence and uncanny darkness fill the land.

A light in this intense darkness ushers in the culminating event of the Book of Mormon: God the Father introduces his son Jesus Christ as the resurrected Savior descends to minister to the people of ancient America. The Savior personalizes his atoning sacrifice by allowing every individual to touch the wounds in his hands and side. He then preaches fundamental Gospel truths: faith, repentance, baptism, and the gift of the Holy Ghost. He administers the ordinances of the sacrament, teaches the people to pray, heals the infirm, and touchingly blesses the little children. He organizes his church on the earth, authorizing men with his priesthood authority.

Christ's appearance results in peace and harmony for two hundred years (4 Nephi), when some minor societal divisions occur. Three hundred years after Christ's birth, both the Lamanites and the Nephites are again wicked (Mormon). The book's editor, Mormon, is leader of the Nephite armies. With anguish he describes the wickedness and mass destruction of thousands upon thousands of his people. The Nephite nation is utterly destroyed: Only Mormon's son Moroni survives. Mormon's concluding words are a testimony of Jesus Christ, a plea that the descendants of these great civilizations will repent and come to Christ.

Mormon hides the records in the Hill Cummorah, where the final combat took place. He delivers a few records to his son Moroni, who makes an abridgment of the Jaredite record and adds his own testimony.

Leaving the Old World at the time of the Tower of Babel (Ether), the Jaredite prophet, referred to as "the brother of Jared," prays so that he and his family and friends will be spared the language upheaval of the time. They are directed to build barges. The brother of Jared, concerned for light in the barges during their submerged oceanic journey, requests that the Lord touch stones to illuminate them. The brother of Jared's great faith enables him to see the outstretched finger of Christ's spirit body, a body "like unto man" (Ether 3.6).

Upon reaching the Americas, the group establishes a productive society. To Jared's sorrow, the people request a king and Jared's son is made ruler. Generations later, Jared's premonition comes to sad fruition when battling clans squabble for the throne. Prophets, including Ether, preach repentance, and peace is intermittently restored— translator Moroni inserts at this point extensive editorial comments on the saving power of faith. The struggle between wickedness and righteousness, between the blood lust of warlords and the fervor of prophets, accelerates until in a terrible last stand Shiz, headless, finally succumbs. The consuming blood lust leaves only one survivor of that great Jaredite nation: Coriantumr, the man who lived with the people of Zarahemla.

Moroni's prolonged life allows him to write a few more words (Book of Moroni). He gives clear instruction on the sacrament of the Lord's Supper and includes his father's eloquent and insightful sermon regarding faith, hope, and charity. The book's culminating chapter contains a testable promise that Moroni makes to all readers: If they will sincerely ask of God, He will reveal the book's truth through the power of the Holy Ghost (Moroni 10.4).

Christian Themes

The Book of Mormon purports to recount a history of the early peoples of the American continents, raising intriguing possibilities about the background of cultural phenomena ranging from the widespread democratic tendencies of indigenous peoples to such specifically quirky practices as "burying the hatchet." The book speaks hauntingly to the American experience, since promises and warnings made to the early inhabitants apply forcefully to modern society, as when the Nephites are repeatedly enjoined to keep the land a land of liberty or face disaster. Through its reiterative cycle of righteousness leading to success, followed by pride triggering wickedness and disaster, each contributor to the Book of Mormon urges readers to repent or suffer the drastic consequences.

The function of the book, however, extends beyond its complex narrative of cultural descriptions, epic journeys, stirring battles, harrowing threats, thrilling escapes, and dramatic conversions. The Book of Mormon itself declares (on its title page) its primary purpose to be "the convincing of the Jew and Gentile that Jesus is the Christ." The book is clearly, as its subtitle insists, intended as "Another Testament of Jesus Christ." Christ is central to the book.

Though its characters are of Jewish provenance (Isaiah is quoted extensively), the book's concerns reach beyond the Old Testament to focus on Christian insights. The climax of the book is 3 Nephi, the coming of Jesus himself to these "other sheep" of his fold (3 Nephi 15.17, 21). His personal appearance on the American continent, particularly when he allows his scars to be touched or when he blesses the Nephite children, is reminiscent of the moving moments of the New Testament.

The Church of Jesus Christ of Latter-day Saints, popularly known as the Mormons, use the Book of Mormon as a companion to the Holy Bible, adhering to the church structure and doctrinal principles described in the book. They find in its journey motifs, struggles between good and evil, and direct theological doctrine on spiritual principles pertinent to modern lives. Mormons believe the Book of Mormon, like the Bible, its own best witness: Any reader can gain confirmation of the book's truth by asking God about the record.

Sources for Further Study

Duke, James T. *The Literary Masterpiece Called the Book of Mormon.* Springville, Utah: CFI, 2003. Duke provides detailed illumination of Richard Dilworth Rust's overview.

Nibley, Hugh. *An Approach to the Book of Mormon.* 2d ed. Salt Lake City: Deseret Book, 1964. This classic study by the foremost academic proponent of the book is particularly good on cultural background and theological insight.

Rust, Richard Dilworth. *Feasting on the Word: The Literary Testimony of the Book of Mormon.* Salt Lake City: Deseret Book, 1997. Rust examines the literary dimensions of the book: its narrative, poetry, sermons, letters, imagery, typology, and epic elements.

Steve Walker

BOOK OF REVELATION

Author: John (first century C.E.)

First published: Apokalypsis, c. 95 C.E. (English translation, 1380)

Editions used: The Greek New Testament, edited by Barbara Aland et al. 4th ed. Stuttgart, Germany: Deutsche Bibelgesellschaft/United Bible Societies, 1983; *The New Oxford Annotated Bible: New Revised Standard Version with the Apocrypha,* edited by Michael D. Coogan. 3d ed. New York: Oxford University Press, 2001

Genre: Holy writings

Subgenres: Spiritual treatise; theology

Core issues: Apocalypse; the Bible; constancy; good vs. evil; hope; martyrdom; persecution; works and deeds

The book of Revelation brings an apocalyptic view of history and of the end of the world directly to bear on the self-understanding of the churches in western Asia Minor toward the end of the first century, with a view to inspiring believers to be faithful to God and the way of life that pleases him, and not to succumb to the temptations of power, wealth, sexual immorality, and tyrannical ruler worship presented by the dominant Roman-Anatolian society.

Overview

Like former prophetic writings in the Hebrew Bible, the book of Revelation (also known as the Apocalypse of John and Revelation to John), the only book of prophecy in the New Testament, summons contemporaries of the prophet to be faithful to God in a time of crisis for the Christian faith. Addressed as a circular letter to the churches of western Asia Minor (now Turkey), probably near the end of the reign of the Roman emperor Domitian (81-96 C.E.), it finds Christians there adopting a variety of stances toward the pagan environment, from accommodation at one extreme to passive resistance at the other. It encourages the resisters to remain loyal to Christ in spite of harassment and warns compromisers to repent lest they fall under judgment together with the world of the godless.

The author gives his name as John. From the middle of the second century onward, in keeping with the testimony of the next generation after the apostles, he has been identified as Saint John, son of Zebedee, member of the twelve nearest to Jesus, author also of the Gospel of John and of the three Johannine epistles. Since the European Enlightenment, critical scholarship has cast doubt on this tradition, and on ancient traditions generally, citing in this case marked differences between the writings in grammar, style, genre, and temper.

During the closing decades of the first century, the Roman province of Asia was enjoying an economic boom, accompanied by spreading acceptance of the Roman peace and its cultural emblems. In particular, popular fervor attached itself to a Roman cult in which officers of the government were accorded rites of worship. The imperial cult was fostered in Asia through the proconsul based in the great port city of Ephesus, with a hierarchy of priests at temples and shrines throughout the interior. The largest concentration of Christians in the empire lived in the populous and prosperous urban centers of Asia, the region having been evangelized almost half a century earlier by Saint. Paul and his associates, though even at the century's end the Christians formed but a minority of the total populace. Out of the many cities and towns, John was instructed to write to churches in seven, selected as representative of all.

Although John uses an array of artful literary devices to shape his prophecy, there is little agreement among interpreters on the details of its structure. Most recognize a prologue (1:1-11) and an epilogue (22:6-21), which mirror each other and sandwich the whole. A reasonable analysis might divide the main body as follows. Introduced by a vision of the resurrected Christ (1:10-20) are seven oracles directed to the angels of the seven churches (chapters 2-3), calling on five of them to amend their worldly ways and promising the two who are holding up under pressure generous compensation for their sufferings. Then John is invited into the sky by a voice that echoes the first vision of Christ, and he finds himself in the throne room of heaven (chapters 4-5). There follow seven apocalyptic revelations of the end of the world: seven seals (6:1-8: 5), seven trumpets (8:6-11: 19), the beginning of a final combat between good and evil (12:1-15:4), seven bowls of divine wrath (15:5-16:21), the judgment of Lady Babylon (17:1-19:10), the conclusion of the final combat between good and evil (19:11-21:8), and the bliss of Lady Jerusalem (21:9-22:9). As before, the scheme of seven breaks down into two plus five: two of the vision sequences focus on persecuted believers, offering encouragements (those that make up the combat story), while the other five show the human race in general moving inexorably toward the judgment at the end of the age, which will assign people either to the doom of Babylon or to the everlasting joy of Jerusalem. Thus the visions of chapters 6-22 reinforce the admonitions of 2-3 by bringing readers face to face with the end-time outcomes of their choices, and together form an unified message.

Central to the gist of the book are the introductory theophanies. In chapter 1, Christ is seen as the living one who has emerged victorious from death and now rules over the kings of the earth. Therefore he is qualified to encourage and comfort or to criticize and threaten the churches, according to the need of each. In chapters 4-5, God is seen as the Almighty whose purpose governs all history from the creation of the world to its fulfilment in the age to come. A visionary scene—in which rank upon rank of angels prostrate themselves before God and the Lamb on the throne, setting in motion a wave of acclaim that eventually encompasses every living thing in heaven and earth and under the earth— reveals that power, wealth, and joy flow from God and not from the cultural icons of the Roman Empire, as many at the time supposed.

Because the visions make lavish use of symbols, the book presents a special challenge. Many figures are explained by clues embedded in the text. Others have roots deep in the prophetic literature of the Hebrew Bible or in the Jewish apocalypses of the second temple period, from which the author draws as one who stands firmly in the prophetic tradition yet reserves the freedom to adapt and recast it for his own purposes. A ground rule for interpreting any symbol is that it must have made sense in the context of John's urgent plea to the churches of his day. The key antagonists are the dragon, the beast, and the false prophet in the combat story (12-14, 19-20) and Lady Babylon (17). These are all linked to "the great city that rules over the kings of the earth" and has "seven mountains" (17:9, 18)—undoubtedly Rome, known during that period as the City of Seven Hills. Thus the dragon represents the satanic inspiration behind Rome's blasphemous, humanistic ideology and propaganda; the beast, its political and military dominance; the false prophet, its religious officers enforcing the imperial cult; these three being parodies of God almighty, his agent the Messiah, and the church witnessing to the truth of the Gospel in the world. Babylon symbolizes the social and commercial engine of Rome as the focal point of an entire civilization embracing Rome's values, in contrast to Lady Jerusalem, consisting of the abstinent people of God.

John's prophetic genius lies in his effectiveness in casting an alternative view of reality that stands as a corrective against the pomp of Rome, which threatened to mislead the church together with society at large. John suggests that Rome's impressive self-vaunting originates from Hell without any legitimacy in the eyes of the true God. Far from being heroes, the emperor and his cronies are caricatured as brute beasts and society's enthusiasm to offer them worship as the most preposterous flattery. Roman culture with its glitter is a whore destined for destruction. God's faithful people, alienated and marginalized, in a few cases imprisoned or even lynched and martyred, stand high in God's estimate. They are the bride of the Lamb, and will shortly be his co-regents.

Although John clearly addressed people of his own day, his pregnant symbols and the schema of final events in which he hyperbolically dressed his immediate situation were by no means exhausted in their first century setting, but tap into principles awaiting fulfilment on a grander scale. Therefore the church reads the Apocalypse not merely as a tract for its own times, but as a clarion call to faith and perseverance as the clock ticks on toward the end of the age.

Christian Themes

The book of Revelation reinforces the theistic worldview of the rest of Scripture. God almighty ordains all events, all choices, and all acts of created beings without exception, not only of those who actualize his moral will, but also of those whom he permits to contravene him, for a time and within limits set by him. All contribute objectively to the eventual achievement of God's plan, some voluntarily and some in spite of their contrary aim, and will be rewarded or punished according to their inner intent. The universality of God's sovereignty reassures rejected and persecuted Christians that nothing they suffer can thwart God's promise to bless them in the end; indeed, their sufferings enhance their future glory.

John calls on Christians to go on bearing witness to the truth and practicing good deeds, even when their integrity brings them into direct conflict with widespread cant and they become objects of hatred and oppression. Jesus is the model martyr who triumphed over death and was exalted to the high station of God's plenipotentiary agent, soon to execute judgment on God's foes. He holds out to his followers whose constancy brings on them the bitterness of martyrdom the promise of sharing his throne, as he overcame and now shares his Father's throne.

No book of the Bible contains more graphic images of the coming end of the world. Ever more intense serial plagues torment humankind in the seals, trumpets, and bowls, leading up to an extended taunt over Babylon's devastation, a gory description of birds feasting on the carcasses strewn at Armageddon, and visions of smoke rising to all eternity from the holocaust of the wicked in the lake of fire and brimstone. Behind such grim depictions is a divine love that spares no expenditure to persuade the impenitent before it is too late of the final consequences of their self-exclusion from the presence of the one God, the only source of happiness. As for those whose names were written in the Lamb's book of life before the foundation of the world, the Apocalypse speaks of a new order, where God will wipe away every tear, and death, mourning, and pain will be no more, and God will dwell among his people, and they shall behold his face and reign for ever and ever.

Sources for Further Study

Bauckham, Richard. *The Theology of the Book of Revelation*. New Testament Theology series. Cambridge, England: Cambridge University Press, 1993. Organizes the theological concepts of the book into a coherent presentation.

Friesen, Steven J. *Imperial Cults and the Apocalypse of John: Reading Revelation in the Ruins*. Oxford, England: Oxford University Press, 2001. A specialist in Anatolian archaeology reconstructs the social and cultural background to the Apocalypse with the help of the material remains.

Kovacs, K., and Christopher Rowland. *Revelation*. Blackwell Bible Commentaries. Malden, Mass.: Blackwell, 2003. A commentary that focuses on the many ways the book has been interpreted or been influential, including references in art and literature as well as biblical studies and theology.

Osborne, Grant R. *Revelation*. Baker Exegetical Commentary on the New Testament. Grand Rapids, Mich.: Baker, 2002. A conventional and insightful commentary on the text of the book, interacting with all the most significant previous commentaries.

Paul A. Rainbow

BOOKS OF THE PROPHETS
Isaiah, Jeremiah, Amos, and Micah

Authors: Isaiah (c. 760-c. 701/680 B.C.E.); Jeremiah (c. 645-after 587 B.C.E.); Amos
(fl. eighth century B.C.E.); and Micah (fl. eighth century B.C.E.)
First appeared: c. mid-sixth century B.C.E. (English translation, 1384)
*Edition used: The Holy Bible: Containing the Old and New Testaments with the Apoc-
ryphal/Deuterocanonical Books* by the National Council of the Churches of Christ
in the United States of America. Nashville, Tenn.: Thomas Nelson, 1990
Genre: Holy writings
Subgenres: Biography; handbook for living
Core issues: The Bible; forgiveness; God; sacrifice; sin and sinners; social action

*The Old Testament prophetic books—Isaiah, Jeremiah, Amos, and Micah—each ad-
vocate the exclusive worship of the God of Israel and the extending of compassion and
justice to other people. Failure to obey God in these matters was sin and would be
punished, but God offered forgiveness to people if they repented and changed. Morality as defined in the Ten Commandments and other laws was expected, but the prophets called Israel to take action to assure social justice as well.*

Overview

The author of the Old Testament book of Isaiah flourished between 760 and 701/
680 B.C.E., but many modern scholars think that much in the book by his name originated c. 540 and later. The author of the book of Jeremiah lived from c. 645 to after
587. A collection of his sermons appeared about 605, but the book was not completed
before 585 at the earliest. Amos's career lasted two years or less, but the book bearing
his name presupposes the collapse of the Davidic dynasty in 587. Micah was a contemporary of Isaiah, but some of the materials in the book of Micah come from the
period of the Exile (586-539) or slightly later.

The book of Isaiah may be divided into three basic parts. It develops chronologically, with chapters 1-39 dealing mostly with people and events between 742 and 697
B.C.E. Chapters 40-55 shift both scene and time, addressing the exiles in Babylon near
the end of the enforced captivity of Jews in that land (539). Chapters 56-66 shift the
focus back to Jerusalem, but many scholars think the time frame is the last quarter of
the sixth century. While the name Isaiah appears fifteen times in chapters 1-39, and
the prophet appears in several narratives (chapters 6-7, 36-39), neither Isaiah nor any
other person or event from the eighth century is mentioned in chapters 40-66.

Within chapters 1-39, the first twelve contain a number of passages reprimanding
Judah and Jerusalem for sinful behavior and for making alliances with other countries. A narrative reporting Isaiah's call to be a prophet (in 742 B.C.E.) appears in chapter 6, followed by the narrative of Isaiah's confrontation with King Ahaz over
whether to support a rebellion against Assyria initiated by small, neighboring coun-

tries (734-732). In that confrontation, Isaiah tells Ahaz that a "young woman" (the Hebrew word used is not the same as the word for "virgin") will bear a son (7:14), and before that son can distinguish right from wrong, the threat posed by neighboring nations will disappear. Christians often see in that verse a prediction of the birth of Jesus, because Matthew 1:22 says that Jesus' birth took place to "fulfill" what God had said through Isaiah. Saying that Jesus fulfilled the passage is one thing; saying the passage predicted Jesus is quite different. Other passages in chapters 1-12 alternate between denunciations of Israel for sin and—following repentance—depictions of a restoration, including a righteous king (9:2-7, 11:1-9). These last two texts help form the Old Testament expectation for a future messiah (that is, Israel's king). Christians often read these passages as predictions of Jesus, though he is never mentioned by name.

Chapters 13-23 consist of a collection of prophetic sayings against foreign nations. Because few foreigners would hear (or read) them, they perhaps served to warn the people of Israel not to form political or other alliances with Judah's neighbors, no matter how powerful they might appear at times. Chapters 24-27 probably arose during the dark days of the Babylonian exile. They envision widespread destruction of the earth and its inhabitants for sin, but they also hold out hope for Israel's future deliverance from its enemies. Chapters 28-32 return to messages against Judah and Jerusalem. Repentance (turning from sin to God) will result in God's forgiveness and blessing; rebellion will result in punishment. Chapters 36-39 narrate the siege of Jerusalem by King Sennacherib of Assyria in 701. It ended in the payment of tribute by Judah's king Hezekiah (2 Kings 18:16, but not mentioned in Isaiah) and the subsequent destruction of the Assyrian army. Isaiah's roles were to advise Hezekiah and to intercede with God for the king's health.

Chapters 40-55 form what many scholars call Second Isaiah because they address the conditions of the Jewish exiles in Babylon. First, they explain the causes for the fall of the Judah—namely, the sinfulness and impure worship of its people. Second, they proclaim that the God of Judah is the only god and that the Babylonian gods are not genuine; these verses constitute the earliest, unequivocal statements of monotheism in the Old Testament. Third, they announce hope for the future. God would use Cyrus the Great, emperor of Persia, to defeat the Babylonians. Fourth, God would use the suffering of a righteous "servant" to effect the rescue of his people. The New Testament also uses some of these passages in its presentation of Jesus as savior, but Isaiah 40-55 cast him as someone living among the exiles.

Chapters 56-66, often called Third Isaiah, are set in Jerusalem, probably in the last decades of the sixth century, around the time of the rebuilding of the Temple in Jerusalem (520-515 B.C.E.). They address the problem of unfulfilled hope. Second Isaiah had predicted a glorious new day after the exile, but conditions in Judah and Jerusalem in the decades after Jews began returning were bleak. The Temple, which the Babylonians had destroyed in 586, was rebuilt, but the monarchy was not restored. Even the wall protecting the city was not rebuilt until the time of Nehemiah (445 B.C.E.). These chapters reflect a struggle over who could worship in the Temple, opting for including all sincere worshipers. They also envision a remaking of the world in peace, where natural enemies (such as wolves and lambs) will live in harmony.

The book of Jeremiah relates the life and message of a prophet who belonged to a disenfranchised priestly family. Much of the book is a third-person narrative, perhaps written by Baruch, Jeremiah's secretary (36:1-32). The narrative flow of this material begins with Jeremiah's call to be a prophet (1:4-10). His most famous message was his so-called Temple sermon, in which he predicted the Temple's destruction if the people of Judah did not obey God's law. He was arrested and tried for treason but acquitted. He remained such a thorn in the side of King Jehoiakim that the king burned a written copy of the prophet's sayings. Jeremiah also saw the siege of Jerusalem by the Babylonians as God's punishment on Judah for infidelity to God and unfairness to the poor. He counseled surrender. Not surprisingly, Jeremiah found himself in prison; he might have died in a pit had not a servant of King Zedekiah pulled Jeremiah from its mud-filled bottom. After the fall of Jerusalem to the Babylonians, a group of Judeans took Jeremiah with them to Egypt, where he repeated his message that Judah suffered because it had sinned.

The book of Jeremiah also contains poetic prophecies, many (such as 2:1-3:5) of doom. Some of those passages (such as 4:5-31) appear to have been pieced together with interpretive prose. The book also contains prophecies of hope, perhaps including some from one or more later prophets. The contours of that hope begin with a letter from Jeremiah to the exiles, telling them they will soon return from Babylon. These passages promise that God will restore the fortunes of the exiles, bring them back to Judah, and rebuild their cities. They announce that the northern kingdom of Israel (which fell to the Assyrians in 722 B.C.E.) will be included in that new day. God will also restore the Davidic monarchy and the Levitical priesthood. The most important of these texts promises that God will initiate a new covenant with God's people, one that is unbreakable and one that they will internalize (31:31-34). It is from this passage that Christians drew the term "New Testament" for its scriptures (the terms for "testament" and "covenant" being synonymous).

The namesake of the book of Amos was a shepherd from the town of Tekoa (1:1), located ten miles south of Jerusalem. He flourished in the northern kingdom of Israel in the eighth century B.C.E., particularly in the sanctuary at Bethel. The book opens with a series of prophecies of disaster against the surrounding cities of Damascus, Gaza, and Tyre, and the small kingdoms of Edom, Ammon, and Moab, primarily for acts of aggression. Such prophecies against foreign nations became a feature of many other prophetic collections.

Most of the remainder of the book addresses the kingdom of Israel, with the prophet insisting on social justice. He complains that the indolently wealthy have taken advantage of the poor (6:4-7), even selling debtors into servanthood for a trifling sum owed them (2:6, 8:6). He complains that the people thought they could sacrifice to God and then live as they pleased. Instead, Amos advocates letting justice "roll down like waters" (5:24).

The book concludes with two positive messages. The first (9:7-10) predicts that

God will destroy a "sinful" kingdom (Babylon) without harming Israel; the second (9:11-15) predicts that God will restore the "booth of David" (the Davidic monarchy) and the fortunes of God's people. The verses clearly look back on the destruction of Jerusalem and fall of the Davidic dynasty in 586, and they envision the restoration of both. These two passages reveal themselves, therefore, to have arisen later than 586. They seem to have been added to bring the book to a positive conclusion. The pattern of doom (1:2-9:6) followed by hope (9:7-15) became a pattern widely used in arranging the prophetic books.

The book of Micah illustrates that pattern. It contains a mixture of passages on doom and restoration: doom in 1:2-2:11, hope in 2:12-13, doom in 3:1-12, hope in 4:1-8, doom in 4:9-5:1, hope in 5:2-15, doom in 6:1-7:7, and hope in 7:8-20. This fourfold repetition of the pattern emphasizes that the punishment of sin—necessary as it may be—is not God's final word. Many scholars think most if not all of the passages of hope derived from someone who lived later than Micah. The prophet himself, a contemporary of Isaiah, lived in Moresheth, a small village located approximately twenty-five miles southwest of Jerusalem. He seems to have distrusted cities, especially Jerusalem.

At least as much as Amos, Micah championed the cause of the poor, but the passages of hope in Micah far exceed the two at the end of Amos. The first (2:12-13) depicts God as a shepherd who will bring Judah home from exile, marching in front of the people like a triumphant king. The second (4:1-8) contains the famous line about men's beating their swords into plowshares and spears into pruning hooks and living on the land without fear of one another. The third (5:2-15) dares to hope for a new king from the line of David in Bethlehem who will defeat Israel's enemics. The fourth (7:8-20) looks beyond the destruction of Jerusalem by the Babylonians to its rebuilding at a time when God forgives Judah for its sins. The promise of the new king from Bethlehem forms a small but essential part of the Old Testament's expectations for the future. In the New Testament, the author of Matthew says that Herod's scholars used the verse to answer the query of the Magi about where the king of the Jews would be born.

Christian Themes

The books of the four prophets advocate an unswerving faithfulness to God, and in the event of sin, they advocate repentance. A proper relationship with God was to manifest itself in three ways. First, the people would experience peace within their community (Isaiah 9:7); what the prophets saw instead was the ruthless pursuit of self-interest. Amos and Micah especially condemn those wealthy people who used their power and wealth to oppress the unfortunate. Isaiah and Jeremiah emphasize that the worship of only God, not the gods of the Assyrian and Babylonian conquerors, is necessary for living as God's people. Although that idea may seem self-evident to modern Westerners, it was novel in ancient biblical times.

Second, living in faithfulness to God would result in justice in the land. Justice was first and foremost the responsibility of the king (Isaiah 9:7; 11:3-5). In Amos (5:21-

24), God rejects worship and sacrifices that are not tied to justice for the poor. Micah (6:8) ties justice to kindness toward other human beings and humility before God. Judeans were to act in ways that guaranteed protection to the poor.

Third, living in faithfulness to God was the means to hope for the future. The prophets were sober in their assessment of the power of Assyria and Babylon vis-à-vis Judah. Its only hope was that God would aid Judah for remaining faithful.

These prophets made predictions. Sometimes they seemed to be without qualifications. Jeremiah, for example, became convinced that Babylon would capture Jerusalem and that the only prudent action, therefore, was for Judah to surrender to the conqueror. Other times, however, prophetic predictions seem to have been conditional. In his Temple sermon, Jeremiah (7:1-15; 26:1-6) warned that the Temple would be destroyed if the people of Judah did not repent. Still other predictions may have been fulfilled in the past (such as the restitution of the Levitical priesthood after the Exile) and others in ways the prophets did not anticipate (such as Isaiah 7:14). Still others perhaps have not been fulfilled (Isaiah 65:17-25), at least not yet.

Sources for Further Study

Brueggemann, Walter. *A Commentary on Jeremiah: Exile and Homecoming.* Grand Rapids, Mich.: Wm. B. Eerdmans, 1998. An exploration of the historical and social milieu of Jeremiah's career that presents a theological interpretation of the book.

Childs, Brevard S. *Isaiah.* Louisville, Ky.: Westminster John Knox, 2001. A critical study of the book of Isaiah that nevertheless examines its shape as determined by the rabbis who validated the books of the Hebrew Bible about the end of the first century C.E.

Holladay, William L. *Jeremiah 1 and Jeremiah 2.* 2 vols. Minneapolis, Minn.: Fortress, 1986, 1989. A two-volume critical and historical commentary on Jeremiah, based on the Hebrew text with Holladay's translation.

Jeremias, Jörg. *The Book of Amos.* Translated by Douglas W. Stott. Louisville, Ky.: Westminster, 1998. Describes how the book came into being with emphasis on its various stages and their meanings and functions.

Mays, James Luther. *Micah.* Philadelphia: Westminster, 1976. Pays particular attention to the meaning of individual sayings based on the author's own translation.

Sweeney, Marvin A. *The Prophetic Literature.* Nashville, Tenn.: Abingdon Press, 2005. A study of the entire prophetic corpus with particular attention to the genres and their interrelatedness.

Paul L. Redditt

BREAD AND WINE

Author: Ignazio Silone (Secondo Tranquilli; 1900-1978)

First published: German translation, 1936 as *Brot und Wein*; Italian original, 1937 as *Pane e vino*; revision, 1955 as *Vino e pane* (English translation, 1962)

Edition used: Bread and Wine, translated by Eric Mosbacher. New York: New American Library, 2005

Genre: Novel

Subgenre: Literary fiction

Core issues: Catholics and Catholicism; communism; good vs. evil; Jesus Christ; justice; social action

Internationally regarded as one of the major political novelists of the twentieth century, Silone here depicts the enduring struggle between individual conscience and repressive ideology. Pietro Spina, the novel's protagonist, refuses to surrender his mind or soul to church, party, or state, as he dedicates his life to the cause of universal brotherhood and peace. In the figure of Spina, Silone offers the faint hope that individual vision and voice may survive the pervasive forces of totalitarianism.

Principal characters

Pietro Spina, the protagonist, a social activist

Don Benedetto, an elderly, socialist Catholic priest, Spina's former teacher, mentor, and role model

Bianchina, daughter of the landlady of the Girasole Hotel

Cristina Colamartini, daughter of the most prominent family in Pietrosecca

Zabaglione, a lawyer and former socialist leader

Battipaglia, the interregional secretary of the Communist Party

Luigi Murica, a socialist and activist

Annina, Luigi Murica's girlfriend, a fellow activist

Overview

As Ignazio Silone's novel *Bread and Wine* opens, Don Benedetto, a Catholic priest, is sitting outside his modest home. It is his seventy-fifth birthday, and he is awaiting the arrival of some former students to celebrate the occasion. Don Benedetto is a socialist in the Fascist Italy of the early 1930's, and he refuses to seek any accommodation with the regime. Talk of a new war of imperial expansion in Africa is in the air.

Three former students arrive. Each has found a place in the new social order, and the priest reflects sadly on the moral compromises people make to survive. Then talk turns to a former pupil and classmate, Pietro Spina, who has not compromised. As a student he was idealistic, compassionate, and fiercely committed to justice. He became a socialist and was later exiled to various places in Europe, where he lived and labored under wretched conditions. He is rumored to have returned recently to Italy, to work on behalf of the communists.

The scene shifts to Spina's home village, to which, in fact, he has returned. He is seriously ill and is being hidden by a former comrade. When he is able to move, Spina leaves the village disguised as a priest with the name Don Paulo Spada. As Don Paulo, Spina sets off for the mountain village of Pietrosecca in the Abruzzi area. On the way, he comes across Bianchina, a young, unmarried woman apparently dying of complications from an abortion and in mental agony from fear of eternal damnation. Moved by compassion, "Don Paulo" tells her that all is forgiven.

The next day Don Paulo travels to an inn in Pietrosecca, where he hopes the mountain air will contribute to his recovery. Life in Pietrosecca is extremely hard; the peasants are poor, intensely superstitious, and politically naïve, and they are without hope of any change in their condition. There is only one family of any material substance, the Colamartini family. The miraculously revived Bianchina arrives in Pietrosecca, seeking the compassionate priest who saved her life, believing him to be a saint or perhaps Jesus. While they talk, Cristina Colamartini arrives, and the two young women recognize each other as former classmates. A complex relationship develops between Don Paolo and the two women. Bianchina is physically drawn to him. Don Paolo is attracted to the radiant, idealistic, and devout Cristina.

Don Paolo later meets Zabaglione, a lawyer and former socialist leader in that area. Zabaglione tells him of the brutal methods the Fascists used to crush the socialist and Christian organizations that attempted to address the plight of the people. Zabaglione's opinion is that the only organized resistance to the regime will come from radical students. Don Paolo arranges to meet with some students and is energized by their idealism and fervor. He prepares to leave for Rome.

In Rome, Don Paulo resumes his identity as Pietro Spina and meets with Battipaglia, the interregional secretary of the Communist Party. Battipaglia is an inflexible ideologue who expects and demands complete orthodoxy from all Party members. There is tension between the two men.

Before he leaves Rome, Pietro tries to find an experienced comrade to accompany him back to work in the area. He looks for a young man named Luigi Murica and learns that he is hiding from the police. Pietro goes to see Luigi's girlfriend, Annina. She tells him of their love, idealism, and commitment to the socialist cause, all destroyed by government persecution.

On his way back to the mountain village, Pietro transforms himself back into Don Paolo, and he hears excited talk about the coming war in Africa. When he arrives, he is shocked at the scene of patriotic parades and drunken celebrations. That night, he scrawls revolutionary and antiwar slogans on buildings, before returning to his room. The next morning, Bianchina tells Don Paolo of the agitation and fear caused in the town by the seditious slogans. He tells her that he has decided to go abroad as soon as he is well. She offers to come with him. Later, Don Benedetto visits Don Paolo. Their meeting is emotionally charged. Both men have felt inadequate to the challenges of their times. Each has taken comfort from the thought of the other, working in the cause of universal brotherhood.

Murica comes to visit Don Paolo. He has rededicated himself to the socialist cause and is preparing to resume party work. The mood is optimistic as they part. The next morning Don Paolo receives a letter from Annina saying Luigi has been arrested. Later he learns that Luigi was tortured and killed in a manner reminiscent of Christ's agony and death. Don Paolo goes to the Murica home to convey his profound sorrow and solidarity. Luigi's father performs a ritual sharing of bread and wine, products of Luigi's love and labor, in a reprise of Christ's offering at the Last Supper of bread and wine as his own body and blood. Bianchina arrives. She tells Don Paolo that his identity is known to the authorities, who are on their way.

Returning to Pietrosecca, Pietro meets Cristina, who asks if the rumor about his real identity is true. He says it is and asks her forgiveness for the deception. He then attempts to make his escape on foot in a snowstorm. Later, Cristina sets out in pursuit, carrying food and clothes. Evening falls, and she loses his tracks. As wolves gather around her for the kill, she makes the sign of the cross.

Christian Themes

Bread and Wine, set in Roman Catholic Italy of the 1930's, focuses predominantly on the struggles of the peasants to survive with dignity in the face of the worldwide depression that followed World War I along with the rise to power of a Fascist government. Don Benedetto is presented as an ideal man and churchman, a follower of the Jesus who loved sinners, challenged the entrenched powers of His time, and held out the promise that the poor shall inherit the earth. In contrast, most of the official Church finds accommodation with the repressive Fascist government.

Pietro Spina is the spiritual son of Don Benedetto. He is an idealistic young man who dedicates his life entirely to the project of universal brotherhood, to creating a just society. From the very beginning of the story, there are parallels between his life and that of Jesus and of the Apostles. When he returns to his home village, he is hidden in a barn reminiscent of Jesus' birthplace; when he leaves, he takes the apostolic name Paolo (Paul) to begin his new ministry; he "raises" Bianchina from the dead; later, Bianchina jokingly refers to herself as the "handmaiden of the Lord"; before his darkest hour, he enters a church and stands by an engraving of Christ being turned over by Pontius Pilate to be scourged.

As Spina is the spiritual heir to Don Benedetto, so is Luigi Murica the true heir to Pietro Spina. Murica's arrest, torture, and murder at the hands of the police echo Christ's agony and crucifixion. When he learns of Murica's death, Spina utters the words "Consummatum est." Finally, Murica's father offers bread and wine to Spina in a scene deliberately reminiscent of the Last Supper.

The many biblical parallels and allusions in the story emphasize a fundamental theme of the novel: that the world is always a place where evil threatens to overwhelm good and therefore the sacrifice of Christ, giving oneself for others, must be repeated in every age in order to keep alive the promise of dignity, brotherhood, and peace.

Sources for Further Study

Leake, Elizabeth. *The Reinvention of Ignazio Silone*. Toronto: University of Toronto Press, 2003. A study of Silone's major works of fiction in the light of his complex, conflicted political philosophy and activity.

Paynter, Maria Nicolai. "Ignazio Silone." In *Italian Prose Writers, 1900-1945*. Vol. 264 in *Dictionary of Literary Biography*, edited by Luca Somigli and Rocco Capozzi. Detroit: Gale Group, 2002. An overview of Silone's life, times, and published works.

_____. *Ignazio Silone: Beyond the Tragic Vision*. Toronto: University of Toronto Press, 2000. A comprehensive study of Silone's life and work, informed by critic Northrop Frye's theories of myth, archetype, and symbol.

Michael J. Larsen

BREAD FOR THE JOURNEY
A Daybook of Wisdom and Faith

Author: Henri J. M. Nouwen (1932-1996)
First published: New York: HarperSanFrancisco, 1997
Genre: Nonfiction
Subgenres: Devotions; guidebook; handbook for living; meditation and contemplation
Core issues: Compassion; daily living; devotional life; discipleship; wisdom

Nouwen provides inspirational thoughts for daily living, covering key topics such as community, forgiveness, friendship, hope, trust, love, joy, Jesus, and God. He provides powerful and stimulating words to guide readers toward a life that we can live peacefully and in harmony with others and, more important, with ourselves.

Overview

Henri Nouwen was a professor who taught at Harvard University and Yale University before becoming the senior pastor at the L'Arche community called Daybreak in Toronto, Canada, a post he held until his death in 1996. L'Arche is a community of people with disabilities living together. Nouwen was a prolific writer and wrote numerous books on spirituality and daily living. *Bread for the Journey* is an important book that gives new hope and inspiration for how to live.

Nouwen first began this book with the intention of writing a devotional work that touched on matters relating to all people of faith. However, the more he wrote, the more he realized that he had to deal with Jesus, the center of his life. This devotional book is therefore Christo-centric; its ideas and images center on Christ as savior, teacher, creator, and peace giver. The book is organized as a calendar: Nouwen provides one short inspirational thought for each day of the year. He covers many important issues to help his readers live authentically, holistically, and in a deeper relationship with the divine. Nouwen tries to open his readers' hearts and minds so that they can focus more intently on God's presence in and purpose for their lives. According to Nouwen, developing a relationship with God is a lifelong journey; this book is intended as spiritual bread for that journey.

Touching on topics both joyous and sad, Nouwen describes human experiences: loneliness, suffering, loss, and how one can deal with such experiences. He advises that, rather than harbor these feelings, we live through and overcome them: In the depths of pain and sorrow, for example, it is better to have risked the work of loving than not to love at all. Rather than hoard material goods for ourselves, Nouwen reminds us that, paradoxically, the more we keep, more we lose, not only in material goods but, more important, in relationships. Nouwen's message reflects the experience of the Israelites, who collect manna and were warned by God not to take more than was necessary for a day. God's message is as true today as it was for the Israel-

ites: We live in a capitalist and a consumer society where enough never seems sufficient. Nouwen warns us of the cost of such overabundance: We need to reflect on the
damage we are causing the earth and one another as we live with more than we need,
at the expense of others. Nouwen's ideas relate to the Asian term *han*, the "unjust suffering" experienced by the poor and the oppressed; the earth also experiences *han* as
human beings take too much from it for their own greed and selfishness. Nouwen asserts that we are living on this earth as one family and must act as stewards, rather than
exploiters, of our precious earth and its resources, including each other.

An inspirational and motivational work, Nouwen's daily meditations offer life-
changing thoughts for approaching one's daily life in a world of suffering, pain, loneliness, separation, and fear. Nouwen's words enter our hearts to warm us with encouragement and strength. Taken meditatively, in tiny morsels like the bread of the book's
title, these words are designed to sustain one's spiritual life as bread sustains one's
physical body.

Christian Themes

Chief among the work's many themes are that Christianity is love. Nouwen emphasizes that love must be reflected in action, not merely feeling. Although our material
culture emphasizes the good feelings of love, love cannot be sustained by feeling
alone. Nouwen advises that we act upon our love—that we create love by our actions;
the feelings will follow.

One of the most important Christian values is to love one's neighbor, and Nouwen
asks the question of how we can do that. Reiterating Jesus' parable of the Good Samaritan, who crossed the road to help a stranger, Nouwen notes that in many cases
people erect barriers against those who are different from them, just as the Israelites
did against the Samaritans. A modern example is the barrier between Western, mainly
Christian, and Middle Eastern, often Muslim, nations. We tend to objectify and vilify
others rather than seeing them as our neighbors. Once we stop objectifying people, we
will realize that they are like us: mothers who care about their children, fathers who
worry about their family's future, and brothers and sisters who want the best for one
another. Like the Good Samaritan, we need to cross the road to become neighbors.

Jesus is central to Nouwen's theology. Nouwen devotes many of his devotional
days to helping readers understand the complexity of Jesus. For example, Nouwen assigns one day to each of the different characters of Jesus based on the Sermon on the
Mount. He describes Jesus as the blessed one, poor, gentle, mournful, hungry, thirst-
ing for uprightness, merciful, pure of heart, a peacemaker, and persecuted. These aspects of Jesus reveal to us what it means to be in the world but not of it. If we follow
the example of Jesus, we too will see God in the present moment. The ability to live
this way will enrich our lives and comfort us in our pain and sadness.

Another theme is God's relationship with us. Nouwen describes this by examining
the difference between a contract and a covenant. Contracts, in which each side promises to keep its part as long as the other keeps to its agreement, can be broken. The
word "covenant," however, means "coming together." God does not make a contract

with us, but a covenant. God comes to us so that we can have a lasting relationship with God. God wants all our relationships to reflect a covenant; thus marriages, friendships, and community should all reflect God's covenant with us. If only our society could see relationships not as adversarial contracts, preventing two sides from splitting, but rather as covenants, broken relationships would be a rarity.

Sources for Further Study

Kushner, Harold. *When All You've Ever Wanted Wanted Isn't Enough: The Search for a Life That Matters*. New York: Summit Books, 1965. A search for a meaningful and purposeful life which is beyond the mere gathering of material goods or material success. A complement to Nouwen's work.

Nouwen, Henri J. M. *Finding My Way Home: Pathways to Life and the Spirit*. New York: Crossroad, 2001. This is a devotional book complementary to *Bread for the Journey*.

_____. *The Road to Daybreak: A Spiritual Journey*. New York: Doubleday, 1988. This book reveals Nouwen's spiritual journey and struggle to decide to live at the L'Arche community in Richmond Hill, Ontario. The book provides strength to the readers as it encourages and helps people who also struggle with life decisions.

Schut, Michael, ed. *Simpler Living Compassionate Life: A Christian Perspective*. Denver, Colo.: Living the Good News, 1999. A compilation of excerpts from contributors such as Henri Nouwen, Richard Foster, John B. Cobb, Jr., Frederick Buechner, and others on how to live an abundant life. These essays touch on many aspects of life, including time, wealth, nature, community, and relationships.

Grace Ji-Sun Kim

BRIDESHEAD REVISITED

Author: Evelyn Waugh (1903-1966)
First published: 1945
Edition used: Brideshead Revisited, with an introduction by Frank Kermode. New
   York: Alfred A. Knopf, 1993
Genre: Novel
Subgenre: Catholic fiction
Core issues: Beauty; conversion; death; friendship; grace; marriage; memory

*Waugh chronicles the memoirs of Captain Charles Ryder, especially the friendships
and loves that draw him toward conversion to Roman Catholicism. Through the voice
of his fictional narrator, Waugh captures the elegiac mood of a religious man who
witnesses the destruction of beauty, high culture, and the Western civilization he
loves. The book reaches through a wealth of particular detail toward an eternal consolation. This movement, consummated by Ryder's assent to a divine purpose behind
human tragedy, depicts the means by which a believer can suffer gladly the ravages of
time.*

Principal characters
   Charles Ryder, the narrator, a British officer in World War II
   Sebastian Flyte, Charles's closest friend
   Lord "Bridey" Brideshead, Sebastian's older brother
   Julia Flyte, Sebastian's sister
   Cordelia Flyte, Sebastian's sister
   Lady Marchmain, Sebastian's mother
   Lord Marchmain, Sebastian's father
   Cara, Lord Marchmain's mistress

Overview

The action of *Brideshead Revisited* describes providence, grace, and the redemption through suffering of a jaded, often hilarious modernism. Evelyn Waugh explores
these themes in the memory of his fictional narrator, Charles Ryder. In the prologue,
Ryder prepares to move from the military camp where he has been stationed for several months. At the age of thirty-nine, he reflects that he has begun to feel old, and his
love for the army has died. His company travels to camp on the grounds of Brideshead Castle, a name that evokes Charles's memories and propels him into the narrative, which comprises the body of the novel.

Charles first remembers his experience of college at Oxford, which essentially begins when he meets Lord Sebastian Flyte, a Roman Catholic of eccentric habits, en-
dearing innocence, and a love of beautiful things. As an apology for his drunken behavior, Sebastian invites Charles to a luncheon in his rooms, and the two quickly form

a deep friendship. On one occasion they travel to Sebastian's home at Brideshead Castle, stopping on the way for wine and strawberries in the countryside. Sebastian explains that his mother, his older brother Lord Brideshead, and his sisters Julia and Cordelia live in the house, while his father lives with a mistress in Venice. On this first visit, Charles begins to note stirrings in himself of his own love of beauty, which will later develop into his artistic career and his religious conversion.

The friends spend the term in decadent misbehavior, which elicits a remonstrance from Charles's cousin Jasper and a different kind of remonstrance from the colorful Anthony Blanche. At the end of the term, Charles returns impoverished to his father, with whom he engages in silent battles of will over the dinner table. Their relationship declines until a summons from Sebastian brings Charles to spend the rest of the vacation at Brideshead. There, Charles indulges his interest in art and aesthetics. He also discovers the central place the Roman Catholic religion holds in the family's life. At the end of the summer, the two friends visit Lord Marchmain and his mistress, Cara, in Venice, where they enjoy the artistic beauties of the city. Cara describes to Charles the hatred Sebastian and his father bear toward their mother and warns him about Sebastian's drinking habit.

In the following term, Sebastian begins to exhibit symptoms of alcoholism. Charles realizes the gravity of his problem at Easter, when Sebastian becomes drunk in front of his family. When the two are arrested for Sebastian's driving drunk, the family responds by treating Sebastian like a child, having him watched and stopping his allowance. Charles sides with Sebastian against the rest and gives him money, although drunkenness and family tension strain their friendship. Finally, Sebastian is sent down from Oxford, and Lady Marchmain sends Charles away from Brideshead.

Charles leaves Oxford for art school in Paris but returns to London for the General Strike of 1926. There, he learns that Lady Marchmain is dying, and the family sends him to search of Sebastian. Finding him in a Moroccan hospital, Charles stays with him until he is discharged and then returns to England alone. He paints the Marchmain family's London house just prior to its destruction, a work that launches his artistic career.

Ten years pass, after which a growing feeling of deadness and an unhappy marriage provoke Charles to flee abroad in search of peace. Returning to England three years later, he meets Julia Flyte on board their ship. She tells him of her stormy romance and unhappy marriage to politician Rex Mottram. Charles and Julia begin a love affair that breaks both of their marriages, though Julia becomes torn between her love for Charles and her conscience.

In the spring before World War II, Lord Marchmain returns to Brideshead Castle to die theatrically at home. Bridey, Cordelia, and Julia ask that a priest be admitted. Although Lord Marchmain refuses at first, in the end he responds to the Sacraments with a sign of the cross. At this sign, Charles feels his last doubts about the reality of the supernatural world give way. He and Julia, still in love, choose to end their affair. At the same time, Charles learns from Cordelia that, despite his continuing alcoholism, Sebastian has entered a monastery in North Africa, where he remains as a pathetic and permanent acolyte. Cordelia explains to Charles that her brother has found holiness through suffering and infirmity.

In the epilogue, Charles returns from his memories to his dismal present, when the beautiful Brideshead Castle has become a soldiers' barracks. He tours the house and finds its artworks ruined and its Baroque fountain dry and filled with cigarette butts. Nevertheless, when he enters the chapel, he sees its sanctuary lamp lit and feels peace and hope despite the prospect of a bleak future. He realizes that he has played a role in a divine plan that will transcend the war and destruction now surrounding him.

Christian Themes

Brideshead Revisited is concerned above all with the operation of divine grace in the modern world. Permeated with grotesque incidents and metaphysical similes and allusions, it incorporates supernatural agency into the conventions of the realistic novel. In this context, both the appeal and the strangeness of Christianity become central themes. Waugh's depiction of a Catholic family through the eyes of a nonbeliever defamiliarizes Christian culture to highlight its paradoxes. The Flytes discuss sacred and profane ideas side by side; they discern supernatural motives and causes in everyday events; even the lapsed members of the family believe firmly in the reality of sin.

Although he presents three rebellious Catholics and an agnostic assent in the end to the existence and providence of God, Waugh consistently maintains that conversion does not solve the painful dilemmas of life. Instead, the author draws on a Catholic understanding of redemptive or sacrificial suffering. Thus, Sebastian's suffering confers the dignity of holiness on his apparently ignominious life, while the fulfillment of Charles's love for Julia requires his separation from her. In the world of *Brideshead Revisited*, genuine happiness and worldly success rarely coincide: The novel is a true tragedy, redeemed by the persistence of faith and not by an outwardly happy ending.

Because Waugh sets his novel in historical time, his portrayal of the intersection of the supernatural with the natural extends beyond individual lives, becoming a mode of interpreting the twentieth century, World War II, and the triumphs and heresies of modernity. Aesthetic themes also flood the novel so that art, like history, becomes infused with supernatural significance. Ultimately, the novel achieves a synthesis between physical and spiritual events, affirming the belief that nothing happens without a purpose.

Sources for Further Study

Davis, Robert Murray. *Brideshead Revisited: The Past Redeemed.* Boston: G. K. Hall, 1990. Summarizes the novel's historical context, importance, and critical reactions, analyzing Waugh's style and narrative technique. Includes chronology of Waugh's life, bibliographical references, index.

Ker, Ian. "Evelyn Waugh: The Priest as Craftsman." *The Catholic Revival in English Literature, 1845-1961.* Notre Dame, Ind.: University of Notre Dame Press, 2003. Discusses Waugh's practical understanding of Catholic life, including the portrayal of Catholicism as a lived faith in *Brideshead Revisited.* Includes index.

McCartney, George. *Confused Roaring: Evelyn Waugh and the Modernist Tradition.* Indianapolis: Indiana University Press, 1987. Explores Waugh's place among authors of the modernist tradition, discussing metaphysical, aesthetic, epistemological, and other themes in Waugh's collected works. Includes bibliographical references, index.

Patey, Douglas Lane. *"Brideshead Revisited."* In *The Life of Evelyn Waugh: A Critical Biography.* Malden, Mass.: Blackwell, 1998. A concise study that addresses the novel's autobiographical aspect as well as its Catholic and aesthetic themes. Includes bibliographical references, index.

Mary Kolner

A BRIGHTNESS THAT MADE MY SOUL TREMBLE
Poems on the Life of Hildegard of Bingen

Author: Stella Ann Nesanovich (1944-   )
First published: Thibodaux, La.: Blue Heron Press, 1996
Genre: Poetry
Subgenres: Lyric poetry; meditation and contemplation
Core issues: Forgiveness; holiness; humility; justice; truth; women

Through a series of lyrical and meditative poems, Nesanovich pays homage to an important historical religious figure, Hildegard von Bingen (1098-1179). Each poem insightfully and artistically depicts a significant moment in Hildegard's life and thus enriches and enlarges the reader's understanding of a courageous and influential medieval woman.

Overview

Born in what is now Germany in 1198, Hildegard von Bingen was tithed to the Catholic church at the age of eight. She lived in abbeys as a nun for the rest of her life and rose to a position of leadership from which she wielded considerable influence within the church hierarchy. Her visionary experiences doubtless contributed to her status as a healer, preacher, writer, and teacher of younger women, who became nuns under her influence. Her life as a female leader in a male-dominated church hierarchy was predictably one of constant struggle and conflict, but also often was one of eventual success. Stella Ann Nesanovich has selected the major struggles and successes of Hildegard's life as the basis for poetic renderings, which creatively and with artistic license bring Hildegard to life for modern readers.

The first several poems, "Prayer," "Entry at Disibodenberg," and "The Child Hildegard at Her Needle," present Hildegard at or near the time of her being tithed to the Church. These are simpler than the later poems, to appropriately reflect the mind of an eight-year-old child. One depicts the child in her loneliness and self-dissatisfaction, seeing herself as a weed outside the abbey. These poems also effectively capture the child's immaturity in her fixation on the smell of leeks on the abbot and the ugly, toothless smile of the servant and in her inability to perceive their more subtle but more substantial inner virtues. However, they also show the child's awareness of her own flaws and need to mature into adult religiousness. In these poems, Hildegard's struggle is with herself.

In the next poem, "The Death of Jutta and Election as Magistra," that struggle has been won. Hildegard is now thirty-eight years old and has been elected magistra, or leader, of the abbey in which she resides. Here, the imagery is complex and sophisticated, reflecting an intelligent, persuasive leader at the height of her powers, including metaphors of the black wing of death, the rose mallow as opening life, the world as God's tapestry visible by only a golden thread, and the deceased former magistra as a star in the firmament. Even more impressive is Hildegard's persuasive, humble depiction of herself as the irritant in an oyster's eye that engenders a pearl, unworthy in herself but working for invaluable ends via service to her religion. Here, Hildegard is presented as having won her first and most important struggle, to become an intelligent, persuasive, powerful leader in her religious community.

The next poems, "First Visions" and "Letter to Bernard of Clairvaux," reflect Hildegard's successful effort to win church approval for her visionary experiences. The same sophisticated and complicated imagery is used here, with an abundance of color references ("greening power," "golden cloud," "shining fire," "Christ in blue," "deepest crimson") to give substance to essentially mystical experiences. Smells also figure prominently ("stench of hell," "sweet perfume of paradise") as does touch ("pain like blows," "gentle touch of angels"). These appeals to the senses bring her visionary experiences into the realm of human, earthly perception.

The next poem, "The Move to Rupertsberg," deals with Hildegard's gaining approval to move her group of nuns to Rupertsberg and establish a new abbey in the relative wilderness. The poem presents Hildegard using her leadership abilities to attest persuasively to the overcrowding of the abbey at Disibodenberg and shows her ambition to fulfill her vision of establishing the new abbey in furtherance of the spread of her religion. The poem ends with the marvelous image of the nuns as uncaged robins in winter, marking a course for others to follow.

After these successes, the next three poems depict a turning point in Hildegard's life: her first real, public defeat. "The Threat of Bremen" reveals that a favorite nun, Richardis, has used the assistance of her brother, a high-ranking church official, to leave Hildegard and become the leader of her own abbey. That Hildegard is distraught and feels betrayed is obvious, and by unicorn imagery Nesanovich subtly suggests that there may have been at least a subconscious, sublimated sexual element in Hildegard's attachment to the younger nun. "The Uprooting" is an address to Richardis's brother, pleading for the return of the younger nun. Although Hildegard overtly states her concern for Richardis's soul, Nesanovich's poem hints that here Hildegard's motives are less admirably clear and consistent than in previous struggles. The next poem, "The Death of Richardis," confirms this by revealing Richardis's death in the midst of this power struggle and by Nesanovich having Hildegard note the importance of begging God's pardon for all involved, including herself.

Hildegard's struggles continue in "The Death of Volmar," her monk secretary. This poem, which depicts the struggle to obtain approval for proper burial of Volmar, foreshadows the final struggle in Hildegard's life. Several of the last poems, "Interdict," "Symphonia," and "The Strength of Air," present Hildegard's struggle with the aftermath of her decision to have a young man buried in the sacred ground of her abbey and her refusal to have him disinterred, based on her conviction that he confessed and reconciled himself to the Church and thus deserved the honorable burial. "Interdict" reflects the punishment she and her nuns received, a prohibition on all religious ritual and celebration, including singing and the important Eucharist. In "Symphonia," Hildegard pleads strongly and persuasively before the prelates for the lifting of the interdiction, but to no avail. Then, in perhaps the most powerful poem, "The Strength of Air," Hildegard persuades the archbishop of Mainz to intercede for her abbey and end the interdiction, with strongly alliterative lines like "now justice seems a juiceless maiden" and "not the noble warrior we know." This poem also memorably ends with alliteration, in Hildegard's admonition that pride rules the prelates. By this judicious alliteration, Nesanovich makes this poem even more effective. The last poems, "Our God Has Come to Save Us" and "Let This Green Earth," capture Hildegard's triumph when the interdiction is lifted but also the price she paid by her death soon thereafter.

Christian Themes

Christian themes abound in Nesanovich's poems about Hildegard von Bingen. By far the most significant of these is Christian forgiveness, established initially in "The Child Hildegard at Her Needle." After admitting her abhorrence of the smell of the abbot and of the toothlessness and other flaws of the servant, even at age ten Hildegard is able to perceive the wrong in fixing on people's flaws without appreciating their virtues. The poem ends with the child praying to be forgiven for her pride, the worst sin, implicit in her criticisms of others. Also, forgiveness figures prominently in "The Death of Richardis," in which the mature Hildegard is presented as aware that all involved in the struggle over Richardis, including herself, contributed to the younger nun's death. Thus, Hildegard indicates that she will ask God's forgiveness for all.

Forgiveness is also central to the final, and probably greatest, struggle of Hildegard's life, that concerning burial of the young man on her abbey's sacred ground, which led to the interdiction against Hildegard's anchorage. This struggle, reflected in several of Nesanovich's poems, derives from Hildegard's conviction that the young may genuinely confess and repent and thus must be forgiven and honored by a proper, sacred burial. That this forgiveness was fundamental to Hildegard is obvious in her refusal to bow to pressure to disinter the young man, her endurance of the interdiction, and her powerful struggle to have it lifted. Although she is more than eighty years old, she goes in person to argue the issue before the prelates and basically gives her life for the principle of Christian forgiveness. Three aspects of the forgiveness— that it is given by a woman leader and her female followers; that it is of a young man probably like most young men, a significant sinner; and that it is against the virtually intransigent authority of male church leaders—shows the importance of the feminine in the Christian forgiveness tradition. Without this feminine element in Christianity, very likely there would not be such a tradition. Through the emotional power and skillful artistry of her poems, Nesanovich has given this Christian forgiveness principle renewed life.

Sources for Further Study

Gottfried and Theoderic. *The Life of Hildegard of Bingen*. Translated by Adelgundis Furhkotter and James McGrath. Collegeville, Minn.: The Liturgical Press, 1995. A biography of Hildegard von Bingen, as related by two monks very knowledgeable about her.

Hildegard of Bingen. *Book of Divine Works with Letters and Songs*. Edited by Matthew Fox. Translated by Robert Cunningham, Terry Dybdal, and Ron Miller. Santa Fe, N.Mex.: Bear, 1987. A diverse collection of writings by Hildegard von Bingen, including sermons, meditations, letters, and songs.

_____. *Mystical Writings*. Edited by Fiona Bowie and Oliver Davies. Translated by Robert Carver. New York: Crossroad, 1990. An extensive collection of writings by Hildegard von Bingen about her visionary or mystical experiences.

John L. Grigsby

BROKEN LANCE

Author: Michele Sorensen (1962-1995)
First published: Salt Lake City, Utah: Deseret Book, 1997
Genre: Novel
Subgenres: Adventure; historical fiction (nineteenth century); Western
Core issues: Alienation from God; connectedness; faith; Mormons and Mormonism;
   Native Americans

*Sorensen's novel displays how people from different cultures and religious traditions
can connect with one another. As Sorensen illustrates, people share the human condition and thus have similar experiences and can empathize with one another. Furthermore, Sorensen also deals with the theme of alienation from God and the problem of
evil.*

> Principal characters
> *Callie McCracken*, the protagonist
> *Angus McCracken*, Callie's husband
> *Jamie McCracken*, Callie's oldest son
> *Duncan McCracken*, Callie's middle child
> *Susa McCracken*, Callie's youngest and only daughter
> *Three Elk*, an Indian who guides the McCracken family to Fort
>   Bridger

Overview

Set in 1857, *Broken Lance* follows Angus and Callie McCracken, emigres to the
United States who have converted to the Mormon faith, as they trek west to join other
Mormons in Salt Lake City. The novel opens with the McCracken family—Angus,
Callie, and their three children—along with other individuals encountering a group of
Cheyenne Indians who are attacking their wagon party. While Callie and her children
remain hidden, Angus and the other men attempt to fight off the Indians. In the process, Angus is killed. In the meantime, Callie and her children have hidden in a secret
compartment in the wagon, safe from harm. Once the Indians have left, Callie
emerges to discover her husband's body. Determined that her children not see her
bury their father, she demands that they stay in the wagon. Callie must then determine
how she and her children, stranded in Wyoming, are to make their way to the closest
fort, which is Fort Bridger.

Thus, Callie and her children, along with what small provisions they have, trek
through the wilderness of Wyoming. At first, she is alone in protecting her children
and making sure they have enough food. However, at one point, Callie comes across a
wounded Indian. When she sees him, "Callie's first impulse was victorious revenge.
Something sweetly exuberant rose inside of her at the sight of a red savage devastated
and defenseless." Even though this particular Indian has done no harm to her, she still

feels hatred toward him. Since her husband was killed by Indians, she views all Indians negatively. When Jamie, her oldest son, asks her what she is going to do with him, she answers, "'Turn him over to the authorities, as soon as we find some. He's a brutal murderer.'" Callie, though, does not know that the Indian is a murderer; she is making an assumption based on what happened to her husband.

When the Indian wakes up, Callie learns that his name is Three Elk. At first, their interaction does not encourage Callie to change her views on him. She becomes angry when she realizes, "That contemptible, illiterate savage thought no more of her than she did of him!" There is a obvious irony in the fact that she does not see the inconsistency of her moral stand: She disdains Three Elk, but when she comes to the conclusion that Three Elk does not think much of her, either, she is upset.

Despite this rocky beginning, Callie slowly starts to see Three Elk differently. It is winter, and when Callie is adamant about continuing their journey, Three Elk decides to stay at their campsite. Once Callie and her children have been out on foot for a while, a snowstorm develops. Callie realizes that it would be best for them to head back to the campsite. As they are returning, they come across Three Elk, who seems happy that they have come back. Another breakthrough moment is when Callie is out hunting:

> Callie breathed deeply and lifted her right foot, and then her left, then her right again. Her mind saw the faces of Jamie and Duncan and Susa—not hunger-pinched, in her memory, but jolly and round. She caressed them, kissed them, showed them what she'd brought. Then she saw Three Elk, and gratitude rushed up inside her, for he had been there with them while she was gone. That was when Callie realized, as she approached the door of their shelter, that she would be glad to see Three Elk, too.

As a result, Callie starts to see Three Elk as a person who can help her and someone whom she can trust.

Three Elk also starts to see Callie differently. Three Elk promises Callie that he will help protect her and her children against those Indians who "hunt his friend." This promise is a breakthrough moment in the novel: Not only is Three Elk committing to help Callie, but he also has revealed that he considers her his friend. No longer do they have disregard for one another; they value each other and have developed a friendship full of compassion and respect.

When Three Elk has finally led Callie and her children to Fort Bridger, they have to say good-bye to one another, which is difficult for Callie. As a parting gift, she gives Three Elk Angus's copy of the Book of Mormon. Even though Three Elk is not a Mormon himself, he very much values the book and handles it gently. Following this, Three Elk takes the lance Callie had used many times to hunt food and breaks it. Callie is confused at first in regard to why Three Elk would break the lance. However, she realizes that the lance is a symbol for violence, and it is violence that caused her to lose a husband and a father for her children. By destroying the lance, Three Elk is showing that violence should not exist in a person's life and people should be more peaceful toward one another.

Christian Themes

One major Christian theme in *Broken Lance* is alienation from God. There are times within the novel when Callie feels abandoned by God and does not understand why she has been placed in various difficult situations. At one point, she reflects: *"How could God have let this happen?* Once again she felt deserted, frustrated even beyond what her own thoughts could define." Her thoughts insinuate that God is responsible for the obstacles people encounter. However, throughout the course of the novel, Callie faces difficulties and is able to overcome them. For example, by overcoming the obstacle of judging Three Elk, she not only becomes a better person but also is able to see all people as individuals and avoid prejudging them as typical of a certain group of people.

What makes it possible for Callie to survive the difficult situations she faces is her continual faith in God. Even though she questions God, she does not lose her faith. For example, when Callie hunts and is able to secure food for her and her children, she "fell on her knees among the bright sun-washed rocks and thanked Heaven." When any good event happens, Callie thanks God. Her gratitude reveals that she firmly believes that every blessing she receives is from God and therefore that she has not lost her faith.

Finally, a significant Christian theme in *Broken Lance* is connectedness. Even though Three Elk is not Christian, Callie learns that she can still connect with him because he is a human being. As human beings, they share similar experiences and similar emotions. At one point in the novel, Callie "felt a sudden unsettling certainty, a startling sure conviction that, like her supplications, his prayers were also heard." Even if they do not practice the same religion, they both have religious beliefs and they both pray to a higher power to help them get through hard times.

Sources for Further Study

Anderson, Lavina F., and Maureen U. Beecher, eds. *Sisters in Spirit: Mormon Women in Historical and Cultural Perspective*. Urbana: University of Illinois Press, 1987. This group of essays, dealing with issues of women and Mormonism within a historical framework, sets the novel in perspective.

Davies, Douglas J. *An Introduction to Mormonism*. Cambridge, England: Cambridge University Press, 2003. A guide and overview of Mormonism, which includes its historical and theological development over the years.

Hudak, Melissa. Review of *Broken Lance*. *Library Journal* 122, no. 14 (September 1, 1997). Brief, positive review of the novel which "highly recommends" it.

Shipps, Jan. "Difference and Otherness: Mormonism and the American Religious Mainstream." In *Minority Faiths and the American Protestant Mainstream*, edited by Jonathan D. Sarna. Urbana: University of Illinois Press, 1998. Discusses early Mormonism in the United States and how it is separate from other mainstream faiths.

Paula D. Krueger

THE BROTHERS KARAMAZOV

Author: Fyodor Dostoevski (1821-1881)
First published: Bratya Karamazovy, 1879-1880 (*The Brothers Karamazov,* 1912)
Edition used: "The Brothers Karamazov": The Constance Garnett Translation Revised by Ralph E. Matlaw—Backgrounds and Sources, Essays in Criticism. New York: Norton, 1976
Genre: Novel
Subgenre: Literary fiction
Core issues: Doubt; faith; good vs. evil; justice; love; suffering

In his last novel, Dostoevski focuses on a family in crisis to explore fundamental issues of religious faith, particularly the question of whether it is possible to find and maintain faith in God despite enormous and inexplicable suffering on earth. Dostoevski critiques the notion of a benevolent God against active models of selfless love to offer a hopeful vision of an authentic Christian spirituality.

> *Principal characters*
> *Fyodor Karamazov,* a father
> *Dmitri Karamazov,* Fyodor's eldest son
> *Ivan Karmazov,* Fyodor's second son
> *Alyosha Karamazov,* Fyodor's youngest son
> *Pavel Smerdyakov,* Fyodor's illegitimate son
> *Grigory,* Fyodor's servant
> *Zosima,* Alyosha's spiritual mentor
> *Grushenka,* Dmitri's beloved
> *Katerina Ivanovna,* Dmitri's fiancé
> *Ilyusha Snegiryov,* a young boy who is seriously ill
> *Kolya Krasotkin,* a charismatic young boy

Overview

The plot of *The Brothers Karamazov* revolves around the murder of Fyodor Karamazov, a grasping Russian landowner with three legitimate children—Dmitri, Ivan, and Alyosha. Each son has a dominant personality trait: Dmitri possesses broad passions, Ivan is a cool intellectual, and Alyosha has a spiritual orientation. Another member of the Karamazov household, a servant named Pavel Smerdyakov, is rumored to be Fyodor's illegitimate son, and he emanates corrosive malevolence.

As the novel opens, Fyodor and Dmitri are in competition for the affections of a young woman named Grushenka. Although Dmitri is betrothed to Katerina Ivanovna, a proud woman of the gentry, he has fallen madly in love with Grushenka, but Grushenka keeps both Dmitri and Fyodor at a distance because she has hopes of a reunion with her first lover, a Pole who abandoned her years earlier. Discovering that

Grushenka has unexpectedly left home one evening, Dmitri suspects that she has gone to Fyodor's house. Frenzied, he snatches up a pestle and rushes off to his father's house. Catching sight of him in an open window, Dmitri feels such revulsion that he is on the verge of striking him, but, at the last moment, he restrains himself. Running away from the house, Dmitri is seized by his father's servant Grigory. Dmitri hits Grigory with the pestle and, believing him to be dead, leaves him behind.

Dmitri learns that Grushenka has gone to an inn in a nearby town to meet her former lover. Dmitri follows her there, planning to see her one more time before he kills himself. Once there, however, he realizes that Grushenka has become disenchanted with the Pole, and she and Dmitri declare their love for each other. Dmitri is torn between joy over his newfound love with Grushenka and grief over the thought that he has killed Grigory. The police arrive and charge Dmitri with murder, not of Grigory but of Fyodor. Grigory's wound was not fatal, but Fyodor was found brutally murdered. Dmitri is interrogated at length and then is allowed to sleep briefly. He has a vivid dream featuring a mother with a suffering child, and he feels a deep determination to help. He awakens with a new sense of resolve. He declares that he is ready to accept responsibility for his father's death, even though he was not the actual murderer, because he had had the intention of killing him.

While Dmitri's experiences represent a major focus of the novel, the other brothers have important roles to play as well. Whereas Dmitri is filled with turbulent passion, Ivan is filled with skepticism and doubt. In a conversation with Alyosha, Ivan cites examples of the suffering of innocent children as the grounds for a searing attack on the idea of a beneficent God. He then narrates his "Legend of the Grand Inquisitor," the protagonist of which declares that humans are too weak to bear the freedom of choice that Jesus asked of them. Ivan's Inquisitor says that he has learned that the way to bind human hearts is through miracle, mystery, and authority, as suggested in the three temptations presented to Jesus by the devil in the wilderness.

Tormented by Ivan's diatribe, Alyosha undergoes a crisis of his own when his spiritual mentor, the monk Zosima, dies. Alyosha had hoped that the man's saintliness would be marked by miracles after his death, but instead, the corpse began to decay and smell at an unusually rapid rate. In an echo of Ivan's position, the grief-stricken Alyosha feels ready to reject God's world, but an unexpected encounter with Grushenka triggers a sharp reversal. Grushenka's compassion for Alyosha's grief leads him to a new appreciation of the instinctual goodness of people. He returns to Zosima's cell and has a radiant vision of the resurrected monk beckoning him to a divine feast. When he awakens, he feels himself to be a new man.

Near the end of the novel, Ivan learns from Smerdyakov that Smerdyakov had murdered Fyodor, and that he had done so because of Ivan's oft-stated conviction that without immortality, all things are permitted. After his last meeting with Smerdyakov, Ivan returns to his lodging and has a conversation with a mysterious figure who claims to be the devil, but Ivan cannot decide whether it is an authentic figure of evil or merely the product of his own fevered imagination. This shabby demon serves to mock and expose the rank cynicism of Ivan's cherished ideas.

The next day, Ivan goes to Dmitri's trial and makes a confession of Smerdyakov's crime and his own complicity in it, but his words strike the public as the ravings of a deranged mind, and the jury is not swayed. Dmitri is found guilty of his father's murder. At the end of the novel, Dmitri's fate is uncertain: Will he accept the verdict and go to prison in Siberia, or will he escape? Ivan's fate is also uncertain: He lies near death with brain fever. Alyosha, on the other hand, has found his calling. In the last scene of the novel, he makes a stirring speech prompted by the death of Ilyusha, a young boy whom he had befriended. Alyosha exhorts the boy's companions, including the charismatic youth Kolya Krasotkin, to use their memories of Ilyusha to lead them to a life of goodness and mutual concern.

Christian Themes

Early in the novel, Dmitri declares that God and the devil are at war, and their battlefield is the heart of man. In *The Brothers Karamazov* Dostoevski sought to depict the battle between God and the devil, good and evil, faith and doubt, in vivid and eminently human terms. In one corner stands Ivan Karamazov, who offers wrenching examples of the senseless cruelty inflicted upon innocent children and uses these examples to cast doubt on the concept that the Christian God is all-good if he is all-powerful. Ivan's posture of corrosive doubt casts a pall on the other characters, and his denial of the notion of immortality and divine justice encourages Smerdyakov in his conviction that he can kill with impunity.

Significantly, Dostoevski does not try to rebut Ivan's attack on the righteousness of God's universe through direct argumentation. Instead, he deploys a series of indirect arguments to present a different view of God's world and the potential for human goodness latent within it. To begin, he introduces the Russian Orthodox monk Zosima, a kind and compassionate man who preaches a doctrine of active love and personal responsibility for the well-being of others. Not only are Zosima's teachings presented in an extended conversation recorded by Alyosha, but the monk is also shown at work among the people, putting into practice what he preaches. His active selflessness contrasts distinctly with Ivan's passive and egocentric peroration.

What is more, Dostoevski uses figures of suffering children, such as Ilyusha Snegiryov, to suggest the ultimate good that can emerge from what at first glance seems to be tragic and painful. Finally, Dostoevski introduces a series of scenes in which the sadness of death is followed by the discovery of a joyful new beginning, and thus the entire novel becomes an affirmation of the basic message of Christ's death and resurrection.

Sources for Further Study

Frank, Joseph. *Dostoevsky: The Mantle of the Prophet, 1871-1881*. Princeton, N.J.: Princeton University Press, 2002. This authoritative critical biography provides detailed information on the intellectual and literary context of the novel's creation as well as a close reading of its main themes.
Scanlan, James P. *Dostoevsky the Thinker*. Ithaca, N.Y.: Cornell University Press,

2002. Scanlan places Dostoevski's views on Russian Orthodox Christianity in the broader context of his philosophic writings.

Terras, Victor. *A Karamazov Companion: Commentary on the Genesis, Language, and Style of Dostoevsky's Novel.* Madison: University of Wisconsin Press, 1981. Offers introductory essays on major themes and techniques as well as comprehensive annotation of literary and religious allusions.

Thompson, Diane Oenning. *"The Brothers Karamazov" and the Poetics of Memory.* Cambridge, England: Cambridge University Press, 1991. Thompson's study of the theme of memory also gives illuminating commentary on the Christian themes in the work.

Julian W. Connolly

THE BURNING FIELDS

Author: David Middleton (1949-   )
First published: Baton Rouge: Louisiana State University Press, 1991
Genre: Poetry
Subgenres: Lyric poetry; meditation and contemplation
Core issues: Attachment and detachment; connectedness; time

These poems, by one of America's leading Episcopalian poets, consider themes of landscape, memory, and devotion on both abstract and experiential levels. Middleton, a poet of the modern South, gives a series of vivid glimpses into the region's past and present, devoting many poems to his ancestors and teachers and pursuing questions fundamental to Christian belief.

Overview

David Middleton has spent nearly all his life in the state where he was born, Louisiana. Growing up in Saline, in the northwestern part of the state, as of 2006 he lived in Thibodaux, in southeastern Louisiana, near the Mississippi Delta. There he composed *The Building Fields.* The poems are short to medium-length and use rhyme and meter. They also, however, have a conversational, personal quality, and Middleton's use of contemporary language avoids archaisms and stilted expressions.

Middleton begins and ends the collection with poems dedicated to the memory of his maternal grandmother, surnamed Sudduth, who died in Saline in 1962. The opening poem, "The Vision," describes the grandmother's memories of her southern past in vivid, sensory terms, describing the plants and birds of the region as well as the grandmother's grace and courtesy. The grandmother's optimism about what awaits her in the afterlife is conveyed charmingly and unpretentiously. The closing poem, "The Family Tree," describes a pecan tree in the grandmother's backyard. The combination of the tree's abundance and mortality, its fertility and its vulnerability to nature's ravages, become symbols for the grandmother, whose bodily mortality is offset by the continuity of the poet's memories of her.

"The Vision" is followed by "The Patriarch," a poem dedicated to the memory of the poet's grandfather. A white, male southerner, he was haunted by the legacy of the Civil War. "His" war, however, was World War I, and Middleton makes the important point that this first major conflict since the battle between the Union and the Confederacy was important for southerners because it enabled them to channel their patriotism into a worldwide battle for democracy, as opposed to a regional resentment.

Another poem of mourning, for Middleton's mother, is much more personal. "The Quiet Garden" is an intimate and moving meditation on the close and essential bond between mother and son. Like the other poems of mourning, this poem invokes nature imagery to stress both the melancholy and consoling aspects of change.

Middleton also looks back to the southern Agrarian writers, such as Allen Tate and the Tennessean novelist Andrew Lyle (who died in 1992, but not before offering a strongly positive blurb for the jacket of the first edition of *The Burning Fields*). In "The Agrarians," Middleton argues that these thinkers, though self-consciously rooting themselves in the southern rural tradition, also were at pains to call upon the entire tradition of the West. They strove, Middleton stresses, to communicate essential truths not fundamentally grounded in any specific culture or place. Some might argue that Middleton fails to mention the Agrarians' strong sympathies for white supremacism and offers an overly optimistic reading of their legacy. Other poems about honored predecessors, including tributes to Father Francis L. Kerne and the scholar of the Victorian era John Hazard Wildman, are more personal, sketching character traits the poet admires and wishes to recommend to the reader.

The title poem, "The Burning Fields," relates the destruction of sugar fields in southern Louisiana by fire that spread from oil refineries. Though fire, not water, is the elemental agent of disaster here, the scene will resonate strongly with post-2005 readers aware of the destruction wreaked by Hurricane Katrina on the same region.

"On the Suicide of the Chairman of the Math Department" contrasts a mathematics scholar's skill at quantitative reasoning with the despair he experiences in his inner life. The poem's clipped, terse pace achieves pathos without being overly sentimental or melodramatic. Similarly evocative of a mentality closed to consolation is "The Stoic," one of the volume's most intriguing poems. Written in the first person but not necessarily in Middleton's own voice, the poem, measured in strict quatrains, succeeds in sketching a sensibility utterly remote from any sort of higher calling, a mindset that refuses inspiration or idealism.

Christian Themes

Middleton is an active Episcopalian, the poetry editor for the *Anglican Theological Review*, and an elected member of the Guild of Scholars of the Episcopal Church. An indication of both Middleton's theological perspective and his sense of the Christian life is the central sequence of *The Burning Fields*, "The Middle World," which is dedicated to Eric Voegelin (1901-1985). Voegelin was a conservative thinker who left Germany during the Nazi era and taught for many years at Louisiana State University, where Middleton was his student. Voegelin was interested in the idea of tradition in both the classical and the biblical worlds—interests that Middleton, who ends this primarily Christian volume with a series of poems on incidents from classical mythology, would maintain.

Middleton writes about the essential generalities of Christian faith, but he examines them through the prism of felt experience. In "The Shepherd," the speaker recalls seeing a Christmas pageant as a young boy. He then traverses the same ground many years later as a mature adult. Instead of being a trivial memory of childhood fun, the Christmas pageant now seems profoundly symbolic of life's meaningful losses.

Middleton shares many of his Christian themes and interests with T. S. Eliot, a poet widely influential on the southern Agrarians, who were his teachers and forebears. In "Epiphany in Baca," Middleton seems to write a deliberate sequel to Eliot's "The Journey of the Magi," describing the return of the three wise men from Bethlehem as Eliot had evoked their arrival. In "The Buried Life," Middleton praises the life of H. J. Sachs, another of Middleton's teachers. Sachs was just the sort of freethinking Jew whom Eliot, in his 1934 essay collection *After Strange Gods*, deplored as unlikely to contribute to an ordered society with a strong sense of tradition. Middleton praises Sachs for acknowledging his religious tradition at the end of his life, but at the same time the poem does not leave the reader feeling as if a lifetime championing secular ideals has been a total waste. A shorter, related poem, on the alleged deathbed conversion of the poet Wallace Stevens, makes a similar point. It testifies to both the honor of a life spent largely without the consolations of religion and the pleasure the soul gives itself upon an acknowledgment of faith.

Middleton is generally optimistic about the ability of art to embody Christian meanings. In "For a Needlewoman" and "The Maker in Lent," both dedicated to women, Middleton celebrates the anonymous craftspeople whose dedication to sacred art has provided an ordinary yet compelling illustration of the way the numinous can surprise and animate the world.

Middleton is not narrowly sectarian. In "Two for Taliessin" he shows the continuity between Celtic paganism and Christian spirituality. Though he is an Episcopalian, in "Thomas Tallis to William Byrd, upon the Late Dissolution of the Abbeys" he laments the seizure of Roman Catholic monastic properties by King Henry VIII of England. Henry VIII was the founding father of the Anglican tradition, from which Episcopalianism derives; Middleton does not, in other words, blindly endorse every aspect of the history of his own tradition. "Lines for the Dormition of the Virgin" uses the image of the Dormition (earthly death) of the Virgin Mary to castigate secular modernity. Middleton suggests that the Virgin Mary's unique combination of fleshliness and abstract spirituality is meaningless amid the vast wasteland of the modern age.

Sources for Further Study

Middleton, David. Review of *Christina Rossetti: The Complete Poems*. *Anglican Theological Review*, January, 2003. In reviewing the great nineteenth century Christian poet Christina Rossetti, Middleton offers his own thoughts on how to achieve spiritual intensity in poetry, as well as on the role the individual sensibility can play in religious poetry.

_____. Review of *Hours/Moon and Sun/A Hymn of Simon Peter*, by Kenneth A. Lohf. *Anglican Theological Review*, Fall, 1999. Middleton's review of his fellow Christian poet gives an overview of Middleton's own aesthetic preferences.

Sampson, Dennis. "The Authentic Voice." *The Hudson Review* 45 (Winter, 1993): 668-676. The reviewer is uncomfortable with Middleton's formalism but praises the vivid portraiture of the people depicted in the poetry.

Stanford, Donald E. "Wintersian Formalism." *Southern Review* 104 (Winter, 1996): 164-167. Although mentioning *The Burning Fields* only briefly, Stanford provides an informative general discussion of Middleton's poetry, his relation to the formalist aesthetic of Yvor Winters, and his debts to previous Christian poetries.
Tota, Frank P. Review of *The Burning Fields*. *The Hollins Critic* 30, no. 1 (February, 1993): 19. Short but perceptive review concentrating on its southern and religious themes.

Nicholas Birns

CALLED TO QUESTION
A Spiritual Memoir

Author: Joan D. Chittister, O.S.B. (1936-   )
First published: Lanham, Md.: Sheed & Ward, 2004
Genre: Nonfiction
Subgenres: Autobiography; handbook for living; journal or diary
Core issues: Asceticism; Catholics and Catholicism; church; clerical life; faith; freedom and free will; religion; women

Benedictine sister Chittister, a prolific author and outspoken advocate for social justice, focuses her attention on the spiritual growth process. She offers insights into her own growth and discusses how our relationships with God and other people, our sexuality, the natural world, and the struggle to find the holy in daily life all shape our spiritual journey. In the end, Chittister concludes that the seeking matters most of all.

Overview

Sister Joan Chittister has been an influential person in the Catholic Church for more than three decades. A former president of the Leadership Conference of Women Religious, she has been a strong advocate for women's ordination and has spoken out on other issues of social justice, such as rights for homosexuals and environmental concerns. A controversial figure, she is held in great esteem by those on the left and is sometimes vilified by those on the right.

In *Called to Question*, Chittister invites the reader to share in her thought processes and her spiritual journey. When she was younger, she was convinced of the correctness of the Catholic Church's position. She tells how she struggled to accept pre-Vatican II teachings concerning Protestants in the light of her own Presbyterian stepfather. She also had difficulty with her mother's not attending Mass. Her questions about the Church were therefore planted in her youth, but she suppressed them and willingly accepted Church teachings. Then, when a cardinal at a conference in Rome made some questionable assertions about the Eucharist, she no longer took the Church's teachings for granted and began to take responsibility for her own spirituality.

Chittister began to keep a journal—a dialogue with other spiritual writers in which she recorded her questions and what others from a variety of faith traditions had to say about each topic. Then she would record her responses. Excerpts from that journal are included in *Called to Question*, which expands on her original ideas.

Chittister begins by questioning the role of religion in our lives, exploring the difference between religion and spirituality. According to Chittister, religion is external; it provides rules and rituals to lead us to the divine. Spirituality is the internal process that takes us beyond religion to the divine. Chittister questions the nature of that divine being. One day she was at prayer with her community and realized that prayers were always addressed to "God the Father," never to "God the Mother." This assumption that God is male barred women from being seen in the image of the divine. Chittister therefore set out to change that understanding of God and received much opposition in the process. She also questions the image of God as an eternal judge, keeping close track of the multiple levels of sin that one might commit. Chittister instead seeks an emphasis on regarding God with awe. She states that the focus should be on God, not on human sin. She values prayer to God and its role in aligning our will with his, but she questions those who pray without corresponding action. In her eyes, prayer should never be used as an escape from life.

She also discusses what it means to be "called." God calls each of us to contribute in some way to creation. God gives us the tools to carry out our particular mission in life. While acknowledging how difficult it can be to strip away all the other voices that speak to us and that try to influence the direction of our lives, Chittister emphasizes the importance of listening to God's direction, no matter where it may lead or what others might say. She also delves into what it means to have commitment and balance in our lives.

The second half of *Called to Question* deals with relationships with other people and the world at large. Chittister encourages us to love with passion, convinced that it is only through human love that we can come to know God's love. Her position on love leads to her emphasis on social action. Love must be taken out into the world and used to make that world a better, more just place for others. We need to find evil in the world, particularly ageism, sexism, and racism, and root it out. Silence does not make things better; we must speak up and work for change. Chittister finds power in the position that one has nothing to lose—one has nowhere to go but up. She speaks for women's rights because without the full contributions of women to the world, the world is using only half its resources. Men, too, will be more complete when women can use all their gifts.

It is also important to respect the natural world. We are part of nature and must treat it and ourselves as such. Nature can teach us much about life's rhythms: growth, death, and rebirth. Chittister attacks asceticism, because it seeks to reject the material world of which we are so much a part. She notes that creation is not a onetime event; we are always changing, becoming something new.

Christian Themes

In *Called to Question*, Joan Chittister explores many of the questions that have haunted her as she has traveled on her spiritual journey. For persons who were raised, as Chittister was, in the era before Vatican II (1963), which reformed some basic Catholic teachings, the Church had all the answers. No one questioned; one merely accepted, or if one could not accept, one left the Church or did not take part in the Sacraments. A Benedictine sister, Chittister is representative of many "women religious" who faced profound changes in the Church after Vatican II. The religious institution in which they had believed no longer was seen as infallible. As a result, almost everything became ripe for questioning.

It is important to note that Chittister did not leave the Catholic Church. She sought change from within and has made both friends and enemies in the process. In the best Christian tradition, Chittister speaks for those who are often considered powerless. She wants a Church that treats women as equals and that will get involved in political issues and social justice causes. *Called to Question* illustrates the reasoning behind her positions. As the title suggests, Chittister believes her God-given role in life is to question everything, to seek God's (not necessarily the Church's) answers.

Chittister has much to offer in her writing for those who struggle in their spiritual lives. Although she offers few answers to the questions and struggles that plague people as they travel on their spiritual journey, she makes a strong case that the struggle itself has value. In the end, she concludes that it may be the journey, the seeking, that is the most important part of life. For Catholics, *Called to Question* also raises the issue of what it means to be faithful to the Catholic Church. Chittister seems to have very little respect for the tradition of which she is a part. While she would no doubt argue that she is trying to make the Catholic Church better, she wants a Catholic Church of her own making. She is attempting to discard two thousand years of authority and spiritual teaching. It is not surprising that many find her ideas controversial.

Sources for Further Study

Chittister, Joan. *Heart of Flesh: A Feminist Spirituality for Women and Men.* Grand Rapids, Mich.: Wm. B. Eerdmans, 1998. Beginning with the presumption that traditional spirituality has not worked, Chittister argues that a spirituality that does not consider the full experience of women is not an authentic spirituality.

_____. *Scarred by Struggle, Transformed by Hope.* Grand Rapids, Mich.: Wm. B. Eerdmans, 2003. Everyone experiences struggle and pain in life. Chittister examines the way struggle defines us and offers hope for those looking to find God through such difficulties.

Johnson, Elizabeth. *She Who Is: The Mystery of God in Feminist Theological Discourse.* New York: Crossroad, 1992. This classic theological text explores the feminine aspect of God. Johnson challenges the traditional depiction of God as male and invites the reader to broaden his or her understanding of God.

Patrice Fagnant-MacArthur

THE CANTERBURY TALES

Author: Geoffrey Chaucer (c. 1343-1400)

First transcribed: 1387-1400

Edition used: The Canterbury Tales, in *The Riverside Chaucer,* 3d ed., edited by
  Larry D. Benson. Boston: Houghton Mifflin, 1987

Genre: Poetry

Subgenres: Narrative poetry; stories

Core issues: Clerical life; confession; marriage; pastoral role; pilgrimage; sin and sinners

*Twice in this work Chaucer asserts that "Al that is writen is writen for oure doctrine,"
an idea that leads him to "retract" many of his works, including a presumed majority
of the narratives in* The Canterbury Tales. *However, Chaucer certainly expected that
serious readers would recognize that the "sinful" works must be seen as part of a total
context of a major work that demonstrates Chaucer's commitment to the truths of
Christianity as he understood them.*

> *Principal characters*
> *Chaucer*, the narrator
> *Harry Bailly*, the host
> *Robin*, the miller
> *Alison*, the miller's wife
> *The Wife of Bath*
> *The Nun's Priest*
> *The Knight*
> *The Summoner*
> *The Pardoner*
> *The Monk*
> *The Friar*
> *The Prioress*
> *The Franklin*
> *The Merchant*
> *The Parson*
> *The Reeve*

Overview

In the "General Prologue" of *The Canterbury Tales,* Geoffrey Chaucer describes
the assembling of a group of pilgrims at the Tabard Inn near London. They plan to
journey to Canterbury to visit the shrine of Saint Thomas Becket, archbishop of Canterbury, murdered by agents of King Henry II of England in 1170. A pilgrimage to this
spot was one of the favorite religious exercises in medieval England, but Chaucer's

work does not deal with an actual pilgrimage. It would have been an impossible feat for about thirty people traveling on horseback to tell a series of tales, mostly in verse. In "The Knight's Tale," one character says:

> This world nys but a a thurghfare ful of wo,
> And we been pilgrymes, passinge to and fro,
> Deeth is an ende of every worldly soore.

(This world is but a thoroughfare of woe/ And we be pilgrims passing to and fro/ Death is the end of every worldly sore.) This pilgrimage, then, is a symbol of the life of human beings.

Their host at the Tabard, Harry Bailey, proclaims that he will accompany the pilgrims and judge the effectiveness of the tales. The scope of the completed work, two tales by each pilgrim on the way out, two more on the way back, would have amounted to about 120 tales. Like Edmund Spenser's *The Faerie Queene* (1590, 1596) and other grandiose literary schemes, the work falls far short of its goal. The pilgrims, in fact, do not reach Canterbury. Chaucer may have run out of time or energy—or he may never have intended to write so many tales. In the symbolic sense, Canterbury represents death, the end of the earthly journey. It is fitting that the pilgrims remain on their pilgrimage of life toward death.

Most of the pilgrims come alive in the descriptions in the "General Prologue." Several colorful ones are in holy orders or are functionaries of the medieval church. These include priests (at least two, possibly four), two nuns, a monk, a friar, a pardoner who sells papal indulgences, and a summoner who issues summonses to an ecclesiastical court. The majority of these officials hardly live up to their vocational ideal. The Prioress is a rich, extravagant woman, the Friar gives very easy penances to confessors to encourage personal gifts, the Monk spends little time in his cloister, and the Pardoner and Summoner are scoundrels. The Parson, however, performs his duties admirably; he preaches well and, more important, obeys the rules himself. He is patient, diligent, generous, a true shepherd of souls.

Another group of pilgrims contributes tales on the subject of marriage. Of these, the most fascinating, though not the most exemplary, is that of the Wife of Bath. She has had five husbands and is now seeking a sixth. Her tale, designed to prove that wives should have sovereignty over their husbands, shocks several of the men and provokes several more marriage tales. The Clerk, a university student who will probably become a cleric, tells of a lord who subjects his wife to years of abuse, all to prove that if she submits patiently to it all, she will be rewarded. The Merchant offers a tale of a young wife who betrays her senile husband. The Franklin, who clearly does not approve of most of what he has heard and seen, offers a romance of two devoted—and married—lovers. Arveragus, the husband, resembles the Clerk's lord in expecting more or less blind obedience from his Dorigen, but extends her torment only minutes instead of years. All these men reject utterly the Wife of Bath's treatise on sovereignty, but Averagus, while no incipient feminist, understands that women, like men, enjoy liberty and temperate behavior from their mates.

The Canterbury Tales exists as a group of ten fragments, containing from one to six tales each. Although some fragments are clearly meant to precede or follow others, no one knows what Chaucer's complete order might have been, but that he wanted the Parson's Tale to come last is obvious. This man's lesson on penance and on the Seven Deadly Sins amounts to a resolution of the points of conflict seen in the marriage tales, for instance, and of controversies that erupt among the pilgrims themselves.

These controversies, for the medieval Christian mind, reflect the Seven Deadly Sins: pride, greed, lust, anger, gluttony, envy, and sloth. The Nun's Priest's Tale is a medieval favorite, the beast fable. A fox invades a barnyard and captures Chauntecleer, a cock, who has wit enough to know that the fox, successfully fleeing from the owner's pursuit, is too proud of his own cleverness to avoid bragging to his pursuers. To brag is to open the mouth in which he clutches Chauntecleer, allowing his escape to the nearest tree. The Pardoner's proposition is simply that greed is the root of all evil. Three men fall victim to their own greed by killing one another, each obsessed with being the possessor of gold coins found under a tree.

Sin breaks out not only in the tales but also in the links between them, in which the pilgrims interact. One prominent sin is anger. Some of the pilgrims either already know and dislike their fellow travelers or quickly learn to dislike them. The Miller tells a tale in which a carpenter is betrayed by his wife and a parish clerk. The Reeve, employed as a foreman on a manor, is a carpenter by trade who sees the Miller's carpenter as a caricature of himself. His response is to retaliate by telling a tale featuring a miller who is humiliated even further. There is no reconciliation between these two or in a similar exchange of tales between the Friar and the Summoner, but in a stormy clash between the Pardoner and the Host, occasioned by the Pardoner's charge that the Host is the greatest sinner of the group, the Knight intervenes and literally makes them kiss and make up.

The fact that sin is not always punished and sometimes might seem to be at least tacitly approved in *The Canterbury Tales* raises the question of the sincerity of Chaucer's insistence that all his writing reflects Christian doctrine. The tale of the Parson goes far in answering this question. The Parson is not Chaucer's most interesting character, and up to the time of his tale, he is an observer. Someone else, the Knight or the Host, steps forward to make peace. The Parson is presented as a man of great integrity in the "General Prologue," but he is silent throughout most of the work. When the Host introduces him rather rudely, he rejects the latter's suggestion of a "fable." The Host then suggests a quick tale; the Parson replies with the longest one of all. His tale, though far from the most popular among today's readers, has qualities that Chaucer's contemporaries surely would have recognized. It would have struck them as less dull than we find it. This tale would have helped the medieval audience understand the entire *Canterbury Tales* more clearly than today's typical reader. It is one of only two tales composed in prose rather than verse, but the prose clearly and vigorously resolves the moral issues posed by the waywardness of the pilgrims and of the characters in their tales. It explains penitence, the process of contrition, confession, and satisfaction that each sinner must undergo. Also, it explains thoroughly the Seven Deadly Sins, which all good pilgrims must strive to avoid.

Christian Themes

Unlike many medieval writers whose backgrounds were religious, Chaucer was a man of the world: a courtier, diplomat, and customs official. Yet his greatest work, *The Canterbury Tales*, containing many worldly elements, is a literary version of a major Christian endeavor, the pilgrimage to a holy place. A pilgrimage could of course attract worldly people, and such types are certainly found among Chaucer's pilgrims, but all medieval people recognized it as a holy exercise. Three of the tales are plainly religious: the Prioress's concerns a miracle of the Virgin Mary, the Second Nun's is a biography of Saint Cecilia (a form that in Chaucer's time was commonly called a "legend"), and the Parson's is a sermon, or perhaps more properly a theological tract. The prominence given to the last of these works in itself supports Chaucer's insistence on the reigning importance of Christian doctrine.

In a number of respects, the medieval Christian perspective permeates other tales. Several are influenced by the *De consolatione philosophiae* (523; *The Consolation of Philosophy*, late ninth century) of Boethius, who lived in the early sixth century, wrote Christian theological tracts, and was honored at least in Italy as Saint Severinus. The Boethian concept most attractive to Chaucer, *gentilesse*, is not precisely a Christian term but signifies virtuous nobility. Because "The Franklin's Tale," the most positive of Chaucer's tales on marriage, has an ancient Breton setting rather than a Christian one, the stress is not on the sacramental nature of marriage, but rather the virtue that makes Arveragus and Dorigen everlastingly true.

In the late fourteenth century, a moral decline in the habits of the religious and the deterioration of religious exercises was causing great concern. The Friar's casual attitude toward confession, the corruption in the granting of papal pardons by the Pardoner, and the worldly interests of the Prioress signal Chaucer's awareness of these shortcomings and highlights dramatically their threats to authentic Christian life. It has even been suggested by some Chaucerians that Chaucer was motivated by the principles of the Lollards, a sect of religious reformers in England in his time. Whatever the value of this interpretation, Chaucer's Parson is an obviously important moral counterweight to this deterioration of religious life. "The Parson's Tale" is an elaborate and authentic statement of the nature of sin and the importance of penitence.

Confession being an obligation of medieval Christian life, it is interesting how often Chaucer's pilgrims misunderstand and misapply it. The Miller confesses that he is drunk when he is asked for a tale, the Wife of Bath's prologue is, despite its defiance of the standards of Christian marriage, a confession of her marital failings. The Pardoner candidly acknowledges his avarice. None of them shows any sign of the contrition for their sins that the Parson insists must precede confession, and none expresses a resolution of dealing with their transgressions as an aftermath to confession. They do not turn their hearts to God, as the Parson insists is necessary. Confession, he tells them, must be to a priest in good standing with the church, and it must be discreet. By implication, the false confessions that some pilgrims have been making reflect vain-glory, not any attempt to heal their souls.

Sources for Further Study

Besserman, Laurence. *Chaucer's Biblical Poetics*. Norman: University of Oklahoma Press, 1998. Interprets the many instances of biblical diction, imagery, and themes in Chaucer's *The Canterbury Tales*.

Brown, Peter. *A Companion to Chaucer*. Oxford, England: Blackwell, 2000. Designed to appeal to inexperienced Chaucerian students, this work contains a section on Christian idealogies.

Correale, Robert M., ed. *Sources and Analogues of the Canterbury Tales*. Rochester, N.Y.: Boydell & Brewer, 2003. Includes information on and selections from many Christian sources used by Chaucer.

Robertson, D. W., Jr. *A Preface to Chaucer: Studies in Medieval Perspectives*. Princeton, N.J.: Princeton University Press, 1962. A standard reference work on Chaucer's acquaintance with, and employment of, early Christian theological works.

Robert P. Ellis

A CANTICLE FOR LEIBOWITZ

Author: Walter M. Miller, Jr. (1923-1996)
First published: New York: Eos, 2006
Genre: Novel
Subgenres: Apocalyptic fiction; Catholic fiction; science fiction
Core issues: Apocalypse; Catholics and Catholicism; devotional life; knowledge; monasticism; reason; sainthood

Miller believes that history repeats itself because people never learn from history and make the same mistakes over and over again. Humans are free but usually make the wrong choices when left on their own. Salvation and redemption can be attained only through Christianity and with guidance from organizations such as the Catholic Church. Miller is pessimistic about most people, but optimistic that at least a few will follow the will of God and be saved.

> Principal characters
>> *Brother Francis Gerard*, a monk at Leibowitz Abbey
>> *Lazarus*, a biblical character whom Jesus raised from the dead
>> *Dom Paulo*, an abbot
>> *Thon Taddeo Pfardentrott*, a secular scholar
>> *Dom Jethrah Zerchi*, a later abbot
>> *Doctor Cors*, an atheist physician

Overview

A Canticle for Leibowitz relates that about six hundred years earlier, a nuclear holocaust occurred, and the only organization to survive, at least in North America, was the Catholic Church. When the war began, Isaac Albert Leibowitz was a Jewish electrical engineer in the defense industry. He survived the war, converted to Catholicism, became a priest, and founded a monastery dedicated to the preservation of knowledge. He based the rules of the monastery on the Benedictines and established it near the remains of a highway that ran between Salt Lake City and El Paso. He named the order after Saint Albert the Great, teacher of Saint Thomas Aquinas and the patron saint of scientists. In the first years following the war, the surviving population hunted down and killed the remaining scientists and engineers because they blamed them for the disaster. They also burned all the books they could find. Leibowitz organized "bookleggers," who smuggled books, and memorizers, who memorized the contents of books. However, he was eventually betrayed by a member of his order, and a mob hanged then burned him. He was later beatified and had become a candidate for sainthood by the time the novel begins.

Part 1, "Fiat Homo" (let there be man), opens with Brother Francis Gerard of Utah, a not-too-bright novice at Leibowitz Abbey, fasting alone in the desert during Lent.

He meets a pilgrim, whom the reader eventually learns is Lazarus of the Bible. Lazarus shows Francis the entrance to a fallout shelter, where Francis discovers several artifacts and a corpse that investigators determine to be Leibowitz's wife, Emily. These artifacts include a grocery list that scholars conclude to be in Leibowitz's handwriting and a blueprint signed by Leibowitz. The discovery of the shelter becomes a key event in the canonization of Leibowitz, and several priests interview and interrogate Francis. After seven years, which is an unusually long time for a novice, Francis finally becomes a full member of the order and begins his life work as a scribe. In his spare time, he makes an illustrated and embellished copy of the blueprint. Francis, of course, has no clue as to the nature of the blueprint, entitled a "Transistorized Control System for Unit Six-B." When Leibowitz's canonization is announced fifteen years later, Francis journeys to New Rome (present-day St. Louis) to present the pope with both the original of the blueprint and his copy. On the way, he meets mutant bandits, who steal both his donkey and the copy. Nonetheless, he makes the rest of his journey on foot, attends the ceremony, and personally delivers the original blueprint to the pope.

Part 2, "Fiat Lux" (let there be light), begins in the year 3174. A scientific renaissance is taking place, and the kingdom of Texarkana is expanding to an empire spanning the continent. Scientists in Texarkana realize that they could speed up their research by examining the archives at the monastery. Thon Taddeo Pfardentrott, a cousin of the king, visits the monastery at the same time that one of the monks has deciphered one of the texts and has constructed an electric light. As he is researching the archives, Taddeo has discussions with Dom Paulo, abbot of Leibowitz Abbey during this time, about the relationship between science and faith.

Part 3, "Fiat Voluntas Tua" (thy will be done), takes place in 3781. By this time, the human race has rediscovered space travel and built on the knowledge of the twentieth century to the point where people have colonized planets in other solar systems. Unfortunately, humans have also rediscovered nuclear weapons, and the two leading superpowers, Texarkana and the Asian Coalition, are on the brink of war. The Catholic Church prepares for another nuclear holocaust by chartering its own starship with the archives of the Leibowitz Abbey and assembling a contingent of priests, nuns, and Leibowitz brothers who have space experience. The abbey is just outside an area hit by a nuclear bomb and, for a time, is used for triage by Green Star, Texarkana's emergency response organization. Dom Jethrah Zerchi, the last abbot of Leibowitz Abbey, and Doctor Cors, the head of the Green Star team, have extensive discussions about the morality of euthanasia with respect to a woman and her child who are terminally ill from radiation poisoning.

Lazarus is the only character who appears in all three parts. Because Jesus has raised him from the dead, Lazarus cannot die, and Walter Miller combines his story with the legend of the Wandering Jew. In part 1, he is a wandering pilgrim, In part 2, he is living close to the monastery as a hermit, and Dom Paulo comes to him for advice. In part 3, he is wandering again and stops by the monastery for a visit.

Christian Themes

Science and Christianity are not inherently adversarial, according to Walter M. Miller, Jr., but science for the sake of science leads to pain, suffering, death, materialism, and bondage to technology. The book implies that Leibowitz was guilty of this sin, but that he repented after seeing the consequences. Dom Paulo is a spokesperson for this position, and his secular opponent is Thon Taddeo, who argues that there is no role for religion in science or any part of society.

Miller believes that humans have freedom of choice and are ultimately responsible for their actions. This includes scientists and engineers who assist their governments in making war, such as Leibowitz. Thon Taddeo's work is supported by a prince who has no interest in science beyond its ability to increase his power. Taddeo tries to wash his hands of his employer's sins just as Pontius Pilate tried to wash his hands. The novel takes the position that Taddeo is just as guilty as any other follower and possibly more so, because he is intelligent enough to know better.

Doctor Cors regards pain as the ultimate evil and advocates euthanasia, but Dom Jethrah and Miller strongly disagree and believe that God does not send people more pain than they can bear. Cors is both eloquent and compassionate. Because radiation poisoning is a very painful way to die, Miller does not give Jethrah an easy position from which to argue. Miller also indirectly engages in a dialogue with Nevil Shute, whose classic 1957 novel *On the Beach* also deals with the consequences of nuclear warfare. Shute's main characters commit suicide when they feel the first symptoms of radiation poisoning, whereas a true Christian, according to Miller, would not.

Sources for Further Study

Miller, Walter M., Jr. *Saint Leibowitz and the Wild Horse Woman*. New York: Bantam Books, 1997. This novel, published posthumously, is not a sequel, as it is set between parts 2 and 3. It contains a map and considerable background information.

Percy, Walker. *Signposts in a Strange Land*. New York: Farrar, Straus and Giroux, 1991. Includes the essay "Rediscovering *A Canticle for Leibowitz*." Walker was an enthusiastic fan of the book but argues that it is impossible to review.

Robertson, William H., and Robert L. Battenfeld. *Walter M. Miller, Jr.: A Bio-Bibliography*. Bio-Bibliographies in American Literature 3. Westport, Conn.: Greenwood Press, 1993. Biography and annotated bibliography for all of Miller's short stories along with commentary, a glossary, and a time line for *A Canticle for Leibowitz*.

Seacrest, Rose. *Glorificemus: A Study of the Fiction of Walter M. Miller, Jr*. Latham, Md.: University Press of America, 2002. Analysis of Miller's fiction organized by topic, including a map, time line, bibliography, glossary, and plot summaries.

Thomas R. Feller

A CAPITAL OFFENSE

Author: Gary E. Parker (1953-　　)
First published: Nashville, Tenn.: T. Nelson, 1998
Genre: Novel
Subgenres: Evangelical fiction; mystery and detective fiction
Core issues: Despair; doubt; faith; innocence; prayer; trust in God

Parker's protagonist, Connie Brandon, has her Christian faith put to the test when it appears that her husband has used drugs, had an affair, and committed suicide, but she places her faith in God and looks to the Bible for answers, overcoming her doubt and despair and using her considerable detective skills to find her husband's murderer.

Principal characters
 Jack Brandon, a bookstore owner and opponent of gambling
 Connie Brandon, Jack's wife
 Katie Brandon, Jack and Connie's daughter
 Wilt Carver, attorney general, an ambitious politician
 Robert Carver, Wilt's father, behind Jack's death
 Luke Tyler, a police detective
 Sandra Lumsford, Jack's cousin
 Justin Longley, Jack's grandfather
 Brit, a psychotic hit man
 Lennie, Brit's superior
 Johnson Mack, Jefferson City's mayor, who has ties to the mob
 Tick Garner, a policeman and Jack's friend
 Tess Garner, Connie's best friend

Overview

A Capital Offense opens when bookstore owner Jack Brandon, after attending a meeting of the city council regarding gambling casinos, stops at his church and then drives his pickup to the Katy Trail, where he meets his death. Initially, the evidence (a suicide note and a mysterious twenty-five-thousand-dollar loan) points to suicide, but his wife, Connie Brandon, a devout Christian, believes that he was killed by the casino people. Other evidence surfaces: Jack died of a drug overdose, and a woman claimed that she and Jack were having an affair.

However, Connie, who has almost finished her law degree, acts as a detective: She spots a problem with the suicide note (which uncharacteristically refers to their daughter as Kate, not Katie) and points out that Jack's office, which he never locked, was locked with the door's deadbolt, but there were no fingerprints. With the help of a policeman friend of Jack, Tick Garner, and his wife, Tess, Connie perseveres. Police detective Luke Tyler is sympathetic but, because of Jack's financial problems, drops the investigation. He also keeps an influential person informed about the progress of the case. Connie finds a canceled check for ten thousand dollars made out to a Reed Morrison and a one-million-dollar life insurance policy, and one of the store employees shows her drugs that were in the store. Meanwhile, Johnson Mack, Jefferson City's mayor, offers her an exorbitant amount of money for the bookstore so that there will be a place for conventions as well as a casino.

Determined to get at the truth, Connie drives to St. Louis, where the remaining fifteen thousand dollars was deposited, and withdraws the money. She realizes that the bank's video cameras must have recorded Jack depositing the money there, so she goes to Wilt Carver, attorney general and longtime friend, for help. Wilt gets the video but first shows it to Luke, who then shows it to Connie. The video shows Jack and Sandra Lumsford kissing; Lumsford is the woman who claimed to be having an affair with Jack, but she has vanished. Furious with Jack and with God, Connie decides to go to Las Vegas, where Morrison lives. A hit man, Brit, however, has been tapping her phone and, knowing her plan, meets his boss Lennie in Las Vegas, where the two kill Morrison. When Connie arrives, the killers are escaping, and the only thing she finds at the private detective's house is a body and a picture of Jack, Sandra, and an elderly man. When she returns home, she is despondent, ignoring her children and wallowing in despair. Tess, her close friend, gets her to go to church, where she finds Jack's black book, which was not found with the other books in his book bag at the murder scene. (The night of his murder he had left it there for her to find.)

Connie follows the enigmatic directions Jack left in his black book to his favorite possession, a baseball with autographs and a barely decipherable note that sends her to the Miller High School yearbook, where she finds photos of Jack and Sandra. Through Tess, Connie traces Sandra to Black Canyon, near Las Vegas, and flies out there. She does not realize that Brit and Lennie are tapping her phone and plan to meet her in Black Canyon. By the time she arrives at the telephone address, a house owned by Justin Longley, the house has been ransacked by Lennie and Brit, and she meets Luke, who has unofficially (after the mayor shut down the investigation) followed other leads to Black Rock. Luke and Connie return to Jefferson City, but Connie is upset by Luke's romantic attention and decides to act on her own. She gets a phone call from Sandra, who comes to take her to Longley, who is near death. Longley explains that Jack's father, who had a gambling problem, promised to kill a man in order to pay off his gambling debts but could not go through with it and ran. The gamblers finally tracked him down, killing him and his wife (Longley's daughter), but Jack got away. When Lennie and Brit appear, Connie, Sandra, and Longley barely escape. Brit, who has abducted Katie, then calls Connie about meeting him at the Katy Trail. Connie agrees. When she arrives, she discovers that Lennie and Brit are acting on the orders of Wilt's father, Robert Carver, who is determined to protect his son's political future. Jack had learned that Wilt had raped Sandra, and Wilt's father feared that Jack would disclose the information if Wilt did not give up his political ambitions. When he orders his men to kill her, he is stopped by Connie's religious community, hundreds of people her pastor recruited to go with her to Katy Trail. Even Wilt appears and admits all, finally receiving the spiritual cleansing he has sought. Brit, however, does not stop, but wounds Wilt before he is shot by Luke. The novel ends with Connie at Jack's grave, assuring him about the future.

Christian Themes

A Capital Offense is representative of the boom in Christian genre fiction (here, mystery and detective fiction) written specifically for a Christian, often evangelical, audience. Gary E. Parker presents Connie Brandon as a kind of Everywoman whose Christian faith is shattered by the idea that her husband, a devout Christian, is not what he seems to be. After encountering a series of problems ranging from despair to sexual temptation she regains her faith and is at peace with her departed husband and God. Like her husband, who realizes that Christians are often at odds with the prevailing culture but believes that God wants him in the fight against the evils of gambling, Connie relies on her church, scripture, and God to persevere. She frequently turns to her Bible for relevant passages to get her through tough times and believes that raising kids is holy work (she was a stay-at-home mom who pursued a law degree only after her children were in school). The frame-up, however, shakes her faith, and she feels, "like Jesus," abandoned by God. Tess persuades her to consider her children, and she again realizes that God's love is perfect. Unfortunately, more disclosures and the futile trip to Las Vegas (depicted as a modern hell) result in another period of despair and anger at her husband and God. Her return to the church, described as "a hurting lamb returning to the sheepfold," results in her finding the missing book. When she learns that Luke is attracted to her, she distances herself from him and from the law. Her problem can be solved only "from above," and the solution comes in the form of a "circle of praise and joy" of her congregation, who surround the evildoers in an ending that strains credibility but affirms God's enduring love.

Sources for Further Study

Hudak, Melissa. Review of *A Capital Offense*. *Library Journal* 123, no. 6 (April 1, 1998): 78. A sympathetic review of Parker's novel, noting the book's Christian emphasis.

Nelson, Marcia Z. "Publishing Faith Fiction: Reeling in the Readers." *Publishers Weekly* 251 (August 4, 2004): S6-S8. Examines the booming business in Christian novels and discusses the book buyers' preferences and the reasons for the growth of the genre.

Parker, Gary E. *Dark Road to Daylight*. Nashville, Tenn.: T. Nelson, 1997. Another Christian novel by Parker, this one featuring Burke Anderson, a former pastor who is forced to act as a detective to solve a murder case.

Thomas L. Erskine

CARE OF THE SOUL
A Guide for Cultivating Depth and Sacredness in Everyday Life

Author: Thomas Moore (1940-   )
First published: New York: HarperCollins, 1992
Genre: Nonfiction
Subgenres: Handbook for living; mysticism; spiritual treatise
Core issues: Acceptance; guidance; healing; redemption; self-knowledge; wisdom

In helping people to deal with the failures and crises of their lives, contemporary psychology has failed to take into account the importance of the human soul in achieving a sense of acceptance and wisdom. Moore believes that the soul is the window to true understanding of one's place in the world. Knowledge of the soul enables people to function at a deeper level and to appreciate the significance of the forces that shape and guide human existence.

Overview

Modern behavioral psychology has denied the existence of the human soul, believing instead that a person's actions are key to understanding. In this way, a "cure" can be found for atypical behavior. Author Thomas Moore believes this neglect of the human soul has led therapy astray. According to Moore, only by looking deeply inward to the soul can a person discover the key to coping with life's problems.

Moore first addresses the question of just what the human soul is. To Moore, it is the center and core of every human being. It is the locus of the spiritual side of a person, beyond the reach of rational inquiry, yet is key to understanding the essence of life and its challenges. The only way to explain the workings of the soul, he says, is through metaphor and myth. Myths have always served to illuminate universal truths about human triumphs and sufferings. Many have to do with love and power. Myths begin to unravel the mysteries of life in a way that rational inquiry cannot. They explain, in a symbolic way, a person's relationship to the world and can produce a profound sense of acceptance and understanding. In contrast, modern psychology has focused on developing a "cure" for life's problems by redirecting patterns of behavior. This empirical approach obscures the fact that there are much deeper origins. Problems of love and hate, jealousy and envy, depression and failure are too complex to be cured by a modification of one's behavior, if they can be cured at all.

To reach the level of understanding of the soul, one must first acknowledge its existence. This requires a journey deep inside oneself. This effort of self-discovery may be painful but is essential. It is a journey taken throughout history by many people, which is why myths have a universal ring. Despite humanity's technological advances, the human condition has not changed. To illustrate how myths can teach us about ourselves, Moore recounts the ancient Roman story of Narcissus, who falls in love with his own image in a pool of water and, in an attempt to merge with that image, falls into the pool and drowns. This is more than a story of self-love; it is also about a journey to self-knowledge. To love oneself selfishly is to have no soul, Moore says, and the myth teaches us that our self-image may not be what it first appears. Thus the myth helps us to unravel a fundamental mystery of the soul and may lead to a transformation of one's self-image.

One of the major themes of the book is self-acceptance. A divorce, the loss of a job, the passing of a loved one—all of these common experiences can pose a tremendous psychological shock. There is no "cure" for such events, only acceptance. To move beyond such problems is never easy and requires considerable soul-searching. To neglect the role of the soul during such times is to deny the depth of the problem. Such times are difficult but in fact may be opportunities to learn and grow. Even those in the grip of psychological depression may emerge from it with new opportunities, if they see the depression as an important and necessary stage in the growth of the soul.

Moore also reflects that modern life moves at a hectic pace, and many times people leave no time for reflection or contemplation; the speed of the outer world often leaves the inner world behind. Removing oneself from the world for a time has been part of the spiritual life of many cultures and, Moore asserts, is an essential part of caring for the soul.

The author's work is deeply influenced by Carl Jung, a Swiss psychiatrist and founder of analytical psychology. Mythology and the analysis of dreams played a large part in Jung's thinking. He saw myth and dreams as important tools in exploring the soul. James Hillman, a disciple of Jung who developed archetypal psychology—a form of therapy that stresses the importance of myths and symbols—is also frequently referred to by Moore. Hillman's thesis of psychology as a "way of seeing" and his humanistic approach are evident in Moore's work.

Another influence was the Renaissance thinker Marsilio Ficino, whom Moore discovered while searching for a topic for his doctoral dissertation. Ficino, a Neoplatonist, wrote about the divinity of the soul and the importance of a spiritual life. Ficino turned to mythology for insight, a practice that contributed to Moore's own work as a therapist.

Knowledge of Greek and Roman mythology are also key to Moore's philosophy. Classical mythology was a way of making sense out of the world through their personification in the actions of the gods. The humanness of the Greco-Roman gods provided Greeks and Romans with a way of conveying universal truths and explaining the triumphs and tragedies of existence in myth. Such myths unlock the mysteries of the soul by symbolically portraying universal themes such as suffering, jealousy, love, hate, and death. Moore's approach is polytheistic; he draws from Asian religious traditions as well. Like Joseph Campbell—perhaps the most the famous writer on the subject of myths—Moore sees the same motifs repeated in all cultures.

Christian Themes

Thomas Moore spent twelve years of his life preparing for the priesthood, although he was not ordained. There is no question, however, that those years had a profound effect upon his thinking. He understands the importance self-denial, a simple life, and contemplation. The Bible, he says, is "a compendium of insight into the nature of the soul." He talks of the importance of ritual and symbolism, which is so much a part of the Catholic Church. Christians understand that spirituality needs to be reinforced by going to church and reserving time for worship.

The Christian conception of the soul and the symbolism inherent in biblical writings are consistent with Moore's idea of soul. He uses the example of Jesus standing in the River Jordan, waiting to be baptized before he begins his life's work. Symbolically, Jesus is standing in the swirling waters of time and fate—a "stream of events"—in which at some point every individual must find a place. The stories in the Gospels can be read for inspiration as we make our way through life. The formal Christian teachings, rites, and stories, Moore says, "provide an inexhaustible source for reflection on the mysteries of the soul."

The title of this work, *Care of the Soul*, may suggest that this is a "self-help" book. The author takes care to explain that this is not the case. "Self-discovery" is a better characterization. As a practicing psychotherapist, Moore relates several times in the book how analysis of the soul has helped his patients. He does not, however claim to "cure" people. Moore is suggesting a new way of thinking about the inner life that brings about understanding, acceptance, and wisdom.

Sources for Further Study

Armstrong, Karen. *A Short History of Myth*. New York: Canongate Books, 2005. An introduction to the history and meaning of myths and mythology in Western culture.

Campbell, Joseph. *The Power of Myth*. New York: Anchor, 1991. A good introduction to the significance of myths in modern life by one of the most famous scholars of the subject.

Hillman, James. *A Blue Fire: Selected Writings by James Hillman*. Edited by Thomas Moore. New York: Harper and Row, 1989. A collection of essays by a modern disciple of Carl Jung and the foremost spokesperson for a soul-oriented psychology.

_____. *Re-visioning Psychology*. New York: Harper, 1978. Hillman's most important work, a primer on his school of archetypal psychology.

Jung, Carl. *Memories, Dreams, Reflections*. Edited by Aniela Jaffé and translated by Richard and Clara Winston. New York: Pantheon Books, 1973. A collection of memories, thoughts, and philosophical reflections compiled shortly before the 1961 death of the founder of analytical psychology.

Moore, Thomas. *Dark Nights of the Soul: A Guide to Finding Your Way Through Life's Ordeals*. New York: Gotham, 2004. A sequel to *Care of the Soul* offering specific advice on dealing with life's challenges.

Raymond Frey

CASTI CONNUBII

Author: Pius XI (Ambrogio Damiano Achille Patti; 1857-1939)
First published: 1930 (English translation, 1931)
Edition used: Christian Marriage: Encyclical Letter of His Holiness Pope Pius XI.
   Boston: Pauline Books and Media, 2001
Genre: Nonfiction
Subgenre: Encyclical
Core issues: Abortion; Catholics and Catholicism; chastity; marriage

In this important encyclical, Pope Pius XI addresses questions of marriage and marital relations. He reaffirms Christian teaching that matrimony was instituted by God as the foundation of human society although it arises from the free consent of the spouses. Marriage is intended to bless the spouses with children, with conjugal love, and for Christian spouses, with sacramental grace. Marriage by its nature is exclusive and indissoluble and divorce is prohibited. Although couples may take advantage of a woman's cycles of infertility, contraceptive acts and abortion are forbidden.

Overview

In 1930, Pope Pius XI wrote the encyclical letter *Casti Connubii*, addressed to Catholic bishops throughout the world, to resolve questions of marriage and marital relations raised by new developments of the twentieth century. The immediate impetus for the encyclical was probably the Lambeth Conference of the Anglican Church in 1930. At this conference, the Anglican Church declared newly refined methods of artificial contraception as permissible for Christian couples—making it perhaps the first major Christian church to do so. Pius XI was also reacting to the relaxation of divorce laws throughout the Western world. In *Casti Connubii*, Pius presented a comprehensive summary and reaffirmation of Catholic teaching on Christian marriage.

Pius XI begins the encyclical by restating the classic Christian teaching that matrimony was not instituted by humankind but by God. Therefore, the fundamental doctrines of marriage, found in Holy Scripture and the tradition of the Church, are immutable and inviolable. However, matrimonial union also relies on human will because it results from the free consent of the spouses. As a consequence, although governments can forbid "base" unions, they cannot alter the basic laws of marriage.

Quoting Saint Augustine, Pius summarizes the three blessings of marriage: children, conjugal faith, and the grace of a Christian sacrament. The first blessing of marriage is offspring, as Adam and Eve are commanded to "increase and multiply, and fill the earth" (Genesis 1:28). This blessing is taken to mean that the duty of parents is not only to bear children but also to educate them. Thus the 1917 code of canon law of the Catholic Church (c. 1013.7) states that "the primary end of marriage is the procreation and the education of children." Also implied in this command is the restriction of the goods of marriage—the conjugal act and procreation—to the married state.

The second blessing is conjugal fidelity, as the Gospel declares that in marriage the spouses are no longer two, but one flesh. Therefore, the spouses are forbidden to engage in any form of polygamy or polyandry, any form of adultery, and any unchaste acts. In addition, a husband and wife are called to a holy and pure love for each other, "as Christ loved the Church" (Ephesians 5:25). In fact, exalting the spiritual over the physical realm, Pius declares that this blessing is so important that the mutual growth of husband and wife in holiness, fostered by the birth and education of children, is the chief reason and purpose of matrimony. The husband is the head of the family, and the wife is not a servant but a companion who is the true heart of the family.

The third blessing of marriage is as a Christian sacrament, conveying grace to the spouses. As a sacrament it is indissoluble, and this character as a perpetual and nonbreakable bond extends even to non-Christian marriages. "What God hath joined together let no man put asunder" (Matthew 19:6). The public order, the spouses, and children all benefit from the stability borne by the indissolubility of marriage. Responding to the rise of divorce, effected in both law and in practice, Pius insists on the traditional teaching on the indissolubility of marriage; this thought informs the most extended and emphatic sections of the encyclical.

After summarizing these three blessings of marriage, Pius condemns novel ideas that degrade marriage. Foremost among these is the belief that marriage was neither instituted by God nor raised by Jesus Christ to the dignity of a sacrament but is a mere human invention. Likewise mistaken is any proposal for temporary or experimental marriage or cohabitation. The chief error arising from the modern era is to render marriage a purely civil act, under the complete jurisdiction of the state, which is free to sanction divorce. Even in the case of adultery, dissolution of the marriage is not permitted, although the parties may be separated, and the civil authorities may legitimately enact laws for the custody of the children and the good of the family.

Pius also condemns any deliberate frustration of the fruitfulness of the marital act, such as by contraception. Pius emphasizes that this represents the unbroken tradition of the Church. However, he also clarifies and makes explicit an important point in the theology of marital relations: A married couple is entitled to make use of the rhythms of the wife's menstrual cycle in maintaining the bond of marital intimacy and union. Pius condemns abortion for any reason. He also condemns any eugenic legislation or act that sterilizes or forbids marriage to people deemed "defective."

Pius concludes this encyclical with exhortations intended to foster the ends and security of matrimony in the modern age. Married couples should cultivate reverence to God for the blessings of marriage. Young people should be prepared in adolescence and courtship for a lifetime of marriage. Although the state is not the master of the institution of marriage, it is responsible for enacting laws that safeguard its dignity and stability. The state should adopt economic and social methods to allow the head of the family to earn a wage sufficient for the rearing of children. In its laws and disposal of public funds, the state must assist families who lack what they need for their wellbeing.

Christian Themes

A papal encyclical is a highly authoritative medium for conveying teachings of the Catholic Church and the papal magesterium. By its nature it represents Catholic doctrinal teaching, and *Casti Connubii* contains three principal Christian themes, each presented in response to what Pope Pius XI saw as a modern threat to the sanctity of matrimony. All three themes have a rich biblical and Catholic history. The first is to affirm, against a purely secular and sociological view, that marriage is indeed instituted by God. Therefore, marriage is made up of divine and immutable rules that no society or individual can break. These include the indissolubility of marriage, its ordering to the procreation of children, and its relative autonomy and freedom from the interference of the state. The state is obliged to carry out its governing functions while respecting the essentially sacral nature of marriage.

The second theme is that marriage is truly a sacrament among the Christian faithful. This reaffirms a long-standing Catholic belief as opposed to numerous Protestant denominations that do not count marriage as a sacrament or Christian ordinance. As a Christian sacrament, it is subject to the higher law of Jesus Christ. It demands an absolute indissolubility when consummated by baptized spouses. It demands chastity and purity by its partners—forbidding not only actual adultery but also impure thoughts and intentions as well.

The third Christian theme is to require spouses to practice chastity according to their state in life. Because the Anglican Lambeth Conference had just given cautious approval to contraceptive use by married couples, Pius explicitly addresses the question of birth control. He cites "uninterrupted Christian tradition" that forbids the deliberate interference with the generation of new life while explicitly permitting couples to make reasonable use of the natural periods of infertility. Pius presents this then as a full, balanced, and noble portrayal of Christian marriage, rejecting unchaste practices while fostering the noble and intimate union of the spouses.

Sources for Further Study

Fabrègues, Jean de. *Christian Marriage*. Translated by Rosemary Haughton. Vol. 54 in *Twentieth Century Encyclopedia of Catholicism*. New York: Hawthorn Books, 1959. This volume is a thoughtful exposition of the Church's teachings on marriage through 1960, drawing deeply from *Casti Connubii*.

Kellmeyer, Steven. *Sex and the Sacred City*. Peoria, Ill.: Bridegroom Press, 2003. A series of reflections on Pope John Paul II's theory of married love, now known as the "Theology of the Body," drawing on a range of papal writings beginning with *Casti Connubii*.

Lawler, Michael. *Marriage and the Catholic Church: Disputed Questions*. Collegeville, Minn.: Liturgical Press, 2002. In addressing contemporary issues in Catholic teaching about marriage, Lawler finds *Casti Connubii* to have shifted church teaching from a procreative to a more personal model of marital love and intimacy.

Howard Bromberg

CATECHISM OF THE CATHOLIC CHURCH

Author: Council of Trent (1545-1563)
First published: Catechismus Catholicae Ecclesiae, 1566 (English translation, 1992)
Edition used: Catechism of the Catholic Church, second edition, edited by the Editorial Committee of the Special Commission of the Holy See for the catechism of the Catholic Church. New York: Doubleday, 2003
Genre: Nonfiction
Subgenres: Didactic treatise; guidebook; theology
Core issues: Catholics and Catholicism; guidance

The catechism of the Catholic Church is a document that attempts to absolutely define the precepts of the Holy Roman Catholic Church in relation to the interpretation of Holy Scripture and adherence to religious tradition, and to establish the limits of lay involvement both liturgical and ministerial. This groundbreaking work is the guidebook for Catholic instruction as well as an invaluable reference for any scholar studying Catholicism or Catholic history. Pope John Paul II recommended a second edition to the original text in 1986 and established a commission headed by Joseph Cardinal Ratzinger to write a compendium edition.

Overview

The need for a catechism for the Roman Catholic Church became critical when Martin Luther in 1517 nailed his ninety-five theses to the door of the cathedral in Wittenberg. As the years passed, the hierarchy of the Church became aware of the need to clarify many items of faith, particularly in light of the scores of tracts and pamphlets that the reformers were writing and distributing. In 1545 the Council of Trent was called and began eighteen years of meetings. The purpose of the council was to find common ground with the reformers and to clarify those issues that marked the differences between Catholics and Protestants. Some of the issues discussed at that council were the role of Mary, the place of devotions and good works in salvation, the number and function of the sacraments, the angels, the primacy of place of Latin in church worship, the reserving of Scriptural interpretation to the clergy, and the primacy of the pope.

As the council progressed, it became apparent that there would be few changes to accommodate the Protestant reformers and that the tradition of the Church would be maintained. At the suggestion of Charles Borromeo, who had been working toward reforming the clergy, the council under the leadership of Pope Pius IV decided to publish a book of instruction in the faith, first to educate the clergy and through them the laity. Under the direction of the cardinals, the first edition of the *Catechism of the Catholic Church* was prepared in Italian and immediately translated into Latin.

Published in 1566 during the papacy of Pius V, the *Catechism of the Catholic Church* became the staple of instruction in the Catholic faith. At first it was intended primarily for parish priests, but then, through them, it was to provide a fixed and stable format for the Mass and the distribution of the sacraments. Moreover, unlike many church documents, the *Catechism of the Catholic Church* was translated into the vernacular of each country. There was also an edition to be used by parish priests as sermon material, since it was divided into sections conforming to the church year.

The *Catechism of the Catholic Church* was divided into four parts explaining the creed, the sacraments, the commandments, and prayers, especially the Lord's Prayer. The documents of the Council of Trent, together with the *Catechism of the Catholic Church*, gave the church material with which to wage the Counter-Reformation for the next two centuries. In addition, it provided the members of the church with a clarity and certainty about their beliefs and practices that stood for four hundred years.

Translations and editions of the *Catechism of the Catholic Church* appeared in various countries in the subsequent centuries. Most American Catholics, especially those educated in Catholic schools, would be familiar with the catechism published in Baltimore in 1885 and used extensively from then until the 1960's. *A Catechism of Christian Doctrine, Prepared and Enjoined by Order of the Third Council of Baltimore* (1885) was in a convenient question-and-answer format that made it easy, especially for children or for those studying the faith, to find the answers to their questions.

In 1962, aware of the need for modernization in church worship and practices, Pope John XXIII called the Vatican Council II. This council met until 1965, and although it lasted only three years, it brought about many and sweeping changes. Within twenty years of that council, clergy and faithful alike saw the need for a second edition of the *Catechism of the Catholic Church*. According to the work itself, the purpose for the second edition was to better present Christian doctrine so as to make it more accessible not only to the faithful but also to all others.

In 1986, a commission of twelve cardinals and bishops prepared a draft of the catechism with the express instruction that the material must be biblical and liturgical, be suited to the present life of Christians, and fully respond to the needs of the universal church. Because one of the first and continuing acts of the Second Vatican Council was the reform of the liturgy (particularly in the use of the vernacular in the Mass and the sacraments), the commission had a lot of work to do. First its members had to compile sections of the catechism using the doctrinal statements and pastoral norms that had been written by the Second Vatican Council. They then had to submit the draft to theologians, scriptural interpreters, and to religion teachers and bishops all over the world for their opinions. The result, the authors hoped, would be a text that was accurate, unified, and coherent. The authors did not intend to make a completely new document, for the church leaders felt that it would be the most beneficial if the new material built on the old. One example of building on the old work can be found in the structure of the second edition: Like the first edition, the new edition is divided into four parts, "The Creed," "The Sacred Liturgy," "The Christian Way of Life," and "Christian Prayer."

An example of the way the *Catechism of the Catholic Church* is set up can be seen in the handling of the term "Christian mystery," explained in sections 1066 to 1073.

Starting in section 1066, the Church expresses its belief in the Holy Trinity and in God's plan for salvation by which God gave his beloved Son and his Holy Spirit for the salvation of humankind and for the glory of his name. God's plan for salvation was revealed and accomplished through the death of Christ on the cross, his Resurrection, and his Ascension into heaven. Through these acts, Christ was able to conquer death and sin. From this mystery proceeds the liturgy, the religious celebration that is the basis of Catholic worship. Sections 1067 to 1070 describe the relationship between the liturgy and the Christian mystery. Then, section 1071 describes how the liturgy engages the faithful—both as prayer and as fruitful action in their lives within the community. Section 1073 describes the participation of the faithful in the Lord's Prayer and other prayers during various parts of the liturgical service. In this section as in all others, ample footnotes supply references to sources from the Bible, the documents of the Second Vatican Council, and other religious writings.

Despite the fact that the second edition is easy to read and has ample notes and scriptural references, in 2002 the International Catechetical Conference asked for a more basic synthesis of the essentials of the faith that would be helpful in its mission to teach the faith. Accordingly, the *Catechismo Della Chiesa Cattolica* (2005, *Compendium of the Catechism of the Catholic Church*, 2005) was created to compile the various sections of the *Catechism of the Catholic Church* and to put them into a prose both easy to read and to comprehend. The editor, Cardinal Joseph Ratzinger, later Pope Benedict XVI, meant the compendium to be brief, clear, and comprehensive. As an example, the section on the Christian mystery, which runs to four pages in small type in the *Catechism of the Catholic Church*, is condensed in the compendium into three questions (218-220), complete with clear and concise answers. As in the catechism, scriptural references are given, and reference numbers to the sections of the *Catechism of the Catholic Church* are set in the margin beside each of the questions. It is easy to reference each section to the appropriate area in the catechism.

The three principal characteristics of the *Compendium of the Catechism of the Catholic Church* are, first, its close reliance on the catechism—all sections are clearly marked as to the section to which the question refers. The second characteristic is its question-and-answer format, and the third is its inclusion of graphic images drawn by artists throughout the ages. Recognizing the power of great art, the editors hoped that reproductions of sacred images could express more than words alone could convey.

Christian Themes

The catechism, as envisioned by Pope John Paul II (Karol Jozef Wojtyła), was to make Catholic doctrine easy to understand by those individuals interested in studying Catholicism and the Catholic Church. It was intended to draw the reader into the study of God and God's mysteries. One of the purposes of the *Catechism of the Catholic Church* is to be an instruction manual for the faithful, furthering their love of God and increasing their understanding of the practice of their faith. In particular, the question-and-answer format of the compendium seems intended to directly address issues and questions commonly held by the laity. However, other purposes, such as providing an official statement of Church doctrine for the perusal of non-Catholic readers, should not be regarded as absolutely secondary to the instruction of the faithful. Dominant themes expressed by the writers of the catechism revolve around the nature of the Trinity of God, Jesus Christ, and the Holy Spirit; the interpretation of the Bible as a sacred text; the role of the clergy; and, most important, the function of the Eucharist. The catechism clearly delineates the role of the Eucharist within the structure of the Mass both as a theological concept that connects the physical presence of Jesus Christ with his followers and as a metaphysical concept that establishes certain roles within the Church for the celebrant, the priest, and the congregation. The Eucharist, the literalized "body of Christ," draws together the three persons of the Trinity along with the assembled congregation of laity in both a remembrance of the Last Supper of Jesus Christ and a celebration of Jesus Christ's ultimate triumph over sin and death by his acceptance of God's Will.

Sources for Further Study

Johnson, Kevin Orlin. *Why Do Catholics Do That?* New York: Ballantine, 1994. This book has an imprimatur indicating that it has the approval of a church official, in this case the bishop of the author's diocese. It is recommended for non-Catholics curious about Catholicism and Catholic tradition.

Keating, Karl. *What Catholics Really Believe: Setting the Record Straight—Fifty-Two Answers to Misconceptions About the Catholic Faith.* San Francisco: Ignatius, 1992. This work suggests possible responses to questions posed by non-Catholics regarding a variety of commonly held rumors about Catholic beliefs and practices.

Neuhaus, Richard John. *Catholic Matters: Confusion, Controversy, and the Splendor of Truth.* New York: Basic Books, 2006. Written by a former Lutheran pastor who converted to Catholicism and then entered the priesthood, this work has a nicely objective voice while discussing the impact of popular issues on the current methodology behind the teaching of Catholic doctrine.

Julia M. Meyers

CATHOLICS

Author: Brian Moore (1921-1999)
First published: Toronto: McClelland and Stewart, 1972
Genre: Novella
Subgenre: Catholic fiction
Core issues: Alienation from God; Catholics and Catholicism; clerical life; conscience; faith; monasticism; obedience and disobedience

Set in a vaguely defined future at the end of the twentieth century, Moore's novel explores the changing role of organized religion, specifically Catholicism, in an increasingly secularized world. At issue is the role of faith in believers' lives and the role that organized religion plays in the metaphysics of belief.

Principal characters
  Tomás O'Malley, abbot of an ancient monastery
  James Kinsella, a young priest sent from the Vatican to secure
      compliance
  Father Manus, an older monk devoted to old traditions
  Father Matthew, another unyielding and independent
      traditionalist

Overview

In *Catholics*, Brian Moore's typical antipathy toward Catholicism is transformed into a tolerant skepticism as he pits two contrasting definitions of the Church against each other. Set in what seemed to be the not-too-distant future at the time of the novella's publication (most likely the late 1990's), Moore's novel depicts a clash between the traditionalists and the progressives, who battle for the devotion of the laity.

It has come to the attention of hierarchy in Rome that monks from a remote abbey off the coast of western Ireland are still celebrating the Latin Mass, and the ritual has become so popular that pilgrims travel from throughout the world to celebrate in the ancient ceremony. The popular press has seized on the phenomenon and plans a major documentary. Seeing a threat to its authority, Rome dispatches a young, radical priest, James Kinsella, to stop the practice and preserve the new orthodoxy.

Kinsella is a disciple of the revolutionary Father Gustav Hartman, a priest who has been tortured by totalitarian regimes for inciting seditious ideas. Kinsella's theology is thoroughly modern and, as he sees it, progressive; he is impatient with the older practices of the monks from the abbey. His foil, Tomás O'Malley, a sixty-nine-year-old abbot on Muck Island, is a practical, hardworking man in charge of twenty priests who live an anachronistic, ascetic life. As strongly as Kinsella believes the old Mass must be abandoned, O'Malley is convinced that it serves a profound theological purpose, and its growing popularity is potent evidence of its efficacy in reaching the laity and reviving flagging congregations.

The body of the narrative is taken up with a debate between the two priests' antithetical notions of the role of religion in the lives of the faithful. Kinsella believes in a church that advances the social welfare, while O'Malley is concerned with the condition of people's souls. In the figure of the humble Father Manus, Moore creates a stirring defense of the old Mass when he argues for the miracle of "God coming down among us," as opposed to the modern ritual of "singing and guitars and turning to touch your neighbor, playacting and nonsense, all to make the people come into church the way they used to go to the parish hall for a bingo game."

Kinsella and O'Malley, through their debates, represent notions of theology that have long been associated with the Catholic Church and that continue to define its future. On one hand, the Church can be seen as an instrument of social revolution, and in Kinsella's post-"Vatican IV" era, private confessions have been abolished and distinctions between mortal and venial sins are moot. Most important, the celebration of the Mass, the cornerstone of Catholic ritual and faith, has been rendered nothing more than a pious act of symbolism; members of the Church hierarchy no longer accept the notion of transubstantiation. By contrast, for O'Malley—and even more so for his monks—the Mass is a daily miracle; through the taking of the body and blood of Christ, "God com[es] down among us."

The novella hinges on two central ironies. The first of these ironies involves a priest dedicated to revolution and world ecumenism who is actually an agent of orthodoxy and conformity. He seeks to stamp out heresy and thus reminds O'Malley of the Grand Inquisitor and an intolerant Church bent on quashing all dissent. The second and more profound irony is that O'Malley, the voice defending the sanctity of individual belief, has lost the security of his faith. Overwhelmed by the commercialism and tawdry spectacle of the "miracle" of Lourdes, O'Malley has come to know "the hell of the metaphysicians: the hell of those deprived of God." All of this begs the question, How can a man who has lost his faith remain in the Church and supervise others? O'Malley's answer is that belief is a gift from God, and if he can nurture and protect that belief in others—his congregation and his brother monks—he has done God's work.

An encounter with a second monk, Father Matthew (a strong, uncompromising figure who holds an all-night vigil, praying that Kinsella's orders are countermanded), encourages O'Malley's ultimate decision. When Father Matthew refuses to terminate his vigil and go to bed, O'Malley stands on his authority and orders the priest to concede. The next morning, when Kinsella braces himself for more debate and dissension, he is shocked to find a compliant O'Malley, who now follows the very demands he placed on Father Matthew: He obeys authority regardless of personal opinion.

After Kinsella's departure, the brother monks are distressed and angry. O'Malley calms them by insisting they pray: "Prayer is the only miracle," he said. "We pray. If our words become prayer, God will come." As the community kneels and offers their supplications, O'Malley is left alone, yearning for faith yet denied its comfort and assurance.

Christian Themes

Moore's principal concern is with the phenomenon of faith, and more specifically with what constitutes that devotion. The novel questions whether faith is a product of instruction, coercion, or the imposition of authority. Certainly Kinsella and his ilk would argue for orthodoxy and conformity. Indeed, the central conflict can be seen as the differences between institutional and private faith. O'Malley well understands that modern people are not typically defined or animated by a deep, abiding sense of spiritual faith. He notes to Kinsella that attendance at Mass has declined with the institution of the vernacular Mass, whereas people flock to the Latin celebration. His argument highlights a central feature of faith: It is not rational, it cannot be legislated, and it will assert itself in often private, highly individualistic ways. Faith is furthermore not antagonistic or seditious, except to those authorities who demand conventionality. Thus a skeptic like O'Malley can yearn for and thoroughly respect the beliefs of the naïve Father Manus and the self-righteous Father Matthew, for he sees in each the radiance of true faith, which is absent from Kinsella's secular demeanor and authoritarian obsession.

A second important concern is with the tension between tradition and modernity and the ways in which religion finds itself torn between these extremes. As the novel makes clear, for a people like the Irish, who endured the Penal Laws of a colonizing nation bent on eradicating their religious beliefs, a dedication to tradition is more than reactionary complacency. For the Irish, to lose their sense of tradition is linked to the serious losses of identity and culture. The appeal of modernity is not only that Catholicism will join other world religions (Kinsella is concerned that the persistence of the Latin Mass will undermine the Vatican's *apertura* with Buddhism at a forthcoming World Ecumen Council) but also that religion can answer directly the most pressing issues of human rights and freedoms. *Catholics* is extraordinary in its evenhanded treatment of these issues, making each compelling and each intellectually and spiritually legitimate.

A last key concern is the tension between individual will and obedience to authority. Once again, Moore gives equal validity to each point of view. Although O'Malley eventually concedes to Kinsella's authority, the debate is never resolved. Perhaps the most concise articulation of the dilemma comes in one of O'Malley's retorts, "Yesterday's orthodoxy is today's heresy."

Sources for Further Study

Craig, Patricia. *Brian Moore: A Biography*. London: Bloomsbury, 2002. The first full-length biography of Moore's life, writing, and fictional concerns.

Dahlie, Hallvard. *Brian Moore*. Boston: Twayne, 1981. A general study of Moore's novels up to the publication of *The Temptation of Eileen Hughes* in 1981.

Gearon, Liam. *Landscapes of Encounter: The Portrayal of Catholicism in the Novels of Brian Moore*. Calgary, Alta.: Calgary University Press, 2002. A book-length examination of Moore's treatment of Catholicism in the majority of his novels.

McSweeney, Kerry. *Four Contemporary Novelists*. London: Solar Press, 1983. A study of four contemporary novelists who share a dedication to the novel as a genre that represents and re-creates lived human experience.

O'Donoghue, Jo. *Brian Moore: A Critical Study*. London: McGill-Queen's University Press, 1991. Perhaps the best critical examination of Moore's works, revealing his deep spiritual concerns as well as an extraordinary understanding of female experiences.

Sampson, Denis. *Brian Moore: The Chameleon Novelist*. Dublin: Marino, 1998. In a work that is part biography and part critical study, Sampson traces Moore's enduring fictional concerns and his ability to immerse himself in whatever tradition or subject he explores.

David W. Madden

CENTESIMUS ANNUS

Author: John Paul II (Karol Jozef Wojtyła; 1920-2005)
First published: 1991 (English translation, 1991)
Edition used: Human Dignity and the Common Good: The Great Papal Encyclicals from Leo XIII to John Paul II. Edited by Richard W. Rousseau, S.J. Westport, Conn.: Greenwood Press, 2002
Genre: Nonfiction
Subgenres: Encyclical; theology
Core issues: Capitalism; freedom and free will; justice; morality; social action

John Paul II's most significant encyclical on economics and politics was written on the one hundredth anniversary of Rerum Novarum, *the first social encyclical. It affirms some of the ideas in earlier social encyclicals but gives greater approval to aspects of capitalism and democracy. This encyclical discusses the fall of communism in eastern and central Europe and the rise of democracy there and in other parts of the world. It rejects totalitarianism but still reserves some role for the state in economics.*

Overview

Cenetisimus Annus (on the hundredth anniversary), the ninth encyclical of John Paul II's pontificate and his third social encyclical, was written on the one hundredth anniversary of Leo XIII's *Rerum Novarum* (1891). It examines the role of the state and the economy from the perspective of Catholic moral theology.

In the brief introduction, John Paul II indicates he will look back to *Rerum Novarum* and forward to prospects for the future. In the first chapter of six, John Paul affirms Leo XIII's teachings that there should be rights for people who work, including the right to private property and the right to a family-supporting wage, and that individuals and families should be served by the economy rather than the reverse.

The second chapter examines the "new things of today," by which John Paul means emerging economic arrangements. He strongly rejects that idea that socialism is the proper response to current economic conditions. He then argues that the state should assist workers as they participate in economic life. The state should adopt measures to help those who become unemployed and encourage proper wage levels. However, the state's role should not be so extensive as to discourage individual initiative in the economy. The state can play a positive role by encouraging authentic development of human beings.

The third chapter, entitled "1989," considers the remarkable events of that year, when many totalitarian governments toppled in a wave across eastern and central Europe. John Paul argues that communism failed not only because it was an inefficient economic system and could not produce sufficient consumer goods but also because it neglected to regard the spiritual nature of humans. The pope states that prospering nations have a duty to assist the former communist countries as they attempt the authentic development of persons. He is hopeful about the various parts of the world that have adopted democracy but is concerned that it may lead some nations to accept moral relativism.

In the fourth chapter, John Paul considers essential themes in Catholic social teachings. He strongly reaffirms the right of private property, saying that "this right, which is fundamental for the autonomy and development of the person, has always been defended by the church up to our own day." He then goes on to defend entrepreneurial action within the economy and says that "the modern business economy has positive aspects." He further says that "the church acknowledges the legitimate role of profit as an indication that a business is functioning well."

John Paul acknowledges that there have been some who have greatly prospered in modern economies. These individuals and nations have a great duty toward those nations and individuals who are less fortunate, especially many in the Third World. Moreover, individuals are asked to reject materialism and consumerism because "what is wrong is a style of life which it is better when it is directed toward 'having' rather than 'being' and which wants to have more not in order to be more."

As for economic systems, John Paul says that the "Marxist solution has failed" and that the church would accept an "economic system which recognizes the fundamental and positive role of business, the market, private property, and the resulting responsibility for the means of production." However, the pope adds that he would not accept an economic system without a moral framework and a "strong juridical framework which places it at the service of human freedom."

In the fifth chapter, "State and Culture," John Paul examines the role of the state in the modern world. He emphatically rejects a minimal state that does not engage the economy, but he also rejects a totalitarian state. He asserts that the state should have a role in protecting workers and providing a framework for economic life. However, the state should not become a complete social welfare state that is so extensive that it prevents private individuals from serving others in need. Families and private organizations have a role in serving others.

John Paul defends the fundamental dignity of humanity in the final chapter, "Man Is the Way of the Church." He says that "the church has constantly repeated that the person and society need not only material goods, but spiritual and religious values as well." The church can teach the world what humans are so that people might better participate in economic life. Human beings, John Paul asserts, must love others because all are made in God's image.

Christian Themes

The most significant theme of this encyclical is capitalism. John Paul clearly asserts that Marxism is not an appropriate economic system and affirms that under appropriate conditions, capitalism is legitimate. A foundational element of capitalism is private property, and the pope strongly affirms the right of private property. That, however, does not mean that he endorses an economic system divorced from moral concerns and where individuals engage only in rapacious economic activity. Economic life should provide a place for individuals to engage in economic initiatives and participate in business life. Under capitalism, individuals have a positive duty toward those less fortunate, and employers a duty toward their employees. The state must promote just economic conditions within its jurisdiction, and developed nations must aid poorer nations.

John Paul examines capitalism within the context of justice, not just economic efficiency and productivity. He argues that private property and the allowance of individual activity is just and that individuals and families must be treated in a just manner. He also argues that individual freedom bounded by traditional morality is the appropriate form of human freedom. True freedom recognizes the inherent dignity of human beings.

Finally, John Paul addresses proper social action when he defends the actions of those who toppled communist regimes and others working for systems that encourage the authentic development of the human person.

Sources for Further Study

Cochran, Clarke, and David Carroll Cochran. *Catholics, Politics, and Policy: Beyond Right and Left*. Maryknoll, N.Y.: Orbis Books, 2003. Includes a chapter that examines a just economic life and therein discusses *Centesimus Annus* and relates it to other encyclicals.

Mott, W. King, Jr. *The Third Way: Economic Justice According to John Paul II*. Lanham, Md.: University Press of America, 1999. Argues that John Paul's views of economics are best understood in light of his philosophic anthropology.

Novak, Michael. *The Universal Hunger for Liberty: Why the Clash of Civilizations Is Not Inevitable*. New York: Basic Books, 2004. Contains chapters that consider the relationship between Catholicism and capitalism as well as a lengthy chapter on how the Catholic Church came to embrace democracy.

Pham, John-Peter, ed. *Centesimus Annus: Assessment and Perspectives for the Future of Catholic Doctrine*. Vatican: Libreria Editrice Vaticana, 1998. This work includes twenty essays dedicated to *Centesimus Annus* and includes discussions of themes and how the work was received around the world.

Pontifical Council for Justice and Peace. *Compendium of the Social Doctrine of the Church*. Washington, D.C.: USCCB, 2005. This work attempts to systematize and synthesize the many documents, including *Centesimus Annus*, that are part of Catholic social teachings.

Weigel, George, and Robert Royal. *Building the Free Society: Democracy, Capitalism, and Catholic Social Teaching*. Grand Rapids, Mich.: Wm. B. Eerdmans, 1993. This work includes eleven essays, each examining a different document. One examines the place of *Centesimus Annus* in the tradition of Catholic social teachings.

Michael L. Coulter

THE CHERUBINIC WANDERER

Author: Angelus Silesius (Johannes Scheffler; 1624-1677)
First published: Geistreiche Sinn-und Schluss-reime, 1657 (English translation, 1909)
Edition used: The Cherubinic Wanderer, edited and translated by Maria Shrady. New
   York: Paulist Press, 1986
Genre: Poetry
Subgenres: Epigrams; lyric poetry; meditation and contemplation; mysticism
Core issues: Death; humility; love; mysticism; time; union with God

In addition to being one of the most popular works of seventeenth century German literature, The Cherubinic Wanderer, *the poems which have been turned into hymns in Catholic, Lutheran, Calvinist, and Methodist hymnals, has intrigued scholars, both literary and theological, with the deceptively simple epigram form and theologically complex content of its little poems. No anthology of German Baroque literature is complete without a selection of poems from this classic collection of verse exploring the nature of the relationship between God and the individual.*

Overview

When Johannes Scheffler, under the pen name and religious name Angelus Silesius ("The Angel," or perhaps "messenger," of Silesia) published *Geistreiche Sinn-und Schluss-reime* (sage rhymes and epigrams) in 1657, his audience was undergoing a crisis in identity in both language and religion. The seventeenth century was fiercely sectarian: For the first twenty-three years of Scheffler's life, his homeland, like the rest of northern Europe, was locked in the Thirty Years' War, ostensibly a religious conflict between Catholic and Protestant Germany. At the same time, a handful of German poets and intellectuals were attempting to forge the German language into a medium for poetry to rival that of France and Italy.

Both the Catholic-Protestant conflict and the struggle to establish German as a literary language met in Scheffler's 1657 masterpiece, later retitled *Cherubinischer Wandersmann* (the cherubinic wanderer). The sectarian struggle is central to its publication history: Scheffler had probably written such verses from his university days but was first moved to publish in 1652, when he was serving as court physician to Duke Sylvius Nimrod at Oels. His work at that time consisted of anthologies of mystical prayer, and as required, he submitted them for approval to the court chaplain, Christoph Freytag. Freytag, a Lutheran like Scheffler (and like the duke of Oels), was horrified by what he considered the "superstitious," Roman Catholic, and, worst of all, mystical nature of the prayers, including some by the Catholic Saint Gertrude. Freytag refused permission to publish. Whether this censorship precipitated Scheffler's conversion, or whether Freytag correctly diagnosed an already Catholic-leaning piety in Scheffler, the young poet was received into the Catholic faith the following year, changing his name to Johannes Angelus Silesius.

The Cherubinic Wanderer consists of five books totaling more than 1,400 short poems (the 1675 edition added a sixth for a total of 1,676 poems) expressing different aspects of the mystical union of God and humanity. A handful are sonnets, but the vast majority are Alexandrine couplets, the extremely concise two-line form known as the epigram. Because the form of the Alexandrine couplet is tied to the content of *The Cherubinic Wanderer*—how it is said is part of what it says—a brief explanation of the form is appropriate here. Although popular piety can sometimes chafe at formalism as a restriction inhibiting expression, mystical poets like Silesius often seek the most restrictive forms. In Catholic sacramental theology, the word "form" has a precise meaning and importance: It refers to the exact wording used in the ceremony. Vary the words beyond prescribed limits, and the Sacrament is invalid. In the couplets of Silesius, the formal tension between perfectly balanced half-lines highlights contradictory elements of mystical paradoxes. The following couplet, poem 80 of book 3, illustrates. "Gott der die Welt gemacht und wider kan zunichten:/ Kan nicht ohn meinen willn die Neugeburth auss richten." ("The God who made the earth, and can destroy the earth/ Cannot, without my will, accomplish my rebirth.") The absolute symmetry of the form is clear in this example. There is only one pair of rhymed lines. Some of the 1,676 poems in the collection are longer, but the majority are in this spare, two-line form. However, even within the line there are subdivisions. The meter is iambic hexameter, six feet of two syllables each, an unstressed syllable followed by a stressed. Because the line has an even number of feet, it can divide evenly, as Shakespeare's iambic pentameter (five feet) cannot. Instead of composing the line as a structural unity, Silesius follows the ancient Germanic poets (and the French neoclassic writers who gave the Alexandrine its name and its vogue) in building in a metrical pause, known as a caesura, in the middle of the line.

The form therefore is tailor-made for the language of paradox, because the two discordant elements that paradox brings into concord can be isolated and yet harmonized. In these two lines, the first presents an image of God's absolute power: He created the world and can destroy it (literally, "bring it to nothing"). The final word in each half-line is half of an antithetical pair of verbs: *gemacht* (created) and *zunichten* (destroy). A second parallelism links the two lines: The root of *zunichten* is *nicht*, "not," which is the second word in the next line. Having established that God can do anything, Silesius then goes on to say what God cannot do: He cannot go against a will he has made free.

The boldness of this seemingly impious statement—presenting God's willing gift of free will as if it somehow limited God's power—is typical of Silesius's method and typical of German Baroque poetry, which deliberately attempts to shock reader's expectations. In his preface to *The Cherubinic Wanderer*, Silesius took care to assure readers of his orthodoxy, however irreverent his mystical language might sound.

The poems are divided into five books (six in the 1675 edition), but there is no principle of organization within or among the books. A number of themes recur, however, and Jeffrey L. Sammons discussed the separate poems of *The Cherubinic Wanderer* under four themes: God, God and I, eternity, and death. The seeming contradiction (or repetition) of the first two topics, God and God and I, again suggests the paradoxical nature of the poet's thought. Although it could be argued that virtually all the poems of *The Cherubinic Wanderer* fall under the topic of God and I, for every expression of the oneness of God and the self, Silesius offers an expression of God's radical otherness. The topic of eternity offers ample opportunity for mystical expression, as humans' minds and languages are finite: The same is true of the poems about death, which are always in the context, whether spoken or not, of eternal life.

Christian Themes

The Cherubinic Wanderer, the title by which this collection is most widely known, is the perfect, succinct expression of two major themes in Christian literature: wisdom and pilgrimage. While "cherubinic" suggests to the twenty-first century mind the chubby little angels of Christian religious art, its implication for the seventeenth century mind involved finding God through reason and thought. The cherubim were the second order of angels in the early Christian tradition; the first order was the seraphim. If the seraph represents coming to God through the heart, the cherub represents coming to God through the mind. "Cherubinic" was the ideal approach not only for seventeenth century theology, when sectarian strife forced a minute intellectual analysis of doctrine, but also for the century's poetry, which was known (and in the following century scorned) for intellectualizing poetic feeling.

The second key word of the title, "wanderer," suggests the fallen individual's role in a fallen world: We are in this world only as pilgrims, on our way to an unfallen, eternal reality. The feelings of exile and alienation are not often invoked by the poems of the collection; instead, the poems suggest the German folk tradition of the "Happy Wanderer," the vagabond who recalls the wandering minstrels of the medieval tradition, the troubadour. Because Silesius joined the Franciscan order before publishing *The Cherubinic Wanderer*, there may also be overtones of Saint Francis's call for Christians to be "troubadours for Christ," transforming secular poetic traditions to religious use. The subversion of the worldly to the divine was a stated goal of many of the German religious poets of Silesius's day: they called the technique *Kontrafaktur*, and it permeates *The Cherubinic Wanderer*.

Sources for Further Study

Faber du Faur, Kurt von. Introduction to *The Cherubinic Wanderer: Selections*, by Willard R. Trask. New York: Pantheon, 1953. A leading American authority on the period places the work in its cultural context.

Flitch, J. E. Crawford. Introduction to *Selections from the Cherubinic Wanderer*, by Angelus Silesius. London: George Allen & Unwin, 1932. One of the first studies in English to look at Silesius's verse as poetry rather than just mystical thought.

Sammons, Jeffrey L. *Angelus Silesius*. Boston: Twayne, 1967. An early entry in a standard series, this work remains the only book-length study of Silesius in English.

_____. "Johannes Scheffler." In *German Baroque Writers, 1580-1660*, edited by James Hardin. Detroit, Mich.: Gale, 1996. Connects Silesius with his contemporaries in German Baroque poetry, particularly poets of mystical religious verse.

Schmidt, Josef. Introduction to *The Cherubinic Wanderer*, by Angelus Silesius, translated by Maria Shrady. New York: Paulist Press, 1986. Places Silesius's work in the wider context of German mysticism.

John R. Holmes

CHRIST
A Crisis in the Life of God

Author: Jack Miles (1942-   )
First published: New York: Alfred A. Knopf, 2001
Genre: Nonfiction
Subgenres: Biblical studies; biography
Core issues: The Deity; Incarnation; Jesus Christ

Miles investigates the character of Jesus as it is presented in the literature of the New Testament. Central to this work is an insistence that, as the New Testament claims, Jesus is the incarnation of God. As such, he can be understood only when his actions are considered as a continuation of the character of God in the Hebrew Bible. Jesus' life exemplifies a "crisis in the life of God" because he must reconsider his past actions as he plots a new course for himself.

Overview

In 1996, Jack Miles wrote a Pulitzer Prize-winning work entitled *God: A Biography*. In that work, he constructed a character analysis of God, based strictly upon a literary study of the Hebrew Bible. He gleaned from the text of the Bible a dynamic and complex deity, and his literary analysis of God's character, because it shunned dogmatic concerns of Judaism and Christianity, proved provocative. In *Christ: A Crisis in the Life of God*, Miles turns to the New Testament and the character of Jesus. As he did in *God: A Biography*, Miles analyzes the character of Jesus, based on the New Testament texts alone. The sequel forms a continuity with the first work, however, because Miles takes seriously the claim that Jesus was God incarnate. Therefore, the complexity of God's character in the Hebrew Bible is brought forward *in toto*, into the person of Jesus as well.

The book divides into four chapters—"The Messiah, Ironically," "A Prophet Against the Promise," "The Lord of Blasphemy," and "The Lamb of God"—presented in roughly chronological sequence, each chapter focusing on a particular characteristic of Jesus Christ. Although he refers to many New Testament books, Miles primarily uses Gospel passages. Because the Gospel of John is the Gospel most emphatic about Jesus as the incarnation of God, it functions as the outline for most of Miles's work.

In his first chapter, "The Messiah, Ironically," Miles highlights passages from the early chapters of the Gospels, especially John. In these passages, Jesus and others make claims for his status as messiah, but their understanding of "messiah" is so strange that it becomes an ironic title. For instance, John the Baptist calls Jesus the "Lamb of God," and Jesus himself uses the image of a bronze serpent to expound on his status. The second image, drawn from Numbers, was an object used to heal the people of Israel from an attack of poisonous snakes sent by God himself. These two animal symbols demonstrate that God has dramatically and voluntarily altered the power he exerted in the Hebrew Bible. God has chosen sacrificial animals as metaphors for his life and death, symbols that point to him as the means of forgiveness, but a forgiveness of a curse that he himself caused.

In chapter 2, Miles calls Jesus the "prophet against the promise" because so much of Jesus' words and actions invert God's actions in the Hebrew Bible. Instead of expressing a concern for justice that includes reward and punishment, Jesus proclaims that "he is no longer a head-smashing kind of God." While he had previously announced himself as a mighty warrior, now the Lord opts for nonviolence. The strict distinction between Jew and Gentile that defined God's relationship to humanity is made obsolete by Jesus' preaching to his hometown. In all these instances, God in the form of Jesus contradicts his prior acts. Moreover, Miles asserts, the actions of God incarnate change so dramatically because Jesus makes a virtue out of necessity. God found that he could no longer live up to the covenant of the Hebrew Bible, so he altered its rules to make it a covenant of unconditional love.

When, in the third chapter, Miles addresses the blasphemous aspects of Jesus, he looks primarily at Jesus' speech. At the center of Jesus' blasphemy is his unequivocal claim, made in John 8:56-58, that he and God are the same. Nothing could be more blasphemous than making oneself equal to God, and when his audience hears Jesus say this, they attempt to stone him (as God in the Hebrew Bible commands them to do). This blasphemy, however, goes beyond hubris. Jesus exalts himself to the level of God, and, concurrently, brings God down to the level of humanity. The crisis that the incarnation solves is a crisis of God's failing to live up to his own assertions about himself. The incarnation obliterates this failure by making a new assertion—namely, that Jesus' victory over death takes the place of the triumph of God's chosen people over their flesh-and-blood enemies.

In the final chapter, Miles treats the passion, death, and resurrection of Jesus. The passion narratives of the Gospels finalize the reversal of expectations that Jesus has been enacting in his public ministry. Jesus' (God's) death on the cross and his subsequent resurrection are the ultimate revisionist acts. God's grandeur and power are exchanged for helplessness and shame. Through the passion, God announces that he "is no longer a warrior prepared to rescue the Jews from foreign oppression but, rather, a savior who has chosen to rescue all mankind from death." Appropriately, Miles closes this chapter with references to Revelation, the book of the New Testament that most graphically depicts the dual nature of God as victim and conqueror when it presents a lamb with its throat slit as the most powerful being in Heaven.

At the end of his book, Miles includes an epilogue and two appendixes that explain his procedure and put his work in conversation with the academic field of New Testament studies.

Christian Themes

Miles's investigation of Jesus startles the reader by making strange (what literary critics call defamiliarizing) the doctrine of the incarnation. Although Christian dogmas have long seen Jesus as a human incarnation of God, elaboration of Trinitarian doctrine usually keeps God and Jesus separate as well. Miles does not. Everything that God has thought, said, or done carries forward into the consciousness of Jesus, and Jesus acts and speaks as if he were reacting to his previous manifestations in the Hebrew Bible. As Miles puts it:

> Jesus being God Incarnate, all of God's earlier words were Jesus' words as well and may—indeed, must—be taken into account as evidence about his character.

Because Miles understands Jesus as arriving on earth with a pre-formed conscious-ness and memory, he engages aspects of Jesus' character that do not often appear in Christian theology. Among these, for instance, is the question of whether the Cruci-fixion is tantamount to God's committing suicide. If Jesus/God had the power over life and death, as he claims in John 10, then his death must be self-inflicted. It matters little what the Romans or Jesus' fellow Jews intended; God can do what God wishes. This suicide/deicide starkly points to the central feature of Miles's work, a feature captured in the "crisis" of the title. The New Testament story of Jesus functions as a narrative of inner conflict in which God is forced, either by himself or by external events, to reformulate his patterns of behavior.

By examining the New Testament only through the lens of the character of God, Miles necessarily omits many facets of the New Testament that Christians hold dear. He has no interest in personal application of the text or its meaning for a religious con-gregation. The book, therefore, ignores Jesus' teaching on these matters. Shorn of its theological qualities, the canon looks strikingly different and even distorted. This dis-tortion, however, allows Miles to sidestep some of the distracting issues that historical and theological interpretations often present as blinders to reading the text. Miles has made plain that the concept of "the Word become flesh" (John 1:14) provides the framework—consciously or unconsciously—for almost all subsequent readings of the New Testament, and his literary acumen delves into the incarnation with a keen perceptiveness that complements theology and history.

Sources for Further Study

Madsen, Catherine. "Jesus Saves Face." *CrossCurrents* 52, no. 1 (2002): 131-136. A review that focuses on Miles's treatment of irony.

Wood, James. "God, Interrupted: Revisiting the Life of Christ." *New Yorker* 77, no. 35 (November 12, 2001): 122-125. Explores the book as a study of theodicy.

Wood, Michael. "Nobody's Perfect." *The New York Times Book Review*, December 23, 2001, p. 8. A critique of Miles's literary reading, centering on Miles's lack of attention to authorial presence.

Kyle Keefer

CHRIST CLONE TRILOGY

Author: James BeauSeigneur (1953-   )
First published: In His Image, 1997; *Birth of an Age,* 1997; *Acts of God,* 2004. New York: Warner Books
Genre: Novels
Subgenres: Apocalyptic fiction; science fiction; thriller/suspense
Core issues: Acceptance; Apocalypse; Gnosticism; good vs. evil; Jesus Christ; reason; scriptures

BeauSeigneur's trilogy tells the story of Decker Hawthorne's journey of decades and examines the question: What is humanity's relationship to God? The plots involve modern political, social, and religious conflicts, paired with natural and supernatural disasters, often footnoted and updated to make the events feel as real as possible. As the world looks for a way out of the spiral of pain, suffering, and death, false and true hopes compete for the soul of each individual.

Principal characters
> *Decker Hawthorne*, a reporter who becomes the stepfather to the cloned Christ
> *Christopher Goodman*, the cloned Christ, who is really the Antichrist
> *Harry Goodman*, a scientist who clones skin cells from the Shroud of Turin
> *Robert Milner*, one of the members of the Lucius Trust, a secret society that wants to control the Christ clone
> *David Bragford*, the wealthy supporter of the Lucius Trust
> *Tom Donafin*, Hawthorne's reporter friend, who is the prophesied hero for Israel
> *John* and
> *Cohen*, two prophets
> *Scott Rosen*, leader of the KDP, a radical messianic group
> *Rhoda Donafin*, Tom Donafin's wife, a new believer in Jesus Christ

Overview

The Christ Clone Trilogy begins with the first of James BeauSeigneur's novels, *In His Image*. The image is that of Jesus Christ on the Shroud of Turin, which reporter Decker Hawthorne is invited to investigate with a team of scientists and scholars in the late 1970's. Years later, scientist Harry Goodman tells his former student, Hawthorne, that he has cloned skin cells from the Shroud and implanted them in his son, Christopher. Instead of seeing the boy as Christ, though, Harry sees him as an evidence of alien life come to earth, an example of what can be done by humankind regardless of the existence of God. These ideas are later used by those following Christopher to promote his authority.

Christopher seems like a wonderful person—caring, considerate, intelligent, and charismatic but humble. When the Disaster results in millions of deaths around the world and both lose their families, Hawthorne accepts Christopher as his stepson. No explanation can be found for the Disaster and the deaths that result, and religious and political leaders start attacking each other around the world. A world in need of leaders allows Christopher to advance politically; as head of the United Nations' World Food Organization, he promotes the cause of fighting hunger around the world. While he is working and Hawthorne is supportive, forces from the Lucius Trust have learned about him and are working to move into position and gain influence over the young Goodman.

With money from David Bragford and the outreach of Lucius Trust member Robert Milner, the Lucius Trust gains Christopher's and Hawthorne's confidence and starts to direct their lives. Around them the world is spinning out of control. Israel is invaded by Russia, then leaves the United Nations. Illegal arms dealing gives Pakistani and Indian extremists the weapons that begin a nuclear war, which China enters. Droughts and radiation cause millions of deaths throughout the Middle East and Asia.

This series of wars, natural disasters, and political corruption force Christopher to make a forty-day journey into the desert, as Jesus did (related in the New Testament books of Matthew, Mark, and Luke), to find his true identity and reason for being. After communing with his Father for this time, Christopher returns to the United Nations and makes a powerful bid for the position of secretary-general. The humility has left Christopher, who now believes he is indeed Jesus Christ, but with a much different mission this time.

The second novel, *Birth of an Age*, presents a world torn apart by continuing war and disaster. Two prophets, John and Cohen, preach in the politically isolated city of Jerusalem. The natural and supernatural disasters are shown in great detail as the world, under the guidance of Christopher, works to avert and then cope with each one. While some people believe that these events are a call to worship God, others see the United Nations and Christopher's ability to cope as signs of humanity's strength.

A new series of supernatural disasters strikes the world in the form of strange infestations and plagues (corresponding to those predicted in the Book of Revelation). Christopher heals some, especially those who have political power, but seems afraid of letting too many people discover who he is too soon. The Lucius Trust tells both Christopher and Hawthorne that there is a time for such things, but the Christ Clone can hardly refuse to heal when approached by various ambassadors in the United Nations. Soon he has made allies he will later need.

In Jerusalem itself, three factions are competing to explain the events: the traditional Jews, the KDP (a radical messianic group), and the Jewish Christians. Having been kidnapped earlier by the KDP, Hawthorne is hostile to their message and suspicious of anyone in that region. His good friend Tom Donafin has been rescued and helped by Jewish Christians, who reveal to Donafin Christopher and Hawthorne's roles in the events around him.

As the world blames the two prophets in Jerusalem for its problems, Donafin uses his friendship with Hawthorne to get into the United Nations, where he kills Christopher on international television before being shot himself. This confusing event is merely a ploy that allows Christopher to be resurrected on international television, which makes his authority even greater. Christopher's desecration of the Temple and his murder of the two prophets were prophesied but ignored by all but the KDP and some Christians.

Christopher and Milner use their new visibility to promote their view of a New Age, where humanity will become like gods and leave behind the need to worship one deity. They do this using Gnostic ideas of the world god as Satan, pointing out contradictions in the Bible and asking whether a loving god would say and do the things they cite. They also draw on religious texts and philosophies from around the world, notably Eastern ones, that teach the idea of cycles of reincarnation until one achieves higher stages of development.

Everything is exposed and explained in the third book, *Acts of God*. Instead of fighting the prophecies of those unable to embrace Christopher's vision of humanity's final stage of evolution, Hawthorne encourages Christopher to play up to them. They create laws and use language that support the images of the Antichrist, though Christopher himself seems to need convincing of the correctness of these steps. They construct a new U.N. building on the site of the ancient city of Babylon, and Hawthorne designs a mark (the Mark) that will be required to take a new medication made from Christopher's healing blood.

Christopher preaches that his ability to heal the sick and injured is not limited to him; people must reach inside themselves to advance spiritually, and as they do, they too will be able to heal and be healed. People start to exhibit their own supernatural abilities for short periods of time as they turn toward Christopher. All of this adds more weight to Christopher's argument that humankind is on the verge of a great evolutionary step and the trauma killing millions is an attack from a jealous God.

Kidnapped again by the KDP, Hawthorne hears the other side of the argument from their leader, Scott Rosen, and Rhoda, the wife of his former friend Tom Donafin. Hawthorne has been too busy or too unsure to take the Mark he designed. Now he is confronted with the opposing argument, and in confusion he witnesses a world suffering through a series of plagues, again predicted in the Book of Revelation. Hawthorne is torn between the destruction he sees, Christopher's words, and those of his kidnappers.

It is only by confronting Christopher that Hawthorne learns the truth from the mouth of the Antichrist himself, who points out that he has never outright lied about who he is to Hawthorne. Refusing to accept the Mark, Hawthorne meets his death at Christopher's own hand. With his stepfather dead, Christopher the Antichrist is now surrounded only by those who fully embrace his message, who allow and encourage him to kill anyone who refuses the Mark.

The rest of the novel presents the final battle between good and evil, a battle not of weapons but of minds, hearts, and souls. Many have come to Megiddo, where the KDP and those with them in Petra will face off against the New Age in a battle of spirits and wills. The cities of the world are destroyed as the Petra camp repents and cites biblical passages. In the end, Jesus Christ and the Antichrist Christopher confront each other. The world watches on television as the Antichrist reveals himself, and everything falls into hellfire.

BeauSeigneur gives us a brief glimpse of the Millennial Kingdom when Hawthorne wakes up not in Hell as he had imagined but in the arms of his Raptured wife, Elizabeth, on a revitalized Earth. They look forward to eternal life, but with the knowledge that human beings will always have the choice to follow God's path or not, a foreshadowing of the true end of the Earth a thousand years in the future.

Christian Themes

The Christ Clone Trilogy interweaves many different references to the scriptures, both Old and New Testaments, as well as texts from other religions. Both sides in this battle for the souls of humanity use sacred texts to make their points. Both sides use logic and reason to argue for their interpretations. Both sides also claim evidence for their arguments from history, science, and logical faith.

The side of good uses arguments primarily focused on accepting God's role in deciding what is wrong and what is right. While there are attempts to back up claims with history and science, the approach is primarily based on faith in God. In contrast, the side of evil uses an argument that refers to texts from a variety of religions and philosophies, including several Gnostic beliefs about the nature of God, Satan, good, and evil. Its primary focus is on humans' faith in themselves.

The trilogy poses a fundamental question: Who is Jesus? Cloned from skin cells that no one denies belonged to the crucified Christ, Christopher Goodman nevertheless becomes the Antichrist, the force of evil. Christopher was created from cells that were part of Christ, but he was cloned is to prove that there is no God; his purpose is to draw people away from God. Clearly, Jesus Christ is therefore more than just a body; he is created from motivation, from an intended purpose. When the motivation is different, the person in the body is different too.

Sources for Further Study

Allitt, Patrick. *Religion in America Since 1945: A History*. New York: Columbia University Press, 2003. Looks at various trends in religion, including millennium fiction such as the Christ Clone Trilogy.

D'Ammassa, Don. Review of *Acts of God. Radford Chronicle* 27, no. 2 (February, 2005): 35. A brief review that concludes the third volume of the trilogy is "well enough written."

Frykholm, Amy Johnson. *Rapture Culture: Left Behind in Evangelical America*. New York: Oxford University Press, 2004. Examines the rising popularity of evangelical fiction and depictions of the Antichrist and Armageddon.

Hartshorn, Laurie. "Sacred Thoughts." *Booklist* 98, nos. 19/20 (June 1, 2002). Includes a review of *In His Image*.

Kirkus Reviews. Review of *Birth of an Age*. 71, no. 10 (May 15, 2003): 694. Comments on the trilogy as a whole (self-published in the 1990's), as well as this volume, considering it "astoundingly intelligent."

_____. Review of *In His Image*. 70, no. 23 (December 1, 2002): 1711. Review of the trilogy's first installment, calling it "silly, cheap, fun" and a potboiler.

Madsen, Niles J. "At the Libraries: Thrillers with a Biblical Flavor." *The Providence Journal*, December 8, 2003, p. B5. Notes that the trilogy describes the "calamitous afflictions" of Christ's cloning "in such scientific detail and accuracy as to require footnotes."

Seed, David. *Imagining Apocalypse: Studies in Cultural Crisis*. New York: St. Martin's Press, 2000. Several articles focus on different aspects of Christian science fiction, especially those that examine modern attitudes toward sex, science, and government.

Smietana, Bob. "Cloning of Christ Powers Three Plots." *The Patriot*, January 17, 2003, p. E4. Review of three novels, including the first installment of BeauSeigneur's Christ Clone trilogy, in the context of the cloning debate.

Zaleski, Jeff. Review of *In His Image*. *Publishers Weekly* 250, no. 1 (January 6, 2003): 38. Considers the first volume awkward and "rickety."

TammyJo Eckhart

CHRIST IN A PLURALISTIC AGE

Author: John B. Cobb, Jr. (1925-   )
First published: Philadelphia: Westminster Press, 1975
Genre: Nonfiction
Subgenre: Theology
Core issues: Incarnation; Jesus Christ

In traditional orthodox Christianity, Christ is understood to be the only way to salvation. In a world of increasing religious pluralism, however, Christianity must find a way to embrace other religions rather than to exclude them. Using Alfred North Whitehead's process philosophy, Cobb proposes that Christ is not the universalization of one way of living religiously over another. Rather, Christ is the image of creative transformation, enabling us to be open to the potential meanings of other religious paths and leading to a deeper understanding of Christian existence.

Overview

By the 1970's, Christian systematic theology had undergone enormous changes. The great systematic theologians of the mid-twentieth century—Karl Barth, Paul Tillich, and Emil Brunner—came under attack in the 1960's on a variety of fronts. Most important, Thomas Altizer's radical theology, which proclaimed the death of God in 1966, challenged the traditional transcendent notion of God (a God over and against us in the heavens) and opened the way for theologies that focused more on God's immanence (God's presence within the world, not outside of it). The 1960's and 1970's witnessed the great flourishing of theologies in which human experience rather than God or Scripture became the sole authority for doing theology. The feminist theologies of Mary Daly and Rosemary Ruether, the liberation theology of Gustavo Gutiérrez, the black theology of James Cone, and the process theology of John B. Cobb, Jr., all grew and developed during these decades.

In addition, the 1960's witnessed the great "turn to the East" in religion. Turning away from the irrelevant religions of their parents, scores of young people sought spiritual direction and enlightenment in various forms of Buddhism and Hinduism. As colleges began to offer programs in the history of religions that offered an objective study of these religions, Christian thinkers were looking for ways to engage with the increasing religious pluralism of the age. One method was simply not to engage and to exclude the beliefs and practices of these other religions as false paths to God. Another method was to include these religions as legitimate in their own right but as merely incomplete manifestations of God. A final method embraced religious pluralism and recognized in it the potential for understanding more richly Christian existence.

Cobb's groundbreaking book, *Christ in a Pluralistic Age*, grows out of his work in process theology as well as his attempt to answer the question, "How can Christians understand the primary image of their faith in a pluralistic age?" Originally delivered as lectures at Austin Presbyterian Theological Seminary in 1972, Cobb's chapters undertake a radical rethinking of the nature of Christ, the relation of the image of Christ to the historical Jesus, and the future of a Christianity in which Christ is understood as a way of creative transformation. If Christ is to continue to be relevant as one religious image among others in a pluralistic age, how can we embrace Christ in a way that fosters pluralism without losing Christ's distinctiveness and without succumbing to the relativism that most people mistakenly attribute to pluralism?

Cobb's answer is a relatively simple one, and he explores it in three distinct parts of his book. He observes that Christ is a process of creative transformation that provides a unity to the many paths of religious meaning and that encourages openness to other religious ways of living.

In part 1, Cobb sets forth his notions of creative transformation and its impact on the idea of Christ. In this section, Cobb uses process philosophy to ground his idea that Christ is an image of an entity that actualized its own potentiality, liberating Christians from the burden of their past and encouraging hope for the future. Thus, Christ transforms our world by moving us from a static concern with the ways things have always been in religion to a more dynamic structure of existence that opens us to others and their experiences of religious life. Christ as creative transformation breaks our relationship with every established doctrine and its mooring in the past to allow us to experience many forms of Christ in the world today, including the presence of Christ in others. In short, Cobb argues in this section of his book that we are all potential Christs to one another.

Part 2 examines the relationship between the historical Jesus and Christ as creative transformation. Because the life and work of Jesus is the primary way that many people come to know anything about the Christ of Christianity, are there qualities in Jesus' life that help us understand Christ as creative transformation? Very simply, Cobb observes, Jesus provides a model of this transformation in his acceptance of God's divine initiative and his human freedom. In the Incarnation, God gave Jesus the possibility of actualizing himself around God's presence. At many times during Jesus' life, he chose freely to allow his own selfhood to coalesce with the presence of God within him. Thus, Jesus becomes an image of the truly successful Christ, a human who is able to respond creatively to God's immanent presence.

Part 3 of the book examines the image of Christ as hope. Christ transforms not only our past and present but also our future. Jesus' structure of existence—his full incarnation of self and God's presence—is the model we imitate as we go forward into our futures. As we transform ourselves by perfecting our love, we become more open to others and to our past and future, and we become more inclusive in our future dealings with others. The perfection of love, demonstrated by Jesus, breaks down our concern with our private selves and with our static doctrine and opens us to embrace others and the future, thus helping us to transform our own faith and understand deeply and compassionately the faiths of others.

Christian Themes

Cobb's *Christ in a Pluralistic Age* deals primarily with the Christian theme of incarnation. The doctrine of the Incarnation asks the question, "How can Jesus, in whom God became flesh, be both human and divine?" Early Christian councils debated fiercely the question of the balance between Jesus' humanity and his divinity. The traditional Christian response to these questions is that Jesus is fully human and fully divine. Yet, this view of Christ became static, isolating Christ to a long-past creedal formulation that Christians repeat tirelessly every Sunday in their churches.

What does this ancient formulation have to do with contemporary religious pluralism, asks Cobb, and is there a more dynamic understanding of Christ that will allow us to embrace the promises of religious pluralism? His answer is to understand Christ as an image of creative transformation. This transformation is a process by which we all—looking to Jesus as the model of the incarnation of the divine—come to understand ourselves as more fully human and to open ourselves to others and all that they have to offer.

Using process philosophy, Cobb presents God's presence, or Logos, as the potentiality of novelty to an ever-changing world. Jesus, a specific entity in this world, became the concrete actualization of this potentiality. Christ, for Cobb, becomes the image of that novelty as it is made real, or incarnated, in the world. Thus, following the model of Christ in Jesus—the incarnation of the novelty of God's presence in the world—Christians can actualize the potential they share to deepen that incarnation. For Cobb, the Incarnation as a way of creative transformation encourages Christians to become more fully human in the same way that Jesus modeled his humanity to respond freely to God's initiative to love others and to embrace them as fully human.

Cobb's rich blend of process philosophy and Christian theology challenges traditional notions of the Christian doctrine of the Incarnation and offers fresh new ways of thinking about how Christianity can embrace religious pluralism.

Sources for Further Study

Cobb, John B., Jr. "Response to Ogden and Carpenter." *Process Studies* 6 (Summer, 1976): 123-129. Cobb argues that Ogden misses the point of Cobb's Christ as the way of creative transformation and that Carpenter confuses Cobb's idea of "structure of existence" simply with "quality of life."

Fackre, Gabriel J. "Cobb's *Christ in a Pluralistic Age*: A Review Article." Review of *Christ in a Pluralistic Age*. *Andover Newton Quarterly* 17 (March, 1977): 308-315. A critical but appreciative review that applauds Cobb's use of art and the imagination as ways of understanding Christ as creative transformation.

Jenson, Robert. Review of *Christ in a Pluralistic Age*. *Interpretation* 31 (July, 1977): 307-311. Jenson criticizes Cobb's image of Christ, arguing for a more orthodox view in which Christ functions as a singular way of salvation for others.

Lewis, John M., and John B. Cobb, Jr. "Christology and Pluralism." *Perspectives in Religious Studies* 4 (Spring, 1977): 63-72. A conversation between Lewis and

Cobb on potential Christian responses to increasing religious pluralism, emphasizing Cobb's notion of a pluralistic Christ.

Ogden, Schubert M. "Christology Reconsidered: John Cobb's *Christ in a Pluralistic Age*." *Process Studies* 6 (Summer, 1976): 116-122. Ogden argues that Cobb's image of Christ as creative transformation misses the point of Christology and is too hypothetical to be useful for theology.

Henry L. Carrigan, Jr.

CHRIST THE LORD
Out of Egypt

Author: Anne Rice (1941-   )
First published: New York: Knopf, 2005
Genre: Novel
Subgenres: Biblical fiction; historical fiction (first century)
Core issues: Catholics and Catholicism; Gospels; Jesus Christ; self-knowledge

Rice tells the story of Jesus Christ's childhood as a first-person narrative, from Jesus' perspective, as his understanding of his divinity and mission grow. She writes from a Catholic viewpoint in conscious opposition to much of the skeptical biblical criticism of the preceding decades. Rejecting much of biblical scholars' demythologizing of Christ's story as presented in the Gospel narratives, Rice still makes abundant use of their work in reconstructing details of the first century Roman Empire and Jewish culture, of which Jesus was a part.

> Principal characters
> *Jesus*
> *Mary*, Jesus' mother
> *Joseph*, Jesus' stepfather
> *James*, Jesus' stepbrother
> *Elizabeth*, mother of John the Baptist
> *Salome*, cousin and beloved friend
> *Cleopas*, Mary's bother, Jesus' uncle
> *Old Sarah*, a relative

Overview

In *Christ the Lord*, Anne Rice presents a narrative of Jesus Christ's youngest years, beginning at age seven. The opening scene is familiar to those who have read any of the infancy narratives. In this story, Jesus strikes a playmate dead and returns him to life, at Salome's urging. The resurrected boy's parents want Jesus and his family to leave Alexandria, Egypt. However, the Teacher comes to his defense, saying Jesus and his brother James are his best students at the House of Study.

Jesus' stepfather, Joseph, decides that it is time for the family to return to the Holy Land, in part because Herod, who had been a threat to Jesus, is dead. The Teacher and another minor character, Philo, try to persuade Joseph to let Jesus stay and continue his studies, but Joseph is firm. The family will stay together and go to Nazareth, where more relatives await. Soon Jesus' family is on a boat, leaving Egypt forever. Throughout this period, little Jesus has far more questions than answers about who he is and why he is different. What happened in Bethlehem? Why did the family leave for Egypt?

The journey homeward includes a visit to the temple in Jerusalem. The family's joy and awe soon turn to horror, however, as soldiers massacre worshipers, putting a brutal end to Passover festivities. Elizabeth tells of the foreordained birth of her son John the Baptist and his father's death at the hands of soldiers and insists her son will be raised by the Essenes. Jesus is struck by the way the solemn John keeps staring at him.

Elizabeth and John remain behind and the family continue on their trek. They pass through unsettled regions and see the effect of war, rebellion, and Roman reprisals on villages. They also fall victim to bandits, who say the money they demand is going to the resistance effort against the Roman Empire. The family reaches Nazareth to find it seemingly abandoned. Fearing soldiers, the townspeople have hidden in tunnels. Soldiers do appear and want to take one of the family members back to Rome in reprisal against the Jewish rebellion in the area. The family's relative Old Sarah emerges and defuses the situation, offering the soldiers food and drink. The rest of the extended family emerges from hiding. Soon Jesus and his half brother James are exploring the countryside. While getting used to the homeland he has never known, Jesus is also coming to terms with some of his unique abilities and accepting that he cannot simply wield the power of life and death by whim. Joseph reminds him of the need to remain hidden, and that means keeping his talents hidden as well.

On the Sabbath, Old Sarah insists that the family go to the synagogue. While in Egypt, Joseph and the others had become accustomed to worshiping at home. There is a tense moment at the door of the synagogue when the rabbi hesitates to let Jesus enter, claiming not to know him. Mary's brother Cleopas mediates, presenting the rabbi with a gift from Egypt, and all go in to worship. Soon Jesus and James are favorite pupils of the rabbi. Jesus learns about Jewish faith and traditions from his family. He also seeks out religious education and discussion not only at the synagogue but also later at the temple, as the family returns for the annual holy days, which were shattered by violence the previous year.

On the Day of Atonement, Joseph and Mary come to the realization that their family's experience parallels the larger story of Israel, whose people were exiled to Egypt and then returned to the Holy Land. Economically, Jesus' family does well in the year following their return from Egypt. Their carpentry skills are sought after as families seek to rebuild their homes after the war's destruction. Joseph and company also refurbish the synagogue.

Questions continue to plague Jesus about his origins. Family members drop hints, but Joseph has forbidden Jesus to ask questions. James finally reveals that angels attended Jesus' birth and that he was called the Son of God. Soon, Mary tells Jesus her part of the story, from the Annunciation to the animals in the stable keeping the family warm on the night Jesus was born. She relates Jesus' early miracles and tells him again to keep his power within himself, to use his divine gifts only when God calls upon him to do so. God sent Jesus into the world as a child so that he might grow in wisdom, Mary tells her son.

The final secret is the Slaughter of the Innocents. Jesus goes to the temple alone and seeks out the oldest teacher he can find. He asks this man what happened to the Christ child and is told that the baby was killed soon after his birth, along with all other children in Bethlehem under the age of two. Jesus is upset by this information but recovers. He realizes that all things live and all die. For now, his role is to be alive.

Christian Themes

The primary theme of *Christ the Lord* is Jesus Christ's growing self-awareness during his early youth. Through interactions with family and friends and by watching events unfold around him, Jesus becomes aware of his Jewishness. Jesus' uncle Cleopas is a frustrated scholar, always telling stories and teaching Jesus what he can of the faith. In fact, education is a strong part of Jesus' upbringing. He seeks out knowledge, particularly religious knowledge, wherever it is to be found. Time is marked by Jewish festivals, such as Passover. Distance and place have a Jewish theme throughout this work. Jesus' foster father Joseph even notes that the family's journey from Egypt to the Holy Land parallels, on a small scale, the journey made by the Jewish people centuries earlier.

Jesus' awareness of his deity grows significantly during the year of his life this novel covers. When the narrative opens, his power over life and death has just been displayed, to the horror of neighbors. At a cousin's prompting, he is able to right a wrong by bringing the boy he has accidentally killed back to life. Foreshadowing the nature miracles of the canonical Gospels, such as walking on water, the child Jesus at one point makes it snow. With his growing self-awareness comes self-control and a turning of his will over to God. Several times Jesus is tempted or asked to provide divine intervention, such as healing a stricken family member. Over time, he gains the wisdom and self-discipline needed to control and manage his divine gifts. Rice shows the Christ child's humanity along with his growing sense of divinity. Some of his most traumatizing moments come when he realizes the impact, even destruction, that his entrance into the human world has caused, particularly in the Slaughter of the Innocents.

Sources for Further Study

Boyd, Gregory A. *Cynic Sage or Son of God?* Wheaton, Ill.: Bridgepoint/Victor, 1995. In an effort to refute the portrait of Jesus offered by John Dominic Crossan, Boyd summarizes and counters Jesus Seminar arguments about Christ.

Crossan, John Dominic. *Jesus: A Revolutionary Biography*. San Francisco: HarperSanFrancisco, 1994. A member of the controversial Jesus Seminar, Crossan portrays Jesus as a social rebel and revolutionary, but a starkly human one, whose birth was natural and whose resurrection was, at best, a metaphor.

Fredrikson, Paula. *From Jesus to Christ: The Origins of the New Testament Images of Jesus*. New Haven, Conn.: Yale University Press, 1988. Examines the historical and cultural background behind images of Christ as depicted in the Gospels and letters of Paul.

Wharton, Gary C. *Jesus, the Authorized Biography: The Eyewitness Accounts by Those Who Personally Knew Him*. Green Forest, Ark.: New Leaf Press, 2005. Brings together in narrative form the various accounts of Jesus' life and ministry as found in the Gospels and Epistles.

Wright, N. T. *The Challenge of Jesus: Rediscovering Who Jesus Was and Is.* Downers Grove, Ill.: InterVarsity Press, 1999. An accessible distillation of Anglican theologian Wright's work on searching for the historical Jesus while remaining within theological orthodoxy.

Elizabeth Jarnagin

THE CHRISTIAN FAITH

Author: Friedrich Schleiermacher (1768-1834)
First published: Der christliche Glaube, 1821-1822 (English translation, 1926)
Edition used: Der christliche Glaube, 1821/22, edited by Hermann Peiter. Berlin: Walter de Gruyter, 1980
Genre: Nonfiction
Subgenres: Meditation and contemplation; philosophy; theology
Core issues: Alienation from God; Creation; devotional life; faith; holiness; humility

The Christian Faith, *the most important of Schleiermacher's nearly two hundred works, attempts to articulate a theory of faith to understand the nature of the relationship between God and the created human world. Schleiermacher states that because God is "entirely different" from humans, the only possible reaction that humans can have to God is a "feeling of absolute dependence," which produces awe, humility, and "pious self-consciousness." Religion is constituted in the immediacy of this feeling of dependence.*

Overview

The second edition (1830-1831) of Friedrich Schleiermacher's major work is quite different from the first (1821-1822). The first edition, except for occasional small excerpts, has never appeared in English. The only English translation of the second edition has been reedited and reissued several times, but remains mostly the same as when it appeared in 1926. It was the first edition, however, that had the greatest impact during Schleiermacher's lifetime.

In 1821 *The Christian Faith* caused a stir in German universities, seminaries, and churches by proclaiming that true religion is nothing more than piety grounded in a simple feeling of dependence on an infinite, eternal, unknown, and unknowable power. This feeling is essential, primal, and unavoidable. Piety is neither a kind of knowledge nor a way of behaving, but only this sincere, basic feeling. The feeling of absolute dependence requires no further sophistication as it develops into an intense devotion through the absorption of church doctrine and the regular practice of meekness and worship.

In 1822 Georg Friedrich Wilhelm Hegel, who was then Schleiermacher's colleague at the University of Berlin and the most famous philosopher in Germany, launched a sarcastic attack against the first edition. In the foreword to *Die Religion im inneren Verhältnisse zur Wissenschaft* (*Religion in Its Internal Relationship to Systematic Knowledge*, 1987) by his student Hermann Hinrichs, Hegel wrote that if Schleiermacher were correct that feeling is the essence of religion and that piety is the highest expression of that feeling, then "the dog would be the best Christian." Hegel's point was that to reduce religion to emotion and to disown its cognitive and intellectual content would be to deny the full humanity of religious individuals as rational beings. Schleiermacher's Romanticism, insofar as it valued faith over reason and piety over philosophical inquiry, was anathema to Idealists such as Hegel who held that God was ultimately knowable and that faith must be subordinate to the God-given reason that is the essence of human spirit.

Despite significant differences in tone and vocabulary between the two editions and other strong textual evidence of Hegel's effect on Schleiermacher, scholars disagree about the extent to which Hegel's criticism of the first edition influenced Schleiermacher's preparation of the second. The second edition plays down the ideas of piety and dependence that dominate the first edition. Terms such as "pious feeling of dependence" in the first become "pious self-consciousness" in the second. Instead of uncritically elaborating the feeling of dependence, as in the first edition, Schleiermacher in the second uses a more systematic philosophical vocabulary centered on self-consciousness. Pious feeling remains the main theme, but Schleiermacher now presents it in a way better able to withstand Hegelian and other philosophical onslaught.

Both editions of *The Christian Faith* begin by explaining the advantages of Protestant dogmatic theology for faithful people. Then follows the *Glaubenslehre* itself in two parts, the first presenting the theory of the feeling of absolute dependence, the second contrasting sin and grace. In sin, the feeling of absolute dependence renders us weak and despondent; but through God's grace, mercy, and omnipotence, this same feeling gives us joy, hope, and strength.

The Christian Faith is a long work in two volumes. In the first edition, the first part of the *Glaubenslehre* is about half of the first volume, while the second part is the entire second volume. In the second edition, the first part is only about the middle third of the first volume, while the second part is both the last third of the first volume and the entire second volume. This formal change is significant for the content of the work. In the first edition, the first part of the *Glaubenslehre* considers the development of the pious feeling of dependence without regard to the opposition between its own lack of power and great power that God has given it. In the second edition, the first part of the *Glaubenslehre* shows the development of pious self-consciousness as it is presupposed in every emotional stimulation of Christian piety. Both versions emphasize how this feeling reveals the attributes of God and the character of the world.

The two editions also differ in their portrayal of sin in the first "side" of the second part of the *Glaubenslehre*. While the first edition deals with the inherent consciousness of God as it evolves into its opposite, sin, the second addresses, more philosophically, the development of the bare fact of pious self-consciousness insofar as its opposite, sin, is determined through it.

Both editions follow the same outline for the second "side" of the second part of the *Glaubenslehre*, on the development of the human consciousness of God's grace, discussing the Christian condition to the extent that Christians feel grace, the character of the world in relation to redemption, and the attributes of God that pertain to redemption. Both editions conclude with an essay on the Holy Trinity.

In both editions, the first part of the *Glaubenslehre* and the two "sides" of the second part of the *Glaubenslehre* together form a triad on feeling, sin, and grace, respectively. Each third of this triad is divided into three sections, one on the human condition, one on the character of the world, and one on the attributes of God, each in relation to its main topic: feeling, sin, or grace.

Christian Themes

Schleiermacher was an ordained minister in the Evangelical Church of the Prussian Union. True to his calling, most of his writings are expositions of church doctrine. They are exercises in dogmatic theology insofar as they attempt to show how church teachings are consistent with our typical feelings for God and each other. Schleiermacher saw dogmatic theology as the unending practical science of how to harmonize each present Christian community with the everyday customs of its particular place and time in history.

The Christian Faith is no exception. Its purpose within dogmatic theology is to show and affirm the spiritually healthy relation of our prereflective consciousness of God to the doctrines of sin, creation, the divine attributes, grace, mercy, the Incarnation of Christ, salvation, the Resurrection, eternity, the establishment of earthly and heavenly churches, and the Trinity. The respective meanings of these doctrines have important roles as personal piety develops out of the feeling of absolute dependence. When properly understood, each separate dogma of the church confirms and strengthens the feeling of absolute dependence on God and enlivens our hope of salvation. For non-Christians who also feel absolutely dependent on an eternal power, this feeling remains sterile and without direction; but for Christians, and especially for pious Protestants, the church, by both its word and its community, guides this feeling toward realizing its most profound result.

Some conservative dogmatic theologians, notably Karl Barth, have accused Schleiermacher of importing too much subjectivity into Christianity at the expense of the enduring truth of the Bible as the word of God. Barth's neoorthodoxy proclaims, against Schleiermacher, that religious feeling should be manifest not as simple piety but as passionate love and thankfulness for the objective truth that the Bible reveals.

Sources for Further Study

Clements, Keith W. *Friedrich Schleiermacher: Pioneer of Modern Theology*. Minneapolis: Fortress, 1991. A good general introduction to Schleiermacher, interspersed with selections from several of his works.

Crouter, Richard. *Friedrich Schleiermacher: Between Enlightenment and Romanticism*. New York: Cambridge University Press, 2005. An indispensable addition to Schleiermacher studies by the dean of anglophone Schleiermacher scholars. Discusses most major topics, including Schleiermacher's revisions of the first edition of *The Christian Faith*.

Curran, Thomas H. *Doctrine and Speculation in Schleiermacher's Glaubenslehre*. New York: Walter de Gruyter, 1994. A clear, detailed, and bold exegesis of both editions of *The Christian Faith*.

Luft, Eric v. d. *Hegel, Hinrichs, and Schleiermacher on Feeling and Reason in Religion: The Texts of Their 1821-1822 Debate.* Lewiston, N.Y.: Mellen, 1987. Contains selections from the first edition of *The Christian Faith*, as well as analysis of the philosophical issues that motivated Hegel's attack on Schleiermacher's theology.

Mariña, Jacqueline, ed. *The Cambridge Companion to Friedrich Schleiermacher.* New York: Cambridge University Press, 2005. A useful anthology of new essays by Robert Merrihew Adams, Frederick C. Beiser, Andrew Bowie, Richard Crouter, Francis Schüssler Fiorenza, Terrence N. Tice, and many other prominent scholars.

Williams, Robert R. *Schleiermacher the Theologian: The Construction of the Doctrine of God.* Philadelphia: Fortress, 1978. A vigorous defense of Schleiermacher against critics such as Hegel, Ludwig Feuerbach, and Barth.

Eric v. d. Luft

THE CHRISTIAN TRADITION
Beyond Its European Captivity

Author: Joseph Mitsuo Kitagawa (1915-1992)
First published: Philadelphia: Trinity Press International, 1992
Genre: Nonfiction
Subgenres: Critical analysis; essays
Core issues: Asian Americans; the divine; imperialism; religion; suffering

Culture has a profound influence on religion. According to Kitagawa, to be unaware of how culture has shaped the faith one holds to be revealed truth is to be unaware of the objective point of view, which he calls the biographical aspect. Western Christianity has been mired in the autobiographical aspect of religion, a subjective point of view that has conflated the content of Christianity with Western cultural values. This volume of collected essays probes the history and meaning of Asian Christianity as well as exploring the spiritual significance of the internment of Japanese Americans during World War II.

Overview

Joseph Kitagawa came to the United States just before the outbreak of World War II to further his studies in theology. He was a student at the University of California, Berkeley, when the government ordered the internment of Japanese and Japanese Americans in the United States. The experience of living in a concentration camp with others of Japanese descent provided Kitagawa with two spiritual insights he could never have gained had history allowed him a peaceful academic career at Berkeley. The first was into the essentially racist nature of Eurocentric culture, including the very Christianity he had embraced before his arrival in the country. The second was into the nature of suffering and the resilience of Asian spirituality as demonstrated by the daily heroism of incarcerated Japanese Americans.

These insights shaped much of Kitagawa's distinguished academic career in theology at the University of Chicago, and they inform *The Christian Tradition*, perhaps the least known of his many publications. The very title invites readers to consider the European enculturation of Christianity as a sort of Babylonian captivity from which a release may be at hand. Kitagawa is never polemical in his treatment of church history; he is thoughtful and deliberate and always careful not to demean the many positive aspects of missionary activity in Asia. Yet this low-key academic approach makes the question he asks all the more tantalizing: What if Christianity had traveled not westward, where it was absorbed into the Greco-Roman civilization, but eastward, where it would have been absorbed into Asian culture? How different would it be?

Kitagawa looks back to the Renaissance and the Reformation, when the powerful new synthesis of culture and religion called modernity first raised its head. Individualism, capitalism, and colonialism were the children of this new synthesis; hand-in-hand with colonialism came the missionary effort. The discovery of Asian civilization at this time was as great a shock to the West as the discovery of the New World. For the rational, pigeonholing West, steeped in a philosophical tradition that systematically categorized human existence, the appearance of a spiritual tradition in which humans and nature were not conceived of as separate entities presented a great challenge. In just the same way that Native Americans were classified as pagans by the European explorers, Asians were seen as heathens who worshiped strange gods but were destined to be converted to the truth of Christianity. No less an envoy than the Spanish missionary Francis Xavier marveled that the people of Japan could have achieved such moral goodness without knowing the Christian God, but such recognition did not lessen his determination to bring the peoples of Asia into the Catholic Church.

In the centuries after such early missionary efforts, European powers colonized most of Asia, subjugating its people politically, economically, and culturally. Missionaries presented Christianity as the spiritual engine that motivated European civilization. The churches founded by missionaries in Asia tended to be slavish imitations of the mother institutions, and positions of ecclesiastical authority were not entrusted to native clergy or church members. Even more damaging, Kitagawa says, was the determination to exclude all native spiritual traditions, which were seen as polluting. The nineteenth century was the culmination of this spiritual colonialism and stands as a metaphor for such blind, subjective domination. In many ways, the legacy of this blindness remained strong until after World War II, when the West gradually became aware of Asia and its traditions as possible resources for its own weakening traditions.

According to Kitagawa, part of this appreciation for the spiritual heritage of Asians and Asian Americans has come from the realization on the part of Western philosophers that the dualistic thinking characteristic of Western Christianity is fatally flawed and no longer tenable in a fragile global community. The damage caused by seeing the world in terms of good and evil is evident with every news broadcast. The Asian tradition of juxtaposing several truths and accepting a multifaceted reality has come to be valued as a more practical way to allow the coexistence of disparate peoples and cultures.

At the same time, Western thinkers have moved closer to an appreciation of the material and are less likely to value the spiritual over the material. Kitagawa argues that feminists have emphasized the importance of embodiment and distanced themselves from the bankruptcy of the logocentric tradition of Western metaphysics, a system that prioritizes the ideal at the expense of the real. Asian traditions have held that spirit and matter cannot be divided; in particular, the Japanese tradition has emphasized the importance of the actual and taken pains to preserve its integrity from the annihilating force of ideology. These cultural changes have highlighted the existence and importance of Asian religions at a time when many Westerners have turned away from Eurocentric Christianity.

The question that remains to be answered is how the Asian Christian churches might take up the challenge of offering a new synthesis, one that no longer rejects Asian spirituality. Kitagawa says the new millennium may well be the one in which Christianity moves out of its European captivity and into a more global setting. What will the new face of Christ be like, divested of its European complexion?

Christian Themes

Perhaps the hardest of all questions for a Christian to answer is to explain the essential features of Christianity apart from the cultural values that surround it and have come to inform it. Kitagawa asks: To be Christian, must an Asian believer endeavor to understand and follow those aspects of European culture that cling to the traditional churches? Is some understanding of the complex synthesis of philosophy and theology achieved in the Middle Ages and in the Reformation necessary for Vietnamese or Chinese Christians? Can the centrality of family and community in Thailand serve as a guiding metaphor for an understanding of the Christian experience? Can the suffering of Japanese Americans in the relocation camps scattered across American deserts be raised up as a light upon the mountain for mainstream American Christians?

At one end of biblical literature is the story of the Tower of Babel, an account that envisages a multiplicity of languages as God's punishment for the sin of arrogance. At the other end we find the description of Pentecost, the great community-forging event of the New Testament, in which the Spirit bestows the gift of tongues, suggesting a Christianity without cultural borders. Other passages from the New Testament, like the story of Peter and Cornelius from the Acts of the Apostles, also involve key elements of going beyond culture in the presence of the Spirit. Of all the apostles, perhaps Paul, the convert from Judaism, aficionado of Greek culture, and citizen of the Roman Empire, demonstrated the most sophisticated sense of the place of Christianity in a Mediterranean civilization populated with a plethora of deities. In this sense Paul displays a biographical awareness of Christianity, as opposed to the merely autobiographical knowledge of the simplistic believer.

Christianity is entering a new global phase, in which the old paradigm of the West as teacher and the East as pupil no longer holds. As the confidence and identity of Asian churches grow, elements of the Christian experience that have not been emphasized in the traditional churches will appear and renew the faith of the global community.

Sources for Further Study

Carnes, Tony, and Fenggang Yang, eds. *Asian American Religions: The Making and Remaking of Borders and Boundaries.* New York: New York University Press, 2004. This book explores the hybrid nature of religious expression in contemporary Asian American culture.

Kogawa, Joy. *Obasan.* New York: Anchor Books, 1994. Kogawa, an Anglican like Kitagawa, explores the theme of Christianity and the Japanese-Canadian wartime experience. This novel embodies many of Kitagawa's concerns in a powerful story of suffering and love.

Moss, David M. "Internment and Ministry: A Dialogue with Joseph Kitagawa." *Journal of Religion and Health* 32:3 (September, 1993). In this dialogue Kitagawa reviews many of his research concerns, including the internment experience of Japanese Americans and the characteristics of Asian religions.

Hideyuki Kasuga

CHRISTIANITY AND DEMOCRACY

Author: Jacques Maritain (1882-1973)
First published: Christianisme et démocratie, 1943 (English translation, 1944)
Edition used: Christianity and Democracy, translated by Doris Anson. New York: Charles Scribner's Sons, 1947
Genre: Nonfiction
Subgenres: History; philosophy; theology
Core issues: Catholics and Catholicism; ethics; freedom and free will; justice

In Maritain's shortest presentation of his understanding of democracy, he argues that true democracy can arise only from a Christian understanding of the person, as one made in the image and likeness of God. Democracy, according to Maritain, is not primarily about mechanisms of public participation and political institutions but about promoting human dignity.

Overview

Noted Catholic philosopher Jacques Maritain spearheaded a Catholic revival in France and the revival of philosophical Thomism in Europe and the United States. Although philosophically a traditionalist, he was one of the foremost proponents of Christian democracy in the twentieth century, and his work paved the way for the reforms of Vatican II. *Christianity and Democracy* consists of about one hundred pages, a preface and eight chapters. In his preface, Maritain identifies the theme of the work: A new understanding of democracy must arise in the light of the destruction of World War II. Maritain expresses great hope that such an understanding will develop.

The first chapter, entitled, "The End of an Age," asserts that fascism and communism have completely poisoned the modern world, which he says was "born of Christendom and owed its deepest living strength to Christian tradition." In the second chapter, Maritain argues that the democracies that emerged by 1942 are weak and not prepared to build a proper civilization. Even though the youth of these democracies have expressed great doubt about society, they have expended much energy on fighting totalitarianism. Democracies have given too much attention to economics and the concern for acquisition of material goods. According to Maritain, the greatest failure of modern democracies is that religion has been ignored.

In chapters titled "Three Remarks" and "Evangelical Inspiration and the Secular Conscience," Maritain presents his understanding of the relationship between religion and democracy. Maritain asserts that "democracy is linked to Christianity" and that the democratic impulse has arisen because of Christianity. Christianity, Maritain argues, promotes an understanding of civic friendship because of its emphasis on brotherly love. This civic friendship will enable justice and peace to exist in political life. Maritain says that Christianity "has taught . . . the unity of the human race, the natural equality of all men . . . , the dignity of every soul fashioned in the image of the God, [and] the dignity of labor and the poor." These ideas have spread to the "secular conscience," by which he means the everyday thinking of the common people. Maritain recognizes that the common people can err, but the common people generally understand these basic truths. Maritain believes that the common people's belief in the consent of the governed is necessary for the legitimacy of the government.

In the chapter titled "The True Essence of Democracy," the longest chapter in the work, Maritain states that others agree with his views about the relationship between Christianity and democracy and then cites U.S. president Franklin Roosevelt's assertion that democracy and human rights have their strongest foundations in Christianity. Maritain notes that Henri Bergson, the noted French philosopher, has similar beliefs. According to Maritain, Christianity is not only the foundation of proper democracy but also the best means to sustain an operating democracy. Christianity will best support the practice of virtue and the seeking after justice in a political order. Christianity, Maritain asserts, will help ensure that the state is not the highest end, which is a fundamental error of politics. Christianity will also help prevent a democratic society from becoming too individualistic. The political order built upon Christianity will enable a consideration of the common good.

There follows a brief chapter about the leadership needed for a proper democracy. That leadership will look to the common beliefs of the people about human dignity, which is not the same as believing every opinion stated by human beings. Maritain says that the "inspirational leadership which the people need must always live in communion with this people."

Another brief chapter recognizes that communism will likely be a continuing threat. Defenders of democracy must realize, Maritain states, that communism is not just about economic distribution; it presents a vision of human life. Defenders of democracy must work to build an attractive society that can undermine the attractions of communism.

The final chapter, "An Heroic Humanism," argues that those who promote an authentic Christian humanism must do so with great courage. Suffering and betrayal have prevailed in Europe for a very long time; hence, courage and heroism are needed to surmount this history if a proper view of the human person is to be inculcated. The French, Maritain notes, can be particularly cynical because of the betrayal by Philippe Petain, who served as the Nazi-imposed Vichy president during the war. Those defending humanism, Maritain states, can look to the case of the United States, where there has been a teaching about the equality of human beings that has pervaded much of society. The "mainspring of American civilization is this dignity of each one in daily existence." Americans so strongly believed in this humanism that the United States abandoned its previous stance of isolationism and defended the rights of others in foreign lands. All peoples can take this example and engage in a heroic defense of humanism, which requires sacrifice and virtuous action, but not necessarily martyrdom. According to Maritain, heroic humanism is needed "if we want civilization to survive."

Christian Themes

The most significant theme of this work is the relationship between Christianity and democracy. Maritain argues that democracy is not primarily about developing political institutions such as legislative bodies and developing habits of political participation; instead, democracy is best understood as a social vision that is built upon a view of the human person as one who derives dignity from bearing the image and likeness of God.

Democratic society, according to Maritain, should promote the common good. That common good will be achieved when people exercise what Maritain calls civic friendship. Once civic friendship is exercised, there will be a true justice and peace. Thus there cannot be true Christianity without democracy, because the two are essentially linked.

A second theme in the work is the spread of Christian notions about the person and the manner in which that influences common humanity. Maritain believes that a Christian notion of the human person has permeated Western society. In this sense, one can be a democrat without being an active practitioner of Christianity. Because notions of human dignity have spread to many people, leaders can look to the beliefs of common humanity. Maritain sees these beliefs being held by many in Europe and, most definitely, by many in America.

A third theme of the work is the need for heroic actions on the part of those seeking to restore democracy. Heroic actions by leaders promoting a new understanding of democracy are particularly needed in Europe, because the destruction in Europe in the wake of World War II will require a new social vision. Maritain says that Americans have exercised some heroic action in coming to the aid of democracy in nations battling fascism, and the optimism and hopefulness of Americans can be a model to others around the world.

Sources for Further Study

Bokenkotter, Thomas. *Church and Revolution: Catholics in the Struggle for Democracy and Social Justice*. New York: Image Books, 1998. Examines Catholics who have promoted social reform; includes two chapters that consider the humanist vision of the Jacques Maritain.

Kraynak, Robert. *Christian Faith and Modern Democracy: God and Politics in the Fallen World*. South Bend, Ind.: University of Notre Dame Press, 2001. Discusses the relationship between the Christian tradition and the development of democracy. Discusses why some recent Christian thinkers, including Maritain, have supported democracy. Kraynak argues that there is no essential connection between democracy and Christianity.

Pontifical Council for Peace and Justice. *Compendium of the Social Doctrine of the Church* Washington, D.C.: United States Conference of Catholic Bishops, 2004. This document is a summary of the Catholic Church's social teaching and includes significant discussion of the Catholic Church's teaching on democracy and the belief in human dignity. This work reflects an understanding of democracy and human rights similar to Maritain's.

Michael L. Coulter

"A CHRISTMAS CAROL"

Author: Charles Dickens (1812-1870)
First published: 1843
Edition used: Christmas Stories, with an introduction by May Lamberton Becker and illustrations by Howard Simon. Cleveland: World, 1946
Genre: Short fiction
Subgenre: Literary fiction
Core issues: Christmas; compassion; poverty; redemption; selfishness; social action

In an age of declining influence for the traditional church, Dickens redefined the familiar conversion narrative in terms that emphasize human kindness and the struggle against poverty and ignorance. The redemption of Ebenezer Scrooge demonstrates the possibility for a miraculous transformation of a selfish and bitter man once such an individual discovers his interconnections with others. Dickens implies that the result of such a conversion leads the individual to live a more moral and compassionate lifestyle and has an immediate impact on social problems and social justice.

> *Principal characters*
> *Ebenezer Scrooge*, the protagonist, a miserly and ill-humored businessman in London
> *Bob Cratchit*, Scrooge's clerk
> *Jacob Marley*, Scrooge's deceased business partner
> *Ghost of Christmas Past*,
> *Ghost of Christmas Present*, and
> *Ghost of Christmas Yet to Come*, three spirits that instruct Scrooge
> *Tiny Tim*, Bob Cratchit's youngest son
> *Fred*, Scrooge's nephew

Overview

Charles Dickens's "A Christmas Carol" opens with the protagonist, miserly businessman Ebenezer Scrooge, working late on Christmas Eve in his London office when his nephew Fred drops by to invite him to Christmas dinner. Fred's Christmas greetings—repeated annually and annually declined—send Scrooge into a rant against the holiday and those who celebrate it. When Scrooge's clerk, Bob Cratchit, quietly applauds Fred's inspirational defense of Christmas, Scrooge threatens to fire him. As Fred leaves, a pair of gentlemen collecting money for the poor call on Scrooge, but he quickly dismisses them with the reminder that he already supports prisons and workhouses for the poor.

At closing time, Scrooge grudgingly gives Cratchit the next day (Christmas Day) off before heading home to a gloomy structure that once belonged to his business partner Jacob Marley, who died on Christmas Eve seven years before. As Scrooge enters, he sees Marley's face on the door knocker. He rushes inside and goes upstairs to his bedroom, seeing a hearse traveling up the stairs in front of him. In the bedroom, he locks the doors and sits down to eat. Suddenly, bells begin to ring, the bedroom door flies open, and in walks Marley's ghost, bound in a chain made of cash boxes, padlocks, and ledgers. Marley tells Scrooge that the spirits of men must walk among their fellow men, if not in life then in death. His chain, he informs Scrooge, was forged, link by link, over a lifetime of ignoring his responsibilities to others, and he warns that Scrooge has forged a chain much more ponderous than the one he, Marley, is carrying. He offers Scrooge one chance to avoid his fate: to be visited by three spirits that night. Marley shows Scrooge one last vision, a sky full of phantoms, but Scrooge concludes that the evening has been a figment of his imagination, perhaps caused by indigestion, and goes to bed.

At one o'clock in the morning, a childlike spirit with a white tunic appears and introduces itself as the Ghost of Christmas Past. The spirit takes Scrooge to an institution where he grew up, where they witness Scrooge's boyhood friends going home to celebrate Christmas, leaving the young Scrooge behind with only imaginary friends from books he has read. The spirit then takes Scrooge to a happier Christmas, when his sister Fan, Fred's mother, came to the institution to bring Scrooge home. They visit yet a third Christmas, a party at the warehouse where Scrooge was apprenticed as a young man. Scrooge reminisces about his kindly boss, Fezziwig, and how meaningful Fezziwig's generosity had been. The spirit then transports Scrooge to the Christmas when his fiancé, Belle, left him because of his preoccupation with wealth and business. Scrooge begs the spirit to take him home, but the spirit shows him one final Christmas seven years before, when Belle's husband tells her he saw Scrooge that day, all alone and still working, even with Marley at the point of death. At that, Scrooge returns to his sleep.

When the clock strikes again, Scrooge awakens to find his room decorated in holly and ivy with a roaring fire in the fireplace. A gigantic spirit wearing a green robe trimmed in white fur, the Ghost of Christmas Present, takes Scrooge on a tour of dingy, soot-covered neighborhoods where, in spite of their poverty, residents are celebrating Christmas. Scrooge and the spirit soon arrive at the Cratchit house, where the family delights in a Christmas meal far nicer than their usual fare but still quite meager for the large family. Scrooge is especially moved by the youngest child, Tiny Tim, who is crippled and will soon die, the spirit tells Scrooge, if nothing changes. Scrooge hears Bob Cratchit offer a toast in Scrooge's name and discovers the disdain in which the family holds him. The spirit then takes Scrooge on brief visits to a miner's home, a lighthouse, and a ship; in each of these lonely settings people are celebrating Christmas. Finally, they arrive at Fred's home, where the party guests are discussing Scrooge's absence. Fred explains that Scrooge's demeanor brings its own consequences and expresses his hope that his Christmas invitations may one day soften Scrooge's bitterness. Scrooge, invisible to the partygoers, becomes absorbed in their party games and has a wonderful time, even though he is only a spiritual presence and in one of the games a joke is made at his expense. As they leave, the spirit shows Scrooge a boy and a girl—Ignorance and Want—sheltered beneath his robe and warns Scrooge of the doom they foretell for humanity.

The clock strikes twelve and Scrooge finds himself in the presence of a phantom shrouded in black, the Ghost of Christmas Yet to Come. They watch people discussing a man's death to which they are completely indifferent, then travel to a seedy neighborhood where men and women are selling goods stolen from the dead man's house. Scrooge, alarmed at the cavalier and heartless response to the unknown man's death, asks to see someone who feels some emotion over the deceased one, so the spirit takes him to overhear a family hopeful that the man's death will bring a kinder creditor. Eventually, they go to the Cratchit home and see the family grieving the death of Tiny Tim. Scrooge inquires about the identity of the dead man, so the spirit takes Scrooge to a cemetery. There Scrooge sees his own gravestone. With that, the spirit vanishes.

Scrooge awakens a changed man and begins making amends for his past. He has a huge turkey sent to the Cratchit house, makes a large donation to the men who visited him the day before, and calls on Fred to accept his invitation to dinner. The next day, he raises Bob Cratchit's salary. Eventually, he becomes like a second father to Tiny Tim, and he is remembered ever after as one who knew how to celebrate Christmas.

Christian Themes

"A Christmas Carol" is deeply rooted in the important nineteenth century question of how Christian morality would survive in the face of an increasingly utilitarian and capitalistic world brought on by the Industrial Revolution. The financial success that Scrooge enjoyed is precisely the goal of capitalism, but a fixation on the accumulation of wealth seduced Scrooge into seeing every aspect of life in such terms. Not only Christmas, but his fiancé, his dying friend and business partner, his reputation, his office staff, and his only living family member are all weighed against their financial cost and found unworthy. The costs of such selfishness and bitterness are not borne by Scrooge alone, however. Dickens's portrayal of the social costs—prisons, workhouses, increased mortality, the creation of ghettos and slums, the miserable state of both wealthy and poor alike—clearly makes a case for morality and social justice on a larger scale.

On the other hand, the solution to social injustice in "A Christmas Carol" is not a social movement but individual redemption. The world becomes a better place almost immediately following Scrooge's conversion. In fact, the story implies that a renewed connection to humanity is, in fact, the very essence of redemption. Though the Christmas setting invites a traditional Christian interpretation of Scrooge's redemption, his change is rooted not in a commitment to deeper spirituality or orthodoxy but in an authentic connection to and investment in the lives of other human beings. This "conversion" is not introspective and personal; it is outward-looking and social. While the results seem to change nothing about the social structure itself, the compassion shown by individual people changes the social relationships they share.

Sources for Further Study

Epstein, Norrie. *The Friendly Dickens: Being a Good-Natured Guide to the Art and Adventures of the Man Who Invented Scrooge*. New York: Penguin, 2001. A light-hearted and enthusiastic biography of Dickens that includes critical summaries of sixteen of his novels, with illustrations and references to popular culture that elucidate Dickens's work and demonstrate his influence.

Gissing, George. *Charles Dickens: A Critical Study*. 1898. Boston: Adamant Media, 2001. A biography and critical analysis written only thirty years after Dickens's death by a prolific Victorian novelist who shared Dickens's concern for exposing social problems.

Newey, Vincent. *The Scriptures of Charles Dickens: Novels of Ideology, Novels of the Self*. Aldershot, England: Ashgate, 2004. An examination of Dickens's view of humankind's options for living in a world of flux, including a chapter exploring "A Christmas Carol's" view of conversion.

Pool, Daniel. *What Jane Austen Ate and Charles Dickens Knew: From Fox Hunting to Whist—The Facts of Daily Life in Nineteenth Century England*. New York: Simon & Schuster, 1993. An engaging look at social customs and everyday objects from the period in which Dickens's novels are set.

Devon Boan

CHRISTY

Author: Catherine Marshall (1914-1983)
First published: New York: McGraw-Hill, 1967
Genre: Novel
Subgenres: Historical fiction (twentieth century); romance; saga
Core issues: Awakening; compassion; friendship; love; service; trust in God

The novel's protagonist, Christy, questions her faith when she immerses herself in the isolated Cutter Gap community located in mountainous eastern Tennessee in 1912. As a young, inexperienced schoolteacher from urban North Carolina, Christy struggles with her reactions to backwoods people and customs, examines her motives to pursue mission work, and constantly seeks God's guidance to reveal the purpose he intends for her. Christy's mentor, Miss Alice Henderson, a Quaker, gently guides Christy through phases of doubt, helping her examine her beliefs by suggesting biblical passages to achieve spiritual awareness and growth.

> *Principal characters*
> *Christy Rudd Huddleston*, the protagonist
> *Alice Henderson*, a teacher
> *Dr. Neil MacNeill*, a physician
> *David Grantland*, a minister
> *Fairlight Spencer*, a mountain woman
> *Ruby Mae Morrison*, a student
> *Lundy Taylor*, a student

Overview

The daughter and wife of Presbyterian ministers, Catherine Marshall fictionalized the religious awakening her mother experienced while teaching in Appalachia. Nineteen-year-old Christy Huddleston—inspired by Marshall's mother, Leonora Whitaker Wood—volunteers to teach after hearing about efforts by the American Inland Mission and Miss Alice Henderson, a Quaker teacher, to establish schools for mountain children discussed at a church conference.

Leaving her Asheville, North Carolina, home by train in January of 1912, Christy ignores the conductor's warnings that Cutter Gap is dangerous because of feuds and vice and that she is unprepared for the extremes she will encounter. Christy walks seven miles from the depot in snow and cold temperatures toward the mission building with Ben Pentland, who delivers mail. On the way, Christy and Pentland stop at the Allen cabin, where men bring unconscious family patriarch Bob Allen, saying he suffered an accident on his way to greet the schoolteacher. Christy meets brusque Dr. Neil MacNeill, who performs emergency surgery, and observes the superstitious ways of the mountain people. Her repulsion at the rustic cabin's lack of sanitation and people's seemingly unenlightened practices test her commitment, but Christy resolves to stay.

Exhausted, Christy arrives at the mission, where she meets preacher David Grantland, his sister Ida, and Ruby Mae Morrison, a student who helps at the mission. Christy welcomes her pupils at the school building, which also serves as a church, and soon learns that they are more complex than she expected. Christy is impressed by their intelligence but not by their hygiene, and holds a handkerchief over her nose. She leads daily recitations of Bible verses, as required by Tennessee law at that time, and develops lessons she can adjust for children of all ages grouped together in her single classroom.

Christy struggles to teach without adequate supplies and books and plans how to secure materials. She visits students' homes and tries to explain proper sanitation to their parents. Frustrated because male and female students insist on sitting separately and children avoid people from rival families, Christy disciplines fighting children and attempts to enforce discipline when older boys, especially Lundy Taylor, play pranks.

Meeting Miss Alice Henderson, Christy confides her disappointment and concerns, questioning whether she should leave. She admires the older teacher, seeking her guidance and addressing practical concerns regarding educational and spiritual issues; Miss Alice reinforces Christy's resolve to continue her work. Christy's endurance of hardships is strengthened by her interactions with adults interested in learning. She begins teaching Fairlight Spencer, with whom she develops a friendship, and attends sewing circle sessions where Miss Alice tells parables. Christy learns about the people she has chosen to teach and live among, enjoying tales explaining their Scotch-Irish traditions. She delights in everyday things and applies the religious understanding she acquires from reading the Bible, evaluating scriptures, and praying. She matures spiritually and emotionally.

Upset that children walk miles barefoot to school despite snowy conditions, Christy decides to create a boarding facility at the mission where pupils can stay during the winter. Praying about how she will fund her project, Christy resourcefully writes potential patrons and boldly travels to Knoxville to discuss her ideas with a rich businessman. Her prayers are answered with an outpouring of donated items and funds.

The brutal murder of a friend's husband, Tom McHone, and Christy's discovery of jugs of moonshine hidden underneath the school shatter her confidence that she can improve the lives of the mountain people. She contemplates her spirituality, reevaluating her philosophy of what religion means to her. Christy ponders secrets confided to her by Miss Alice, realizing that Miss Alice resists some of the Quaker ways she considers incompatible with her work. As Miss Alice advises, Christy studies the Bible and thoroughly evaluates her beliefs. She is shaken when Dr. MacNeill comments that Christy merely repeats what Miss Alice tells her, pressuring Christy to state her opinions. He says that, although he believes God exists, he dislikes how God lets people suffer and refuses to embrace faith.

A typhoid epidemic initiates Christy's greatest spiritual crisis. Frustrated by how ignorance perpetuates the spread of that disease by contaminated water and food, Christy nurses afflicted students and adults, grieving when they die and rejoicing when remedies she uses save Ruby Mae and other victims. The death of Fairlight Spencer profoundly affects Christy; she doubts her faith and is angry at God. Miss Alice suggests that Christy read the Book of Job, who also was frustrated with God. Miss Alice instructs that God allows people to suffer troubles but is present and supportive, suggesting Christy talk to God and trust in God, submitting to his wishes in order to become stronger.

Christy falls ill and, while unconscious, in her mind retreats to a secluded mountain site that resembles Heaven. There she sees her deceased students and friends, including Fairlight. Tempted to stay in Heaven, Christy awakens when Dr. MacNeill tells her he loves her and she hears him apologizing to God, begging for forgiveness, and professing faith in him. Her faith reaffirmed, Christy realizes her compassion for her mountain community and the purpose God gave her to serve them with both her heart and her soul.

Christian Themes

Prior to writing about Christy, Marshall underwent a spiritual crisis following the death of her first husband. She was ill for two years with tuberculosis. She sought guidance from ministers and prayer, asking questions, much as Christy does, to establish a personal connection by talking to God. Marshall developed a great joy and enthusiasm for God, writing *Christy* to share her deep love for and closeness to Jesus Christ, to reinforce her faith, and to help others achieve knowledge of God.

Marshall's evangelical nature resulted in her incorporating in *Christy* the message that every individual, regardless of denominational or religious affiliation, can develop a personal relationship with God through prayer and trust him as a guide, seeking a deeper understanding through faith, as Christy does. Marshall hoped to help people see Jesus Christ as an approachable and genuine source of comfort and inspiration, not simply as an abstract idea.

Through her evaluation of her beliefs, Christy realizes that God gives people strength when their faith is tested and weaknesses threaten to divert them from their path. She discovers that God has a plan for each person, a design for each individual's purpose and duties in life. Despite despair, doubts, and hardships, good prevails over evil. God answers prayers in ways most suitable for each individual, although his response may not seem appropriate initially.

Christy also finds that people's spirituality is reflected more in how they live and how they treat others than in whether they attend church. Comparing churches, Christy notes her home church did not inspire her to the degree that mountain services and work do. Christy's actions emphasize that God values the richness of people's spirits, not their material wealth. Christy unselfishly tends to her neighbors, regardless of their wealth or poverty, sophistication or lack of education, discovering that those who give and share are blessed. She welcomes God's instructions on how she can best serve her community, accepting responsibilities and being accountable to both God and her fellow human beings.

Finally, Christy learns that unconditional love is a gift from God, whether it is her altruistic affection for others or the romantic love that develops between her and Dr. MacNeill, with its potential for companionship, family, and service.

Sources for Further Study

Goin, Mary Elisabeth. "Catherine Marshall: Three Decades of Popular Religion." *Journal of Presbyterian History* 56, no. 3 (Fall, 1978): 219-235. Examines how Marshall developed her writing to help readers meet God and seek salvation as a goal, stressing her focus on the individual's spiritual experiences.

McReynolds, Kathy. *Catherine Marshall*. Minneapolis, Minn.: Bethany House, 1999. Explores Marshall's spiritual beliefs and practices while writing *Christy* and how that book affected her spiritually after publication. Incorporates excerpts from her journals.

Marshall, Catherine. *A Closer Walk*. Edited by Leonard E. LeSourd. Old Tappan, N.J.: Chosen Books, 1986. Marshall's second husband, a religious publisher, re-marks on his editorial input while she wrote early drafts of *Christy*. Includes Marshall's spiritual lifeline.

_____. *Meeting God at Every Turn: A Personal Family Story*. Grand Rapids, Mich.: Chosen Books, 2002. A chapter discusses Marshall's mother, her religious viewpoints, her mission work, and how she influenced the characterization of Christy.

Elizabeth D. Schafer

THE CHRONICLES OF NARNIA

Author: C. S. Lewis (1898-1963)

First published: The Lion, the Witch, and the Wardrobe, 1950; *Prince Caspian,* 1951;
The Voyage of the "Dawn Treader," 1952; *The Silver Chair,* 1953; *The Horse and His Boy,* 1954; *The Magician's Nephew,* 1955; *The Last Battle,* 1956

Edition used: The Chronicles of Narnia. New York: HarperCollins, 1994

Genre: Novels

Subgenres: Adventure; alternate universe; fantasy

Core issues: Faith; good vs. evil; guidance; pilgrimage; salvation; time

This series of seven fantasy novels for children and young adults depicts the parallel universe of Narnia, telling the story of the Pevensie children's travel to Narnia from World War II England through a magic wardrobe in the country mansion where they are staying. Lewis relates their discovery of Narnia, battles against evil, Narnia's rise and fall, and final demise of Narnia within two generations of earth time. Heroes and villains play roles that can be strongly identified with counterparts in the Bible, particularly the story of Jesus Christ.

Principal characters

Aslan, the great lion of Narnia and its divine being

Peter Pevensie, the oldest of the Pevensie children

Susan Pevensie, the oldest girl, who loses faith in the end

Edmund Pevensie, the younger brother, who initially succumbs to the witch's temptations

Lucy Pevensie, the youngest, whose faith remains the keenest

Digory Kirke, the old professor, who as a boy witnessed the creation of Narnia

Polly Plummer, Digory's companion

Jill Pole, another traveler to Narnia

Eustace Scrubb, the Pevensies' disbelieving cousin

Prince Caspian, a young prince whose kingdom is returned to him

Prince Rilian, a prince enchanted by a witch

King Tirian, the last king of Narnia

Jadis, the last queen of Charn and the first witch, who enters Narnia at its creation

The White Witch, a reincarnation of Jadis after she has taken command of Narnia

The Green Lady, another reincarnation of Jadis

Reepicheep, a soldier-mouse, the epitome of chivalry

Puzzle, a donkey who is made to impersonate Aslan

Shift, an ape whose act of treachery leads to Narnia's downfall
Bree and
Hwin, talking horses in exile from Narnia
Shasta, an abducted prince
Puddleglum, a marsh-wiggle
Uncle Andrew, an amateur magician, Digory's uncle

Overview

C. S. Lewis was a celebrated academic in the field of medieval literature, first at Oxford University, then at Cambridge, where he held the first chair in medieval and Renaissance literature. He also was a noted convert to Christianity who in the 1940's established himself as a popular Christian apologist with a series of wartime radio talks, later collected under the title *Mere Christianity* (1952). Between 1938 and 1945 he wrote a trilogy of science-fiction books (the Space Trilogy, consisting of *Out of the Silent Planet*, 1938; *Perelandra*, 1943; and *That Hideous Strength: A Modern Fairy Tale for Grownups*, 1945) with underlying Christian themes. He was still unmarried in the early 1950's, living with his brother and an elderly widow and her daughter.

It is perhaps surprising, then, that Lewis is best known by those other than academics as a children's writer. The seven novels in his fantasy series the Chronicles of Narnia have remained consistent best sellers ever since their publication, and have inspired several film and television series. Although children evacuated from London did stay at his house in Oxford during World War II, the main inspiration for the stories came from memories of his own childhood reading, as recounted in his autobiography, *Surprised by Joy: The Shape of My Early Life* (1955), as well as by certain recurring images he had had, some for many years. Lewis had once bemoaned to his colleague J. R. R. Tolkien (a fellow Christian academic at Oxford and later author of the Lord of the Rings series) the lack of stories he had enjoyed as a boy. Such books included the animal stories of Beatrix Potter and the children's stories of E. Nesbit. The only solution, they felt, was to write such stories themselves.

The result for Lewis was the publication of *The Lion, the Witch, and the Wardrobe* in 1950. Lewis wrote six more stories over the next three years. However, the publishers, Geoffrey Bles, like today's filmmakers, decided to space them out to one per year. He had found a young illustrator, Pauline Baynes, for the first book and asked her to stay with the series. After the series was published, Lewis received the 1957 Carnegie Medal, Britain's most prestigious award for children's literature, for the last chronicle, *The Last Battle*. Some have argued the award was really for the whole series, but in many ways, *The Last Battle* really is the best of the seven stories.

The order of reading the Chronicles which Lewis recommended is not the order in which they were written or published. Lewis suggested that new readers start with *The Magician's Nephew*, which tells of the creation of Narnia. This should be followed by *The Lion, the Witch, and the Wardrobe*, then *The Horse and His Boy*, *Prince Caspian*, *The Voyage of the Dawn Treader*, *The Silver Chair*, and finally *The Last Battle*, which tells the story of the Narnian world brought to an end. Four of the stories deal with children entering the parallel, or secondary, world of Narnia, setting disorder to right, and then returning to their own world, only to find that no time at all has elapsed there. One of the novels presents an adventure that happens purely within Narnia; one tells a story of secondary world spilling over into the children's primary world of England; and in one, *The Last Battle*, all the previous "friends of Narnia" (except for one) never return to their own world but find themselves in an after-death state in a new Narnia.

The entrances to the world of Narnia are different each time: magic rings; a wardrobe; a picture of a ship at sea; a gate in a wall; a waiting area at a railroad junction. Three are journeys, two of which are quest journeys, one an escape. All feature the rulership of humans over a land of talking animals and mythical creatures, but the rule is still largely democratic and consensual, a pastoral and medieval acceptance of a certain order. From the start, however, evil—in the form of a series of witches or piratical invasion—threatens and usurps this order. Lewis leaves as a mystery the hostile southern land of Calormen: how its inhabitants got there and how that society evolved.

One of Lewis's recurring images was of a huge lion. The image became the character Aslan, the divine being who creates Narnia and overlooks its affairs. He appears in each of the Chronicles to guide and encourage the children. He is also the one who ends Narnia. Another fascination for Lewis was talking animals, as in the Beatrix Potter books; hence, the Chronicles are populated by talking animals, though nontalking animals exist as well. A final image was of a faun walking through woods, carrying parcels. This image became incorporated into *The Lion, the Witch, and the Wardrobe*.

In that chronicle, the Pevensie children have been evacuated from London during the bombings of World War II to live in a rambling old country house. (Lewis was also evacuated, though the house of the novel is more like his boyhood house in Belfast, Northern Ireland, than the residence to which he was relocated.) Temptations of the various children take place, the most famous being when Edmund, one of the Pevensies, is deceived by the White Witch. Aslan has to sacrifice himself to save Edmund from the curse laid on Narnia by the witch and to redeem him from her. Aslan is resurrected, however, and defeats the witch in a pitched battle. Narnia is now ruled by the Pevensies as kings and queens until it is time for them to return to earth. Other battles take place in *Prince Caspian* and *The Last Battle*, something for which Lewis was criticized by non-Christians, usually left-wing critics. The Chronicles of Narnia have themselves become sites of conflict in the world of children's literature.

The Voyage of the Dawn Treader and *The Silver Chair* are quests. Eustace Scrubb, an obnoxious cousin of the Pevensies, is featured in both, being transformed by an encounter with Aslan in the former. Eustace and Jill Pole are unhappy students at a boarding school, and in *The Silver Chair* they have to rescue a lost prince. *The Horse and His Boy* has no time travel at all, being set during the Pevensie reign within the neighboring countries of Calormen and Archenland. This chronicle is again about a lost prince rightfully restored. *Prince Caspian* and *The Last Battle* involve miraculous interventions when the rightful young ruler is usurped and Narnia seems lost. In the latter, Narnia is indeed ended, as Aslan intervenes to roll up the Narnian universe, then takes those who acknowledge him into a heavenly Narnia, which joins a new earth. In fact, all the human entrants to Narnia, apart from Susan Pevensie, enter this new Narnia/earth, because on earth they have all simultaneously been killed in a train wreck.

Christian Themes

Although not allegory, the Chronicles of Narnia do convey Christian themes systematically. The most dramatic of these is the death of Aslan as a substitute for Edmund, and Aslan's resurrection. While not a "one for all" death (as was Jesus' crucifixion in the Bible), it does show the substitutionary aspect of Christian atonement and the inability of evil to overcome a sinless individual by death. Aslan is a type of Christ, who is seen as "the Lion of the Tribe of Judah" in biblical symbolism (Revelation 5:5).

Aslan reveals himself from time to time. He is not a hidden god, and his self-disclosures are real and life-changing. Eustace Scrubb, although turned into a dragon in *The Voyage of the Dawn Treader*, has a revelation of Aslan that transforms him, as happened to Edmund in *The Lion, the Witch, and the Wardrobe*. Although Aslan is divine, the "Emperor over Sea" is clearly the ruling divinity. Hence, there is a partial depiction of the Christian doctrine of the Trinity.

Lewis presents a possible mode of Creation and "Last Day" Judgment, as well as a glimpse into what "a new heaven and a new earth" (Revelation 21:1) could be like. While Lewis states at the end of *The Voyage of the Dawn Treader* that Narnian theology is different from earth theology, at an imaginative level Lewis is showing how such divine acts are conceivable.

In Lewis's use of parallel time, there is a biblical sense of "one day as a thousand years and a thousand years as one day" (2 Peter 3:8) in God's sight. Events that transpire over weeks, months, and years in Narnia have consumed, in the "real" world of England, little or no time at all. Lewis also demonstrates a doctrine of election: Some animals are chosen by Aslan to be talking animals. However, it is possible for the talking animals to lose their gift of speech, as happens in *The Last Battle*, just as it is possible for Susan to lose her faith. Elsewhere, as in *The Silver Chair*, the children are "chosen" and empowered for various quests and tasks (as in Ephesians 2:10), being given suitable helpers. Lewis marries fairy-tale motifs with biblical truth. There is also a Christian sense of temptation as testing, especially strong in the Edenic parallels at the end of *The Magician's Nephew*.

While some commentators have denied any overt Christian meaning or message in the Chronicles, others have claimed the novels present a fully fledged Christianity. It is important, therefore, to recognize what Christian truths Lewis does not address. There is no reference to the Holy Spirit, the third person of the Trinity, nor is there any real sense of the fatherhood of God. There is no incarnation: Aslan remains always a lion; there is no suggestion that he has taken on the form of a lion in order to enter Narnia (as there is in Christian teaching the notion that God takes the form of a human being, Jesus Christ, his manifestation on earth). Last, no religious practice of any sort is presented in the chronicles: no church, no spiritual leaders, no holy book. Nevertheless, the spirituality of Narnia cannot be denied as expressed in the numinous feeling at times, such as in Lucy's encounters with Aslan and at the end of *The Voyage of the Dawn Treader* and in the sense of design, purpose, and destiny that runs throughout the plotting.

Sources for Further Study

Barratt, David. *Narnia: C. S. Lewis and His World*. Grand Rapids, Mich.: Kregel, 2005. A useful introduction to Lewis for the general reader. The first two chapters deal with the Narnia stories.

Duriez, Colin. *The C. S. Lewis Encyclopedia*. Wheaton, Ill.: Crossway, 2000. Every name in the Narnia chronicles is listed here; longer entries on genres and themes explain Lewis's ideas.

Ford, Paul F. *Companion to Narnia*. Rev. ed. Foreword by Madeleine L'Engle. San Francisco: HarperSanFrancisco, 2005. An updated edition of this popular guide to the places, characters, and themes of Narnia.

Hooper, Walter. *Past Watchful Dragons: The Narnian Chronicles of C. S. Lewis*. New York: Macmillan, 1974. Hooper was Lewis's main editor and guardian of his works. Here he examines the Narnia chronicles as children's literature, showing how Lewis's Christian message is conveyed.

Manlove, Colin. *C. S. Lewis: His Literary Achievement*. New York: St. Martin's Press, 1987. A leading scholar of fantasy literature assesses the quality of Lewis's fantasy writing.

Sayer, George. *Jack: A Life of C. S. Lewis*. Wheaton, Ill.: Crossway, 1994. The fullest and most sympathetic account of Lewis's life.

David Barratt

THE CHURCH

Author: Jan Hus (1372/1373-1415)
First published: wr. 1413, pb. 1520 as *De ecclesia* (English translation, 1915)
Edition used: The Church, translated by David S. Schaff. Westport, Conn.: Greenwood Press, 1974
Genre: Nonfiction
Subgenre: Didactic treatise
Core issues: Catholics and Catholicism; church; faith; obedience and disobedience; persecution; predestination

The Church *is one of the central ideological treatises of the fifteenth century Hussite religious reform in Bohemia. Its author, Hus, defines the universal church as a community of all individuals predestined for salvation under the leadership of Jesus Christ. He challenges the Roman pontiff's claim to spiritual supremacy and asserts every Christian right to disobey what he terms unlawful commands. Calling attention to the decline of moral discipline within the Roman curia, in particular to the sale of indulgences, he urges a return to the virtues of the primitive church.*

Overview

In 1412, Jan Hus, Jerome of Prague, and other prominent members of the Czech reform movement mounted a vigorous campaign against the sale of indulgences under Antipope John XXIII. As a result of this and other signal acts of disobedience, Hus was placed under major excommunication on October 18 of that year and quickly left Prague so that the city would not fall under a papal interdict. He completed *The Church* in May of 1413 and then returned to Prague to offer a public reading of its contents at the city Bethlehem chapel.

Hus divided the work into twenty-three chapters. The first ten chapters were most likely completed by February, 1413, and deal mainly with the constitution of the church, its headship, and its divisions. The remaining thirteen chapters, in which Hus defends his stance on controversial issues and refutes charges levied against him by his opponents, are more polemical in nature and appear to have been written for the most part after February, 1413.

Hus defines the holy, catholic, and universal church as a community of all individuals predestined for salvation throughout time. He calls these individuals the predestinate (*predestinatos*) and distinguishes them from those who cannot become true members of the universal church because they lack grace. He calls this latter group the reprobate (*reprobatos*) or the foreknown (*prescitos*). Just as spittle, phlegm, ordure, and urine are not parts of the body, so, too, the foreknown are not members of the universal church. Even if they are temporarily in the church, he says, they are not of it. Membership in the church is determined not by human election or office but by divine grace.

On the basis of that definition of the church, Hus takes issue with Pope Boniface VIII's bull *Unam Sanctam* (promulgated November 18, 1302; English translation, 1927), which advocates of the Roman papacy frequently cited in Hus's time in support of Rome's claim to spiritual supremacy. The bull proclaimed the unity of the church and identified the pope as the legitimate head of the church and the cardinals as its body. It asserted that obedience to the Roman pontiff was necessary for eternal salvation. Hus rejects these claims, arguing that the Roman Catholic Church represents only a particular church and is no different in that respect from the churches of Jerusalem, Alexandria, Constantinople, or Antioch. In his view, only the universal church—which consists of all the predestinate in Heaven, on Earth, and in Purgatory—can be considered unified, holy, catholic, and apostolic. That church is Jesus Christ's mystical body, and Christ is its sole legitimate head. For this reason, he continues, Christians need not obey papal bulls that are at variance with Holy Scripture:

> For to holy Scripture exception may not be taken, nor may it be gainsaid; but it is proper at times to take exception to bulls and gainsay them when they either commend the unworthy or put them in authority, or savor of avarice, or honor the unrighteous or oppress the innocent, or implicitly contradict the commands or counsels of God.

To strengthen his argument against the authority of the Roman pontiff, Hus calls into question the legitimacy of Constantine the Great's donation to Pope Sylvester I. He points out that unworthy individuals have occupied the papal office in the past, and he cites Liberius, Constantine II, and the legendary Pope Joan as historical examples. Barring some act of revelation, he adds, there is no way for Christians to know for certain if a pope even belongs to the predestinate. However, it seems clear in his mind that an avaricious pope whose lifestyle conflicts with Christ's commandments cannot be a true successor of Peter. The same critical reasoning applies to cardinals who, like thieves and robbers "devour and consume in luxurious living the goods of the poor."

There are similar abuses at all levels of the priesthood, says Hus. Those who put a price on the sacraments or who trade in episcopates, canonries, and parishes for profit are unworthy of their office. How, he asks, can priests take credit for the binding or loosing of sins? It is divine work that only God performs. A priest merely announces its eventuality in a ceremonious fashion.

The final chapters of *The Church* provide insight into Hus's clash with church authorities. In 1409, says Hus, the archbishop of Prague, Zbyněk Zajíc of Hazmburk, obtained from Antipope Alexander V a bull forbidding local priests from preaching in private chapels. In defiance of that injunction, however, Hus continued to preach at Prague's Bethlehem chapel and was threatened with excommunication. At present, Hus says, Štěpán Páleč, Stanislav of Znojmo, and other university doctors have turned against him and invent lies to destroy him. They even threaten him with execution, calling him a heretic. They claim that Hus swears only by Holy Scripture, interprets it according to his own fancy, spurns the opinion of the apostles and of the holy doctors, opposes God's law, and incites the people to disobedience. Hus rejects all these assertions and affirms that "there is no such thing as obedience in the case of things unlawful." In his view, Alexander's bull against the use of private chapels for preaching was contrary to Christ's teachings and hence invalid.

Christian Themes

Many of the ideas and Scripture-based arguments contained in *The Church*, especially in the early chapters, were directly inspired by writings of the fourteenth century English theologian John Wyclif. It has been estimated that Hus "borrowed" about 23 percent of his material for *The Church*, much of it verbatim or near verbatim, from fourteen of the Englishman's treatises. In 1403 and 1412, theologians at the University of Prague critically examined Wyclif's writings and derived from them a list of forty-five articles that they considered to be heretical. Hus strongly disagreed with their assessment, and in the final pages of *The Church* he insisted that the university's theologians had failed to prove that a single one of the forty-five articles was in fact erroneous.

Church historians are quick to note that Wyclif was only one of several influences on Hus's thought and that the Czech reformer was a discriminating reader. Placed on trial at the Council of Constance in 1415, Hus refused to condemn Wyclif's teachings en bloc, but he did expressly reject the Englishman's views on absolute necessity and remnance in the Eucharist. Although he reserved the right to disobey church officials whose commands were contrary to the lessons of Holy Scripture, he did not seek to abolish the institutional church. It would be naïve to think that Hus had intended for the borrowed passages to escape the notice of his curial opponents in Prague, especially as most of them were already intimately acquainted with the original texts. It seems far more likely that the Czech reformer's insightful presentation of Wyclifian views was part of an intertextual strategy, a provocative barb of sorts, intended to deflate the theologians' case against Wyclif and Wyclif's admirers within the Czech reform movement.

Whatever his strategy may have been, history shows that Hus—not only in *The Church* but also in some of his other works—willfully linked his fate to that of his English predecessor. The Council of Constance reached this conclusion when it condemned Hus to burn at the stake by declaring him a heretic and a disciple of Wyclif.

Sources for Further Study

Fudge, Thomas A. *Magnificent Ride. The First Reformation in Hussite Bohemia*. Aldershot: Ashgate, 1998. An in-depth study of the Hussite reform movement in Czech society from about 1410 to 1437; places Hus in a larger historical context.

Herold, Vil. "Jan Hus Heretic, a Saint, or a Reformer?" *Communio Viatorum* 45 (2003): 5-23. Examines the nature and extent of Wyclif's influence on Hus.

Shelley, Marshall, and Elesha Coffman, eds. *Christian History* 68 (2000): *Jan Hus. The Incendiary Preacher of Prague*. A richly illustrated issue devoted to Hus and his contemporaries, with brief articles by eight Church historians; intended for the general reader.

Spinka, Matthew. *John Hus: A Biography*. Princeton, N.J.: Princeton University Press, 1968. An authoritative study of the events that shaped Hus's life; discusses Hus's major writings in Czech, his opposition to the sale of indulgences, and events at Constance.

_____. *John Hus' Concept of the Church*. Princeton, N.J.: Princeton University Press, 1966. A survey of the Czech reformer's life and his major works, with special emphasis on *The Church*; recommended reading.

Jan Pendergrass

CHURCH FOLK

Author: Michele Andrea Bowen
First published: New York: Warner Books, 2001
Genre: Novel
Subgenre: Romance
Core issues: African Americans; chastity; church; clerical life; marriage; pastoral role; racism

Christian life carries even more challenges for a pastor and his spouse than the layperson suspects. For the first year of their marriage, Theophilus and Essie Simmons struggle to meet each other's expectations while negotiating the treacherous shoals of denominational politics. Theophilus faces his biggest test at the Triennial Conference, as he reveals that some church big shots are running a brothel. The resulting furor shows Theophilus that God has a purpose that goes beyond human frailties and plans.

> *Principal characters*
> *Theophilus Henry Simmons*, the young pastor of the Greater Hope Church
> *Essie Lee Lane Simmons*, Theophilus's wife
> *The Reverend Murcheson James*, Theophilus's mentor and friend
> *Coral Thomas*, a deaconess at Greater Hope Church
> *Glodean Benson*, an outrageously flirtatious woman
> *Sister Willie Clayton*, the owner of a funeral home chain
> *Cleotis Clayton*, Willie's son
> *Marcel Brown*, a cunning, ambitious young minister
> *Sonny Washington*, another ambitious minister
> *Bishop Otis Caruthers*, a disgraced and suspended bishop
> *Mother Laticia Harold*, a very proper elderly lady
> *Saphronia McComb*, Mother Harold's granddaughter, romantically involved with Marcel
> *Precious Powers*, also romantically involved with Marcel
> *Bishop Percy Jennings*, a senior bishop in the Gospel United Church

Overview

Church Folk is a Christian romance novel that relates the story of the marriage of a young pastor, Theophilus Simmons, and his calling. Filled with fire to preach the Gospel, Theophilus Simmons is nonetheless dismayed by his first pastoral assignment. Greater Hope Church is in Memphis, and is the home church of Glodean Benson, whose exuberant sexuality held him in thrall during their college years. When their affair ended before he went off to seminary, an angry Glodean promised to "get" him someday—but only to become first lady of a congregation, not because she loved him. His rigorous studies enabled Theophilus to push away his treacherous images of Glodean during seminary years, but he is not so sure he can resist her in person.

He is being tested, the Reverend Murcheson James tells him—tested in the fiery furnace as Shadrach, Meshach, and Abednego were long ago. Bishop Percy Jennings, their superior, has high hopes for Theophilus, but first he wants to make sure the young minister can resist the net of desire that Glodean still weaves around him. Theophilus, knowing his call to ministry means facing such tests, agrees to go to Greater Hope.

His first year as pastor there is a success. The church's membership grows, the choir and usher boards' performances are "spiffed up," and the young pastor gains a reputation for brilliant preaching. He is sent as guest preacher to a revival in Mississippi. On his trip home, he stays overnight at a tiny Delta town with a locally renowned restaurant, Pompey's Rib Joint. Although Theophilus avoids wild behavior—and thankfully has not seen Glodean since coming to Memphis—he decides to relax and slip out of his clerical role long enough to try Pompey's barbecued rib-tip sandwiches and hot blues music.

At Pompey's he meets Essie Lane, the cook. He is immediately attracted to her; she is just as drawn to him, but her basic seriousness and experience of life have made her cautious. When he asks her out, she counters with an invitation to lunch at her mother's house. Their initial rapport survives the chaperonage and, later, the miles between Mississippi and Memphis. On Saturday nights, Theophilus calls Essie to seek inspiration for his next day's sermon. Coral Thomas, a deaconess at Greater Hope Church, overhears enough of these calls to know the young pastor is smitten. She makes sure Essie can attend an upcoming annual conference in Memphis and arranges for Theophilus's responsibilities there to allow them time together. The plans are almost wrecked, however, when Glodean appears, and slick Marcel Brown makes public references to Theophilus's former affair with her. Theophilus tells Essie that Glodean was a mistake from his past, but he fears that he has not seen the last of her.

After another visit, and another crisis with Glodean, Essie and Theophilus finally marry. Their happiness in their realized passion and closeness is evident. Still, living in the center of church life is full of problems. Theophilus loses a large pledge from Sister Willie Clayton after he scolds her for overcharging a poor family for their baby's funeral. Essie offends Mother Laticia Harold by ignoring invitations to join her "exclusive ladies' clubs." The couple has to define boundaries between clerical confidentiality and sharing a spouse's burdens.

Meanwhile, the denomination's Triennial Conference is approaching. Theophilus's friend Murcheson James is a candidate for an episcopal seat. Other plans afoot, though, are less straightforward. Bishop Otis Caruthers misses having a regular bishop's district, with all its perquisites and power, and is sure that, with enough money to spread around, he can buy his way back into one. With pastors Sonny Washington and Marcel Brown, men who have a sharp eye for the main chance, Theophilus works out a scheme to provide "hospitality" at a price to preachers attending the conference. Sister Willie Clayton's son Cleotis provides the quarters in his family's lavish new funeral home.

By coincidence, Essie's Uncle Booker and his friend discover what is going on at the conference, and they report to the Reverend Murcheson James and Bishop Jennings. All agree that more proof is needed to take any action. At the same time, Tee, a cook at the "club," decides that Marcel Brown's two-timing ways deserve exposure. She tells Saphronia McComb and Precious Powers—each of of whom is, unknown to the other, romantically involved with Marcel. Together they devise a scheme to sneak Saphronia into the club to embarrass Marcel. In a hilarious scene, she does just that.

Embarrassment is not the end of it. On the evening before the new bishops are chosen, Bishop Jennings asks Theophilus to speak to the whole conference and reveal the club's existence. Theophilus, already shaken by the degree of politicking and influence trading that goes into making church decisions, wants to refuse. He knows, however, that this is something he has to do. He tries to put it in nonvulgar terms, speaking of a "club of ill-repute" operating at the conference. Essie's down-to-earth Uncle Booker interrupts to make sure everyone gets the point: "He's talking about a ho' house, folks!" The conference erupts into chaos and near-violence.

In the aftermath, the denomination's group of newly elected bishops includes some surprises for everyone. Murcheson James and another, quietly faithful pastor are elected. So is a man whose name was on the roster of "preacher's club" customers. The rascally Bishop Caruthers's situation stays unchanged; Theophilus consoles himself that the situation is God's way of keeping other church leaders wary of the devil at work. Glodean finally gets a clergyman husband. She marries Marcel Brown after Saphronia and Precious both tell him off. Theophilus and Essie leave for a bigger, more challenging church in St. Louis, charged with building it into a true community center filled with God's presence.

Christian Themes

As the story of a marriage, *Church Folk* is nonexplicitly but realistically concerned with sexuality in a Christian context. Glodean's unwholesome use of her sexuality to manipulate men contrasts with Theophilus and Essie's joyful coming together in marriage. Theophilus even preaches a sermon on the goodness of such a bond, saying that husbands should love their wives "with juice." Not only does such loving sexuality hold families together; it helps give African Americans strength for their struggle against injustice. However, minor lapses resulting from unmarried men's and women's natural attraction to each other do not draw heavy condemnation. Sexual sins occur when people turn sexuality to other purposes: Glodean's flaunting of it to manipulate and punish men, and the preachers' brothel venture using sex to make money and provide "entertainment."

Racism is an implicit but powerful theme. Although the foibles, temptations, and strengths of the characters could occur in any group of Christians, racist restrictions confine these Christians' lives. In the 1960's south, blacks could not stay at regular motels, so when Theophilus travels he must find a boardinghouse that accepts blacks. Racism has deformed some characters' self-image. Mother Harold is so proper that she cringes when people use even clean slang or contractions—yet for all her sense of propriety, she has no dignity in the eyes of prejudiced white people. The Civil Rights movement functions in this novel as a vehicle for the church's redemptive work in the world. Ironically, Theophilus and Essie cannot work for it as openly as their hearts desire. In deference to their church superiors, they provide background support for civil rights efforts as leaders in the respectable black community.

God's plan is bigger than man's plan, and not always understood by mere mortals. Most of Theophilus's big decisions are made in the light of this truth. Thus he answers repeated "calls" that are not his own choice, secure in his trust of the Lord's will.

Sources for Further Study

Bowen, Michele Andrea. *Second Sunday*. West Bloomfield, Mich.: Walk Worthy Press, 2003. Another absorbing novel of African American church life, this one set in 1970's St. Louis.

Lewis, Lillian. Review of *Church Folk*. *Booklist* 97, no. 18 (May 15, 2001): 1730. A brief, descriptive review.

Mason, Felicia. *Testimony*. New York: Kensington, 2002. The story of a traveling black gospel music group and its struggle to carry the good news to far-flung audiences.

Raboteau, Albert J. *Canaan Land: A Religious History of African Americans*. New York: Oxford University Press, 2001. Concise and perceptive history of religious experience and institutions in African American life.

Emily Alward

THE CIRCLE TRILOGY

Author: Ted Dekker (1962-　　)
First published: 2004
Editions used: Black, 2004; *Red*, 2004; *White*, 2004. Nashville, Tenn.: WestBow
　Press
Genre: Novels
Subgenres: Adventure; apocalyptic fiction; evangelical fiction
Core issues: Apocalypse; doubt; the Fall; good vs. evil; love; sin and sinners; union
　with God

In The Circle Trilogy, Dekker creates a Christian, biblical picture of a prelapsarian
world in a new, Eden-like Earth populated by unfallen humans. He then takes this
world and its inhabitants through a Fall into sin and evil and a redemptive solution
provided by God through a sacrifice much like that of Jesus Christ's. He compares
this future Earth with twenty-first century Earth through two parallel and interdepen-
dent plots linked by a single protagonist. In so doing, Dekker offers readers a creative,
compelling, and Christian vision of romance, pleasure, human creativity, innocence,
sacrifice, and above all, relationship with God.

>*Principal characters*
>　*Thomas Hunter*, the protagonist
>　*Kara Hunter*, Hunter's sister
>　*Carlos Missirian*, an assassin
>　*Valborg Svensson*, the man who seeks to release a deadly virus
>　　upon the world
>　*Monique de Raison*, a vaccine developer
>　*Rachelle*, Hunter's romantic interest and wife in future Earth
>　*Johan/Martin*, Rachelle's brother and a member of the Circle
>　*Elyon*, the name for God used by the inhabitants of future Earth
>　*Michal* and *Gabil*, Roush counselors and messengers of Elyon
>　*Teeleh*, the leader of the Shataiki, the evil and fallen Roush
>　*Tanis/Qurong*, the first born of unfallen humanity and later,
>　　leader of the Horde
>　*Justin*, an incarnation of Elyon
>　*Makil*, Hunter's military lieutenant in future Earth and later a key
>　　member of the Circle
>　*William*, a military leader and key member of the Circle
>　*Ciphus*, a high priest of the Great Romance religion as corrupted
>　　by the Scabs
>　*Chelise*, the daughter of Qurong
>　*Woref*, the military leader of the Horde and suitor of Chelise

Overview

In *Black*, the first volume of Ted Dekker's Circle Trilogy, Thomas Hunter, a twenty-five-year-old in twenty-first century America, finds himself in another reality whenever he falls asleep or loses consciousness. He is told that this alternate world is Earth, far in the future following an event called the Great Deception in 2010, in which most of the world's population was destroyed by the Raison strain, a deadly virus mutated from a vaccine of the same name.

After waking up, Tom reads a newspaper article about a vaccine just developed by Raison Pharmaceutical. Tom realizes he must warn the world before it is distributed. With his sister's help, he begins a quest to convince authorities that the vaccine—touted as a revolutionary solution to multiple worldwide diseases—is actually destined to become a worldwide killer. His quest requires him to learn more about the virus, so he seeks to return to future Earth frequently in hopes of learning details that will enable him to thwart the villainous effort to destroy the world. Tom's efforts to warn the world work paradoxically in the plot: His urgent report to the Centers for Disease Control (CDC) becomes the very means whereby Valborg Svensson learns (via an informant at CDC) that the seemingly safe Raison vaccine has the potential to mutate into a deadly virus, setting in motion the very chain of events Tom is working to thwart.

In Tom's frequent return visits to future Earth, he learns from the white, batlike Roush named Michal and Gabil that Elyon has returned the world to a prelapsarian state in which evil—personified by thousands of black, batlike creatures called Shataiki—is entirely contained on one side of a river, opposite untainted goodness lived out by humans who are experientially ignorant of evil. In this new Eden, the unfallen humans worship and commune daily with Elyon through a ceremony at a nearby lake with restorative waters that serve as a metaphor for Elyon's presence. The people of future Earth pursue every desire of their hearts without internal sin or negative consequences. Only one act is forbidden them: to drink the water of the Shataiki on the other side of the river. Should any one of them do so, Elyon's protection from evil will be lifted, and the humans will be at mercy of the evil bats.

From his first visit onward, Tom begins engaging with future Earth in ways that begin to change both him and its residents. He meets and begins courting Rachelle, receiving lessons in their unfallen courtship process from other men in the village. Tom also has a personal encounter with Elyon at the lake. Overcome with an unexplainable desire to immerse himself, Tom dives into the lake when others merely drink. He hears Elyon's voice calling lovingly to him, and through the water, he feels both Elyon's love for him and hatred for sin.

Just as Tom is beginning to embrace the goodness of this unfallen world, Tanis, the firstborn, Adam-figure of future Earth, becomes increasingly fascinated with the evil Shataiki and the knowledge of "ancient Earth" that he believes—incorrectly—Tom has gained from them. Despite a lifetime of warning, Tanis allows Teeleh, the leader of the Shataiki, to tempt him; he then crosses the river and drinks the forbidden water. Future Earth and its inhabitants are immediately infected with the loss of innocence, and the Shataiki are able to cross the river and attack. All the people become infected with a skin and mind disease, and many are killed by Shataiki; a few, including Tom, Rachelle, and Rachelle's brother Johan escape across the desert. They are led by a boy who speaks for and represents Elyon to a forest with a lake. The boy instructs them to bathe every day in the lake to keep the disease away and to never forget him.

In *Red*, the second volume, Tom's efforts to preserve goodness in future Earth and his quest to stop the Raison strain from destroying present Earth's population continue. He must rescue Monique de Raison, the vaccine developer who has been kidnapped by Svensson so that he can obtain the key to creating an antidote for the Raison virus, which has been released and threatens to destroy most of Earth's population in ten days. Tom's rescue attempt becomes a critical part of the worldwide effort to discover an antidote; meanwhile, Svensson and his allies seek to obtain global power by demanding the surrender of all military weapons in exchange for the antidote.

In his existence in future Earth, fifteen years have passed, and Tom has become the leader of the Forest People, a community of people faithful to the commands of Elyon in the wake of the exile from the Colored Forest and the infection. All who would follow him must bathe in the lake water of one of the forests at least once every two days; otherwise, their minds will become dull and scabs will form on their skin, and eventually the person will become a Scab, joining the ranks of the Horde. Tom leads the army's resistance to the Horde, who significantly outnumber the Forest People and seek to destroy them.

The future Earth plot centers around a young man named Justin who is teaching a new way of peace, urging mercy and understanding toward the Scabs. His ideas seem heretical to the Forest People, who believe they must remain enemies with the Scabs to be faithful to the Great Romance, and many fear Justin plans to betray them so that they fall under the Horde's power. *Red* culminates in the wrongful execution by drowning of the innocent Justin, who is revealed to be an incarnation of Elyon. His death turns the water of the lake red like blood. Tom's love for and trust in Justin leads him to follow Justin into the lake, voluntarily inhaling the bloody water. He, Rachelle, and a few others all do so and find they can breathe the water. They hear Elyon's voice speaking to them under the water, and they surface. After this death-and-resurrection-like experience, they no longer need to bathe regularly; their disease and scabs have vanished. Surrounded by Scabs and forest dwellers who condemned Justin, they are in danger and race to escape. Most succeed, but Rachelle is killed by the Scabs. *Red* concludes as these few depart the forest to dwell in the desert. At the command of Justin, who appears to them alive, they call themselves the Circle.

In *White*, the final novel of the trilogy, those in the Circle led by Tom are no longer at war with the Horde. Their mission is to avoid capture and death and to convince as many Scabs as possible to willingly drown and then find new life in the red pools Justin has revealed to them. Those who do this find freedom from the disease and join the Circle. Tom singles out one particular Scab, Chelise, daughter of Tanis/Qurong, to woo and win to the Circle, risking his life and friends to convince her. Woref, whom she detests but who has been promised her hand in marriage by Qurong, opposes Tom and the Circle with an intensity fueled by his lust for Chelise and by the hatred of the Shataiki for the Circle.

Meanwhile, in 2010 in Tom's present Earth, people are showing symptoms of the disease, and panic spreads globally as word of the nature of the virus becomes known. The world looks to Tom for a solution, and he seeks to find one through his experiences in future Earth. Like most of the events in the two realities, the solution to the dilemma in 2010 is intimately tied to Tom's knowledge of and existence in future Earth and his identity as part of the Circle.

Christian Themes

The Circle Trilogy weaves together numerous themes that are either foundational or central to Christian life. In *Black*, through his unfallen future Earth, Dekker imagines the intangible as tangible: God (Elyon) speaks directly to humans, and they can literally—not just metaphorically—bathe in the water alive with his presence. Organized religion practiced by the community is vibrant for each person and brings delight and spiritual refreshment daily. Fruit provides nourishment not only to the palate and body but also to the soul. Relationships between humans are free from jealousy and strife, and individuality is no threat to the community: People reflect God's creativity in their distinctiveness without expressing that individuality in self-exaltation or selfishness.

One of the most vivid materializations of spiritual truth in the novel is the Great Romance, the name used in future Earth both for Elyon's means of relating to humans and for the courtship of a man and woman. In *Black*, Tanis teaches Tom that a man follows the same steps to win a woman's heart that Elyon takes to rescue "everything that is his . . . he chooses . . . he pursues . . . he rescues . . . he woos . . . he protects . . . he lavishes." By depicting religion as a romance between humans and God with God as initiator, Dekker portrays passion and desire—not simply duty and decision—as essential elements of a true relationship with God.

Evil, too, is more visibly a corruption of something originally intended by God to be good, and the consequences of exchanging evil for good, of desiring the creation instead of the Creator are incalculably disastrous. As with Adam and Eve's disobedience in Genesis, the essence of the first sin in future Earth is a desire for knowledge that grants godlike power. Dekker also portrays a Christian understanding of God's hatred of and grief over sin when, during Tom's conversion-like experience in the lake, Elyon gives him a glimpse of the ugliness of his own sin followed by the sound of Elyon's voice screaming in pain as a consequence of that sin.

In the second and third volumes, *Red* and *White*, the events in future Earth parallel and become a metaphor for the practice of religion that is merely ceremonial versus the mercy, faith, suffering, and joy that are at the heart of biblical Christianity. *Red* portrays those obedient to Elyon (God) at war with the disobedient, but many of the obedient have lost sight of love and mercy. Justin's death and resurrection at the end of *Red* offer a vivid picture of Christ's death and resurrection, and the implications of the new life and community this sacrifice makes possible for Elyon's followers are demonstrated by the members of the Circle in *White*. Their new freedom through drowning and living anew in the red water of the pools parallel several biblical teachings central to Christianity, perhaps most explicitly expounded by Paul in Romans, chapters 6-8: the Christian's appropriation of forgiveness and new life by dying to self and sin through baptism into the death of Christ, the resulting experience of a second birth and new life, and the mercy and love toward others that this process is to produce in the Christian as one becomes like Christ.

Throughout the trilogy, Dekker presents a clear contrast between unfallen, fallen, and redeemed humanity. The dual plot provides a vehicle for the reader to appropriate these biblical teachings to daily life. The tale encourages readers to apply to twenty-first century Earth what Dekker has taught them through the creative images of unfallen (and then, recently fallen) future Earth and its inhabitants.

Sources for Further Study

Butler, Tamara. Review of *Red*, by Ted Dekker. *Library Journal* 129, no. 10 (June 1, 2004): 114. Looks at the second in the series, finding it a somewhat unsettling mix of politics and religion.

_____. Review of *White*, by Ted Dekker. *Library Journal* 129, no. 18 (November 1, 2004): 70. Praises the concluding book in the series and calls the author a "master of suspense."

Dekker, Ted. *The Slumber of Christianity: Awakening a Passion for Heaven on Earth*. Nashville, Tenn.: Thomas Nelson, 2005. This nonfiction work by Dekker criticizes the Church for its reluctance to pursue pleasure in God. Dekker calls the Church—believers in Christ—to awaken to God-centered pleasures in the midst of the darkness and dryness that can dull the spiritual senses to God's goodness and hinder the Christian from walking in freedom, hope, and joy.

Fowlds, Sean. "Ted Dekker: Black, White, and Read." *Publishers Weekly* 250, no. 37 (September 15, 2003): S11. This article focuses on Ted Dekker's rise to prominence as a writer and describes his style as well as the then upcoming trilogy.

Holm, Kelsey. "Hollywood Plot Holds Deeper Message." *Knight Ridder Tribune Business News*, January 5, 2007, p. 1. Article deals with the release of the film *Thr3e*, based on one of Dekker's novels. It is the first release of Fox Faith, a division of Twentieth Century Fox Home Entertainment, and a Christian film company.

Kennedy, Douglas. "Selling Rapture: The Rise of the Christian Right in American Politics Has Added Impetus to an Already Huge and Growing Market in Evangelical Fiction." *The Guardian*, July 9, 2005, p. 4. Kennedy examines the growth of Christian fiction in a variety of genres. Includes discussion of Dekker and his works.

Christopher E. Crane

THE CITY OF GOD

Author: Saint Augustine (354-430 C.E.)

First published: De civitate Dei, 413-427 C.E. (English translation, 1610)

Edition used: City of God, edited by Philip Schaff, in *Nicene and Post-Nicene Fathers*, series 1, vol. 2. Peabody, Mass.: Hendrickson, 1994

Genre: Nonfiction

Subgenres: History; theology

Core issues: Church; God; life; love; obedience and disobedience; peace; pilgrimage; salvation; sin and sinners

Saint Augustine's most mature, comprehensive, and influential work of theology, political philosophy, and salvation history was written in response to pagan charges that Christianity was responsible for the decline in Roman power. Augustine posits the existence of two invisible cities: the city of man, rooted in the love of self, and the city of God, rooted in the love of God. All human history can be explained by recourse to these two opposing loves, which compete for the attention and loyalty of the human heart.

Overview

In 410 C.E. Alaric and the Goths sacked Rome, shocking the Mediterranean world and raising charges by pagans, then chafing under the rule of Christian emperors, that Christianity was responsible for weakening the once powerful Roman Empire. Saint Augustine's *The City of God* was a sophisticated answer to these charges, pointing out, contrary to the teaching of ancient philosophers, that no earthly political system could be relied upon for the satisfaction of the most important human needs, which are ultimately spiritual rather than material ones. The first ten of the twenty-two books expose the false teachings of the pagans as found in the writings of their poets, politicians, and philosophers, while recognizing the truth that can be observed in them. The second part of *The City of God* presents a Christian understanding of the origins, progress, and ultimate ends of the two cities: the earthly city of man, represented by Babylon, rooted in vice and sin, governed by selfish love, and destined to conflict, destruction, and eternal death; and the heavenly city, represented by Jerusalem, rooted in grace and virtue, governed by love of God, and destined for peace, salvation, and eternal life.

Augustine asserts that Rome's problems were of its own making, not a result of Christian teaching. Rome's own gods did not come to the city's protection, and Roman pagans sought and found protection from the Goths only by fleeing to Christian churches, which the pagan hordes dared not enter or burn. The mythic gods of Romans actually degraded the civic and moral virtues that once characterized the Roman republic. No less a figure than Plato had banished the poets and their mythic gods from his ideal republic for these reasons. Pagan gods, then, failed to protect human souls, to prevent human evils, or to guarantee human happiness even in the possession of the goods of this life. Some pagans understood, more properly, that the gods should be worshiped for the sake of happiness in life after death. By God's providence, civic virtues of prudence, justice, temperance, and courage marked the early Romans, but even these early Romans were oriented toward fabulous and nonexistent gods—to the embarrassment of Roman philosophers such as Seneca, who observed pagan rituals but did not believe in the gods. Enlightened by degrees of wisdom, even the philosophers failed to see that human wisdom and virtue are gifts from God rather than strictly human efforts. Thus, while the natural philosophy of the Presocratics, Socrates, Plato, Aristotle, and even the Roman Stoics made significant advances (even in the understanding of the divine), these philosophers also trusted too much to human virtue for its own sake and not enough to the love of God, author of all virtue. Philosophers therefore sought but could not find the full truth, and so genuine happiness eluded them.

In parts 3 and 4, Augustine turns to a full account of true salvation history and the quest for human happiness, found only in the beatitude of God. Following the proclamation of Psalm 87 ("Glorious things are said of you, O City of God"), Augustine begins by discussing the origins of the city of God. Out of love, God created time and space, the whole visible universe, and the invisible world of angelic spirits. Human beings were made in his image, capable of knowing, loving, and choosing to serve him with free will. However, angelic and human intellect and will, though capable of knowing God, can and do, out of pride, freely choose to reject God. Perverse wills choose evil and death, falling into sin, though by their very nature all things created were good. Weakness of will and sin turn the human heart toward disordered love of self instead of life-giving love of God. This Original Sin is the foundation of the city of man. From this bad use of the will—this Original Sin—flows every evil known to man, evils that can be healed only by God's grace. Amid the city of man, therefore, are those who in humble obedience strive for virtue and the love of God and neighbor, seeking to avoid the endless death of the soul.

In part 4, Augustine traces biblical history, showing how Cain, having killed his brother Abel in envy, built a city in which the wicked make war both with one another and with the good. Abel, a shepherd, built no city, living in charity as a pilgrim in, but not of, the world. Even a good man, amid the city of man, can be at war with others and with himself, as he strives for virtue. Down through the descendants of Cain and Seth, scripture describes the proud, who love themselves, and the humble, who love God. The city of God claims Noah, Abraham, Isaac, Jacob, and Moses, King David, and the prophets who worship God and seek his promise of eternal life, to be fulfilled in the coming of Christ. The city of man rises and falls in the ephemeral empires of the Egyptians, Assyrians, Babylonians, Greeks, and Romans, who idolize themselves and worship false gods. With the coming of Christ, the members of his pilgrim Church strive to advance the city of God.

Finally, in part 5, Augustine treats the ends of the two cities. The city of God, begging God's grace to avoid vice, seeks eternal life; the city of man, believing in its own virtue, is destroyed by pride. Real human happiness is possible only in abandonment of the will to complete trust in God, rather than in trusting one's own pitiful strength, which is itself a gift from God. The Christian must live in the earthly city and must obey lawful authority while advancing earthly peace as far as possible. Eternal happiness, however, rests in faith, hope, and love, not in human industry and policy. Those who trust in the latter run the risk of eternal death, which is the fruit of sinful pride. True happiness is attained in the ultimate joy of heaven and eternal life with the God who made us and calls every person back to his heavenly home, where the city of God abides in fullness of praise and joy.

Christian Themes

Saint Augustine's two cities are ultimately mystical in nature, each containing a visible component among the living generation struggling in this world for either material or spiritual goods. Those striving for the city of God live in, but are not of, the city of man, seeking rather to transcend the material order by living in obedience to God's commands.

In Augustine's view, the Church, though amid the city of man, serves as the visible sign of God's love among the living and as a means of grace to strengthen its members' life of charity and virtue. It teaches obedience to the moral law and offers sacraments of life-giving grace as it seeks to advance the city of God, calling all people to obedience and away from sin. It cooperates with the city of man to advance peace through justice in human affairs. It urges the punishment of evil, even to the point of just war, in order to preserve and protect the innocent and establish a just and fruitful peace. It serves as a sign of God's mercy, offering sinners a haven from a world too often mired in violence and selfish disregard of the common good.

Augustine's ultimate message is that Christ died for the redemption of this sad and sinful world, and his resurrection points to the final judgment, in which God will separate the two cities. Those proud citizens of the city of man will suffer eternal separation from God, in the second death of hell, while the sojourners who loved and obeyed God on pilgrimage in the city of man will be rewarded with eternal bliss.

Sources for Further Study

Augustine. *Augustine: Major Writings*. Edited by Benedict J. Groeshel, C.F.R. New York: Crossroad, 1995. Offers a chapter on Augustine as historian and political philosopher, emphasizing his teachings on spiritual and civic life and earthly war and peace as treated in *The City of God*.

Brown, Peter. *Augustine of Hippo: A Biography*. Berkeley: University of California Press, 1967. The standard biography of Augustine, which devotes significant space to the composition and themes of *The City of God*.

Fortin, Ernst. *"De Civitate Dei."* In *Augustine Through the Ages: An Encyclopedia*, edited by Allan D. Fitzgerald, O.S.A. Grand Rapids, Mich.: Wm. B. Eerdman's, 1999. A fine summary of the basic themes and historical and political significance of *The City of God*.

Trapè, Agostino. "Saint Augustine." In *Patrology*, edited by Johanness Quasten. Vol. 4. Westminster, Md.: Christian Classics, 1992. A superb summary of the life, works, writings, philosophy, and theology of Augustine, with an extensive bibliography.

Robert F. Gorman

THE CLOUD OF UNKNOWING

Author: Unknown; attributed to the "Cloud-author"
First transcribed: Late fourteenth century
Edition used: The Cloud of Unknowing, edited with a preface by Simon Tugwell and
    an introduction by James Walsh, S.J. New York: Paulist Press, 1981
Genre: Nonfiction
Subgenres: Didactic treatise; instructional manual; spiritual treatise
Core issues: Contemplation; faith; God; love; prayer

The linguistic and manuscript evidence seems to indicate that The Cloud of Unknowing *was written in the northeast Midlands of England in the last half of the fourteenth
century. Among other works are explicitly said to be the work of the author (commonly known as the Cloud-author), the key texts are* The Book of Privy Counseling,
The Epistle of Prayer, *and* Denis Hid Divinity. *The internal evidence of his writings
indicates that the author was a priest, dedicated to the contemplative life, and recognized as a spiritual father. He was a competent theologian, with a great knowledge
of patristic and monastic literature. He knew some elements of the teaching of Saint
Thomas Aquinas.*

Overview

The Cloud of Unknowing is not an orderly treatise. It is repetitious. It has its share
of digressions. It is primarily addressed to an enthusiastic young disciple, age twenty-
four, who is prone to overdo things even while he struggles with some natural fickle-
ness and laziness. It inserts basic human and Christian teaching at random points. The
treatise leaves us with a sense of helplessness in the face of our divine aspirations, but
it also leaves us with a certain comfortableness with that sense of helplessness, for
here the author—a wise spiritual father who clearly seems to have found his way—
keeps reassuring us that this confusion is all right, quite to be expected. We really
have to do only one thing, and that is to leave things in the hands of God, to turn ourselves over to him, to accept his gift of himself which is the union of contemplation:

> But if you strive to fix your love on him, forgetting all else, which is the work of contem-
> plation I have urged you to begin. . . . I am confident that God in his goodness will bring
> you to a deep experience of himself.

The father tells us for whom he has written *The Cloud of Unknowing*:

> I have in mind a person who, over and above the good works of the active life, has re-
> solved to follow Christ (as far as humanly possible with God's grace) unto the inmost
> depths of contemplation . . . who has first been faithful for some time to the demands of
> the active life.

The father sees some Christians called primarily to a life of active service, but these must at times lay aside their activity and give time to meditation and communion with God. Others are called primarily to a Christian life centered on prayer and contemplation, but these too must lay aside their primary concern at times to attend to human and social affairs. Thus he speaks of two degrees in each life, a higher and a lower, and he sees the higher degree of the active life coalescing with the lower degree of the contemplative. It is here where most good Christians are situated but each with his or her proper call with its particular emphases.

One must be a person of faith, sufficient faith to believe in the Divine Presence hidden beyond in the cloud of unknowing. One must have turned from sin toward God in love, a love strong enough to make one seek God in the darkness of his incomprehensibility, leaving behind other attractions and desires. When the father comes to express concretely what this means, he is not as demanding as we might have expected:

> If you ask me when a person should begin his contemplative work I would answer not until he has first purified his conscience of all particular sins in the Sacrament of Reconciliation as the Church prescribes. . . . Once having done what the Church requires, he should fearlessly begin the contemplative work.

The past does not matter, the author insists ("Some who have been hardened habitual sinners arrive at the perfection of this work sooner than those who have never sinned grievously"), nor even present weakness ("In choosing your present way of life you made a radical commitment to God and this remains despite temporary lapse"—the father seems decidedly up to date in speaking here about a fundamental option), but only one's true desire: "It is not what you are nor what you have been that God sees with his all-merciful eyes, but what you desire to be."

Going on to close the treatise with a passage from Saint Augustine that reads, "The entire life of a good Christian is nothing less than holy desire," the father seems clearly to indicate that this way of contemplative prayer is for all Christians. However, in prescribing the contemplative way, he respects the diversity of ways within it, a position well developed with biblical imagery in the previous chapter, where he says: "It is important to realize that in the interior life we must never take our own experiences (or lack of them) as the norm for everyone else." Earlier he has affirmed: "How often it happens that the grace of contemplation will awaken in people of every walk and station of life, both religious and lay alike."

Far from excluding anyone from seeking to develop the contemplative dimensions of life, the father seems to imply that its development is essential for the fulfillment of human life:

> It is God, and he alone, who can fully satisfy the hunger and longing of our spirit which, transformed by his redeeming grace, is enabled to embrace him by love.

The activities of the lower degree of the active life (the corporal works of mercy) in themselves leave much of our natural human potential untapped. At this stage one lives, as it were, outside oneself and beneath oneself. As one advances to the higher degree of the active life (which merges with the lower degree of the contemplative life) one becomes increasingly interior, living more from the depth of oneself and becoming, therefore, more fully human. For the fulfillment of the human spirit one must have a spiritual life; for fulfillment of the Christian spirit that has been given us at baptism, one must have a full Christian life, one of intimate communion with God.

One of the objections against this work of contemplation is its emptiness; it is an experience of nothingness, of being nowhere—it is idleness, a quietism. The first to raise this objection is the contemplator: "Who do you suppose derides it as an emptiness? Our superficial self, of course." Those closest to us quickly join in: ". . . family and friends descend upon them in a storm of fury and criticism, severely reproving them for idleness."

Right from the start the father assures his son of the preeminent fruitfulness of contemplation:

> What I am describing here is the contemplative work of the spirit. It is this which gives God the greatest delight. for when you fix your love on him, forgetting all else, the saints and angels rejoice and hasten to assist you in every way—though the devils will rage and ceaselessly conspire to thwart you. Your fellow men are marvelously enriched by this work of yours, even if you may not fully understand how; the souls in purgatory are touched, for their suffering is eased by the effects of this work and, of course, your own spirit is purified and strengthened by this contemplative work more than by all others put together.

The father continues: "For I tell you this, one loving blind desire for God alone is more valuable in itself, more pleasing to God and to the Saints, more beneficial to your own growth, and more helpful to your friends, both living and dead, than anything else you could do." But—"It cannot be explained, only experienced." Our Master has said: "Judge a tree by its fruit." There should be some fruits that the objective observer should be able to experience. The father speaks of these:

> Moreover, in contemplation the second and subsidiary command of charity is also completely fulfilled. The fruits of contemplation bear witness to this even though during the actual time of prayer the skilled contemplative has no special regard for any person in particular, whether brother or stranger, friend or enemy . . . when he speaks or prays with his fellow Christian at other times, the warmth of his love reaches out to them all, friend or enemy, stranger and kin alike.

"Genuine goodness is a matter of habitually acting and responding appropriately in each situation as it arises, moved always by the desire to please God," the father writes. Other norms he notes are the general good use of time and the regard for communal prayer: "The true contemplative has the highest esteem for the liturgy and is careful and exact in celebrating it, in continuity with the tradition of our Fathers." These fruits of contemplation can be readily perceived and might therefore reassure some, looking in from the outside, as to the value of contemplative prayer—but probably not many. Moreover, they do not touch the more significant meaning and value of contemplative practice for the human community. There is a bonding, transcending time and place, with Jesus, "creator and dispenser of time," which enables the contemplative to "share all Jesus has and enter the fellowship of those who love Him," including "the communion of the blessed." Each member "must do his share however slight to strengthen the fellowship as it strengthens him."

The father is not, in this work, offering a full systematic treatment of the spiritual life. His concern here is about a way of prayer, but that is a part of a whole life and a whole attitude. This latter is important. Nonetheless, he does offer a very simple, traditional method of prayer that can be drawn out from his work.

Simply sit relaxed and quiet. Center all your attention and desire on God, and let this be the sole concern of your mind and heart. If you want to gather all your desire into one simple word that the mind can easily retain, choose a short word rather than a long one, but choose one that is meaningful to you (such as "God" or "love"). Fix the word in your mind so that it will remain there, come what may. The father's advice involves words of encouragement and the reminder that the darkness of the cloud of unknowing comes between the contemplator and the God one desires to reach; despite the darkness, one wills to reach out to God.

The father admonishes us to be careful in this work: Never strain mind or imagination, for truly one will not succeed in this way; leave these faculties at peace. It is best when the word chosen for contemplation is wholly interior, without a definite thought or actual sound. Let this little word (the father enjoins) represent to you God in all his fullness; let nothing except God hold sway in your mind and heart. One may be distracted by remembering some task undone or one may find that some disrupting thought is clouding one's attention, the father comments—but, he advises, if one answers with the word chosen, if one resists intellectualizing about its meaning and, instead, holds the word before oneself in all its simplicity, one may escape distractions. Put all thoughts of other creatures—past, present, and future—under a "cloud of forgetting." If in this way one strives to fix one's love on him, forgetting all else, which is the work of contemplation, God in his goodness will provide a deep experience of himself.

Christian Themes

The anonymous author of *The Cloud of Unknowing* urges us to to fix our love on God while forgetting all else, which is the work of contemplation. If we do so, God in his goodness will bring us a deep experience of God. Even Christians called primarily to a life of active service must at times lay aside their activity and give time to meditation and communion with God. One must be a person of faith, sufficient faith to believe in the Divine Presence hidden beyond the cloud of unknowing. One must also have turned from sin toward God in love, a love strong enough to make one seek God in the darkness of his incomprehensibility, leaving behind other attractions and desires. It is not what we are or what we have been that God sees with his all-merciful eyes, but what we desire to be. It is God, and he alone, who can fully satisfy the hunger and longing of our spirit, which, transformed by his redeeming grace, is enabled to embrace him by love.

Sources for Further Study

Hodgson, Phyllis, ed. *The Cloud of Unknowing and Related Treatises*. Analecta Cartusiana 3. Salzburg: University of Salzburg, 1982. This volume includes Hodgson's edition of *The Cloud of Unknowing* and the related texts on contemplative prayer that are argued to come from the same author: *The Book of Privy Counselling*, *The Epistle of Prayer*, *The Epistle of Discretion*, *Hid Divinity*, *Benjamin Minor*, *The Study of Wisdom*, and *Of Discerning of Spirits*. It also contains six pages of bibliography.

Johnston, William. *The Mysticism of "The Cloud of Unknowing."* 1967. 4th ed. Foreword by Thomas Merton. New York: Fordham University Press, 2000. The author gives an extensive study of the mysticism of the period and also compares the teaching of *The Cloud of Unknowing* with that of Saint John of the Cross and other apophatic mystics. There is a good introduction by Thomas Merton.

Pennington, M. Basil. *Centering Prayer: Renewing an Ancient Christian Prayer Form*. 1980. New York: Doubleday, 2001. This study places *The Cloud of Unknowing* in its full historical context within the ever-renewing Christian tradition and gives a very practical, modern presentation of its basic teaching.

Szarmach, Paul E., ed. *An Introduction to the Medieval Mystics of Europe: Fourteen Original Essays*. Albany: State of University of New York Press, 1984. This collection of essays contains a good study of *The Cloud of Unknowing* by John P. H. Clark.

M. Basil Pennington

THE COLOR OF FAITH
Building Community in a Multiracial Society

Author: Fumitaka Matsuoka (1943-   )
First published: 1998
Edition used: The Color of Faith: Building Community in a Multiracial Society. Cleveland, Ohio: United Church Press, 1998
Genre: Nonfiction
Subgenre: Critical analysis
Core issues: African Americans; good vs. evil; hope; justice; racism; reconciliation; redemption; social action

After presenting the view that American society is inherently and thoroughly racist in nature and that all American societal institutions are run by the agents of Satan, the powers and principalities of evil, Matsuoka calls for the constitution of an indigenous religion originating from the fringes of American churches that will bring forth a reconciliation of the races after the pain and bewailing of the oppressed races has been heard in the United States.

Overview

From the outset of *The Color of Faith*, Fumitaka Matsuoka expresses his belief that people of Western European descent in the United States practice an ongoing racism against all the other people living in the country. He contrasts this vision of racism with the Christian faith, which invites all people, regardless of race or ethnicity, to join. According to Matsuoka, although Christian religion is communitarian, inclusive, just, and righteous, American society is racist and segregated, and it caters to the interests of the dominant Caucasian population.

When discussing various theoretical and practical aspects of race in the United States, *The Color of Faith* uses politically correct academic jargon that may quickly deter readers not used to this language. Moreover, although the author is quick to critique conservative and moderate views, he does not exercise authorial censorship over extreme views, including the belief that a jury should not convict a person such as O. J. Simpson, even if they believe him to be guilty of murder, in order to send a signal against perceived racial oppression.

Rather controversially, Matsuoka states that the devil controls American societal institutions. He argues that hordes of fallen angels, the "powers and principalities" of evil, run U.S. institutions and have created a "monopoly of the imagination" that shapes public opinion and seeks to control how American people think. The agents of Satan thrive in "the hostile soil of larger institutions" that they have created, and the righteous are in an almost hopeless struggle against evil. For Matsuoka, racism runs rampant in an American society where Satan is manifested in all societal institutions.

Matsuoka seeks to validate this dark vision by referring to the testimony of twenty people in Chicago at a 1994 hearing that had church groups among its sponsors. By quoting from the hearing, sometimes repeating the same quotes within a few pages, *The Color of Faith* strives to paint a very dark vision of racial relations in the United States. Matsuoka quotes, for example, the belief of one writer that the health care needs of African Americans "differ from the needs of European Americans."

Throughout *The Color of Faith*'s discourse on race and racism in the United States, which makes up about three quarters of the work, Matsuoka paints a grim picture. For him, membership in any race but the Caucasian comes with "memories of historical wrongs" suffered, never of past achievements or triumphs. While acknowledging that contemporary physical anthropology has severely questioned the scientific validity of the term "race" as used to categorize people, Matsuoka argues with those who believe that the general American populace fails to accept this scientific verdict and still clings to unscientific racist beliefs. Thus, according to Matsuoka, U.S. institutions such as the criminal justice system are still inherently racist.

Against his belief that the devil holds American institutions in a firm grip, toward the end of *The Color of Faith*, Matsuoka identifies some signals for Christian hope. Beginning with "Signs of Repeopling in Christian Churches," the final twenty-five pages of his book are devoted to describing churches and communities that have risen against the powers and principalities of evil that Matsuoka views as running the United States. *The Color of Faith* praises Christian congregations that allow the "voices of the pain and bewailing of devalued people" to be heard. Matsuoka expresses his hope that out of this testimony, a new "indigenous religion" will arise and give freedom to all who participate in this process.

The Color of Faith closes by describing instances of redemption in which non-Caucasian congregations have offered reconciliation to European American Christians. Matsuoka places great hope in this "vision of reconciliation," which he views as "a clear demonstration of the power and vitality of the Christian faith." For him, the ability of African American Christian faith communities to forgive European Americans for their historical sins of slavery and racism points in the direction of new hope for a truly integrated, communitarian, and multiracial neighborhood-based Christianity in the United States. Matsuoka says people and small community groups who attempt to build neighborhoods across racial divides act as models.

Although American churches still suffer from segregation, Matsuoka concludes that there are positive fringe churches that defy this trend. One example is Messiah Housing in Michigan, where a band of people is deliberately living together and equally "dividing all resources" brought into the collective home.

The Color of Faith ends on a guardedly optimistic note that the work of the devil in the United States can be overcome despite the creation of a racist society intended to last forever. The work of Christians on the fringes of the established churches—those who work through the power of reconciliation after airing their just grievances and invite all members of multiracial neighborhoods into their community of faith—represents a vision of hope for Matsuoka that American society may be "repeopled" with new Christians.

Christian Themes

Matsuoka bases his objection to racism on the belief that the Christian God accepts all people into his community of the faithful. God stands for justice and righteousness, and every human being is invited to join God's community through baptism. Every time Christians celebrate the Eucharist, coming together at the table of Christ to commemorate with bread and wine the Last Supper of the Savior, they reaffirm this belief in an all-encompassing, race-transcending God whose divine sovereignty transcends any racial barrier, preference, or law. This is why for Matsuoka, a true Christian can never be a racist.

The Color of Faith insists that the devil, in his ceaseless devious struggle to alienate humans from each other, has infiltrated all American societal institutions with his legions of fallen angels, the powers and principalities of evil. Acting as agents of Satan, these demons have infested U.S. institutions and seek to perpetrate the evil of racism.

In this struggle of good versus evil, from Matsuoka's point of view, many Christians are tempted to fall into the trap sprung by Satan and re-create in their own congregations a separation of the races that prevents the establishment of social justice and the rule of the righteous. Social action that leads to societal justice is stifled when the evil of racism invades Christian faith communities.

Matsuoka ends on a note of hope. Satan's grip on U.S. institutions can be challenged, he argues. If persecuted and oppressed non-Caucasian Christians are allowed to voice their grievances and offer reconciliation and thus redemption to their European American fellow faithful, redemption is possible. He states that further redemption can be achieved through the churches at the margins of mainstream America, in which some Christians go as far as the Christian communitarians in the first centuries after Christ's death who shared all their resources. When non-Caucasians forgive Caucasian Christians their historical sins, Matsuoka's text argues, there is hope for a new, indigenous American religion. This religion will not be tainted by the work of the devil. Instead, America can be repeopled with Christians who live close in the spirit of God. These Christians obey God's inclusive rule that does not distinguish people on the base of their race but rather welcomes all believers into God's faith community, where each and every one of them will find redemption.

Sources for Further Study

De Young, Curtiss Paul, et al. *United By Faith*. New York: Oxford University Press, 2004. Authors strongly support multiracial congregations for which they make a theological as well as a sociological point; they also show that American churches are still strongly divided by race.

Matsuoka, Fumitaka, and Eleazar S. Fernandez, eds. *Realizing the America of Our Hearts: Theological Voices of Asian Americans*. St. Louis: Chalice Press, 2003. A collection of essays on Asian American theology and experiences of Asian Americans with Christianity.

Ortiz, Manuel. *One New People: Models for Developing a Multiethnic Church*. Downers Grove, Ill.: InterVarsity Press, 1996. Articulately promotes the idea of an ethnically diverse congregation based on racial reconciliation and celebrating Christian faith across racial divides; offers models for achieving this goal, which Matsuoka believes holds hope for the future.

Yancey, George. *One Body, One Spirit: Principles of Successful Multiracial Churches.* Downers Grove, Ill.: InterVarsity Press, 2003. Offers practical examples and case studies to create the kind of racially inclusive community churches that Matsuoka envisions.

R. C. Lutz

THE COLOR PURPLE

Author: Alice Walker (1944-   )
First published: New York: Harcourt Brace Jovanovich, 1982
Genre: Novel
Subgenre: Literary fiction
Core issues: African Americans; compassion; connectedness; faith; God; racism; self-knowledge

Walker explores ways in which the role of faith and differing views of God affect the lives of blacks in the rural South and in Africa. She uses one extended family to illustrate a traditional Christian, a pantheistic, and a native African tribal perspective on God's role in human lives.

> Principal characters
> > *Celie*, the protagonist, who tells her life story in letters to God and her sister
> > *Nettie*, Celie's sister, a missionary in Africa
> > *Shug Avery*, a glamorous blues singer, whom Celie loves
> > *Mr.——*, Celie's husband, who mistreats her and loves Shug
> > *Harpo*, Mr.——'s son
> > *Sofia*, Harpo's wife, a strong and confident woman
> > *Samuel*, a missionary, who takes in and later marries Nettie
> > *Corrine*, Samuel's first wife
> > *Olivia*, Celie's daughter, raised by Samuel and Corrine
> > *Adam*, Celie's son, raised by Samuel and Corrine

Overview

The Color Purple consists of a series of letters describing the complex life of Celie and her extended family as they deal with poverty and racism in the rural South in the early part of the twentieth century. The first fifty-one letters are written by Celie, a fourteen-year-old girl who has been repeatedly raped by her father. They are addressed to God, the only one to whom she can tell this secret and mourn the fact that her two infant children were taken from her.

Another major worry in the early letters concerns her younger sister Nettie. Because their father has stopped molesting her, Celie believes he will start abusing Nettie. However, Celie is unable to protect her sister because of her forced marriage to Mr.——, a widower, who needs a wife to take care of him and his unruly children. Her life in this new family is dismal because no one treats her with kindness or affection. She briefly gains relief from worry, as well as companionship, when Nettie arrives, living with Celie briefly. However, Mr.——'s lustful attitude toward Nettie forces her to leave. Celie advises Nettie to seek refuge with a minister and his wife because the couple has enough money to employ her. Celie also believes that this couple has adopted her lost children.

In spite of her mistreatment by her new family, Celie tries her best to create a good home. Eventually Harpo, Mr.——'s son, marries Sofia, a strong, confident woman who will not be dominated by any man. Celie, at first, supports Harpo and encourages him to beat Sofia since this is the only type of relationship she has ever known. However, reading the Bible makes her feel that she has wronged Sofia, and the two women become friends. Sofia encourages Celie to stand up for herself against Mr.——'s tyranny, but she is unable to follow this advice.

A first step in Celie's growth occurs when Mr.—— invites his old mistress Shug Avery, a nightclub entertainer, to his house to recover from a venereal disease. Both Shug's appearance and behavior fascinate Celie. Even more than Sofia, Shug demonstrates that women can control their own lives. Meanwhile, Sofia and Harpo continue to fight for dominance. Finally Sofia goes back to her family. After her departure, Harpo suddenly gains self-confidence and turns their home into a juke joint, a nightclub, which becomes very popular, particularly after Shug agrees to sing there. When Sofia eventually returns with her new boyfriend, the mayor's wife offers her a job as a maid. After Sofia violently refuses, she is beaten and jailed. Ironically, she is eventually released when she agrees to work for the mayor's family. She is treated like a slave, forbidden to see her family except on rare occasions.

Shug also returns with a new husband, Grady. However, she and Celie become even closer, beginning a sexual relationship. While she is there, Shug discovers several letters from Nettie that Mr.—— had hidden from Celie. These letters, recounting what happened to Nettie over the years, form the next section of the novel. Samuel and Corrine, the minister and his wife who adopted both of Celie's children, take in Nettie. They are missionaries, and Nettie accompanies the family to Africa, where they live with a native tribe, the Olinka, until the tribe is almost destroyed by English rubber manufacturers. When Corrine dies, Nettie and Samuel marry.

While Celie is pleased to know that Nettie had written, the discovery that Mr.—— hid the letters causes Celie to question her faith. She stops addressing her letters to God because in her mind God is just another man who will betray her. Shug comforts her with a different view of God, a pantheistic one in which God is present in all of nature.

Shug convinces Celie to move to Memphis, thus providing a life of comfort and happiness for Celie, who shows her appreciation by designing some clothes for Shug. This eventually leads to a successful business, Folkpants Unlimited.

When Celie returns home again, she has money and confidence. In fact, Mr.—— doesn't even recognize her. He, too, has changed and is working hard and treating others with respect. In addition, she learns that she has inherited the family store. The man who raped her was only her stepfather, and therefore she is entitled to the family property.

Unfortunately, Celie's comfortable world falls apart. Shug falls in love with a younger man and leaves to be with him. The Department of Defense reports that

Nettie and her family were killed. In spite of all this, Celie learns to accept her life. She and Mr.—— discover that they enjoy each other's company. Each of them has grown to value the people and things around them. By the novel's end, Shug returns and even seems a little jealous of the relationship between Celie and Mr.——. Nettie and her family come home as well; the letter about their death was incorrect. She and Samuel hope to found a church that preaches the spirit of God not just his image. In the last letter, Celie once again writes to God; however, this time God includes the trees, the sky, and everyone. This letter celebrates her extended family, finally together, finally happy.

Christian Themes

In *The Color Purple*, Alice Walker explores the nature of God and religion. Celie shares a traditional Christian view of God with the rest of her community. The church is an essential part of this society, although there is a clear hierarchy within the congregation. The Bible is a guide for correct behavior, and the local preacher uses it to help shape the moral values of the community as a whole. The early letters demonstrate the key role that religion plays in determining Celie's behavior, even to the point where she refuses to criticize her father for raping her because the Bible says she should honor her father. God, to whom Celie addresses her letters, is both a confidant and a source of protection. She pictures God as he appears in many Christian images, an Old Testament patriarch with long hair and flowing robes. However, after the revelation that Mr.—— withheld her letters for all those years, God suddenly seems a representative of the two groups that abused and betrayed her all her life, men and white people.

Shug Avery, a self-confessed sinner who is denounced by the churchgoing community, defends God. God is not "him" to her, but rather "it." She espouses a pantheistic view of the world in which all nature is God, and God appears in all nature. God is a joyful and loving being. The novel's title reflects this as Shug tells Celie that she thinks God may become angry when people walk past a field and fail to appreciate the color purple. In her view, God appears in church only when the people themselves bring him in. Her religion stresses love, compassion, and pleasure.

This contrast between the conventional Christianity of established churches and more nontraditional views is also reflected in Nettie's letters from Africa. Although the Olinka worship nature and pay homage to the rootleaf plant, the crop that sustains their lifestyle, they listen to stories about the white Christian God. However, the destruction of the rootleaf and their village by the white colonialists causes the Olinka to question all religion because no God has been powerful enough to save them. Samuel and Nettie, too, find failures in conventional religion. They eventually wish to establish a new church in their community, one that honors the spirit of God rather than the image.

Sources for Further Study

Bloom, Harold, ed. *Alice Walker's "The Color Purple."* Philadelphia: Chelsea House, 2000. Includes essays that analyze the views of the main characters concerning

God and religion as well as discuss social and moral interpretations of Walker's work.

Gates, Henry Louis, Jr., and K. A. Appiah, eds. *Alice Walker: Critical Perspectives Past and Present*. New York: Amistad, 1993. A good overview of Walker's work, including the role of God and the spiritual quest in *The Color Purple*. Bibliographical references, index.

Winchell, Donna Haisty. *Alice Walker*. New York: Twayne, 1992. The role of sex, race, and class in religious imagery is analyzed. Includes a very helpful annotated bibliography.

Mary Mahony

COME SWEET DEATH
A Quintet from Genesis

Author: Bunyan Davie Napier (1915-   )
First published: Philadelphia: United Church Press, 1967
Genre: Poetry
Subgenres: Narrative poetry; spiritual treatise; theology
Core issues: Alienation from God; attachment and detachment; Creation; redemption; suffering

With a barrage of rhetorical questions and emotional, ethical, and rational appeals, a modern-day fugitive Job charges a bungling, anguished Creator with abandoning his promise to create a people who will inherit a blessed land. The quintet is a negative theodicy based on five major stories from Genesis 2-12: the garden, the brothers, the flood, the tower, and the call of Abraham. Come Sweet Death *may be viewed as a Christian existentialist's treatment of themes found in William Butler Yeats' "The Second Coming," Ezra Pound's cantos, and T. S. Eliot's "The Waste Land."*

Overview

Bunyan Davie Napier, a minister, theologian, and seminary professor, published Old Testament theological research between 1955 and1964 and the later Rockwell Lecture, *On New Creation* (1971). Napier's first single-volume poem, *Come Sweet Death*, appeared in 1967, followed by two additional poems, *Time of Burning* (1970) and *Word of God, Word of Earth* (1976). These three poems compose *The Best of Davie Napier.*

Napier values myths, especially theologically refined mythical stories found in Genesis, for what he terms their "isness" more than their "wasness." Genesis was orally transmitted from the tenth century B.C.E. before it was recorded in the sixth century B.C.E., so it is both informed by and informing to the rest of the Old Testament. As such, Napier calls Genesis "a meditation on history" that reveals how Creation shaped the faith and life of first the Jews and then the nations. Like Genesis, *Come Sweet Death* may be viewed as an act of "prophetism," which Napier defines in *Prophets in Perspective* (1963) as "a way of looking at, understanding, and interpreting history."

Napier introduces *Come Sweet Death* as a colloquial retelling or "existential interpretation" of Genesis 2-12 in the present tense. He excerpts from Genesis 2-12, with additional verses from Isaiah, Jeremiah, Hosea, the Psalms, and Luke. The poem closes with John 1:1, returning to the creative word in the beginning. With its present-day "isness," the quintet is suprahistorical, moving from Gilead to Geneva or from Noah to Unamuno in the same line. The omnipresent point of view is purposely disconcerting but nevertheless representative of the timeless audience for whom the Bible was intended.

Apart from the dated technology—Napier cites computers and rockets as the latest innovations—the 1967 poem still feels current with its Joycean compendium of both popular and literary allusions and its cynical, Nietzschean tone. Like the Lost Generation after World War I, Napier also writes in the shadow of nations at war, this time in Vietnam. His own intense frustration is evident in his persona's assessment: "A lousy, lying land;/ a dirty, stinking, bleeding, schizoid land!" Napier's speaker is a fugitive addressing an anguished Creator.

In the quintet's five parts, the speaker is a symbolic Adam, Cain, Noah, architect, and, finally, Abraham. He is the disobedient, murderous, inebriated, self-sufficient god of his own life. However, like Abraham, the wanderer ultimately finds solace in God's promise—a future event to be hoped for today. Because myth has meaning for all of history, the reader's role in this existential trial is to reinvent the five major events from Genesis.

Suggestive of scriptural format, each of the five parts is subdivided into ten sections, each with a version of the phrase, "come sweet death," emerging somewhere in the last three stanzas. The five chapters are variations on a theme that Napier refers to in *The Song of the Vineyard* (1962) as "the etiology of etologies": alienation, which he offers as the explanation for distorted, aborted creation. Unlike the book of Job, "Come Sweet Death" is an antitheodicy. The anthropocentric poem allows an exile to justify his annoyance with "a godforsaken, catastrophic mess" he calls "Yahweh's yo-yo," begging God to cut the string for good.

All remorse, repentance, and humility is absent on the speaker's part, as evident in a typically sarcastic remark: "Congratulations, God and Man. Well done." However, the offensive position is only a mask for the speaker's fear. He admits to being scared, armed with nothing more than "puny theological peashooters," such as the claim that God is responsible because he started the whole thing by electing and creating a people and establishing a covenant.

The speaker can no longer accept the yet-to-be-fulfilled covenant: God promised to bless and multiply his people, and yet the world is broken and humanity is full of hate. Because this season of personal despair feels universal, the speaker assumes that the horrific present is the consummation of history, and as a universal finale, it has fallen flat.

Although he is accused of being an extremely harsh judge, Napier's God is an active listener, incredibly tolerant and responsive to the accusations levied line after line by his accuser, of whom God says: "I hear the Adversary coming now./ A busy and ambitious Son of God." The man asks for a word with God, adding, "Now hold your fire, let me finish—Sir," and continues to enumerate God's misdemeanors for several more stanzas without interruption.

The narrative free verse uses obvious end rhymes to accentuate the dark humor in the present absurdity: "remnant-maker" and "drown the taker"; "unsteady" with "too heady"; "weapon and palm" with "Vietnam." Admittedly, the profound level of discourse found in Job is hard to equal. Napier's quintet relies on clever connections and sarcasm for effect: "Eden schmeeden/ tillit schmillit." "Suffering Lord and gentle

Schemer,/ here's the dream—you be the Dreamer." The visual form is important in the fourth part on the tower; the initial quatrains are funneled into a V-shape as if descending toward or burrowing into earth, while the final quatrains are inverted, assuming the form of a tower rising toward heaven.

Christian Themes

Come Sweet Death is a case study of a desperate people in need of a Redeemer, or at least a miracle, without specifying a deus ex machina. The speaker's complaint is resonant with the Hebrews' charge that God took them out of Egypt to die in the wilderness, a violation of the binding covenant established between the elector and electee.

The embittered Adversary sneers that following God is only easy for fundamentalists who simply respond to an altar call and then live happily ever after. In his view, people are proud and rebellious, and God is bemused, and suspected of being ill, asleep, or dead.

Although the conversation is between a man and God, the subtext is also about relationships among people. Whether they are facing God or a neighbor, people are "estranged, embittered, lonely." The poem describes a world of Babel that has produced J. D. Salinger, Jean-Paul Sartre, Bertolt Brecht, and Edward Albee—writers who expose how "wordless words" fail to communicate. The citizens of Babel have lost Logos as well as language. The speaker taunts: "O come, O come Immanuel/ and ransom captive, Wordless Israel."

In turning to God as a last resort, the speaker plays out the call and response of Abraham. In *The Song of the Vineyard*, Napier argues that once a land is possessed and named, it is lost, which explains why his persona is finally satisfied with the promise of what seems to be a "never-never land," which is actually a future-but-present land that only faith can make present. Babels fall; only God can form and continually uphold a community.

In part 3, the "sweet death" is scorned as a "macabre" and "bloody crucifixion." In part 5, section 9, a portrait of faith emerges as Abram is transformed into the faithful Abraham. Finally, in section 10, the full articulation of "come sweet death" is pronounced with a serenity facilitated by a humble, receptive posture.

The crucifixion is mirrored in the speaker's resolution to die to the "ancient land" and enter "the Land." By his acquiescence, the speaker attests that his own misguided will is responsible for placing Jesus on the cross, requiring his daily repentance. Confessing his need to put his proud will to death on a daily basis, he submits: "Come fresh again, sweet death, in us." Like Abraham, we cannot possibly understand this, but we can continue to inherit and re-create this promise afresh.

Sources for Further Study

"Napier, B(unyan) Davie." *Contemporary Authors: New Revision Series*. Vol. 4. Detroit: Gale Research Group, 1981. A short biography of the author, listing his published works. Bibliography.

Napier, Bunyan Davie. *From Faith to Faith: Essays on Old Testament Literature.* New York: Harper, 1955. Five essays demonstrate the essential unity of the Old Testament; the first treats brokenness in Genesis 1-11, and the second considers Abraham's faith as counterpart.

_____. "On Creation—Faith in the Old Testament: A Survey." *Interpretation* 16, no. 1 (January, 1962): 21-42. God shaped preexistent chaos into Creation and formed slaves into his elect people, which, Napier argues, shows that Creation substantiates God's saving power.

_____. *Prophets in Perspective.* Nashville, Tenn.: Abingdon Press, 1963. Napier draws on Gerhard von Rad's research in his 120-page study that examines the prophetic giants who proclaimed God's plan to judge and then redeem Israel and the world.

_____. *Song of the Vineyard: A Guide Through the Old Testament.* Rev. ed. Philadelphia: Fortress Press, 1981. An inductive introduction to the Bible's literary, historical, and theological meaning in the life and faith of ancient Israel and the present state. Brief bibliography, detailed indexes.

Pam Fox Kuhlken

THE COMING OF THE COSMIC CHRIST
The Healing of Mother Earth and the
Birth of a Global Renaissance

Author: Matthew Fox (1940-   )
First published: San Francisco: Harper & Row, 1988
Genre: Nonfiction
Subgenres: Meditation and contemplation; theology
Core issues: Jesus Christ; mysticism; wisdom

Fox makes a case for mysticism that unfolds a spiritual path for humans to experience God's grace across traditional barriers of culture, race, religion, and gender. He reiterates the importance of both male and female principles in celebrating the complete human being and notes the need for a global awakening that seeks wisdom and understanding as proof of God's presence in his creation. The mystical experiences of Christ include the full cycle of events from his death on the cross to his resurrection as the ruler of the universe and the embodiment of divine wisdom.

Overview

In *The Coming of the Cosmic Christ*, Matthew Fox addresses mysticism as an essential part of spirituality and Christian faith. The prologue, "A Dream and a Vision for a Global Renaissance," underscores the importance of the language of mysticism in communicating spiritual matters beyond physical reality.

The book is organized into six parts with several subheadings. Each begins with quotations or citations from the Bible and writers who have captured the ecstasy of experiential mysticism in their works, including Christian saints (such as Hildegard von Bingen and Thomas Aquinas), poets (such as Jalāl al-Dīn Rūmī, Kabir, and Walt Whitman), and other writers (such as Henry David Thoreau and Dorothea Soelle). At the end, an epilogue sums up the book's ecumenical scope. It relates a dream about the Third World nations and the United Nations' plans to prepare for the year 2000 as a jubilee year, when spiritual leaders from both West and East will gain appreciation for cosmic wisdom in their relationships. The new era will be marked with possibilities for experiential mysticism and excitement and will dismantle the institutions of abusive power. Old divisions of race, gender, and culture—often promoted through religion—will cease to exist.

In part 1, Fox interprets the Crucifixion story in a modern global context by using Mother Earth to represent the primal elements of humanity, which are threatened in many ways. He then shows how separation from the primitive cultures and primeval elements of religion deprives humanity of "Mother Love." He adds that universal wisdom is dying along with native peoples, their religions, and their cultures.

In part 2, Fox describes mysticism as the expression of renewal and resurrection for our times. He deplores the rise of pseudomysticism in Christianity, which separates the mystical experience from the natural state of a living creature. Taking a more inclusive approach to mysticism, he suggests "twenty-one experiential definitions of mysticism" that embrace the changing conditions of human life and cultural diversity without losing the balance between the parts and the whole being through universal connections. Experiential mysticism resists a compartmentalized approach, blends human reasoning with emotional understanding, includes both the right and the left brain, and resists reductive visions. Fox refers to the historical Jesus as a mystic, a storyteller whose preferred form of teaching through parables encouraged his followers to seek wisdom by connecting natural contexts to spiritual understanding.

In part 3, Fox shows that a quest for the Cosmic Christ requires a paradigm shift: a search for the renewal of fixed traditions of the past, traditions that have promoted exclusion based on gender, race, culture, and religious differences. This paradigm shift is necessary to understand various biblical references to the Cosmic Christ as the ruler of the universe and the embodiment of the wisdom of all world religions.

In part 4, Fox takes a close look at the Cosmic Christ's role as the redeemer of humankind in the "Third Millennium of Christianity." Christ's suffering, crucifixion, and resurrection represent the mystery of faith that connects the human condition to the power of divine will and word. Fox proposes that pain and suffering are an inevitable part of human life on earth; however, sensitivity to pain not only teaches compassion but also leads to a realization of the need to explore possibilities for relief from pain through creative means. The Cosmic Christ is the mediator between God the Creator and his creation, especially human beings. The Cosmic Christ inspires creativity among humans and restores the connection between mind and heart through spiritual experiences. His divine wisdom shows new connections between world religions that have remained distant and unexplored because of factionalism based on cultural differences. Instead of promoting anthropocentrism and rationalism, the Cosmic Christ moves religion toward spirituality, from rationalism to mysticism, from asceticism to the aesthetic, for art, like science, is transcultural.

In part 5, Fox concludes with an optimistic vision for a global renaissance and the beginning of a healing process with the Second Coming of the Cosmic Christ, when deep divisions will give in to deep ecumenism. This transformation will require a change in human outlook and a new worldview. For example, as a starting point, Fox refers to sex as a topic that must be dissociated from a negative frame and reconnected to its primal roots of a mystical experience of love. Sexual love must be part of a cosmic context in which justice becomes the ultimate test of mystical experience. Fox acknowledges the complexity of connecting sexuality and questions of justice, but the key is to take a balanced approach through a sacramental stance; there is a need to learn how to embody the sacred and the physical together again in human relations.

The book concludes with three appendixes. Appendix A contains the text of an apology to Native Congregations by the United Church of Canada. Appendix B includes a joint letter of apology to Tribal Councils of Indians and Eskimos of the Northwest. Appendix C is an apology for "religious imperialism" to the Indian Community

of the United Church of Christ by the United Church of Christ, which expresses penitence and hope for reconciliation. Appendix D is a litany of deliverance from patriarchy that separates parts from the cosmic whole.

Christian Themes

Fox's reference to Mother Earth furnishes a powerful image for a creation-centered
theology; it is also an acknowledgment of the significance of the maternal attributes
of God, who has traditionally been imaged as a male patriarch. Fox argues for a theology that embraces maternal love as a sustaining force in God's creation on earth. He
begins with the ecological surroundings of humans and connects Mother Earth to the
process of renewal and new birth. He regrets Western societies' emphasis on science
and rationalism and their disregard for the role of mysticism in natural phenomena,
which underscores unity and interconnectedness in God's creation. Since reverence
to Mother Earth is lacking, humans have abandoned Mother Earth to a painful condition of toxic contamination. "The maternal is the place of new birth" and new beginnings, but instead of connecting to the possibilities for a healthy and wholesome future, humans are inflicting pain on Mother Earth by polluting the holy water, which is
symbolic of spiritual rebirth during baptism.

Fox describes the historical Christ as a mystic who would retreat to quiet places for
prayer. Christ fasted in the wilderness for forty days and overcame Satan's temptation.
His miracles are evidence of his human compassion, but as a mystic he also knows
God's will and carries it out to the point of death. However, his death was an apocalyptic event, culminating in his resurrection with the promise of his Second Coming.

Fox aims to revive the experiential mysticism of the early Christian saints and martyrs; he contrasts it with modern pseudomysticism (found in nationalism, consumerism, asceticism, and fundamentalism), which "lacks integrality of justice," promotes
divisions, and is deficient in the prophetic energy and ecumenical wisdom of the Cosmic Christ.

Sources for Further Study

Fox, Matthew. *Creativity*. New York: Penguin, 2002. After breaking away from the
Roman Catholic Church, Matthew Fox became the founder and president of the
University of Creation Spirituality and serves as an Episcopalian priest. This book
reiterates his argument for combatting the ecological and spiritual crisis. He sug-
gests that humans need to assume the role of co-creators to preserve and to enjoy
God's creation.

_____. *A New Reformation: Creation Spirituality and the Transformation of
Christianity*. Rochester, Vt.: Inner Traditions, 2006. This book includes Fox's
ninety-five theses that Fox nailed to the church door in Wittenberg, Frankfurt, Germany. He emulated Martin Luther (who in 1519 had nailed his ninety-five theses
on the same church door). The ideas expressed in Fox's theses have already appeared in his books: for example, "Religion is not necessary, but spirituality is"
(Thesis 11) and "Cosmos is God's only temple and our holy home" (Thesis 58).

_____. *One River, Many Wells: Wisdom Springing from Global Faiths.* New York: Putnam, 2000. In this book, Fox discusses the common aspects of world religions while acknowledging the diversity of sources for spiritual wisdom. He strings together excerpts from various religious books to emphasize the power of spirituality to inspire reverence for the natural order.

Mabel Khawaja

A COMPLICATED KINDNESS

Author: Miriam Toews (1964-   )
First published: Toronto: Alfred A. Knopf Canada, 2004
Genre: Novel
Subgenres: Humor; literary fiction
Core issues: Coming of age or teen life; doubt; freedom and free will; love; Menno-
nites; obedience and disobedience

*The cultural divide between a traditional Mennonite community and the much more
liberal society outside it tempts a sixteen-year-old Mennonite girl to rebel against her
religion. While leading the life of a rebel, however, she longs for the security of her
former way of life.*

Principal characters
    Nomi Nickel, a teenager living in a Mennonite community
    Tash Nickel, Nomi's older sister
    Trudie Nickel, Nomi's mother
    Ray Nickel, Nomi's father
    Hans Rosenfeldt, Nomi's uncle and a Mennonite minister
    Travis, Nomi's boyfriend
    Lydia, Nomi's best friend
    Mr. Quiring, Nomi's English teacher

Overview

Teenager Nomi Nickel's loose narrative consists of anecdotes and observations
about her Mennonite community that are often comic but that also reveal a young
woman who is struggling to cope with the sudden defiant departure from the community three years earlier of her sister Tash and her mother, Trudie. Like her mother and
sister, Nomi finds life in her traditional Mennonite town increasingly oppressive.

Although Nomi yearns to live in New York City's bohemian East Village, she lives
in the Canadian town of East Village, which is populated by a conservative branch of
the Mennonite faith. The town's economy is based on a chicken processing plant,
where most of its young people will end up working, and a museum village that reflects
the community's history of avoidance of the worldly and the modern. The reality of
working in this living history museum, however, suggests the difficulty of keeping modernity at bay. Nomi works playing the part of a traditional Mennonite villager. However, an incident in which she inadvertently sets fire to her bonnet with one of her ever-
present cigarettes demonstrates the gap between what Nomi's life as a Mennonite is
supposed to be and what it really is. Similarly, even though there are rules prohibiting
dancing, drinking, swimming, wearing jewelry, or staying up past nine o'clock, Nomi
and her friends ignore them. They are up on the latest music, and they purchase drugs

from dealers who have set up business in a trailer on the edge of town.

The most prominent among the town rebels was Nomi's adored older sister, Tash, who was the first to leave. After Tash left, her mother, Trudie, was furious that her brother, church minister Hans Rosenfeldt, may have led his niece Nomi to believe that Tash's departure for the outside world with her boyfriend has consigned her to eternal damnation. Trudie quarreled with Hans, accusing him of knowing nothing about the love that is ideally the basis of the Mennonite faith and instead establishing a punitive regime calculated to frighten and control his community. Hans, disturbed by his own brief experience with modern society during a time of youthful experimentation, is trying to shield the community from the outside world and is determined to preserve the traditional Mennonite lifestyle. Hans is a lonely, defeated man, and as a minister, he has the power to punish and exclude those who deviate from the Mennonite way. He is partly responsible for driving off his niece Tash and his sister Trudie. Hans formed an alliance with another authority figure in East Village, Nomi's English teacher, Mr. Quiring, and the pair decided to subject Trudie to a shunning.

The reader learns that Nomi's entire narrative is the fulfillment of a writing assignment for Mr. Quiring's class. By the end of this writing assignment, Nomi has disclosed to the reader and to Mr. Quiring that she knows the dark reality that has been lurking underneath her story the entire time: When her mother, Trudie, attempted to break off her secret love affair with Mr. Quiring, he denounced her to Hans, compounding his betrayal with lies about Trudie's sexual conduct with other men of the town. The hypocrisy of Mr. Quiring, his sanctimonious retaliation against Trudie, and the conspiratorial patriarchal power he and Hans assume over the women of the Nickel family are at the heart of Nomi's quarrel with her Mennonite community.

Nomi does not leave her community, but like Tash and Trudie, she struggles against all things Mennonite. She makes a major departure from the ways of her community when she acquires birth control pills in preparation for her first sexual experience with her boyfriend Travis; his loss of interest in her afterward is an abandonment that is particularly shattering in the wake of the departure of her sister and mother. Nomi engages in a kind of prostitution when she finds herself trading sex for drugs with the local drug dealer. More feelings of abandonment beset Nomi when her best friend Lydia, who is suffering from an illness that is somehow related to her upbringing in East Village, leaves for an extended stay in a distant hospital. As Tash, Trudie, Travis, and Lydia disappear from her life, all that remains is her father, Ray, a dedicated grade-school teacher and devout Mennonite. When Nomi's outrageous behavior and provocative manner of dress finally lead to an official shunning, Ray leaves town to avoid the pain of having to coldly ignore his most beloved and most dutiful daughter.

However, unlike the rest of her family, Nomi does not go away. Although Nomi packs her bags and gets in her car, she does not leave the community; she is instead filled with good memories of her childhood in East Village. Appropriating the Mennonite expectation of a family reunion in Heaven, Nomi hopes her family will one day reunite on earth. There is also a tacit hope that somehow her Mennonite community will find a way to look on the Nickel family with sympathy and understanding.

Christian Themes

One of the major themes in *A Complicated Kindness* is the practice of the ban, or shunning, common to Mennonite and related Christian communities. This form of excommunication is at the heart of what led to the breakup of the Nickel family. Originally a way to avoid bloodshed, the pacifist tactic of shunning is, as Miriam Toews's title suggests, "a complicated kindness." By excluding those who come into conflict with the community, shunning can destroy the relationship between neighbors and, as in the case of the Nickel family, cruelly divide family members.

Author Miriam Toews, who grew up in a Mennonite community, also questions the Mennonite religion as practiced by intolerant leaders such as Hans, whose conservative policies had intensified in response to the loosening and liberalizing of the larger culture in the 1970's. Hans presides zealously over a central tenet of the Mennonites, which is to remain outside the mainstream of modern life and practice self-denial and austerity in the expectation of eventual heavenly reward. The dangers of a consequent rigidity and repression, Toews suggests, may ultimately damage the integrity of the Mennonite way of life. Although the pressures of feminism and modern individualism, with its emphasis on personal choice and gratification over social obligations and family responsibilities, certainly had a role in fragmenting Nomi's family, Toews suggests that the unforgiving and controlling Mennonite community may also be responsible for the disintegration of the Nickel family and its estrangement from its community.

Even as the Mennonite community is subjected to Toews's wit and irreverence, she also affirms the aspect of the Mennonite faith that emphasizes the love of family and community. The reprobative Hans contrasts with Nomi's father, Ray, whose gentle, loving nature and devotion to his family stand for all that Nomi values about her little Mennonite town. Nomi demonstrates a similar empathic core, caring for both members of the older generation such as her lonely father and the little children in neighboring families. Rejecting the Mennonite suspicion of the worldly, Nomi counsels adherence to that side of the Mennonite faith that affirms the Christian law of love for all things, including her time on earth.

Nomi's crisis has as much to do with the evaporation of her family and the loss of her community as with the nature of the Mennonite religion; these are losses for which the liberal benefits of modernity cannot compensate. In this regard, the novel is an open dialogue with her community, in which the hope is for changes that will allow a bridge to be built between herself and her Mennonite roots.

Sources for Further Study

Birns, Margaret Boe. Review of *A Complicated Kindness*. *Canadian Ethnic Studies* 37, no. 1 (October, 2005): 163-165. Review that emphasizes the effect of the social changes of 1970's on the Mennonite community.

Herbert, Marily. *Bookclub-in-a-Box Discusses the Novel "A Complicated Kindness" by Miriam Toews*. Toronto: Bookclub-in-a-Box, 2006. Reader's guide with notes on the Mennonite religion, facts about the author, and an examination of the character of Nomi.

Shillinger, Liesl. "A Prairie Home Companion." Review of *A Complicated Kindness*. *The New York Times Book Review*, January 23, 2005, p 18. Notes the mix of irreverence and compassion in Nomi's narrative; emphasizes the sympathy Nomi expresses for her community even as she struggles against it.

Toews, Miriam. *Swing Low: A Life*. New York: Arcade, 2001. Sympathetic examination of Toews's Mennonite father, whose strict Mennonite upbringing may have made it difficult for him to treat the bipolar disorder that led to his suicide.

Williams, Zoe. "The One Who Got Away." *The Guardian*, July 24, 2004, p. 30. Includes material from an in-depth interview with Toews. Explores the novel in terms of Toews's own background as a Mennonite and her more liberal current life in Winnipeg.

Margaret Boe Birns

CONFERENCES

Author: John Cassian (c. 360-c. 435 C.E.)

First transcribed: Collationes, c. 420-429 C.E. (English translation, 1867)

Edition used: Conferences, edited by Colm Luibheid. Mahwah, N.J.: Paulist Press, 1985

Genre: Nonfiction

Subgenres: Church history; spiritual treatise; theology

Core issues: Asceticism; contemplation; monasticism; prayer; union with God

Cassian was one of the early founders of coenobitic, or communal, monasticism in southern France in the early fifth century. He spent a number of years studying monasticism in Bethlehem and with the Desert Fathers in Egypt. His Conferences provides advice and guidelines for developing and living in a monastic community in a European context. These guidelines are adaptations of his own monastic experiences.

Overview

In the early fifth century C.E., when Christianity was not only legally recognized but also the preferred religion for advancement in social and political circles in the Roman Empire, many people with only the most rudimentary knowledge of Christianity flooded into the Church. Although monasticism had long been practiced by Christians in Syria, Palestine, and Egypt, the practice had not spread to Christians in southern France where John Cassian spent the last decades of his life. Devoting oneself full-time to the practice of monastic Christianity was a new idea in the Western Roman Empire. Cassian's monastic writings, *De institutis coenobiorum* (419-426 C.E.; *The Institutes of the Coenobia*, 1894) and *Conferences*, are among the earliest writings in Latin to explain what monasticism is, what the purpose and motivation for a monastic life are, and how to organize a community centered on monastic practices.

Cassian had spent a number of years visiting and studying the lifestyles of the Egyptian Desert Fathers, each of whom struggled in his own way to find a path to God. He was convinced that such idiosyncratic patterns of fasting, harsh physical asceticism, and prayer would not help establish monasticism in southern France. What was needed was general guidance to gain the proper understanding of the monastic life as an example of living out the Christian faith. Day-to-day details about how long to pray, what prayers to say, when and how much to eat, were not Cassian's main concern. He thought all these details could be worked out as a community of like-minded individuals grew, provided each member of that community had a shared and correct understanding of the purpose and goal of the monastic life.

Cassian's twenty-four *Conferences* are retellings of his experiences during his studies with the Egyptian Desert Fathers. Each conference is retold in the name of the particular hermit with whom Cassian conversed on a specific topic. The *Conferences* take the form of interviews rather than systematic, scholarly discussions and contain general guidance on friendship, prayer, and discerning God's will as distinct from one's own will rather than precise regulations to be followed. Cassian argued that coenobitic, or communal, monasticism was the best form of monasticism, as a community could encourage individuals to follow time-tested forms of asceticism rather than to take an anything-goes attitude as sometimes was prevalent among the Egyptian hermits. Cassian considered the monastic lifestyle to be a lifelong, communally based process of spiritual growth. Only after a long period of communal monasticism should individuals even consider the eremitic life, and then only in rare cases.

Cassian thought that monastic life had a twofold goal. It taught an individual how to live spiritually as a member of community and provided a means for an individual to reach union with God through contemplative prayer that grew out of communal worship. A monastic community had a common moral aim and was able to provide support and direction for individual members.

The first conference is among the most important in that it deals with the goal or objective of a monk, movement of the soul toward God. Cassian was convinced that once that goal is properly understood, there exist a multitude of pathways to achieve it. Conferences 2 to 8 deal with various virtues that monks should try to cultivate. A sense of humility and discretion are required, otherwise the entire monastic life would be lived for human recognition and reward rather than for the sake of heaven. Conference 3 discusses the need to renounce most possessions to concentrate on the beauty of the soul rather than material things. This conference also touches on the relationship between human free will and divine grace. This topic is taken up at greater length in conference 13, in which Cassian hints that an individual can make a free choice to move toward God before any action on the part of God. Many later Christian writers considered Cassian theologically suspect because he seemed to argue that grace was not initially necessary to begin the process leading to possible union with God. A sympathetic reading of Cassian's writings on free will and grace shows that what Cassian meant was a person just starting to turn toward God might not recognize the presence of grace in the initial movement and would ascribe the decision to individual initiative. A more mature person of faith would be able to look back and recognize hints of grace from the very beginning.

Also problematic for later Christian writers is conference 17 in which Cassian discusses the conditions under which it is permissible to lie. Cassian uses as a scriptural example Rahab the Harlot in Joshua 2. Rahab hid the Israelite spies from the Canaanite soldiers and lied about their whereabouts when asked. She did so because she discerned the will of God with respect to the Israelites, not because she expected any type of reward from the Israelite spies. Cassian suggests that if a greater good is served by lying in exceptional cases, then no sin is imputed to the one who lies. Moral theologians have been arguing over this line of reasoning for centuries.

Conferences 9, 10, and 11, on prayer and perfection, form the heart of Cassian's writings. Prayer is a constant turning of the soul toward God. Gradually the mind ceases to be concerned abut anything else. This prayerful concentration, provided by God's grace, leads to a process of purification of the heart, which leads to perfection or union with God, intimations of which are possible even in this life.

Conference 20 deals with the notion of penitence and forgiveness of sins. Excessive penance, the idea that one's own sins are so numerous or serious that they are beyond even God's ability to forgive, is itself a sin. Cassian suggests one should always try to cultivate an attitude of humility and contrition of heart, coupled with a sincere determination to avoid further occasions of sin. The rest depends on God's grace.

Christian Themes

Throughout his monastic writings, *The Institutes of the Coenobia* and *Conferences*, Cassian repeatedly stresses that living a Christian life, whether monastic or lay, is a lifelong process of prayer, discernment, and mental and physical discipline. These actions will eventually lead to glimpses of union with God. Proper mental concentration in communal prayer, by using the Psalms, coupled with both a literal and a metaphorical reading of Scripture, will help purify the heart and the mind so that the human will is not mistaken for the divine will. This entire process of spiritual movement toward union with God is a result of grace that initially impels the soul. Although an individual has a moral responsibility to recognize and protect that movement, the initial impulse illustrates complete human dependence on God, from whom the initial impulse originated.

It was left to Saint Benedict of Nursia in the sixth century C.E. to lay down specific rules for how a monastic community should conduct itself. However, it was Cassian's insistence on the communal aspects of monasticism that established coenobitic monasticism throughout Western Europe.

Sources for Further Study

Merton, Thomas. *Cassian and the Fathers: Initiation into the Monastic Tradition.* New York: Liturgical Press, 2005. This volume is a printed version of lectures Thomas Merton gave to novices at Gethsemani Abbey in Kentucky in the early 1960's when Merton was novice master. Students of Merton will want to read this volume to see how Merton understood later monasticism as an offshoot of the Desert Fathers.

Ramsey, Boniface, ed. *John Cassian: The "Conferences."* Ancient Christian Writers 57. Mahwah, N.J.: Paulist Press, 1997. Ramsey provides a useful introduction to the state of Christianity in Western Europe at the beginning of the fifth century, as well as Cassian's contributions to later monastic history.

Stewart, Columba. *Cassian the Monk.* New York: Oxford University Press, 1999. Stewart discusses Cassian's somewhat controversial teachings on grace and free will. He also analyzes Cassian's contribution to Latin Christianity as a monk, a theologian, and a bishop.

Victoria Erhart

CONFESSIO AMANTIS

Author: John Gower (c. 1330-1408)
First published: 1386-1390
Edition used: The English Works of John Gower, edited, with introduction, notes, and
a glossary by G. C. Macaulay. London: Early English Text Society, 1900-1901
Genre: Poetry
Subgenres: Morality tales; narrative poetry
Core issues: Confession; contemplation; love; morality; sin and sinners

*In this long narrative poem, Gower uses the frame of a lover's confession to present
stories drawn from classical, historical, biblical, and contemporary sources. The stories provide instruction in the morality of Gower's society, which is determined by the
strictures of Christian doctrine. A tension in the morality of the poem exists in the opposing interests of nature and reason.*

> *Principal characters*
> *Amans*, the persona of poet John Gower, a lover who seeks relief
> from unrequited love
> *Confessor/Genius*, the priest of Venus who hears the confession

Overview

Although little is known about the life of John Gower, records indicate that he was
born between 1327 and 1330 into a landholding, Kentish family, associated with the
royal court while living near London, and died in 1408 as a respected poet. Gower
also had a documented friendship with another well-known London poet, Geoffrey
Chaucer.

The works of John Gower as well as those of Chaucer initiated a new tradition of
vernacular English poetry relying on a syllabic verse structure. *Confessio Amanitis* is
approximately thirty-three thousand lines, most of which are octosyllabic couplets
rhymed *aa bb cc* in the London dialect of Chaucer. Prior to the Norman Conquest of
England (1066), Old English poetry depended on a four-stress, alliterative line as its
primary organizing device. With French as the official language between the eleventh
and fourteenth centuries, the English language and its poetic forms changed dramatically. When English again gained literary currency in the late 1300's, continental influences produced in the works of Gower and Chaucer a type of poetry that employed
set syllable counts and rhyme patterns. The dialect used by these two poets became
the basis for Modern English.

Confessio Amanitis is the last of Gower's long works and the only one written in
English. Gower's two other long works are *Mirour de l'Omme* (1376-1379; mirror of
mankind), written in French, and *Vox Clamantis* (1379-1382; the voice of one crying
out), written in Latin. He began work on *Confessio Amantis* around 1386 and pub-

lished the first recension dedicated to Chaucer and Richard I in 1390. Gower published a new version of *Confessio Amantis* known as the third recension in 1392, this one dedicated to Henry of Lancaster. There is also an intermediate version that demonstrates a limited return to the original form. Of the forty-nine known manuscripts, thirty-one follow the first recension. Gower most likely oversaw the corrections to his manuscripts.

In the lengthy prologue to *Confessio Amantis*, Gower announces his intention to write a book in English that gives both pleasure and instruction to his audience. Gower uses his prologue to convey an urgent message about the present state of society, which has declined from a golden age of wealth, honor, and peace, a common theme in medieval English literature. Gower divides his complaint among the three estates of medieval society—the nobility, the clergy, and the laborers. It is clear that the lessons that follow in the body of the poem—warning against wrath, greed, and sloth, for example—apply as much to England and English society as to the lover.

In the body of the poem, the voice of the poet changes from the moralizing Gower to the love-struck Amans ("the lover") who begs Venus, the goddess of love, and her son Cupid for relief from the woe of unrequited love. Venus asks first that Amans confess his sins against love to her priest Genius, the Confessor. Amans and the Confessor engage in a dialogue that lasts through the eight books of the poem. In each book, the Confessor questions Amans about his guilt in one of the seven deadly sins (pride, envy, wrath, sloth, avarice, gluttony, and lechery) as they pertain to love. Each sin is personified and subdivided into five attendants, or aspects, of the sin. Genius typically offers one or two *exempla*, or stories, to illustrate the dangers of each aspect of the sin. Book 7 addresses "The Education of a King" and includes lessons—also illustrated through *exempla*—valuable to both rulers and lovers. The tales are drawn from contemporary, historical, biblical, and classical sources, significantly Ovid's *Metamorphoses* (c. 8 C.E.; English translation, 1567). However, in his presentation of the tales, Gower does not merely recite them as they appear in his sources but adapts his *exempla* from their original form, and using rhetoric, he guides the audience's response to his poem. The Confessor's questions and admonitions along with the lover's denials, admissions, and explanations offer a glimpse of medieval life similar to though less boisterous than that found in Chaucer.

At the end of book 8, Genius finally advises Amans to follow the path of truth, give up vain pursuits, and trade love for reason. The lover writes a letter to Venus with his tears, asking that either his lady ascent to his wooing or that Cupid remove his arrow from the man's heart. The voice of Gower returns as Genius delivers Gower's petition and he waits for a reply. Arriving before Gower, Venus declares that she acquits him of being a false lover but condemns him as an old man past the age of love. Though the revelation of Gower's age seems to come as a shock, some critics argue that the medieval audience would have known this all along because of their knowledge of Gower's life, the moralizing tone of the prologue, or Cupid's scorn for the lover. Gower immediately loses his desire for the lady and sees two processions, one of Youth and the other of Age. A debate ensues as to whether Gower is to blame for his condition or needs help. Ultimately, Cupid removes his arrow, and Venus anoints the wound, gives Gower a rosary and a final warning, and departs. After again reviewing the condition of England, Gower concludes his poem with an apology for any lack of artistry and a call for divine rather than earthly love.

Christian Themes

Confessio Amantis is not an overtly Christian poem and does not always seem to present tales that accord with a Christian sense of morality. English medieval society, however, was intensely religious, so this work cannot be dismissed as lacking in any significant treatment of Christianity.

Gower organizes his conventional courtly love poem around the seven deadly sins of Christianity. The warning to avoid behavior that falls into the category of these sins is sound Christian advice; however, the Confessor advises Amans that they will deal only with his sins as they apply to love.

Many critics view the poem as a psychomachia with the dialogue of the poem taking place between two competing aspects of Gower's consciousness, Amans and Genius, or love and reason. Throughout the confession, it becomes apparent that the sexual love found in nature does not conform to either rationality or Christian doctrine. There is an ultimate movement to subordinate the natural impulse of sex to the Christian standards of reason.

The figure of Genius as a priest of both Venus and orthodox Christianity provides tension in the morality of the poem. This dual identity puts the Confessor in the precarious position of defending incest against Christian belief as in the story of Canace and Machaire and virginity against the interest of the goddess Venus. The priest represents the opposition between the body and soul, the earthly and divine that confronts each human. In this way, the poem deals with the medieval theme of the role of Christianity within a Christian world that is still of this world. There is a mixing of the sexual and the spiritual so that natural impulses are satisfied within Christian limits. The morality that emerges is a middle ground between the extremes of nature and reason.

Ultimately, the poem concludes with a more traditionally Christian recognition by Gower that only divine love brings true and unwavering bliss to the heart that possesses it.

Sources for Further Study

Baker, Denise N. "The Priesthood of Genius: A Study of the Medieval Tradition." *Speculum* 51 (1976): 277-291. Considers Genius's dual role in the poem as both a Christian priest and a priest of Venus in the context of contemporary literature.

Echard, Siân, ed. *A Companion to Gower.* Cambridge, Mass.: D. S. Brewer, 2004. A collection of essays analyzing Gower's life and work. Includes a chronology of Gower criticism from 1778 to 2003 and an index.

Gower, John. *Confessio Amantis.* Translated by Terence Tiller. Baltimore: Penguin Books, 1963. A translation into modern English with both verse and prose summary to condense the poem into a manageable form and length for nonspecialists. Includes an informative introduction.

Mitchell, J. Allan. *Ethics and Exemplary Narrative in Chaucer and Gower*. Cambridge, Mass.: D. S. Brewer, 2004. This book examines Chaucer and Gower's use of exemplary rhetoric in the context of medieval narrative ethics. Includes bibliography and index.

Leah R. Krynicky

"CONFESSION" AND "THE NEW BIRTH"

Author: Menno Simons (1496-1561)
First published: Confession, 1554 (English translation, 1871); *Die nieuwe creatuere,* 1539 (English translation, 1871)
Edition used: "Confession of My Enlightenment, Conversion, and Calling"; The New Birth and Who They Are Who Have the Promise, translated and edited by Irvin Buckwalter Horst. Lancaster, Pa.: Lancaster Mennonite Historical Society, 1996
Genre: Nonfiction
Subgenres: Exegesis; hermeneutics; theology
Core issues: Amish people; Baptism; Communion; conversion; faith; grace; Mennonites; the Sacraments

"Confession" reports Menno's struggle with the Catholic theology and practices of Communion and baptism and his departure from the priesthood of the Catholic Church as a result. It briefly explains his transition to and life as an Anabaptist preacher as well. In "The New Birth," Menno outlines his view of the characteristics of the true Christian. Both articles were based on his study of the New Testament and were intended to explain his spiritual and theological positions on the subjects treated.

Overview

The book contains two articles and an introduction to each by the editor. The two articles are considered to be among the most important contributions made by Menno Simons, a Dutch priest and subsequently an Anabaptist preacher and an important figure in the Reformation. "Confession" was written to explain Menno's decision to leave the Catholic priesthood and to counter accusations that he was part of the extreme radical arm of the Reformation exemplified by the Anabaptist group that captured and held the German city of Münster from 1534 to 1535. "The New Birth" was written to explain the behavior that should characterize a follower of Christ and to challenge the established religious leaders with regard to their behavior.

In "Confession," Menno described his service as a Catholic priest, starting in 1524. Early in his Catholic career, it troubled him that the bread and wine used in the Communion service did not appear to change into the flesh and blood of Jesus. The Catholic Church's doctrine of transubstantiation argued that such a change took place. He tried to allay his doubts but could not escape them no matter how much he prayed. As a result, he was inspired to study the New Testament, in which he found no basis for the literal transformation.

When Menno heard that an Anabaptist was beheaded for being baptized as an adult, he studied the New Testament with regard to baptism. The word Anabaptist means "baptized again or rebaptised" and was coined to describe a loose group of Reformation activists who believed the Bible taught that baptism should come after a person had declared his or her belief in Christ, not as an infant before that decision could be made. Infant baptism was the policy and theology of the Catholic Church, and most infants were baptized. Therefore, baptism as an adult was generally a second baptism and was held to be a capital offense. Menno's study led him to agree with the Anabaptists.

As Menno searched the New Testament for information on these questions, he was also bothered by his life as a priest. He found it too comfortable and too loose morally. The Bible seemed to teach that followers of Christ should live a much more meaningful life of sacrifice, service, and moral uprightness. He explored the thoughts of Martin Luther and other leaders of the Reformation on these and other questions, and after struggling with them for some time, he began teaching his convictions while continuing to serve as a priest. Later, in 1536, about twelve years after he began his New Testament studies, he abandoned his position as a Catholic priest.

Menno used the "Confession" to refute the accusation that he was allied with the Münster Anabaptists. In 1534, an Anabaptist group took control of the German city of Münster and ruled it for about a year. Münster was freed from the Anabaptists' control in 1535, but the policies and actions of the group while controlling the city gave all Anabaptists a bad name. They embraced a number of questionable practices, including the community of goods (in which individuals turned everything they owned over to the group, for use by the group), polygamy, and violence, often killing their opponents. In refuting the accusation, Menno describes his many arguments against the Münster Anabaptists. He also outlines the events leading to his association with the Anabaptists as follows. Shortly after he left the priesthood, members of a group not associated with Münster in any way asked him to take a leadership role with them. After considerable discussion, prayer, and meditation, he agreed and was ordained as an Anabaptist preacher, probably in late 1536.

In the final part of the "Confession," he describes his life as an Anabaptist preacher, including the lack of resources and prestige, and the danger of persecution and death because of his beliefs. He spent much of his Anabaptist life hiding from authorities. Still, he declares his primary concern to be the salvation of those he taught and his satisfaction with his position in the center of God's will.

"The New Birth" describes what Menno believed were the characteristics of the true Christian and contrasts them with the characteristics of the majority of professing Christians of his day. The New Testament compares Christian salvation to a second birth, hence the "new birth" terminology. Menno says that salvation is attained through faith in Jesus Christ and given by the grace of God, not earned by human behavior. However, he also argues that true Christians will demonstrate their faith and salvation by their behavior. That behavior includes honesty, sobriety, faithfulness to one's spouse, charity to those in need, repaying evil with good, nonviolence, the baptism of believing adults, use of Communion as a symbolic reminder of Christ's suffering, and separation from those who behave otherwise. He argues that professing Christians who do not demonstrate these behaviors are not among those "who have the promise."

Christian Themes

In these two papers, Menno challenged the church of his day on many of the fundamental issues that have been debated throughout church history. His beliefs include that the Bible is the word of God and should be literally applied as instructions for Christian life and that baptism is for believers on confession of faith, not for infants who could make no such confession. The bread and wine of the Communion are symbols of the body and blood of Jesus, not literally converted into such during Communion. Salvation is not earned but granted by the grace of God, dependant only on the faith of the believer and not earned in any other way. However, true believers demonstrate their faith by living as they are commanded to live in the writings of the New Testament. Those who profess belief but live in opposition to the principles taught in the New Testament are not Christians at all and have no claim on the promises made to Christians.

The principles espoused by Menno in these and other works were embraced by some Anabaptists, who later identified themselves as Mennonites in honor of Menno. The Mennonites disagreed on the interpretation of these and other issues and split repeatedly. In one of these splits, in 1693, Jacob Amman and his followers separated from the Mennonites to form the Amish community. One question leading to the split was that of separation from the world and maintenance of a simple life more or less free of worldly technology. Subsequently, the Amish split into several groups, the most fundamental of which still reject or restrict the use of many modern conveniences (such as automobiles, televisions, and telephones) to maintain their separation from the world and proximity to God. The Christian themes of forgiveness and repaying evil with good were profoundly demonstrated by a Pennsylvania Amish group in 2006. A non-Amish man took ten Amish schoolgirls hostage. He shot all of them, killing some and seriously injuring the others, then shot and killed himself. The response of the relatives of the dead and injured girls was to forgive the perpetrator and to pray for him and his relatives. The principles and spirit of the "Confession" and "The New Birth" were still affecting lives four and one half centuries after they were written.

Sources for Further Study

Goertz, Hans-Jurgen. *The Anabaptists*. Translated and revised by Trevor Johnson. New York: Routledge, 1996. Sets the historical stage for Menno Simons and his writings. Includes a table that outlines the chronology of the Anabaptists' early years.

Kraybill, Donald B. *Who Are the Anabaptists?* Scottdale, Pa.: Herald Press, 2003. A brief history of the Anabaptist movement and its offspring groups, the Hutterites, Brethren, Mennonites, and Amish.

Menno Simons. *The Complete Works of Menno Simons*. LaGrange, Ind.: Pathway, 1983. Contains alternate translations of the two papers considered here. Lends itself to a complete study of all Menno's written ideas.

Urry, James. *Mennonites, Politics, and Peoplehood.* Winnipeg: University of Manitoba Press, 2006. Traces the development of the organizations most closely linked to Menno Simons's name, the Mennonite churches.

Voolstra, Sjouke. *Menno Simons: His Image and Message.* Newton, Kans.: Mennonite Press, 1997. Considers the contributions of Menno Simons to theology and his place in religious history.

Carl W. Hoagstrom

CONFESSIONS

Author: Saint Augustine (354-430 C.E.)

First transcribed: Confessiones, 397-400 C.E. (English translation, 1620)

Edition used: Confessions, translated by R. S. Pine-Coffin. New York: Penguin Books, 1961

Genre: Nonfiction

Subgenres: Autobiography; spiritual treatise

Core issues: Confession; conversion; faith

One of the doctors of the Catholic Church, Saint Augustine was raised a Christian but resisted participation in life from that perspective for many years. His mother, Saint Monica, nurtured him in the faith as best she could in spite of his mistresses (one of whom bore him a son), his attraction to generally pagan learning, and later his immersion in heretical (Manichaean) religions. A professor and author in his early thirties, Augustine encountered Saint Ambrose in Milan, converted to orthodoxy, and was baptized. He later became a priest, then bishop of Hippo. Confessions is the first, and some will consider the greatest, of autobiographies as we know them in the modern sense.

Overview

Books 1 through 9 of Saint Augustine's *Confessions* are a kind of backward reflection, covering the period from the author's birth to his religious conversion to Christianity. In books 10 through 12, Augustine no longer tells us about his past life but exercises a theological inquiry into memory, time, and creation. The final chapter, book 13, is also on the creation theme but as a confession to God, in rather direct style, of his faith.

Augustine begins by wondering whether one should first pray to God for help or to praise him and whether a person must first know God before calling on him for aid. In humility the author asks if there is something in himself that is fit to contain the infinite God. Also, he asks, why does God show such concern for this finite person? We learn that Augustine came from a household of believers (with the exception of his father) and learning was an important aspect of his early life. However, we read of what Augustine considers the sins he committed as a baby: crying too much over insignificant things, being selfish, and experiencing jealousy. Later he sinned by disobeying his parents. Even when his learning went well, he was guilty of more concern over the fate of characters in classic literature than in the state of his own soul. In games he cheated to win and asks, ironically, if this is the innocence of childhood. His sin, he concludes, was in looking for pleasure, beauty, and truth not in God but in himself.

In the second book Augustine confesses two failings, lust and thievery. He admits to having run wild sexually, because he could not distinguish between true love and mere casual sexuality. He thinks that he should have listened more carefully to the scriptural admonition that he who is married will be more concerned with pleasing a wife than with God's claim. His lust gripped him in his sixteenth year and was to trouble him for some time to come. The youth apparently had it too easy, partly because his father provided for too many of his wants, caring more for his son's earthly success than for his spiritual growth. As for stealing, Augustine tells of robbing from a pear tree near his family's property, glorying not in the eating of the fruit but in doing that which was forbidden.

In book 3 we learn that the narrator moved to Carthage and found himself "in the midst of a hissing cauldron of lust." Friendship became perverted by lewdness and then, caught in "a snare of my own choosing," he fell in love. This led to jealousy, fear, anger, and quarreling. At the same time the theater, looked on with great suspicion by the Church, attracted him. Yet in the midst of this, Augustine recognizes that God watched over him faithfully. While pursuing his ambition to be a good speaker, Augustine was introduced to the work of Cicero, and this encounter with the pagan writer had an enormous impact on the future saint. It altered his prayers, and his search turned from empty dreams to the "passion for the wisdom of eternal truth." With the financial support of his mother, his father having died two years previously, when Augustine was seventeen, he pursued the study of Scripture with something beyond the understanding of the proud. The youth kept to many of his bad habits, however, but his mother, Monica (later to be canonized as a saint), prayed for him unceasingly, particularly after a dream that consoled her about her son and after a bishop told her to persevere in her prayers and they would be answered.

The years from age nineteen to twenty-eight are the time span covered in book 4. During this period, Augustine taught the art of public speaking. It was a time, he writes, when he was led astray and when he led others astray as well. He also had a mistress then, whom he does not name, and she was his only lover at the time—he remained faithful to her. As a writer his skills developed, and he won a poetry competition while flirting with astrology, which he later dropped. The severe illness of a friend was the cause of much reflection for Augustine. What baptism meant to the ill young man impressed the author deeply, and when the friend died, Augustine became frightened in contemplating his own end. This did not keep him from writing a multivolume work he called *Beauty and Proportion*, the manuscript of which was lost and never recovered. Some thoughts on those topics, however, are shared with the reader of the *Confessions*. Among the conclusions is Augustine's notion that in goodness, there is unity, but in evil, some kind of disunion.

The next segment of the *Confessions* represents the autobiographer's twenty-ninth year, a time when he was drawn ever closer to God. Initially his interest was in Manichaean theology. (Mani, the founder of this heretical sect, advocated a dualistic doctrine that regarded matter as evil, the spirit as good.) For nearly nine years, Augustine had hoped to hear Faustus, the Manichaean bishop of great reputation, develop the theory of Mani. When at last the opportunity came, great disappointment accompanied the event. "He was a great decoy of the devil," Augustine decided, one who was able to win disciples through charm rather than reason, his scholarship being very weak.

After this experience, Augustine decided to teach in Rome, and he left Carthage. On arrival in his new home, he became very ill but still had no desire to be baptized. On recovery, he began teaching literature and public speaking but later applied for work in Milan where he met Bishop Ambrose, who was to have a profoundly positive impact on him. Augustine's interest in the Church grew, and he became a catechumen but chose not to go beyond that preparatory step at that time.

The faith and faithfulness of Augustine's mother is told in book 6. Her remarkable devotion to her son is indicated, as is the influence of Bishop Ambrose, which was hinted at in the previous chapter. Augustine went to hear the great preacher every Sunday, and he came to realize that the web of deception woven around him by others could be broken. "From now on I began to prefer the Catholic teaching." However, there was no instantaneous change in Augustine's habits. He calls himself eager for fame, wealth, and marriage. An obstacle to this last was his mistress, who left him, with their son, vowing to accept the affections of no other man as she returned to Africa. Now thirty, Augustine was increasingly attracted to the Church, "But not so fast! This life is too Sweet." So Augustine prepared to marry; his proposal was accepted, but the nuptials were put off for two years. Returning at least in part to his old ways, he took another mistress.

The author recognizes in the next book that his adolescence was gone and he was approaching maturity, yet his behavior grew more disgraceful and his self-delusion greater. From such introductory remarks, Augustine makes the transition to a discussion of the nature of evil, concluding that evil is the absence of good, and not caused by God. As this segment ends, Augustine tells how he was slowly being drawn into Christ's orbit, particularly through intensive reading of the Scriptures.

The story of the episode that finally led to Augustine's total embracing of Christianity comes in book 8. He writes of the influence that he felt from talking with Ambrose's spiritual father, Simplicianus. Augustine was moved, too, in reading the story of Saint Anthony, the Egyptian monk who struggled so long and successfully to remain chaste, a condition the narrator admits to having approached this way in prayer: "Give me chastity and continence, but not yet." A terrific struggle, sometimes manifesting itself physically, took place in Augustine as he seemed to undergo a spiritual tug-of-war for his soul's commitment. He got to the point where he tore his hair, hammered his forehead with his fists, and the like. The future saint was at once both attracted to heaven and resisting the call. The final push came when he randomly opened up a book containing the epistles of Saint Paul and read the first lines his eyes fell on, lines counseling against reveling and drunkenness. Needing no further sign, Augustine rushed to tell his mother of his newfound strength in faith, much to Monica's great joy.

Book 9 may be considered the last chapter of the first—and considerably longest—section of the *Confessions*. Here Augustine describes his surrender to God: through Ambrose, through the Scriptures, and through like-minded companions who were baptized into the faith as Augustine was. This proved an emotionally overwhelming experience for him. He also tells of particular miracles: of Ambrose's vision telling him where the uncorrupted bodies of two holy martyrs were to be located and how these "relics" were the occasion of cures of various physical maladies for a number of persons. While once again praising the virtues of his mother—who, like other good women of that era, understood her subservient role to her husband (master, according to the author)—Augustine renders a quite unflattering description of his father. However, the writer believes that through the efforts of the former, who died at age fifty-six, the latter was "won" for Christ.

There appears to be quite a break in the Augustinian technique beginning with book 10. The emphasis now is not so much on what happened but on examining what certain experiences might mean. What is God? he asks, having searched among all the things of the earth, the sea, the chasms of the deep, even into himself. The conclusion is that "He is the Life of the life of my soul." Then comes a relatively long reflection on memory, where Augustine sees all as being preserved separately, according to category. He marvels at this ability to store up enormous treasures of knowledge and the senses, even suggesting that certain things must have been in his mind even before he had learned them. However, God lies beyond memory, in himself, above us, because "You are Truth." God's existence is not established by logic but must be accepted as a premise. Augustine asks the question why it is that when he preaches truth it sometimes engenders hostility, "although men love happiness which is simply the enjoyment of truth"? He decides that we love what is not true by pretending that it is.

One of the best-known sections of the *Confessions* is next, containing the author's attempt to come to grips with the idea of time. He is moved to deal with this question because the Bible mentions creation but does not say what came before it. He concludes that time is nothing except in relation to temporal events.

Books 12 and 13 both contain analyses of creation with a look also, into the validity of the Scriptures. Most of Augustine's efforts here are concentrated on the opening of Genesis. Yet the two chapters are quite different in approach. In the first part of this volume (1-9), the author describes his life as if he were an objective viewer, almost another person looking in on himself. In the next part (10-12), the narrator and the person whose life is being retold are one. The final section (13) still finds the "two Augustines," but the tone here is considerably altered. As critics have observed, the writer is no longer presented as one in pursuit of a heavenly goal but rather as one who communicates and confesses to God directly his own understanding that faith is wisdom. The entire volume leads to this final point. Some have suggested that the last book, perhaps even the final four, was appended to Augustine's work in later editions. However, the lack of unity of tone and voice is diminished in importance when the unity of approach leading up to the final confession of faith is noted.

Christian Themes

Saint Augustine focuses on three major themes in his autobiography: the nature of evil, time, and wisdom. According to Saint Augustine, God cannot be the cause of evil. For God, he says, "evil does not exist." Evil is a lack, an absence of good. Anything that has substance is good, therefore evil can have no substance. Furthermore, anyone who finds fault with any portion of God's creation is bereft of reason. They fail to comprehend that wickedness is not a substance but a perversion.

Saint Augustine addresses the nature of time because in the Bible the concept of creation out of nothing is revealed. This, some had said, raised the issue of an absolute beginning, something that human experience simply could not conceive. (What happened before the creation always comes to mind.) Augustine responded by explaining that time does not have the same kind of being as events that occur in time. It is appropriate to ask particular questions about a sequence of events but not what happened before all events. Time, he observed, has no substantiality outside of its relation to temporal events. Time is nothing except in relation to temporal events.

Much of Saint Augustine's life was involved in what he saw as a search for "the wisdom of eternal truth." He spends years pursuing this wisdom while encountering doubt and temptation. He also is disappointed by the Manichaeans, whom he regards as lacking in wisdom. Gradually he comes to the understanding that faith is wisdom, and all values stem from God.

Sources for Further Study

Clark, Mary T. *Augustine*. 1994. Reprint. New York: Continuum, 2005. A biography of the saint that deals with the theology of the saint and the early church.

Matthews, Gareth B. *Augustine*. Malden, Mass.: Blackwell, 2005. This work, part of the Blackwell Great Minds series, looks at questions such as Augustine's thoughts on time and creation. Focuses on his theology.

O'Donnell, James Joseph. *Augustine, Sinner and Saint: A New Biography*. London: Profile Books, 2005. This biography of Saint Augustine contains a chapter on the *Confessions*.

TeSelle, Eugene. *Augustine*. Nashville, Tenn.: Abingdon Press, 2006. This biography, part of the Abington Pillars of Theology series, deals with Saint Augustine's life and theology.

Harry James Cargas

THE CONFESSIONS OF NAT TURNER

Author: William Styron (1925-   )
First published: 1967
Edition used: The Confessions of Nat Turner. First vintage international edition. New York: Vintage Books, 1993
Genre: Novel
Subgenre: Historical fiction (nineteenth century)
Core issues: African Americans; atheism; homosexuality; redemption; scriptures; social action

The Confessions of Nat Turner, *which Styron in a prefatory note calls a "meditation on history," is a highly fictional account of Nat Turner, who organized and led the only successful slave rebellion in U.S. history. Although set in Virginia in 1831, the novel serves as a 1960's timepiece because of its controversial depiction of the slave Nat Turner and its embedded social commentary about race relations.*

> *Principal characters*
> *Nat Turner*, the protagonist, a self-ordained minister of the slaves
> *Thomas Gray*, lawyer and magistrate who elicits the confessions
> *Hark*, fellow slave and Turner's first in command,
> *Samuel Turner*, Nat Turner's first owner
> *Reverend Alexander Eppes*, an intermediary guardian of Turner
> *Thomas Moore*, Turner's second owner
> *Joseph Travis*, Turner's third owner
> *Catherine Whitehead*, owner of neighboring plantation who hires Turner,
> *Margaret Whitehead*, Catherine's young daughter and the only person killed by Turner during the rebellion
> *Willis*, young slave with whom Turner has a homosexual encounter
> *Ethelrad T. Brantley*, a white homosexual whom Turner baptizes
> *Jeremiah Cobb*, judge at Turner's trial

Overview

William Styron's *The Confessions of Nat Turner* is a lengthy book organized into four chapters, three of which take biblical allusions for titles. In the opening chapter, "Judgment Day," the attempted rebellion has already occurred, and Turner and his fellow slave friend (and second in command) Hark have been imprisoned and are awaiting trial and the inevitable hanging. Turner is tormented by his inability to pray or read the Bible, two matters that Thomas Gray, an atheist lawyer and magistrate, uses to coax Turner into making his "confessions." Styron constructs an imagined dialogue between Turner and Gray, which turns into something of a personal debate between Christian belief and atheism. Turner is tormented, not knowing why the rebellion ultimately failed if God were indeed on his side; and Gray successfully transforms these doubts into proof that the black race is inferior and that, as he says several times in refrain, "[N]igger slavery is going to last a thousand years."

The second chapter, "Old Times Past: Voices, Dreams, Recollections," is essentially a fictional biography of Turner. Styron takes the bare facts of Turner's life and embellishes them with relentless and bountiful license. This account of Turner's life records the horrors of slavery in the context of his family history and his life under his four owners. Styron also gives readers imagined insight into Turner's spiritual development, beginning with his teaching himself to read and then his relentless study of the Bible. Fascinated most centrally with the prophets of the Old Testament, particularly Ezekiel, Turner comes to fancy himself a prophet whose God-appointed destiny is to lead his people out of bondage. This section records one of the most controversial scenes in the novel, as Styron creates a homosexual relationship between Turner and Willis, another young slave on Samuel Turner's plantation. After their first encounter, Turner baptizes Willis.

"Study War," the longest chapter of the book, records concocted details of the actual rebellion itself. Replete with an endless number of quotations from the Old Testament prophets, it shows Turner transforming himself into a modern-day Ezekiel—one who has visions, receives signs from God, meditates on his actions, and fasts to prove himself fit for what he believes to be God's mission: to start a rebellion and murder every white person possible. Again, Styron rarely departs from what he calls the "known facts" of the rebellion in which 55 white people were killed and subsequent to which 131 black people were killed by white people in fear and retaliation. Of the rebellion itself, Turner's participation as leader is portrayed as weak and ineffectual; he himself is initially unable to kill, and the one person he does kill, Margaret Whitehead, is symbolically the white, innocent virgin who actually has been kind to Turner and is the only white person to treat him with decency and respect.

The shortest and final chapter, "It Is Done," echoes the words of Jesus on the cross when he utters, "It is finished," shortly before his death. Styron returns here to the debate between Gray and Turner in the first chapter, where the seeming subject is the success or failure of the rebellion, but the actual subject is the struggle between belief and atheism. Turner broods about his actions, not sure whether he was carrying out the will of God or of himself in conducting the insurrection. Being a rational creature, Gray overwhelms Turner in his argument but still does not crush his will.

Christian Themes

Central to Nat Turner's mission is the question of how one can distinguish between the will of God and the will of the self. Turner becomes first a self-appointed minister of God and then a self-ordained prophet of God—that is, the God of the Old Testament. It is only logical and natural that the slaves of the American Old South would identify forcefully with the Israelites as slaves in Egypt, but Turner seldom reflects on this comparison. Rather, he focuses on the Old Testament prophets Ezekiel and Jeremiah and broods on references to the Babylonian Captivity and the Apocalypse. In so doing he chooses destruction and damnation rather than progress and salvation.

Turner is left at the end in a totally ambiguous dilemma: Can he be redeemed and forgiven of his sins (the responsibility for the deaths of some two hundred persons, white and black alike) or is he eternally damned for them? He is unable to make peace with this question, because to receive forgiveness from God presumably he would have to admit that he was acting of his own will and volition in carrying out the atrocities and that God had never directed him to take these actions. The lawyer Gray repeatedly points out that if God had given his blessings to the insurrection, it would surely have succeeded. Whereas, its failure is manifest proof that God was not involved. Hence, Turner is left in a fixed state, like limbo, of denial paired with an attempt at belief. He is unable to pray and read the Bible as he approaches his execution. Moreover, Gray's atheism seems to triumph in trouncing Turner's belief.

Also of importance here is the issue of social action: How does a Christian fight against the evils of an institution so inherently wicked as slavery? Does God want Turner to kill its perpetrators to eliminate it? Or should he stay within the system to fight against it with whatever effect he can muster? It is the choice of understanding Jesus as the God who drove the money changers out of the temple or as the preacher who delivered the Sermon on the Mount. Styron's novel raises this question but does not attempt to answer it. Finally, Turner will simply be hanged.

Sources for Further Study

Clarke, John Henrik, ed. *William Styron's Nat Turner: Ten Black Writers Respond.* Boston: Beacon Press, 1968. A collection of articles by ten black critics that appeared one year after the publication of the novel. Most take Styron to task for his characterization of Turner as a weak and ineffectual man with homosexual proclivities.

French, Scott. *The Rebellious Slave: The Image of Nat Turner in American Memory.* New York: Houghton Mifflin, 2004. This scholarly study places Nat Turner and the rebellion he led within the broader context of American history. It includes the actual document of the "Confessions," which Turner supposedly wrote.

Greenberg, Kenneth S., ed. *The Confessions of Nat Turner, and Related Documents.* Boston: Bedford Books of St. Martin's Press, 1996. These documents and essays emphasize the historical context of the novel and provide much information about other attempted slave rebellions.

_____. *Nat Turner: A Slave Rebellion in History and Memory.* New York: Oxford University Press, 2003. A collection of sundry critical essays by various scholars of literature and history, one of which is an interview with Styron.

Herion-Sarafidis, Elisabeth. *Mode of Melancholy: A Study of William Styron's Novels.* Uppsala, Sweden: Uppsala University Press, 1995. One chapter of this study is devoted to *The Confessions of Nat Turner.* The critic interprets the novel in a broad context of the author's biographical psychology.

Oates, Stephen B. *The Fires of Jubilee: Nat Turner's Fierce Rebellion.* New York: HarperCollins, 1990. While this work has little to do with Styron's novel, it does chronicle actual known, historical events of the uprising that can be set against the fictional account in the novel.

Carl Singleton

CONSTANTINE'S SWORD
The Church and the Jews, a History

Author: James Carroll (1943-   )
First published: Boston: Houghton Mifflin, 2001
Genre: Nonfiction
Subgenres: Church history; history; theology
Core issues: Catholics and Catholicism; guilt; Judaism; persecution; racism

The issue of Catholic responsibility for the Nazi mass murder of Jews during World War II has been a contentious one. In recent years, a number of authors have claimed that the Church, under the wartime leadership of Pope Pius XII, did little to save the Jews from the German death camps. Carroll retraces Christian-Jewish relations throughout the history of the Church to argue that anti-Semitism is deeply rooted in Christianity and that this anti-Semitic heritage created the conditions that made the Nazi crimes possible.

Overview

James Carroll begins *Constantine's Sword*, a history of Catholicism's treatment of Jews, with a reflection on the cross made of railroad ties erected at the Auschwitz death camp. Pope John Paul II, still alive this book was published, visited the camp in 1979 and prayed for the Catholic martyrs who died at the camp, including Edith Stein, a Jewish convert to Catholicism whom he declared a saint in 1998. During his visit to Auschwitz, the pope stated that he would like to see something established there to honor the Catholic martyrs of Auschwitz. Five years later, a group of Carmelite nuns moved into a theater at the camp's gate, fulfilling the pope's wish and intending to pray especially for Sister Teresa Benedicta, the name given to Edith Stein after she joined the Carmelite order. Many Jews responded by protesting what they saw as a Christian takeover of a place that had been dedicated primarily to the murder of Jews.

For Carroll, the story of Catholic-Jewish tensions at Auschwitz is more than a struggle over whose tragedy should be recognized. He takes the Christian emblem of the cross as a symbol of the history of the anti-Semitic trend in Christianity. During the early centuries of the Christian faith, believers began to focus on the death of Christ, represented by the cross, rather than on Christ's life and teachings. This focus on the Passion was also an early expression of hostility toward Jews, who were blamed for the death. Carroll interprets the history of the Catholic Church, including the wider history of Christianity after the Reformation, as a long series of movements in the wrong direction, ultimately ending in the Shoah, the Nazi attempt to exterminate the Jews of Europe. Throughout his examination, Carroll inserts his own memories of growing up Catholic, connecting the personal to the historical.

Christianity began within the Jewish religion at a time when this religion was redefining itself in response to pressure from the Roman Empire. One of the conflicting groups within the Jewish faith was the Pharisees, who eventually evolved into rabbinic Judaism, and another group was the followers of Jesus. Therefore, early relations between those who were becoming the Christians and those who were becoming the Jews had something of the nature of sibling rivalry. As Christianity moved away from its original Jewish base and into the broader Roman world, though, Christians tended to downplay the brutality of Rome and to emphasize their rivalry with the Jews. They did this through focusing on the story of the death of Jesus. Because the Gospels were being written at this time, their authors took the story of the Passion of Christ, with primary responsibility attributed to the Jews, as central to their religious narratives. Although Saint Paul attempted to join Christians and Jews together, in Carroll's view, Christianity came to adopt the doctrine of supersessionism, which held that the new religion of Christianity had replaced the old religion of Judaism.

Carroll identifies the reign of Emperor Constantine (324-337 C.E.) as a critical time in the history of Christianity and of church relations with the Jews. Constantine adopted the cross as his symbol and united the Roman Empire under official Christian dominance. From that time on, what became the Catholic Church had secular as well as spiritual power, and it identified itself closely with the death of Christ. Jews were defined as outside of Christendom and continually held responsible for Christ's death.

Carroll follows Christian hostility toward the Jews through the Crusades of the Middle Ages, discussing the bloody episodes when the holy wars turned against Jewish populations. He finds antagonism toward Judaism in such major thinkers as Saint Anselm and Saint Thomas Aquinas, arguing that Saint Anselm's focus on the death of Christ on the cross reinforced anti-Jewish tendencies in Christianity. The controversial Peter Abelard, with his emphasis on the life of Christ and on God's mercy and acceptance of all, is one of the few medieval figures Carroll sees in a positive light.

Although many historians have seen racist, as opposed to religious, anti-Semitism as a product of modern times, Carroll traces this racism back to the Inquisition. As Jews were forced to convert, especially in Spain, this created a category of suspect Christians. Thus, Jews began to be defined less by their beliefs than by their ancestry. Modern anti-Semitism, then, emerged from the Inquisition. The emancipation of Jews during the nineteenth century followed from the fears produced in European populations by assimilated Jews, in somewhat the same manner that earlier Christians had felt threatened by converted Jews.

In considering the Catholic Church's relations with Adolf Hitler, Carroll agrees with those who argue that the Church had little interest in protecting the Jews from Nazi extermination, rather than with those who argue that the Church simply had no power to protect the Jews from the Nazis. He points out that the Church was, in fact, effective in opposing German chancellor Otto von Bismarck's persecution of German Catholics during the late nineteenth century. Carroll maintains that the popes during the late nineteenth century and the first part of the twentieth century continually opposed modernity as a threat to papal power and that Catholic authorities frequently identified modernity with the Jews. Thus, he claims that Christianity in general, and Catholicism in particular, helped set the stage for the Shoah.

Carroll ends with a call for a Vatican III, a council of the Church that would enact fundamental reforms. He would like this council to go back to the New Testament and critically reconsider the anti-Semitism of the Gospels. Further, he would like the Church to use this council to renounce its efforts at worldly power by formally repudiating the late nineteenth century doctrine of papal infallibility. Further, he believes this council should adopt a new Christology, repudiating the doctrine of atonement through the death of Christ and celebrating a Christ whose life and teachings brought salvation to all. The council should adopt a new and more democratic approach to Church government. Finally, Carroll believes that the council needs to express repentance for its long history of anti-Semitism.

Christian Themes

In addition to a history of Christian relations with Judaism, Carroll offers an interpretation of the significance of Jesus that differs radically from the traditional view of the Catholic Church and the views of other major Christian denominations. He not only rejects the predominant concept of atonement, the doctrine that Christ saved humanity by dying for human sins, but also maintains that this concept of atonement has been the source of centuries of wrongdoing. Carroll's call for a Vatican III to consider his interpretation, then, is a call for an event that would be not only more radical than Vatican II but also far more radical than the Reformation. Some critics may question why Carroll believes that a Church that needs to repudiate almost all of its own heritage should seek to continue to exist at all.

The idea that Christianity developed within Judaism after the death of Christ is closely connected to the work of a group of scholars known as the Jesus Seminar. These scholars have maintained that the historical Jesus differed from the Christ who emerged in the minds of believers and who was described in the New Testament. Thus, from this point of view, one can find teachings of Jesus that predate Christology.

Finally, the theme of the role of the Church in promoting anti-Semitism is one that a number of modern thinkers have considered. The topic of how the beliefs and politics of the Church may have either resisted or contributed to the mass murder of Jews during World War II has been a subject of intense debate.

Sources for Further Study

Cornwell, John. *Hitler's Pope: The Secret History of Pius XII.* New York: Viking, 1999. This biography of Pope Pius XII argues that the pope failed to oppose the Nazi attempt to exterminate the Jews of Europe.

Gilmour, Peter. Review of *Constantine's Sword. Religious Education* 97, no. 2 (Spring, 2002): 184-198. Transcription of an online symposium with Jewish and Christian participants on the importance of Carroll's work for religious education.

Küng, Hans. *Judaism: Between Yesterday and Tomorrow.* Translated by John Bowden. New York: Crossroad, 1992. An examination of the past and present of Judaism and of the relationship of Judaism with Christianity by a Catholic theologian who has been an outspoken and controversial critic of the Church.

Pagels, Elaine. *The Origin of Satan*. New York: Vintage, 1996. Pagels argues that the figure of Satan in the Christian tradition emerged from the efforts of Christians to distinguish themselves from Judaism in antiquity. By identifying Jews and unorthodox Christians with Satan, early Christians sought to demonize their opponents.

Carl L. Bankston III

THE COUNTRY PARSON

Author: George Herbert (1593-1633)
First published: wr. 1632, pb. 1652 as *A Priest to the Temple: Or, The County Parson, His Character, and Rule of Holy Life*
Edition used: The Country Parson, The Temple, edited with an introduction by John Nelson Wall, Jr. New York: Paulist Press, 1981
Genre: Nonfiction
Subgenres: Didactic treatise; handbook for living
Core issues: Baptism; Communion; prayer; preaching

Herbert's The Country *Parson is both a handbook for pastors and a kind of gloss on his* The Temple, *a celebrated book of religious poems written at the same time. Herbert focuses on prayer and preaching, as well on the necessity of conducting a model life that will bring congregations closer to God. This modeling includes a parson's library, church furnishings, family, and servants; and particular attention is paid to the nature of a country congregation.*

Overview

George Herbert, who had served Cambridge University in positions of increasing importance, culminating in his appointment as university orator, left Cambridge in 1627, thereby forsaking a future career in diplomacy. Instead, he pursued a life devoted to religion. In 1630, at Archbishop William Laud's urging, he took the position of rector at a small church at Bemerton, near Salisbury. There he wrote *A Priest to the Temple: Or, The Country Parson, His Character, and Rule of Holy Life* in 1632. The work was written in conjunction with *The Temple*, 1633, an organized collection of holy poems. In his preface, Herbert describes his book as an attempt to set high standards for the priesthood, while acknowledging his own shortcomings and allowing for other pastors to add information and observations to produce a true "pastoral," a word suggestive not only of the curing of souls but also of the image of the pastor as a shepherd with his flock or congregation. Because his was a country congregation, shepherding and agricultural metaphors permeate the book.

Herbert begins by defining the pastor as the "deputy of Christ," whose role is to bring his flock to a closer relationship with God. Quoting extensively from the Bible, he discusses how different clergy have varied gifts and how, regardless of the nature of their assignment, they are to serve God first. Acknowledging that nobles may have undue influence, Herbert nevertheless states that clergy should not kowtow to the wealthy but should walk a tightrope between correction and civility. The ideal way to bring people to God is to serve as a model by using self-control, avoiding covetousness, keeping one's word, and exercising moderation in food and drink. Appearances are important, both in church and in person, because there can be no instruction without respect for the teacher. Aware of the importance of maintaining a good reputation, hc cautions against involvement with women; and while he subscribes to the notion that unmarried clergy are superior to married ones, he admits that a good wife (he himself married Jane Danvers in 1629) may be a helpmate. However, he advocates marrying women whose behavior, not appearance, is excellent (he advises choosing a wife "by ear, not eye"). The parson's family and servants should also serve as models for the congregation. In a sense, modeling behavior for a congregation provides the flock with a kind of "sermon," a word he uses to describe charity, not just gifts, but charity in the sense of loving kindness.

Herbert's parson is a busy fellow. He visits not only the sick but also all members of his congregation and usually in the afternoon in midweek, when parishioners do not wear their "Sunday best" in terms of behavior. His charity is not confined to his own parish; mindful of the less fortunate in neighboring parishes, he also reaches out to them. When he travels, he does not leave his pastor's hat behind. He takes the parish with him in spirit, offers prayers at the inns where he stays, tends the spiritually afflicted, and discreetly reproves offenders. He not only is his parish's "father" but also serves, with his wife's assistance, as physician and as lawyer, referring his flock to professionals only when their problems are out of his depth.

At the core of Herbert's desire to bring his flock closer to God is his belief that the parson should know his congregation. He does this by visiting them, counseling them, and catechizing them. His is a country congregation, a fact that influences his behavior, his teaching, and his preaching. According to Herbert, they are "thick, heavy, hard to raise to a point of zeal" and are the kind of people who are prone to take offense at a slight, real or imagined, so it is important to treat them equitably, to visit and receive all of them, regardless of their rank. In terms of rewarding virtue and punishing vice, the wise parson makes his rewards and reproofs in the present rather than in the vague future because the people do not think in terms of their long-term salvation. They are also liable to see sins in others rather than in themselves. To teach by catechizing the young, the parson uses the exact words from the Book of Common Prayer (1549), but to reeducate the older members of the congregation, the parson looks for answers that reflect understanding. These can be obtained by the use of agricultural and rural metaphors and illustrations. Therefore, to take the good from the bad is to "pare the apple." To counter his congregation's belief that all things come from natural causes, the parson uses crops as the metaphor to demonstrate how God works in their lives and affects their livelihood.

Prayer and preaching are Herbert's two main concerns, and he offers at the end of his book a prayer for before the sermon and one for afterward. Before the sermon, Herbert acknowledges humankind's fall, praises the Lord for salvation through Christ, and then announces that he, a sinful man, must feed his flock the word of Christ's love. He prays that God will enable him to deliver a message faithfully, reverently, and readily, and then leads his congregation to the Lord's Prayer. The prayer after the sermon is one of thanks for "the bread of life" and God's continuing love for people and ends with a reference to the Trinity.

Christian Themes

Herbert's "sample" prayers reflect his twin concerns, praying and preaching. When he prays in church, the parson acts in such a manner that his whole being suggests true devotion, because he desires that the congregation will be as affected as he is. He speaks deliberately but fervently, and he expects that the congregation will behave reverently—not sleeping, talking, or half-kneeling, but sitting attentively and providing responses that are heartfelt rather than rote. Herbert follows Anglican tradition regarding prayer (the necessity of praying three times a day) and encourages his flock to maintain a prayer life. Knowing that people sometimes fail to pray because they are embarrassed or feel guilty, he reminds them of their need for prayer. His concerns even extend to advising the church-wardens (those responsible for maintaining order during worship) to admonish those who do not behave properly during prayers or those who arrive too late for prayers, whatever their social status may be.

For Herbert, the parson's life is preaching in action; his life is a sermon. He does offer some suggestions for reaching a congregation. The parson knows his flock, maintains eye contact, and speaks earnestly: He aims to inform and to inflame his audience. Clever eloquence and learned speech, which might be "over the heads" of his audience, are secondary to holy content and attitude. He relies on stories and metaphors tied to their lives, and he frequently interrupts the sermon with addresses to God and requests for his blessings on the congregation. (This same concern about letting one's learning and wit interfere with a holy message appears in several poems in *The Temple*.) Finally, Herbert urges "preaching in friendliness."

Herbert's attitude toward the Sacraments is that of a typical Anglican pastor. For him, baptism is a solemn ceremony conducted only on Sundays and special occasions, and he instructs the godparents about its significance as the first step for a Christian. It is also a time for a congregation to reexamine their own baptisms and lives. Holy Communion should not be administered until a person understands the difference between the sacramental and ordinary bread and knows and understands the catechism (not just memorizes it). It is the understanding, not the age, of the person that determines fitness for Communion.

Sources for Further Study

Bloch, Chana. *Spelling the Word: George Herbert and the Bible*. Berkeley: University of California Press, 1985. Bloch discusses the figurative language in the Bible and relates it to the kinds of metaphors that Herbert used in his poetry and in *The Country Parson*.

Guibbory, Achsah. *Ceremony and Community from Herbert to Milton*. New York: Cambridge University Press, 1998. Depicts Herbert as taking a conformist, anti-Laudian attitude toward religious ceremony and clerical attire but exhibiting an open attitude toward receiving Communion.

Malcolson, Cristina. *Heart-Work: George Herbert and the Protestant Ethic*. Stanford, Calif.: Stanford University Press, 1999. Chapter 6, which is devoted to *The Country Parson*, contrasts Herbert as country priest with his life as a chaplain at court.

Singleton, Marion White. *God's Courier: Configuring a Different Grace in George Herbert's "Temple."* New York: Cambridge University Press, 1987. Discusses *The Country Parson* in light of how it relates to Herbert's focus on his calling, or choice of a vocation, and the necessity of serving humankind.

Stewart, Stanley. *George Herbert.* Boston: Twayne, 1986. Uses *The Country Parson* as a gloss with which to discuss Herbert's attitudes toward Catholicism and Presbyterianism. Provides a time line and a bibliography.

Thomas L. Erskine

THE COURAGE TO BE

Author: Paul Tillich (1886-1965)
First published: 1952
Edition used: The Courage to Be. 2d ed. Introduction by Peter J. Gomes. New Haven,
    Conn.: Yale University Press, 2000
Genre: Nonfiction
Subgenres: Handbook for living; history; theology
Core issues: Acceptance; death; despair; doubt; faith; guilt

To address the problem of existentialist anxiety, Tillich traces the history of anxiety and explains how faith and the courage to be can overcome it. He calls for transcending traditional notions of God, denies the immortality of the soul, and says faith does not mean believing unbelievable things but is a state of being in which one is grasped by the power of "being-itself."

Overview

In 1950 the German-born theologian Paul Tillich, who had fled the Nazis in 1933 and become a lecturer in the United States, was invited to give the Terry Foundation lectures at Yale University. Two years later Tillich published an expanded version of the lectures as *The Courage to Be* and became something of a celebrity. The book struck a chord and became a best seller as well as a text used in college courses and at religious seminaries.

The book seemed to speak to its time, a time of disruption and uncertainty, the beginning of the Cold War, and the spread of modernist despair and existential doubt, at least among the intellectuals. The book itself, though coming from a well-respected Christian theologian, focuses on the secular philosophy of existentialism, and not until its concluding chapter does Tillich attempt to connect his analysis of society to religious themes.

He begins by tracing the history of courage, referring to Socrates and other early Greek philosophers as well as to the stoic philosophers of ancient Rome and such later thinkers as Thomas Aquinas, Baruch Spinoza, and Friedrich Nietzsche. He argues that courage is connected to being, that it is the affirmation of one's being, and distinguishes this sort of self-affirmation from the courage of soldiers.

In his second chapter, Tillich introduces the concept of nonbeing, saying that being embraces both itself and its negation, adding that being is eternally overcoming nonbeing. He then moves on to discuss anxiety, which he describes as the awareness of one's own potential nonbeing, and he says nonbeing threatens being in three different ways, producing three different forms of anxiety.

The first form of anxiety is related to fate and death, the fact that human beings are subject to a variety of accidental factors that can change the direction of their lives and the fact that ultimately all human beings must die. The second form of anxiety is related to emptiness and meaninglessness, something that arises when there no longer seems to be a clear explanation of the meaning of existence. In such a situation, which Tillich equates with the loss of a spiritual center, doubt arises and leads to despair. The third form of anxiety relates to guilt and self-condemnation, which arises from the feeling that one has not fulfilled one's potential.

Tillich associates the three forms of anxieties with three different eras. The anxiety related to fate and death was dominant at the end of the ancient period in Europe, when the rise and fall of empires, the destruction of old city-states, and the tyranny of the later Roman emperors made life seem beyond control.

The anxiety associated with guilt became dominant in Europe at the end of the Middle Ages. The rise of the middle class, the economic disruption caused by the European discovery of America, and other aspects of the breakdown of the medieval order led to the undermining of medieval religion and concern over how to appease the wrath of God and avoid being condemned to hell.

The anxiety associated with meaninglessness arose in the modern era, but before dealing with it, Tillich spends a chapter describing what he calls neurotic or pathological anxiety. He distinguishes this sort of anxiety from the existential sort he has been describing. Existential anxiety for Tillich stems from the human condition, whereas pathological anxiety is an individual matter affecting those who seek to deal with existential anxiety by escaping in some manner.

Courage for Tillich is self-affirmation in spite of anxiety over the threat of nonbeing. It is the taking of anxiety into oneself. Those who succumb to pathological anxiety cannot take anxiety into themselves but instead seek to flee it and in doing so flee life itself.

Tillich also spends a chapter describing the relation of self and world, seeing two sorts of self-affirmation: affirmation of the self as self and affirmation of the self as a part of a larger whole. He notes the attraction of immersing oneself in a group to combat anxiety, referring to the medieval Catholic Church in Europe, to twentieth century fascism and communism, and to conformism in the United States.

In reaction to the desire to be a part of a group, Tillich points to the rise of individualism, beginning with the Protestant Reformation, continuing through the Enlightenment and the nineteenth century Romantic movement, and culminating in the existentialist movement in the twentieth century.

For Tillich, the existentialist movement derives from the attack on God and religion by Karl Marx and Friedrich Nietzsche in the nineteenth century. He says this attack felt like a liberation in a way, but it also meant the destruction of a whole system of values, leading to an upsurge in anxiety and despair.

Tillich sees existentialist writers and philosophers such as Jean-Paul Sartre, Albert Camus, and Franz Kafka as creatively expressing the despair associated with the anxiety of meaninglessness, but he does not follow the existentialists in their human-centered solution to the despair. For Tillich, human beings are too limited to provide the solution, and in his final chapter, finally turning to Christian themes, he explains how the courage to face the anxiety of meaninglessness must rely on a power beyond human beings.

Christian Themes

Having summarized the course of Western history to show that it has culminated in despair over the meaninglessness of existence, Tillich proceeds to show how religious faith can provide the courage to cope with this despair and meaninglessness.

In doing so, Tillich adopts an idiosyncratic terminology that led some orthodox Christian commentators to criticize him and even to accuse him of not being a Christian. For one thing, he speaks of the "power of being," the "ground of being," and "being-itself" as apparent synonyms for God, making God less a being than a condition. In fact, Tillich specifically opposes any approach, such as the arguments for the existence of God, that would make of God a mere being among other beings rather than being-itself.

For Tillich there is a religious root to the courage to be, based on the relationship to being-itself. This relationship can be mystical if the emphasis is on uniting with ultimate reality, or it can be personal if the emphasis is on the individual encounter with God. He sees Martin Luther as an example of the personal approach, not dependent on institutions or collectives.

In Luther and the Protestant Reformers, Tillich sees the means to conquer the anxiety associated with guilt by accepting God's acceptance, allowing oneself to have one's sins forgiven by God. This requires courage because it means confessing one's sins and accepting one's guilt.

Similarly, Tillich sees a need to accept one's death to deal with the anxiety associated with death. He does not support the popular belief in immortality of the soul, which he says is not truly Christian and which he says seeks to evade the fact of death. Instead, he emphasizes communion with God.

Tillich also argues against the popular notion that faith means believing unbelievable things. He sees faith as a state of being in which one is grasped by the power of being-itself and through which one can deal with the anxiety of meaninglessness by accepting it.

Tillich ends his book with a controversial discussion of the "God above God." This is the God above the all-powerful tyrant that Tillich sees as the conventional God. He says it is necessary to go beyond this conventional God to be grasped by the God above God, faith in whom provides the courage to be.

Sources for Further Study

Carey, John J. *Paulus Then and Now: A Study of Paul Tillich's Theological World and the Continuing Relevance of His Work*. Macon, Ga.: Mercer University Press, 2002. Discusses the composition and popularity of *The Courage to Be*, highlights its controversial notion of a God above God, and discusses Tillich's relevance in the postmodernist era. Includes photographs.

Gilkey, Langdon. *Gilkey on Tillich*. New York: Crossroad, 1990. Sees Tillich as an unusual theological writer, being as much interested in philosophy and culture as theology. Includes personal reminiscences.

Thomas, John Heywood. *Tillich*. New York: Continuum, 2000. Sees *The Courage to*

Be as Tillich's message to America. Includes biographical material and a general survey of Tillich's thought.

Wheat, Leonard F. *Paul Tillich's Dialectical Humanism: Unmasking the God Above God*. Baltimore: Johns Hopkins Press, 1970. Surveys Tillich's critics. Says that the obscurity of his language is the result of his hiding the fact that he was a secular humanist masquerading as a Christian.

Sheldon Goldfarb

CRAWL WITH GOD, DANCE IN THE SPIRIT
A Creative Formulation of Korean Theology of the Spirit

Author: Jong Chun Park (1954-   )
First published: Nashville, Tenn.: Abingdon Press, 1998
Genre: Nonfiction
Subgenres: Church history; critical analysis; theology
Core issues: Asians or Asian Americans; Awakening; evangelization; Holy Spirit; social action

Drawing heavily on the Korean Christian experience, Park proposes a "third theology" of the Holy Spirit that centers on "divine-human participation." According to Park, God walks with the downtrodden and promises a jubilant future for the faithful. Although not always historically accurate and with some unorthodox theological views, Park's book promotes his theology as an alternative to the established Protestant churches of South Korea.

Overview

The goal of *Crawl with God, Dance in the Spirit* by South Korean theologian Jong Chun Park is to propose a new theology of the Holy Spirit. This new theology is to move beyond the previous two Christian theological approaches that Park deems unfit for guiding Christians in the twenty-first century. According to Park, the first theology of the Christian church fathers encompasses a view of an absolute, omnipotent God that "does not resemble the God of the Bible and is not relevant to the modern person's" life. He also states that the second theology, which emerged from the Reformation, is no longer appropriate. The second theology, Park says, focused on the subjective religious feelings of Christians and was promoted by nineteenth century theologians such as the German Friedrich Schleiermacher.

Park's third theology emphasizes divine-human participation, with the two partners being almost equal. For this theology, Park draws heavily on the history of Christianity in Korea and also takes into account the pre-Christian Korean spiritual and historical experience. Park calls his endeavor an ecumenical enterprise that will bring the Korean Christian in closer communion with God. Central for the overall Korean spiritual experience, Park states, is the concept of the mountain of Arirang, a mythical mountain that is the subject of many popular folk songs. In the version referred to by Park, the Korean people symbolically crawl over Arirang to demonstrate resistance to injustice and suffering. Even though the righteous are executed at the top of Arirang by the minions of feudalism, there is triumph in their sacrifice. Park sees this as being like the experience of Christ at Golgotha.

Park grounds his theological view of divine-human participation as the next wave of Christian theology in his discussion of the history of the Christian church in Korea. According to Park, the Methodist missionaries of the late nineteenth century initiated a liberating wave during the Great Revival movement in Korea that lasted from 1907 to 1910. However, he faults Western missionaries for their "demonic endorsement" of the Japanese-American noninterference pact of 1905 that paved the way for Japan's colonization of Korea from 1910 to 1945. For the twenty-first century, Park exhorts Korean churches to "overcome a neocolonialist missiology which is coopted by the Korean capitalist system." Instead, they should learn from the first Korean Christians and "work for cosmic and historical divine-human participation" that strongly centers on social action to create a more just world.

Unfortunately, some of Park's most moving examples of the people's embracing of the Holy Spirit to overcome memories of deep suffering are marred by his acceptance of a historical falsehood. Park writes about "the tragic massacre which took place in Cheju island on April 3 in 1948" and in which "South Korean soldiers killed several hundred thousand innocent people on Cheju island." However, in reality, as Korean and American historians and eyewitnesses concur, on April 3, 1948, some rebellious villagers on Cheju, Korea's southernmost island, killed some fifty police officers representing the nascent South Korean government that had oppressed the villagers. In retaliation, from 1948 to 1954, South Korean forces killed between 30,000 to 80,000 of Cheju's roughly 240,000 inhabitants. Unfortunately, Park uses a historical falsehood when the facts already bespeak a great human tragedy.

Crawl with God, Dance in the Spirit gives a critical review of the history of Korean churches in the twentieth century. In opposition to the established churches, which Park blames for having an "intra-ecclesiastical structure of patriarchy and mammonism," he sympathizes with "*Minjung* theology." Unfortunately for non-Korean speakers, he never directly translates the term *minjung*. Instead, the author defines it by stating that it is synonymous with the Greek term *ochlos*, which he translates as "large crowd." Another translation of *minjung* would be "masses," a term often used in communist rhetoric. Clearly, *minjung* theology stands at the left side of the Korean religious spectrum, but to discover this requires a reader's careful attention. Park also examines socially engaged South Korean religious readers, closely tying his reviews to his presentation of his Holy Spirit theology.

Park finishes his book by giving his own autobiography. Born in 1954 just after fighting ended in the Korean War, Park developed from a fanatical Christian who at age seventeen disturbed shamanistic rituals by throwing stones at a ceremonial pig's head into a seminary student and assistant army chaplain by the end of the 1970's. By the mid-1980's, Park had aligned himself with the radical forces calling for greater democracy in South Korea. He recollects the division among *minjung* theologians and fanatical supporters of North Korea's communist system. He acknowledges that in 1989, "the breakdown of the Eastern bloc became a major blow to most progressive theologians in Korea," including himself.

Park closes by quoting the founder of Methodism, John Wesley, to stress the importance of Christian charity. For Park, key goals for Korean churches should be to promote peace and the reunification of Korea, just as Christians should work globally for peace and justice. In the end, humanity may be able to "reconcile heaven and earth" if the guidance of the Holy Spirit is accepted.

Christian Themes

Park's Christology stresses the suffering of Christ and his sympathy with the disadvantaged. One of Park's central theological visions is the idea of crawling with God and Christ over the mythical hill of Arirang and experiencing suffering. This leads to the subsequent revelation that humanity is invited to dance with the Holy Spirit in an equal divine-human partnership. Some may take issue with some of Park's unorthodox views such as Jesus' being a "slave." This view could be at most a metaphor because the historical Jesus was a free Jew and was never legally enslaved. Park's assertion that "the Word of God is more than the Bible" is also a challenging position.

Park places great emphasis on the Pentecostal ideas of revival and awakening. He believes the Korean church was first uplifted by the faithful gathering at meetings to express their belonging to Christ through collective prayer and the confession of sins. Then the Christians found new life-giving repentance. Park sees this process as a model for the future.

Park strongly encourages the ecumenical inclusion of Korean spiritual practices in his third theology of the spirit. He also sides with some more extreme Christian groups such as the historic "national-socialist united front," who from 1927 to 1931 opposed the Japanese colonialism of Korea.

Park strongly argues that Christians should ally themselves with the "democratic masses" he elsewhere calls the *minjung*. Christians, he says, should fight against their souls becoming "demonically distorted to become the prey of communist or military chauvinism." This statement appears to see the work of the devil both in North and South Korea. Yet Park also writes mysteriously of "a devil such as anticommunism." This may startle readers, who may wonder why Park sees the devil's work in opposing communism, an ideology that condemns all religious activity.

Park embraces a feminist interpretation of theology, writing of "God the motherly Father" who transcends human gender. He supports Christian ecology and liberation theology but comes down hard on American New Age philosophy. He quotes without objection the Reverend Cho Yong-gi, who claims that "transcendental meditation and Buddhist mysticism . . . belong to a Satanic effort." Without comment Park reports the surprising view of Ham Suk-hun that "the Soviet Union is an Apollos, who cultivated the more authentic character of Korean Christians."

Throughout *Crawl with God, Dance in the Spirit*, Park presents his theology of the Holy Spirit as an alternative to the mainstream Korean church and mainstream Christian beliefs. His deep sympathy for the poor occasionally leads him into rather idiosyncratic theological and political territory.

Sources for Further Study

Buswell, Robert E., and Timothy S. Lee. *Christianity in Korea*. Honolulu: University of Hawaii Press, 2005. Comprehensive, accessible, and balanced review of two centuries of Christianity in Korea. Provides background information on people, events, and theological and historical issues discussed by Park that put his views in broader perspective.

Kang, Wi Jo. *Christ and Caesar in Modern Korea: A History of Christianity and Politics*. Albany: State University of New York Press, 1997. This concise, balanced discussion of how political and social events in Korea affected Christian movements there covers well the period discussed by Park and provides an excellent frame of reference.

Yu, Chai-shin, ed. *Korea and Christianity*. Fremont, Calif.: Asian Humanities Press, 2004. Seven essays cover the history of Christianity in Korea and are linked by preface and epilogue by the editor. A good look at issues important to Park's theology such as the Christian response to Japanese colonialism and the history of the Protestant Church in Korea with discussion of its possible future.

R. C. Lutz

THE CREATION

Author: Bruce Beasley (1958-   )
First published: Columbus: Ohio State University Press, 1994
Genre: Poetry
Subgenre: Lyric poetry
Core issues: Creation; healing; love; prayer; suffering

According to Beasley, physical existence separates us from God and, therefore, re-sults in pain and suffering. Our own creation wounds us, leaves us helpless and in need of healing. This healing can occur only through the grace of God. Language, though imperfect, serves as a tool to pray for this grace.

Overview

Bruce Beasley loosely organizes *The Creation* chronologically around Old and New Testament narratives and Christian rituals. In the book, which received the 1993 Ohio State University Press/*The Journal* Award, the poet intertwines materials from Greek mythology, history, and science, and personal contemporary imagery with references to Christian myth and devotion. Beasley, a Roman Catholic with an M.F.A. and a Ph.D., publishes regularly in prestigious literary journals such as *Poetry*, *Virginia Quarterly Review*, and *Southern Review*.

The Creation, his second volume of poetry, depicts God as an estranged father and is representative of the poet's work. The first poem is "The Creation of Eve," a recollection in the voice of Adam, dusted with the red of blood and seeds. This creation of Eve is portrayed as a rather violent and painful one, through the use of the verbs "hacked," "split," "squeezed," "crushed," and "splayed." God appears distant in this poem, and both Adam and Eve are left weak and wounded by creation. Similarly, the divine Christ child, after his birth in "After an Adoration," is described as "cold" and "helpless," while his mother "flails her arms in her sleep." These birth stories prepare the reader for the book's final poem, "The Conceiving," which narrates the impending birth of the child of the speaker of the poem. The child is welcomed to "an earth/ almost too physical to endure." However, unlike Adam, Eve, and Christ, this newborn has a father to guide the child through the pain of earthly existence.

Poems referencing Beasley's childhood suggest the absence of a warm parental presence. "Going Home to Georgia" announces that his parents, though now dead, suffered lives plagued by alcoholism. "The Instrument and Proper Corps of the Soule" reveals an estrangement between father and son, possibly because of the father's "years of liquor." However, though his mother apparently drank as well ("vodka killed her"), the poet does not experience the same estrangement from her: "Someone I love/ has wept/ for days, with no reason." "January Thaw" is presented as an elegy to the poet's mother and serves as a vehicle to detach himself from her, ten years after her death.

Ironically, the use of human language spiritually diminishes us, according to Beasley. "Eve, Learning to Speak" presents an Eve hesitant to use the language taught her by Adam. Eve complains, "He wanted everything/ common, reduced, so we could/ exchange it." By the conclusion of the poem, she laments, "I'd feel the world diminishing, name by name/ as we talked through the long hours." Similarly, "The Conceiving" indicates the poet's own reticence: "I have always wanted to be/ anonymous, unbidden into speech/ withdrawn/ into what remnant of the spirit's left in me." However, language also gives us the means to pray, as demonstrated by "Utter," a meditation on prayer.

Although winter predominates, the four seasons and liturgical calendar provide the book with a sense of movement and time. "Black Wednesday with Ashes" presents Ash Wednesday as particularly cold and dismal, with its pervading sense of spiritual loss. Easter arrives in "Longing." Here the poet is saddened by our inability to know God through the senses. In a Christmas poem, "Noel," the birth of Christ is overshadowed by the setting of a cemetery and the beating wings of hundreds of blackbirds.

Death permeates *The Creation*. "Eternal Spring" recalls the day of a miscarriage. Starting with the image of a slaughtered cow's brain, "The Instrument and Proper Corps of the Soule" recounts the death of the poet's mother. Through the voice of Orpheus, Beasley travels to the underworld in "Eurydice in Hades." In addition, the book includes two elegies and numerous images of ash, burial, and various stages of rot and decay. Creation itself demands a corresponding death in that a physical creation results in a spiritual death or diminishment. As the poet argues in "Consolation," "*to be full of created things/ is to be empty of God.*" In "The Conceiving," he warns, "This life of the body, this ceaseless prayer . . . costs distance, and diminishment."

Not having traveled such distance, the child, unlike the adult, attains some link to the spiritual in Beasley's work. A poem about Sunday School, "Sins," reminds us that "only/ children [can] enter/ the Kingdom of Heaven." The young boys in "Tracing the Angel" show no lack of faith. The boy who wins the prize for best drawing spins and sings, "I see heaven,/ I see God." In contrast, the adult, having "hardened into form," can only pray, "Savior,/ stranger, enter me again."

Human intelligence and the use of reason also distinguish the child from the adult. These faculties give us the freedom to view the world as either sacred or profane. As Beasley argues in "Doxology," "Only we have the soul/ to reject you . . . and only we have the intelligence to expose you/ in the workings of what you've made." Early scientists, for the most part, still found a deep connection to religion. As Beasley suggests in "Consolation," "In *Natural Theology*, William Paley/ detected God's omnipotence/ everywhere. . . . Everything surrendered God to him." However, contemporary science more often alienates us from God. The absence of mystery tends to distance us from the spiritual. As Beasley accuses in "Longing," "We bleed/ the world of mystery, settle/ among its elements instead."

Christian Themes

The poems collected in *The Creation* can be read as an extended prayer, a plea for healing. Creation results in a wound, and physical existence itself is equated with suffering. God, as Father, is addressed directly throughout the volume, most notably in the first poem, "The Creation of Eve." However, the relationship between God and the speaker of these poems is one of great distance. This is a transcendent God. God and poet communicate only through dreams. Although we know that the poet dreams of interacting with God, poems such as "Utter" and "Zeta Hercules" leave us to wonder if God ever hears the poet at such a distance. Ironically, love, rather than healing us, only serves to wound us more deeply, according to Beasley. Love serves to attach us to the earth and worldly things; hence, it diminishes us spiritually. This particular vision of love seems more Buddhist than Christian.

The physical and spiritual landscape of Beasley's poems is cold and harsh. Things often appear "lopsided," while God (in reference to Saint Augustine) is compared to a circle. The colors red and black dominate the imagery, though occasionally, a hint of heavenly blue or pink tints the landscape with hope. Although a dove appears once, in remembrance of a childhood lesson about Noah, blackbirds occur more often. In "Sleeping in Santo Spirito," even the wings of an angel are black, and accusatory religious authority greets the poet harshly.

From Beasley's bleak poetic landscape, we hear a voice crying for immanence and the ability to experience God through the senses. So, in addition to a prayer for healing, these poems might be read as a call for scientific evidence of the spiritual, a return to the historical perspective of Paley. Furthermore, they can be read as a plea for direct communion with God rather than a relationship though memory or dream. The experience itself would provide healing, Beasley suggests. Reminiscent of Ralph Waldo Emerson, Beasley perceives language as defective, and Beasley prays for the ability to use language more purely, possibly to serve God, the Father, more worthily.

Sources for Further Study

Beasley, Bruce. *The Corpse Flower: New and Selected Poems*. Seattle: University of Washington Press, 2006. A collection of poems that contains some from *The Creation*. Provides an overview of the poet's work through his poetry. Contains some information about the author.

"Bruce Beasley." *Contemporary Authors Online*. Farmington Hills, Mich.: Thomson Gale, 2007. Provides an overview of Beasley's first four volumes of poetry. Includes biographical details and a bibliography.

Platt, Donald. Review of *Summer Mystagogia*, by Bruce Beasley. *Christianity & Literature* 47 (1997): 114-116. Although Platt describes the poetry of Beasley as largely poststructuralist, he compares it to the work of Emily Dickinson, Robert Lowell, and the religious poets John Donne, George Herbert, and Gerard Manley Hopkins.

Wallenstein, B. Review of *The Creation*. *Choice* 32, no. 2 (1994): 278. Wallenstein suggests that *The Creation*, though centered in Christian imagery and themes, will appeal to an audience of non-Christian readers as well.

Nettie Farris

CREDO

Author: William Sloane Coffin (1924-2006)
First published: Louisville, Ky.: Westminster John Knox Press, 2004
Genre: Nonfiction
Subgenres: Sermons; theology
Core issues: Ethics; faith; justice; nonviolent resistance; peace; service; social action

This collection of excerpts and quotations gleaned from the sermons and unpublished writings of Presbyterian minister and social activist Coffin highlights his thoughts on the topics of faith, justice, peace, politics, economics, the environment, nuclear disarmament, the Church, a pastor's responsibility, and mortality. At the heart of his perspective on social and political justice is his commitment to the teachings and example of Jesus Christ.

Overview

In historian James Carroll's moving introduction to William Sloane Coffin's *Credo*, he outlines Coffin's career as a college chaplain, a Presbyterian minister, and an activist. A chaplain at Yale University in 1961, Coffin became an outspoken leader in the Civil Rights movement and was jailed as one of the first Freedom Riders, a group that fought segregation in the South by riding interstate buses. In 1967 during a protest against the Vietnam War, he encouraged young men to turn in their draft cards at a church service in Boston. He and fellow protestor Benjamin Spock were indicted and convicted of conspiracy charges. The conviction was later overturned. In 1977, he became pastor of Riverside Church in New York City, a congregation known for its leftist bent. Influenced by the activism of Henry David Thoreau, Mahatma Gandhi, Martin Luther King, Jr., and Jesus Christ, Coffin emphasized the responsibility of individuals—especially Christians—to speak out against unjust social and political structures. In 1987 he stepped down from the pulpit at Riverside Church to become president of SANE/Freeze (Committee for a Sane Nuclear Policy), an organization that advocated the elimination of nuclear weapons. After his retirement and until his death, he continually castigated the U.S. government for what he viewed as imperialist ambition, and he vigorously opposed the Iraq war that began in 2003.

Credo presents Coffin's thoughts and observations on subjects as varied as "Faith, Hope, and Love," "Patriotism," "War and Peace," "Nature," and "The End of Life." Whether crafted to convict, encourage, provoke, or inspire, the reflections in *Credo* are grounded in the Gospel as Coffin understood it. Speaking truth to the powers that be on behalf of the poor, the disenfranchised, the oppressed, and others who have little or no voice in society was fundamental to Christ's mission and the hallmark of Coffin's own ministry.

Coffin's commitment to justice and peace is reflected in his understanding of the word "credo." Usually it is translated simply as "I believe," but Coffin interprets it to mean "I have given my heart to." Although he values reason and claims that "faith is no substitute for thought," he argues that a Christian's commitment to political and social activism can be sustained only by love, not by intellectual or theological convictions. Doctrines and creeds, while useful as vehicles to shape belief, are "only signposts. Love alone is the hitching post." Yet, he does not advocate a sentimental love or a love that passively accepts the status quo. Instead Coffin warns that we must not "ignore the power of anger in the works of love; for if you lessen your anger at the structures of power, you lower your love for the victims of power." This type of angry love is reminiscent of the emotion that Jesus felt when he expelled the money changers from the temple.

It is also the type of love that is at the heart of Coffin's inclusive worldview. He claims that "we all belong to one another" and that "diversity may be both the hardest thing to live with and the most dangerous thing to be without." He eloquently advocates gay rights, women's rights, affirmative action, a woman's right to choose, and justice for the poor and oppressed—all issues that have sparked debate among conservative and liberal Christians who are concerned about biblical interpretation. The Bible informs Coffin's views, but he takes an open-ended approach to the text. For example, in his opinion, the conservative attitude of some believers toward homosexuality is too narrowly defined by "a few sentences from Paul" and "passages from an otherwise discarded Old Testament law code."

In addition to commenting on social issues, Coffin also criticizes the politics of patriotism and war. He writes, "Don't just salute the flag, and don't burn it either. Wash it. Make it clean," and he assails those who would declare "My country, right or wrong." He notes that unquestioning love for one's nation can be equated with blind obedience to one's parents, neither of which Jesus endorsed. He turns the conventional notion of patriotism on its head when he berates the United States government for carrying on an "illegal and unjust war" in Iraq. While the government contends that fighting in Iraq demonstrates a love for one's country, Coffin argues that men and women serving in Iraq are "not called to die for, but rather *kill* for their country. . . . What more unpatriotic thing could have we asked of our sons and daughters serving in the military?" War and the prevalence of terrorism are the fault of the "structures of power" because at the heart of international conflict lies economic inequity. Coffin believes that "attacking worldwide poverty could be our best defense policy" against terrorist assaults.

If the world is to be free of terrorism and war, then the Church must take an active role in working for peace and economic justice. Coffin reprimands white middle-class American churches for "lacking the vigor to deal with big problems" and instead focusing on issues of no consequence. To recover their God-ordained prophetic role in society, churches must "quarrel far more with the governments of their own countries" in order to move administrations in the direction of justice and peace.

Christian Themes

Coffin asserts that "Christianity is a worldview that undergirds progressive thought and action." His notion of Christian activism is founded on what Carroll notes in his foreword as Coffin's firm belief that "God exists and that God's existence matters." If God exists and God is love as 1 John 4:16 says, then Christ's followers are called to exhibit an active love by feeding the hungry, clothing the naked, providing for the homeless, fighting against prejudice, and working for peace.

For Coffin, practicing love takes precedence over adhering to traditional Christian doctrines. In terms of spiritual priorities and how they relate to social action, Coffin looks to 1 Corinthians 13:13: "And now faith, hope, and love abide, these three; and the greatest of these is love." He calls Paul's declaration a "radical statement of ethics" and exhorts his readers to "Make love your aim, not biblical inerrancy, nor purity nor obedience to holiness codes."

Coffin's treatment of the Bible—considered by most believers to be the definitive arbiter of Christian values—is often paradoxical. He employs illustrations from Scripture to support his views and begins each chapter in *Credo* with quotations from the Bible as well as from literary and religious figures. Yet he claims that "any belief in biblical inerrancy is itself unbiblical," and then defends his contention by citing the story of Peter and Cornelius in Acts 10 as an example of the Hebrew scriptures being overturned after God reveals to Peter that an uncircumcised Roman soldier is an acceptable convert to the Christian faith. Coffin sees the Bible as an important tool to aid believers in living a godly life, but he does not regard it as the final authority on spiritual matters because God's inscrutable thoughts ultimately transcend the words on the page.

Coffin's view that the spirit of the law trumps the letter of the law is not unprecedented in biblical history. His passionate call to cast aside stale traditions and embrace a new understanding of how God is working in the world follows in the footsteps of both Jesus and the Old Testament prophets who habitually demanded that religious and government leaders look beyond their narrow, self-righteous interpretations of Scripture. True religion is dynamic and responsive, always evolving to address vital issues that threaten or suppress the rights of minorities.

Sources for Further Study

Coffin, William Sloane. *An American Prophet*. Louisville, Ky.: Presbyterian Publishing House, 2005. A DVD documentary about Coffin's remarkable life, including illuminating interviews with fellow activists Arthur Miller, James Carroll, and others.

_____. *The Heart Is a Little to the Left: Essays on Public Morality*. Hanover, N.H.: Dartmouth College, 1999. A collection of seven sermons encouraging believers to challenge the Christian Right's stances on issues such as homophobia, biblical literalism, and military spending.

Foley, Michael S. *Confronting the War Machine: Draft Resistance During the Vietnam War*. Charlotte: University of North Carolina Press, 2006. Well-researched study of the protests against the Selective Service System during the Vietnam War. Includes coverage of the trial and conviction of Coffin and Benjamin Spock on conspiracy charges.

Goldstein, Warren. *William Sloane Coffin, Jr.: A Holy Impatience*. New Haven, Conn.: Yale University Press, 2006. A compelling, honest look at Coffin's public and private lives. Details his journey from a son of privilege to a tireless advocate for social justice and world peace.

Pegge Bochynski

THE CRUCIFIED GOD
The Cross of Christ as the Foundation and Criticism of Christian Theology

Author: Jürgen Moltmann (1926-   )
First published: Der gekreuzigte Gott, 1972 (English translation, 1974)
Edition used: The Crucified God: The Cross of Christ as the Foundation and Criticism of Christian Theology, translated by R. A. Wilson and John Bowden. New York: Harper & Row, 1974
Genre: Nonfiction
Subgenres: Biblical studies; theology
Core issues: Atonement; the cross; God; Jesus Christ; redemption; the Trinity

Moltmann see the Crucifixion of Jesus as both a criticism of conventional religion (even theism itself) and the basis for constructing a more nuanced vision of God as Trinity. When God gives himself on the cross, we see God's inner self-differentiation, and in the Resurrection, we can reinterpret the past and find grounds for hope throughout history. Jesus' forsaken state echoes our suffering and the Father's grief, and his resurrection gives us promise for the future and energy for active ethics.

Overview

In *The Crucified God,* Jürgen Moltmann states that though often misunderstood, the crucifixion of Jesus is central to the identity and the relevance of Christian faith. Because of the cross and Christ, people's entire perception of God as well as humanity must be reinterpreted. Moltmann argues that this change in perception would rejuvenate Christology. Rather than sterile arguments about whether Jesus was "truly God" or "truly man," which set the wrong framework, Christians should enter into dialogues with Jews about the meaning of "Messiah." Who Jesus is must be defined by the Messianic future; Christology remains forever unfinished until the new Creation arrives, according to Moltmann.

Jesus' trial and execution put his message into question. Coming as it did at the end of years of conflict with the law and the authorities, Jesus' final cry of dereliction echoed a conflict even of God against God. Although close to God, Jesus was abandoned and then resurrected. In that terrible hour, the very deity of God was at stake, and believers were forced toward a new and more nuanced concept of the divine. Surprisingly, however, through the cross and the Crucifixion, God was disclosed in his very opposite. Moltmann concludes that not continuity and analogy, but contradiction and struggle, are sources both for people's faith and moral life.

Moltmann states that the Resurrection indicates that we are in the midst of unfinished history; in that light we should reevaluate both the past and the future. Because Jesus was raised from the dead, we look back on his sacrifice as an act of liberating love done for our sakes. We look forward because the "promise" is far more than just a resuscitation, rather it is a summons for us to the future already dawning.

Simple theism has proved inadequate, according to Moltmann. Together the cross and Resurrection drive us beyond even the monotheism revered in Christian heritage. Conventional theism is far too easily misused by worldly Caesars and institutional religions for their own purposes. Theology drawn from a "natural" knowledge of God is manipulated by human perversity and pride. However, the cross changes everything, shattering our self-serving presumptions. When we see God suffering in his despised humanity, it frees us to a new kind of love: love for the "other," for those different from ourselves. This pivotal event has become the groundwork, both for a doctrine of Trinity, God's self-differentiation amid unity, and also for a social ethic of compassion, as we seek solidarity with the wretched and those unlike ourselves.

Moltmann says that here atheism can render a service by unmasking the dubious foundations of conventional theism and insisting that the world is not yet transformed. However, atheism and theism alike make the mistake of viewing humanity and God through identical categories, so that whatever attribute is ascribed to the one must be subtracted from the other. That is, atheism depicts humans at the expense of God, so that divine traits are implicitly reassigned to feed our egos, while theism depicts God at the expense of humans, reducing us to alienated and compliant subjects of a cosmic emperor. It is only "protest-atheism" that should be taken seriously, because it agonizes over injustice and cries out on behalf of innocent suffering. Such protest, even from nonbelievers, helps us appreciate the triune life of God disclosed by the cross.

Traditional doctrines of the Trinity often lapsed into formalities of church dogma. However, as stated in *The Crucified God*, the true meaning is grounded in Jesus' cross and his cry to God. At heart it reflects the painful separation yet mutual empathy of Father and Son, the profound self-sacrifice that was marvelously transformed through Easter. This interior event within God's triune life also marks the life of Christians, for disciples are summoned to become vulnerable and impassioned for the sake of the unfinished created world. The inner division within God must take up into itself all the unfolding story of humanity, providing dynamism for our cooperation until the new creation arrives. Thus Moltmann sees parallels between the inner life of the divine Trinity and the outward progression of mortal history.

Because of the world's suffering, human sin must be taken very seriously. Yet Moltmann is confident that the future, as illuminated by God's promise, will bring fulfillment and salvation. Such confidence is far from humanistic optimism; rather it is rooted in implicit divine grace that has surmounted even the cross. "Dialectical panentheism" is a term Moltmann has used in describing our salvific destiny, a phrase almost hinting at divinization as we mortals retrace the inner history of the Trinity.

However, according to *The Crucified God*, this destiny requires a profound liberation of human nature on two fronts, psychological and political. The psychological liberation entails dialogue on analyzing how childish religion cloaks human anxieties and apathy. From this we are freed by hope grounded in God's pathos on the cross.

The political dimension of liberation calls for demythologizing state religions and grasping an iconoclasm empowered by the Spirit and eschatological hope. Liberation on this level is interdisciplinary as it addresses several interlocking vicious circles: economic poverty, political violence, racial/cultural alienation, industrial pollution, and the dread of meaninglessness in life. Genuine freedom must begin now, and it is enabled by God's trinitarian history that points beyond itself to a glorious consummation of divine and human fellowship.

Christian Themes

Moltmann's epistemology mistrusts simple analogy, the conventional "like is known only by like." Instead he relies on dialectical thinking: paradoxes of seeming opposites. Revelation is not dogma or proposition but an event happening in contradiction; God is able to make use of whatever appears furthest from the divine. Thus Jesus' cross becomes not an embarrassment but the epitome of God's selfhood.

History is not to be defined by the positivists or materialists but is open-ended, an indeterminate flow until the grand climax of all things. Historical criticism should be welcomed, including studies of the historical Jesus, but criticism by itself proves inadequate. That is because historical and eschatological methods are reciprocal, each casting new light on the other. Jesus' history must be read both forward and backward, relating him both to his Jewish heritage and his (and therefore our) resurrected future. The end calls forth the beginning.

Critiques of religion from various quarters are embraced by Moltmann, who sees how often in history religiosity has supported alienation. As his allies, he cites critics such as the psychoanalyst Sigmund Freud and especially liberal Marxists (Ernst Bloch, the Frankfurt school of social analysis), who detail how institutions and civil religion manipulate religion whenever it loses its primal dimension of hope. Theistic faith is hardly immune from this critique, but for years it has been the most susceptible to unholy alliances with autocratic regimes or mystical privatism.

So who is God? Not polytheism, of course, but the subtleties of trinitarian vision have shaped Moltmann's doctrine of God—especially with the horrific tensions of Good Friday, first analyzed in this book. Because the triune One is both vastly transcendent and intimately present, and it encompasses from the far reaches of ancient Israel to our own daily lives, only a doctrine of Trinity can serve adequately. Moreover, it not only clarifies the inner life of God but also marks a paradigm for the unfolding of earthly history toward its goal. Moltmann has adopted the term "panentheism" to navigate between the extremes of austere theism and shapeless pantheism, and he openly admires Eastern Orthodoxy with its heritage of a "social Trinity" of divine persons (contrasting to Augustinian/Western emphases on divine unity). This vision undergirds Moltmann's social ethic, for which he is well known, because humans are empowered by God's presence and stretched beyond their failings by the gospel of hope.

Sources for Further Study

Bauckham, Richard. *The Theology of Jürgen Moltmann*. Edinburgh, Scotland: T&T Clark, 1995. Irenic British exposition of the major themes found in Moltmann, set against the background of his dialogue partners.

Meeks, M. Douglas. *Origins of the Theology of Hope*. Foreword by Jürgen Moltmann. Philadelphia: Fortress Press, 1974. The best summary of early influences on the young Moltmann, by a colleague who helped introduce him to the English-speaking world.

Moltmann, Jürgen. *Theology of Hope: On the Ground and the Implications of a Christian Eschatology*. London: SCM Press, 1967. The author's first major work, which has influenced all his subsequent writings. Across the world, this is one of the most significant theological works of the late twentieth century.

Müller-Fahrenholz, Geiko. *The Kingdom and the Power: The Theology of Jürgen Moltmann*. Minneapolis, Minn.: Fortress Press, 2001. Weaves biographical details and some mild criticism with the most comprehensive analysis of Moltmann's lifelong work.

Wakefield, James L. *Jürgen Moltmann: A Research Bibliography*. Foreword by Moltmann. ATLA Bibliography Series. Lanham, Md.: Scarecrow Press, 2002. Exhaustive, definitive listing of works by and about Moltmann, including doctoral dissertations and an essay by Moltmann, "What Is a Theologian?"

G. Clarke Chapman

CUR DEUS HOMO
Or, Why God Was Made Man

Author: Saint Anselm (c. 1033-1109)

First published: 1098 (English translation, 1854-1855)

Edition used: Anselm of Canterbury: Major Works, edited by Brian Davies and G. R. Evans. Charlottesville, Va.: InteLex Corp., 1999

Genre: Nonfiction

Subgenre: Theology

Core issues: Atonement; God; guilt; Incarnation; sacrifice; sin and sinners

According to Saint Anselm, because humanity was intended for perfect and sinless happiness, the sins of humanity dishonor God, who would be false to himself if he allowed the falling away of humanity to continue without redress. However, as humanity is incapable of achieving liberation from sin, only God, by becoming human, could "ransom" sinners, and through a death voluntarily suffered, pay the debt owed to himself. Even if we knew nothing of Christ through revelation, reason alone would demand that God must have, of necessity, assumed human flesh to redeem humanity.

Overview

Within a few years of his appointment as archbishop of Canterbury in 1093, Saint Anselm found himself caught up in a number of theological controversies. One of these hinged on the following question: Why was it necessary that God become human and, through his death, redeem the world from sin, when it would seem that God in his omnipotence might have accomplished this saving act in any number of ways or simply by an act of divine will? This question reached Anselm from two sources: the so-called secular schools (nonmonastic Christian seminaries) of Northern Europe and a group of learned rabbis and Jewish scholars recently settled in London for whom the very idea of divine incarnation was an intellectual and theological affront.

For the secular schools, interest in the question was largely a matter of formulating a theology of the Incarnation in keeping with the dominant trend of the age, which was to place Christian doctrine on a more rational foundation. For the Jews, the question arose out of a concern with the nature of God. For them, the idea of the Incarnation was an assault on the dignity of the Supreme Being. How could an utterly transcendent being be required to suffer the ignominy of human suffering and death on a cross? While the Jews shared with Christians the view that humanity lived in a condition of Original Sin and was therefore in need of divine forgiveness, they could not accept the notion that human restoration to the perfection lost with the Fall could be accomplished only through God's assumption of human flesh.

The key term in Anselm's statement of the question is "necessary." Earlier Christian apologists had assumed that God's decision to take on the human condition was not governed by necessity but was simply an act of the divine will; God had merely chosen this manner of saving humanity by some mysterious preference but could have chosen some other method to achieve the same end. For Anselm this inherited notion that God's assumption of human flesh was, in effect, a purely contingent act was unacceptable. It was a violation of the "rightness" (*rectitudo*) of things—that is, of the justice that is the essence of the created order. Thus, if fallen humans were to be restored to their original perfection, that could be accomplished only in conformity with the eternal moral order.

Because humans were created with freedom of will—their essential dignity—they could have fallen only by their own choice. In succumbing to the devil's temptation, people failed to render to God what was owed him: perfect obedience freely given. This failure was a violation of God's justice and of the fundamental moral order. Moreover, that same justice required that humans' restoration be accomplished in a way that was consistent with the free will God had ordained for them. Thus, human redemption could be accomplished only by a sacrificial act of perfect human obedience. To use the biblical metaphor, by their failure of obedience, humans owed a debt to God that required payment. However, fallen humans are incapable—by virtue of the radical insufficiency that mars their nature as a result of Original Sin—of paying such a debt, of rendering to God the perfect obedience that was still possible before the Fall. Moreover, simply to absolve humans of their debt by fiat (by an arbitrary act of divine will) would not accord with God's justice, because it would involve God's perfection in an inconsistency—a contradiction in terms.

The Anselmian solution to this dilemma is paradoxical. The injustice done to God required "satisfaction" by humans, but fallen humans were incapable of paying such a debt. It is true that God might have restored the moral order by simply condemning fallen humans to an eternal punishment that would have "satisfied" God's justice. Yet such a vindication would have required God to abandon his original purpose for humans and, more important, would have been inconsistent with the Christian view of God as infinitely merciful. Clearly, then, if humans are incapable of giving God what his justice required, then only God himself could accomplish that work of restoration. However, how could God do so in a way that was consistent with a moral order that required free human consent to God's perfect authority? Only one answer was possible: God must assume the human condition and, through the agency of the Son, Christ Jesus, submit himself to the punishment of death. To the objection that God could not assume the human condition without abandoning his divinity, Anselm reasserts the traditional Trinitarian view that God suffered the indignity of suffering and death only in the person of Christ, while in his essence remaining transcendent. As for Christ, while he willingly subjected himself to death, he remained divine in the sense that his assumption of the human condition did not include sin. Had it done so, then truly God's divinity would have been fatally compromised. So, also, would human salvation have been compromised, because only a perfect offering to the Father could compensate for the perfection that humans cast away in their original act of disobedience.

Christian Themes

The central theme in *Cur Deus Homo* is atonement (the reconciliation of humanity to God), which in turn can be divided into a number of subsidiary themes. Anselm brings a high degree of originality to his treatment of two of these: The first involves the question of humanity's subjection to the devil; the second, the "necessity" whereby God became human. In the early part of the work, Anselm disposes of the traditional view that God became human because the sin of Adam had delivered the human race to Satan. In this understanding of atonement, the devil held "rights" over humanity that God was obligated to recognize. The Incarnation was seen as a kind of divine trickery because in conspiring to bring about Christ's death, the devil forfeited his right of possession over humanity. Anselm's refutation of this notion of Satan's "rights" established what would be the cornerstone of his argument throughout *Cur Deus Homo*: The Fall of the human race in no way diminished God's dominion over his creation. To accept the view that the devil possessed any "rights" whatsoever would have been to accept a compromised idea of God's omnipotence. Both faith and a rigorous reason demanded that the devil be reduced to a minor player in the drama of atonement.

In diminishing the devil's role, Anselm places atonement on a new doctrinal basis, one in which the central theme became the story of how God's mercy is reconciled to his justice. In Anselm's aesthetic vision, the perfectly ordered universe must reflect a flawless harmony of divine attributes: a perfection of power, justice, order, and beauty. If any of these attributes is diminished in the slightest degree, the harmony of the whole is distorted. Therefore, while God is a merciful God, an arbitrary act of divine mercy that failed to accord with God's justice would be impossible. Even in his will to forgive, God cannot, of "necessity," act inconsistently against his own *rectitudo*. To find scope for his mercy, then, it was "necessary" that God become human and be punished for humanity's sin. For justice and for the universal harmony to be restored, compensation had to be made. Therefore Anselm introduced into the theological tradition a rational coherence that would shortly give rise to what is known as Scholasticism.

Sources for Further Study

Holmes, Stephen. "The Upholding of Beauty: A Reading of Saint Anselm's *Cur Deus Homo.*" *Scottish Journal of Theology* 54, no. 2 (Spring, 2001): 189-203. Focuses on Anselm's contribution to medieval debates concerning rational understanding of Christ's Incarnation.

Leftow, Brian. "Anselm on the Necessity of the Incarnation." *Religious Studies* 31, no. 2 (June, 1995): 167-185. Argues that while Anselm's view of atonement seems to diminish God's omnipotence, this is not so. "Necessity" in Anselm's argument arises from God's prior actions and does not restrict his power.

McMahon, Kevin A. "The Cross and the Pearl: Anselm's Patristic Doctrine of the Atonement." In *Saint Anselm: His Origins and Influence*, edited by John R. Fortin. Lewiston, N.Y.: Edwin Mellen Press, 2001. Shows that, despite the usual claims that in *Cur Deus Homo* Anselm breaks radically with the tradition of the church fathers, he was in fact much influenced by them.

Southern, R. W. *Saint Anselm: A Portrait in a Landscape*. New York: Cambridge University Press, 1990. Contains a lengthy discussion of *Cur Deus Homo* within its historical context and stresses especially the aesthetic dimension of Anselm's rationality.

Jack Trotter

CURE FOR THE COMMON LIFE
Living in Your Sweet Spot

Author: Max Lucado (1955-   )
First published: 2005
Genre: Nonfiction
Subgenres: Guidebook; handbook for living
Core issues: Daily living; faith; guidance; self-knowledge; service

Scripture claims that each person is unique, wonderfully and carefully designed by God to reveal a part of his glory. Lucado's guidebook calls on people to believe that description fully and to examine their lives for the clues God has placed there that reveal the work he intended each carefully crafted person to do. Pursuing one's particular path, Lucado explains, will glorify God and bring personal joy and fulfillment. For those in an employment situation that must be endured, Lucado provides spiritual guidance that will infuse common work with uncommon joy.

Overview

The premise behind minister and Christian writer Max Lucado's *Cure for the Common Life* is that all people have what he calls a "sweet spot," a unique service for God that they were created to fulfill. More particularly, Lucado defines this spot as the point at which an individual's personal strengths and successes converge with glorifying God and everyday life.

In the first section of the book, "Use Your Uniqueness," Lucado sets about helping readers understand that each of us was crafted by a master designer who prepackages his designs, wiring us in a particular way so that we can fulfill our individual purpose. Introducing a concept he calls "unpacking our bags," Lucado encourages us to examine our own skills and predispositions and those moments when we knew we were performing well (when, he explains, we were in "the zone") to discover exactly how it is that each of us is packed. Lucado attacks the common secular concept that we can be anything we want to be and replaces it with a Scripture-based mandate to first seek the maker so that we can then learn who it is we were uniquely crafted to be. Unpacking our bags is important spiritual work, Lucado asserts, because strengths and interests visible in even our youngest childhood memories suggest to us who we were designed to be. One boy's proclivity with model airplanes, for example, and another boy's love of art point to God-designed penchants for particular fields of interest.

Incorporating Scripture, exegesis, and everyday examples, the first section of *Cure* ultimately underscores the value of all work. The point is not, according to Lucado, to do what the secular world defines as valuable work but to discover our irrepressible passions to pursue what God intended for us to pursue. Despite secular claims to the contrary, the pursuit of financial gain or prestige will not lead us to personal joy; in fact, Lucado argues, such pursuits will lead us away from our true selves.

So that we will not lose our way but find it, Lucado has appended a version of the System for Identifying Motivated Abilities (SIMA) technology, an assessment tool used by People Management International that guides users through an examination of their STORY (strengths, topics, optimal conditions, relationships, and the Yes! factor, those times when we have consciously felt God's pleasure).

In the second section, "To Make a Big Deal Out of God," Lucado focuses on the reason he feels we should make such a discovery. This he calls the "why" of our sweet spot. When we know who we are, who crafted us, and what we were shaped to do, then we can discover why we were thus shaped. We come to know who we are, says Lucado, to be fully the expression of Christ that God designed us to be. If, according to Lucado, we chase after financial gain or fame, or if we are afraid of stepping out of our comfort zones into a new life, we risk missing our own purpose, thereby wasting our God-given talents. Are we here to glorify ourselves or God? Lucado asks. Because we are designed to glorify God in the unique way that he crafted us to do, Lucado insists, our work is immensely valuable because it is God's work. We are not designed to be the answer to every social evil, Lucado cautions; neither are we given an unimportant role. When our spiritual gifts meet with our God-given mission, we feel our God-centered worth. When this happens, Lucado says, we worship God, and when that happens, all moments of our daily life are moments of worship.

The main thrust of section three, "Every Day of Your Life," is the "when" of our sweet spot. The work we do glorifies God the instant we recognize that ultimately it is God for whom we work. By seeing this reality, Lucado argues, we remember that it is God who confirms the work of our hands, regardless of who signs the paycheck. Thankfully, Lucado adds, a grinding nine-to-five, dead-end job that we simply cannot escape because of poor choices, financial responsibility, or through no evil of our own can still be our sweet spot. For this to happen, Lucado suggests, we must remember that God is always with us, that all work, even small deeds, if surrendered to our Lord, glorify him. Thus, even when we do jobs that we simply must perform, such as cleaning bathrooms and changing diapers, tasks that perhaps are no one's sweet spot, we glorify God.

Christian Themes

Lucado's *Cure for the Common Life* is a daily living guidebook that encourages us to study our everyday lives for practical answers to our employment questions. By completing the STORY assessment, Lucado claims, we will see the areas in our life where satisfaction and success meet.

Ultimately, though, Lucado's text is about faith. As Scripture suggests, most things in life come down to this one issue. Believing the promises of God lies at the heart of this guidebook. At one point, both Abraham and Sarah laughed at the outrageous promise of God. What about the stuttering murderer Moses? Could he believe his call? Lucado's book asks us a similar question. Do we believe the radical claims of such Scripture as Psalm 139? Does our God know us that intimately? How about the first chapter of Ephesians? Did God really pick us, imperfect as we are, and create what Lucado defines as a sweet spot for each of us? Perhaps some of us will believe that God designed this thing Lucado calls a sweet spot for each of us that will reveal a part of his glory. Lucado's book calls us beyond merely believing in God to believing God, to trusting him, to surrendering all that matters to his care.

At its core, Lucado's guidebook asks us the really hard questions of Christian surrender and faith. Will we fall into the secular sickness of disbelief, doubt, and depression? Or will we seek a cure? Do we trust God not only with our souls in the afterlife but also with our everyday lives in the here and now? Do we trust his gifts, his guidance? What about our hopes for our children? Lucado asks. Do we trust God to give our children sweet spots? Do we believe in the power of the Resurrection in our everyday life? Like the Israelites of long ago, we question whether God will make good on his promise to guide us to a sweet spot. Can our Lord transform the mundane tasks of a mundane job into the stuff of miracles? Reading Lucado's chapter titles one after the other leads us to Lucado's answer to that question of faith: "Use your uniquesness to make a big deal out of God every day of your life." If we do, Lucado affirms, we will live in a sweet spot.

Sources for Further Study

Lawrence, Brother. *The Practice of the Presence of God*. Translated by John J. Delaney. New York: Doubleday, 1977. This work, available in many editions, is one of a handful of classic devotional works that reveal the transforming power of the Resurrection in our everyday lives.

Lucado, Max. *It's Not About Me*. Nashville, Tenn.: Integrity, 2005. A powerful complementary text to *Cure for the Common Life* because both deal with what seems a contradiction: In the secular world, each Christian has a role to play, but life is not about the individual.

Moore, Beth. *Believing God*. Nashville, Tenn.: Life Way Press, 2002. A text that, like Lucado's, calls people to the radical faith of stepping beyond merely believing in God to believing him.

Publishers Weekly. Review of *Cure for the Common Life*. 252, no. 40 (October 10, 2005): 57. Review of the work that notes the author's traditionally evangelical yet easy-to-read style.

Warren, Rick. *The Purpose-Driven Life: What on Earth Am I Here For?* Grand Rapids, Mich.: Zondervan, 2002. Warren's text defines the five purposes for existing and makes the claim that people are uniquely shaped for serving God. Like Lucado's STORY, Warren's SHAPE is an assessment tool for discovering God's purpose for one's life.

Anna Dunlap Higgins

THE DA VINCI CODE

Author: Dan Brown (1964-   )
First published: New York: Doubleday, 2003
Genre: Novel
Subgenres: Catholic fiction; literary fiction
Core issues: Catholics and Catholicism; church; Gnosticism; Jesus Christ; obedience
and disobedience; truth

The Da Vinci Code presents a fictional hunt for the Holy Grail. It ends in a discovery of a lineage that claims to be descended from Jesus and Mary Magdalene, who is the Grail. The novel is important because it has brought the recent discoveries of the Apocrypha to popular awareness. It is controversial because it fabricates its own art and religious history, misleading many readers.

> *Principal characters*
> *Robert Langdon*, protagonist, murder suspect
> *Sophie Neveu*, Robert's best friend, collaborator
> *Jacques Sauniere*, murder victim
> *Leigh Teabing*, villain, appearing as friend to Robert
> *Rémy Legaludec*, Teabing's co-conspirator
> *Bezu Fache*, antagonist, chief investigator of murder
> *Manuel Aringarosa*, antagonist, head of Opus Dei
> *Silas*, murderer, Opus Dei member, friend of Aringarosa

Overview

As *The Da Vinci Code* opens, the protagonist Robert Langdon, a renowned Harvard symbologist lecturing in Paris, is awakened late at night. Jacques Sauniere, curator of the Louvre, has been murdered, and Langdon must lend his expertise to the investigation. Chief Investigator Bezu Fache has summoned Langdon partly because he regards Langdon as the prime suspect because he and Sauniere had an appointment to meet that night. Also, a cryptic message that Sauniere left behind included a phrase, which Fache had erased before summoning Langdon: "P.S. Find Robert Langdon."

Sophie Neveu, a beautiful cryptographer, interrupts Fache and Langdon, announcing that Langdon has a phone call from the American embassy. On dialing the number, Langdon hears instead a warning from Neveu, who subsequently explains that she is Sauniere's estranged granddaughter, who broke off contact with her grandfather when as a young girl she witnessed him participating in a sexual ritual for a secret society, the Priory of Sion. Langdon and Neveu escape after finding the key that Sophie's grandfather left her. It belonged to him as Grandmaster of the Priory, a sect that guards the secret of the Holy Grail. The Grail is said to be the cup that Christ used at the Last Supper.

   While Langdon and Neveu try to decipher an ever-expanding list of Grail clues, others besides the police pursue them. Bishop Manuel Aringarosa, head of Opus Dei, a conservative Vatican prelature, has been told by Vatican lawyers that his organization will lose its status of independence from local control in six months. Desperate, Aringarosa agrees to pay a fortune in Vatican bonds to a man calling himself The Teacher, who promises that he will bring Aringarosa the Holy Grail. Aringarosa must also entrust The Teacher with Silas, an albino monk whom he took under his wing years ago. Silas has a preconversion history of violence. The Teacher orders Silas to interrogate the four top leaders of the Priory, find out where the keystone to the Grail is hidden, and then kill the leaders. Getting the same confession out of all of his victims, Silas hurries to Saint Sulpice to find the Grail keystone, but this is a decoy that had long before been set out for would-be Grail hunters. An enraged Silas kills Sister Sandrine, the keeper of Saint Sulpice and a Priory sympathizer.

   The real keystone is a cryptex within a cryptex, allegedly invented by Leonardo Da Vinci and manufactured by Neveu's grandfather: a small container with a five-letter dial for the password. If forced open, a cryptex breaks a vial of vinegar around which the papyrus script is wrapped, destroying it. After finding the cryptex, Langdon consults Sir Leigh Teabing, an extremely wealthy independent Grail researcher and former British royal historian. Teabing explains that Mary Magdalene, wife of Jesus and mother of the French Merovingian line, is the real Holy Grail. Silas, guided by The Teacher, invades Teabing's estate, threatening to kill Neveu unless the keystone is handed to him.

   Despite having physical limitations, Teabing trips Silas and takes charge of an illegal flight to London with Langdon, Neveu, Silas, and Rémy Legaludec, Teabing's butler. In England, Legaludec helps Silas escape. Legaludec introduces himself as The Teacher and tells Silas to hide in the Opus Dei headquarters. The real Teacher shares a peanut scrap-laden victory cognac with Legaludec, who dies because of an allergy to peanuts.

   Meanwhile, Silas feels uneasy in the Opus Dei headquarters. Seeing a police car behind a hedge, he comes out fighting and shooting; but to his horror, he accidentally shoots Bishop Aringarosa, who had offered his apostolic ring as a bribe to an airplane pilot in return for flying illegally to London. The dying Silas vows vengeance against the one who has betrayed them, but Aringarosa counsels forgiveness.

   The Teacher, Teabing, visits the tomb of Sir Isaac Newton, where other clues exist. He lures Langdon and Neveu to a deserted area, where he threatens to kill Neveu unless Langdon helps him decipher the code and reveal that the Catholic Church has been lying. Langdon appears to comply, taking the cryptex and turning aside in an attempt at a solution. However, he returns the cryptex to Teabing by tossing it in the air. In his scramble to save the falling cryptex, Teabing falls and the vial breaks, but Teabing sees at that instant that Langdon has deciphered the code. Fache, realizing that all are innocent except Teabing, rushes in to arrest Teabing; Langdon reads the final clue.

   In closing, Fache meets with the bishop and gives him back his ring. Neveu meets her family, the hunted Merovingians of Grail lore. Langdon closes by making a pilgrimage to the resting place of Mary Magdalene, whose remains are under a small pyramid sculpture in the Louvre that opens into a huge underground pyramidal chamber. The visible tip of this giant pyramid meets a giant upside-down glass pyramid, representing the union of masculine and feminine divinity. In a manuscript that Sauniere saw, Langdon had observed that the small pyramid suggested a larger underground structure. This initiated Sauniere's contact with Langdon and led to the subsequent events.

Christian Themes

It is important to be aware that *The Da Vinci Code* is literary fiction; the appearance of historical accuracy is only superficial. Brown's book is a minefield of disinformation for the unwary reader. He disturbs scholars of history and theology alike with his claims to legitimate scholarship, when evidence suggests that his sources are often from latter-day mystics rather than from reliable academic research. There is, however, a consistent reality behind Dan Brown's fictionalized Church and art history: For instance, the Church has, indeed, suppressed alternative Gospels, many written by sects denounced as heretical a few centuries after Christ.

The discriminating reader may notice that the book is a somewhat formulaic mystery, and not a notably executed representative of the genre. Still, it was on *The New York Times* best-seller list for more than two years and was made into a film starring Tom Hanks. Brown's achievement is that he has made ecclesiastical history exciting for the general public. He has also created a cottage industry of refutation against his claims regarding apocryphal writings. While these early writings do suggest that Jesus intended a more active role for women than what subsequently developed, none claim that Jesus was married as the novel does. A married Jesus is, at best, an unlikely possibility among serious students of early biblical history.

As a story, *The Da Vinci Code* considers the relationship of authority and conscience. All the characters transgress at some point, but the outcomes depend on their motives. Sir Leigh Teabing, although apparently heroically supportive of reinstating the divine feminine in Christianity, is the true villain of the novel, arrogating divine authority to himself. Opus Dei's tortured Silas, although a victim, chooses to descend to the level of brutality that he experienced in his youth to gain status. Yet Bezu Fache, also an Opus Dei member, does not abandon his conscience, even though his professional standards as a detective oblige him to support those whom he considers heretical: Langdon and Neveu. Langdon challenges his students not to fear truth, and Langdon's disarming sincerity tempts the reader to accept his account of early Christianity in the novel. However, unquestioning acceptance of any form of authority is being challenged. Like Fache, readers must follow their consciences yet be open to fortuitous revelations (especially those available outside of the book) of what authority to trust with the truth.

Sources for Further Study

Burstein, Dan, ed. *Secrets of the Code: The Unauthorized Guide to the Mysteries Behind "The Da Vinci Code."* New York: CDS Books, 2004. Burstein, a journalist, has created a compendium of scholars and popular writers discussing pros and cons of the novel. The glossary is especially recommended.

Ehrman, Bart D. *Truth and Fiction in "The Da Vinci Code."* New York: Oxford University Press, 2004. This is a balanced rebuttal of Brown's book; the author is a distinguished scholar from the University of North Carolina at Chapel Hill.

Estruch, Juan. *Saints and Schemers: Opus Dei and Its Paradoxes*. New York: Oxford University Press, 1995. This is a scholarly report on Opus Dei published before *The Da Vinci Code* came out.

Robinson, James McConkey. *The Coptic Gnostic Library: A Complete Edition of the Nag Hammadi Codices*. Boston: Brill, 2000. Brown consulted this resource for *The Da Vinci Code*. It is worthwhile to compare the contents with what was made of them.

Suzanne Araas Vesely

A DANGEROUS SILENCE

Author: Catherine Palmer (1956-   )
First published: Wheaton, Ill.: Tyndale House, 2001
Genre: Novel
Subgenres: Evangelical fiction; romance; thriller/suspense
Core issues: Death; faith; forgiveness; love; Native Americans; Protestants and Prot-
    estantism; responsibility

*Using the thriller genre, Palmer shows how faith helps people get through crises and
how important the ability to forgive and the willingness to take responsibility are to
becoming a true Christian. By contrast, the inability to forgive and the unwillingness
to take responsibility leave a person vulnerable to the temptation to do harm to others.
The romantic aspect of the novel emphasizes that the love of God must be present before someone can truly love another person.*

> *Principal characters*
> *Ed Morgan*, a Kansas farmer
> *Marah Morgan*, Ed's oldest daughter, a pediatrician
> *Milton Gregory*, a former doctor posing as an archaeologist
> *Judd Hunter*, an undercover FBI agent posing as a farmhand
> *Pearl "Perky" Harris*, the seven-year-old daughter of Ed's next-
>   door neighbors

Overview

Catherine Palmer tells the story of *A Dangerous Silence* through four point-of-view
characters. At the beginning of the novel, Ed Morgan is working alone on his Kansas
farm when he has a disabling accident. His daughter, Dr. Marah Morgan, is working
on the staff of a pediatric clinic in St. Louis at the time. Dr. Milton Gregory closes his
remote Wyoming laboratory and announces that he and a few associates will be relo-
cating to Kansas. Finally, Judd Hunter is wrapping up a case for the Federal Bureau of
Investigation (FBI) in which he infiltrated a group conspiring to use fertilizer to blow
up government buildings.

After losing two burn patients under mysterious circumstances, Marah agrees to
her father's demand to come home and take over the farm. Her mother has been dead
for many years, and her three sisters live even farther from Kansas than she does. She
has no brothers, for which Ed blamed her mother and punished his daughters by with-
holding his love. Marah has no intention of moving home permanently, however. She
plans to get Ed admitted to a retirement community and sell the farm. Although she is
a devout Christian, she observes the letter, but not the spirit, of the commandment
"Honor thy father."

Gregory and two of his associates arrive at the farm and pose as archaeologists for the Bureau of Indian Affairs. In exchange for doing some work around the farm, they get permission to live in Ed's bunkhouse while they conduct a search for an Osage village known to have existed somewhere on Ed's property. In the bunkhouse, they set up a laboratory.

When Marah finally arrives, her first project is to clean up and paint the house. She renews her acquaintance with one of the neighbors and meets Pearl (Perky), their seven-year-old daughter, a bright, precocious child whose actions drive much of the plot. When Judd arrives, he asks Marah for a job, and she hires him. His latest assignment is to infiltrate Gregory's team.

When a tornado passes over the farm, Marah takes refuge in the cellar, only to find an intruder there. The intruder escapes and locks the door to the cellar behind him. Fortunately, there is a window, and Judd helps her climb out. When Judd reveals knowledge of anatomy too advanced for an ordinary farmhand, she begins to suspect that he is not what he seems. They also start to fall in love and to talk about Christianity and faith.

Perky finds a Native American grave while searching for wildflowers. She falls into a pit and comes face to face with the mummified remains of an Osage woman. The arid climate has kept the body from complete deterioration. Gregory and his team remove the corpse and take it to the lab. However, instead of preparing the corpse for reburial, they determine that the woman died of smallpox and harvest the body for the virus, which has been their plan all along.

Marah finally confronts her father. Although never physically abusive, he was always verbally abusive, emotionally distant, and self-centered. Furthermore, he forced her to take care of her younger sisters when her mother died, although Marah was only eight years old at the time. She had left home for college after graduating from high school eighteen years previously and had never looked back. She finally learns the circumstances of her mother's death, including the facts that Ed cheated on her mother and has a son by another woman.

Judd takes a few days off to visit Gregory's former laboratory in Wyoming as part of an FBI team. However, an associate of Gregory is maintaining surveillance and informs him that Judd is an FBI agent. Gregory arranges for a bomb to be attached to Judd's pickup truck when he returns. Fortunately, Judd survives the blast. Marah finds him in the barn and helps him walk to the house. At his request, she calls the FBI. Leaving Judd with Ed, she drives to Wichita to a Native American museum, where she learns that the Osage village formerly on the farm was wiped out by smallpox in 1865. At Wichita's main hospital, she learns the medical reasons for her mother's death.

While she is gone, Perky visits the bunkhouse. Gregory exposes her to the smallpox virus because he needs to test it on a human. From there, Perky goes to Ed's house and informs Judd and Ed. They call her parents and tell them she will be staying with them. Marah finally gets home after midnight, and Judd informs her of Perky's exposure. Just as they are leaving, Gregory and his men capture them. A short time later,

FBI agents arrive. Gregory and his cohorts then hold their captives as hostages.

The situation continues through the next day as Gregory's group remains confined in the house with their hostages. When Judd and Marah attempt to get Perky out of the house through the bathroom window, they are discovered. In all the commotion, members of the FBI SWAT team crash into the house to rescue them.

Christian Themes

In *A Dangerous Silence*, past and present meet to bring disparate characters' lives together and to demonstrate their different responses to past wrongs (or perceived wrongs) and how those reactions shape their futures. Those who are able to forgive, accept responsibility, and move on in a Christian manner fare best; those who remain bitter grow worse.

The name of the protagonist, "Marah," in fact means "bitter" in Hebrew, and her name describes how she feels about her father at the beginning of the story. She eventually forgives him for his adultery, verbal abuse, neglect, and other transgressions, however. Marah grows and changes. She and Perky have strong Christian beliefs that help them through the crisis.

Marah's father, Ed, has always regarded preachers as confidence artists and has always hated going to church. His wife died at home in considerable pain, but he regarded doctors, including his daughter, as overpaid pill pushers. Judd, similarly, has no religious beliefs. Fortunately, both Ed and Judd eventually see the errors of their ways. Ed takes responsibility for his unhappy marriage and for refusing to take his wife to the hospital when she became ill. He finally realizes that there may actually be something to churchgoing and praying. Judd realizes that his first marriage failed because it was centered on sex rather than love.

Dr. Gregory, by contrast, considers Christians to be fools. He previously ran a successful obstetrics and gynecology practice in Los Angeles, including a discreet abortion clinic. However, he never took responsibility for a late-term abortion that went badly and led to his suspension. He has never forgiven the state of California and the medical community for having taken away his medical license and affluent lifestyle. His pride blinds him to his own contributions to his current situation in life, and he instead seeks revenge against the medical community in particular and the United States in general.

Although the novel has a romantic subplot between Marah and Judd, their romance is not consummated, because Judd is not yet a Christian. He has not learned to love God, and he is therefore incapable of truly loving another human being, although he has shown a capacity for friendship and affection. The story does, however, end on an optimistic note: Judd appears ready to leave the FBI and give his life to God.

Sources for Further Study

Duncan, Melanie. Review of *A Dangerous Silence*. *Library Journal* 126, no. 6 (April 1, 2001). Emphasizes Marah's relationships with the other characters in the novel.
Palmer, Catherine. *The Happy Room*. Waterville, Maine: Thorndike Press, 2002. The

daughter of missionaries, Palmer uses her upbringing as background material for this novel.

_____. *Sweet Violet*. Wheaton, Ill.: Tyndale House, 2005. Palmer cites the title character as her most autobiographical.

Zaleski, Jeff. Review of *A Dangerous Silence*. *Publishers Weekly* 248, no. 11 (March 12, 2001). Points out that the action is character-driven and that Palmer does not preach but integrates her Christian beliefs into the story.

Thomas R. Feller

THE DAWNING OF DELIVERANCE

Author: Judith Pella (1948-   )
First published: Minneapolis, Minn.: Bethany House, 1995
Genre: Novel
Subgenres: Adventure; historical fiction (twentieth century); saga
Core issues: Conversion; doubt; faith; God

*This historical novel centered on the Fedorcenko family in pre-revolutionary Russia
deals with faith in God and the difficulty of maintaining it in a bewildering or cruel
world. Its reassuring message is that our spiritual struggles and failures matter less
than our spiritual successes to a God who will patiently continue to love us and wait
for us to approach him in confident faith.*

> Principal characters
> *Mariana, Countess Remizov*, the protagonist
> *Dmitri, Count Remizov*, Mariana's father
> *Prince Sergei Fedorcenko*, also known as *Sergei Christinin*,
>   Mariana's foster father
> *Anna Christinin*, Mariana's foster mother
> *Daniel Trent*, an American journalist who becomes Mariana's
>   fiancé
> *Cyril, Count Vlasenko*, a cousin of Sergei's father and enemy of
>   the Fedorcenkos
> *Basil Anickin*, a would-be lover of Mariana's mother
> *Nicholas II*, czar of Russia
> *Alexandra*, the wife of Nicholas II
> *Misha*, a Cossack, friend of the Fedorcenkos

Overview

The Dawning of Deliverance is the fifth book in The Russians series about the
Fedorcenko family and other individuals in pre-revolutionary Russia. Judith Pella
collaborated with Michael R. Phillips on the first four novels, then Pella continued the
series on her own. The book, after a prologue that summarizes the earlier installments
in the series, opens with Mariana traveling by train across the vastness of Russia to
Manchuria to take up a position as nurse during the Russo-Japanese War of 1904-
1905. Twenty-three and unmarried, she is troubled by memories of Daniel Trent, an
American journalist who betrayed her trust nearly four years ago. Mariana is conscious of a desire to help the suffering and is aware that her physical journey has a
spiritual dimension.

When she arrives at the north end of the Liaoyang Peninsula, she is immediately
needed to nurse wounded Russian soldiers. In the midst of this exhausting labor, she

meets Daniel again and wonders if God is giving her a second chance with him. She learns that his father has died, but Daniel does not reveal that his search for God has lapsed.

Meanwhile in St. Petersburg, Mariana's foster father, Prince Sergei Fedorcenko has escaped from exile in Siberia and is living under the name of Sergei Christinin. He decides he must teach working men to read and write to compensate God for his goodness to his family. Cyril, Count Vlasenko, now in possession of Sergei's St. Petersburg estate, schemes to become minister of the interior. The scene moves to Geneva, where Vladimir Lenin works for revolution, before it returns to Manchuria.

Mariana, now in Port Arthur, saves the war hero Captain Barsukov from the unnecessary amputation of his leg by the incompetent Dr. Vlasenko, son of Count Vlasenko. Daniel, in search of a story, bribes his way to Port Arthur, where, during a shelling by the Japanese, he comforts Mariana, although he himself is frightened. Mariana suddenly has an insight that she will marry either Barsukov or Daniel.

The scene shifts back to St. Petersburg, where the delight of the czar and his wife at the birth of a son, Alexis, is shattered when the baby seems subject to mysterious bleeding. There is social unrest as well: Father George Gapon, although loyal to the czar, is founding unions for workers. The scheming Count Vlasenko thinks he may be able to further his aims through Basil Anickin, a fugitive recently returned to Russia and half-mad with hatred of the Fedorcenkos. Basil has recognized in Anna, Mariana's foster mother, the person whose intervention prevented him from killing Mariana's mother after she rejected him.

Conditions in Port Arthur grow worse as water, food, and medical supplies run low. Mariana blames herself for the death of an uncle, a patient in the hospital where she works, and seeks out Daniel for comfort. He tells her that God would have cured her uncle if he had wanted to, and she responds that God sent Daniel to her at just the right moment. They declare their love for each other, but Daniel silently wonders if it will be strong enough to survive the wartime trials ahead.

Mariana attends her uncle's funeral. Although she is sad, her knowledge of Daniel's love enables her to keep going. She gently rejects a proposal of marriage from Captain Barsukov. Under the influence of professional ambition and the desire for adventure, Daniel makes a serious blunder. He agrees to smuggle a report regarding Japanese troop movements onto a Red Cross ship permitted to leave Port Arthur, a ship on which Mariana is a nurse and which is unexpectedly boarded and searched by a group of Japanese. In the ensuing confusion, Mariana is accidentally shot by a Russian patient embittered by a serious war wound and seeking revenge against the boarding party; Daniel is betrayed as a spy by Dr. Vlasenko and arrested. Before being led away, he kisses Mariana and promises her they will be together again.

Incarcerated in a Japanese prison camp, Daniel has a religious awakening. He realizes that he had been happiest in the days following his father's death when he had been actively seeking God. He stops feeling guilt at the sporadic nature of his pursuit of God and accepts that God loves him despite his imperfect nature. He then discovers that he is to be released. Strings have been pulled on his behalf, and the Japanese do not wish to offend their prisoner's family, who own a firm that is a major producer of the steel on which the Japanese navy relies. Daniel and a recovered Mariana are soon reunited in St. Petersburg and plan marriage. As an authentic Russian heroine, she is granted an interview with Nicholas and Alexandra. In gratitude for Mariana's selfless work, the czar pardons Sergei, her foster father, who can now live openly as a Russian prince.

Once again private happiness and misery take place against the backdrop of sweeping historical events. Sergei is killed when the authorities fire on a peaceful demonstration led by Father Gapon. This bodes ill for the future of Russia, as the marchers would have been satisfied by a simple appearance by the czar, absent from St. Petersburg on the fateful day. An attempt by Basil to bomb the flat where Sergei's mourners gather is thwarted by the technical expertise of Misha, a Cossack and longstanding friend of the Fedorenkos. Dmitri, Mariana's father, who has lived irresponsibly, regains some self-respect as he risks his life to capture Basil. The novel ends on an optimistic note with Anna deciding she wishes to go on living despite the death of her husband Sergei.

Christian Themes

The Dawning of Deliverance uses its characters' struggles and triumphs to examine questions of doubt, conversion, faith, and the nature of God. A rapidly moving story is set against dramatic events and a simply sketched background. Characterization can be superficial (Pella's Russian aristocrats are more like twentieth century Americans), dialogue is wooden, and the style is pedestrian. Also, the historical background is not utilized in any depth. This book is clearly a historical romance designed to entertain, with no literary pretensions, although it does bear a message for its readers.

The message, designed to uplift a people in a difficult world, is that God understands people's doubts and questionings. Daniel seeks God for some time after the death of his father, then loses focus in the everyday busyness of his life. Ashamed of seeming a foul-weather Christian, one who only approaches God when life is painful, he hides his spiritual failures from Mariana, whose tranquility he envies. In the Japanese prison camp, Daniel dreams of a tentmaker and the line "It's not easy to kick against the pricks." He is reminded of the references to the apostle Paul's conversion on the road to Damascus and realizes that the God who had steadily pursued him, even in sleep, will not condemn him for unavoidable human weaknesses. He accepts his human fallibility and God.

Anna, Mariana's foster mother, had been told by her father in a previous volume in the series that she is to bear the family's burdens but will not be called on to do so unaided by God. The death of her husband makes her angrily question God's treatment of her, a woman who loves God. Only in the novel's last scene does she accept that she still has much for which to live.

Sources for Further Study

Hudak, Melissa. Review of *Passage into Light*, by Judith Pella. *Library Journal* 123, no. 18 (November 1, 1998): 66. A review of the seventh novel in The Russians series takes the Fedorcenko family in 1917 and the start of the Russian Revolution.

_____. Review of *White Nights, Red Mornings*, by Judith Pella. *Library Journal* 122, no. 2 (February 1, 1997): 68. This review of the sixth book in The Russians series focuses on Anna's children and their differing political views.

Mort, John. Review of *Mark of the Cross*, by Judith Pella. *Booklist* 102, no. 16 (April 15, 2006): 28. A review of one of Pella's numerous historical romances, which may be compared with those in The Russians series.

Pella, Judith. http://www.judithpella.com. The author's personal Web site, with sections headed "Book List," "About Judith," "FAQ," and with details of a newsletter and links.

M. D. Allen

DEAR AND GLORIOUS PHYSICIAN

Author: Taylor Caldwell (1900-1985)
First published: Garden City, N.Y.: Doubleday, 1959
Genre: Novel
Subgenres: Catholic fiction; historical fiction (first century)
Core issues: Alienation from God; compassion; despair; healing; Judaism; pilgrimage

The Roman Lucanus, today known as Saint Luke, loses his faith after the death of a loved one and spends his life as a physician wandering in search of the unknown God. During his journeys, he encounters others who tell him of their firsthand experiences concerning the life and death of Jesus. Lucanus begins to record these experiences and in the process regains his own faith. In time, his records become the Gospel according to Saint Luke, the third book of the New Testament.

> Principal characters
> *Lucanus*, Saint Luke, the protagonist
> *Diodorus*, Saint Luke's Roman stepfather
> *Iris*, Saint Luke's mother
> *Rubria*, a girl Saint Luke loved
> *Priscus*, Saint Luke's brother
> *Sara ben Solomon*, a woman Saint Luke loved

Overview

At the start of *Dear and Glorious Physician*, the child Lucanus looks at his father's hands, covered with scars from his years of servitude before he was freed from slavery by Diodorus's father. Lucanus decides that he loves his father despite his prideful attempts to forget his former lowly status. Meanwhile, the lonely Diodorus is in need of a companion with whom he can discuss philosophy. He grew up with Iris, the mother of Lucanus, and remains in love with her despite his happy marriage to Aurelia, the mother of his sickly daughter, Rubria. One evening he comes across Lucanus praying for Rubria in the garden. He is fascinated by the boy's quick intelligence and mature demeanor and especially impressed when he tells Diodorus that he prays to the unknown God, who is kind and loving unlike the vengeful Roman gods. Lucanus gives Diodorus herbs for his daughter, and Diodorus decides to send him to Alexandria to attend medical school when he is older.

From the beginning, the physician Keptah realizes that Lucanus is an exceptional student. While gazing on a star from the east one evening, they share their common love of the unknown God. One day the young man Lucanus accompanies Keptah to a temple, where the Magi predict Lucanus will live a life of deep sorrow. Lucanus suffers terribly after Rubria dies, and he begins to hate God. However, he cannot deny his gift as a healer and comes to defy God by saving his people's lives in the study of medicine. After Diodorus's wife Aurelia dies in premature childbirth, he miraculously saves the infant's life. Diodorus returns from Rome, asks Iris to marry him, and adopts Lucanus.

At medical school in Alexandria, Lucanus cannot reconcile how God can inflict pain on mortals and not offer them consolation in the form of salvation. He has no time for fun and shuns company, but his heart is filled with pity and love for all those who suffer. He miraculously cures a leper, and after he has finished his studies and is returning to Rome, Lucanus cures plague-infected slaves on the ship. All Lucanus wants from life is to heal people, and he realizes he can best serve humankind in this regard by going among the poorest of the poor. Even Sara ben Solomon, a woman with whom he falls in love, cannot move him to do otherwise. He promises during his travels to look for her brother who was kidnapped as a child.

Before Lucanus arrives in Rome, Diodorus dies after taking the senate to task for corruption. Lucanus refuses a job as chief physician, and when he is called before Tiberius Caesar, he explains that he would rather cure the poor. Impressed, Tiberius forces him to remain in the luxurious but morally corrupt Imperial City for six months, believing Lucanus will also fall into corruption. Soon, Julia, the bare-breasted, wanton wife of Tiberius, attempts to seduce the young Lucanus, but he spurns her and is forced to flee Rome. Tiberius writes and vows eternal friendship.

In Greece, Lucanus works as a physician. One day in the slave market, he buys a suffering young African man named Ramus only to free him and save him after he is blinded by a mob. Lucanus miraculously restores his sight, and they travel together and care for the sick. When they hear of Jesus of Nazareth, Ramus leaves for Israel to ask Jesus to remove the biblical curse of Ham that plagues his people. Lucanus also saves another slave named Arich, Sara's missing brother.

In the final section of the novel, Lucanus encounters a wide variety of people who inform him about Jesus. One patient, the wealthy Hilell ben Hamram, informs him how Jesus died and insists that Lucanus accompany him to Israel. At this point, Lucanus begins to write an account, which grows as he talks to others. In Israel he meets the Romans Pontius Pilate and Herod Antipas, and his own brother Priscus, a Roman centurion who was present at Christ's crucifixion. Finally, Lucanus travels to Nazareth to visit Mary, Jesus' mother, who, in the form of the Magnificat of John the Baptist, tells him about the Annunciation and her joy over being the mother of God. The account Lucanus created became the Gospel according to Saint Luke, the third book of the New Testament.

Christian Themes

In *Dear and Glorious Physician*, Taylor Caldwell writes enthusiastically about how the Roman gentile Lucanus, who later became Luke, goes on a search for God. The story of Saint Luke is the story of Everyman's pilgrimage. Taylor's text provided a characterization of Saint Luke that critics never appreciated, but she intertwined in it homilies that teach and inspire. For example, Iris says to her son that now he must put aside "childish things" and be a man, a quote from the first letter from Paul of Tarsus to the Christians at Corinth (1 Corinthians). Also, when Diodorus lies dying, he replies to Tiberius that a higher power to whom he "must commend [his] spirit" calls instead. Here Caldwell casts Diodorus as a holy character because his statement mirrors Jesus' final words on the cross: "Father, into your hands I commend my spirit." In short, *Dear and Glorious Physician* is a didactic novel—it instructs and forces the reader to think.

Caldwell's popularity has been attributed to her support of traditional American domestic and ethical values by portraying male characters as strong and successful and female characters, especially wives and mothers, as the heart and moral center of the home. Men might go out into the world and excel, but in the evening they return to strong women for nurturance and guidance. The tired governor Diodorus goes first to Aurelia for comfort and, after her death, to Iris. Lucanus repeatedly turns to women for comfort, ultimately to Mary, Jesus' mother. Men are heroes, Iris thinks, after Aeneas drowns attempting to save the financial records, but women are sensible. After a young woman undergoes a horrific operation, Keptah remarks to Lucanus that the surgery was harder on her husband. However, Caldwell's good and generous women suffer. Sara waits patiently, never once looking at another man, and when Lucanus finally does propose, she realizes that he belongs to God instead. Mary's sufferings are beyond description.

Caldwell also preaches against intolerance, speaking out in particular against slavery. The characters who free slaves are blessed. In addition, she makes a parallel between the conflicts experienced between the powerful Romans and Rome's subservient colonies with those experienced by majority and minority groups in twentieth century America. Rome's decline, she suggests, is due to its increasing moral laxity and posits this as a warning to the United States.

Sources for Further Study

Detweiler, Robert. *Uncivil Rites: American Fiction, Religion, and the Public Sphere.* Champaign: University of Illinois Press, 1996. Scholarly analysis that demonstrates how religious works influence American society and culture, especially during times or crisis and war. Includes a discussion of Caldwell's *Dear and Glorious Physician.*

Jasper, David. *The Sacred Desert: Religion, Literature, Art, and Culture.* Malden, Mass.: Blackwell, 2004. Engages the works of various authors to explore the depth of spiritual meaning in works of literature, film, and art.

Stearn, Jess. *In Search of Taylor Caldwell.* New York: Stein and Day, 1981. Deals with reincarnation and past-life regression. Caldwell starts out a skeptic but under hypnosis recalls past lives that explain the psychic revelations from which many of her books originate, including *Dear and Glorious Physician.*

M. Casey Diana

DEATH COMES FOR THE ARCHBISHOP

Author: Willa Cather (1873-1947)
First published: 1927
Edition used: Death Comes for the Archbishop. New York: The Modern Library, 1931
Genre: Novel
Subgenres: Historical fiction (nineteenth century); literary fiction
Core issues: Bishops; Catholics and Catholicism; clerical life; evangelization; faith; Native Americans; pastoral role; priesthood; sin and sinners

Bishop Latour and Father Vaillant are two French missionaries transferred from Ohio to organize the diocese of the new U.S. territory of New Mexico. Resolute yet sensitive, they reform the diocese, removing materialistic and authoritarian priests. They recognize and respect the ancient pre-Christian religious traditions of the indigenous population. As Frenchmen, they are alien figures to Mexicans and Americans, but their dedication and sincerity build admiration. The completion of the cathedral of Santa Fe is a symbol of the success of Bishop Latour's pioneer episcopate.

Principal characters
Bishop Jean Marie Latour, the "archbishop" of the title, a French missionary who founds the frontier diocese of New Mexico
Father Joseph Vaillant, a French priest who is Latour's friend since youth and serves as vicar general of the diocese
Jacinto, an experienced Pueblo guide who accompanies Latour on many pastoral journeys
Manuel Lujon, a wealthy rancher who gives his best mules, Contato and Angelica, to Vaillant
Kit Carson, the historic frontier guide
Father Antonio José Martínez, a lapsed and authoritarian priest of Albuquerque
Father Lucero, a miserly priest in Arroyo
Father Gallegos, an indulgent priest of Sante Fe
Friar Baltazar Montoya of Ácoma, a priest who "lived for the people or on the people"
Doña Isabella Olivares, the refined wife of wealthy rancher Don Antonio Olivares
Eusabio, the Navajo guide of Latour who is a defender of these people

Overview

Death Comes for the Archbishop opens with a prologue in which three cardinals and a French missionary bishop from the Great Lakes are gathered for dinner while watching a radiant Roman sunset. The bishop has come to plead for the episcopal appointment of a man of vigorous faith to the newly annexed U.S. territory of New Mexico. The bishop's candidate is a fellow countryman, Father Jean Marie Latour, a missionary priest in Ohio. As the dinner ends, the host, head of the Propagation of the Faith, wanly accedes to the bishop's request.

After a yearlong, hazardous trek from Ohio, Bishop Latour arrives as apostolic delegate in Santa Fe, accompanied by his boyhood friend, Father Joseph Vaillant, the vicar general. The local Mexican clergy does not accept his authority, so he must travel to the former head of the jurisdiction, the bishop of Durango. He loses his way during this journey and is befriended by an isolated Mexican family with whom he stays, observing the syncretism that has occurred between Catholic and local religious practices. Returning to Santa Fe, he finds that Father Vaillant has secured a house and furnishings for them, even a bell for the church.

For their missionary journeys, Father Vaillant persuades a local rancher, Manuel Lujon, to give them two mules, Contato and Angelica. On a pastoral trip to Mora, the priests rescue a woman, Magdalena, who has been made a domestic prisoner by her scoundrel Yankee husband. They take her to live happily in a convent with a newly arrived group of nuns. The bishop meets the historic figure Kit Carson and establishes a lasting relationship.

Latour begins to visit his parish priests. At Albuquerque he meets the good-living and no longer celibate Father Gallegos, whom the bishop resolves to dismiss. At Isleta the bishop meets an aged, kindly, and austere priest, the opposite of Father Gallegos, who lives a faithful and humble priestly life. Traveling further, the bishop arrives at the Indian village of Ácoma. There he hears the legend of Friar Baltazar Montoya, a cleric so self-indulgent and arrogant that his parishioners killed him.

The bishop has an Indian guide, Jacinto, and visits his pueblo and family, thereby learning more of local religious ways, coming to respect them. Once lost in a snowstorm, they find refuge in a sacred Indian cave.

The most troublesome priest for the bishop is the curate at Taos, Padre Martinez. Born locally, the priest has become an authoritarian, astute, and materialistic anomaly, and the bishop replaces him. A compatriot and archrival of Martinez is the miserly Father Lucero, at Arroyo Hondo. The two form a schismatic church. Trinidad Lucero, a dim-witted nephew, supposedly studying to be a priest, accompanies them. Martinez dies, remaining in schism. After knifing a thief who gets into his house, Lucero dies, reconciled to the Church. It is discovered that he has left a fortune of twenty thousand American dollars.

Bishop Latour had grown up in a refined French provincial family. He and Father Vaillant find some of the quality of this life through Doña Isabella, second wife of the wealthy rancher Don Antonio Olivares. Educated at a French convent, Doña Isabella establishes a salon atmosphere on her husband's ranch. They both greatly admire the bishop and frequently receive and support him. When Don Antonio dies, his will is contested. The two clerics successfully advise her, encouraging a convenient manipulation of the truth at a trial, and her inheritance is secured.

Often ill but ever resilient, Father Valliant becomes quite sick and recovers only as the bishop promises to allow him to move further into the frontier to do missionary work. Bishop Latour falls into a period of depression but recovers after a midnight conversation in his church with a poor Indian housekeeper, in bondage to her Protestant employers. Young French priests come to work with Bishop Latour, and he reflects on what had been the loving and special character of Father Vaillant. The bishop's guide is now Eusabio, whose people Latour defends from frontier advances.

The discovery of gold at Pike's Peak rapidly increases the population within Bishop Latour's jurisdiction. Father Vaillant is eager to go to Colorado to support the spiritual needs of the raw frontier settlement. Bishop Latour reluctantly appoints him to the parish of Denver. The bishop talks about the golden yellow stone he has found in the mountains, which he believes most appropriate for building of a French-style cathedral.

Raised to an archbishop but now in his seventies, Latour retires to a small estate near Santa Fe. A young French seminarian, inspired by the bishop's life, comes to be his close companion. Debilitated by illness, the archbishop expresses the desire to return to Santa Fe. Shortly after arriving, he dies and his body is laid in the cathedral he built.

Christian Themes

At the heart of the Christian religion is the virtue of faith. The archbishop reflects this quality not only in the integrity of his own life but also in the extent to which he preserves, revives, and expands it among his clergy and laity. Numerous characters, such as Father Gallegos, Martinez, and Lucero, are examples of those who have lost faith because of corrupting vices. Others, such as Father Vaillant, Magdalena, and numerous others, reflect those who humbly continue in their faith.

Integral to faith is perseverance. The long arduous pastoral journeys of Bishop Latour and Father Vaillant demonstrate this devoted application of their labor in the spread of the faith. Perseverance requires courage, the ability to continuously confront and deal with hostilities and hardships.

Faith, however, sustains hope, the virtue of confidence in redemption. Through the faith that the bishop and his vicar spread, they mean to give hope to the varied and conflicted peoples among them, the numerous Indian groups, the settled Mexican cultures, and the advancing American ones.

However, within Christian moral theology, the most important virtue is love. In general, the archbishop's life of devotion and labor reflects his love for his flock. Most important, his love is reflected in his personal relationships. Father Vaillant is his lifelong friend, someone whom he knows very well, admires, respects, and cares for. The bishop is especially alert to and respectful of the religious sensitivities of the indigenous populations, even curious and admiring of how they have synthesized both Catholic and native tradition. He is attentive to the most humble of his parishioners. His love is also "tough." He knows how to patiently, diplomatically, and effectively remove clerics whose vices have become the antithesis of virtue.

Sources for Further Study

Lindemann, Marilee, ed. *The Cambridge Companion to Willa Cather*. Cambridge, England: Cambridge University Press, 2005. Compilation of thirteen articles, including John N. Swift's "Catholic Expansionism and the Politics of Depression in *Death Comes for the Archbishop*."

Murphy, John J., ed. *Willa Cather and the Culture of Belief: A Collection of Essays*. Vol. 22 in *Literature and Belief*. Provo, Utah: Bringham Young University Press, 2002. Compilation of nearly two dozen articles includes three focusing on religious aspects of *Death Comes for the Archbishop*.

O'Connor, Margaret Anne, ed. *Willa Cather: The Contemporary Reviews*. American Critical Archives. Cambridge, England: Cambridge University Press, 2001. A compilation in excess of five hundred pages of all the contemporary reviews of Willa Cather's novels. More than forty pages concentrate on *Death Comes for the Archbishop*.

Rosowski, Susan J., ed. *Willa Cather's Ecological Imagination*. Vol. 5 in *Cather Studies*. Lincoln: University of Nebraska Press, 2003. Collection of articles focusing on aspects of land occupation, frontier borders, agriculture, horticulture, ecology, and the environment in Cather's work.

Edward A. Riedinger

A DEATH IN THE FAMILY

Author: James Agee (1909-1955)
First published: 1957
Edition used: A Death in the Family. New York: Vintage Books, 1998
Genre: Novel
Subgenre: Literary fiction
Core issues: Alienation from God; death; doubt; faith; good vs. evil; religion

The tragic death of a small boy's father in a traffic accident forces him to face the conflicts in his parents' marriage, especially with regard to his mother's scrupulous religious belief, which threatens to alienate him both from her and from the Christian faith that is so central to her life. The dominating presence of his middle-class, puritanical mother, combined with the loss of his empathic and easygoing backwoods father, leads the small boy to be apprehensive not only about his own future manhood but also about the possibility of ever achieving an authentic spiritual life.

> Principal characters
> *Rufus Follet,* six-year-old boy
> *Jay Follet,* Rufus's father
> *Mary Follet,* Rufus's mother
> *Catherine Follet,* Rufus's sister
> *Ralph Follet,* Jay's brother
> *Hannah Lynch,* Mary's aunt
> *Andrew Lynch,* Mary's brother
> *Father Jackson,* an Episcopal priest
> *Joel Lynch,* Mary's father
> *Walter Starr,* a family friend

Overview

A Death in the Family opens with a poetic meditation that introduces the perspective of Rufus, who is at once both boy and man and is looking back on his childhood in Knoxville, Tennessee, in 1915, as a time of both innocence and mystery. The actual narrative, however, begins as he and his father, Jay, enjoy a companionable evening together at a Charlie Chaplin movie; this and Jay's stop at a local saloon after the movie are both activities of which Jay's wife, Mary, does not approve. Other differences between mother and father also surface; Jay is from a poor country family, while Mary is from a middle-class city family. An even greater conflict concerns religious differences that the narrative will develop in the wake of the sudden death of Jay in an automobile accident.

After Jay has rushed out to the family farm in the mistaken belief that his father has died, Mary receives a phone call telling her that her husband has been involved in a serious automobile accident. This news ushers in a central section in the novel, in which Mary and her family gather to await further news. Each member of the family reacts differently to the crisis, but the narrative concentrates in particular on Mary's reaction. A pious Anglo-Catholic, Mary's response to the distinct possibility that her husband has died is made problematic by an evasive religiosity. Although Mary's aunt Hannah is also a deeply religious woman, we see that Hannah finds Mary's histrionic religious rhetoric disturbing and even malign. When Mary persuades Hannah to kneel and pray with her, what Hannah begins to perceive in Mary is not devout belief but spiritual pride and pretension that, ironically, appears to prevent the development of any true religious feeling. Hannah, however, understands how deeply vulnerable Mary is and how devastating the loss of her husband is to her, and she wisely allows Mary to take her own time in accepting the fact of Jay's death, a course of action that recalls an earlier time in which she presided over Rufus's purchase of a cap. The gaudy cap Rufus chose expressed his desire to abandon the babyish identity encouraged by his mother in favor of a more mature identity like that of his free-spirited father. Although the cap was not one to his great-aunt Hannah's taste, she wisely allowed him to make up his own mind. Similarly, Hannah does not impose her ideas on Mary, realizing that she will come to accept Jay's death in her own time and in her own way.

Mary's brother Andrew eventually confirms that Jay has died. The family draws together, but each family member reacts to the death and to the meaning of death itself in his or her own way. Mary at first interprets the accident as a punishment from God and then flees into affirmations of determined religious faith, which, ironically, make her appear increasingly heartless. Mary's brother Andrew disdains organized religion; their father, Joel, goes further by expressing doubts about the nature or existence of God. The division between Mary and Hannah on one side and Joel and Andrew on the other is also suggested by an enigmatic episode in which only Mary and Hannah appear to feel the spirit of Jay returning home to say a last good-bye. In addition to these differing spiritual perspectives, Jay's sullen brother Ralph is haunted by the guilty feeling that his drunken telephone call to his brother began the chain of events that led to his death. Finally, among this confusion of voices are those of neighboring boys, who taunt Rufus with suggestions that Jay had been drinking or perhaps driving too fast, possibly in a self-destructive way.

Jay's funeral is the province of a priggish Anglo-Catholic priest, Father Jackson, who visits the house soon after Jay's death and tells Mary he will not read a full burial service because Jay was not baptized in the Church. Father Jackson emerges as a censorious and insincere man whose purpose is to subjugate the anguished Mary to his authority and who notices the bereaved children only long enough to lecture them on deportment. While Rufus is infuriated by the priest's sanctimony and his presumptuous attempts to exert paternal authority, he is reassured by the family friend Walter Starr, who remembers Jay as a strong, good man with a natural sympathy for everyone.

As the narrative begins with Jay and Rufus walking together, the novel concludes with Andrew and Rufus taking a similar walk after Jay's funeral. Andrew expresses deep hostility to the Church and to Father Jackson, taking pains to impress on Rufus that his loving and lively father was neither genteel nor religious. However, although Andrew is not a believer, he tells Rufus about a miracle he felt he witnessed at Jay's graveside. He notices a butterfly in the coffin as it is lowered into the earth, which he takes as a sign from Jay himself and a hopeful symbol of the soul's transfiguration. This is the one thing, the bitter Andrew tells Rufus, that could make him a believer; but he will share this story only with Rufus, not with Hannah and Mary, who would of course welcome this spiritual moment. Andrew's intense but conflicted feelings of real love and resentful hatred for Hannah and Mary act as a mirror for Rufus's own developing emotional life. As they walk back to the house where the women are waiting for them, Rufus's conversation with Andrew has defined for him the ambivalent relationship both with his mother and with religion that Rufus understands will trouble him for the rest of his life.

Christian Themes

All the key Christian issues are explored within the context of the Anglo-Catholicism in which James Agee was raised in the early years of the twentieth century in the American South. Agee particularly examines Mary Follet's religion as a crucial ingredient in how she faces the sudden death of her young husband. Her reaction to the death, however, indicates that she may be the captive of a mistaken Christianity that fails to cope with grief or loss and instead feeds the sin of spiritual pride.

In addition to exploring Mary's religious convictions, Agee uses the novel to explore an entire family that is divided on the issue of religion. Hannah is a stoical believer; Mary is a grandiose believer; and Joel is angry at God. Andrew, in contrast, is angry at the Church but seems to be in touch with spiritual impulses. The individual nature of each family member's view of religion tells Rufus that beliefs and values ultimately come down to the single self. As Rufus begins to work things out for himself, however, he struggles with the problem of evil, which surfaces within his family in the wake of the death of his father and also in his neighborhood through issues such as racism and bullying.

Even as Agee's novel explores false or hypocritical religiosity, the novel's pervasive mood is one that suggests that the ordinary days and hours of our lives possess a sacred aspect. Similarly, Agee also introduces into his narrative a sense of spiritual humility in the face of the mystery of life and death.

Sources for Further Study

Doty, Mark A. *Tell Me Who I Am: James Agee's Search for Selfhood*. Baton Rouge: Louisiana State University Press, 1981. Examines the theme of identity and the centrality of religion in Agee's life and works.

Folks, Jeffrey J., and David Madden, eds. *Remembering James Agee*. Athens: University of Georgia Press, 1997. Essays and recollections by people who knew Agee, including his widow.

Kramer, Victor A. *James Agee*. Boston: Twayne, 1975. Covers all of Agee's work including a lucid and insightful discussion of *A Death in the Family*.

Lafaro, Michael A., ed. *James Agee: Reconsiderations*. Knoxville: University of Tennessee Press, 1995. Collection of essays that considers the Agee legacy; extensive consideration of *A Death in the Family* and of Agee's narrative techniques.

Spiegel, Alan. *James Agee and the Legend of Himself: A Critical Study*. Columbia: University of Missouri Press, 1998. Important study of all of Agee's work; in-depth consideration of *A Death in the Family*, including discussion of the book as a transcendental novel infused with a sacramental vision.

Margaret Boe Birns

THE DEATH OF IVAN ILYICH

Author: Leo Tolstoy (1828-1910)
First published: Smert' Ivana Il'icha, 1886 (English translation, 1887)
Edition used: The Kreutzer Sonata, and Other Short Stories, edited by Stanley
   Appelbaum. Mineola, N.Y.: Dover, 1993
Genre: Novella
Subgenre: Literary fiction
Core issues: Acceptance; death; forgiveness; repentance; self-knowledge; suffering

Tolstoy presents the sterile life and painful death of a Russian Everyman who has focused on material gain and almost lost his soul. On his deathbed, Ivan Ilyich realizes that he has lived badly, asks forgiveness from his family, and perhaps gains self-knowledge and redemption.

> *Principal characters*
> *Ivan Ilyich*, a Russian magistrate
> *Praskovya Fyodorovna*, Ivan's wife
> *Piotr Ivanovich*, Ivan's colleague
> *Gerasim*, Ivan's servant

Overview

Leo Tolstoy's tale of Ivan Ilyich begins with his death at age forty-five, which is reported by his law colleagues, who read about his demise in the newspaper. Immediately Ivan's colleagues begin to wonder how his death might affect their own positions in the court bureaucracy. Several colleagues attend Ivan's wake, but reluctantly because it interferes with their weekly bridge game.

At the wake, Piotr Ivanovich, Ivan's closest colleague, is engaged in conversation by Praskovya Fyodorovna, Ivan's widow, who tells Piotr that Ivan suffered greatly during the final days of the long illness that ultimately took his life. Praskovya then asks Piotr about Ivan's pension, which she has already calculated, wondering whether she possibly could extract an additional widow's stipend from the government. When Piotr suggests that Praskovya's effort probably would not be successful, Praskovya quickly ends the conversation, and Piotr leaves to attend his bridge game.

After this brief opening scene, Tolstoy's narrator begins to recount Ivan's life, which he identifies as both ordinary and terrible. Ivan, the son of a Russian government official, has lived a life of relative privilege in nineteenth century Russia. He graduates from the state school of law, then moves up the legal bureaucracy, receiving promotions and accompanying increases in salary. After achieving the position of examining magistrate, Ivan begins to consider marriage, mainly on the advice of highly placed law associates. He marries a woman whose family has property and social position. Initially, Ivan and Praskovya seem happy with each other, but she becomes jealous and demanding during her first pregnancy. To avoid conflicts, Ivan withdraws from family life into his work and bridge games with colleagues. The Ilyich marriage produces five offspring, three of whom die in childhood.

Because his marriage is less than satisfactory, Ivan focuses on his career, driven by the power that he holds over individuals and by his salary, which does not increase as quickly as Ivan desires. When Ivan finally receives a good promotion and substantial salary increase, he seems happy. He purchases a large house and fusses over its furnishings. After Ivan and his family settle into their spacious new home, however, he complains that it is just one room short. Nonetheless, Tolstoy's narrator describes the life of Ivan Ilyich as thoroughly pleasant and proper.

Ivan's pleasant life takes a downward turn when he falls off a ladder while showing an interior decorator how new draperies should be hung. Ivan suffers a painful bruise on his side. The wound seems to heal quickly, but Ivan feels a lingering pain in his side and a foul taste in his mouth. He consults several doctors, none of whom correctly diagnoses Ivan's problem. As his health deteriorates and his mood sours, Praskovya begins to hope that Ivan will die, then prays that he will live so that his salary will not cease. She fails to provide Ivan with any care or show any concern for him as his condition worsens. Medications offer no relief for Ivan. Only Gerasim, one of Ivan's servants, provides any relief. On a particularly bad day, Ivan asks Gerasim to lift his legs and insert a pillow under them, and Ivan feels his pain ease when the young man raises his legs. He sometimes calls on Gerasim to lift his legs and place them on Gerasim's shoulders until his pain eases.

As Ivan's health continues to deteriorate, he falls into despair. He begins to hate his wife, who virtually ignores his suffering. He becomes frustrated with the medical specialists who attempt to treat his illness. Looking back on his career accomplishments and on the wealth that he has accumulated provides no satisfaction for Ivan. A priest who hears Ivan's confession provides only temporary relief. Eventually Ivan's damaged spirit causes more pain and anguish than his deteriorating body, and he begins to sense that he is dying. In desperation, Ivan calls on God, asking why he has brought this endless suffering on Ivan, who still believes that he has lived a pleasant and proper life. The response to Ivan's question comes in the form of an inner voice that asks whether indeed Ivan has lived life correctly.

Ivan begins to review his entire life and realizes that his fondest memories are from his childhood. He has some good memories of his time at the school of law, but no more after the start of the deadly period that produced Ivan's current situation—his preoccupation with his salary and promotions, a loveless marriage, and the boring duties of a public official. Ivan recognizes that as he was rising in professional stature, his life was actually slipping away from him. He starts to think that he has lived improperly, even while he was rising in position and public opinion. As he looks into the eyes of Gerasim, the happy and healthy peasant, Ivan senses that his entire life might have been false.

Tolstoy's novella concludes by relating the physical suffering and mental anguish that Ivan experiences during the final three days of his life. Screaming in anguish,

Ivan wonders where his life went wrong and how he might have corrected it. Hours before Ivan's death, his son visits his deathbed. Momentarily calm, Ivan reaches out to the boy, who grabs his father's hand and kisses it. At that instant, Ivan sees a light and realizes his errors. He has made his family miserable; he has treated his wife and children wretchedly. Ivan tries to ask forgiveness and mutters "forego" instead of "forgive," but he believes that God will understand what he intended to say. Ivan realizes that he must die to release his family members from the suffering that he has caused them. At that moment, Ivan sees light and experiences joy. Seconds later, Ivan says to himself that death is no more and dies.

Christian Themes

The Death of Ivan Ilyich is a story of sin and redemption. Ivan had been blindly building what he thought was a good and proper life. He had completed his education, landed professional positions with increasing responsibilities and salary, married well, and surrounded himself with the outward signs of wealth—a large estate with handsome and stylish furnishings. However, Ivan's obsession with work, money, and possessions, and his neglect of his family, brought on Ivan a personal crisis from which he could not recover. Ivan's physical problems—which began when he fell from a ladder while obsessing over draperies—provoked the spiritual crisis that caused his anguish and eventually led to his death.

Ivan's suffering, however, prompts a self-examination that leads ultimately to his redemption. That self-examination begins when Ivan asks God why he is allowing Ivan, who believes he has led a pleasant and proper life, to suffer. An inner voice questions whether Ivan has lived a good life, provoking Ivan to review his entire life, from his childhood to the time of his illness. This self-examination results in an epiphany for Ivan, as he realizes the sterility of a life of materialism and meaningless work, a life without love and human contact. On his deathbed, Ivan asks his son's—and God's—forgiveness for his errors and accepts his own death. His admission of guilt and acceptance of death relieves his suffering, allowing him to see light before he closes his eyes for the final time.

Ivan's redemption, however, is private, recognized by no one else in Tolstoy's tale. In the novella's opening frame, Ivan's colleagues go about their business, obsessing over their positions in the Russian law court bureaucracy; some are too busy to attend Ivan's wake and funeral. After Ivan's death, his widow, having learned nothing from her husband's sufferings, is mainly concerned with receiving Ivan's pension so that she can continue living a life devoted to material possessions.

The publication of *The Death of Ivan Ilyich* occurred during a period in Tolstoy's life in which he became increasingly concerned with religious issues and closely studied the Gospels of the New Testament. Following a personal religious crisis during the late 1870's, Tolstoy embraced a radical form of Christianity that is expressed in *The Death of Ivan Ilyich* and other works published during the 1880's.

Sources for Further Study

Jahn, Gary R. *The Death of Ivan Ilich: An Interpretation*. New York: Twayne, 1993. A monograph-length study of Tolstoy's text, containing character analyses and discussions of major themes.

Orwin, Donna Trilling, ed. *The Cambridge Companion to Tolstoy*. Cambridge, England: Cambridge University Press, 2002. A collection of essays on Tolstoy's major works.

Tolstoy, Leo. *Tolstoy's Short Fiction*. Edited by Michael R. Katz. New York: W. W. Norton, 1991. Contains critical essays on *The Death of Ivan Ilyich* and other Tolstoy stories.

James Tackach

DEATH ON A FRIDAY AFTERNOON
Meditations on the Last Words of Jesus from the Cross

Author: Richard John Neuhaus (1936-   )
First published: New York: Basic Books, 2000
Genre: Nonfiction
Subgenres: Biblical studies; meditation and contemplation; theology
Core issues: Atonement; the cross; death; hope; Jesus Christ; Lutherans and Lutheranism; sacrifice; salvation

The suffering and death of Jesus Christ on the cross on Good Friday afternoon is both the defining narrative and the central mystery of Christianity. Neuhaus examines the seven passages Christ is reported to have spoken as he died, words that reveal the layers of implications in the Crucifixion, which in turn help define the meaning of redemptive sacrifice, the difficult reality of death, the dynamic of Christian justice and punishment, and the ramifications of the Passion as a consummate act of divine love.

Overview

Richard John Neuhaus first came to national prominence in the mid-1960's when, as a Lutheran pastor, he participated in both the Civil Rights and antiwar movements. Later, after a much documented conversion to Roman Catholicism and ordination into the priesthood, he emerged as a staunchly conservative Church commentator on social and political issues. In the early 1990's, Neuhaus survived a catastrophic health crisis; a tumor ruptured in his intestines, and several mishandled procedures led to further complications. That near-death experience encouraged the theologian to explore the implications of mortality and specifically the difficult mystery of a Christian death. Those speculations led Neuhaus to focus on the words Christ spoke during the three-hour public execution on the cross (Christianity, he points out, is alone in centering its faith on the death of its God). The seven passages, as recorded by the four Evangelists, are: "Father, forgive them; for they know not what they do"; "Truly, I say to you, today you will be with me in Paradise"; "Woman, behold your son. Son, behold your mother"; "My God, My God, why hast thou forsaken me?"; "I thirst"; "It is finished"; and "Father, into your hands I commend my spirit."

Neuhaus devotes a chapter to each utterance. Drawing on a wide range of relevant biblical passages and traditional scholarship, Neuhaus explicates the import of each passage and extends its argument to reveal the mysteries that are central to the cross, mysteries that Neuhaus contends are not designed to be resolved but rather contemplated until they yield not answers but wonder. His exegesis is directed particularly to contemporary Christians who have not sufficiently examined the Passion or who have been persuaded by the faddish optimism of New Age revisionism to embrace the joy of Easter at the expense of confronting the complicated love at the heart of the ghastly sacrifice on Calvary.

Neuhaus's premise is that Christians must begin by accepting that they are all, by reason of their pride, implicated in the sin that demanded divine intervention. Meditation on the Crucifixion, thus, is not a morbid exercise in sadomasochism or a clinical study of victimhood. Rather it is a profound speculation on the vastness of God's plan for his creation and how God determined to set right the fall of Adam, to reassert the joyful dependency of humanity (Neuhaus contends the sacrifice on Good Friday is meant to redeem all creation), and to celebrate the mercy and love of the Creator. Although revisionist readings of the Crucifixion often dismiss the subtleties of the act by seeing Christ as a God playacting at death or by seeing God the Father as an unreasonable, even sinister paterfamilias tormenting an innocent son, Neuhaus sees Good Friday as a powerful reminder that Christians have only their helplessness to offer to God. He uses the figures of Mary and the disciple John at the foot of the cross to suggest the opportunity for the faithful of all eras to witness the glory of Christ's surrender and, there amid the evident pain and agony, to find the premise of a sustaining hope. Only by accepting that witnessing role (and not hurrying to the obvious joys of the Resurrection) can Christians begin to approach the surrender to death itself as a Christian experience.

Neuhaus is perhaps his most powerful when he explicates the apparent despair of Christ's disconcerting cry of abandonment, drawn from Psalm 22, accusing God of forsaking him. Neuhaus, dismissing the appropriation of the line as a bumper sticker for postmodern alienation, returns the modern Christian to the fullest implications of those last agonizing moments. He argues that in those moments, Christ accepted his role as a creature, and his words mark a joyful, albeit difficult, surrender to a silent but loving God. Glory, Neuhaus finds, comes from obedience, a position at odds with modern feel-good self-aggrandizing Christianity. God, Neuhaus argues, is very much at Calvary, thus providing that act of uncompromising surrender its widest possible context. The responsibility of the modern Christian (which Neuhaus draws from Christ's distressed call for drink) is not only to accept the mystery of the cross but also to witness to that mystery, to practice the zealous missionary protocol to extend the word of God, to thirst for souls with a fervor that Neuhaus sees as flagging since the close of the great era of Christian evangelizing more than a century ago.

Thus, when Christ, shortly before his death, proclaims, "It is finished," Neuhaus says that, far from indicating resignation, the words indicate that the project of redemption has been fulfilled, that the sacrifice of Christ's love signaled that God has again invested hope in the human project. It is an act that cannot be revoked. Far from a scapegoat, Christ has mended the relationship between humanity and God in a conspiracy of love conducted through the agency of the triune Christian God.

Christian Themes

Throughout the Christian era, the seven utterances of Christ on the cross have been, as Neuhaus points out in *Death on a Friday Afternoon*, the subject of numerous interpretations, Catholic and otherwise, ranging from Ludwig van Beethoven to Samuel Beckett, from James Joyce to Pope John Paul II. Given the stark confrontation with his own mortality and his long publishing career examining the troubling implications of Christianity in a contemporary culture unwilling, or as Neuhaus fears, uninterested, in accepting the fullest responsibilities of its faith, Neuhaus brings to the genre a singular voice that offers a reading of these words that although solidly girded by biblical scholarship is immediate and accessible. To establish its relevance, the argument draws from personal anecdotes and popular culture without abandoning its gravitas. Although in the 1980's Neuhaus had established a reputation as an uncompromising archconservative columnist for *Commonweal* and as the editor of provocative critiques of modern culture, he offers these chapters not as scholarly exegeses or as incendiary diatribes but rather as occasions for reflection, arguing that only in pondering the essential mystery of the sacrifice at Calvary (a God accepting the ignominy of such a brutal and public execution) can a contemporary Christian begin to appreciate the gift of hope that is central to the Christian conception of the universe as creation.

Thus, there is nothing groundbreaking in Neuhaus's commentaries. He places the Crucifixion at the core of the Christian story, grounded in the Jewish concept of atonement, and then locates the agony of Christ, rather than the Resurrection, as the defining act of redemption for humanity. His reading of the implications of the Crucifixion, specifically the obligation of Christians to accept complicity in the need for their own salvation (to gather, metaphorically, at the foot of the cross) and the obligation, in turn, to witness the power of Calvary to those still unconvinced of its centrality in human history, gains its impact by being offered to a contemporary nominally Christian world too fearful of death, too obsessed with ego, too enthralled by the fetching busyness of today, and too easily persuaded by theological readings that have softened the Crucifixion.

God is unknowable, Neuhaus concedes, but Christians are invited to approach the unfathomable mystery of the execution of Christ with patience and faith and to see there amid evident hopelessness the beginnings of Christians' perfect surrender to God's unfolding plan for salvation.

Sources for Further Study

Brown, Raymond. *The Death of the Messiah: From Gethsemane to the Grave—A Commentary on the Passion Narrative in the Four Gospels.* New York: Doubleday, 1994. A standard work in the genre of Passion commentaries. Although Neuhaus draws on commentaries since Saint Augustine, Brown's reading, a traditional exegesis, is a frequent subject of Neuhaus's critique.

Neuhaus, Richard John. *As I Lay Dying: Meditations upon Returning.* New York: Perseus, 2002. An indispensable companion volume that brings together eschatological theology with personal testimony by exploring the implications of mortality and Christianity through Neuhaus's own medical crisis.

_____. *Catholic Matters: Confusion, Controversy and the Splendor of Truth.* New York: Basic Books, 2006. Neuhaus examines the state of the Catholic Church, especially after Vatican II, and describes why he became a priest.

"Richard John Neuhaus, 1936-." *Contemporary Authors Online*. Farmington Hills, Mich.: Thomson Gale, 2006. Overview of Neuhaus's spiritual journey from Lutheran pastor and political activist to archconservative voice of Catholicism. Includes helpful biographical timeline and bibliography.

Joseph Dewey

A DECLARATION OF THE SENTIMENTS OF ARMINIUS

Author: Jacobus Arminius (1560-1609)
First published: Corte ende grondighe verclaringhe uyt de Heylighe Schrift . . . over het swaerwichtighe poinct vande cracht ende rechtvaerdicheyt der voorsienicheyt Godts ontrent he quade, 1608 (English translation, 1657)
Edition used: The Writings of James Arminius, translated from the Latin by James Nichols and W. R. Bagnall. 3 vols. Grand Rapids, Mich.: Baker Book House, 1977
Genre: Nonfiction
Subgenre: Theology
Core issues: Arminianism; Calvinism; Methodists and Methodism; salvation

Arminius thought Calvin's ideas of predestination as taught in seventeenth century Holland were injurious to the glory of God and repugnant to Scripture. He wrote this book to explain the Bible more clearly.

Overview

In 1608, when theological differences arose over predestination and threatened civil war, the Dutch national legislature called Dutch Reformed minister and professor of theology Jacobus Arminius to explain why he rejected Calvinism. After hearing both sides of this issue, the government decided that since the controversy had no bearing on the main points pertaining to salvation, each side should tolerate the other. Arminius died the following year, but his ideas were developed and championed by the founder of Methodism, John Wesley. Later thinkers who opposed Calvinism called themselves Arminians and advocated Unitarianism (the rationalistic belief that God exists only in one person) and Pelagianism (the denial of Original Sin and the belief that human beings have perfect free will to do either right or wrong), two movements that Arminius himself had repudiated.

In *A Declaration of the Sentiments of Arminius* (also known as the "Just Man's Defense"), Arminius explains the doctrine of predestination as taught by his opponents. It has four main points:

(1) Before the creation of the world, God chose to make certain individuals in order to give them eternal life in heaven, and others in order to destroy them in hell. He did this to show his mercy and his power, and nothing in the individuals themselves can account for the destiny God chooses for them.

(2) In order to carry out his plan, God created human beings and then made them commit sin.

(3) God brings those whom he has chosen to save to faith in Christ by irresistible grace, so that it is impossible for them to avoid going to heaven.

(4) God withholds grace from those whom he has chosen to damn, so they cannot believe and be saved.

Arminius then gives twenty reasons for rejecting this view of predestination. They may be condensed into eleven:

(1) No council of the early church, church father, or contemporary church creed holds this doctrine.

(2) It is repugnant to the nature of God, especially his justice and goodness: to his justice, because it teaches that God determined to punish some people even before they became sinners; to his goodness, because it states that from eternity God willed the greatest evil to some of his creatures.

(3) It is contrary to the nature of humanity, which God created in his image, whom he endowed with free will, and in whom he instilled the disposition and aptitude for enjoying eternal life.

(4) It is diametrically opposed to the act of creation, because the purpose of creation is to communicate good. According to predestination, some people are created only for the purpose of damnation, so creating them does not communicate any good.

(5) It is at open hostility with the nature of eternal life, which the Bible calls "the reward of obedience" (Hebrews 6:10).

(6) It is opposed to the nature of eternal death, which the Bible says is "the wages of sin" (Romans 6:23).

(7) It is inconsistent with the nature and properties of sin, which the Bible calls "disobedience" and "rebellion," because a person who has no choice cannot disobey or rebel.

(8) It is repugnant to the nature of divine grace, because predestination understands grace to take away free will and to be irresistible, but the Bible says people have free will and that they can resist God's grace.

(9) It is injurious to the glory of God, because it makes God the author of sin, and in fact, the only one real sinner in the universe.

(10) It is hurtful to the salvation of humanity, because it states that humans can contribute nothing toward their own salvation, and if that were true, they need not even try.

(11) It is in open hostility to the ministry of the Gospel because it implies that nothing the minister does—not preaching, not baptizing, not praying—will make any difference in anyone's salvation.

After rejecting predestination, Arminius explains two attempts to avoid the problems it raises. The first is to say God made all humans mortal and incapable of any supernatural activity, even of simple obedience to God. God then chose some of them to be made spiritual, capable of a relationship with him, and favored with eternal life. This kind of predestination believes in election but rejects reprobation, saying that God merely passes over those who end up being damned. The second attempt to escape the objections to predestination says God did not choose to elect and reprobate people until after he had decided that all should fall into sin. Thus God is not predestining people who are guiltless, but out of all of sinful humanity, he graciously saves some. By each of these explanations, the holders of predestination hope to avoid making God the author of sin.

Arminius rejects these two modifications, pointing out that both of them attribute the fall of humanity to God's decree, either by making humans naturally incapable of obeying him or by willing that all humanity should fall. Neither of these schemes solves the problem of making God responsible for sin.

Finally, Arminius explains what he believes the Bible teaches about predestination. Mirroring his presentation of his opponents' belief, he makes four points about it.

(1) The first absolute decree of God is to appoint his son, Jesus Christ, to mediate salvation to the world.

(2) The second absolute decree of God is to save those who repent and believe in Christ and to damn those who refuse to believe.

(3) The third divine degree is to administer the means for salvation according to divine wisdom and justice.

(4) The fourth divine decree is to save those particular individuals whom God through foreknowledge knows will come to faith and will persevere.

Arminius finally shows how this understanding of predestination fulfills the conditions which his opponents' understanding does not.

Besides predestination, Arminius deals with nine other topics related to it, briefly saying that God's providence means that nothing happens in the world by chance but that the good happens by God's direction and the bad happens by God's permission. God orders the events of the world in a way that glorifies him and saves believers. Of human free will, Arminius says that people were originally endowed with free will but lost it in the Fall. However, by God's grace, the regenerate are capable of freely doing the good. About God's grace, Arminius states that his only disagreement with the predestinarians is whether one can resist it or not. He says the Scripture clearly teaches that people may reject the Holy Spirit and reject the grace of God. Arminius says that in the matter of the perseverance of the saints, some Bible passages seem to affirm it and some seem to deny it, and he is still considering the matter. Likewise Arminius considers the assurance of salvation to be a matter of further discussion, because the Scripture is not clear on this topic. Another matter for further consideration is the perfection of believers in this life.

On a wholly different topic Arminius treats the question of whether God the Son can properly be termed *autotheos*, or "God in himself." After a long discussion, he concludes that he cannot, because the Son has the divine essence from the Father. Next, he refuses to take sides in the question of whether the active obedience of Christ justifies humanity as well as his passive obedience. Finally, he opposes those who say the Dutch Confession and the Heidelberg Catechism should never be subject to examination or revision, pointing out that only God's word is immutable.

Christian Themes

Arminius's main concern is to protect the justice and goodness of God, which are compromised by the idea that God created certain individuals solely for the purpose of damning them. The idea that people do not have free will but only follow the course that God predestined for them also impugns God's character. While Calvinists believe the foundational truth of the Bible to be God's sovereign grace in the predestination of individuals to heaven or hell, Arminius says it is God's love for the sinner and his gracious salvation for all who believe.

Sources for Further Study

Bangs, Carl. *Arminius: A Study in the Dutch Reformation*. Nashville, Tenn.: Abingdon Press, 1971. A theological biography explaining Arminius's work in its historical setting.

Forster, Roger T., and V. Paul Marston. *God's Strategy in Human History*. Wheaton, Ill.: Tyndale House, 1974. A modern presentation of Arminian theology.

Hunt, Dave. *What Love Is This? Calvinism's Misrepresentation of God*. 2d ed. Bend, Oreg.: Berean Call, 2004. A somewhat simplistic refutation of Calvinism.

Peterson, Robert A., and Michael D. Williams. *Why I Am Not an Arminian*. Downers Grove, Ill.: InterVarsity Press, 2004. A modern presentation of the objections to Arminianism.

Slaatte, Howard A. *The Arminian Arm of Theology: The Theologies of John Fletcher, First Methodist Theologian, and His Precursor, James Arminius*. Washington, D.C.: University Press of America, 1979. A work showing how Fletcher's theology influenced Arminius and John Wesley and Methodism.

Walls, Jerry L., and Joseph R. Dongel. *Why I Am Not a Calvinist*. Downers Grove, Ill.: InterVarsity Press, 2004. A modern presentation of Arminian and other objections to Calvinism.

Charles White

THE DESTINY OF MAN

Author: Nicolai Berdyaev (1874-1948)
First published: O naznachenii cheloveka, 1931 (English translation, 1937)
Edition used: The Destiny of Man, translated by Natalie Duddington. New York: Harper, 1960
Genre: Nonfiction
Subgenres: Critical analysis; spiritual treatise; theology
Core issues: Creation; freedom and free will; good vs. evil; love; redemption; time

Traditional theological explanations of the origin of good and evil, Berdyaev contends, are demeaning to humanity and posit an Aristotlean monotheistic Creator, thereby failing to attribute a sufficient sense of creative freedom to God or humankind. Instead, God the Creator must strive with a mystic realm of freedom called the "Ungrund" in order to exercise his freedom in making the world. As free spirits, human beings are at their most spiritual and godlike when they exercise their freedom in acts of creativity. When humanity learns to overcome the limitations of historical time to live in partnership with God in existential time, then humanity in alliance with the divine will create the last days or the end of time and bring about the fulfillment of human life in an apocalyptic conclusion to history.

Overview

Nicolai Berdyaev wrote *The Destiny of Man* as an exile in Paris, following a long philosophical journey that began in his native Russia. Born in czarist Russia in Kiev to an aristocratic father who was a skeptical disciple of Voltaire and to a mother of French descent sympathetic to Catholicism, Berdyaev gradually moved from skepticism to Christianity in the form of the Russian Orthodox faith, following a brief infatuation with Marxism as a youth. From the first he rejected the materialism of Marxism, and he had turned to philosophic idealism before embracing the passion for spiritual freedom in certain Russian thinkers, most notably in Fyodor Dostoevski's impressive fiction.

After reactionary forces in czarist Russia exiled him to a rural province near Kiev, Berdyaev began to engage in religious speculation with intellectual groups during residence in St. Petersburg, Paris, and Moscow before accepting the Orthodox faith. Despite his conversion, however, he explored Christian theology from a critical position, an approach that brought him into conflict with his church's conservative hierarchy, and his lifelong support of social reform and liberal causes caused friction first with the czarist government and later with the Soviet administration.

An energetic writer, Berdyaev published numerous articles and books on religion and social issues during his fourteen years in Moscow, despite much opposition. However, after the Russian Revolution, his work brought him into irreconcilable conflict with the Communist government, thereby causing permanent exile in 1922. After a brief residence in Berlin, he settled permanently in Paris, where he became a lecturer and prolific author on theological themes and often worked to bring about rapprochement between French Catholics and French Protestants.

Berdyaev considered himself to be an existentialist because he did not believe in the validity of building a philosophical system like those constructed by traditional philosophers who had been attacked for this practice by Søren Kierkegaard. As, however, he claimed to have discovered the writing of the Christian existentialist Kierkegaard rather late, Dostoevski, particularly his novels, was a greater influence than Kierkegaard. In fact, Dostoevski was the subject of one of Berdyaev's early books *Mirosozertzanie Dostoievskago* (1923; *Dostoievsky: An Interpretation*, 1934). Another major influence was German mysticism, especially the writings of Meister Eckhart and Jakob Böhme.

Rapidity of composition tended to make Berdyaev's books seem somewhat repetitious and unsystematic, though the concept of a book often came to him as a single, unified imaginative vision. As illustration, he revealed in his posthumous autobiography *Samopozhaniye* (1949; *Dream and Reality*, 1950), that the idea for *The Destiny of Man* came to him while he was watching a ballet in Paris.

Not only is *The Destiny of Man* one of the most coherent and unified of Berdyaev's books, but also its synthesis of his major themes makes it a central event in the development of his thought. The work looks both back to his influential early work, *Smysl tvorchestva* (1916; *The Meaning of the Creative Act*, 1955), and forward to his analysis of the obsessions that enslave the human spirit in his later masterpiece, *O rabstvie I svobodie chelovieka* (1939; *Slavery and Freedom*, 1944).

The nominal subject of *The Destiny of Man* is a study of ethics from the perspective of Berdyaev's theology, but in reality, the book takes on a cosmic perspective, since Berdyaev begins with a theory of the creation of the world and the origin of evil and proceeds to a visionary and eschatological conclusion. Hence the book is divided into three well-defined parts.

The first section of Berdyaev's work is concerned with the theme of creation and the fall of humanity into a world of good and evil. Here Berdyaev rejects static theological conceptions of God in favor of a creator who must strive for perfection by creating the world from the mystic realm of the *ungrund* or realm of potential, a concept that Berdyaev took from the writing of Jakob Böhme. In Berdyaev's thought, God is a striving spirit, and human beings are also free spirits who must struggle with the limitations of matter.

In the second part of *The Destiny of Man*, Berdyaev proceeds to discuss specific problems of ethics, focusing on such themes as social reform and sexuality. In essence, he sees human existence largely as a tragic conflict between spiritual striving and the material realm, but unlike thoroughgoing Gnostics, Berdyaev does not naïvely attribute evil to the concrete world of matter.

Finally, in the third and most inspiring section of *The Destiny of Man*, Berdyaev discusses death, immortality, and the apocalyptic transformation of life. Rejecting Greek ideas of the immortality of the soul, Berdyaev contends that Christianity must seek a transformed world, beyond the commonplace notions of good and evil, a realm created at the end of time involving the complete resurrection of the body in a spiritual form.

Christian Themes

At first glance, Berdyaev's thinking may remind readers of the heterodox vision of the English poet William Blake, and this resemblance should not be entirely surprising, since both thinkers shared a common influence—the mysticism of Jakob Böhme. Moreover, both were passionately dedicated to the ideals of human freedom and creativity, and both believed in the need for positive action to transform society.

Though remaining close to the boundaries of orthodox Christian theology, Berdyaev's work offers strong criticisms of certain traditional theologies, such as Thomism, that posit a creator who is omnipotent but who seems remote and dispassionate toward humanity. For Berdyaev, such a conception is overly rationalist and derives ultimately from Aristotle, not from Christian sources. Berdyaev shows a particular scorn for theologies that emphasize human weakness and are demeaning to the dignity of human beings. In this regard, both Roman Catholicism and classical Protestant Calvinism become targets of Berdyaev's attack.

In the final summation, Berdyaev places the highest value on human personality and its potential to be creative in every sphere of life. Thoughtful Christians should find Berdyaev's eschatological thought intriguing and provocative. Berdyaev does not present his vision of the final days in a superstitious tone or picture it as a coming event that inspires terror, as in Medieval Christianity or some forms of Christianity today. Rather, Berdyaev's vision of the end is based on his concept of the different modes of time in which humans may live, and the achievement of eschatological events results from the partnership between the striving of human spirits and the action of God.

Sources for Further Study

Berdyaev, Nicolai. *Dream and Reality: An Essay in Autobiography*. Translated by Katherine Lampert. London: Geoffrey Bles, 1950. Berdyaev's autobiography, whose Russian title means "self-knowledge," focuses on intellectual issues and spiritual values, though it is rather slight in its treatment of personal details, such as comments on his marriage.

Dye, James. "Berdyaev." In *A Companion to the Philosophers*, edited by Robert L. Arrington. Malden, Mass.: Blackwell, 1999. Brief but insightful article on Berdyaev describes the theme of spirit in his work. Many of the other entries in this volume, such as the essay on Henri Bergson, should be of interest to readers of Berdyaev.

Lowrie, Donald A. *Rebellious Prophet: A Life of Nicolai Berdyaev*. London: Victor Gollancz, 1960. A sympathetic biography by a translator and disciple of Berdyaev, describing major intellectual themes in the work. Lowrie treats Berdyaev's turn to the Russian Orthodox faith as an "evolution" rather than a conversion.

Ree, Jonathan, and J. O. Urmson, eds. *The Concise Encylopedia of Western Philoso-phy*. 3d ed. New York: Routledge, 2005. Contains an excellent brief entry on Berdyaev, describing major concepts in his work. Also offers helpful if terse es-says on philosophers who had some influence on him as well as on major philo-sophical movements such as existentialism.

Slaatte, Howard A. *Time, Existence, and Destiny: Nichoas Berdyaev's Philosophy of Time*. New York: Peter Lang, 1988. Readable and perceptive description of central themes in Berdyaev's philosophical theology.

Vallon, Michel Alexander. *An Apostle of Freedom: Life and Teachings of Nicholas Berdyaev*. New York: Philosophical Library, 1960. A very informative biography in English. Vallon's work presents Berdyaev in the context of Russian cultural his-tory and deals in detail with his conversion.

Edgar L. Chapman

DEVOTIONS UPON EMERGENT OCCASIONS

Author: John Donne (1572-1631)
First published: 1624
Edition used: Devotions upon Emergent Occasions: Together with "Death's Duel."
  Ann Arbor: University of Michigan Press, 1959
Genre: Nonfiction
Subgenres: Devotions; meditation and contemplation
Core issues: Connectedness; death; fear; God; healing; prayer; regeneration; the Sacraments; soul; suffering

A great poet in an age of great poetry and a great preacher in an age of great preaching, Donne studied at Oxford and at Lincoln's Inn; joined the famous expedition to Cadiz (1596); aspired to preferment at court until James I pressed him into Anglican orders (1615); and was appointed dean to London's Saint Paul's Cathedral (1621), where he served until his death. His meditative imagination is evident in both his religious poetry and his prose. Among his best-known works are the two Anniversaries *(1611, 1612), the* Divine Poems *(1633), and "Death's Duel," the most celebrated of his 160 extant sermons.*

Overview

"No man is an island." However familiar this observation, few except students of English literature would recognize it as coming from John Donne's *Devotions upon Emergent Occasions*. That may be because today Donne is remembered more for his metaphysical poetry than for his spiritual exercises, and we are more inclined to think of a rakish Jack Donne than of an earnest dean of London's Saint Paul's Cathedral and author of the devotions. Nevertheless, the dean had the temperament of the poet, and his spiritual exercises exhibited the imaginative concreteness, intellectual tautness, and dramatic immediacy of his poetry. As in the poetry, puns and metaphors abound; images build on images; analogies and correspondences between the material and the spiritual world are discovered and elaborated. Even the poetry's familiar themes are evident: the transience of human existence, the illusory character of the phenomenal world, and the ubiquity of death and dissolution.

There was, however, no work with more personal immediacy for Donne than *Devotions upon Emergent Occasions*. Their circumstance was a sudden sickness, thought to have been either typhus or relapsing fever, that brought him near death in the winter of 1523. Donne was then in his third year as Saint Paul's dean and in the tenth year of his ministry. Not that Donne had aspired to church or pulpit. He contemplated holy orders at first reluctantly and then principally at the urging of the king, James I. Nevertheless, the interpretation he gave to this first vocational crisis is consistent with the thoroughness with which he gave himself to the Church. "[T]hou who hadst put that desire into [the King's] heart didst also put into mine, an obedience to it." His almost exclusive occupation with sacred themes after his ordination indicates how earnest he was when in his own words he turned from "the mistress of my youth, Poesie, to the wife of mine age, Divinity." Because he believed himself called to God's service, the serious illness of his fifty-first year had a vocational as well as a personal significance for the author. "Why callest thou me from my calling?" "In the door of the grave, this sickbed, no Man shall hear me praise thee." The author's "calling" to the Church intermingles with thoughts about the soul's vocation and final destiny.

So vividly presented are the successive stages of the sickness that one is tempted to take the contemporary biographer Izaak Walton at his word, that the devotions were composed on the sickbed. The probability is that they were written during Donne's convalescence. The work consisted of a dedication to Prince Charles, later king; the Latin *Stationes*, or table of contents in the shape of a poem; and the text proper, containing twenty-three devotions, which are further divided into meditations, expostulations, and prayers. The meditations open each devotion with a report on the sickness or with a reflection on the human condition; the expostulations anatomize the soul's spiritual condition; and the prayers express the soul's willing conformity to God's proceedings. Collectively, the devotions chart the disease and its treatment over the twenty-three days of sickness, beginning with the first evident alteration in the patient's condition. Almost as if making diary entries, Donne details each day. The patient takes to his bed; the physician is called. Other physicians are brought in for consultation, and these are joined by the king's own physician. The disease worsens imperceptibly; a cordial is administered for the heart, and pigeons are applied to the feet to draw off humors from the head. Spots appear and the crisis deepens. Tolling bells of a nearby church signal the death of a neighbor. The physicians detect hopeful signs, and at last the patient rises from bed, as Lazarus from the grave, but with warning of the danger of relapsing.

The meditations thus detail the patient's physical state or his treatment; they take the body as a type or figure for the self and the human condition, and they usually reflect not directly on religious themes but on secular ones. The third meditation, for example, focuses on the patient taking to his bed, on the likeness of the grave to the sickbed, and on the contrariness between the prone position of the sick and the natural upright position to which God created us. The Renaissance commonplace that "man is a little world" is the motif for the fourth meditation. How much greater than nature are human beings, whose thoughts reach around the globe and from earth to heaven, and how strange it is that they have need of physicians, when even wild creatures are physicians to themselves. At every point, we are confronted by our paradoxical nature, at once a wonder of the world and a fickle, variable thing, prone to sudden alteration, dissolution, decay, and decomposition. "Let [the self] be a world," we read in the eighth meditation, "and him self be the land, and misery the sea." The waters of the sea swell above the hills, whelming kings and commoners alike, for all are dust, "coagulated and kneaded into earth, by tears."

The meditations take measure of the human condition: "Variable, and therefore miserable condition of man!" Throughout, the human condition is discovered in the condition of the human body, the principal analogue for the meditator's larger text,

God's Second Book, the historical world of time and space. The expostulations repeat the themes or the motifs of the meditations for, in Donne's words, "the body dost effigiate my soul to me." The expostulations, however, are more passionate, more urgent than the meditations. In the expostulations, for example, the meditator exegetes Scripture and anatomizes the spirit's health: The soul hangs in the balance. Thus, nature's inconstancy is the theme of a meditation arising from the sudden weakening of the body's faculties with the first approach of the sickness; the expostulation turns on the soul's vulnerability. His prostrate body occasions a meditation on human dignity; the expostulation focuses on spiritual impotency. The prospect of universal ruin accompanies the "insensible" or imperceptible progress of the disease; the expostulation wrestles with Eve's temptation and Adam's sin, with the serpent within the human heart and the lie that conceals the heart's guilt.

The devotions progress from a general meditation in the first section to the soul's concrete expostulation of God in the second, from thoughts on the condition of humankind to the private afflictions of the individual soul, from contemplation of the world of humanity to an anxiety about the state of the spirit. A resultant energy and passionate intensity characterize Donne's exegesis of God's Third Book, the Bible, in the middle section of each devotion, and this level of intensity sets these spiritual exercises apart from most traditional meditations. Rather than spiritual colloquies, the soul's conversations with God, the expostulations take the form (as the Latin of "expostulation" indicates) of urgent demands or passionate interrogations. The biblical text is interrogated for answers to the exegete's own bewilderment in face of the text's ambiguities or the soul's doubts and uncertainties. In the sixth devotion, for example, the patient marks the apprehension in his physician and the mounting fear in himself. In the expostulation he searches Scripture to resolve his mind that fear need not be evidence of despair. He reads in Scripture that "fear is a stifling spirit," and asks: "Shall a fear of thee take away my devotion to thee?" He discovers also that fear of the Lord is the beginning of wisdom and that a holy fear is an antidote against "inordinate fear." From start to finish, the exegete scrutinizes biblical texts and presses God for a clarification of his meaning ("Dost thou command me to speak to thee, and command me to fear thee?"), pressing the demand at times very near complaint, "too near murmuring." In the end, the questions are answered, the ambiguities and doubts are resolved, and the expostulations attain a kind of equilibrium in what amounts to an intellectual assurance, propaedeutic to the affective or emotional acceptance of the prayers, which conclude each devotion.

Taken separately, the expostulations move from ambiguity and doubt to clarity and assurance. Collectively, they chart the soul's conversion from a self-preoccupation and a "care" for its own preservation to a concern for the neighbor, from anxiety and fear to patience and assurance. By the sixth devotion, absorption with sin, God's anger, spiritual impotency, and isolation have been somewhat mollified intellectually—if not affectively—by an acceptance of a wholesome fear of the Lord. In the seventh devotion we hear also of the "multiplication" of divine assistances and of Donne's profound dependency on the Church and its Sacraments. We become aware too that the spiritual exercises, while they are intensely personal, are not private. The Church is never far from the meditator's mind, nor are the Sacraments—confession, baptism, Eucharist—ever without a place in his devotion. Even confinement to the sickbed in the second devotion causes Donne anxious concern for his soul's safety. "It is not a recusancy," protesting his absence from church, "for I would come [to thy holy temple], but an excommunication, I must not come." Thus, when the seventh devotion notes the consultation of his physicians, the meditator's mind turns to God's manner of proceeding with the soul afflicted with spiritual disease. "Thy way from the beginning," he announces, "is multiplication of thy helps." Helps multiply for the assistance of human weakness, but not as schismatics multiply. God's health-giving Word is not to be sought among "comers or conventicles or schismatical singularies but from the association and communion of thy Catholic church." Divine assistance is multiple, though the Church principally administers that assistance in the form of the divine Word and the Sacraments. Donne's own personal Easter—"my quickening in this world, and my immortal establishing in the next"—is in fact associated with the reappropriation and interiorization of the Church's sacramental life during the course of the spiritual exercises. Though confined to a sickbed, he experiences anew the Sacraments that chasten, quicken, and communicate Christ's mystical body to the diseased soul.

Donne's universalism is also the expression of this Catholic view of the Church. At the devotions' spiritual center, in devotion 17, the meditator hears the bells of a nearby church, tolling the passing of one who, perhaps like Donne, had fallen victim of the fever that swept through London. Earlier, in the seventh devotion, preoccupation with the self had been temporarily interrupted with thought for the need of others more destitute and with great reason to complain of aloneness, and the meditator interrogates himself: "Is not my Meditation rather to be inclined another way, to condole, and communicate their distress, who have none [to aid them]?" Now the enlarging of this meditation in the seventeenth devotion comes about when thoughts of the neighbor, audibly present to the meditator in the bells, are joined with thoughts of the universal fellowship of Christians in the mystical body of Christ. The Church, he says, is universal; "so are all her actions; all that she does belongs to all." The baptism of a child—"That action concerns me; for that child is thereby connected to that body which is my head too." The burial of a man—"That action concerns me." All of humankind is of "one author, and is one volume," and in the last day God will "bind up all our scattered leaves again for that library where every book shall lie open to one another." As if by anticipation of that eschatological age, where "every book shall be open to one another," we are given Donne's consummate expression of universalism and Christian charity:

No man is an island, entire of itself; every man is a piece of the continent, a part of the main. If a clod be washed away by the sea, Europe is the less, as well as if a promontory were, as well as if a manor of thy friend's or of thine own were: any man's death diminishes me, because I am involved in mankind, and therefore never send to know for whom the bell tolls; it tolls for thee.

Here is no gloomy obsession with death but rather confirmation that even in seeming isolation, the isolation of a sick man's closet, God has us speak to and serve one another.

After the meditations and the expostulations, where the emotional experience of the devotions is sustained by taut historical description, argument, and exegesis, the prayers give us the measured assurance of one who is planted firmly in the Church. Beginning with an invocation to the eternal and gracious God, the prayers call to mind God's mercy and eternal ways and make petition for the soul's needs. Above all, the meditator asks for a will obedient to God's directives and for the soul's conformity to Christ's example. In the seventeenth prayer the meditator, having given thanks for divine instruction mediated through "this sad and funeral bell," makes priestly intercession for the one, "the voice of whose bell hath called me to this devotion." The meditator's prayers, in short, revolve on God's mercy and God's power to communicate grace to the members of his Church, and by stages the meditator arrives at an ever-deepening conviction that his sickness is a "correction" and a preparation of his spirit, that it might be "conformed to thy will."

In conforming the soul to the pattern of Christ's affliction, Donne does not promise a spirituality of safe harbor. Yet, though the waters of destruction mount, the Church, a type of the Ark, is envisioned as a refuge when the flood grows "too deep for us." Like Noah, members of Christ's mystical body have God's Word and the divine Sacraments, rising above the Flood's destruction, and in a personal confession of gratitude the meditator says "to the top of these hills, thou hast brought me." Still the rigor of the spiritual exercise does not dissipate with the prospect of recovery. In the last devotion, Donne asks for assistance against presumptuous security, mindful that, as his physicians counsel watchfulness against the fever's recurrence, so strict vigilance is also wise counsel against a future lapsing of the spirit from grace.

Christian Themes

Devotions upon Emergent Occasions addresses the Christian response to the human condition: Sudden illness occasions the thought of life's variableness and of the soul's imminent danger in face of the body's death. Meditations on the misery of the human condition, on spiritual impotency and isolation, and on the mysterious ways of God confront the self with its own spiritual destiny. Finally, meditative insight reveals to the soul a God who multiplies aid for human spiritual assistance and above all makes us ministers in mutual assistance to one another in Christ and Christ's body, the Church.

Sources for Further Study

Frost, Kate Gartner. *Holy Delight: Typology, Numerology, and Autobiography in Donne's "Devotions upon Emergent Occasions."* Princeton, N.J.: Princeton University Press, 1990. Frost argues that the work, despite its idiosyncrasies, belongs to the tradition of English devotional literature and spiritual autobiography.

Guibbory, Achsah, ed. *The Cambridge Companion to John Donne*. New York: Cambridge University Press, 2006. Provides a comprehensive survey of essays on Donne's life and writings. Of particular interest are "Donne's Religious World," by Alison Shell and Arnold Hunt; "Devotional Writing," by Helen Wilcox; and "Facing Death," by Ramie Targoff.

Mueller, Janel. Introduction to *Donne's Prebend Sermons*. Cambridge, Mass.: Harvard University Press, 1971. The superb introduction treats the sermons from the period following Donne's illness, a period informed by Donne's conviction that he had been restored to health so that he could preach.

Raspa, Anthony. Introduction to *Devotions upon Emergent Occasions*. Edited with commentary by Anthony Raspa. New York: Oxford University Press, 1987. Provides an interesting review of the scholarly conjecture concerning Donne's illness and an excellent discussion of Donne and the meditative tradition.

Weber, Joan. *Contrary Music: The Prose Style of John Donne*. 1963. Reprint. Westport, Conn.: Greenwood Press, 1986. An insightful discussion of Donne's religious prose with a concluding section on the *Devotions upon Emergent Occasions* and its tripartite division.

Thomas E. Helm

THE DIALOGUE

Author: Saint Catherine of Siena (Caterina di Giacomo di Benincasa; 1347-1380)
First transcribed: Libro della divina dottrina, c. 1377 (English translation, 1896)
Edition used: The Dialogue, translated with an introduction by Suzanne Noffke, O.P.,
  with a preface by Giuliana Cavallini. New York: Paulist Press, 1980
Genre: Nonfiction
Subgenres: Dialogue; meditation and contemplation; mysticism; spiritual treatise
Core issues: Jesus Christ; love; obedience and disobedience; peace; perfection; salva-
  tion; sin and sinners; truth; union with God

The Dialogue, *which consists of several petitions to God and God's responses, was
dictated by Catherine while she was in a state of ecstasy and was recorded by members of her religious community.*

Overview

Catherine begins *The Dialogue* by discussing the intimate relationship of truth and
love, then goes on to discuss the beauty and dignity of each person who becomes perfect in proportion to union with the Creator. She then makes four petitions to God: for
herself (to be permitted to suffer so as to atone for her sins); for reformation of the
Holy Church; for peace in the world, and for the entire world in general; for the effects
of Providence in everything, but particularly for a special intention. She indicates that
she is relying on God's promise to Saint John and others that God will show himself to
those who love him.

There is a brief reply from God to the first petition. She is told of the need for infinite desire in relation to works even though they are finite, because sin done against
God is sin done against the Infinite Good. So God wishes infinite grief in his creature
concerning her own sins and through the sorrow she feels for sins that she sees committed by her neighbors. However, she is promised that the pain she feels through
love will nourish rather than dry up the soul.

God then explains in some detail what the role of the neighbor is in regard to a person's spiritual development. Pride destroys charity and affection toward the neighbor
and is the main source of every evil. When we deprive a neighbor of that which he or
she ought to be given, a secret sin is committed. God gives each person a special virtue that draws to the soul all others bound by love. However, unless we make our act
of love through God, it is meaningless. The virtues such as faith, patience, benignity,
kindness, fortitude, and perseverance are then extolled. It is discernment or holy discretion that is the light of all the other virtues, Catherine is told.

Thus end what some call the prologue and the section titled (not by Catherine herself but by later editors) "The Way of Perfection." The next series of chapters—and
here the lead of those editors is followed—is called "Dialogue." Here the future saint
lists three petitions to which God gives a short reply. These petitions correspond

roughly to the second and fourth petitions of the prologue (Church reform and the role of Providence in all things). Catherine seeks mercy for God's people and for all aspects of the life of the Church, to its very core. She is concerned with all grace that is manifested through material things and temporal experiences. To this God answers by reminding Catherine that the world has already received the great gift it needs for redemption and that is Christ, the Redeemer, himself. However, this gift brings with it a tremendous responsibility of which we must be aware.

Catherine implores God to be merciful to the entire world. He says, in return, that selfish love is a poison that can undermine all, and he recalls to her that he is the God of all, of the evildoer as well as of the good. Then the fourteenth century mystic asks specifically for grace for her spiritual director, Raymond of Capua (later her biographer), and God tells her of the way of truth, using the metaphor of Christ as bridge. He also speaks of the twofold vineyard, which is composed of the individual's soul and the Church. For spiritual growth this vineyard must be nurtured by all who wish to serve God. This "dialogue" section closes with praise rendered divine love and Catherine's expressed desire to learn more about Christ as the necessary bridge. "I remember that you wanted to show me who are those who cross over the bridge and those who do not. So, if it would please your goodness to show me, I would gladly see and hear this from you."

The heart of the book follows and has been signified as "The Bridge." Christ, the only begotten Son, is the bridge that spans heaven and earth. This, God says, is one result of the union that he has made with man, the creature fashioned out of clay. The approach is in three steps: Two were made with the wood of Jesus' cross. The third— which still retains its bitter taste—is the gall and vinegar he was given to drink. These three steps symbolize the states of the soul, and they are likened to the Crucifixion experience in this account. In the first step, when the soul lifts her feet from the affections of the earth, she strips herself of worldly vice. As a result of step two, the soul is filled with love and with virtue. In the final step she tastes the peace of God.

The Bridge is built of the stones of true and sincere virtues. On the Bridge is an inn where food is given the travelers. Those who go over the Bridge go to eternal life, while those who travel beneath the Bridge go to everlasting death. These latter suffer four pains: the deprivation of seeing God, the worm of Conscience, the vision of the Devil, and the torment of a fire that burns but does not consume. Those who make spiritual progress pass from a state of imperfection (acting in servile fear) to arrival in the state of perfection (filial love).

This section may be regarded as God's response to Catherine's plea for his mercy to be extended to the entire world. Nor does this response end here but continues at some length. At this point, however, Catherine observes that she has seen several kinds of tears, and she asks for instructions about each of these types. God tells her that there are those of the wicked as well as of those who fear God; there are the tears of those who imperfectly love him, and of those whose weeping is perfect because they love God in total abandon. Finally, there are the sweet tears of great peace that are joined to the fourth.

Catherine then thanks God, praising him for the gift of love. From this she feels she has the permission to ask for grace and mercy while searching for his truth. She requests further guidance from God at this point, concerning how she should advise others who come to her for counsel and how she can tell whether a spiritual visitation truly comes from God or is a deception of which she should be wary. (Regarding this last, Catherine recalls that she has been told if the visitation left her spirit glad and encouraged her toward virtue, then this was indeed a divine intervention, but she wishes assurance on this point.)

Truth is what the seeker in this book yearns for, and the next pages are devoted to such an inquiry. She learns that there are three kinds of lights by which we may see reality. These are called the imperfect, the perfect, and finally the most perfect lights. First is ordinary light which all human beings need, regardless of their earthly situation. Those who walk in perfect light do so in two separate ways: Some men and women rise above this world and practice the mortification of their bodies; some kill their own self-wills and "find their nourishment at the table of holy desire." Others should be reproved only gently. When they are clearly living sinfully, that is another matter, but in general God counsels that neighbors' apparent vices must not be harshly judged nor are their degrees of perfection to be judged. Furthermore, not all are expected to live their spiritual lives in the same manner or to follow the same path to holiness.

There is some repetition here of previous advice and admonitions; then Catherine is urged to ask for more and is given a new promise of mercy. She then again praises God, particularly for his truth, and beseeches God anew. The ecstatic requests the grace necessary to remain totally faithful to God's truth. She asks this not only for herself but for her companions as well, particularly for two priests who were her confessors, "those two pillars, the fathers you have appointed for me on earth to guide and teach me, who am so wretchedly weak, from the beginning of my conversion until now." One of these men is Raymond of Capua, who was to become the mystic's first biographer. The other is probably Tommaso della Fonte, an earlier confessor and a man who was a companion to her throughout her relatively brief life.

She then asks for some indication of the extent of the sins of evil clergymen so that she may increase her sorrow and desire for mercy. This recalls her earlier petition on behalf of the entire sacramental life at the heart of the Church. God promises an answer and tells Catherine that her "two pillars" will receive the grace they need from God through her. However, he warns her, "never fail to trust Me for my providence will never fail you."

The next section begins with God's praise for his ministers, the priests through whom the sacraments are administered, particularly the Eucharist. Something of the nature of the Eucharist is also discussed. The host given in Holy Communion loses none of its glory upon being divided, just as fire divided remains fire. When Catherine receives this sacrament she lives in God and God in her, she is told. Then God tells her of the sins of the clerics, but not until he first notes that those who persecute the clergy are working against God himself. Nevertheless, in some priests, "selfish love is alive in them." Some do not correct people in order to curry favor with them; others exemplify great pride. Certain clerics are ruled by their senses, some by an acquisitiveness of material things. Drunkenness, too, is a sin for many of them, and some are lustful in word and deed. Catherine reacts to all that she has heard with a prayer of praise for God. She portrays him as light and fire, as the supreme charity, and as the great fulfiller of all that is honestly desired. Again she begs God for mercy for the world in general and for the Church in particular.

God's providence is the subject of the next several segments of *The Dialogue*. He speaks of his general providence in creation, in redemption, and in the Sacraments, as well as in his gift of the virtue of hope and in the Law. He then relates his special providence in particular events in history and in the lives of people. God indicates that he allows the world to bring forth many troubles to prove the virtue of people and "that I may have reason to reward them for their suffering and the violence they do themselves." Subsequently, Catherine says that she wishes to be instructed concerning obedience. She wants to know how perfect it is, where she can find it, what might cause her to lose it, who gives it to her, and by what sign she might know whether or not she has it.

The woman is told that the sign that one has the virtue of obedience is patience; the impatient have it not. The fullness of obedience, God says, is found in the gentle, loving Word, his only begotten Son, for Jesus' obedience was even to a shameful death on the cross. Pride causes us to lose that virtue. This caused Adam's sin, and it was not only he who fell here but the whole human race as well. Jesus left this key of obedience to the gate of heaven, and whoever fails to avail himself of it risks living in damnation. Perfect obedience is found in those who bind themselves to the obedience of a religious order or in those, outside such orders, who submit their wills to a spiritual teacher who will help them to advance more speedily to unlock the gate of heaven.

The work ends with a recapitulation by God of all that has gone before, followed by Catherine's final hymn of praise to the Trinity and a prayer that she may be clothed in God's truth.

Christian Themes

During her lifetime, the future patron saint of Italy, Catherine of Siena, was a fourteenth century ascetic, mystic, and activist who worked for peace within the Church when Florence was placed under an interdict by the pope. She visited Pope Gregory XI in Avignon to mediate in the political dispute; there, she also promoted a crusade against the Muslims. When the papacy returned to Rome, Catherine participated in the reorganization of the Church under Urban VI.

Catherine dictated *The Dialogue* while she was in a state of ecstasy to members of her religious community, who recorded it for posterity. The main Christian themes can be summarized as follows:

- Love is the way to perfection.
- Christ is the bridge between heaven and earth.
- Five kinds of tears correspond to the conditions of the soul.
- Love involves grief for one's own sin and that of others.
- Obedience to the Word is the remedy to the sin of Adam.

Sources for Further Study

Cavallini, Giuliana. *Catherine of Siena*. New York: G. Chapman, 1998. A solid overview of Catherine, with coverage of her writings, her search for truth, her Christology, and her politics. Chronology, bibliography, index.

Gardner, Edmund G. *Saint Catherine of Siena*. London: Dent, 1907. Covers the background as well as the life of Catherine through a study of the religion, literature, and history of fourteenth century Italy.

Hilkert, Mary Catherine. *Speaking with Authority: Catherine of Siena and the Voices of Women Today*. New York: Paulist Press, 2001. Examines Catherine in the context of modern women's issues. Bibliography.

Luongo, F. Thomas. *The Saintly Politics of Catherine of Siena*. Ithaca, N.Y.: Cornell University Press, 2006. Counters the notion of Catherine as isolated mystic and considers her in a sociopolitical context—including the Black Death, social revolutions, Florence versus the papacy—by examining her letters and juxtaposing her words to those of contemporary political and social movements. Bibliography, index.

Noffke, Suzanne. *Catherine of Siena: Vision Through a Distant Eye*. Collegeville, Minn.: Liturgical Press, 1996. The author, a Dominican of Racine, Wisconsin, considers Catherine as a rare authoritative woman of her time, the first to be published in one of the emerging Italian vernacular dialects. Part 1 covers her theology and spirituality; part 2 presents resources on her person and thought, her world, and others writings in English. Annotated bibliography.

Raymond of Capua. *The Life of St. Catherine of Siena*. Translated by George Lamb. New York: Kennedy, 1960. The first biography of the saint, written by her confessor, who shared many of her experiences.

Harry James Cargas

"A DIALOGUE OF SELF AND SOUL"

Author: William Butler Yeats (1865-1939)
First published: 1933
Edition used: "A Dialogue of Self and Soul," in *The Variorum Edition of the Poems of*
   W. B. Yeats, edited by Peter Allt and Russell K. Alspach. New York: Macmillan,
   1957
Genre: Poetry
Subgenres: Debate; dialogue; lyric poetry
Core issues: Heart; life; morality; soul; spiritual warfare

In this variation on a traditional Christian poetic form, Yeats turns the Christian mes-
sage almost upon its head in order to affirm our human life as it is lived rather than as
it should be lived.

Overview

William Butler Yeats was born into a middle-class Church of Ireland family—that
is, he was a product of Protestant and English descent. His grandfather and great-
grandfather were members of the clergy. His father, however, rebelled against the
family's religious life, so Yeats was not reared in the traditional Christian faith, although Christian imagery and beliefs, especially moral, remained a continuing and
powerful element in his poetry. For instance, his Crazy Jane poems thematically echo
the conflicts between Christian morality and human desire which are the concerns of
"A Dialogue of Self and Soul." Too, Yeats used the form he used in "A Dialogue of
Self and Soul" in the seventh section of "Vacillation," although in the latter poem the
debate is between the "Soul" and the "Heart." Certainly, a knowledge of the story of
the conception and birth of Christ, as well as of that birth's religious significance, is
necessary for the reader of the antithetical images of Yeats's "The Second Coming."
However, Yeats's own "religious" life was a committed interest in, faith in, and even
practice (largely synthetic) of various occult beliefs, from his early involvement with
the Rosicrucians and Theosophy to his acceptance of aspects of Eastern religions. He
was far from being a rationalistic unbeliever.

Yeats was also an Irish patriot and regarded Irish culture as his own; his earliest
works are steeped in Irish myth. At the same time, however, he was intensely proud of
his English ancestry (to the point of exaggerating its status) and felt himself a part of
historical European high culture. He would never really leave Irish myth behind, but
his committment to the European tradition, based as it was on the Christian religion,
was almost everywhere in his writings. Too, he made direct use of his own life, especially in his later works—a use that gives solidity, facts, and images to his poetry,
making them more alive.

In "A Dialogue of Self and Soul," Yeats employs the traditional Christian-based form of a dramatic poetic *débat*, or debate, between the Soul (or heart) and the Self (or body), reversing the usual Christian message of works in which the soul laments what the body has done. Sinning has condemned both body and soul to hell. Traditionally, sin originates with the body, since that body desires pleasure—the pleasures of the egoistic present and so not of the future in heaven in contemplation of God. Paradoxically, Yeats's poem chooses the body and life—with all its failures, sins, and humiliations—over the morality of the soul.

Because Yeats's poem echoes and responds to this debate tradition, its place in that tradition is a necessary part of its meaning. For example, the fifteenth century French poet François Villon's "Le Débat du corps et du cœur de Villon" (1461; the debate of the body and the heart of Villon) is a concentrated and emotional series of short exchanges between body and heart, "heart" meaning here the soul. Villon's "heart" speaks the truth and so "wins" the argument. Yeats, too, is concrete, his poem rich with imagery, although his poem lacks that quick interchange of argument and so is less dramatically presented. However, the "argument" that Yeats gives the Soul, although powerful emotionally in its imagery, is also more enigmatic in meaning than what he gives the Self.

"A Dialogue of Self and Soul" is also built upon traditional patterns: Most of the lines are iambic pentameter, although with great variants, plus rhyme, although not all the rhymes are perfect; the effect is to emphasize the chanting human voice. The rhymes are *abbacddc*, a modification of another traditional pattern, the ottava rima. Thus, if this pattern of repetitions controls as well as emphasizes the emotion, behind the intensity of the imagery the pattern tells us there is order in the world. Still, that order is problematic: Is it divine or is it simply imposed by humankind?

The poem is divided into two main sections. In the first section, the Soul and the Self alternate, the Soul beginning and ending the exchange. In giving the Soul an extra stanza, Yeats would seem to be coming down on the side of the Soul, but the second part of the poem is one long speech by the Self alone, emphasizing that it chooses, has chosen, to live life in all its pains and difficulties, since that is what life is. The Self would be "content to live it all again":

> I am content to follow to its source
> Every event in action or in thought;
> Measure the lot; forgive myself the lot!
> When such as I cast out remorse
> So great a sweetness flows into the breast
> We must laugh and we must sing,
> We are blest by everything,
> Everything we look upon is blest.

Christian Themes

The most striking comment on Christian themes in "A Dialogue of Self and Soul" is the attitude toward the human body and experience, which reverses the traditional

Christian stance. For instance, the English poet Andrew Marvell (1621-1678), in his "A Dialogue, Between the Resolved Soul, and Created Pleasure" (1681), has his Created Pleasure present the things of this earth as beautiful, pleasurable, and tempting. Human knowledge is powerful, although by implication much less so than heaven; so too the pleasures of heaven are far beyond our human existence.

Yeats's Self, by contrast, promises nothing of this, saying rather that the experiences of this world are ignorance, pain, difficulty, and humiliation but nevertheless asserting that "I" would suffer it all again. Here the poem is filled with painful memories and images from Yeats's life, including a reference to his long and unrequited love for Irish actress Maud Gonne ("A proud woman not kindred of his soul"). Too, the image of the Japanese sword and the old and ragged but still beautiful embroidered cloth in which it is wrapped emphasizes both the violence (which can also be seen as courage) and the power of sex in human life, reversing two aspects of a once widely held ideal of the Christian life, peace and asceticism.

Yeats is arguing that life itself is—paradoxically, because of its difficulty—our reason for existence. The Self's arguments can be read as laying out the Eastern religious belief that the soul is born again and again, on the slow path to escaping the individual existence. However, Yeats, even in using these images, is still arguing against treating the body as something that leads only to sin. Yeats's poem also differs from the usual *débat* in that the *débat* normally begins at the end of life, when hell threatens and has, usually, won the struggle through the sins of the body. Although the Self in Yeats's poem is obviously no longer young, the poem still celebrates physical life, life as individual existence, and furthermore asserts it to be "blest."

Neither hell nor punishment enters into Yeats's poem. Nor, for that matter, does any vision of heaven: There is no promise of eternity in the presence of God, as in the standard Christian teaching. Indeed, Yeats's Soul offers a mystery, almost more threatening than comforting. The Soul urges the Self to climb the staircase of the tower on Yeats's Irish property, mounting toward death but not to see a landscape that somehow speaks of a Dantean heaven—rather to see only the darkness, the mystery, of the night. What that night may mean cannot be discerned. Indeed, the Soul's last speech closes with "Only the dead can be forgiven;/ But when I think of that [what follows life] my tongue's a stone." Heaven, in brief, hardly seems a reward. The Soul itself in not speaking, or being unable to speak, cannot therefore prove that it is right.

Sources for Further Study

Foster, R. F. *W. B. Yeats: A Life*. 2 vols. New York: Oxford University Press, 1997, 2003. A biography in two volumes, *The Apprentice Mage, 1865-1914* and *The Arch-Poet, 1915-1939*, giving the facts of Yeats's life and connecting those facts with his works.

Jeffares, A. Norman. *A Commentary on the Collected Poems of W. B. Yeats*. Stanford, Calif.: Stanford University Press, 1968. Commentary on the poems, giving explanations of people, places, and sources in each poem treated.

Rosenthal, M. L. *Running to Paradise: Yeats's Poetic Art*. New York: Oxford University Press, 1994. Careful chronological working through of Yeats's poems.

Unterecker, John. *A Reader's Guide to William Butler Yeats*. New York: Noonday Press, 1959. Offers a short biographical sketch along with themes and explications of the poems, worked through chronologically.

L. L. Lee

THE DIARY OF A COUNTRY PRIEST

Author: Georges Bernanos (1888-1948)
First published: Journal d'un curé de campagne, 1936 (English translation, 1937)
Edition used: The Diary of a Country Priest, translated by Pamela Morris. New York: Macmillan, 1954
Genre: Novel
Subgenre: Literary fiction
Core issues: Catholics and Catholicism; contemplation; daily living; pastoral role; priesthood; trust in God

A young priest is assigned to his first parish and faces the day-to-day duties of a village priest. He deals with peasant parishioners who judge him as too young to fulfill the role of spiritual leader and with aristocrats who view him as too simple and poor to understand or appreciate their place in life. The country priest struggles with his own prayer life and duties as well as the commitments of a parish priest: mass, teaching the catechism to the young, counseling the parishioners in their family and personal life, and burying the dead. During his duties, he comes to terms with his own health problems.

> *Principal characters*
> *Naïve priest*, the protagonist, who earnestly struggles with his duties
> *Seraphita*, young catechism student
> *M. le Comte*, a carnal nobleman, interested in appearance rather than spirituality
> *Mme. le Comtesse*, the mother of an unruly daughter
> *Mlle. Chantal*, their young daughter and the instigator of most of the conflict

Overview

The Diary of a Country Priest presents the journal of a recently ordained priest in his first year in the parish of Saint Vaast in the French countryside. The priest is an ordinary young man from a working-class background with a decidedly intellectual bent and an above-average preoccupation with his physical health. He began writing for comfort, but more than likely also as a substitute for contemplative prayer, a spiritual requirement that he is not completely comfortable with, but which he would never admit the journal replaces. He determines this writing exercise will be his experiment for only the next year and vows, "On the 25th of November I'll stuff these pages in the fire and try to forget them."

His approach to helping with the spiritual well-being of his parishioners consists of an intellectual debate. He approaches his young catechism students in this manner and views them as adults of miniature stature, a fact that endears him neither to the children nor to their parents. On one occasion, the mother of one of his students declares to the priest that he is treating her daughter Seraphita entirely too harshly. The young priest, confident in his sacred duty to guide the girl down the correct path to God, tells the woman that her daughter is far too advanced for her age, a trait that is causing her to be a problem in class and implies future problems of a much more severe nature. In the process of the discussion, the priest makes the mistake of describing Seraphita as "coquettish," a word that her mother objects to because of the priest's youth and inexperience. Later it is this very girl who befriends the priest when he falls ill on the road near her home. Seraphita, who had been sent out that night to deal with the cattle, literally stumbles across the priest. After seeing the priest is not dead as she had originally feared, the girl decides not to inform her brutish father of the priest's condition. She is very understanding as she bring cold pond water to wash his face of blood and vomit and cleans him up until he is somewhat presentable. She stays with him until he gets some strength back and walks with him down the rough road toward his home until her father comes to the door of her house and calls to her to hurry up and come inside.

The youth of the priest and his habit of not eating but rather living on wine and bread are the principal complaints against him. The priest also makes hasty assumptions concerning another young woman, Chantal, daughter of the local aristocracy. As with Seraphita, these judgments are superficial and simplistic. Chantal is a headstrong young woman who is determined to have her way. When her mother decides she is to be sent away to boarding school, Chantal reacts wildly, telling the priest that she will kill herself if her mother sends her away. The young priest confronts the Comtesse and becomes involved in a religious debate with the woman about love, forgiveness, and God's will. In the process of trying to convince her that her attitude is not at all Christian, the priest makes the mistake of telling the woman that because of her trenchant attitudes against God's way, she will never again be with her beloved dead son. In the end, the Comtesse comes around. The priest leaves, unaware that Chantal has heard the entire discussion from underneath the window. Later that night, the Comtesse dies. Chantal uses the incident to her advantage. The priest looks not only young but also insensitive, inappropriate in his course of action, and not at all Godlike.

The youthful priest's health worsens; he is blacking out and hemorrhaging. He is close to being fired when he decides it is prudent to see the specialist that a local doctor had suggested soon after the priest came to the village. While the priest is packing for the trip, Chantal visits him and declares her decision to do as she wishes even at the peril of hell. Although her words make it seem otherwise, the priest has won at least a small part of the battle in hearing Chantal admit she is aware of the ultimate consequences for her actions.

Soon thereafter the priest sees the specialist, who is quick to give advice. That advice is that the priest should do as he wishes, eat or not as he wishes, and carry on with his day-to-day activities as normally as possible. The doctor recommends an X ray and gives the young man a prescription for a pain medication, but in the priest's haste to leave and the doctor's haste to be finished with the exam, the priest leaves without the prescription. The two men return to the examining room and have a lengthy discussion about God and faith. The doctor decides to tell the priest the true nature of his ailment, which is not tuberculosis but rather advanced stomach cancer, for which there is no real treatment and no hope for a cure. The priest leaves in a daze, misses the train home, and ends up at an old friend's flat—an old friend who is also seriously ill and once was a priest. The country priest collapses and loses a lot of blood, so he is put to bed in the friend's flat. He dies in the night after having asked the old friend for absolution. The friend hesitates and is then reassured by the young priest's final remark that God's grace was and is all around them.

Christian Themes

The major theme in the novel is that nothing is as it seems on the surface or as it seems after being explored in depth. Only God can judge. The villagers observe their new priest and judge him as too young. The aristocrats view him as unsophisticated; the commoners view him as remote and harsh. At times both groups attribute to him the ability to see into souls and to discern a person's innermost secrets.

The priest observes the villagers and often attributes to them a depth and sophistication that could not be further from the truth. He judges the children by adult standards and assigns to them motives far beyond the childhood whims that dictate their actions.

The priest judges with his head, through his philosophy, logic, and debated alternatives. The villagers judge from what they observe, assuming that things are always as they seem. The priest is young and a drunkard to the villagers, and the villagers are willful and unrepentant to the priest.

At his death, the priest concludes that God's grace is everywhere. Readers are led to hope that when the villagers learn of the death of the priest and its cause, they too will realize that God's grace has been and remains among them.

Sources for Further Study

Curran, Beth Kathryn. *Touching God: The Novels of Georges Bernanos in the Films of Robert Bresson*. New York: Peter Lang, 2006. A look at the themes of the Catholic novelist and the spiritual filmmaker and their attempts to articulate grace and redemption through the suffering and death of characters in their works.

Heher, Michael. *Lost Art of Walking on Water: ReImagining the Priesthood*. Mahwah, N.J.: Paulist Press, 2004. Heher describes the modern plight and perils of the priesthood.

Molnar, Thomas. *Bernanos: His Political Thought and Prophecy*. Somerset, N.J.: Transaction, 1997. Bernanos' work went beyond commentary on religion and had political implications for his day and the future.

Lesa Dill

DIRECTED VERDICT

Author: Randy Singer (1956-   )
First published: Colorado Springs, Colo.: WaterBrook Press, 2002
Genre: Novel
Subgenres: Evangelical fiction; thriller/suspense
Core issues: Ethics; evangelization; justice; persecution; religion

Attorney Brad Carson assists Christian missionary Sarah Reed in suing the Saudi Arabian government and the head of its religious police for crimes committed against Reed and her late husband. As the case unfolds, the Reeds' quiet, nonviolent methods of evangelization are contrasted with both the tyrannical methods used to enforce the practice of Islam in Saudi Arabia and the secular, sometimes antireligious practices of the American justice system.

> *Principal characters*
> *Brad Carson*, an attorney
> *Sarah Reed*, a Christian missionary
> *Leslie Connors*, a law student
> *Nikki Moreno*, a paralegal working for Carson
> *Bella Harper*, Carson's administrative assistant
> *Ahmed Aberijan*, head of Saudi Arabia's religious police
> *Mack Strobel*, noted international law expert
> *Cynthia Baker-Kline*, a federal judge

Overview

Directed Verdict won a Christy Award for best suspense story in 2002, launching the writing career of attorney Randy Singer, who manages in this novel and subsequent ones to combine his legal skills with his deep religious commitment. In *Directed Verdict*, he created a story that pits the forces of evangelical Christianity against both radical Islam and the modern, secular world. Though at some points he resorted to stereotypes to accentuate these contrasts, Singer managed to construct a story that is both a courtroom drama and an international political thriller.

Set in Saudi Arabia and in the Tidewater region of Virginia, *Directed Verdict* is about an American Christian missionary's attempt to restore her late husband's reputation and obtain justice for his murder at the hands of religious fanatics. As the novel opens, Sarah and Charles Reed, American missionaries working in Saudi Arabia, are attacked by the Muttawa, the country's religious police, in an effort to break up their tiny church. Muttawa leader Ahmed Aberijan, zealous in enforcing laws prohibiting the practice of religions other than Islam in his country, directs his men to torture the Reeds to get them to reveal the names of church members. To discredit the couple further, he has them both injected with cocaine. Charles, already suffering from a weak heart, dies hours later. Sarah is deported.

After returning to her home in Norfolk, Virginia, Sarah determines to clear her husband's name. Acting on the suggestion of the pastor of her church, she seeks legal advice from Brad Carson, an ambitious, worldly attorney who had defended the Reeds' pastor against charges of trespass and assault stemming from a protest in front of an abortion clinic. Carson has built a highly successful practice working alone, aided only by his domineering administrative assistant Bella Harper. Though not religious himself, Carson believes international laws have been violated and that Sarah is entitled to compensation from the Saudi government. He agrees to file a civil suit on her behalf in the United States federal court. To assist him in preparing his case, he hires Leslie Connors, a law student at William and Mary whom he meets while helping to evaluate a moot court case. He also hires Nikki Moreno, a paralegal known for getting good deals for her clients through questionable methods.

The Saudi government and Aberijan are represented by Mack Strobel, senior partner in a large firm specializing in international law. The case is heard before federal judge Cynthia Baker-Kline, a feminist with a reputation for ruling against religious conservatives. She had sent Carson to jail for contempt during the trial of the Reeds' pastor. Baker-Kline's dislike for Carson leads her to run roughshod over him during the Reed trial, sometimes at the expense of allowing the facts of the case to be presented. To make matters worse for the plaintiffs, both before and during the trial, Aberijan works behind the scenes to intimidate witnesses in Saudi Arabia and bribe jurors in the United States. These activities stymie Carson's team as they try to assemble their case and occasionally put one or more of them in danger.

Sarah's case is heard before a jury empaneled to determine Aberijan's culpability for Charles Reed's death. Both attorneys are aware, however, that Judge Baker-Kline alone will decide if the Saudi government also bears responsibility. Therefore, both hope at some point for a "directed verdict"—a ruling by the judge that will either exonerate the defendants or award damages to the plaintiff. This and other legal maneuverings occupy the attorneys' time—and the readers' attention—for the majority of the novel.

Although the action in *Directed Verdict* revolves around preparations for trial and courtroom dynamics, Singer further complicates his narrative in several ways. He creates a romantic subplot by having the divorced Carson and widowed Connors gradually fall in love. Additionally, as the plaintiffs prepare their case, readers learn of the presence of a mole within Carson's team. One of the women working for him begins to negotiate with Aberijan, apparently to sabotage the case, and it is not until the final pages of the novel that readers learn her identity and the reasons for her actions. At the same time, the illegal activities of both Aberijan and the government of Saudi Arabia are exposed in such a way that Carson gets the coveted directed verdict, awarding millions in compensation to his client.

While legal action dominates the story line in *Directed Verdict*, other activity is going on as well—activity that is of equal importance to Singer as an evangelical writer. As the trial progresses, Carson, Harper, Connors, and even Moreno come to admire the simple faith Sarah Reed exhibits. Her insistence on justice rather than vengeance and her declaration of forgiveness for her husband's tormentors have a noticeable effect on these worldly members of the legal establishment. Sarah is even able to convert Harper, who has not been religious since childhood, by befriending the woman's mother, who is in a nursing home. The occasional insertion of biblical lessons that Sarah provides to the members of her legal team are reminders that this novel is intended as more than mere entertainment.

Christian Themes

Unquestionably, the most notable Christian theme in *Directed Verdict* is the idea that Christians may be forced to suffer persecution for their beliefs. The Reeds' missionary work in Saudi Arabia puts them in constant danger, but they continue to work quietly to lead others to Christ until Charles dies and Sarah is expelled from the country. The theme of persecution is reinforced in the novel by depictions of the treatment evangelical Christians receive from the U.S. legal system, which Singer depicts as predisposed to deny them justice, especially when their moral stance puts them at odds with the perceived freedoms of other citizens.

A second major Christian theme is the requirement for toleration of others' beliefs. The Reeds are able to convert Muslims in Saudi Arabia and Americans in Virginia through a combination of quiet example and gentle encouragement; they never coerce those with whom they speak but instead let Christ's message speak for itself. There is no room for such toleration in the Muslim world as Singer portrays it; government agents resort to the most heinous and immoral tactics to guarantee there will be no challenge to Islam in Saudi Arabia. At the same time, Singer infuses the novel with a sense of recognition that the American government's position of tolerance toward all forms of religious worship is far better than the intolerance practiced by the Saudi Arabian government.

Directed Verdict also highlights the disparity between the simple life Christians are supposed to lead and the extravagant modern lifestyle considered the mark of success in the United States. Singer brings out this notion by contrasting subtle descriptions of the attorneys on both sides of the civil suit with depictions of the lifestyles of Sarah Reed and Carson's administrative assistant, Harper. Also under scrutiny are the ethics of the American legal profession. The attorneys in the novel—including the protagonist at times—all seem motivated as much by the desire to win cases and reap material benefits from their profession as they are by any zeal to promote justice. Throughout the novel, Singer sets up numerous situations in which characters are required to make ethical choices, often involving highly questionable acts taken to achieve noble ends. By doing so, he calls attention to his belief that in the modern, global society, even good people are sometimes forced into making objectionable choices to follow the dictates of their conscience.

Sources for Further Study

Herald, Diana Tixier, and Wayne A. Wiegand, eds. *Genreflecting: A Guide to Popular Reading Interests*. 6th ed. Westport, Conn.: Libraries Unlimited, 2006. Traces the historical development of Christian literature, focusing on its adoption of various genres of mainstream fiction in the twentieth century. Cites *Directed Verdict* as an example of the Christian thriller.

Mort, John. *Christian Fiction: A Guide to the Genre.* Greenwood Village, Colo.: Libraries Unlimited, 2002. Contains a chapter explaining how Christian literature differs from mainstream fiction; a separate chapter discusses the contemporary Christian thriller, the genre in which Singer works.

Singer, Randy. *The Cross Examination of Jesus Christ.* Colorado Springs, Colo.: WaterBrook Press, 2006. This work combines a fictionalized account of the trail of Jesus and a nonfictional examination of the interactions between Jesus and his critics as noted in the Gospels, plus personal anecdotes from Singer's life.

White, Terry, ed. *Justice Denoted: The Legal Thriller in American, British, and Continental Courtroom Literature.* Westport, Conn.: Praeger, 2003. Annotated bibliography of works in the genre; an introductory essay describes the conventions of legal thrillers and provides background for examining Singer's work.

Zaleski, Jeff. Review of *Directed Verdict. Publishers Weekly* 294, no. 36 (September 9, 2002): 41. Brief summary of the story line and major themes of the novel.

Laurence W. Mazzeno

DIVINE AND HUMAN

Author: Leo Tolstoy (1828-1910)
First published: "Bozheskoe I chelovecheskoe," 1906 (English translation, 1906)
Edition used: Divine and Human, and Other Stories, translated by Peter Sekirin. Grand Rapids, Mich.: Zondervan, 2000
Genre: Short fiction
Subgenres: Biblical fiction; evangelical fiction; morality tales
Core issues: Alienation from God; atonement; awakening; the Beatitudes; conversion; Gospels

Tolstoy presents the thoughts and actions of three revolutionaries in the 1870's in Russia. When they are incarcerated for their plans as well as for their actions, they are forced to think about their intent to topple the czarist government. In such fateful moments, they reveal their innermost thoughts, some of which lead to changes of heart and mind.

> Principal characters
> *Anatoly Svetlogub*, a young revolutionary
> *Ignaty Mezhenetsky*, a leader of a revolutionary group
> *Roman*, a new kind of a revolutionary, precursor of the Bolsheviks
> *Old Believer*, a member of the old Russian Orthodox sect

Overview

Leo Tolstoy wrote "Divine and Human" as a chapter in the novel *Voskreseniye* (1899; *Resurrection*, 1899), but it was omitted when the novel was published, then rewritten and expanded. It is one of many pieces of shorter fiction Tolstoy wrote in the last decade or so of his life, with pronounced religious and Christian content, intended as educational incentives.

The three revolutionaries presented here differ in their approach to their zeal. The youngest of them, Anatoly Svetlogub, is of a rich family and is very intelligent and ambitious. He tries to help the disadvantaged as much as he can, but his heart is not fully in it; strangely, he even feels some shame while helping. His mother had high hopes that he would eventually attain a reasonably good position in society. Instead, as a young man he manages to get involved in the struggle for justice and reforms that marks the second half of the nineteenth century. He wants to help the poor and disadvantaged, but he is also attracted to the dangers involved in his revolutionary engagement. When explosives left in Svetlogub's house by the leader of his revolutionary circle are discovered, the young man is imprisoned, convicted without definitive proof of a direct criminal act on his part, and hanged in the public square. As he presses the New Testament to his heart, he dies in peace and in the belief that all men are good and that all is well with the world. However, his mother, whose hopes that he would be set free are dashed, voices her disbelief in the kind of God that would allow such injustice to happen.

The irony of this injustice is that during the long incarceration, after Svetlogub had a chance to read the New Testament, he underwent a genuine conversion to Christianity and was ready to start a new life free of rebellion and terrorism. Another prisoner, who belonged to the Old Believer sect of the Russian Orthodox Church, made friends with Svetlogub and influenced him to the point of conversion. Svetlogub embraced the basic tenets of Christianity, even the hardest one to accept, "love thy enemy." He not only admitted to his wrongdoings but also learned to love the authorities in their zeal to persecute and eventually kill him.

That is not the case with the second revolutionary, the leader of Svetlogub's revolutionary circle, Ignaty Mezhenetsky. He has no qualms about the cruelty of his activity, believing firmly, like Svetlogub, in the justice of the revolutionaries' desire to lift their poor brethren from the pits of poverty, overthrow the despotic government, and establish a free, elected government. However, because his fanaticism lacks any spiritual fervor, Mezhenetsky's beliefs are purely rational. He is spared capital punishment and sent to a labor camp in Siberia. There, he meets another revolutionary leader, Roman, who is even more "rational" than he.

Roman and his group belittle Mezhenetsky's revolutionary tactics as inadequate and ineffective. They advocate instead an almost "scientific" approach to the revolution. They believe that the peasants of Russia are stupid and will never understand the struggle for their own betterment until they all become proletarians. The peasants' attachment to the land they have just received from the government after liberation from serfdom makes them conservative and unwilling to change. Therefore the land must be collectivized. In this belief, Roman's revolutionaries resemble the Bolsheviks, who would soon take over the revolutionary movement and eventually succeed in their efforts only eight years after Tolstoy's death. Tolstoy, like Fyodor Dostoevski, prophesied that the Bolsheviks would change the face of Russia. The coldness of Roman and his followers surpasses even Mezhenetsky's calculative approach. Mezhenetsky is so unnerved by the lack of recognition and gratitude on the part of this extremely radical group that he hangs himself in the labor camp. Before he commits suicide, he sees the Old Believer, who tells him that the lamb, a symbol of love, peace, kindness and humility (Svetlogub is with the lamb), will conquer the kings of this world—clearly having Jesus Christ in mind.

Christian Themes

The Christian themes in "Divine and Human" are woven firmly into the work. The first word of the title, "divine," refers to the behavior of Svetlogub, while the last word, "human," refers to the revolutionaries, Mezhenetsky and Roman. The divine element in Svetlogub is reflected in his transformation from a nonbeliever, even an enemy of believers, into a follower of the New Testament tenets. The other two revolutionaries remain "human" in that they refuse to rise above the basic concerns of human beings—a better material life—even though they too have potential for doing good because they want to help the poor. Yet, their transformations in the course of the work were "human" in the worst way.

Tolstoy is pointing out that a desire to do good is not enough. Although Svetlogub firmly believes that he is doing the right thing by wanting to eliminate social injustice, his desire lacks firm foundation. Only after he repeatedly reads the New Testament while in prison does he realize the true meaning of his efforts. Faced with death, he now believes that he will not die but will just start a new life after death. That new life will be full of joy and, most important, of love for fellow human beings. As for the authorities who are putting him to death, they know not what they are doing. Above all, they must save their souls, for what good does it do a man to gain the whole world and lose his own soul? Many other sayings from the New Testament now connote a new, Christian way of life for Svetlogub.

On the other hand, Mezhenetsky does not show any interest in reading the New Testament, even though every prisoner is given a copy. It has no meaning for him and for his practical frame of mind. However, when faced with a real challenge by Roman's group, he has nothing to fall back on, and he commits suicide.

The third revolutionary, the leader of the radical group, Roman, likewise shows no interest in the New Testament. Instead, he relies on the "scientific" approach to the toppling of the government. The story ends before the readers learn what happens to him, but the assumption is that Tolstoy was fearful of Roman's triumph.

The Old Believer, another prisoner, best personifies Christian virtues. He notices Svetlogub before he turns to Christianity. Yet the old man loves Svetlogub and always asks for him. He teaches him by example how to love even your enemy. After all, it was the wife of the governor-general of the province—the enemy—who gave Svetlogub and all the other prisoners copies of the New Testament.

Sources for Further Study

Berlin, Isaiah. *The Hedgehog and the Fox: An Essay on Tolstoy's View of History*. New York: Simon and Schuster, 1953. A standard essay on Tolstoy's view of history and the role of individuals in it, as applied to Tolstoy's works, especially *Voyna I mir* (1865-1869; *War and Peace*, 1886).

Egan, David R., and Melinda A. Egan, eds. *Leo Tolstoy: An Annotated Bibliography of English Sources from 1978 to 2003*. Lanham, Md.: Scarecrow Press, 2005. Indispensable, though time limited, for students of Tolstoy, including sources on religion and all other aspects of his works.

Levin, Michael L. *A Signature on a Portrait: Highlights of Tolstoy's Thought*. New York: Levin Press, 1994. Criticism and interpretation of major aspects of Tolstoy's thinking, including spiritual and Christian aspects.

Matlaw, Ralph E., ed. *Tolstoy: A Collection of Critical Essays*. Englewood Cliffs, N.J.: Prentice-Hall, 1967. Essays on different aspects of Tolstoy's life, works, and art, by various authors. With chronology of important dates and selected bibliography.

Poggioli, Renato. *The Phoenix and the Spider*. Cambridge, Mass.: Harvard University Press, 1957. An astute analysis of psychological aspects of Tolstoy's approach to literature.

Simmons, Ernest J. *Leo Tolstoy*. Boston: Atlantic, Little Brown, 1947. One of the best biographies of Tolstoy in English.

Vasa D. Mihailovich

THE DIVINE COMEDY

Author: Dante (1265-1321)

First transcribed: La divinia commedia, c. 1320 (English translation, 1802)

Edition used: The Comedy of Dante Alighieri, the Florentine, translated by Dorothy
  L. Sayers. Harmondsworth, Middlesex, England: Penguin Books, 1967

Genre: Poetry

Subgenres: Allegory; didactic treatise; narrative poetry

Core issues: Catholics and Catholicism; the divine; good vs. evil; salvation; union
  with God

*Dante travels through the afterlife, where he witnesses souls being punished or re-
warded for their deeds. This is a necessary result of divine justice: In Dante's comprehensive medieval vision of the divine order, the world is an expression of divine
thought, which is justice itself. Therefore, Dante's individual union with God is an allegory of every soul's journey toward salvation.*

> *Principal characters*
> *Dante*, protagonist and first-person narrator, symbolic of every
>   man
> *Beatrice*, his love and guide through Earthly Paradise and most of
>   Heaven, symbolic of divine revelation
> *Virgil*, the Roman writer and Dante's guide through Hell and to
>   Earthly Paradise in Purgatory, symbolic of human reason

Overview

Dante's *The Divine Comedy* is the beginning of Italian literature and the single
most significant work of the Middle Ages because its allegory emphasizes the importance of salvation and divine love in a work that is inclusive and tightly structured. It
is so thoroughly infused with Christian ethics that any overview has to touch on major
Christian themes, beginning with the plot being set during Easter week 1300.

The work is a complex narrative with many allusions to biblical stories, classical
myths, history, and contemporary politics; however, the plot's symbolism provides
clarity in that it celebrates the ideal of universalism, where everything has its place in
God's world, and its ultimate goal of salvation triumphs over the contemporary reality of the power struggle between worldly and religious leaders.

The structure of the entire work, as well as of its parts, is symbolic of the story it
tells, as the use of numbers shows. The number 3 (symbolic of the Trinity: God as the
Father, the Son, and the Holy Ghost) and the number 10 (the "perfect" number: 3×3
+ 1) are the most conspicuous examples. *The Divine Comedy* has three "cantiche," or
parts (Hell, Purgatory, and Heaven). Each cantica has thirty-three cantos, or songs,
with the exception of the first cantica, which has thirty-four cantos, adding up to a to-

tal of one hundred (the perfect number squared: 10×10). Each canto is written in *terza rima*, that is, in tercets that rhyme in an interlocking manner.

The first canto, "Inferno," is considered to be an introduction to the whole work (making the structure even more symmetric: $1 + 33 + 33 + 33 = 100$) because all three parts of *The Divine Comedy* are present in the first canto's symbolic landscape. Dante finds himself lost in a dark forest. Looking for orientation, he decides to hike up a mountain, whose sunlit top represents Purgatory, while the sky and the sun represent Heaven. However, Dante's path is blocked by three animals on the mountain's slope: a leopard, a lion, and a she-wolf, which represent the three main types of sin that correspond to the three main divisions of Hell.

The spirit of Virgil appears and promises to get Dante to salvation the long way: through Hell, Purgatory, and Heaven. Dante's doubts are assuaged because Virgil has been sent by three heavenly ladies (the Virgin Mary, Saint Lucy, and Beatrice); in the combination of human reason with divine grace, Dante's salvation may yet be achieved. After they enter Hell in the third canto, Dante learns through conversations with Virgil and individual souls that each sin is punished according to its severity, systematically going from the lighter sins of incontinence (giving in to one's desires) to the more severe sins of violence (actively willing evil) and fraud (adding malice). Hell, which is presented as a huge funnel-shaped underground cave, extends in ever-smaller and more-constricting circles to the middle of the earth; there, in the pit of hell, sits Satan himself, forever stuck frozen in the ice of the lake Cocytus, chewing on the three worst human traitors: Judas, Brutus, and Cassius.

Climbing past Satan, Dante is headed toward salvation. While all sinners in Hell will remain there forever to suffer their horrible punishments because they did not admit their sins, souls in Purgatory are already saved and eventually will go to Heaven because they confessed their sins before death. Therefore, the mood has completely changed: The souls are not stuck in everlasting isolation but learn in groups from examples of the virtue and vice that correspond to their penance. Purgatory is presented as a huge cone-shaped mountain and the only landmass in the southern hemisphere. Purgatory proper is organized in seven rings according to the traditional seven deadly sins (pride, envy, wrath, sloth, avarice, gluttony, and lust). At the top of the mountain is earthly paradise (the Garden of Eden); this is as far as human reason can lead, so Virgil leaves and Beatrice becomes Dante's guide.

Cleansed of his own sins, Dante rises naturally toward Heaven. In keeping with the Ptolemaic worldview, Heaven is organized in spheres with the earth in the center. Dante identifies ten spheres that he relates to the so-called four pagan virtues of fortitude, justice, temperance, and prudence in varying degrees (first to seventh Heavens), the three Christian virtues of faith, hope, and charity (eighth Heaven), the Primum Mobile (the ninth heaven, which moves all others), and the Empyrean (the tenth Heaven outside of time and space, where God dwells). The Empyrean as a state of being also contains the Celestial Rose, where all blessed souls reside. The souls do not reside in the individual heavens where Dante encounters them but are put there so that he may more easily understand their place in the divine order. The blessed souls in Heaven form a true, though strictly hierarchical, community that exists in an all-permeating feeling of love and bliss, which comes from the joy and peace of being in the proper place in God's creation. Dante evokes in images of light what lies beyond human experience, such as the radiance of the blessed souls and Dante's vision of God.

Christian Themes

Dante's work, while largely in keeping with fourteenth century Catholic teachings, reveals the vision of an individual. For example, Dante's tripartite division of the afterlife into Hell, Purgatory, and Heaven follows standard dogma, but his depiction of Purgatory as a soaring mountain in the southern hemisphere was his own invention. Dante is never antireligion, although he is at times anticlergy. He sometimes criticized religious leaders because he had a clear personal concept of the spiritual role of the church and the worldly role of the empire, each of which he saw as divinely ordained in its specific role.

Dante also had a clear concept of Christian ethics. In his work, he shows the tradition of courtly love as transcended by divine love. He also portrays love as the root cause of all human vices and virtues. Dante uses the idea of *contrapasso* (retribution) to provide the rationale for dealing with good and evil actions during life and finding everybody's proper place in the afterlife. Every human deed receives a punishment or reward that is not only in proportion but also symbolically in kind. For example, the repentant sinners in Purgatory walk through fire to burn away the earthly fire of lust. Dante uses the image of fire sparingly to keep it symbolically appropriate and to avoid glamorizing sin; he prefers to show the bone-chilling coldness of evil.

Salvation, according to Dante, can be achieved only through divine grace. Human reason may be enough to lead a virtuous life on earth (as in the case of the so-called virtuous pagans), but it alone cannot lead to salvation. Because humans have free will, salvation starts with human reason but depends on grace. Beatrice, by transcending human love for divine love, is a source of revelation for Dante, and by her acts, she makes divine grace accessible to him.

Dante imagines God as moving everything in the universe. His union with God reveals to him that, paradoxically, the universe is in God, taking the form of God's thought, and because God is love and justice, the universe is also just, even if it is not fully understood by humans. The complex character of Dante's union with God suggests that full understanding may not be necessary because the experience itself is joyful and puts him at peace with himself and God. Dante's final union with God is, for a Christian, the most happy ending; therefore, his using the word "comedy" in the title of a tale that begins with sin makes sense because the story leads to the ultimate good news of salvation.

Sources for Further Study

Bemrose, Stephen. *A New Life of Dante*. Exeter, England: University of Exeter Press, 2000. Biography that includes a discussion following the plot of *The Divine Comedy* and differentiating between the real-life Dante and the character.

Cogan, Mark. *The Design in the Wax: The Structure of the Divine Comedy and Its Meaning*. Notre Dame, Ind.: University of Notre Dame Press, 1999. Argues that a complex system of interrelated values of sin, redemption, and blessedness is embedded in the work's structure.

Hollander, Robert. *Dante: A Life in Works*. New Haven, Conn.: Yale University Press, 2001. Uses a thematic approach to *The Divine Comedy* by focusing on main characters; also thorough discussion of allegory.

Ingo R. Stoehr

THE DIVINE CONSPIRACY
Rediscovering Our Hidden Life in God

Author: Dallas Willard (1935-   )
First published: San Francisco: HarperSanFrancisco, 1998
Genre: Nonfiction
Subgenres: Biblical studies; exegesis; handbook for living; theology
Core issues: The Beatitudes; daily living; discipleship; faith; Jesus Christ; sanctification

In The Divine Conspiracy, *selected as Book of the Year by* Christianity Today *in 1999, Willard discusses influential and sometimes harmful trends present in contemporary society and the Christian church. He considers the Gospel to be good news not just for securing eternal life in heaven but also for securing an eternal kind of life here on earth, through apprenticeship to Jesus Christ. The book contains an extended discussion of the Sermon on the Mount as a picture of life in Christ.*

Overview

According to Dallas Willard, part of our nature as human beings is to want to live lives that have deep significance, which is a reflection of our God-given creative impulse. Modern society contains several hindrances to experiencing this type of significance: skepticism about the possibility of moral knowledge, scorn for the profound, and the belief that the only two elements of reality are particles and progress. That is, reality is ultimately physical, and all that matters socially is that we make progress, whatever that may be. Absurdity and cuteness are admired in society. For Willard, they are fine to laugh and even think about, but absurdity and cuteness fail to lead us into lives of satisfaction and significance. Jesus, however, possesses enduring relevance because he relates to human beings in ways that produce wholeness.

The Church also erects barriers to human flourishing, especially in its espousal of what Willard calls the gospels of sin management. Christians of a conservative theological persuasion hold that Christianity is about only forgiveness of sins and eternal life after death. This is problematic, because it seems impossible to trust Jesus to provide eternal life in the hereafter but not trust him for new life, an eternal kind of life, in the here and now. For the more theologically liberal, the Gospel is not about securing life after death in heaven with God, but rather the focus is on social ethics. In recent times, the idea is that the good news is that Jesus died to promote liberation, equality, and community and that this was his message.

In Willard's view, the true good news communicated through the Scriptures and displayed in the life of Jesus is that we can have our lives and characters transformed now, as we seek to live under God's rule. Both privatized forgiveness of sins as well as the social Gospel have failed to produce deep and lasting transformation of either individual human lives or of our lives together. The Gospel is about eternal life and life in the present, and it does have social implications, but according to Willard, the kingdom of Christ is not essentially a social or political kingdom. Rather, his kingdom is about extending God's rule in human hearts in a way that pervades the entire universe.

Because there is more to reality than particles and progress, Willard describes the nature of spiritual reality. God is spiritual, and people are spiritual beings who live in a spiritual reality. Spiritual reality is not physical. It is not perceivable by the physical senses. The spiritual is powerful, however. It works via the mind and will. The spiritual also has to do with thought, and people, unlike any merely physical object, by their nature think. Finally, the spiritual as it exists in people is concerned with value and valuing. We are favorably disposed to some things and not so favorably disposed to others.

Willard argues that Jesus is truly the smartest man in the world; therefore, he explores Christ's teachings in the Sermon on the Mount as an intellectually sound and practically viable approach to life. In the Sermon on the Mount, Jesus is concerned with two questions of perennial interest to human beings: What kind of life is truly good? and Who is truly a good person? In response to the first question, Willard says Jesus would answer the kind of life led by a person who accepts God, is intimately related to God, and works with God to further his kingdom. Regarding the second question, Jesus would answer that the truly good person is the one who actively promotes the good of all.

Willard goes on to discuss the need to escape the deceptions of both wealth and a good reputation. For him, pursuit of these things will not lead to a good life, nor is such a pursuit conducive to becoming a good person. He also discusses individual and corporate prayer. He marshals biblical support that was meaningful in his own spiritual journey in favor of the claim that prayer is at its most basic level a request and that God does respond to prayer. God may grant or refuse requests made to him in prayer, based on what is good. Next, Willard examines life as a student of Jesus and offers a practical curriculum for becoming like Christ. The primary objectives of such a curriculum should not be mere external behavior nor profession of precisely and perfectly correct doctrine. Rather, the main objectives in the pursuit of Christ-like character should be to develop a love of God and deep trust in God's goodness and to undergo a transformation of body and soul such that one's automatic responses are in line with the rules of God's kingdom. Finally, Willard concludes the book with a description of what human existence will be like in an eternity with God.

Christian Themes

In the chapter entitled "What Jesus Knew: Our God-Bathed World," Willard discusses the belief that God is present in the air that surrounds our bodies. He argues that the biblical phrase "the first heaven" refers to this. Therefore, God does not inhabit the heavens in a distant sense, but rather God is present in the space that surrounds our bodies. The significance of this lies in the fact that when we conceive of God and heaven as existing in some far-off place or even beyond outer space, God and his kingdom seem remote and distant, which is damaging to our spiritual lives. However, a proper understanding of the experience of people as recorded in the Old and

New Testaments reveals a God who is present in the space around our bodies and with whom we can enter into an intimate, powerful, and loving relationship.

A second key issue dealt with in *The Divine Conspiracy* is Willard's understanding of the Beatitudes. The prominent understanding of the Beatitudes is that they are pre-scriptions for how human beings should live. For example, humans should be poor in spirit, meek, and persecuted for the sake of righteousness. Willard's view is that the point of the Beatitudes is that God's kingdom is available to all people, right now, through Jesus. The descriptions given in the Beatitudes are of the people who were present during Jesus' Sermon on the Mount, and he was describing the inclusiveness of God's kingdom.

Willard argues that Christians should not seek to be meek or poor in spirit but rather should seek out the meek and poor in spirit so that they too can understand the availability of God and his kingdom. Once rightly related to God, the poor in spirit become indescribably rich in spirit because they are blessed by God.

Finally, there are many other Christian issues dealt with by Willard in ways that are new to the modern mind but not to the biblical record or to Christian history. Part of the value of this book is the biblical and historical case Willard makes for his views not only on God's presence and the availability of God's kingdom but also on the true content of the Gospel, the nature of life together among followers of Christ, and the aim of the Christian life as one of union with God and automatic response in line with the rules of God's kingdom.

Sources for Further Study

Foster, Richard. *Celebration of Discipline*. San Francisco: HarperSanFrancisco, 1998. Contains a description of many of the classical spiritual disciplines, as well as several practical applications for each of them.

Moreland, J. P., and Klaus Issler. *The Lost Virtue of Happiness*. Colorado Springs, Colo.: Navpress, 2006. Discusses how the worldview assumptions of modern culture undermine the Christian pursuit of true happiness and offers practical guidance in how to experience such happiness in life.

Van Der Wheele, Steven. Review of *The Divine Conspiracy*. *The Christian Century* 116, no. 20 (July 14-21, 1999): 719-721. Praises Willard's work for its command of Scripture, comprehensiveness, and accessibility.

Willard, Dallas. *Hearing God*. Downers Grove, Ill.: InterVarsity Press, 1999. Focuses on developing a conversational relationship with God. Useful as a guide for practical spirituality but includes theoretical content as well.

————. *Renovation of the Heart*. Colorado Springs, Colo.: Navpress, 2002. Contains a discussion of human nature and how true discipleship to Jesus affects the character of human beings.

————. *The Spirit of the Disciplines*. San Francisco: Harper and Row, 1988. A biblical, theological, and philosophical case for practicing the classical spiritual disciplines, such as solitude, fasting, and silence.

Michael W. Austin

THE DIVINE MILIEU
An Essay on the Interior Life

Author: Pierre Teilhard de Chardin (1881-1955)
First published: Le Milieu divin, 1957 (English translation, 1960)
Edition used: The Divine Milieu: An Essay on the Interior Life, translated by Bernard
  Wall. New York: Harper, 1960
Genre: Nonfiction
Subgenre: Meditation and contemplation
Core issues: Asceticism; attachment and detachment; awakening; church; Commu-
  nion; the divine; Jesus Christ; psychology; soul; union with God

*The son of a farmer who inherited his father's interest in geology, Teilhard de Char-
din was ordained a priest in 1912 and chose to serve as a stretcher-bearer, proving
very courageous, rather than as a chaplain in World War I. After study in Cairo and
teaching in Paris, the Jesuit spent a number of years doing paleontological and geo-
logical research in China. He returned to France in 1946 amid theological controversy. Since Teilhard de Chardin was forbidden by religious superiors to publish
during his lifetime, his important works all appeared after his death on Easter Sunday, 1955.*

Overview

Pierre Teilhard de Chardin's well-known book *Le Phénomène humain* (1955; *The
Phenomenon of Man*, 1955) contains the core of his scientific thought. *The Divine Milieu* is its counterpart on the spiritual level. It is a meditation book for intellectuals and
is addressed primarily to those who waver rather than to Christians who are firmly established in their beliefs. However, as the author writes in the preface, there is not
much in this book on moral evil and sin. Teilhard de Chardin assumes that he is dealing here with souls who have already turned away from such errors. The subject to be
treated in these pages is actual, supernaturalized human beings, seen in the restricted
realm of *conscious* psychology.

Humankind is involved in a collective awakening, Teilhard de Chardin notes in his
introduction. This will inevitably have a profound religious influence on humanity.
Teilhard de Chardin sets out to consider human beings in the double aspect of their
experience: active and passive—that which the person does and that which is undergone.

Part 1, "The Divinization of Our Activities," begins with a note that what is most
divine in God is that "we are nothing apart from him." All persons are impelled by the
will to be and to grow; the particular problem that Christians face is to sanctify their
actions. How is one to make important contributions to the world, though, when one is
constantly warned by spiritual writers to preserve an attitude of detachment toward
the world? There are three responses, traditionally, to this dilemma, according to Teil-

hard de Chardin. One is to center oneself on specifically religious acts; another is to devote oneself to strictly secular pursuits; finally, and usually, one merely throws up one's hands at the inability to understand the problem and makes a weak compromise that results in one's belonging neither wholly to God nor wholly to things.

All three responses are dangerous, Teilhard de Chardin writes, but there is a fourth way to resolve the situation that will provide mutual nourishment for love of God and a healthy love for the world. This will combine a striving for detachment with a striving for development. There are two solutions that can be employed when facing this Christian problem of the divinization of human activity. The first is an incomplete solution and is based on the concept that our actions have no value except in the intentions that motivate them. However, this solution is not fully satisfactory because it does not give hope for the resurrection of our bodies. The more satisfactory solution is found in this: that all work, all striving, cooperates to complete the world in Christ Jesus. Teilhard de Chardin illustrates this point by use of a syllogism. At the heart of the universe, every soul exists for God, but all reality exists for our souls; therefore, all reality exists, through our souls, for God. God's creation, after all, was not completed long ago; it is a continuing process and we serve to complete it by what we do. The task is no less than bringing Christ to fulfillment.

The divine so permeates our every energy that our action is the most appropriate milieu for embracing it. In action we cleave to God's creative power; we coincide with it and prolong it. There is a specifically Christian perfection to human endeavor. We cripple our lives if we see work as only an encumbrance. Because of the incarnation of Christ, nothing on this earth is profane for those who see properly. Too many Christians are not conscious enough of the responsibilities to God that we have for our lives.

There is, of course, the need for detachment through action, Teilhard de Chardin adds. By its very nature, work may be seen as an important factor in detachment. First, work indicates an effort beyond inertia. Then, too, it is always accompanied by painful birth pangs. The worker becomes more avid in his or her efforts, wanting to blaze new paths, to create more widely. Thus one belongs no longer exclusively to oneself, but the spirit of the universe gradually insinuates itself in the person. The Christian, as described in this section, is at once the most detached and the most attached of human beings.

"The Divinisation of Our Passivities" is the title and content of part 2. In the encounter between humanity and God, Teilhard de Chardin writes, humanity—because it is the lesser—must receive rather than give. Our passivities comprise half of our existence, as has been said earlier, but it is important to realize that the passive parts of our lives are immeasurably wider and deeper than the active.

Growth itself is essentially passive, is undergone. Teilhard de Chardin writes that we probably undergo life more than we undergo death. All of our desires to realize ourselves are charged with God's influence. However, the forces of diminishment are our true passivities, and we should recognize their twofold origins: those passivities whose origin lies within us and those whose origin is found outside ourselves. The passage of time is an important diminishment. Death is the consummation of all our diminishments, but we can overcome death by finding God in it. We must ask ourselves how our deaths may be integrated into God's milieu.

One of the most difficult of all mysteries is found in the problem of attempting to reconcile our failures with creative goodness, Teilhard de Chardin argues. Providence may be seen as turning evil into good in three main ways. Occasionally one of our failures will divert our energies into another channel that will be a more virtuous one. Sometimes the loss we experience will cause us to turn, out of frustration, to less material areas. The third and most common way, because we see diminishment all around us, almost continually, is by uniting with God and transfiguring our sufferings within the context of a loving annihilation and union. God carves out a hollowness in us in order to make room for his entrance into our innermost being. Thus everything can be taken up again to be recast in God, even our failures.

In a separate section, "Some General Remarks on Christian Asceticism," Teilhard de Chardin appends a conclusion to the first two parts of his treatise. He thinks that the question very often facing people is not well put when dichotomies are implied. For example, when someone asks if activity or passivity is better for the Christian, the question is unfair because misleading. Other contrasts are set up as well: growth or diminishment; development or curtailment; possession or renunciation. Why, Teilhard de Chardin responds, should we separate what should be recognized as two natural phases of a single effort? We must develop ourselves and take possession of the world *in order to be*; he advises us that once that is achieved, the time to think about renunciation has come, as well as the time to begin diminishment for the sake of being in God. This is the way to complete Christian asceticism, Teilhard de Chardin contends.

Previous writings on spiritual perfection usually fail to emphasize enough the need for self-development first. This is a serious flaw, Teilhard de Chardin believes. The effort of humanity, even in what are incorrectly felt to be solely secular areas, must assume a holy and unifying function. In the Gospel, Christ says that we should leave our possessions and follow him. We must do penance as a way of organizing and of liberating the baser forces within ourselves. We have no right, however, to diminish ourselves solely for the sake of self-diminishment. The general rhythm of the life of a Christian indicates that development and renunciation, attachment and detachment, are not mutually exclusive. They are, rather, harmonized, like inhalation and exhalation.

What is true of individuals is true of the Church, as well, which goes through phases in its existence. At times it projects a great care in the duties of its earthly tasks; at other periods it emphasizes the transcendental nature of its activities.

The section on asceticism ends with the typically Teilhardian view of the spiritual power of matter. To despise matter, as the Manichaean heretics did, is to err gravely, he contends. Matter can represent a continual aspiration toward failure, but by its nature, and particularly by Christ's incarnation (wherein he took on a physical, material existence), matter can be a partner in the quest for spiritual perfection. Just like humanity, the world has a path to follow to reach its final goal.

"The Divine Milieu" is the heading for part 3, implying as it does that it is toward this point that what has gone before has prepared us. This may be seen as Teilhard de Chardin's major mystical statement. According to his account, all created things are penetrated by the divine. The world is, in truth, a holy place. The basic attribute of the divine milieu is the ease with which it is able to gather into harmony within itself various qualities that appear to be contradictory. God shows himself everywhere as a universal milieu, Teilhard de Chardin argues, because God is the ultimate point toward which all realities tend or, to use an important word for Teilhard de Chardin, "converge." Regardless of the tremendous size of this divine milieu, it is in fact a center in which all for which we strive is reunited. We should, therefore, attempt to establish ourselves in that divine milieu. Moreover, the French theologian insists, one who travels in this center is not a pantheist. Our God, he assures us, preserves the individuality of things in their fulfillment, whereas in pantheism they would lose their differentiation.

This true spiritual milieu is formed by the divine omnipresence, Teilhard de Chardin writes. It is charged with sanctifying grace, the fundamental sap of the world. The great communion is found in the universal Christ; there is a profound identification of the Son of man and the divine Eucharist. Teilhard de Chardin suggests that not only are all the communions of a lifetime one single communion and all the communions of all now living a single communion, but all the communions of all who have lived and who will live are but one single act of adoration.

When we come to realize that the divine milieu has been revealed to us, it is possible to make a pair of important observations, Teilhard de Chardin suggests. First, the manifestation of the divine causes no apparent changes on the outward nature of things as perceived by our senses—though their meanings may be accentuated. Second, the persistence of the revelation is guaranteed by Christ himself. No power can keep us from the accompanying joys.

Individual growth in the divine milieu stems from purity, faith, and fidelity. Purity is not merely a negative, an abstention, but an impulse introduced by the love of God. One's purity is measured by the intensity of the attraction pulling one to the divine center. Faith is not a mere intellectual exercise but rather a belief in God that is charged with total trust in goodness. If one believes, then everything is illuminated with the light of understanding. What we thought was chance is seen as order, and suffering is recognized as the caress of God. Through fidelity, one situates and maintains oneself in God. If a person has this quality, greater desire follows lesser ones, and eventually self-denial will gain ascendancy over pleasure.

Teilhard de Chardin argues in closing that it is through love that the divine milieu will be intensified. Christian charity is the conscious cohesion of souls engendered by their convergence, communally in Jesus Christ. There is a tendency toward fusion among the good, and in this association their ardor increases. In fact, Teilhard de Chardin concludes, the history of God's kingdom is a history of reunion.

In the epilogue, "In Expectation of the Parousia," Teilhard de Chardin writes of segregation (of the evil elements) and aggregation (of the good). There will come a time, the Gospels promise, when the tensions that are accumulating between humanity and God "will touch the limits prescribed by the possibilities of the world, and then will come the end." Such, he says, will be the consummation of the divine milieu. The enchantments of the earth, we thus see, will not harm us because we can see, in truth, it is the body of Jesus who is and who is coming.

Christian Themes

In *The Divine Milieu*, Teilhard de Chardin expresses his fundamental Christian beliefs that (1) the earth is Christ's body; (2) the human endeavor is to be sanctified through embracing rather than rejecting the world; (3) both our activities and our passivities can be sanctified; (4) attachment and detachment are not adversarial experiences; and (5) the divine milieu is in the communion of Christians in the Universal Christ.

Sources for Further Study

Cuénot, Claude. *Teilhard de Chardin: A Biographical Study*. Translated by Vincent Colimore, edited by René Hague. Baltimore: Helicon, 1965. One of the best biographical studies of Teilhard de Chardin.

Deane-Drummond, Celia, ed. *Pierre Teilhard de Chardin on People and Planet*. Oakville, Conn.: Equinox, 2006. A diverse collection of essays covering Teilhard de Chardin's theology as it relates to human relations (feminism, diplomacy, mysticism) and the planet's environment.

Faricy, Robert L. *Teilhard de Chardin's Theology of the Christian in the World*. New York: Sheed and Ward, 1967. Faricy speaks directly to the issues presented in *The Divine Milieu* as he explores Teilhard de Chardin's theology.

Teilhard de Chardin, Pierre. *The Future of Man*. Translated by Norman Denny. New York: Image Books/Doubleday, 2004. Teilhard de Chardin's reflections on the direction and goal of the world.

_____. *The Phenomenon of Man*. Translated by Bernard Wall, with an introduction by Julian Huxley. New York: Harper & Bros., 1959. A scientific and philosophical inquiry into the spiritual meaning of evolution.

Harry James Cargas

THE DIVINE RELATIVITY
A Social Conception of God

Author: Charles Hartshorne (1897-2000)
First published: New Haven, Conn.: Yale University Press, 1948
Genre: Nonfiction
Subgenre: Theology
Core issues: The Deity; knowledge; reason

Hartshorne presents a logical analysis of the nature of God, which attempts to account for the involvement of a perfect, unchanging being in a contingent, relativistic world by arguing that God is simultaneously absolute and relative.

Overview

In *The Divine Relativity*, Charles Hartshorne states that he aims to show that God can be conceived without logical absurdity and that the idea of God does not involve self-contradiction. Some theologians have spoken of the nature of God as paradoxical or mysterious because belief in the Deity implies faith in a being that is both absolute and unchanging and also part of the relativistic, shifting universe. Hartshorne maintains that allowing this kind of paradox contributes to atheism because it allows contradiction at the center of faith. He argues that analysis of the definition of God can solve the apparent problem of self-contradiction.

Hartshorne writes that God is relative in most aspects because God exists in relation to his creation. This is in the nature of God's existence as a subject rather than as an object. The subject, which knows things, is relative to the object, which is known. Because God knows all things, God must be relative to all things. Hartshorne labels the supremely relative nature of God "surrelativism." God is also relative as a social being because persons in a society are defined by their relations to other persons, and God is related to all persons.

The belief that the perfection of God is inconsistent with divine relativity is caused by mistaken thinking in the tradition of the absolute. In the intellectual tradition that has come down to Christianity from antiquity, unchangeability and a lack of relation to other things have been considered superior qualities, while dependence and contingency have been considered inferior qualities. Therefore, this tradition has portrayed God, the being superior to all things, as of necessity absolute and beyond relation and change. However, Hartshorne argues, the relative may legitimately be regarded as superior to the absolute. A person, perceiving an object, is superior to a mere object. The person is affected by the perception, though, and exists in relation to the thing being perceived. The object exists independently of the perception and is therefore not relative to it. Hartshorne maintains that the long tradition of the superiority of uncaused, independent beings is an error and that the relative is, in fact, superior to the unrelated and unchanging. God, the supreme being, must be the most relative of all.

While God is related to all things and therefore the most changing and relative of all beings, he is at the same time the most absolute, according to Hartshorne. Individuals are abstract to the extent that they have enduring qualities that do not relate to any particular time or circumstance. Abstract qualities such as goodness and wisdom consistently characterize God. These are the qualities that give God reliability, because they are the same in all particular connections between God and the world. The omniscience of God means that God knows all facts and therefore does not vary according to any set of facts. Hartshorne argues that God is not only the most relative of all beings in most aspects but also the most absolute of all beings in the aspect of consistency and reliability of abstract attributes.

Hartshorne maintains that the attributes of God are expressions of the types of relationships God has with the world and with humanity. For this reason, he argues that errors about the attributes of God inherited from the religions of the past have led to misconceptions about God that have had negative effects on the ways that people act in the world. The supposed otherworldliness of God has led people to avoid the task of human welfare in favor of seeking entry into Heaven. The separation of divine influence from divine sensitivity to human affairs has led to power worship. Asceticism has prevented churches and believers from recognizing the proper combination of the physical and the spiritual, leading to an inability to deal with the problems of marriage. Abstract moralism has led to an underemphasis on charity and on creative solutions to social problems. Optimism about the ultimate nature of the universe has resulted in the failure to deal realistically with matters such as war and tyranny. Obscurantism, the dedication to paradox and logical contradiction, has prevented clarity in religious and daily lives. These misconceptions about God, in Hartshorne's view, stem from the failure to recognize God's relative nature.

Christian Themes

The question of the nature of God is one of the oldest questions in Christianity. A core part of this question has been the relationship of God to the created world. The pre-Christian Greek philosopher Plato professed the historically influential view of dualism, with the universe split into unchangeable, ultimately real ideas and constantly shifting, relativistic things. Plato's student Aristotle rejected or modified many aspects of Plato's teaching but carried on the tradition of an unchanging absolute beyond the realm of the everyday world. Aristotle, developing an idea that would have a great impact on Christian thinking about God, described the supreme deity as an unmoved mover, a cause of the world but beyond the world. Aristotle's god was eternally concerned with the perfection of unchanging self-contemplation and therefore had no active involvement with the created world.

In the third century, the Neoplatonist Plotinus further developed ideas about the relation between the divine absolute and the relativity of the physical world by describing human beings as existing in a gross material world but ascending toward the divine world of pure mind. In the view of Plotinus, the movement consisted entirely of the human toward the divine; the absolute could have no motivation for a relationship with the mundane.

Neoplatonic and Aristotelian thought became deeply embedded in Christian ideas of the nature of God and the relationship of God to the world. Early medieval Christian philosophers conceived of the universe in Neoplatonic terms as a hierarchy from divine spiritual perfection to the relativistic, changing world. Medieval Christian thinking reached its high point in the thirteenth century in the Aristotlean philosophy of Saint Thomas Aquinas.

Perfection as the nature of God was also the central feature of one of the primary medieval arguments for God's existence, the ontological argument of Saint Anselm in the twelfth century. Anselm maintained that God is defined as the greatest and most perfect of all conceivable beings and that a god who does not exist would not be the greatest being conceivable because one can conceive of a still greater being: A god who does exist.

The connected themes of the perfection of God and the absolute, unchanging nature of God posed major problems for Christianity. Christianity is based on faith in a grace offered by God to humans and on the unceasing activity of God in the world. If perfection is so central to God that it establishes divine existence and perfection is a matter of absolute unchangeability, then how can God be connected to a perpetually changing world? If God is in the world, then how can God exist separate from the world as a source of grace? Hartshorne attempts to address these problems by reanalyzing the concept of God as perfection and arguing that relativity is not contrary to perfection and that perfection entails both absolute and relative aspects.

Sources for Further Study

Connelly, Robert J. *Whitehead vs. Hartshorne: Basic Metaphysical Issues.* Washington, D.C.: University Press of America, 1981. A comparison of the thought of Hartshorne on the temporality and atemporality of God with the thought of Alfred North Whitehead, a great influence on Hartshorne.

Dombrowski, Daniel A. *Analytic Theism, Hartshorne, and the Concept of God.* Albany: State University of New York Press, 1996. A critical examination of Hartshorne's approach to the nature of God by a prominent American philosopher.

Gragg, Allan. *Charles Hartshorne.* Makers of the Modern Theological Mind series. Waco, Tex.: Word Books, 1973. This excellent overview of Hartshorne's professional life and thought covers the influence of Whitehead on Hartshorne's career, Hartshorne's views on what is real, his account of what it means to be human, and his argument on the nature of supreme reality. It also gives a critical evaluation of Hartshorne's thought and a valuable, if somewhat dated, bibliography.

Viney, Donald W. *Charles Hartshorne and the Existence of God.* Albany: State University of New York Press, 1985. An explication of Hartshorne's arguments for the existence of God, based on an argument derived from Saint Anselm that God's conceivability implies God's existence, plus arguments to establish God's conceivability.

Carl L. Bankston III

DIVINI REDEMPTORIS

Author: Pius XI (Ambrogio Damiano Achille Ratti; 1857-1939)
First published: 1937 (English translation, 1937)
Edition used: Seven Great Encyclicals. Glen Rock, N.J.: Paulist Press, 1963
Genre: Nonfiction
Subgenre: Encyclical
Core issues: Alienation from God; atheism; Catholics and Catholicism; communism;
   persecution; religion; social action

In the encyclical Divini Redemptoris, *Pope Pius XI condemned communism and the persecution of Christians under communist governments, including the Soviet Union, Mexico, and potentially Spain. The Church's championing of human rights required that it take a vocal stance against secular forces that sought to replace the Gospel with a worldly perversion of Christ's message. Because of the persistence and spread of communist totalitarianism after World War II, the articulation of the Church's resistance resonated for decades after the encyclical's issuance.*

Overview

Pope Pius XI's message in *Divini Redemptoris* (also known as *On Atheistic Communism*) is addressed to the Church's leadership worldwide. Pius XI states that "bolshevistic and atheistic Communism" threatens "Christian civilization" everywhere and promises a new barbarism worse than that of Jesus' time. It aims at "upsetting the social order" and undermining Christianity's foundations. He states that the Church cannot remain silent and must defend truth and justice.

Pius XI had already condemned communism in five encyclicals beginning in 1924 when he wrote the 1937 encyclical. In this encyclical, he relates how as early as 1846, Pius IX had condemned communism, and Leo XIII labeled it a "fatal plague." However, from its center in Moscow, communism continues to "struggle against Christian civilization." Bishops also have spoken out against communism, but the pope says that "clever agitators" and their "subversive ideas" only grow in influence. In the encyclical, he states that he will present communism's most corrosive ideas, uncover its method of action, and refute its claims with the truth of the Church.

The first tenet he sets out to debunk is communism's "false messianic" ideas of "justice, equality, and fraternity in labor." Claims of progress merely mask exploitation of resources and industrial development unrelated to communism. The second tenet is the historical materialism articulated by Karl Marx, which has "no room for the idea of God," no spiritual life, and no afterlife. The human-centered class struggle leading to history's end is characterized by greed, violence, and hate. Moral restraint, dignity, and personal liberty are lost in the collectivity, and the lack of private property gives the lie to proletarian control. Marriage and the family are subsumed by the collective, and parents lose the right to educate their children. Communist idealism is utterly materialistic, atheistic, and dominated by economic concerns. The state, which is ultimately to disappear, in the meantime is given totalitarian powers. This system defies both human reason and divine revelation.

Yet, the pope says, communism has spread because of its false promises to remove injustice and establish equitability and its manipulation of political and racial antagonisms; already it was taking root in universities. In addition, capitalism has oppressed the working classes, leaving them vulnerable to the communist message. Communist propaganda is well organized and relentless, while the noncommunist secular press has failed to confront the menace, preferring silence. Communism directly targets the Church, physically destroying communities and murdering its leaders, especially those devoted to helping the poor and workers. This is a permanent part of the communist program, because it disdains religion. Its goals, as has been witnessed, can be attained only by violence and terror.

Conversely, the pope argues, Christianity acknowledges God and his truth. Humans are physical and spiritual, having been stamped by the divine and obtaining all human rights from this divine source. Marriage, family, and rightly ordered civil society flow from the Creator to raise humanity: Only people (not societies) have reason and free will. With revelation, humanity is truly raised up. Social justice rather than state terrorism will correct the injustices of liberal (capitalist) society, bringing the rights and duties of all parties in society into harmony. The Church is clearly concerned with social welfare and political justice, though it has never posited a specific system. Its recent social doctrines provide a sound and recognized platform for reform: Labor is provided dignity and workers, rights. However, this doctrine must be both taught and applied in action.

This positive task must start with dedication to God and spiritual renewal, according to the pope. Pius XI emphasizes charity and "detachment from earthly goods" as fundamental: The wealthy have a Scriptural obligation to the poor, but both must look first to God in humility. The poor and the workers must be shown God's love in action, and then they will abandon the false promises of communism. The pope turns to capitalists, begging them to operate justly and with humanity: Providing fair salaries and decent conditions are only part of this.

To help everyone understand this Christian teaching, the pope promotes education on social doctrine and right action from the pulpit and in the Catholic press as the only way to inoculate Catholics against communist subversions. To further this end, Pius XI recommends "a world-wide crusade of prayer and penance" and invocation of the aid of Mary. He addresses priests, asking them to work specifically with the poor and the laborers in their flocks and among those hostile to the Church. The priests are to model the Church's love and charity for the working classes and poor, rather than to act as a hindrance whose control of wealth alienates those groups. The pope turns then to laity in organizations known as Catholic Action who work to spread the Gospel among the laity, especially in families. With training and dedication these people can be the "first and immediate apostles" to the working classes and aid the clergy. Other lay Catholic associations must likewise dedicate themselves and work as they can, and so, too, should the average Catholic "workingmen." From all he asks for prayer and unity and a cessation of dissent. For its part, the state must allow the Church and its members to fulfill their mission and must establish such justice and opportunity as is possible. Finally, to those Catholics who have embraced communism, he expresses the hope that they may "abandon the slippery path on which they tread."

Christian Themes

Pius XI opens with an analytical critique of atheistic communism and proceeds to exhort the members of the Church to take action to confront the seductions and violence of communism. He stresses the ways in which communism is antithetical to Christianity: its basis in materialism, its false ideals and promises, its rejection of the spiritual life and proper religion, and its undermining of Christian-influenced society. It is a critique that at once attacks communism and exalts the Church's Gospel message. In developing the Church's positive message to those attracted to communism, Pius emphasizes Christian social justice rooted in humanity's divine paternity and love. If properly understood, taught, and acted on, Christian social justice is superior in every way to that of the communists. Love provides the template and means, rather than violent revolution, repression, or state terrorism. However, the Church and society have failed to provide for the working people and the poor, opening the door to communism. In his program, Pius outlines the roles and responsibilities of each segment of Catholic society: All must be harnessed to the aim of truth and the opposition to deceit and degradation. The pope makes it clear that the rich cannot disdain the poor and need to take on a mantle of humility and justice in dealing with workers and the poor. Neither class nor race nor wealth can divide God's people. Mere opposition to communism is not enough: The Nazis, condemned in the pope's encyclical *Mit brennender Sorge* (March, 1937), do as much. Opposition must be founded in Christian charity and built on the love of truth that is rooted in the Gospel.

Sources for Further Study

Ferree, William. *The Act of Social Justice*. Washington, D.C.: Catholic University of America Press, 1942. Published dissertation that explores concepts of social justice as stated by Thomas Aquinas and places the *Divini Redemptoris* in the historical context of Catholic social philosophy.

Holland, Joe. *Modern Catholic Social Teaching: The Popes Confront the Industrial Age, 1740-1958*. New York: Paulist Press, 2003. Chapter on Pius XI's "Leonine" encyclicals places *Divini Redemptoris* and its anticommunism in the context of papal writings against modernism, industrial warfare, and economic dictatorship.

Lerhinan, John Patrick. *A Sociological Commentary on "Divini Redemptoris."* Washington, D.C.: Catholic University of America Press, 1946. Examination of the papal encyclical in light of the contrasting secular and Catholic social and political philosophical constructs that were emerging in the 1940's.

Joseph P. Byrne

THE DIVINITY SCHOOL ADDRESS

Author: Ralph Waldo Emerson (1803-1882)
First published: 1838
Edition used: "An Address," in *The Complete Essays and Other Writings of Ralph Waldo Emerson*, edited with a biographical introduction by Brooks Atkinson. New York: The Modern Library, 1940
Genre: Nonfiction
Subgenres: Essays; philosophy
Core issues: Beauty; the divine; God; Incarnation; Jesus Christ; life; nature; preaching; religion; revelation; soul

Breaking with the theological traditions of Puritan forebears and affronting many Unitarian contemporaries, Emerson began his work in controversy and became perhaps the most influential thinker in the American cultural tradition. As preacher, poet, lecturer, and essayist over the course of his career, he sought to articulate a new vision of spirit in the world and a conduct of life appropriate for the citizenry of the young nation. His address to Harvard's divinity students in 1838 articulates this vision.

Overview

With the publication of *Nature* in 1836, Ralph Waldo Emerson found himself the center of controversy with the Unitarian community at Harvard. In the introduction to that essay, he had insisted that his contemporaries discover their own "original relation to the universe" instead of living out the history of the forefathers' understanding. Those "dry bones" of the past ought to be discarded, he declared, in favor of a "religion of revelation to us" in which one could behold God and nature face to face in a new immediacy of spiritual life. In the remainder of the essay, he outlined a vision of the created order in which currents of divinity, stemming from an "Over-Soul," were immanent in the natural world and described a form of the essential human "self," the soul, and the forms of its potency and striving that could take possession of such a world for those people daring enough to seize such possibilities for personal spiritual fulfillment.

In more particular terms, as a "self" enjoyed its most glorious prospects, Emerson argued, it would ascend through the world of nature by approaching it not only for its "commodity," its practical uses, and not only for its "Beauty," its aesthetic and moral uses, but for its "Spirit," its revelation to the self of that presence of world-soul that corresponded to the human soul. Thus would the human spirit be nurtured by self-reliance, the active independent seeking of the soul in the realm of direct experience, through the medium of intuition, for that which would answer it and on which it was ultimately dependent, the immanence of Spirit.

This early, visionary piece of writing, foundational for virtually every feature of

Emerson's subsequent thinking, removed him from his intellectual and religious lineage in the American Puritan tradition and disaffected all but the most radical members of the Unitarian community he served in his own generation. Thus, when Emerson was approached in 1838 to speak to the senior class at the Harvard Divinity School, the invitation came neither from the Unitarian clergy nor from the officers of the school but, rather, from the seniors themselves, eager to get a look at this challenging new figure on the New England scene. He did not disappoint them: The challenge to the doctrinal tradition, generalized and muted in *Nature*, now became decidedly more specific; the hints in the earlier essay about divine capacity in humans were now spelled out more explicitly; the new vision, proposed in broad cultural terms in 1836, was directed during that July of 1838 to inspire a particular community of religious belief.

If the senior divinity students might have been stirred by the speech and if it was highly regarded by men such as William Ellery Channing and Theodore Parker, many others, however, resented this little talk, entitled simply "An Address." If for his part Emerson had delivered a clear remedy for the overemphasis on formalist and rationalist aspects of religion (which he spotted most especially in Unitarianism and which he would elsewhere refer to as its "pale negations"), and if he had done so in what he thought a congenial and constructive manner, one prominent Unitarian, Andrews Norton, vigorously attacked the address as "the latest form of infidelity," expressing a sentiment apparently shared widely among the clergy since only after nearly three decades was Emerson invited again to address the Harvard community.

Planning his talk (later to be called "The Divinity School Address") fully in continuity with the vision of the world articulated in Nature, Emerson opens his remarks with a melodious description of the New England summer and suggests how the plenitude and beauty of nature, its breadth and variety, invite the participation of human life in such abundance. Quickly, however, he turns from the questions of subduing the world for the realm of commodity and of enjoying the world at the level of beauty in order to raise the question of "the laws which traverse the universe" and which contain and unite all of its "infinite relations."

This is the ultimate question the human spirit has sought to answer, Emerson insists, because the human intuition of the spiritual unity of the world has always been the source of morality and worship. To sense the unifying laws of the world is also to have an "insight of the perfections of the laws of the soul" which insight, in turn, leads to "the sentiment of virtue" as the soul seeks to live in harmony with the universal principles of life. If the human soul realizes its implication in the spirit of the universe, it attempts to practice that "reverence and delight in the presence of . . . divine laws" that constitute moral essence. The intuition of these spiritual laws also, however, leads the open soul to the perception that "all things proceed out of the same spirit," to the recognition of "the sublime creed that the world is not the product of manifold power, but of one will, of one mind; and that one mind is everywhere active" in the created order. With the perception of this "law of laws," there is awakened "the religious sentiment" that is both "divine and deifying" because it makes the human soul illimitable in its communion with this Supreme Mind. While the Supreme Mind cannot be fully comprehended by human rationality, it can be approached through the intuitions of a human soul enlarged by worship.

To be opened to and infused by the divine law of the natural world is to exhibit such worship and to practice faith in "the doctrine of soul," which gives full release to the moral and religious sentiments potential in all people. While these sentiments have been embodied fully and uniquely only in Jesus Christ, they are capable of realization by everyone, Emerson thinks, even if now all seem to struggle in darkness and limitation. Were people to enter the world fully open to the currents of spirit flowing through it, they might move in delight and reverence and worship through a confluence of divine spirit with human spirit, and this new conduct of piety would bring to them "the privilege of the immeasurable mind" to seize a world brimming with the miracles of natural life "in the blowing clover and falling rain," a world now seen as revelatory of spirit at every turn, a world forever to be beheld in astonishment by that form of human response to which that world corresponds and for which it is made perfect.

This vision of the world, the doctrine of soul at its heart, and the new conduct of life it would create are yet to be born in his time, Emerson believes, because the age is suffering under a lower estimate of human spiritual potential and under forms of religious understanding and practice that clouded the spiritual horizons. Only one man, Jesus Christ, has ever been true to the doctrine of soul, Emerson argues: Jesus "saw with open eye the mystery of the soul. . . . He saw that God incarnates himself in man, and evermore goes forth anew to take possession of his World." What was open to Jesus, the realization of God in him, is open to all people because the principle of incarnation is structured into the divine laws of the world, Emerson notes, but "alone in all history he [Jesus] estimated the greatness of man." Such an estimate cannot be taught to the rational understanding; it can arrive only through the example of those who have themselves intuited the spiritual unity of the universe by worshiping within the doctrine of soul. Sadly, however, the ages have not followed the soul-principle evident in Jesus Christ but have instead followed his "tropes" to worship with "a doctrine of church."

Thus, historical Christianity itself has erred in two considerable ways, Emerson declares, which further prevent the recognition of people that they have and can do all that Jesus had and did, that by "coming again to themselves, or to God in themselves, can they grow forevermore." First, Christianity errs by confusing the *person* of Jesus with the soul of Jesus. In such a misunderstanding, people are urged to subordinate their own natures to the person of Christ and are not inspired to recognize that the capacity of soul in Christ is duplicated in themselves, in their essential selves, their souls, given by the divine mind for the venturous reach for complete spiritual fulfillment. "The soul knows no persons," Emerson boldly states, and the invitation to the soul is for "every man to expand to the full circle of the universe," not to shackle the self in imitation of another. The second defect of the Christian Church is a related one. By emphasizing the unique person of Christ, Emerson points out, "men have come to speak of the revelation as somewhat long ago given and done, as if God were [now] dead." So long as the Supreme Mind flows through the world of nature and history, however, the principle of revelation centered in Jesus Christ must be seen as a continuing principle—indeed a divine law—that beckons the soul to enter into that "original relation to the universe" Emerson craved in *Nature*. To regard revelation as having gone out of the world after Jesus is to cripple efforts to make the doctrine of the illimitable soul the wellspring of religion and society. Such an "injury to faith throttles the preacher," Emerson thinks, and gives the Church "an uncertain and inarticulate voice."

With these errors of historical Christianity exposed, Emerson becomes more explicitly mindful of his audience, a group of young men poised to take up the vocations of Christian ministry. He challenges them directly: "In how many churches, by how many prophets, tell me, is man made sensible that he is an infinite Soul; that the heavens and earth are passing into his mind; that he is drinking forever the soul of God?" The pulpit has been usurped by formalists, Emerson argues, while the necessities of the age require a preacher "on whom the soul descends, through whom the soul speaks." At a moment in which "the need was never greater of new revelation," the pulpit was being mounted too often by those as yet unawakened to the real presence of spirit in the world, by those cloaked so securely in the doctrinal garments of the Church that they remained untouched by those miraculous currents of life that answer to the struggle of soul for the realization of spirit. Against this deformity in the ministry, Emerson tells the divinity students, the new preacher must "live with the privilege of the immeasurable mind," must not confuse the soul with the Church, must deal with men and women in the immediacy of their experience, which would be to "acquaint [them] at first hand with Deity" by now cheering "their waiting, fainting hearts . . . with new hope and new revelation." In order to accomplish this, he asserts, the young preachers will need to "cast behind . . . all conformity" in favor of their own souls' intuitions of the laws in the world of divine immanence. "I shall look for the New Teacher," Emerson closes, "that shall follow so far those shining laws that he shall see them come full circle; shall see their rounding complete grace; shall see the world to be a mirror of the soul."

Finally, then, Emerson sought in "The Divinity School Address" to instill in the ministers of the young American nation a sense of the revelatory dimensions of the abundantly spiritual world he thought awaited their possession. In this, he spoke with a vibrancy of soul, a hope of heart, an attitude of spiritual conviction that made him less interested in being accredited in terms of the doctrinal measurements of historical Christianity than he was committed to respond out of his own sense of life's mysterious plenitude and humankind's potential spiritual dominion. Above all, he thirsted for an immediacy in spiritual existence. At the last, although he would vaunt the enlarged soul over any constricted sense of the person, Emerson's own passionate voice proposed him as the "New Teacher," captivated by the doctrine of soul and poised to find revelation restored to nature and history.

Christian Themes

Emerson's Transcendental message can be said to be more spiritual than doctrinally Christian. Nevertheless, it grew out of his Protestant New England roots. As Emerson saw it, the world is infused with currents of spirit, emanating from Supreme Being, to which all people have direct access if they will turn themselves to the ways the world answers to the cravings of the human soul. To sense the presence of this divine law in the natural order is to awaken the genuine religious sentiment and to participate in such a perfect world of spirit is to grasp new "miracles," new sources of revelation. Jesus Christ was the only one who fully practiced the religious sentiment and grasped the divine law, who followed out the ultimate reaches of the soul, and who thus participated in the Supreme Mind—but all others have such possibilities open to them in a world permeated with influences of divinity. All people have within them the same capacity of soul, but that spiritual potential is dimmed in an age that fails to comprehend the great unrealized dominion of humankind.

Emerson took issue with historical Christianity in its tendency to assume or teach or practice the idea that such possibilities, centrally evident in Jesus Christ, ended in nature and history with him. Instead, Emerson called for a new kind of preaching that recognizes this "doctrine of soul" and that urges a corresponding conduct of worship in a world understood in its complete spiritual dimensions.

Sources for Further Study

Allen, Gay Wilson. *Waldo Emerson: A Biography*. New York: Viking Press, 1981. Allen's magisterial critical biography treats Emerson's thought in the contexts both of the age and of the personal life history with which Emerson's ideas were so deeply intertwined.

Cameron, Kenneth Walter. *Emerson at the Divinity School: His Address of 1838 and Its Significance*. Hartford, Conn.: Transcendental Books, 1994. A full study devoted exlusively to the "The Divinity School Address."

Geldard, Richard G. *The Spiritual Teachings of Ralph Waldo Emerson*. Foreword by Robert Richardson. Great Barrington, Mass.: Lindisfarne Books, 2001. Explores Emerson's spiritual life and religion in literature.

Robinson, David. *Apostle of Culture: Emerson as Preacher and Lecturer*. Philadelphia: University of Pennsylvania Press, 1982. Following the evolution of Emerson's thought over the course of his career, Robinson studies the shifts of mode involved in Emerson's movement from preacher to lecturer to essayist.

Rowland A. Sherrill

DOCTOR FAUSTUS

Author: Christopher Marlowe (1564-1593)
First produced: pr. c. 1588, pb. 1604
Edition used: Doctor Faustus, edited by Russell A. Fraser, in *The Tudor Period,* vol. 1
   of *Drama of the English Renaissance.* New York: Macmillan, 1976
Genre: Drama
Subgenres: Legends; morality tales
Core issues: Alienation from God; good vs. evil; obedience and disobedience; salvation; sin and sinners; spiritual warfare; suffering

Drawing on medieval legend and a translated German account, Marlowe dramatizes the story of a man who sells his soul to the devil in exchange for the promise of twenty-four years of earthly power and unfettered self-indulgence. Despite his own alleged atheism, Marlowe portrays Faustus's bargain as fundamentally erroneous and evil, the product of overreaching pride and sensuality. Accordingly, the play serves as a moral object lesson, emphasizing the minuscule rewards and dreadful penalties attached to such Faustian bargains.

Principal characters
   Doctor Faustus, the protagonist, who sells his soul to demonic
      forces
   Wagner, Faustus's servant
   Valdes and *Cornelius,* friends to Faustus
   Good Angel and *Bad Angel,* who contest for Faustus's allegiance
   Mephistophilis,
   Lucifer, and
   Belzebub, devils who manipulate Faustus into keeping his unholy
      bargain
   Old Man, a personification of divine mercy who, even at the end,
      seeks to turn Faustus back to God
   Helen, a tantalizing demonic evocation, in spirit form, of the
      legendary beauty Helen of Troy

Overview

In *Doctor Faustus,* Christopher Marlowe supplies a nearly diagrammatic study of damnation—of the decline and fall of a human soul—growing out of excessive pride and overreaching ambition. The well-schooled Faustus, with his unbridled curiosity, skepticism, and knowledge, stands as the epitome of the Renaissance "new man." On his graduation from the German university at Wittenberg, Faustus casts about for a suitable profession. He rejects, in turn, philosophy, medicine, law, and theology, finding that all these fields fall short of what amounts to his supra-human desires. For example, medicine ("physic") promises the possibility of temporary healing but not of bestowing everlasting life or of raising the dead. Accordingly, Faustus at last lights upon necromancy—magic and the black arts—as providing the sole means whereby he can achieve "omnipotence" and become a "mighty god."

In the company of his like-minded friends Valdes and Cornelius, Faustus summons up the demon Mephistophilis and informs him that, in exchange for twenty-four years of earthly pleasure, wealth, and honor, he is ready to abandon his soul to Lucifer, the evil one himself. Immediately, Good Angel and Bad Angel appear to Faustus, the former urgently pleading for the scholar's repentance, and the latter airily dismissing the efficacy of prayer. Willfully determined, Faustus stabs his arm and writes out his agreement with the devil in his own resisting blood.

Almost immediately, however, it becomes clear that there are limits to demonic power: For example, Faustus asks for a wife only to learn that holy matrimony, a sacrament of the Church, is not open to him now. In place of a wife, Mephistophilis promises Faustus a succession of prostitutes, an adjustment that the lascivious Faustus finds congenial. The demon then converses with Faustus about astronomy and cosmology. Throughout this long discourse, Faustus is tempted to repent from time to time; but Mephistophilis, Belzebub, and Lucifer are each time able to distract him with entertaining (if insubstantial) "shows"—for example, with a diverting parade of the personified Seven Deadly Sins—so that the enthralled scholar forgets any misgivings and hews to his bargain.

In a subsequent series of relatively brief and decidedly farcical vignettes—first at the Vatican at Rome, then at the imperial German court, and finally in the swindling of a lowly horse seller—Faustus, aided by the devils who accompany him, demonstrates the arguably paltry powers he has attained at the cost of his soul. In Rome, for example, he assumes invisibility in order to strike the pope about the head, set free the pontiff's enemy Bruno, and befuddle a host of Ecclesiastes. At the royal court, he beguiles Emperor Charles by evoking the forms of such historical figures as Alexander the Great and Darius—all the while reminding the monarch that these apparently tangible manifestations are in fact "but shadows, not substantial." Finally, he provides out-of-season grapes for the duchess of Inhaled and, in the role of court jester, amuses himself and the ducal assembly by cruelly hoodwinking some rustic yokels.

At last, however, as the end of Faustus's life draws near, the mood of the play inevitably lurches from the farcical to the terrifying and demonic. Back in the magician's study, a pious Old Man, representing God's infinite mercy, warns Faustus of the eternal agonies of hell and entreats him, even at this late hour, to repent. Shaken, Faustus nonetheless gives way to the sin of despair and begs Mephistophilis to summon up the distracting image of Helen of Troy, a mythic figure metaphorically associated with fire—in this case, the fires of hell. Kissing Faustus, her "lips suck forth [his] soul." By willfully embracing this demonic figure, Faustus permanently seals his fate, and even as he cries out pitifully for more time, the unholy trinity of Lucifer, Belzebub, and Mephistophilis lead the magician offstage to the unending torment that awaits his spirit. Two scholars later discover his earthly body, horribly torn and dismembered.

Christian Themes

Marlowe's *Doctor Faustus* has been called Renaissance England's "last avowedly religious drama." While that assertion might be contested, it is certainly true that the play supplies the clearest and most emphatic representation of the psychomachia—the struggle between God and the devil for the fate of an individual human soul—that was available to English playgoers since the equally straightforward morality plays of the Middle Ages (with which *Doctor Faustus* bears many similarities.)

It is not that Faustus is unaware of this war between good and evil, between flesh and spirit, that is going on all around and within him. "Oh, I'll leap up to my God!—Who pulls me down?" Faustus cries out at play's end. What pulls him down is his obdurate pride, the habitual pattern of sins from which he cannot or will not release himself, and his condition of despair. Essentially, Faustus is convinced (wrongly, according to orthodox Christian thought) that his sins are so manifold and serious that they are beyond even God's redress and forgiveness; accordingly, he cannot truly repent. To many Renaissance minds, such conscious embracing of despair constitutes the "sin against the Holy Spirit," warned of in Scripture that alone resides outside the circumference of God's mercy.

Faustus finally understands that he has long suspected on some level—namely, that "for the vain pleasure of four and twenty years," he has "lost eternal joy and felicity" in the presence of God's glory. He had dreamed of world conquest but ends up as little more than a court clown, fetching grapes for a bored and dissipated duchess. He had thought to acquire all knowledge but is at last left praying for the sublime oblivion of the bestial and even mineral worlds. This alarming declension—this devolution—of a human soul receives a powerful dramatic treatment in Marlowe's famous play.

Sources for Further Study

Frye, Roland M. "Marlowe's *Doctor Faustus*: The Repudiation of Humanity." *South Atlantic Quarterly* 55 (1956): 322-328. Frye is one of the few critics to identify Faustus's lust for power—not sensuality or curiosity—as his most central and defining sin.

Greg, W. W. "The Damnation of Faustus." *Modern Language Review* 41 (1946): 97-107. An early assertion that Helen of Troy and the other spirits evoked by Faustus are actually devils; Faustus's damnation, therefore, is finally sealed by his outright demon worship. Greg also defends the play's comic episodes, arguing that their triviality underscores the absurdity of evil.

Kirschbaum, Leo. "Marlowe's *Faustus*: A Reconsideration." *The Review of English Studies* 19 (1943): 225-241. Kirschbaum focuses on Faustus's sensuality, his habitual substitution of lower values for higher ones. Nonetheless, this critic insists that the possibility of repentance is open to Faustus from first to last.

Kocher, Paul. *Christopher Marlowe: A Study of His Thought, Learning, and Character*. Reprint. Chapel Hill: University of North Carolina Press, 1974. Sees curiosity as Faustus's primary drive—a curiosity that does not recognize or honor the limitations placed by God on human inquiry. Kocher denies (against the philosopher

George Santayana) that Faustus ever truly repents. In addition, he denies (against many critics) that Faustus is in any sense predestined to fall.

Lucking, David. "Carrying Tempest in His Hand and Voice: The Figure of the Magician in Jonson and Shakespeare." *English Studies* 85 (August, 2004): 297-310. Explicates the influence of the theme of magic in Marlowe's *Doctor Faustus* on such subsequent plays as Ben Jonson's *The Alchemist* and William Shakespeare's *The Tempest*.

Pettigrew, Todd H. J. "'Faustus . . . for Ever': Marlowe, Bruno, and Infinity." *Comparative Critical Studies* 2 (2005): 257-269. Argues that Faustus falls and persists in his damnation largely because, for all his learning, he fails to comprehend fully a punishment that will persist without temporal limits. In this way, he betrays a willed ignorance of the ideas of the Italian thinker Giordano Bruno, a contemporary of Marlowe.

William R. Drennan

DON'T THROW AWAY TOMORROW
Living God's Dream for Your Life

Author: Robert H. Schuller (1926-   )
First published: San Francisco: HarperSanFrancisco, 2005
Genre: Nonfiction
Subgenres: Guidebook; handbook for living
Core issues: Faith; hope; life; time; works and deeds

After publishing his autobiography at the age of seventy-five, Schuller soon realized he had gained a new perspective in what he calls the fourth quarter of his life. When he reflected, he realized that while he planned in the present, the action involved in actualizing those plans took place in the future, and that regardless of what quarter of life people are in, they should always create a plan for tomorrow. These realization form the basis of Don't Throw Away Tomorrow.

Overview

When Robert H. Schuller wrote his autobiography, *My Journey: From an Iowa Farm to a Cathedral of Dreams* (2001), at the age of seventy-five, he thought it would be his last book. However, he realized that being in what he called the fourth quarter of his life gave him a new perspective. He looked back on his life and discovered that he had always lived for tomorrow. While he planned in the present, the action that transformed those plans into reality took place in the future, his tomorrow.

This new perspective revealed to Schuller how many people throw away their future, and he decided to pass along the benefits of his knowledge and experience in a new book, *Don't Throw Away Tomorrow*. Schuller writes that this book is his "testimony" on how to stay focused on dreams and how not to throw away the future.

According to Schuller, people throw away their tomorrow by not being ready to receive ideas as they come along, not accepting challenges and working through problems that arise, letting priorities get skewed, and letting goals get distorted. Other reasons he believes people throw away their tomorrow include being disappointed, tired, rejected, afraid to fail, and frustrated. The result is that people lose control of their lives and are influenced by negative thinking. With God's help, people can use what Schuller calls possibility thinking to save their tomorrow.

"Positive thinking plus possibility thinking equals optimism" is a formula Schuller has developed to transform people into optimists. He believes that an optimist who believes in God has the power to do or to become anything and anyone that person wishes. The formula begins with positive thinking because it is necessary to first eliminate negative thinking and to develop a positive attitude. Possibility thinking, the next element in the formula, puts the dream into action. The result of these two elements coming together is optimism, which begins, continues with, and makes it possible to surmount problems.

Using that optimism is important in finding what mission each person has in life. When there is a goal, or mission, for the future, life takes on meaning and has purpose. Schuller also discusses the importance of choosing the values by which to live. He states that because people's values will shape their destiny, they should choose them carefully so that they support the positive possibilities in life and suppress the negative aspects that arise.

Schuller explains that in addition to optimism, a mission, and values, people need rules in their lives. These rules form people's moral conscience and enable them to be responsible enough to do the right thing and be a good person.

All this involves taking risks, and risks have costs. However, if fear prevents people from taking risks, they will throw away tomorrow, Schuller says. He suggests that people determine what investments in time, energy, emotion, and money are necessary for a particular risk, then ask themselves if the risk is worth it. Although some risks can be handled alone, there are times when it is necessary to ask for assistance, including help from God.

Other factors that come into play in Schuller's formula for optimism include keeping the lines of communication open, dealing with life's contradictions, and using assumptions positively, and he deals with each in a separate chapter.

Communication is an important element of any relationship, whether with a spouse, preacher, prisoner of war, missionary, or any other person. Sometimes, communication is used to form a positive relationship with an adversary. When dealing with a possible adversary, Schuller immediately finds an area of agreement with the person. This provides a positive starting point for their relationship.

Another factor addressed by Schuller is contradictions. Life contains a significant number of contradictions that need to be faced and dealt with rather than disregarded. How this is accomplished determines if tomorrow will be thrown away. Handling contradictions through creative compromise brings about positive results. Although compromise can have a negative meaning (such as when it involves compromising morals and ethics), positive compromise creatively deals with contradictions.

People live with assumptions; just as with contradictions, they are everywhere. Assumptions are usually considered to be negative; however, there are positive assumptions. An assumption is taking something as a fact or as a truth before it has been proven to be a fact or a truth. This is where faith enters. Schuller explains that faith and assumption "describe the same mental activity." In addition, he describes people as "faith-driven or assumption-compelled creatures." Thus, faith is a positive assumption.

Schuller does not assure people they will change the world, but he does believe they can change their personal world. This is accomplished by believing in tomorrow. He asserts his belief in God and in tomorrow through these words: "I don't know what tomorrow holds, but I know who holds tomorrow."

Christian Themes

Don't Throw Away Tomorrow is a book based entirely on faith, as demonstrated by the title. The word "tomorrow" indicates belief in a future. When the media is filled with accounts of war, death, disease, starvation, environmental destruction, and cruelty, it is difficult to get past the present and look forward to or expect a future. According to Schuller, this type of negative thinking results in throwing away tomorrow.

Schuller believes this type of negative thinking is countered through faith in God along with an optimistic attitude. Faith in God is the foundation, and an optimistic attitude forms the pillars that hold the future (tomorrow). It is evident through Schuller's writing that he believes everything rests on faith in God. The subtitle of the work includes the words "God's dream," which is a reference to the future. Dreams may occur in the present, but they are about the future. Schuller's message is that God has a future (dream) for your life.

The issue of faith also includes faith in oneself. Again, the title is an indication of the importance Schuller places on faith. The subtitle includes the self through the word "your." The word "tomorrow" in the title indicates your tomorrow, not anyone else's. According to Schuller, for you to fulfill God's dream for your life, you need to have faith that there will be a future.

Faith is not without hope. Schuller's formula, which combines positive thinking with possibility thinking to form optimism, is his way of producing hope. The opposite of optimism is pessimism. Pessimists do not believe they can do anything worthwhile; they feel that anything they attempt is doomed to fail and there is nothing right with life. In other words, there is no hope. Schuller provides his formula for hope and, throughout his book, gives examples of people who have made their lives meaningful through faith and hope.

Schuller wrote this book to help people live God-centered, optimistic lives. He uses the experiences of a variety of people to show how others have achieved this lifestyle. Many of these people have had to overcome terrible obstacles; however, through their works and deeds, they prove that such a life is attainable.

Sources for Further Study

Booth, Mark, ed. *What I Believe: Thirteen Eminent People of Our Time Argue for Their Philosophy of Life*. New York: Crossroad, 1984. This book presents Schuller's philosophy of life along with those of other notables such as Albert Einstein, Bertrand Russell, Martin Sheen, James Thurber, and H. G. Wells.

Schuller, Robert H. *My Journey: From an Iowa Farm to a Cathedral of Dreams*. San Francisco: HarperSanFrancisco, 2001. Schuller's inspirational autobiography tells of his successes and the painful ordeals he and his family experienced and overcame by turning them into possibilities.

_____. *Tough Times Never Last, but Tough People Do!* New York: Bantam-Random, 1983. In *Don't Throw Away Tomorrow*, Schuller recommends that people read or reread this work, in which he tells how to weather hard times and how to build a positive self-image.

Linda Adkins

THE DOUBLE SEARCH
Studies in Atonement and Prayer

Author: Rufus M. Jones (1863-1948)

First published: 1906

Edition used: The Double Search: God's Search for Man and Man's Search for God, Studies in Atonement and Prayer. Chicago: John C. Winston, 1937

Genre: Nonfiction

Subgenres: Meditation and contemplation; spiritual treatise

Core issues: Connectedness; God; Jesus Christ; love; mysticism; psychology; soul; union with God

Author of more than fifty books and numerous short writings, Jones was renowned in his lifetime as a Quaker, a mystic, a philosopher, and a social activist. He was born to a family of Maine farmers who had identified themselves with intense Quaker piety for generations. His mysticism was emphatically moralistic and led toward social action. He founded the American Friends Service Committee in 1917.

Overview

At the outset of *The Double Search*, Rufus M. Jones invokes the myth in Plato's *Symposion* (c. 399-390 B.C.E.; *Symposium*, 1701) that man in his original nature was a round being with four legs, four arms, one head, and two faces. Plato defines love between humans as the longing to return to this original state, in which each human was perfectly joined to another. While Plato argues that there is a higher love—namely, the soul's longing to return to eternal Truth—Jones believes that our love for God is radically similar to our love for other people. Thus Plato's parable of human love can also be taken as a parable of religious love. God and humanity were originally one, a "divine whole" divided at human birth by the emergence of our individuality. God longs to be reunited with us as much as we long to be reunited with God. Christ represents the fulfillment of this double search; Christ is the round man in whom God and humanity are one.

Jones believes that his view of Christ is not undermined by modern science or biblical criticism. While other views of Christ are called into question by scientific rejections of supernatural claims and by literary critical rejections of the simple unity of biblical texts, Jones believes that his approach avoids these problems. His approach to Christ is an expression of the psychology of New Thought that began to be popular in America in the mid-nineteenth century. Like Ralph Waldo Emerson, the father of New Thought, Jones regards the historical Christ primarily as an example of how persons can realize the presence of God in their own lives. He believes that the outward, historical revelation of Christ is an important guide to God, much as Ludwig van Beethoven is an important instructor in music. Christ, however, is fundamentally an inward reality for Jones. The incarnation is an ongoing psychological event.

Like founder of Christian Science Mary Baker Eddy, the most famous proponent of New Thought, Jones understands Christ as the idea of divine love. He further believes that having the idea of divine love enables human beings to represent Christ to others. Also like Eddy, Jones believes that religious idealism amplifies without contradicting modern science. However, while Eddy focused on the health-giving effects of Christian idealism, in *The Double Search* Jones is primarily interested in reflecting on the role that God and Christ play in the human psyche. He defines God as the spiritual personality that human persons develop through their love of God. He uses the term "Christ" as a means of discussing the evolution of the human personality.

Viewed in relation to the evolution of human society, Christ represents the historical moment when humankind became fully aware of God as the ideal toward which it should rightly strive. Jones believes that the Hebrew prophets were dimly aware of this Christ ideal but that their primitive culture prevented them from fully realizing this ideal. The birth of Christ represents a new era of cultural maturity. Christ is the great divide in the history of human evolution. He embodies humanity's successful striving for the ideal self that pulls it out of its lower nature.

The spiritual evolution of humankind is the result of cooperating forces. On one side, as we strive for an ideal self, we push ourselves upward. God is this ideal self. On the other, by opening ourselves to the compelling force of our ideal self, we are drawn upward by its embrace. This is the point Jones continually reiterates: the uplifting pull of the ideal self cooperates with our effort to push ourselves upward from below. Human beings' efforts to improve themselves are met by spiritual cooperation from above; God is always reaching down to draw us upward. Jones pictures God as a universal force permeating human personalities, much as sunlight permeates the natural world, infusing all organisms with the power of life. Just as in the natural world the capacity to absorb sunlight differentiates a giant oak from a daisy, so in the human world, persons who open themselves fully to God and his uplifting love grow spiritually stronger and more loving than persons who absorb less of his love.

Some confusion results from the fact that Jones sometimes speaks of God as the Divine Other and of his love as a force outside the individual, and at other times he speaks of God and his love as aspects of human personality. Although by identifying him as the person's ideal self Jones implies that God can be understood in terms of human psychology, he ultimately relinquishes this line of thought in favor of mysticism. His experiences of God's love are so fundamental to his worldview that, like other mystics, he ultimately defines himself and others in terms of God.

In his chapter on Christian atonement, Jones defines sin as our disobedience of our own good intentions. He believes that persons seek deliverance from the selfish drives that prevent them from following their own visions of goodness. He argues furthermore that sin corrupts not only the sinner but also the sinner's view of God. The idea of an angry God who demands appeasement is the erroneous but inevitable by-product of the guilt persons feel when they fail to obey the higher principles they know to be right.

The correlation between religious faith and childhood experiences of parental authority is essential to Jones's religious views. In his chapter on the atonement, he compares the disobedient and frightened child's desire to appease his father with the primitive religious belief that an angry deity requires human sacrifice. In both cases the felt experience of sin colors perceptions of authority, causing it to seem stern and distant rather than warm and loving. Although Jones interprets primitive religious fear in terms of childhood guilt and compares a sinner's relation to God with a child's relation to its father, he stops short of discussing the possible relationship between guilt and love.

From the perspective of Jones's mysticism, the Gospel dissolves the pagan fear of God and reveals him to be an inherently loving and tender Father. This does not mean that the Christian God either blinks at disobedience or does not require repentance for sin. The divine Father no more overlooks sin than any responsible parent overlooks errancy in a child. However, like the remonstrances of every loving parent, God's corrections and rebukes are expressions of his love for his children. God actually suffers with his children just as other parents suffer with their children when they fail.

The idea that our sin draws down God's suffering is essential to Jones's whole view of the relationship between God and humankind. Jones believes that sin is not confined to the sinner; every act of sin affects every other part of the organic whole that God and humanity comprise. When a person sins, God reacts; he feels the sin himself and suffers on behalf of the sinner. Thus Jones identifies God's love with vicarious suffering. Furthermore, he believes that this suffering defines holiness. Holiness always involves sacrificial acts in behalf of others. Holiness is the vicarious suffering that is spiritual love.

In the final analysis, holiness is a means of compelling holiness in others. While Jones rejects the idea that God demands human sacrifice as appeasement, he argues that God willingly sacrifices himself for humanity and that everyone who realizes this is compelled by that sacrifice. He also argues that we represent God to each other by acts of holiness that embody vicarious suffering. This process of being compelled by the vicarious sufferings of another is not a matter of involuntary assent but compels our active and total responsivity. The realization that God sacrifices himself for us prompts a radical transformation in our will and stimulates a lifelong faith in the goodness of God. Although Jones does not discuss it fully, guilt plays an essential role in the internal logic of this religious psychology and is not limited to its primitive phases. Just as a child's love for its father can be stimulated by the guilt it feels when the father suffers on its behalf, so guilt is essential to the underlying process by which human beings feel compelled to return the love of their divine Father.

In the final chapter of *The Double Search*, Jones turns to the subject of prayer. He defines prayer as the opening of the soul to God and argues that the effort to communicate with God elicits his response and actually establishes fellowship with him. Jones objects to the idea that prayer is an effort to interrupt the chain of physical causation, and he welcomes scientific critiques of such primitive conceptions. In Jones's view, prayer is not a means to some utilitarian end but an end in itself. Prayer is the spontaneous outreach of the soul toward the circle of life beyond itself. Although opening the soul to larger forces of energy may have utilitarian benefits, such as increased health or perspicacity, the real meaning of prayer is in the act of praying itself. The process by which one opens oneself to God is its own reward.

In Jones's view, there can be no subjective need without "an objective stimulus which has stimulated the need." Extended theologically, this view translates into the theory that longing for communication with God is proof of the existence of his personhood and of his capacity to communicate with us. The soul's outreach toward God inevitably leads to enjoyment of immediate fellowship with him. Prayer in its highest form is "actual social fellowship." God is not a lonely sovereign but a person who, like all other persons, exists in relation to other persons.

Interwoven throughout Jones's testimony to the organic social relationship between God and human beings are statements about the organic spiritual relationships among human beings. The theory that social relationships are central to the spiritual life is the theme of Jones's influential *Social Law in the Spiritual World* (1904), to which he refers the reader of *The Double Search* for philosophic groundwork. In Jones's mysticism, the ties between God and humanity are often manifest in relationships among persons. He believes that we find God in our relationships with other human beings. Thus social life is essential to the mystic's apprehension of God.

Christian Themes

Jones teaches that one does not seek God alone; God is equally fervent in his search for each human being. This double search is represented in the person of Jesus Christ, who is both God reaching down toward humankind and humankind reaching up toward God. The "double search" is characterized by atonement and prayer: Atonement is the process by which God loves and suffers with us and, in so doing, compels our devotion; prayer is the process by which we open ourselves to God and, in so doing, establish fellowship with him.

Sources for Further Study

Fuller, Robert C. *Mesmerism and the American Cure of Souls*. Philadelphia: University of Pennsylvania Press, 1982. An excellent study of the close relationship between psychological theory and American religious thought in the late nineteenth and early twentieth centuries.

Hedstrom, Matthew S. "Rufus Jones and Mysticism for the Masses." *Cross Currents* 54, no. 2 (Summer, 2004): 31-44. A fourteen-page essay that addresses Jones's efforts to bring spirituality to everyday people and their problems.

Jones, Rufus M. *The Later Periods of Quakerism*. Westport, Conn.: Greenwood Press, 1970. An important study of the history of Quaker spirituality.

_____. *Rufus Jones Speaks to Our Time: An Anthology*. Edited by Harry Emerson Fosdick. New York: Macmillan, 1951. A good collection of excerpts from Jones's writings organized by religious themes.

_____. *Social Law in the Spiritual World: Studies in Human and Divine Inter-Relationship.* New York: George H. Doran, 1923. A pioneer study in New Thought exploring the relationship between mysticism and social life.

Meyer, Donald. *The Positive Thinkers: Popular Religious Psychology from Mary Baker Eddy to Norman Vincent Peale and Ronald Reagan.* 1965. Rev. ed., with a new introduction. Middletown, Conn.: Wesleyan University Press, 1988. A good overview of the history and issues involved in the New Thought tradition from Emerson to Norman Vincent Peale.

Amanda Porterfield

THE DRAMA OF ATHEIST HUMANISM

Author: Henri de Lubac (1896-1991)
First published: Le Drame de l'humanisme athée, 1944 (English translation, 1949)
Edition used: The Drama of Atheist Humanism, translated by Edith M. Riley. New
   York: Sheed and Ward, 1950
Genre: Nonfiction
Subgenres: Critical analysis; didactic treatise; history
Core issues: Alienation from God; atheism; God; good vs. evil; Gospels; redemption;
   religion

*De Lubac examines the antitheistic and anti-Christian intellectual climate created by
nineteenth century European thinkers Ludwig Feuerbach, Friedrich Nietzsche, and
Auguste Comte. He contrasts their thoughts with those of novelist Fyodor Dostoevski,
who believed that human beings cannot understand fully or act ethically in a world
without God, to demonstrate that atheist humanism is destined to be defeated by the
spiritual truths in the Gospel of Jesus Christ.*

Overview

Although Henri de Lubac's *The Drama of Atheist Humanism* is a work of nonfiction, he structured the work as a play. He analyzes the drama of atheist humanism in
terms of conflicts between such philosophers as Friedrich Nietzsche and Søren
Kierkegaard and between antitheist Auguste Comte and Christianity, the religion he
opposed. Lubac resolves these conflicts through a person who, unlike the atheist humanists, was not a philosopher but a novelist—Fyodor Dostoevski. This Russian Orthodox Christian used the teachings of Jesus Christ to assuage the alienation and sufferings of those trapped in a world seemingly without providential succor.

De Lubac structures his drama in three parts: "Atheist Humanism," "Auguste
Comte and Christianity," and "Dostoevsky as Prophet." He writes from the perspective of theocentric humanism, and this work can be seen as a meditation on these
words from Genesis: "God made man in his own image and likeness." The humanism
in the book's title refers not to the Renaissance literary movement that emphasized
freedom and tolerance but to a modern movement that makes human nature the measure of all things. Atheist humanists excised the transcendental God from their thinking to free humans from religious shackles and thus to establish genuine human greatness. However, by excluding God from their analysis of the human being, these
atheist humanists denied what de Lubac believes is a human being's spiritual nature
and immortal destiny.

Two German thinkers, Ludwig Feuerbach and Friedrich Nietzsche, are de Lubac's
primary examples of antitheist humanists (neither liked to be called an atheist).
Feuerbach, who argued that God was nothing but a mental projection or idealized ab-
straction, wanted to create a new religion based not on God but on the human being.

He once stated that all his works were based on the idea that humans must have faith in themselves. Karl Marx, the creator of the modern communist movement, was critical of Feuerbach's new religion and wanted to replace it with a science of the historical development of actual human beings. Nietzsche, too, was critical of Feuerbach, believing that God's death must be passionately claimed so that he and other heroic individuals could become fully human.

Nietzsche's emphasis on existential humans as specific individuals in a material world was also a theme in Søren Kierkegaard's writings, and de Lubac contrasts Nietzsche the iconoclast and Kierkegaard the Christian. They were both enemies of philosophical systems, but Kierkegaard was a "herald of transcendence," and he tried to convince an increasingly faithless world of the great value of faith in Jesus Christ. De Lubac sees this conflict between faith and faithlessness as pivotal to the future of the modern world. He says that without God, secular humanism can easily be transformed into such inhuman totalitarian systems as communism, fascism, and Nazism. For example, Nietzsche's "slave morality" developed in the twentieth century not in Christianity but in these atheistic political systems.

Like other atheist humanists, Auguste Comte strove to analyze the human being without any reference to God, and his famous "Law of the Three States" associates theistic thinking with the most primitive stages of human development. This theological or fictitious phase must be followed by a metaphysical or abstract stage, which is little more than a bridge to what Comte truly admired, the scientific or positive stage, the realm of "social physics," which he would later call "sociology," the highest science. In this new society, scientists would be the priests in what would essentially be a "religion of humanity." Though he admired the "social genius" of Catholicism—its powerful ways of organizing human behavior—Comte wanted to replace Jesus Christ and the Christian saints with a "cult of great men," people such as scientist Isaac Newton. Comte believed that this new faith in positivism would not be subject to abuse because positivistic truths must always be demonstrable. However, de Lubac thinks that, in practice, Comtean positivism would lead to the dictatorship of a party or sect. By denying that the human being is a creation of God, Comte, the worshiper of humanity, tragically misjudges genuine human nature, which is spiritual as well as material.

The principal protagonist in de Lubac's drama of atheist humanism is Dostoevski, whom he sees as a prophet because this novelist not only understood the spiritual depths of human beings but also realized what evil would happen if humans had to live in a world without God. De Lubac realizes that both Nietzsche and Dostoevski understood the implications that the disappearance of God would have for humankind; but Dostoevski believed that Jesus Christ could rescue humans from the abyss of despair and meaninglessness. Some of Dostoevski's characters despised Christian morality and admired those who rose above religious restrictions and gloried in their indomitable will to power, for example, the Nietzschean murderer Rodion Raskolnikov in *Prestupleniye I nakazaniye* (1866; *Crime and Punishment*, 1886). One of Dostoevski's most famous atheists is Ivan Karamazov in *Bratya Karamazovy* (1879-

1880; *The Brothers Karamazov*, 1912), who tells the story of the Grand Inquisitor, whose devastating critique has fascinated many readers and critics. In the confrontation between Jesus Christ and the Grand Inquisitor, Ivan proposes that rejecting God means the affirmation of human freedom. Dostoevski's response is well known: If God does not exist, then all is permitted. Against the atheist humanist vision of a paradise on earth, Dostoevski offers hope of the kingdom of God, which would also help create a humane society on earth. De Lubac agrees with Dostoevski that the Christian God-man provides an answer to the physical and spiritual sufferings of the modern world, and he ends his book with a hymn of hope: Another life exists for a troubled humanity—the eternal life of love and happiness promised by Jesus Christ to his faithful followers.

Christian Themes

The atheist humanists attacked faith in God, and de Lubac felt that it was important for people to recognize the important issues at stake in this battle between godlessness and God. Although these atheist humanists reduced the human being to the natural level (and denied the supernatural), de Lubac is famous for his belief in the spiritual grandeur of human nature. He accepted the distinction between the natural and supernatural, but he also believed in the supernatural origin, support (through grace), and destiny of humanity. The spirituality of the human being is thus a principal theme of his book and the reason he believes the teachings of the atheist humanists are dangerously wrong. Christians must fight the false atheist humanist vision of humanity and intensify their faith in God and in their own spiritual nature. A human is a creature with a divine ancestry, for, as Saint Augustine wrote, humans were made in the image of God to grow into the image of Christ. This introduces another important theme in de Lubac's book: No true humanism exists apart from the Gospel of Jesus Christ, which has to be rediscovered and relived age after age.

The themes that de Lubac developed in *The Drama of Atheist Humanism* had an influence on its many readers through several editions and many languages. As a participant in the Second Vatican Council, de Lubac helped make his analysis of atheism and humanism part of such important documents as *Gaudium et spes*, a pastoral constitution on the Church in the modern world promulgated by Pope Paul VI in 1965, and after de Lubac's death the themes of his book appeared in the publications of many philosophers and theologians. They also became part of the debate about the new constitution of the European Union, when many religious Europeans were shocked that no mention of the influence of Christian ideas and values appeared in the document. Although Christianity has certainly declined in many European countries, modern followers of de Lubac have stated that only in the mystery of the incarnate word is the mystery of the human being revealed in its true light.

Sources for Further Study

Balthasar, Hans Urs von. *The Theology of Henri de Lubac: An Overview*. San Francisco: Ignatius Press, 1991. Balthasar, a former student of de Lubac who became a prominent theologian, analyzes his teacher's principal works to show how they insightfully present the truths of Catholicism to contemporary readers.

Hollenbach, David. *The Global Face of Public Faith: Politics, Human Rights, and Christian Ethics*. Washington, D.C.: Georgetown University Press, 2003. An exploration of the relationship between humanism and Christian belief, a theme that concerned de Lubac, with an emphasis on the role that Christian ethics should play in the discussion about what constitutes a good global society.

Lubac, Henri de. *At the Service of the Church: Henri de Lubac Reflects on the Circumstances That Occasioned His Writings*. San Francisco: Communio Books, 1993. This memoir, originally published in French in 1989, contains de Lubac's explanation of the provenance, meaning, and influence of his books along with compassionate responses to his critics.

Milbank, John. *The Suspended Middle: Henri de Lubac and the Debate Concerning the Supernatural*. Grand Rapids, Mich.: Wm. B. Eerdmans, 2005. A brief study of an important theme in de Lubac's writings by one of his British disciples.

Robert J. Paradowski

"THE DREAM OF THE ROOD"

Author: Unknown

First transcribed: "The Dream of the Rood," before c. 700 C.E.; earliest extant manuscript, c. 1000

Edition used: The Dream of the Rood, edited by Michael Swanton. New York: Barnes and Noble, 1970

Genre: Poetry

Subgenre: Narrative poetry

Core issues: Contemplation; the cross; evangelization; Jesus Christ; redemption; salvation

"The Dream of the Rood" retells the Crucifixion of Christ from the perspective of the cross within the frame of a dream vision and ends with a sermon declaring the cross the means of salvation. The poem presents a distinctly Anglo-Saxon variety of Christianity along with eschatological themes. Ultimately, it provides a meditation on the Crucifixion and the symbol of the cross.

Overview

"The Dream of the Rood" is the most widely studied Old English poem with the exception of *Beowulf* (first transcribed c. 1000 C.E.). As with many works of Old and Middle English, it is not possible to determine precisely when "The Dream of the Rood" was written or by whom. Linguistic evidence indicates that the poem was written in the late seventh or early eighth century, and its transmission in several forms attests to its popularity. A fragment of the poem is inscribed on the Ruthwell cross, a twenty-two-foot Celtic ornate high cross that dates to the eighth century and was originally erected at Ruthwell in what is now Scotland. The late tenth century Brussels cross, a small silver reliquary cross, has a two-line inscription similar to the Ruthwell cross's speech. Only one manuscript copy of the 156-line poem exists in the late tenth century Vercelli Book, which also contains three other poems and eighteen homilies.

"The Dream of the Rood" is written in the Late West Saxon dialect of Old English. Although some Old English words survive in modern English, one cannot read Old English without first studying the vocabulary and grammar of the language. When relying on a modern English translation of "The Dream of the Rood," it is important to understand whether the translator is providing a verse or literal translation and to what extent the translator's interpretation influences his translation.

Anglo-Saxon poetry adheres to a set of conventions different from those used by the later English poetry with which most people are familiar. Alliteration, the repetition of an initial consonant sound, is the primary ordering structure of Old English poetry. The poetic line is divided into two half-lines by the caesura. Each half-line contains two stresses, providing four metrical positions in each line, and any number of unstressed syllables. The alliteration occurs on the stressed syllables and links the two half-lines so either one or both of the stressed syllables in the first half of the line must alliterate with one, usually the first, stressed syllable after the caesura. Medieval manuscripts do not divide works into stanzas and lines.

The poem opens with the dreamer's midnight vision of the rood, or cross, alternately adorned with gold and jewels or drenched in blood, representing the redemptive and violent aspects of the Crucifixion. The rood begins to speak to the dreamer and tells the story of its participation in Christ's death. "Enemies" ripped the rood from the ground when it was a tree and turned it into what is first described as a gallows and later a cross for the execution of prisoners. The rood then describes Christ's willingness to ascend the cross as well as its own feelings of fear and a desire to defend the Lord against his enemies. Instead, the rood obeyed Christ, standing firm, and it tells with great pathos how it shared in Christ's torment as nails pierced the wood and blood poured onto the cross. Friends of Jesus removed him from the cross, and the bloody rood watched as they prepared a tomb and sang funeral songs. The three crosses were taken down and buried. Now Christ has honored the rood with the ability to heal those who make supplication to it. The rood instructs the dreamer to make his vision known to others so that they might understand Christ's sacrifice for their sins and prepare for the final judgment. The dreamer then declares his devotion to the cross and desire to share in the Kingdom of Heaven. The poem concludes with a recapitulation of the triumph of Christ's crucifixion.

Christian Themes

The poem as a whole functions as a meditation on the redemptive power of Christ's crucifixion. The dreamer as well as the audience is confronted with a retelling of the Crucifixion from the perspective of one who was not only a witness to but also a participant in the Lord's suffering. The cross, the dreamer, and the audience experience a transformation from confusion to comprehension as anticipated in a medieval dream vision. As a work of affective devotion, the poem also causes movement from uncertainty to faith through the emotional description of Christ's willing suffering and the assurance of salvation through veneration of the cross.

"The Dream of the Rood" belongs to the strong Old English tradition of Christian literature intended to guide the faithful through their lives. Saint Augustine brought Roman Christianity to the Anglo-Saxons in 597, and by the end of the seventh century, monastic life was well established in Britain. The poem exemplifies the fusion of Germanic and Christian-Mediterranean cultures found in Old English literature.

This poem takes up the cult of the cross theme popular in Christianity since the fourth century recovery of the True Cross by Saint Helena. The image of the cross provided a reminder of Christ's sacrifice for the salvation of humankind. The dreamer's experience leads him to a stronger devotion to the cross, and he accepts the command to embark on a mission of evangelization, revealing what he has learned in his dream. "The Dream of the Rood" adds a distinctly Anglo-Saxon dimension in its personification of the cross as a loyal retainer to Christ, standing with his lord even in the deadly battle. For example, the cross expresses its willingness to suffer wounds along with Christ, its refusal to disobey its lord's command even to save him, and its sorrow at the Lord's passing.

The mixture of Christianity and Anglo-Saxon culture is also evident in the portrayal of Christ as a heroic warrior rather than the tormented, suffering figure represented in most Christian art. Christ willingly climbs onto and embraces the cross to sacrifice himself for humankind's redemption. The poet, in fact, comments on Christ's "great courage." The relationship between Christ and the cross as thane and retainer described above is further seen in Christ's rewarding of the cross's loyalty.

Christ also functions in the traditional harrowing of Hell as a Germanic warrior according to the pre-Anselmian belief that Christ battled and defeated Satan to save our souls from Hell. The dreamer in the poem describes Christ as being victorious or conquering in his expedition to retrieve the souls from Hell. In the eleventh century, Saint Anselm argued that Christ in his Crucifixion repaid the debt to God that humankind incurred for its sins and secured our salvation in that way.

Like many works of Anglo-Saxon Christian literature, "The Dream of the Rood" includes the theme of eschatology or "end things." The cross speaks of the final judgment of humanity according to how each person lived. The dreamer accepts the rood's instruction that salvation comes to those who carry the cross in their hearts. He acknowledges the transience of life as he anticipates the joys of the heavenly feast.

Sources for Further Study

Carrigáin, Éamonn. "Crucifixion as Annunciation: The Relation of 'The Dream of the Rood' to the Liturgy Reconsidered." *English Studies* 63, no. 6 (December, 1982): 487-505. This article argues for a correlation between the Crucifixion and the Annunciation in the poem and equates the actions of the rood with those of the Virgin.

Cherniss, Michael D. "The Cross as Christ's Weapon: The Influence of the Heroic Literary Tradition on 'The Dream of the Rood.'" *Anglo-Saxon England* 2 (1973): 241-252. This article discusses the personification of the cross in the context of the weaponry personification in the Anglo-Saxon heroic tradition.

Harbus, Antonina. "Dream and Symbol in 'The Dream of the Rood.'" *Nottingham Medieval Studies* 40 (1996): 1-15. This article argues that the poetic form of the dream vision balances the paradoxes in the poem.

Johnson, David F. "Old English Religious Poetry: *Christ and Satan* and 'The Dream of the Rood.'" In *Companion to Old English Poetry*, edited by Henk Aertsen and Rolf H. Gremmer, Jr. Amsterdam: VU University Press, 1994. The second half of this article discusses the dream vision technique and use of eschatological imagery in "The Dream of the Rood."

Thieme, Adelheid L. J. "Gift Giving as a Vital Element of Salvation in 'The Dream of the Rood.'" *South Atlantic Review* 63, no. 2 (Spring, 1998): 108-123. This article explores the relationship between Christ, cross, dreamer, and audience in the context of the Germanic cultural practice of gift giving.

Leah R. Krynicky

THE DREAM SONGS

Author: John Berryman (John Allyn Smith; 1914-1972)
First published: New York: Farrar, Straus and Giroux, 1969
Genre: Poetry
Subgenres: Lyric poetry; narrative poetry
Core issues: Alienation from God; death; despair; memory

Berryman's narrator Henry seeks spiritual answers and solace after the suicide of his father and the deaths, many by suicide, of close friends. Questions about and addressed to God are left unanswered.

Principal character
Henry, the poems' narrator

Overview

The life of Henry, the main character and narrator of John Berryman's *The Dream Songs*, echoes in many critical ways that of the poet. Most notably, Henry's father's suicide is a recurring preoccupation of the poems; repeatedly, Henry revisits his father's death, seeking ways to cope with the loss. Like Henry's father, Berryman's father shot himself. His mother remarried quickly, and Berryman, born John Allyn Smith, took his stepfather's name.

As Berryman began publishing poetry and teaching at universities, including Harvard and Princeton, he became friends with many of the major poets of the time. His work is generally classed in the movement of confessional poetry. Robert Lowell, Delmore Schwartz, Randall Jarrell, Sylvia Plath, and Theodore Roethke, who are all referred to in the poems, were also among the most famous confessional poets. The term "confessional poetry" derives from the poets' use of deeply personal subject matter in their poems and from the raw emotion the poems reveal.

Henry, in *The Dream Songs*, laments the deaths of several of these promising and still young poets. Berryman did not know Plath, but her death by suicide touched him deeply and is the subject of several of the poems. Schwartz and Jarrell were close friends of both Berryman and "Henry," and their suicides are lamented in the poetry. Read as a whole, the poem cycle presents a literary history of the period as well as an extended and emotional elegy that underscores the tragedy of the deaths. The poems capture more, however, than the private details of the lives and deaths of the poets of the time. Henry copes with the events and issues of the day, including the Vietnam War and racial injustice. The narrator describes great personal loss but also an effort to make sense of the social dilemmas surrounding him.

The structure and narrative voice of *The Dream Songs* challenge many readers. Berryman began work on the poetry cycle in 1955. The earliest poems, published in

1964 as *Seventy-Seven Dream Songs*, earned Berryman the Pulitzer Prize. The later poems were published as *His Toy, His Dream, His Rest* in 1968; this volume received the National Book Award. The two volumes of poetry were combined into *The Dream Songs*, published in 1969. Within *The Dream Songs*, the 385 poems are divided into seven books. As the title suggests, the movement within and among poems proceeds on the level of dream logic.

Henry is a middle-aged white man who sometimes speaks in the first person and sometimes refers to himself in the third person. Many poems draw on the conventions of vaudeville. In these poems Henry takes the role of a performer in blackface and speaks in black dialect. He has an unnamed friend who plays the vaudeville role of the interlocutor and talks to him, sometimes calling him "Mr. Bones."

The choice of vaudeville as a structuring device for the poetry serves several functions. It offers a way of distancing Henry from his often tragic subject matter. Grief and anxiety are performed by Henry for an audience. By the time the poems were written in the 1950's and 1960's, most readers would have been familiar with vaudeville blackface acts but would also have recognized the racist overtones of the convention. The overlying vaudeville theme adds a grotesque aspect to Berryman's delivery. In poem 168, the narrator refers to the "hellish vaudeville turns" that life can take; vaudeville becomes a metaphor for the exaggerated horror recorded in the poetry. Despite its unsavory aspects, however, audiences in vaudeville's heyday earlier in the century found the productions highly entertaining and humorous. Berryman commented that he thought the poems of *The Dream Songs* were very funny as well. The combination of horrific subject matter with deep and sometimes surprising humor is one of the poems' most fascinating qualities.

Berryman's scholarship and craftsmanship as a poet can serve as hurdles to readers; however, *The Dream Songs* rewards the reader's effort. The poems contain numerous references to people Berryman knew, figures from literary history, and events of the time. Written in a time when blank verse was the norm and attention to formal issues was not a major concern of most poets, *The Dream Songs* showcases Berryman's lifelong study of poetic form.

Poets writing in the mid-twentieth century faced the challenge of following the modernist era, when the poetry of T. S. Eliot and Ezra Pound was enshrined by the founders of literary criticism and by English departments as the standard to be met. In a time when short, personal verse was the most common expression of poetry, Berryman produced an epic-length poem cycle that captures both the interest in the deeply personal that was the hallmark of poetry of the time and a desire to grapple with the big questions of living in the world.

Christian Themes

At its most basic level, *The Dream Songs* records the search for spiritual meaning and solace of a man who has suffered devastating losses. Henry never finds what he is searching for, but the poems are full of Christian references, pleas for spiritual enlightenment, and anger at God over the suicides of Henry's father and beloved friends. In poem 168, Henry notes the horrific parallels between his own life, Christ's life, and vaudeville theater. "God has many other surprises," he notes, and later in the poem elaborates:

> hellish vaudeville turns, promises had
> & promises forgotten here below,
> the final wound of the Cross.
> I have a story to tell you which is the worst
> story to tell that ever once I heard.

Henry decides to "pass to the next Song" because that story is too much for him to tell; it is unclear whether he refers to his own story or that of Jesus. *The Dream Songs* as a whole, however, tells of a man filled with horrible stories who is unable to come to terms with the tragedies of his life or to find the understanding he seeks from religion.

The tone of the poems ranges from despair to supplication to outright indignation with God. Dream Song 153 blames God in harsh language for the deaths of Theodore Roethke, Richard Blackmur, Randall Jarrell, Delmore Schwartz, and Sylvia Plath:

> I'm cross with god who has wrecked this generation.
> First he seized Ted, then Richard, Randall, and now Delmore.
> In between he gorged on Sylvia Plath.
> That was a first rate haul.

Henry revisits his father's suicide repeatedly through the poem cycle, with emotions ranging from despair to anger. Even by the end of the poems, he has not accepted the death. In number 384, the second to last of the book, Henry describes himself visiting his father's grave, imagining himself hacking down to the body with an ax and annihilating his own beginning.

In the four years that remained of his life after *The Dream Songs* was published, Berryman began the novel *Recovery*. Published posthumously in 1973, the unfinished work has been hailed by some critics as evidence that Berryman found Christian peace in his final years. His own suicide by walking off a bridge on January 7, 1972, leaves such a claim in doubt.

Sources for Further Study

Bloom, Harold, ed. *John Berryman*. New York: Chelsea House, 1989. Contains several of the most influential essays written on Berryman.

Kirsch, Adam. *The Wounded Surgeon: Confession and Transformation in Six American Poets—Robert Lowell, Elizabeth Bishop, John Berryman, Randall Jarrell, Delmore Schwartz, and Sylvia Plath*. New York: W. W. Norton, 2005. Provides a retrospective assessment of how Berryman's transformation of life into art fits with that of the generation of confessional poets.

Mariani, Paul L. *Dream Song: The Life of John Berryman*. 2d ed. Amherst: University of Massachusetts Press, 1996. Comprehensively researched account of the poet's influences, life events, and personal and professional associations.

Meyers, Jeffery. *Manic Power: Robert Lowell and His Circle.* New York: Arbor House, 1987. Places Berryman's work in terms of literary history and the poetry of his own contemporaries.

Thomas, Harry. *Reflections on the Poetry of John Berryman.* Boston: Northeastern University Press, 1988. Anthologizes many of the best essays written on Berryman. Includes interviews with the author and a concise time line of the poet's life and works.

Joan Hope